WITH

HISTORICAL DICTIONARIES OF RELIGIONS, PHILOSOPHIES, AND MOVEMENTS

Edited by Jon Woronoff

1. *Buddhism,* by Charles S. Prebish, 1993
2. *Mormonism,* by Davis Bitton, 1994
3. *Ecumenical Christianity,* by Ans Joachim van der Bent, 1994
4. *Terrorism,* by Sean Anderson and Stephen Sloan, 1995
5. *Sikhism,* by W. H. McLeod, 1995
6. *Feminism,* by Janet K. Boles and Diane Long Hoeveler, 1995
7. *Olympic Movement,* by Ian Buchanan and Bill Mallon, 1995
8. *Methodism,* by Charles Yrigoyen Jr. and Susan E. Warrick, 1996
9. *Orthodox Church,* by Michael Prokurat, Alexander Golitzin, and Michael D. Peterson, 1996
10. *Organized Labor,* by James C. Docherty, 1996
11. *Civil Rights Movement,* by Ralph E. Luker, 1997
12. *Catholicism,* by William J. Collinge, 1997
13. *Hinduism,* by Bruce M. Sullivan, 1997
14. *North American Environmentalism,* by Edward R. Wells and Alan M. Schwartz, 1997
15. *Welfare State,* by Bent Greve, 1998
16. *Socialism,* by James C. Docherty, 1997
17. *Bahá'í Faith,* by Hugh C. Adamson and Philip Hainsworth, 1998
18. *Taoism,* by Julian F. Pas in cooperation with Man Kam Leung, 1998
19. *Judaism,* by Norman Solomon, 1998
20. *Green Movement,* by Elim Papadakis, 1998
21. *Nietzscheanism,* by Carol Diethe, 1999
22. *Gay Liberation Movement,* by Ronald J. Hunt, 1999
23. *Islamic Fundamentalist Movements in the Arab World, Iran, and Turkey,* by Ahmad S. Moussalli, 1999
24. *Reformed Churches,* by Robert Benedetto, Darrell L. Guder, and Donald K. McKim, 1999
25. *Baptists,* by William H. Brackney, 1999
26. *Cooperative Movement,* by Jack Shaffer, 1999
27. *Reformation and Counter-Reformation,* by Hans J. Hillerbrand, 2000
28. *Shakers,* by Holley Gene Duffield, 2000

Historical Dictionary of Lutheranism

Günther Gassmann

In cooperation with
Duane H. Larson and Mark W. Oldenburg

*Historical Dictionaries of Religions,
Philosophies, and Movements, No. 35*

The Scarecrow Press, Inc.
Lanham, Maryland, and London
2001

SCARECROW PRESS, INC.

Published in the United States of America
by Scarecrow Press, Inc.
4720 Boston Way
Lanham, Maryland 20706
www.scarecrowpress.com

4 Pleydell Gardens, Folkstone
Kent CT20 2DN, England

British Library Cataloguing in Publication Information Available

Library of Congress Cataloging-in-Publication Data

Gassmann, Günther.
  Historical dictionary of Lutheranism / Günther Gassmann ; in cooperation with Duane
H. Larson and Mark W. Oldenburg.
    p. cm.—(Historical dictionaries of religions, philosophies, and movements ; no. 35)
  Includes bibliographical references.
  ISBN 0-8108-3945-8 (alk. paper)
    1. Lutheran Church—Dictionaries. I. Larson, Duane H. (Duane Howard), 1952- II.
Oldenburg, Mark W. III. Title. IV. Series.

BX8007 .G37 2001
284.1'03—dc21

00-063745

Contents

Series Editor's Foreword

Although it is tempting to insert the religions in this series in a somewhat narrower slot than the social movements, all of them had much broader social, economic, and political dimensions along with the more specifically religious and moral ones. This is rarely quite as evident as for the Lutheran church, which was at the center of a radical rethinking of the role of the church in general and gradually affected most other relationships as well while inducing a new way of thinking of God, and man, among its supporters. This is what made Lutheranism such a vigorous force in the Reformation and the following centuries. And it has remained a living and lively entity to the present day, undergoing vital changes in its relations with other churches and the world around it.

This *Historical Dictionary of Lutheranism* sheds light on the many and varied concerns of the church, from its earliest manifestations in the 16th century (and before) to its latest decisions on the eve of the 21st century. This is done through numerous entries on important persons, not only Martin Luther and his co-reformers but also their more distant successors, over these five centuries. Other entries deal with major events and institutions, the broad social and cultural impact of Lutheranism and its worldwide expansion, crucial aspects of theology and ethics, significant concepts and technical terms, decisive issues, and sometimes conflicts. This is grounded in a broad introduction laying out the scope of Lutheranism and a chronology tracing its evolution. No less important is the comprehensive bibliography, which can help readers deepen their knowledge of specific subjects.

This volume was written by an excellent team of authors, Günther Gassmann, Duane H. Larson, and Mark W. Oldenburg. All three are presently academics: Dr. Oldenburg is a professor of liturgics at the Lutheran Theological Seminary in Gettysburg, Dr. Larson is president of the Wartburg Theological Seminary at Dubuque, and Dr. Gassmann is a visiting professor at the Gettysburg Seminary. Dr. Gassmann in particular, who has overseen and contributed heavily to this project, has played an extremely active and unusually varied role, first as professor, then president of the Central Office of the United Evangelical-Lutheran Church of Germany, next associate director of the Department of Studies of the Lutheran World Federation, and finally director of the Commission on Faith and Order of the World Council of Churches, this commission being the most representative theological forum in the world. This exceptional insight into the workings of the Christian church worldwide could hardly be exceeded and provides an institutional breadth that goes well with the theological depth.

Jon Woronoff
Series Editor

Notes to Users

Cross-references. Words printed in bold indicate another entry in this book that can provide further information. Cross-references are sometimes not completely identical with the title of the entry referred to, for example, **Orthodoxy** refers to "Orthodoxy, Lutheran," **worship** refers to "Worship, History and Structure" or "Worship, Theology of."

Quotations. Only very few and short quotations are used in this book. Biblical references are taken from the *New Revised Standard Version* of the Bible. References to the Lutheran confessions are taken from *The Book of Concord*, edited by Theodore E. Tappert (Philadelphia: Fortress, 1959).

Abbreviations. Very few abbreviations are used. Other than common ones such as "e.g." or "i.e.," abbreviations are introduced in each entry by the full term (e.g., Lutheran World Federation [LWF]). Abbreviations of biblical books are the now widely used ones such as Gen (Genesis), Is (Isaiah), Mt (Matthew), Mk (Mark), Lk (Luke), Jn (John), 1 Jn (1 John), and so on. Other abbreviations include Ger (German), Lat (Latin), Gk (Greek), and so forth.

Italics. *Italics* are used for titles.

Preface

This *Historical Dictionary of Lutheranism* seeks to provide information and orientation on one of the major Christian communions. What were the foundational theological and historical events and developments that led in the 16th century to the emergence of the Lutheran movement within the broader context of the Reformation? Who were the reformers who surrounded Martin Luther, the most important and influential figure of the Reformation era? What were the circumstances that led the Lutheran movement, against its original intention to reform the existing church, to develop its own ecclesiastical structures, later to be called the "Lutheran church"? In what ways has the emerging Lutheranism in the 16th century reformulated and reaccentuated the one common Christian tradition of faith and life to which Lutherans clearly felt committed?

It is such questions, but not only such questions, that make this a "historical" dictionary. Wherever possible, the book draws lines of historical development from the time of the Reformation and its biblical and historical background to the present. Such lines run through the periods of Lutheran Orthodoxy, Pietism, Enlightenment, Liberalism, and Neo-Lutheranism to the constitution of world Lutheranism in the 20th century. References to influential Lutherans, developments in theology, new movements in church life engaging in missionary and social work, and fidelity and failure of Lutherans in the exercise of their public responsibilities draw the outlines of a picture of Lutheran history and presence during the four centuries after the Reformation. Much more could have been said in many entries, and there are additional persons, events, and issues that could or should have been included but for limitations of space. However, it is hoped that necessary corrections and certain additions will be possible in future editions.

When I was asked to write this book, I joyfully and optimistically accepted, not only because of my own professional involvement with world Lutheranism, but also and mainly because I considered such a task the ideal preoccupation of a retired person with much free time. However, when it turned out that I became a rather permanent visiting professor (one semester per year since 1995) at the Lutheran Theological Seminary in Gettysburg, Pennsylvania, as well as—for shorter periods—at several European universities, I cried out for help. I was fortunate that two of my Gettysburg colleagues responded to my cry: Duane H. Larson, now the president of Wartburg Theological Seminary, and Mark W. Oldenburg, the professor of liturgics at Gettysburg. Together, they took over approximately one-third of the entries in the areas of their special competence. We experienced a joyful and fruitful style of cooperation, and they gave me the liberty to shorten or expand their entries. I am most grateful to Mark and Duane.

Yet even with the help of these colleagues, the task of writing such a multifaceted book meant a heavy workload for me during the free days, weekends, and nights between 1998 and 2000. My deep gratitude, therefore, goes to my wife, Ursula Gassmann, who had to bear with me during this period—untiringly supportive and a most helpful partner in conversation on many topics. I thank my Gettysburg historical colleagues, Gerald Christianson and Scott H. Hendrix (now at Princeton), for their advice, and the staff of the libraries of the Gettysburg Seminary and the Ecumenical Center in Geneva for their kind assistance. For the technical production of the bibliography, I thank my two Slovak students at Gettysburg, Michal and Katka Valco. In the process of finalizing the manuscript, I received most helpful suggestions concerning form and content from Jon Woronoff, the editor of the series.

Since I had to write in a foreign tongue, my Germanic English (still noticeable in the text) was revised in a number of entries by several friends, and I thank them. The great majority of my entries, however, were corrected by my former Gettysburg student, the Rev. Louise L. Reynolds. Rev. Reynolds not only corrected mistakes, clumsy formulations, and overly long sentences, but also suggested small additions and clarifications. She was a most thoughtful and engaged helper to whom I owe immense gratitude.

The authors of the entries are aware of the many weaknesses and failures of their Lutheran tradition. But they are convinced and grateful adherents of this tradition and highly value its rich theological and spiritual heritage and present-day ecumenical commitment. It is in appreciation of this heritage that they have written their entries. The entries are signed by our initials: D.H.L. for Duane H. Larson, M.O. for Mark W. Oldenburg, and G.G. for Günther Gassmann.

List of Acronyms

American Lutheran Church (ALC)
Christian World Communions (CWC)
Church of the Lutheran Brethren of America (CLBA)
Evangelical Lutheran Church in America (ELCA)
Evangelische Kirche in Deutschland (EKD)
General Evangelical Lutheran Conference (AELK)
International Lutheran Council (ILC)
International Missionary Council (IMC)
Lutheran Church in America (LCA)
Lutheran Church-Missouri Synod (LC–MS)
Lutheran World Convention (LWC)
Lutheran World Federation (LWF)
National Lutheran Council (NLC)
United Bible Societies (UBS)
United Nations High Commissioner for Refugees (UNHCR)
World Council of Churches (WCC)

Chronology

All dates are A.D.

30/33–63	Formation of the first Christian communities.
c.63–200	Expansion of Christianity within the Roman Empire; consolidation of its faith and life by means of the threefold pattern of ordained ministry with bishops in apostolic succession, credal formulas (baptismal creeds), and process of adopting the Canon of Holy Scripture.
c.95–500	Period of the great Greek and Latin church fathers.
313	Toleration and soon privileged status of Christianity in the empire.
325	First Council of Nicea, which opens the sequence of the seven ecumenical councils, recognized by both the Eastern and Western church: 381 Constantinople I, 431 Ephesus, 451 Chalcedon, 553 Constantinople II, 680/81 Constantinople III, and 787 Nicea II. The councils clarified and defined fundamental Christian dogmas.
354–430	Life of St. Augustine, bishop and theologian, who decisively shaped the theological orientation of the church in the West, including Reformation thinking.
440–461	Reign of Pope Leo I "the Great," decisive for the development of the power and authority of the papacy.
c.500–1300	Development of the church in the West and of the papacy into a powerful ecclesiastical and political institution.
1054	Final step in the growing division between the Eastern (Orthodox) and Western (Roman Catholic) church.

c.1100–1350   Flowering of scholastic theology with its synthesis of Aristotelian philosophy and Christian theology: Anselm of Canterbury (1033–1109), Peter Lombard (c.1100–1160), Thomas Aquinas (c.1224–1274), Duns Scotus (1265/66–1308), and William of Ockham (c.1285–1347). They prepared official definitions of Roman Catholic teaching.

c.1200–1545   Reform and renewal movements in the Catholic church, later influenced by Humanism. Pre-Reformation movements: Wycliffites/Lollards (John Wycliffe, d. 1384), Waldensians (Peter Valdes, d. c.1217), and Hussites (John Hus, d. 1415).

c.1300–1517   Decline of papacy, theology, and spiritual life of the late medieval church.

1483–1546   Life of Martin Luther, leading German reformer and formative theological mind of the Lutheran tradition, together with other reformers such as Mikael Agricola, Nikolaus von Amsdorf, Jakob Andreae, Johannes Brenz, Martin Bucer, Johannes Bugenhagen, Martin Chemnitz, Philipp Melanchthon, Laurentius Petri, Olavus Petri, and Urbanus Rhegius.

1484–1531   Life of Ulrich Zwingli, who initiates the Reformation in Zürich in 1523.

1509–1564   Life of John Calvin, leading reformer of Geneva in 1536 and together with Zwingli, the founding theological mind of the Reformed/Presbyterian tradition, often called Calvinism.

1512   Luther joins the theological faculty in Wittenberg, which will soon become the main theological center of the Lutheran Reformation.

1517–1580   Emergence of Anglican, Lutheran, Radical (Anabaptist and Spiritualist), and Reformed/Presbyterian Reformation movements.

1517   Luther makes public on October 31 his *Ninety-five Theses* against indulgences; generally regarded as the beginning of the Lutheran movement.

1518   Philipp Melanchthon, Luther's colleague and important reformer, arrives in Wittenberg. Beginning

1530/31	Melanchthon responds to the *Confutation* with the *Apology of the Augsburg Confession*.
1531	Formation of the Smalcald League, a defense league of the evangelical estates.
1532	Luther publishes his famous commentary on Romans.
1534	Act of Supremacy. Separation of the English church from Rome.
1536	*Wittenberg Concord*. Unites different tendencies within the Lutheran movement concerning the interpretation of the Lord's Supper.
1537	Luther's *Smalcald Articles*, requested by Elector John Frederick of Saxony. Melanchthon's *Treatise on the Power and Primacy of the Pope*, requested as a kind of addendum to the *Augsburg Confession*.
1539	Luther writes *On the Councils and the Church*.
1540–1700	Counter-Reformation. Lutheranism loses much ground in eastern and southeastern Europe.
1541	Colloquy of Regensburg. One of the last—not successful—attempts to mediate between Lutherans and Catholics.
1545–1563	Council of Trent. Responds to the Reformation, seeks to reform the Catholic church, seals the Protestant-Roman Catholic division.
1546	Luther dies in Eisleben. Buried in the Castle Church at Wittenberg.
1547	Smalcald War. Emperor Charles V defeats Smalcald League.
1548	Augsburg (and Leipzig) Interim. Seeks to impose again certain Catholic liturgical traditions. Controversy about adiaphora.
1555	Religious Peace of Augsburg. Provides legal sanction in the empire to Roman Catholicism and adherents of the *Augsburg Confession*.

1560	Philipp Melanchthon dies at Wittenberg. Buried in Castle Church.
c.1548–1576	Intra-Lutheran theological controversies on adiaphora, good works, free will, justification, law and Gospel, and real presence in the Lord's Supper. The differences were resolved between 1568 and 1576, especially by the work of Jakob Andreae and Martin Chemnitz. The outcome of their efforts and of consultations of theologians was the
1577	*Formula of Concord*, the—so far—last Lutheran confession.
1577–18th century	Lutheran Orthodoxy.
1580	Publication of the *Book of Concord*. Collection of all Lutheran confessions: *Three Ecumenical Creeds*, *Augsburg Confession*, its *Apology*, *Smalcald Articles*, *Treatise on the Power and Primacy of the Pope*, *Small Catechism* and *Large Catechism*, and *Formula of Concord*. Conclusion of the confessional formation of Lutheranism.
1618–1648	Thirty Years' War. Peace of Westphalia in 1648 with imperial recognition of the Catholic, Lutheran, and Reformed confessions.
17th and 18th centuries	Main period of Pietism. Strong Lutheran involvement.
1639	First Lutheran congregation in North America (Swedes in Delaware).
1663–1727	Life of August Hermann Francke, leading Lutheran pietist, educator, mission organizer, and social reformer.
1706	Danish-Halle Mission. First Lutheran missionary overseas: Bartholomäus Ziegenbalg arrives 1706 in India.
1741	First Lutheran congregation in Latin America (Surinam).
1742	Arrival of Heinrich Melchior Muhlenberg in America, the "Patriarch of North American Lutheranism."

1685–1750	Life of Johann Sebastian Bach, a genial Lutheran composer of church music.
1748	Ministerium of Pennsylvania, the first North American Lutheran church body.
Early 19th century	Influence of the Awakening on Lutheran theologians and groups. Link between Pietism and Neo-Lutheranism.
19th century	Period of the expansion of Lutheran social, inner mission, and home mission work. Foundation of Lutheran deaconess orders.
c.1817–20th century	Neo-Lutheranism or Confessional Lutheranism.
1820	Foundation of the Evangelical Lutheran General Synod of the United States of North America. First association of several synods.
1820	Beginning of Lutheran mission work in Africa.
1821–1874	Establishment of main Lutheran mission societies in Germany and Scandinavia.
1837/38	Arrival of the first Lutheran groups in Australia.
1847	Formation of the Lutheran Church-Missouri Synod.
1867	Formation of the General Council of the Evangelical Lutheran Church of North America.
1867/68	Foundation of the General Evangelical Lutheran Conference (AELK) in Hannover. It initiates efforts to bring together worldwide Lutheranism.
1883–today	Publication of the "Weimar Edition" of Luther's works.
1910	First World Mission Conference at Edinburgh. Considered the beginning of the modern ecumenical movement.
1918	End of World War I. German churches no longer state churches.
1918–1967	National Lutheran Council (in the United States).
1920 and 1929	First ordinations of women in Lutheran churches (Holland and Alsace).

1923	First meeting of the Lutheran World Convention at Eisenach. The convention becomes the first structured expression of international Lutheran fellowship, theological exchange, and cooperation.
1929	Second meeting of the Lutheran World Convention at Copenhagen.
1935	Third meeting of the Lutheran World Convention at Paris.
1933–1945	Participation of Lutheran groups and churches in the church struggle in Nazi Germany.
1934	*Barmen Theological Declaration* of the German "Confessing Church" against the collaboration of the "German Christians" with the Nazi regime.
1940–1945	Lutheran churches participate in resistance under German occupation in Denmark and Norway.
1945	Following the end of World War II, extensive material aid, rehabilitation, and migration programs are set up by North American and Swedish Lutheran churches for the suffering populations in Europe.
1945/48–1989/90	Lutheran churches under communist regimes in Eastern Europe and China. In the Soviet Union already since 1917.
1946	Last meeting of the Executive Committee of the Lutheran World Convention. Prepares foundation of the Lutheran World Federation.
1947	First Assembly of the Lutheran World Federation at Lund. Offices at Geneva. Becomes one of the largest confessional organizations.
1948	First Assembly of the World Council of Churches at Amsterdam. Many Lutheran churches become members.
1951	New confession of the Protestant Christian Batak Church in Indonesia. Recognized by the Lutheran World Federation as a Lutheran confession.
1952	Second Assembly of the Lutheran World Federation at Hannover.

1957	Third Assembly of the Lutheran World Federation at Minneapolis.
1960s	Lutheran churches in Africa and Asia receive their independence.
1960s	Beginning of official national and regional theological conversations between Lutheran and other churches.
1962–1965	Second Vatican Council. Entry of the Roman Catholic Church into the ecumenical movement.
1963	Fourth Assembly of the Lutheran World Federation at Helsinki. Decision to create a Lutheran Foundation for Inter-Confessional Research. Its Institute for Ecumenical Research was set up in Strasbourg in 1965.
1967	Beginning of official international Lutheran-Roman Catholic dialogue.
1970	Fifth Assembly of the Lutheran World Federation at Evian. Beginning of official international Lutheran-Reformed and Lutheran-Anglican dialogues.
1973	Leuenberg Agreement. Recognition of full church fellowship between Lutheran, Reformed, and United churches in Europe.
1977	Sixth Assembly of the Lutheran World Federation at Dar es Salaam. Its much debated *Status Confessionis* declaration rejects the apartheid regime in Southern Africa on the basis of the Lutheran confession. Beginning of official international Lutheran-Methodist dialogue.
1981	Beginning of official international Lutheran-Orthodox dialogue.
1984	Seventh Assembly of the Lutheran World Federation at Budapest.
1986	Beginning of official international Lutheran-Baptist dialogue.
1987	Foundation of the Evangelical Lutheran Church in America, uniting the great majority of Lutherans in

the United States outside the Lutheran Church-Missouri Synod.

1990	Eighth Assembly of the Lutheran World Federation at Curitiba.
1992	Election of the first two Lutheran women bishops in Germany and the United States.
1992–1996	Signing and acceptance of the *Porvoo Common Statement*, establishing full church fellowship between the four Anglican churches in Great Britain and Ireland and six of the eight Scandinavian and Baltic Lutheran churches.
1997	Ninth Assembly of the Lutheran World Federation at Hong Kong.
1999	Acceptance by the Evangelical Lutheran Church in America (ELCA) of the proposed full communion between the ELCA and the Episcopal Church.
1999	Signing on October 31 at Augsburg of the Lutheran-Roman Catholic *Joint Declaration on the Doctrine of Justification.*
1999	The Lutheran World Federation has 128 member churches with over 59.4 million members. Altogether, there are 63.1 million Lutherans in the world. [G.G.]

Introduction

A NEW ACTOR ON THE HISTORICAL SCENE: LUTHERANISM

The Reformation of the 16th century was not, as some modern historians claim, the conclusion of the medieval era but the inauguration of a new period: that of modern Europe, an era that has also affected much of the rest of the world. We are more aware than before that the Reformation was a complex and multifaceted political, social, cultural, and religious process. Most historians agree, however, that in the framework of this process it was the religious and theological efforts to reform and renew the late medieval church, decadent and irrelevant in much of its life, that were the initiating forces that set a broad historical movement in motion. Among these reforming religious and theological forces, the Lutheran reform movement was the most important and influential one. It was the historical impact of the theological genius of the Wittenberg professor Martin Luther (1483–1546), as well as his and his co-reformers' sense of what was historically necessary and possible that, despite their nonradical, nonrevolutionary intentions, profoundly changed and shaped the face of central and northern Europe and beyond.

The transforming impact of the Lutheran reform movement was prepared and enabled by several major factors. On the one hand, the Lutheran theological focus turned much of the late medieval system upside-down simply by restating and reinterpreting the biblical and faith tradition of the church. No longer central was the human movement toward God through intellectual efforts to gain a knowledge of God and through religious efforts to merit God's salvation; rather, it was God's movement toward human beings, through the revelation of God's nature and will in Jesus Christ, and through God's unconditional and justifying acceptance of sinners for Christ's sake. This change resulted in an immense sense of liberation of human consciences burdened by innumerable imposed religious observations and the uncertainty of salvation. This renewed theological vision led to a reform of the hierarchical, pyramidical system of the church with a powerful, absolute pope at the top, much to the relief of all who already for some time had yearned for a reform of the church's structures and forms of life. One of the most significant religious and secular consequences of these reforms was the liberation of lay members of

1

the church from their subordinate nonposition, their empowerment through education, the assurance that their status and dignity was on a par with the clergy, and the affirmation of their responsibility as God's coworkers in church and society. This, in turn, led to new concepts of and relationships between church and state and church and society, as well as to a transformation of the whole political, social, and cultural fabric of a large part of Europe. Such a broad impact was also possible because Lutheranism emerged as the most significant Reformation movement, thus carrying its theology and ethos to many parts of Europe and later also to other continents.

Today, Lutheranism has become a worldwide communion of churches that reaches from Wittenberg to Siberia, Papua New Guinea, Madagascar, and Surinam. It is no longer a predominantly European and North American phenomenon. This communion of churches represents one of the largest confessional families that has rather late, in the second half of the 20th century, consolidated its own inner coherence and realized its unity with the help of the Lutheran World Federation. At the same time, it has begun to open its windows and doors for closer relations with other churches and worldwide communions of churches. Thus, Lutheranism, despite its failures and weaknesses, claims continuity with its biblical and confessional foundations, while at the same time expressing and living these foundations in new geographical and cultural contexts and seeking to heal the divisions that were one of the bitter consequences of the Reformation.

LUTHERAN CHURCH, LUTHERANISM, AND LUTHERAN: SOME TERMINOLOGICAL CLARIFICATIONS

Before considering the rise, main characteristics, and expansion of Lutheranism, it is necessary to say something about three essential terms. The term "Lutheran church" serves as a general description of churches that belong to the Lutheran confessional tradition. The term "Lutheranism" is used as a general description for the ecclesiastical, theological, spiritual, social, and cultural tradition related to the Lutheran Reformation. And there is the word "Lutheran," which appears in innumerable combinations: Lutheran theology, Lutheran-Anglican dialogue, Lutheran Quarterly, Lutheran Theological Seminary, and so on. It is a rather unique phenomenon within Christianity that the name of a theologian and reformer, Martin Luther, has become part of the identification and designation of a major confessional tradition; the only exceptions are those of John Calvin and the founders of some newer African independent churches.

The original intention of Luther and his co-reformers was to reform their church, not to create the new Christian reality that was subsequently called

"Lutheranism" and institutionalized as the Lutheran church. But during the Reformation period, the followers of Luther and his co-reformers were called by their adversaries *Lutherani* or *Lutherana secta* in order to associate them with their heretical leader. Luther himself, for this and other theological reasons, was against the use of his name as a banner for the movement and the resulting churches. He would have preferred the designation "evangelical," and, indeed, the Lutheran confessions use "evangelical churches" or "churches of the Augsburg Confession." However, a self-identification was needed to distinguish the movement of the Wittenberg reformers from other Reformation movements. Thus, "Lutheran" came to be used. But it was not until 1586 that the term "Lutheran church" appears in Württemberg and Electoral Saxony.

Lutheran Orthodoxy and even more so Neo-Lutheranism in the 19th century firmly established the term "Lutheran church." At the same time, the term "Lutheranism" came into use as a general formula of self-identification. Today, the terms "Lutheranism" and "Lutheran" are widely used, while the term "Lutheran church" is used both in a more general sense (like "the theology of the Lutheran church") and in a more specific sense as part of the name of a particular church (as in "Mexican Lutheran Church"). However, only a few churches use "Lutheran" without any addition in their name. The majority use "Evangelical Lutheran Church of/in . . ."; many others, especially in eastern Europe, call themselves "Evangelical Church of the Augsburg Confession of/in . . ."; and still others carry in their name no direct reference to their being part of the Lutheran confessional tradition (as the "Church of Sweden").

THE RISE OF LUTHERANISM

The Lutheran churches have their origin in the early Christian communities of the time of the New Testament, and they seek to live in continuity with the fundamental theological insights, doctrinal decisions, and spiritual and liturgical developments of the church throughout the centuries since the time of the apostles. The Lutheran churches received their separate existence and particular confessional identity as an institutional outcome of one of the several movements—Anglican, Reformed/Presbyterian, Lutheran, and Radical—that together formed the Reformation of the 16th century. The Lutheran movement was initiated and shaped by Martin Luther and his co-reformers. They criticized what they regarded and experienced as unbiblical theological interpretations and church practices that flourished in the church of their time. Such interpretations and practices included the whole penitential system with its idea of human satisfaction for sin, the ability of humans to cooperate with God's grace in earning their own salvation, the claims of the papal office, or the understanding of the Lord's Supper as a sacrifice offered by the priest. They rejected the many practical abuses and the general miserable estate of the late medieval church, thereby responding also to a widespread longing for reforms in the church. This explains, together with the new possibilities of communication offered by the printing press, the incredibly fast expansion of the Reformation, which, however, was also due to the fact that the message of the Lutheran reformers immediately touched the hearts and minds of countless people. It was a liberating and consoling message that people need no longer worry about and desperately struggle for their own salvation. They were assured that the estrangement between God and human beings has been overcome through the human-divine mediator Jesus Christ. He has become the advocate for all humans and has taken them with him in his suffering and victorious resurrection. For his sake, God accepts people, forgives their sins and failures, and accounts and makes them righteous in his sight. This Gospel of the gift of God's grace and justification is offered to all people unconditionally, free, gratuitously.

Luther's publication of his *Ninety-five Theses* on October 31, 1517, at Wittenberg is generally regarded as the beginning of the Lutheran reform movement. By criticizing in his theses the practice of selling indulgences, Luther, in fact, also rejected their underlying theological assumptions within the late medieval theological and ecclesiastical system, namely, that people cannot be assured of their salvation and therefore had to make their own contribution toward salvation and eternal life. Furthermore, through their financial contributions they had to support the power and wealth of the church. From then on, the Lutheran movement began to spread to many territories and towns in Germany and beyond its borders, and Luther became the most influential and formative theological mind of the movement. He had an enormous sense for the challenges of the moment and responded to them by his biblically informed, deep and fascinating theological insights, genial linguistic abilities, massive literary output, untiring teaching and preaching activity, reforms of the structure and practice of worship, burning concern for the dignity and education of the laity, his life-affirming earthiness, as well as his joyful and searching piety—in all these and other gifts and activities supported by his wife since 1525, Katharina von Bora (1499–1552). Luther did not produce a comprehensive systematic theology; rather, he developed and expressed his ideas always within a particular context (and often confrontation). As a result, quite different emphases can be found in his writings according to the situation of their origins. He enjoyed debate and employed witty, ironic, extreme, and sometimes obscene formulations. He was, not always uncritical, a child of the feudal and paternalistic social conditions and norms of his time, and he made irresponsible and indefensible statements about the Jews and the revolting peasants. Yet despite all the incredible complexity of his personality and work—or perhaps because of it—Luther was and, through the impact of his ideas, continues to be one of the most formative personalities of modern history. Not surprisingly, therefore, he has probably become the most widely studied, written about, misunderstood and misrepresented, portrayed (in art and kitsch), and memorialized (names of streets, schools, church buildings, institutions, and so on) theologian and churchman since the 16th century.

However, Luther was not alone the "father" of the Lutheran Reformation and of ensuing Lutheranism. There were important co-reformers who helped to spread, shape, and consolidate the Lutheran Reformation. Among them were his closest colleague Philipp Melanchthon (1497–1560) and reformers such as Johannes Brenz (1499–1570), Martin Bucer (1491–1551), Johannes Bugenhagen (1485–1558), Martin Chemnitz (1522–1586), as well as the reformers in Scandinavia and eastern Europe. Their intention was not to create a new church, but to reform the existing church on the basis of the normative biblical witness and the positive tradition of the church. However, the Lutheran reforming movement was forced by historical circumstances to develop its own confessional position and institutional expression. The confessional and institutional foundations of Lutheranism were laid in a process extending from the condemnation and banning of Luther and his followers by the 1521 Edict of Worms, the Catholic rejection at the Diet of Augsburg in 1530 of the *Augsburg Confession*, the confession of faith presented by the reform-minded evangelical estates together with their plea for preserving the unity of the church while allowing freedom for reforms, to the legal recognition of Lutheranism as one of the two religions of the empire by the 1555 Religious Peace of Augsburg.

Of decisive importance in this process were the formulation of the Lutheran confessions as well as their successive official reception by evangelical estates and free cities and their churches. A clear priority was attributed to the *Augsburg Confession* of 1530 as the central Lutheran confession. Other contributing factors in the process of introducing the Lutheran Reformation were the church orders (the first one in 1528 by Bugenhagen for Braunschweig) that helped to consolidate in the different territories the confessional basis, forms of worship, and the doctrinal and educational requirements of pastors and teachers. The life of ordinary people was directly touched by reforms of the structure, language, and theology of worship and by Bible translations (the famous German translation by Luther, but also into languages other than German). Study in Wittenberg by many future Lutheran leaders from different countries and the effective use of the new print media contributed to the spread of the Lutheran Reformation. The emerging profile of Lutheranism was further sharpened by the (provisional) settlement of intra-Lutheran controversies in the form of the *Formula of Concord* of 1577 and the official collection of the Lutheran confessions in the *Book of Concord* of 1580. These signaled the conclusion of the clarification and formulation of the Lutheran confessional stance. However, the controversies leading up to the *Formula of Concord* and other theological and practical differences were already in the 16th century an indication that Lutheranism did not represent a uniform reality but a pluriform one, held together by commitment—in various degrees—to the confessions and fundamental common theological convictions.

The process of the Lutheran Reformation led to the establishment of Lutheran territorial churches in Germany, national churches in Scandinavia, and diaspora churches in other parts of Europe. It was most important, however, that the Lutheran movement, despite broad popular support, could only gain space and possibilities for developing its own ecclesiastical existence where secular estates (countries, territories, and free imperial cities) joined and protected the Lutheran Reformation or tolerated it during its early period as in eastern and southeastern Europe. Thus, church history and political history became closely intertwined on the Lutheran side, and the Smalcald League of evangelical estates was founded in 1531 to defend Lutheranism by political and military means. With the establishment of Lutheran churches and the theological response of the Roman Catholic Church to the Reformation at the Council of Trent (1545–1563), the Catholic church lost its privileged place as *the* church in the West and became one of several churches: the *Roman* Catholic Church.

Not only in its origins, but also in its early development, Lutheranism continued to be marked by its distinction from and often sharp criticism of the late medieval Catholic church. Though Lutherans continued to affirm that also in that church there were true Christians, true faith, and real sacraments wherever the Gospel was proclaimed, basically the relationship to that church was considered by Lutherans in terms of the distinction between the true and the false church. This was not only a distinction of degree, but also a radical one before God and in the perspective of eternity. From there follow the harsh judgments on the Roman Church as being in the service of the Antichrist, of Satan, and so on. Conversely, the Roman Catholic Church regarded the emerging Lutheran churches as a breakaway schism and heresy that was destroying the unity both of the church and of the empire and that, in obedience to God and the Catholic faith, had to be suppressed or reconverted back to the one true church, if necessary by force. This project was undertaken, with the help of the secular arm, in the context of the Counter-Reformation. Here, Lutheranism in some areas of Europe, especially in the Austrian-Hungarian Habsburg lands, was reduced by persecution, discrimination, and enforced emigration to minorities living in the "diaspora" (to mention just one example: in the territory of present-day Slovakia alone, over 800 churches were taken away from Lutheran congregations between 1681 and 1691).

After the Counter-Reformation, bitter theological controversies between Lutherans and Catholics still continued. Furthermore, the division between the two churches had many repercussions on the political, social, and cultural life in countries where Roman Catholics and Lutherans increasingly lived side by side (e.g., limited religious liberty for one or the other side, or discrimination of Lutherans or Roman Catholics in the appointment to public offices). While Lutherans and Catholics in other parts of the world were free from such a painful heritage, Europeans had to wait until the second half of the 20th century to experience a radical change in Lutheran-Roman Catholic theological, ecclesiastical, and social relationships. This change was enabled, among other factors, by a far-reaching revision of the Roman Catholic interpretation of the Reformation, a new and intensive Roman Catholic study of the person and work of Martin Luther, convergences in theological thinking, and a common recognition that the conflicts and controversies at the time of the Reformation were also partly the result of mutual misunderstandings and misinterpretations. The new Roman Catholic-Lutheran relationship found one significant symbolic expression at the end of the last century when a basic agreement on the doctrine of justification by faith alone, 450 years ago one of the major reasons for Lutheran-Catholic division, was signed on October 31, 1999, at Augsburg by representatives of the Lutheran World Federation and the Roman Catholic Church.

But also among the different Reformation movements there was not always sheer harmony in pursuing their common cause. This was most dramatically the case when it came to the relations between the Lutheran movement and the radical Reformation movements. Though originally springing up from similar reform concerns and even being part of the Lutheran or Reformed movements, the radical movements soon took their own courses. The Anabaptists rejected the baptism of infants and took up other radical positions. The Spiritualists claimed direct inspiration by the Holy Spirit, which led them to abolish outward means like sacraments and ministries. All of these groups sought to establish a pure church composed only of true believers, and they either refused to be involved in the public affairs of society or sought to establish, by force if necessary, a perfect society already reflecting the Kingdom of God. It is no wonder Lutherans vehemently criticized and condemned these positions and occasionally encouraged the secular arm to persecute adherents of these movements. This tragic part of their history was critically reviewed by Lutherans in the 20th century.

There were many similarities between the Lutheran and the Reformed/Presbyterian Reformation movements. They shared the basic theological presuppositions that undergirded their criticism of the late medieval church and agreed in many points of their positive Reformation teaching. But there were also differences. The Reformation led and shaped by Ulrich Zwingli (1484–1531) in Zürich and John Calvin (1509–1564) in Geneva was much more radical than the Lutheran movement, for example, in the abolition of church usages (the removal of images from church buildings and so on) and in the simplification of forms of worship. Differences in the understanding of Christ's presence in the Lord's Supper were, finally, decisive in dividing the two Reformation movements that went their separate ways. Yet, in many places there survived a sense of common Reformation roots and attributes, and in the 20th century Lutheran and Reformed churches reestablished closer relations or even full fellowship.

The Lutheran and English/Anglican wings of the Reformation were initially more divided by the English Channel and different political contexts than by theological convictions. There were remarkably close contacts and relations between Lutheran reformers and the emerging Rome-free Church of England during the early phase of the English Reformation. The first *Book of Common Prayer* (1549), the theology of leading English reformers such as Archbishop Thomas Cranmer, the theological terminology of new English Bible translations, and the *Thirty-nine Articles of Religion* (1563/71) were profoundly influenced by Lutheran theological perspectives. After separate developments that ensued during the following centuries, Anglicans and Lutherans have rediscovered each other and the many common elements of their faith and church life in the 20th century. In some parts of the world they have established full communion with each other.

Lutheranism in its ecclesiastical, confessional-theological, and spiritual forms of expression, but also in its cultural and social impact (e.g., in the areas of music, literature, art, education, ethos, customs, and social work), was much influenced by the sequence of its own various theological and spiritual movements as well as by the great intellectual movements that followed the 16th century. The influence of Lutheran Orthodoxy, which sought to consolidate and defend Lutheranism by working out a doctrinal system that returned to scholastic concepts, continued through the time when the warm, personal faith of 17th- and 18th-century Pietism extensively marked Lutheranism and the beginnings of its missionary and social activity, while the rationalistic Enlightenment had a more limited influence. Continuing influences of Orthodoxy, Pietism, and Lutheran expressions of the international movements of the late 18th- and early 19th-century Awakening merged into Neo-Lutheranism of the 19th century in central and northern Europe and in North America. During the first half of the 19th century the term "Evangelical-Lutheran Church" was used for the first time in church constitutions, while the second half of the century witnessed the awakening of a new desire for Lutheran unity beyond one's own ecclesial and national boundaries (e.g., by the foundation of the General Evangelical Lutheran Conference in 1867/68 at Hannover). There was a growing recognition that common confessional commitment inherently implies agreement in proclamation of the Gospel and administration of the sacraments, the classical Lutheran conditions for church unity, and should, therefore, enable Lutheran unity. This recognition led to the formation of the Lutheran World Convention in 1923 and the Lutheran World Federation in 1947.

THE EXPANSION OF LUTHERANISM

The expansion of the Lutheran churches beyond their German homeland took place in three phases: during the Reformation; through emigration to other continents; and through mission work in Africa and Asia.

EXPANSION DURING THE REFORMATION

Formative events in the formal establishment of Lutheran churches in Germany and other parts of Europe were the acceptance of the *Augsburg Confession* in 1530 and the formulation and gradual reception of the other Lutheran confessions, finally assembled in the *Book of Concord* in 1580. In Germany, Lutheranism was recognized by imperial law at the Religious Peace of Augsburg in 1555 as one of the two religions of the empire. Lutheran churches were established between 1521 and 1585 in those territories and imperial-free cities in central, northern, eastern, and southwestern parts of the country, where princes or town councils had accepted the Lutheran Reformation. Today, Germany still has the largest Lutheran presence in the world. The 10 territorial Lutheran churches in Bavaria, Braunschweig, Hannover, Mecklenburg, North Elbia, Oldenburg, Saxony, Schaumburg-Lippe, Thuringia, and Württemberg have 14 million members. Many Christians, congregations, and institutions in the United churches in other parts of Germany also regard themselves as Lutherans.

The movement of Lutheranism beyond Germany had already begun during the first few decades of the Reformation. In northern Europe, all churches became Lutheran national churches. In 1536/37 the Lutheran church was established in Denmark (to which Norway and Iceland also belonged at that time), and in Sweden (to which Finland belonged). Here, the introduction of the Lutheran Reformation came to a preliminary conclusion in 1593 and a final conclusion in 1686, when the whole *Book of Concord* was accepted. In these five countries, more than 85 percent of the present-day population belong to the national Lutheran churches; the Church of Sweden with its 7.6 million members being the largest Lutheran church in the world. By way of Germany and Scandinavia, Lutheranism was introduced in the 16th century to Estonia and Latvia in the Baltic region. In these countries, the majority of the population also belonged to the Lutheran churches before World War II. These churches are now in the process of rebuilding church life after a half-century of Soviet oppression.

In eastern and southeastern Europe, the Lutheran Reformation was accepted during the 16th century by large groups of the population in the Habsburg lands, present-day Austria, Croatia, Czech Republic, Hungary, Slovakia, Slovenia, and Yugoslavia, as well as in Poland. The state-supported Counter-Reformation, however, reduced Lutheranism to minority and diaspora churches in this region. During the second half of the 20th century, all these churches, with the exception of Austria, were severely restricted in their life and work by the socialist regimes of their countries during more than 40 years of repression until 1989/90. Most of these churches, the larger ones being in Austria, Hungary, Poland, and Slovakia, refer to the *Augsburg Confession* in their name (e.g., the Evangelical Church of the Augsburg Confession in Poland). In western Europe, Lutheran churches emerged at the time of the Reformation in France (in the regions of Alsace-Lorraine and Montbeliard) and in the Netherlands. Today, there are 37 million Lutherans in Europe.

EXPANSION OF LUTHERANISM THROUGH EMIGRATION

From the 17th to the 20th centuries, Lutheranism was brought to North and South America and Australia, as well as to parts of eastern Europe, by millions of immigrants. In North America, Lutheran congregations came together to form a "ministerium" (Pennsylvania and New York) and then numerous synods since the second half of the 18th century. These synods, formed on a regional or ethnic basis, in the 19th century initiated a process of Lutheran cooperation and formation of larger church bodies—a process that eventually led to the creation of the Evangelical Lutheran Church in America in 1988. The more conservative Lutheran Church-Missouri Synod has participated in Lutheran cooperation but has not yet agreed to pulpit and altar fellowship. There are, in addition, a number of smaller Lutheran churches. Lutheranism in Canada is predominantly made up of 20th-century immigrants and is today represented by the Evangelical Lutheran Church in Canada and the Missouri-related Lutheran Church-Canada. In North America there are 8.5 million Lutherans.

In Latin America, Lutheranism is a minority reaching back to the first Lutheran congregations in Latin America's northern parts of Surinam (1741) and Guyana (1743), while larger groups of Lutheran immigrants came to Argentina, Brazil, and Chile during the 19th century. After World War I and II, more groups of European Lutherans came to various countries on this continent. The largest Latin American Lutheran churches today are the Evangelical Church of the Lutheran Confession in Brazil with 700,000 members and the Missouri-related Evangelical Lutheran Church of Brazil. These two churches and smaller Lutheran churches in several other countries presently make up

1.1 million Lutherans in Latin America. About 10,000 Lutherans have moved to and live in the Caribbean region where there has never been Lutheran mission work or major immigration.

German Lutherans who did not accept the imposed union of Lutherans and Reformed in Prussia emigrated in 1838 and 1841 to Australia where they laid the foundations of Lutheranism in their new country that is today represented by the Lutheran Church of Australia. German Lutherans also emigrated in the 18th and 19th centuries to eastern Europe and settled in Russia, Hungary, Romania, Slovakia, and Yugoslavia. During and after World War II, most of the descendants of these Lutheran immigrants were forced to return to Germany where many of them then emigrated to other continents. A small section of the formerly large Lutheran church in Transylvania (Romania) is still living in its homeland. In the territory of the former Soviet Union, ethnic Germans who remained there have reestablished congregations that now make up the geographically largest Lutheran church in the world, the Evangelical Lutheran Church in Russia and Other States.

EXPANSION OF LUTHERANISM THROUGH MISSION

European and North American mission societies began an intensive phase of mission work in the second half of the 19th century. This work led to the formation of Lutheran churches in Africa and Asia that became independent in the 1960s. In Africa, mission work started after 1820 in South Africa and was extended later to the wider southern and eastern African regions. During the 20th century, Lutheranism moved to western Africa. Today, some of the fastest growing Lutheran churches in the world are to be found in Africa. From 1987 to 1999 membership has grown from 5.6 million to 9.7 million. The largest churches are in Tanzania (2.5 million), Ethiopia (2.6 million), and Madagascar (1.5 million). Fairly large or smaller Lutheran churches are now active in most African countries.

In Asia, Lutheran mission work started as early as 1706 in South India with the arrival of Bartholomäus Ziegenbalg. But most Lutheran churches had their beginnings and growth in the second half of the 19th century and in the 20th century. The largest Lutheran missionary involvement was in China until 1951, when it was stopped by the Chinese revolution. In 1930 the Protestant Christian Batak Church in Indonesia was the first church to become independent. This church, like seven other churches in Indonesia that became members of the Lutheran World Federation, was founded by a united mission society in Germany. It has formulated and in 1951 accepted its own confessional document that is considered to be in agreement with the Lutheran confessions. The other Lutheran churches in Asia achieved independence after

World War II. The largest presence among the 6.6 million Lutherans in Asia is found in Indonesia (3.7 million), followed by India (1.6 million), and Papua New Guinea (910,000).

Apart from the special situation in Indonesia, all Lutheran churches in the world have accepted the *Augsburg Confession* and the *Small Catechism* of Martin Luther as part of their confessional basis. Many churches have also accepted the other confessions. These churches are related with one another through many forms of cooperation, exchange, and partnership. Many of them actively participate in the ecumenical movement. Through their participation in the life and work of the Lutheran World Federation, 128 member churches with over 59.4 million members (out of 63.1 million Lutherans altogether) express and practice their worldwide communion and interdependence in faith, life, witness, and service.

LUTHERAN IDENTITY

Today, Lutheranism can be identified by a number of characteristics. First, Lutheranism has moved far beyond its European roots and has become a worldwide communion of Lutheran churches. Second, since the time of the Reformation Lutheranism has occupied within Christianity a middle position between Roman Catholicism/Eastern Orthodoxy and the Reformed/Presbyterian and other Protestant churches. Third, Lutheranism contains within itself a diversity of theological orientations, prefigured by the Gnesio-Lutherans and the Philippists in the 16th century, moving between a stricter or "milder" Lutheranism or between a confessional and a more liberal one. And fourth, such diversity exists also with regard to the institutional types of Lutheran churches: territorial and state churches in Germany and Scandinavia; minority/diaspora churches in other parts of Europe; immigrant churches in Australia, Namibia, and North and South America; and mission churches in Africa and Asia. The organizational and ministerial structures of the different Lutheran churches also vary.

What holds Lutheranism together and provides it with a common profile or identity is the shared commitment to the fundamental trinitarian and Christological dogmas as clarified and defined by the early church and to the Lutheran confessions, especially the *Augsburg Confession* and the *Small Catechism* of Luther. This is accompanied by an ongoing high appreciation of Luther's theology. Based on this tradition and reinterpreted in new times and contexts are fundamental theological and spiritual convictions and forms of expressions. Among them, as regards to their presupposition and basis, are the understanding and use of Holy Scripture, with the Gospel at its center, as the norm of the church's teaching and life and, under this norm, the appreciation and reception of the theological and spiritual traditions of the church since the first centuries. The focus on the historical study and contemporary interpretation of Holy Scripture and the theological tradition of the church led to the practice of intensive theological research, study, and training that has both graced Lutheranism with an extensive academic-scholarly tradition and famous theologians, liberal as well as more conservative, and has burdened it with theological quarrels and divisions.

The theological foundations of Lutheran identity include the confession of the primary and exclusive initiative of the Triune God, Father, Son, and Holy Spirit, as the only way of salvation and eternal life, the central place of the doctrine of justification by faith alone and through grace alone, and the criteriological distinction between the Word of God as law and Gospel. Essential to the Lutheran concept of the church are the constitutive role in the church of the proclamation of the Word and the administration of the sacraments of baptism and the Lord's Supper as the means of grace necessary for salvation. The church, both visible and hidden, is understood as the living, worshiping, and serving community of believers brought together, enlivened, and sanctified by the Holy Spirit and characterized by an emphasis on the priesthood of all believers served by an ordained ministry instituted by God. As regards to the life of the church, a central place is attributed to all forms of Christian education and a highly developed and rich tradition of church music and hymnody, while a great liberty (and diversity) is upheld concerning the institutional structures of the church and such aspects of church life that are considered nonessential (adiaphora).

When it comes to Christian life in the world, it is part of basic Lutheran convictions to affirm the world as God's good creation and to consider the exercise of the secular calling and responsibility of Christians, using their reason and professional competence, as participation in God's sustaining work in the world. Such involvement also includes an impressive heritage and contemporary exercise of social work (diakonia), a concern for human rights, peace and social justice, and one of the most extensive involvements within Christianity in emergency and development aid. A further mark of Lutheranism today is the rediscovery of its ecumenical calling, expressed through active involvement in national and international ecumenical work, especially and so far most significantly through bilateral theological dialogues with other churches and worldwide communions of churches. These dialogues have helped to establish closer relationships with many churches and, in several cases, full fellowship with some of them. At the dawn of a new millennium, Lutheranism shares with the rest of Christianity the challenge to confess its sins and failures in the past and to renew its thinking and life in the present in order to contribute to the future of humanity in accordance with God's purpose. [G.G.]

The Dictionary

– A –

ABSOLUTION. *See* FORGIVENESS.

ADIAPHORA (Gk "indifferent matters"). A term used in Christian history to indicate areas of Christian belief and life that are useful but not essential because they are neither commanded nor forbidden by Christ or Holy Scripture. This concept allowed **Martin Luther** and other reformers to continue certain traditional rites, ceremonies, and customs as long as they served the **Gospel** and could be changed or abolished. However, when the (Leipzig) **Interim** of 1548 demanded the reinstatement of certain **Roman Catholic** rites and practices, these were considered by **Philipp Melanchthon** and others as adiaphora and, accordingly, acceptable. The **Gnesio-Lutherans** protested vigorously: under no circumstances can this be done when the adversaries are attempting to introduce again their false **doctrines** into the Lutheran churches. The debate continued until it was settled by the *Formula of Concord* of 1577: Adiaphora "have been introduced into the church with good intentions for the sake of good order and propriety." But they cannot be accepted "in a period of **persecution** and a case of confession" (*see* STATUS CONFESSIONIS) when such matters of indifference are imposed by those who regard them as essential. The concept of adiaphora has been used throughout Lutheran history until today. [G.G.]

ADVENT. Period in the **church year** leading up to **Christmas**. After Gallican precedents from the fourth century of a fasting period before **Epiphany**, clear reference to the season of Advent comes from the sixth century. Pope Gregory I (590–604) shortened the six-week season to one of four weeks and the *Gelasian Sacramentary* in Rome contained the first Advent liturgy. Between the ninth and 13th centuries this season became generally considered as the beginning of the church year. The Advent season joyfully celebrates, with special emphasis also on Old Testament prophecies, the first coming of Christ in his **incarnation** and looks forward in solemn anticipation to his second appearing for judgment and the fulfillment of redemption. In Lutheran churches the Advent season is observed with a rich hymnology, much **church music**, and many popular **customs**, of which the Advent wreath in homes and churches is the most beloved. *See also* CHRISTOLOGY; HYMN AND HYMNODY. [G.G.]

AFRICA, LUTHERAN CHURCHES IN. Lutheran mission work (*see* MISSION HISTORY) in Africa began in the 19th century—after 1820 in South Africa, about 1860 in Liberia, Eritrea/Ethiopia, and Madagascar, soon after in South-West Africa (Namibia), and after 1880 in (what is today) Tanzania. In the 20th century, mission work was extended to Nigeria (since 1913), Cameroon (since 1920), and other countries. In connection with the emergence of independent African states, especially in the 1960s, the Lutheran churches received their independence. They are marked by a vital church life and strong missionary activity and seek to contribute to the alleviation of the overwhelming social, ethnic, and political problems in their countries. They are in close contacts with their European and North American partner churches and agencies. These partner churches and the **Lutheran World Federation** support them in their work that includes **emergency and development aid**, service to **refugees**, education, theological formation, social and medical services, communication, and inter-Lutheran as well as ecumenical relations.

Some of the fastest growing Lutheran churches in the world are in Africa. From 1987 to 1999 their membership has grown from 5.6 million to over 9.7 million. The largest Lutheran churches on this continent are those of Tanzania (Evangelical Lutheran Church in Tanzania) with 2.5 million members, Ethiopia (Ethiopian Evangelical Church Mekane Yesus, over 2.6 million), and Madagascar (Malagasy Lutheran Church, 1.5 million). Churches with 100,000 to 1 million members can be found in Cameroon (206,000), Democratic Republic of Congo (former Zaire) (136,000), Namibia (740,000), Nigeria (800,000), South Africa (884,000), and Zimbabwe (100,000). There are smaller churches in 15 other African countries. In the midst of armed conflicts, oppressive underdevelopment, and much human suffering, the Lutheran churches in Africa exercise their ministry in word and deed. [G.G.]

AGRICOLA, MICHAEL (c.1510–1557). Lutheran **bishop** and leader of the **Reformation** in Finland. The bishop of Turku, Finland, sent Agricola in 1536 to **Wittenberg** where he began in 1537, influenced by **Martin Luther**, to translate the New Testament into Finnish. In 1539 he returned to Turku and became headmaster of the famous school there until 1548. In that same year, his translation of the New Testament was printed. During the 1540s he introduced the Lutheran Reformation chiefly through his literary activity. Besides the New Testament, he translated from 1551 onwards the Old Testament Psalter and Prophets. He edited a biblical prayer book

(1544), a Finnish manual of **worship** and a missal (1549, taken over from the Swedish one of **Olaus Petri**), and wrote a manual for **pastors** in 1545 as well as other books. Already in 1542 or 1543 he had published an ABC book that became, together with his other publications, the foundation of the written Finnish language. In 1554 Agricola became bishop of Turku where this deeply pious man continued his many activities.

The cautious reformer with his humanistic appreciation of traditional customs and ideas in the church (*see* HUMANISM) helped to reorganize the Finnish church and to renew its worship and life. Thus, the basis was laid for his church to become truly a Finnish church (at a time when Finland was still part of Sweden). The "reformer of Finland," as he is called, and the leading figure for Finnish language and culture died on the journey back from Moscow where he had been sent by the Swedish king on a peace mission between Sweden and Russia. *See also* WORSHIP. [G.G.]

ALTHAUS, PAUL (1888–1966). One of the pioneer leaders in 20th-century **Luther research** and original Lutheran dogmatic theologian, ethicist, preacher, and pastoral counsellor. Althaus concluded his student career in Göttingen (1913) with a *Habilitationschrift* on reason and revelation. He was called as a university professor to Rostock in 1919, then to Erlangen in 1925. He declined subsequent offers from Leipzig, Halle, and Tübingen, remaining loyal to Erlangen and committed to original Luther research and **dogmatics** that would emphasize the interconnections of the doctrines of **creation**, **anthropology**, and the central Lutheran **doctrine** of **justification**, as well as lead in the publication of monographs on the theology and ethics of **Martin Luther**. Althaus was concerned to engage Luther's thought with the contemporary situation. He extended Luther's insight on the sole gracious initiative of **God's** justification of sinners into anthropology and soteriology by emphasizing that a real relationship between God and the saved person results from such justification. Furthermore, Althaus's recapitulation of Luther's **theology** of the **cross** brought the hermeneutical implications of **revelation** and experience into a more mutual relationship.

Althaus's work on other themes (e.g., the **Lord's Supper** and the doctrine of the **church**), proved to be of great ecumenical significance. His **Christology** would lead toward a reemphasis on the historicity of the resurrection of Christ that one sees in the work, for example, of **Wolfhart Pannenberg**. As an ethicist, Althaus commended a theology of natural orders that would rightly employ Luther's **two kingdoms** theology and severely criticize national socialism, though at first he sympathized with Nazism. Althaus was a devoted, careful preacher, committed to his students and an oft sought pastoral counsellor. He thus demonstrated that a careful stewardship of the Lutheran tradition must not become mere reclamation, but careful extension and application to the personal and corporate lives of contemporary humanity. [D.H.L.]

AMSDORF, NIKOLAUS VON (1483–1565). Influential Lutheran reformer. Nikolaus von Amsdorf was born at Torgau, Germany, and studied in Leipzig and **Wittenberg**. Appointed Canon in 1508, he taught theology at Wittenberg and became a follower and soon one of the closest collaborators and friends of **Martin Luther**. In 1519 Amsdorf accompanied Luther to the Leipzig Disputation and in 1521 to Worms (*see* WORMS, DIET OF). In 1524 Amsdorf introduced the **Reformation** in Magdeburg and soon after in several other towns in central and northern Germany. From 1524–1539 he served as **superintendent** in Magdeburg. Elector John Frederick appointed him as the first **evangelical bishop** of Naumburg and Luther installed him in 1542. Amsdorf lost this position five years later (1547) when, for church-political reasons, a Roman Catholic bishop took his place. Amsdorf went to Jena and participated in the founding of the strictly Lutheran university there. He also initiated the Jena edition of Luther's works.

From his Jena base, Amsdorf fought against the **Interim** and those who accepted it (e.g., **Philipp Melanchthon**). He had become a stern defender of pure Lutheran doctrine and was involved in the inner-Lutheran controversies that found their conclusion with the *Formula of Concord* in 1577. His extreme thesis that **good works** are detrimental to salvation was not accepted by the *Formula of Concord*. This representative of the very few reformers who came from the upper class of the nobility was one of the influential leaders of the **Gnesio-Lutheran** movement, fighting for the faithful transmission of the genuine heritage of Luther and his **theology**. The learned and combative Amsdorf died at Eisenach. [G.G.]

ANABAPTISTS (i.e., "rebaptizers"). Term applied by their opponents to several 16th-century groups organized around the **baptism** of mature believers and aimed at a more radical reform of the **church** than the Lutheran and **Reformed** movements had undertaken. These highly diverse groups in Germany, Switzerland, the Netherlands, and Austria (including Moravia) included the so-called mainline Anabaptists, consisting of the Swiss Brethren, Mennonites, and Hutterites, who rejected infant baptism and sought to establish communities of the regenerated according to biblical precepts; the quite different **Spiritualists** who appealed to a direct inspiration by the **Holy Spirit**; the so-called Revolutionaries like the Münsterites who wanted to bring in the **kingdom of God** with the sword; and the so-called Rationalists or Socinians who read Scripture in the light of reason. The first openly celebrated adult baptism (rebaptism) took place at Zürich in 1525. Some radical groups advocated and practiced a social radicalism (**Peasants' War**) and insurrectionary militancy (in Münster and the Netherlands 1534/35) acting in the horizon of apocalyptic expectation, while other groups aimed at total separation from the evil world and its institutions (government, military, and so on) in order to live a life in purity and holiness.

The Lutheran **Reformation** rejected the position of the radical groups and movements because of their refusal to baptize infants, their biblical interpretations in line with their own ideas, claims of direct personal inspiration, and biblically based social revolutionism or social isolationism with its claim to Christian perfection. An imperial mandate (Speyer 1529) made Anabaptism a crime punishable by death. This led to an estimated number of 1,000 to 4,000 martyrs among the several tens of thousands of followers in these groups. *See also* LUTHERAN-BAPTIST RELATIONS AND DIALOGUE. [G.G.]

ANATHEMA (Gk "accursed"). Strongest form of condemnation of heretical **doctrines** and teachers. Since the beginnings of Christianity, forms of rejection, condemnation, and exclusion of teaching and teachers were used when these were regarded as contradicting the true **faith** of the **Gospel** (cf. Gal 1:8f.; 1 Cor 16:22). This condemnation was seen as a means to preserve both the purity of faith and the bonds of community. The early church was in constant struggle against **heresies**, and after about 300 A.D. the pronouncement of an anathema by a synod or council, implying excommunication, was formalized. The Lutheran confessions (*see* CONFESSIONS, LUTHERAN) contain several condemnations of early heretical teachings from the first centuries and of contemporary **Roman Catholic**, **Anabaptist**, **Spiritualist**, and **Reformed** teachings. Lutheran Orthodoxy (*see* ORTHODOXY, LUTHERAN) enjoyed condemning contrary teaching, while **Enlightenment** and **Pietism** abhorred doctrinal controversies.

The German **church struggle** in the 1930s faced the challenge of false teaching, and the ***Barmen Theological Declaration*** (1934) of the **Confessing Church** contains a number of anathemas. Today, the need to reject false teaching, after careful consideration, is still acknowledged. However, there is also the common declaration of Pope Paul VI and (ecumenical) Patriarch Athenagoras (in 1965) in which the mutual excommunications of 1054 were "erased from the memory" of the church. Likewise, in official ecumenical dialogues of Lutherans with **Baptists**, Reformed, and Roman Catholics the conclusion is drawn that the doctrinal condemnations of the 16th century no longer apply to the present teaching of the partners. *See also* ORTHODOXY, LUTHERAN. [G.G.]

ANDREAE, JAKOB (1528–1590). Prominent German Lutheran reformer. Born in Tübingen, Andreae was 17 years old when he graduated from the University of Tübingen and was ordained one year later. He became pastor (1553) and later **superintendent** at Göppingen and assisted in introducing the **Reformation** in several cities and territories during the 1550s and 1560s. He participated in numerous colloquies with **Reformed**, **Roman Catholic**, and **Anabaptist** theologians and was involved in several efforts to end intra-**Protestant** controversies. In 1561 Andreae became professor, provost, and chancellor of the University of Tübingen where he remained until his death.

In 1569 Andreae joined **Martin Chemnitz** and Nicholas Selnecker (among others) to become the leading force in the efforts to overcome the bitter theological struggles within the Lutheran movement. In 1573, after several unsuccessful initiatives in this direction had been undertaken, Andreae preached his famous six sermons on the disputed issues (such as **law and Gospel**, **justification**, the **Lord's Supper**, **free will**, **good works**, and **adiaphora**). These sermons set in motion a process towards a solution. They formed the basis for a series of documents that eventually became the *Formula of Concord* (1577), for which Andreae also prepared a short version, the *Epitome* (1576). This untiringly active theologian was an outstanding and competent proponent of the Reformation and of Lutheran unity. [G.G.]

ANGLICANISM. *See* LUTHERAN-ANGLICAN RELATIONS AND DIALOGUE.

ANTHROPOLOGY. The theological definition and **doctrine** of what it means to be human. **Martin Luther's** theological view of the human being must be understood in the context of his doctrine of **creation**, having its origin, of course, in the biblical affirmation that **God** created humankind as good and gave humanity a special place and **vocation** in the world. It is also intimately and necessarily connected with the doctrines of **sin** and **justification**. Luther's greatest emphases about the distinctiveness of humanity lay in his view that the human being bears the image of God (*imago dei*). For Luther, this image was divine inasmuch as it bore the possibilities of immortality, reasoning, and understanding (the latter two were denoted in the Latin *ratio*). This latter capacity of *ratio* indeed was what demarked humans as having a special place between angels and beasts; it also was an integral predicate in the notion of orders of creation (*see* NATURAL LAW). Furthermore, bearing (and reflecting) the image of God means for the human being that its abiding energy is always outside the human being per se and comes from God. The authentic or full human being, in other words, is "eccentric"; life comes from God (*see* PROVIDENCE, DIVINE), while **sin**, degeneracy, and death are consequences—as **Augustine** put it—of the human being turned in on itself (*curvatus in se*) in sheer egocentricity. And, as having life from outside themselves so to serve others in appropriate Christian life, human beings are also God's representatives, energized as communal beings in the **church** for the sake of the world (*see* CHURCH AND WORLD).

While Luther understood his (unsystematic) doctrine as having ontological or metaphysical consequences—and this remained so through early generations of **Lutheranism** through the period of Lutheran **Orthodoxy**— 19th-century Lutheranism, typically, gave theological anthropology more of a moral than ontological cast. The ecclesial character of the intended human being was replaced by an understanding of the human individual as a person morally guided by the example of Jesus Christ (*see* IMMANUEL KANT; LIBERALISM). This nascent individualism was exacerbated by Liberalism's tendency to interpret the *imago dei* with more emphasis on *ratio* as "reasoning" than otherwise, and to the relative exclusion of **communion** and immortality. Furthermore, there was a tendency to interpret the human being as a dichotomous sum of matter and spirit, rather than the unitary and integrated being of matter, soul, and spirit that Luther advocated, in continuity with Augustine. More contemporary representatives of this latter train of thought include Paul Tillich, **Dietrich Bonhoeffer**, and **Wolfhart Pannenberg**, who, having borrowed significantly from contemporary German and American **social sciences**, particularly emphasize the "exocentricity" (i.e., something being constituted from outside the self) required for full human health. Expanding upon these near and real contemporaries, Lutheran theologian Philip Hefner has written of the human being as the "created cocreator" who is unitary in terms of origin and destiny, having been created from the communion of God the Trinity (*see* TRINITY, DOGMA OF) for communion with God, humanity, and all creation.

Significant new challenges face Christian theological anthropology, especially from the globalistic alliance of **technology**, materialism, and consumerism. New technological applications derived from genetic and information sciences (*see* SCIENCE AND CHRISTIANITY), like psychopharmaceuticals, gene therapy, and cloning, pose severe questions to human self-understanding as bearers of the *imago dei* who live in justified **faith**, hope, and love. We can be tempted to understand ourselves in reduced ways as creatures merely designed by the "blind watchmaker" of nature for survival through feeding, fighting, and reproducing. Even what we understand as love has been argued to have only biochemical bases. Such reductionistic arguments are easily extended into neo-Darwinian rationales for all sorts of sinful activities like sexism, racism, and ecological insensitivity (*see* ETHICS). The specifically Christian challenge will be to maintain and commend the perspective that God intends the human being to be transcending, communal, and justly creative, employing the fullness of gifts given to the human being in its distinct sphere of freedom. [D.H.L.]

ANTICHRIST. The enemy of Christ and the Christians. The idea that at the end-time a mythological, despotic pseudomessiah will appear attempting to rob **God** and his Messiah of power and authority and, thus, claim the place of God, has roots in Old Testament and late Jewish-apocalyptic thinking. Holy Scripture speaks about the Antichrist as both the great enemy of God at the end of time and as a present reality. The Antichrist (or Antichrists) is an existential threat through activity even within the **church**, and is personified by all false messiahs, and by those who tempt the church to follow the path of glory instead of Christ. Since the 13th century certain popes were identified with the Antichrist because of their unchristian lives.

Martin Luther became "famous" for applying the term Antichrist to the papacy (not to popes personally). Since the mid-1520s Luther saw in the **papacy** a tyranny deserving of the title because the papacy had usurped authority over and above the **Word of God**. The pope had thereby elevated himself to be Lord over the church in the place of Christ and against Christ. The other side of the papacy's tyrannical power was its claim to supremacy over kings and nations. Luther and **Philipp Melanchthon** both express this interpretation in the Lutheran confessions. Lutheran **theology** in the 19th century spoke more reluctantly about the papacy as forerunner of the Antichrist, and some theologians began to refrain altogether from applying this terminology to the papacy. Today, such references are interpreted as an expression of a particular historical context and conflict. *See also* CONFESSIONS, LUTHERAN. [G.G.]

ANTI-SEMITISM. *See* JEWISH-LUTHERAN RELATIONS.

APARTHEID. *See* RACISM.

APOLOGY OF THE AUGSBURG CONFESSION (1530/31). **Philipp Melanchthon's** defense of the *Augsburg Confession* (*CA*) that became a confession itself. At the **Diet of Augsburg** in 1530, the **evangelical** estates presented their *Augsburg Confession*. The **Roman Catholic** party responded with its *Confutation*, which was regarded by Emperor Charles V as a convincing rebuttal of the *CA*. The evangelical side refused to accept the *Confutation*. Instead, Melanchthon prepared this detailed defense of the *CA* and critique of the *Confutation* that was presented to the diet on September 22, 1530. The emperor did not accept it. After having finally received a copy of the *Confutation*, Melanchthon wrote an expanded and revised version of his *Apology of the Augsburg Confession* that was published in April–May 1531. Together with the *CA*, the *Apology* was accepted as an official confession in several **church orders** and became part of the collection of Lutheran confessions, the *Book of Concord*. The *Apology* follows the structure of the 28 articles of the *CA* and is an important commentary on it. It is written in the form of a theological treatise and has its center in article 4 (over 60 pages) on the fundamental **Reformation** doctrine of **justification** by **faith** and **grace** alone. *See also* CONFESSIONS, LUTHERAN. [G.G.]

APOSTOLIC CREED. *See* CREEDS.

APOSTOLICITY. Refers to the teaching or practice that is in accord with the teachings of the apostles. Apostolicity avers that the witness of the apostles and prophets, to whom the **revelation** of Christ was first directed, are foundational for the **church** (cf. Eph 2:20 and 3:5). Lutherans emphasize that the teaching of the apostles, centering on Christ and the **Gospel**, is to be distinguished from the apostles themselves, and that it is Christ and the Gospel that are normative for subsequent teaching and practice. While this intersects with the topics of Gospel, biblical authority, and the affirmation of **tradition**, apostolicity also pertains to how the church currently reflects upon and translates the apostolic tradition into contemporary practice. Apostolicity denotes how a church actively exhibits itself as Christ's church in changing historical circumstances, that the church is accountable to its apostolic tradition, and lives from that tradition. Thus, apostolicity includes the recognition that the church will necessarily decide at given and changing times what is and is not apostolic, and how apostolicity is reaffirmed, and so decides upon **dogma** and **doctrine**. *See also* BIBLE, AUTHORITY OF; CHRISTOLOGY. [D.H.L.]

APOSTOLIC SUCCESSION. The succession of episcopal consecration and **ordination** as well as the succession of the **church** in the apostolic **faith**. From the late first century Clement of Rome's concept that the **ministry** of the church arose from and was authenticated by a continuous line of **bishops** whose authority could be traced linearly back to the original apostles. This continues to be, with some modification, the teaching and practice of the **Roman Catholic**, **Orthodox**, and **Anglican** churches. The Lutheran understanding of apostolic succession refers, however, to the succession of the **Gospel** through the church, first explicitly attested by the apostles and thereafter guaranteed by the **Holy Spirit** at the ordination of **pastors** to **Word** and **sacrament** ministry. **Martin Luther** alluded to the foundation for this pneumatological understanding in his Lectures on Genesis, in which he wrote that the **Word** alone brings the apostolic church into existence. Where there is the Word, there is the church, though the presence of a form of the latter does not necessarily ensure the existence of the former. Therefore, Lutherans affirm that there is a succession of the apostolic tradition— of **faith**, **worship**, life, **mission**, and service—in the church as a whole.

In addition to the primary understanding of succession, the Lutheran confessions do express openness, however, to the continuation of the succession of bishops. This is a narrower understanding of apostolic succession, to be affirmed under the condition that the bishops support the Gospel and are ready to ordain **evangelical** preachers. This form of succession, for example, was continued by the Church of Sweden (which included Finland) at the time of the **Reformation**. Today, the concept of apostolic succession is a major issue in ecumenical dialogue. In **Lutheran-Anglican relations and dialogue**, an understanding of this succession as sign and instrument of the unity and continuity of the church is emphasized. *See also* CONFESSIONS, LUTHERAN. [D.H.L.]

AQUINAS, THOMAS. *See* THOMAS AQUINAS.

ARNDT, JOHANN (1555–1621). German **pastor**, theologian, and author of devotional works, who has been called the "Father of **Pietism**." Arndt attended the University of Helmstedt to study medicine, an interest that lasted throughout his life. His interests and problems with his own health, however, diverted his studies to **theology**, which he continued at **Wittenberg**, Strasbourg, and Basel. Ordained in 1583 to serve the parish at Badeborn, he was deposed in 1590 when he refused the Reformed duke's orders to omit prayers of exorcism from the baptismal service. He then served **parishes** at Quedlinburg (where he began a life-long friendship with **Johann Gerhard**), Braunschweig, and Eisleben, before becoming *Generalsuperintendent* in Celle in 1611.

He is best known as the author of *True Christianity*, which he expanded from four books to six and which has been, except for **Martin Luther's** *Small Catechism* and **hymnody**, the greatest sourcebook for Lutheran devotions. Among his other works, *The Little Paradise Garden of Christian Virtues* and his postils have also been influential. Arndt edited the devotional work and developed the devotional thought of Luther, Tauler, Thomas à Kempis, and the *Theologia Deutsch*. With his appeal to the emotions and expectation of the active, virtuous life, he clearly foreshadowed the work of Philipp Jakob Spener and **August Hermann Francke**. His major theological contribution, in the fifth book of *True Christianity*, clarifies the concept of the *unio mystica*. Like Luther, he considers the **mystical union** of the believer with Christ as the beginning, rather than as the goal, of the Christian life. Arndt places greater emphasis than the reformer, however, on love, expressed in service to the neighbor, as the necessary fruit of this union. *See also* ORTHODOXY, LUTHERAN. [M.O.]

ART, LUTHERAN ATTITUDE TO. There have been Lutherans who, except when considering **Worship and the Arts**, have held a rather negative attitude toward the arts, believing that paying attention to art was poor **stewardship**. While such activities as attending the opera or writing a novel might themselves neither nurture nor destroy **faith**, they were still to be avoided in a world of finite resources, when they took time and energy away from caring for the poor or proclaiming the **Gospel**. Most arguments against this position have been based on the place of the arts in **worship** or proclamation. That is, the arts provide not only for the expression of faith, but also for the clear, honest description of the human condition in all its ramifications, an understanding that is the precondition for faithful proclamation. In other words, the arts are valued because they can proclaim both **law and Gospel**.

But a consistent Lutheran position will value art even beyond such homiletical, liturgical, and devotional uses. The Lutheran understanding of **creation** implies that beauty, **truth**, and other earthly delights are not simply temptations that lead away from **God**; rather, they are gifts whose enjoyment God intended in creation, and that sin never entirely mars. It is further true that, if the incarnation is a paradigm for all of God's self-revelation (*see* CHRISTOLOGY), then the created order, most certainly including human fabrications, must be treated with respect and joy, not only as the gift of the Creator, but also as a potential bearer of the **Word**. Thus, the occupation of artist is a calling (*see* WORK), not because it involves a higher, more direct communication with God, but because it is, like other occupations, a weaving together of our lives for mutual benefit by the **grace** of the Creator. Even when Lutheran theologians have not affirmed this understanding, Lutheran artists, from **Johann Sebastian Bach** in music to **Kaj Munk** in drama to **Johann Gottfried Herder** and Selma Lagerlöf in **literature**, have practiced it. *See also* CHURCH MUSIC; CULTURE; MUSIC IN THE LUTHERAN CHURCH. [M.O.]

ASIA, LUTHERAN CHURCHES IN. Early Lutheran missionary initiatives (*see* MISSION HISTORY) started in 1706 in Tranquebar, South India, but most Lutheran churches on the Asian continent had their beginning and growth in the second part of the 19th century (e.g., China 1840s, Indonesia 1861, and Japan 1892) and in the 20th century. Several of them grew out of the mission work of United churches in Germany. One of the churches with this united background, the Protestant Christian Batak Church in Indonesia, was the first church to become independent in 1930, while other Lutheran churches achieved independence after World War II. The Batak church was also the first church in the modern mission movement that formulated its own official Confession (1951). It was considered to be in agreement with the Lutheran confessions (*see* CONFESSIONS, LUTHERAN) and enabled the acceptance of this church into the **Lutheran World Federation** (1952). China was the country with the largest Lutheran missionary presence in Asia during the first half of the 20th century (600 missionaries). Since 1920 the Lutheran Church of China brought together the different mission groups. It had over 100,000 members in 1951 when it was cut off from the Lutheran community after the Communist takeover in China. The church was integrated into the Communist-imposed and euphemistically termed "postdenominational" Three-Self-Movement and has lost its independence.

Living in the midst of other strong religious traditions, the growth of churches in Asia has been less rapid than in **Africa**. This situation has challenged Lutheran churches in several Asian countries to engage in

interreligious dialogue and to seriously consider their relationship to Asian history and culture (*see* INCULTURATION). In a number of countries, several Lutheran churches exist side by side because of ethnic and linguistic diversity. These churches, even the very small ones, have developed remarkable social and educational activity far beyond their constituency. The largest presence among Asia's 6.6 million Lutherans can be found in Indonesia, which has eight churches with 3.7 million members, among them the largest Lutheran church in Asia, the Protestant Christian Batak Church with 2.9 million members. Second comes India. Its 10 Lutheran churches with 1.6 million members together form the United Evangelical Lutheran Church in India. The two Lutheran churches in Papua New Guinea have 910,000 members. Smaller Lutheran churches exist in Bangladesh, Hong Kong, Japan, Korea, Malaysia, Myanmar, Philippines, Taiwan, and Thailand. [G.G.]

ATONEMENT. The redemptive work of Christ, by which humankind is made again to be "at one" with **God**. There is a variety of interpretations of the work of Christ, which contemporaries view as having evolved from different primary interpretations in the New Testament itself. Lutheran thinking about the atonement today is characterized, however, by the combination of an eschatological (*see* ESCHATOLOGY) perspective with **Martin Luther's theology** of the **cross**. Yet for Lutheran grammar, atonement—like **justification**—is "done" in and with words about it; it cannot be allowed to remain as "theory," but assumes the character of event even while it is necessarily "theorized."

If majority opinion counts, Anselm of Canterbury's (1033–1109) theory of vicarious satisfaction stands as the de facto, though never ecumenically ratified, dogma of the atonement. By asking why God had to become man (*Cur deus homo?*), Anselm was the first to recognize that one must probe why the crucifixion was necessary. His answer was that though God is **love**, God's mercy simply could not negate the law of God in a unilateral judgement of **forgiveness** upon all the **sin** of humanity. Furthermore, the consequences of sin in the universe need redress. Since humankind could not provide the redress or compensation, God had to provide it in his own person of the God-Man, thus bringing the human compensation for sin into communication with divine mercy in the substitute person of the Son of God, Jesus Christ. The Anselmian concept has come to be called the "objective" theory of the atonement, because it places the atoning work outside human possibility.

Because of scholastic arguments in favor of human **free will**, however, the Lutheran reformers accented a forensic side to **justification** that became more juridical than Anselm's theory. In this climate, stronger emphases on the substitutionary character of the atonement and the satisfaction of God's wrath were inserted into theology. Early Protestant orthodoxy, for example in the work of **Johann Gerhard**, distinguished between Christ's active and passive suffering; in addition to his passively suffering under divine law and wrath, Christ was also interpreted to fulfill the law actively in his life for humankind. Atonement theory in Lutheran **Orthodoxy** finally reached its fullest expression with the idea of the threefold office (*triplex munus*) of Christ (*see* CHRISTOLOGY) as the ultimate Prophet, Priest, and King, though in the "post orthodoxy" period this codification was much criticized.

With the atonement theory of Albrecht Ritschl (1822–1889), we see the most influential of Lutheran **Liberalism**. For him, the atoning work of Jesus lay in the fact that in him God took the final historical step with humankind in founding the church-kingdom, in which humans are reconciled to God. In this community, the consciousness of human sin is intensified as is the greater love of God. So atonement, for Ritschl, is in the perfect revelation and religion of Jesus. This liberal stress on the love of God, nevertheless, commended Jesus more as a hero, and accommodated the biblical witness to the religious sentiment of the times. Early postliberal Lutherans argued that God's **holiness** gave shape to God's love, and established criteria for divine **justice**, all of which must be met in an adequate atonement theory. In brief, the category of the "moral" replaced what stood in Liberalism as feeling or sentiment.

It is the Swedish Lutheran theologian Gustaf Aulén (1879–1977) who most intentionally steers this course in his famous model of the Christus Victor, wherein Christ triumphs over the powers of sin and evil and releases humankind from its bondage. Aulén's model accents that it is God who has done all the work, and that God is both reconciler and reconciled, the giver and receiver of sacrifice, and humankind's only liberator. As popular as this model was for a time, it nevertheless could not overcome the criticism that its dramatic, mythological imagery could not communicate to the modern mind. It did provide some inspiration and impetus, though, to subsequent atonement theories—as in **liberation theology**—wherein believers would be conscienticized to politically seize upon the freedom that God has already won for them.

A renewal of **Luther research** that paralleled Aulén's work recaptured Martin Luther's original insights of the "happy exchange" between Christ and Christians and the "theology of the **cross**," however. These foci are the subjects of contemporary theological construction, especially in the work of Gerhard Forde and **Wolfhart Pannenberg**. The theology of the cross, as Luther put it, redirected the question of atonement from what must happen for God to be "satisfied" to what must and can happen for God to get through to humankind. Thus the "great reversal": God in Christ gives himself on the cross, in history, so that humankind is forgiven and made God's own. While historical, this is also an eschatological event, because it both issues from God in God's eternity and its consequences will not be fully consummated until the last days (*see* ESCHATOLOGY). Even so, what is a down payment on the future is also an historical fact: A real exchange of God's life for the human curse is made. Humans are thus reclaimed as God's own people. Thus, the central matter in the Lutheran perspective is that the objective work of God done for humankind historically with the cross and **resurrection** is an intensively objective occasion that, with equal intensive subjectivity, creates **faith** in the hearer. When this faith occurs, God is indeed "satisfied," atonement is "done," and the believer is moved by God's love to live the life described by **sanctification**. [D.H.L.]

AUGSBURG, DIETS OF (1518–1555). Six assemblies of the estates of the (German) Holy Roman Empire called by the emperor. Emperor Maximilian I (1483–1519) introduced the diets as a regular institution within the imperial constitution. During the **Reformation** period, they became the most important occasions for dealing with issues of the empire. The three constituent groups of the diets were electors, princes, and, with lesser authority, free imperial cities. There were 20 diets between 1518 and 1555. Four of the six diets held at Augsburg were especially significant for the development of the Lutheran churches. At the first in 1518 **Martin Luther** was interrogated by Cardinal Cajetan, the papal legate at the diet. Luther refused to recant. The second was in 1525/26. The third in 1530 saw the presentation of the *Augsburg Confession* of the Lutheran princes and cities to Emperor Charles V and its Roman response, the *Confutation* (*see* APOLOGY OF THE AUGSBURG CONFESSION). The fourth in 1548 prepared the Augsburg **Interim**, the unsuccessful attempt at a religious settlement. The fifth took place in 1550/51. Finally, it was at the sixth diet in 1555 that a settlement was reached that legally recognized **Roman Catholicism** and Lutheranism as the two religions of the empire. *See also* AUGSBURG, RELIGIOUS PEACE OF. [G.G.]

AUGSBURG, RELIGIOUS PEACE OF (1555). Political settlement of religious issues and struggles in the German empire. At the Augsburg diet of 1555 (*see* AUGSBURG, DIETS OF) a peace agreement was reached between Ferdinand I (brother of Emperor Charles V) and the electors representing the "Estates belonging to the Augsburg Confession." Lutheranism (i.e., the adherents of the *Augsburg Confession*) and **Roman Catholicism** (but no other confessions) were legally recognized as the two religions of the empire. This settlement included the famous provision that in each territory the subjects had to follow the religion of their ruler: the principle *cuius regio, eius religio*, "whoever rules, his religion." Other provisions were that Roman Catholic spiritual jurisdiction in Lutheran territories was suspended and that in the free imperial cities both religions, if already established, could continue. People who did not accept the religion of their land had to emigrate. Catholic spiritual princes (bishops) who changed their religion would lose their possessions and privileges.

The settlement provided Lutherans with legal security, but any further advance was checked. The confessional lines were clearly drawn according to territorial lines. Thus, the territorial character of religion—and not tolerance—was strengthened. The system of Lutheran territorial churches, still recognizable today, came into existence together with the reinforced religious authority and governance of princes and magistrates in their lands. The Religious Peace of Augsburg was the most permanent settlement of confessional coexistence in the 16th and 17th centuries until the Peace of Westphalia in 1648. *See also* CHURCH POLITY; THIRTY YEARS' WAR. [G.G.]

AUGSBURG CONFESSION (*Confessio Augustana* [*CA*], 1530). Most central and important Lutheran confession. In 1530 Emperor Charles V summoned an imperial diet to take place at Augsburg, Germany. Its purpose was to establish a united front against the Turks by overcoming the religious and political division in the empire. Both sides were asked to present their positions. The **evangelical** party asked **Philipp Melanchthon** to prepare a document that would include in a first part basic doctrinal statements and in a second part a defense of reforms that had been introduced in Lutheran territories and cities. On June 25, 1530, the German text of what was to become the *Augsburg Confession* was read in front of the emperor, the princes, and the representatives of free cities. The Roman Catholic side responded with its *Confutation* to which Melanchthon reacted with a detailed *Apology of the Augsburg Confession*. The *CA* was signed by seven princes and the representatives of two free cities. It was gradually accepted by the Lutheran estates and their churches as their public **confession** of **faith** and was considered as the central confession within the collection of Lutheran confessions. In 1555 the *CA* received legal status in the empire as the basic document of one of the two Christian religions legally recognized in the empire: the Roman Catholic Church and the estates and churches of the Augsburg Confession. In 1540 Melanchthon produced a revised version of the *CA*, the so-called *Altered Augsburg Confession*. The **Formula of Concord**, however, declared the text of 1530 to be the authoritative one.

In line with its original purpose, the content and language of the *CA* emphasize the agreement of the evangelical teaching with the biblical witness and the faith tradition of the church through the centuries. Today, the *CA* is seen as an **ecumenical** text and is, together with **Martin Luther's** *Small Catechism*, the most widely accepted Lutheran confession. Some Lutheran churches refer to the *Augsburg Confession* in their name. *See also*

AUGSBURG, DIETS OF; AUGSBURG, RELIGIOUS PEACE OF; *BOOK OF CONCORD*; CONFESSIONS, LUTHERAN. [G.G.]

AUGUST, ELECTOR OF SAXONY (1526–1586). Prince who played a major role in the consolidation of Lutheranism in Germany. August became elector of Saxony in 1553. He reformed in an exemplary manner the economy, agriculture, and the forest and mining administration of his lands and he supported the arts. He assumed a position of leadership in German Lutheranism and helped to bring about the **Religious Peace of Augsburg** (1555). When **Crypto-Calvinists** gained influence in his territories, he removed them (1574). In order to protect Lutheranism from Calvinism and to bring an end to theological controversies within the Lutheran movement, he supported the process leading up to the *Formula of Concord* (1577) and urged its wide subscription. On June 25, 1580, the 50th anniversary of the *Augsburg Confession*, the *Book of Concord* containing the collection of the Lutheran confessions for which August had secured many signatures, was presented at Dresden. Six years later August died in Dresden. *See also* CONFESSIONS, LUTHERAN. [G.G.]

AUGUSTINE (354–430). Bishop of Hippo in North Africa and one of the great theological teachers of the Christian church. His theology and writings had an extraordinary influence throughout the Middle Ages and on **Reformation** thinking, especially on **Martin Luther's theology**. It was primarily Augustine's theology of **grace**, but also aspects of his teaching on the **sacraments**, the **ministry**, and the **church** that had such an impact on the theological perspectives of the reformers. Luther became acquainted with Augustinian thought during his time as a member of the order of Augustinian hermits. He read Augustine widely and used 35 of Augustine's writings during the preparation of his own lectures and writings in 1509/10. While preparing his lectures on the Letter to the Romans, Luther was particularly interested in Augustine's interpretation of St. Paul as help for his own interpretation. Later, Luther referred to Augustine mainly to confirm his own theology and he used the great theologian selectively, sometimes out of context. Beyond Luther, the Augustinian tradition left its mark on the thinking of many reformers, including Lutheran, **Reformed**, and even radical ones (among others: **John Calvin**, **Ulrich Zwingli**, and **Andreas Karlstadt**). [G.G.]

AUSTRALIA, LUTHERAN CHURCHES IN. The earliest beginnings of a Lutheran presence in Australia go back to three groups of immigrants from Germany that came in 1837/38. These groups were accompanied by a few missionaries. However, the first organized Lutheran **emigration** to Australia was provoked by the imposed **union** between Lutheran and Reformed in Prussia in 1817 (Frederick Wilhelm III). Two groups of Lutheran "dissidents" emigrated with their pastors to South Australia in 1838 and 1841. They formed **congregations** and schools, then synods, and after theological disputes with one another, founded the United Evangelical Lutheran Church in Australia in 1921 and in 1944 the Evangelical Lutheran Church of Australia. After World War II, Lutheran immigrants joined the two churches. They undertook **mission** work among Australian Aboriginals and in Papua New Guinea. After long negotiations, the two churches united in 1966 and formed the Lutheran Church of Australia. The church is actively engaged in educational and social work and has a number of Aboriginal congregations. There are contacts and exchanges with several Lutheran churches in Asia and a series of important theological dialogues with the **Anglican**, **Reformed**, **Roman Catholic**, and Uniting churches in Australia have been undertaken and are continued. The Lutheran Church of Australia has 94,000 members. *See also* DIALOGUES, BILATERAL. [G.G.]

AUTHORITY. Authority in the **church** to lead and govern its life. (This entry is complemented by the one on **teaching authority**). In the New Testament, we encounter a mix of personal charismatic authority of apostles and leaders and the beginnings of institutional authority. The expansion and consolidation of the early church necessarily led to a formalization both of personal authority to lead the churches, exercised by **bishops**, and of institutional authority to express and maintain the unity of the church through synods and councils (*see* COUNCILS, ECUMENICAL), **church discipline**, and the beginnings of **canon law**. The Middle Ages saw a continuing increase of spiritual as well as secular power of the **papacy**.

The **Reformation** and especially **Martin Luther** came into direct conflict with the exercise of papal authority and radically criticized the late medieval system of ecclesiastical power. The right "hierarchy" of authority had to be reestablished with the supreme authority belonging to the **Word of God** and its application through the proclamation of the Word, the administration of the **sacraments**, and the exercise of the **office of the keys** (*see* CHURCH DISCIPLINE). **Church orders** in the Lutheran territories ordered the life of the churches. Bishops, **superintendents**, and **pastors** exercised leadership in **congregations** and churches. Congregations had the right to call and dismiss pastors. The 16th and 17th centuries saw in some Lutheran churches the beginnings of synodical forms of ecclesiastical authority, while in many cases the territorial princes continued to carry out (through consistories) administrative authority (*see* SUMMUS EPISCOPUS).

Today, authority in Lutheran churches is carried out by synodical bodies, church councils, bishops' conferences, and the different ordained ministries. Institutionalized authority, often bureaucratized, finds decreasing acceptance by church members, while they appreciate authority legitimized by competence and spiritual authenticity. *See also* CHURCH POLITY. [G.G.]

AWAKENING, LUTHERAN. The diverse, global reactions to **Enlighten-ment** rationalism. The Lutheran Awakening dominated church life throughout the 19th century, not only in the university and study, but also in the pulpit, the pew, the home, and beyond. While hardly a unified movement, it was marked by a desire to return to confessional subscription, fervent rather than purely rational **faith**, and movements for social improvement and **evangelism**. Its leadership included such varied personages as Claus Harms, **Theodor Fliedner**, **Samuel Simon Schmucker**, **Hans Nielsen Hauge**, and **Nicolai Grundtvig**. It should not be confused with the American waves of "Great Awakenings." The Lutheran Awakening, rather, is a part of the great international intellectual, artistic, and practical movement that has been labeled as "romanticism."

Germany led the way in the Lutheran Awakening in which the triumph over Napoléon Bonaparte and the national rise in spirit that accompanied it seems to have played almost as much a part as the ennui with the Enlightenment, of which the early Napoléon was so much the embodiment. At the beginning of the movement, Friederich Schleiermacher gave encouragement to renewed attention to the place of the affect in faith, the underlying unity of Christianity, and the place of Christological faith, rather than human religiosity, as the center of the theology. On the other hand, Claus Harms with his striking call to confessional arms at the 300th anniversary of the posting of the *Ninety-five Theses* began a confessional revival that gave shape to Lutheranism around the world (*see* NEO-LUTHERANISM). Academically, the Lutheran Awakening in Germany found expression in two schools—"Repristination," which looked to a return to 17th-century orthodoxy, and "Erlangen," centered at the university of the same name, which took modern critical tools and Hegelian historical thought more seriously. The Awakening, however, did not only express itself in a revival of Orthodoxy, but in a return to the best of Pietism as well. The movement saw an explosion in hymnody and devotional literature for home use. Furthermore, the ventures for evangelism and social improvement of such institutions as Halle (*see* FRANCKE, AUGUST HERMANN) were imitated and surpassed, with the formation of **mission societies**, communities of **deaconesses** and **deacons**, orphanages, schools, and hospitals.

In Scandinavia, the Awakening was linked most strongly with the nationalist folk movements. In Norway, Hans N. Hauge was the most famous representative of a lay-led revival of church life, setting a commitment to **mission** and the daily practice of faith against the more ethereal and passive teachings of **Rationalism**. While the orthodox party disagreed with Haugeans on the clerical office and the centrality of objective faith, they formed a united front in opposition to the Enlightenment and in support of missions and the establishment of institutions for social improvement. The

Awakening in Denmark also benefited from the dynamic tension between two schools. Grundtvig was the exponent of an optimistic faith, linked very strongly with the revival of folk culture. **Søren Aabye Kierkegaard**, on the other hand, exemplified a dark, almost individualist appropriation of the **Gospel**. Both rejected the easy optimism of Rationalism, one in favor of a continued growth in faith under the leading of the living faith of the congregation, the other in favor of the heroic leap of the knight of faith.

American Lutherans were touched by the Awakening as well. Certainly the groups of immigrants who came during the 19th century continued the loyalties and understandings they had expressed in Europe. The followers of Harms, **Johan Konrad Wilhelm Löhe**, Fliedner, Hauge, Grundtvig, and many others brought to the New World the renewed liveliness as well as the polemics of their fatherlands. But the Awakening affected older, established groups as well. The confessionalism, piety, and commitment to evangelism of the Tennessee Synod were already remarkable in the 1820s. William Passavant, **Charles Porterfield Krauth**, Henry Eyster Jacobs, and many others were not simply students of contemporary Europe, but drank from the same sources as their continental and immigrant contemporaries. Even S. S. Schmucker's American Lutheranism may be seen, not as a betrayal of neoconfessionalism (which it predated), but as a particularly contextualized expression of the Lutheran Awakening. *See also* CONFESSIONS, LUTHERAN; ORTHODOXY, LUTHERAN. [M.O.]

– B –

BACH, JOHANN SEBASTIAN (1685–1750). One of the most famous composers of all times and the most significant Lutheran church musician. Bach was a Lutheran by conviction and served his church as a composer of an enormous number and wide variety of short and long pieces of **church music**. Born in Eisenach, Germany, he became in 1703 the organist at a church in Arnstadt, Thuringia, and after four years (1707) took a similar position in Mühlhausen. In 1708 the duke of Weimar made him court organist and in 1714 concertmaster. In 1717 Bach followed a call to the court of the prince of Anhalt-Köthen as conductor of the orchestra there. From 1723 until his death he served as cantor at St. Thomas in Leipzig and director of music of this town.

Significant for the musical history of the Lutheran church—and beyond— are his many **cantatas** for all Sundays of the year and other occasions, his masses, motets, **oratorios**, passions, **hymns**, and **chorale**-related organ music. The selection or writing of texts for these works reflect the influence of Lutheran Orthodoxy and the beginnings of Pietism upon his religious orientation. Most of his church music was written for worship services and consciously intended to be a form of proclamation. His motto, *Soli Deo gloria*, witnesses to this basic conviction concerning his work, even for the last two decades of his life when with contrapuntal artifice "absolute music" like *Art of the Fugue*, *Goldberg Variations*, *Welltempered Clavier II*, and *A Musical Offering* was at the center of his creativity. Sometimes called the "fifth evangelist," Bach was brought back to wider audiences in the 19th century by the great composer of the Romantic period, Felix Mendelsohn-Bartholdy, and since then has seen an even wider and truly international renaissance. Bach is one of the eminent contributions of Lutheranism to humanity's **culture**. *See also* ART; MUSIC IN THE LUTHERAN CHURCH; ORTHODOXY, LUTHERAN; PASSION MUSIC. [G.G.]

BAPTISM (Gk *baptizein*, "to dip" or "to immerse" in water). **Sacrament** of initiation to the Christian **faith** and community. Jewish ritual washings and especially the baptism administered by John the Baptist prefigure the various biblical references to the emergence of baptism in relation to Jesus and the first communities of his followers. These biblical references indicate an understanding of baptism as a ritual of initiation or incorporation into the primitive Christian communities (1 Cor 12:12). The development of baptismal **theology** and practice as witnessed by the Scriptures includes the trinitarian baptismal formula and Jesus' mandate of baptism (Mt 28:29), the elements of repentance, **faith** and **forgiveness** of **sins** (Acts 2.38.41), the close connection between baptism and the gift of the **Holy Spirit** (Lk 3:21–22), the intimate communion of the baptized with the life, death, and resurrection of Christ (Rom 6:3ff), and the promise of **salvation** for those who believe and are baptized (Mk 16:16).

The baptismal practice of the early church is described in the *Apostolic Tradition* (c.215/217 by Hyppolytus of Rome. It included a fairly long (up to three years) period of catechetical instruction, the baptismal rite itself including the trinitarian confession and formula with immersion in water, followed by anointing with blessed oil (chrism) and laying-on of hands by the bishop together with prayer for the gift of the Holy Spirit, and, finally, first participation in the **eucharist**. The first part of this practice, the catechumenate, fell out of use as infant baptism, attested around the year 200, became universal in the fourth and fifth centuries. Following the foundational teaching of **Augustine** that in baptism guilt and original sin are remitted, in 418 the Synod of Carthage decreed that infants must be baptized in order to be freed from original sin. When in the expanding church bishops could no longer participate in every baptism, the fourth part of the baptismal rite, the episcopal anointing and laying-on of hands, had to be postponed to a later stage in the life of a young person and became, since the sixth century, a distinct rite of **confirmation**. Key elements of Augustine's baptismal theology and subsequent theologians were: the emphasis on the action of the Triune **God** in baptism for the remission of sin, regeneration, incorporation into the church, the gift of **grace** and the Holy Spirit, and insistence on the validity of baptism by heretic, as well as the rejection of rebaptism.

Martin Luther and the Lutheran confessions continued to affirm the practice of infant baptism—that infants and children should not be excluded from the command of baptism and promise of God's grace—and condemned the rejection of baptism by radical movements, as well as the rejection of infant baptism by the **Anabaptists**. Luther and the confessions also continued much of traditional baptismal theology within the new conceptional framework of the **Reformation**. This includes: baptism is necessary for salvation and requires faith, through God's action in baptism the baptized receive the Holy Spirit and forgiveness of sins, they are brought into the church and led to a new life with Christ, they receive grace and consolation, and they are called to a life-long awareness of their baptism as their adoption as children of God. Today, infants and young persons, as well as adults are baptized in Lutheran churches. In continuing the Reformation teaching, baptism is affirmed as fundamental for a Christian life and as a life-long calling to repentance and renewal in a life of service to others. Baptism leads into the universal **communion** of Christ's church and is the basic sign of its **unity**. Ecumenical **dialogues** have led to basic agreements on baptismal theology and mutual recognition of baptism between most churches that practice both infant and adult baptism. However, the separation between churches that reject infant baptism and other churches that do not has yet to be overcome. *See also* CONFESSIONS, LUTHERAN. [G.G.]

BAPTISTS. *See* LUTHERAN-BAPTIST RELATIONS AND DIALOGUE.

BARMEN THEOLOGICAL DECLARATION (1934). Foundational statement on the relationship between **church and state**. At the beginning of the German **church struggle** about accommodating to or rejecting the Nazi ideology, representatives of 25 territorial churches assembled for the First Confessing Synod at Barmen. On May 31, 1934, they adopted a confessing statement that became known as the *Barmen Theological Declaration*. Its six theses, formulated by the eminent **Reformed** theologian Karl Barth, together with two Lutheran theologians, strongly rejected the ideological stance of the "German Christians" confessing Jesus Christ as the only **Word** and **revelation** of **God** and Christ's sole, exclusive lordship in the **church** and over all realms of life (*see* AUTHORITY). The declaration underlined the church's call to remind the state of the priority of God's **kingdom**, law, and **justice**. The declaration marked both the beginning and the spiritual basis of the **Confessing Church**. It provided an impetus for closer relations between Lutheran, United, and Reformed churches, even though the

Lutheran churches were not able to accept it as a new confession. As a basic and critical statement on the relationship between church and state, the *Barmen Theological Declaration* has served as a model in later situations of conflict such as the struggle against apartheid in southern Africa. *See also* BONHOEFFER, DIETRICH. [G.G.]

BERGGRAV, EIVIND (1884–1959). Norwegian Lutheran **bishop**, patriot, and ecumenist. Berggrav became bishop of North Norway in 1929 and in 1937 was elected bishop of Oslo and primate of Norway, a position he held until 1959. Already widely known in Norway through his literary activities (e.g., editor of *Church and Culture* for 50 years), the crucial time came for him with the German occupation of Norway during World War II. Supported by the other bishops and leading church representatives, Berggrav became the leader of the Lutheran Church of Norway's struggle (1941–1945) against the totalitarian claims of the German occupation regime and against Norwegian collaborators with the Germans led by Vidkun Quisling. Confined to house arrest from 1942–1945, Berggrav was still able to continue to lead the people of his church in their resistance. After Norway's liberation, he guided the restoration of church life.

Berggrav entered the **ecumenical movement** at an early stage. In 1914 he participated in the foundation of the World Alliance for Promoting International Friendship through the Churches, and was involved in peace negotiations on the eve of World War II. In 1946 he became the first president of the United Bible Societies, in 1948 he was elected a member of the Central Committee of the new **World Council of Churches**, and from 1950–1954 was one of its presidents. In a lasting contribution to Lutheran social thinking, Berggrav restated the Lutheran understanding of the relationship between **church and state**. Moved by his own experience during the war, he underlined the right to resist against unjust and tyrannical civil authorities as well as the duty to defend lawful democratic government. [G.G.]

BIBLE, AUTHORITY OF. Supreme norm of Christian **faith** and life. The acknowledgment of the decisive authority of Holy Scripture as norm and final judge of Christian **doctrine** and practice has been the common basis of the Christian church through the centuries. In the course of history, other authorities, seen as being in agreement with Scripture, were added: confessions of faith (**creeds**); decisions of councils (*see* COUNCILS, ECUMENICAL); teachings of the church fathers (*see* PATRISTICS); collections of **canon law**; decisions of general councils and synods; and the rulings of popes, based on an emerging concept of infallibility (*see* PAPACY), which became the decisive authority in the church in the late Middle Ages. The **Reformation** protested against the devaluation of the authority of the Bible by these other authorities and its implications for the church at that time.

The appeal to Scripture alone became the basis of the reformers' criticism against abuses in church life and distortions of the apostolic faith.

In their argumentation, the Lutheran reformers and confessions (*see* CONFESSIONS, LUTHERAN) clearly affirm the authority of Scripture, even though the confessions contain no specific article on the authority of Scripture, as do Reformed confessional documents. The confessions appeal constantly to the Bible and use scriptural references to justify, underline, and develop their arguments and doctrinal positions. However, biblical authority is not based primarily on claims about its literal truth, the authenticity of its texts, or a direct verbal inspiration (*see* BIBLE, INSPIRATION OF). Rather, the authority of the Bible rests in its content as authentic witness to the **Gospel**, and this authority becomes a living reality in the proclamation and application of this Gospel in **Word** and **sacrament**. There is, then, a distinction and a reciprocal relationship between Holy Scripture and Gospel. Scripture is the normative witness to the Gospel, while the Gospel is the heart and center of Scripture. The Gospel as the message of **salvation** and **justification** in Jesus Christ is the light in which the texts of the Bible are to be interpreted. All texts have to be seen in their relative closeness or distance to the saving event of Christ for us or, quoting **Martin Luther's** criterion, according to the degree in which they "convey Christ" (Ger *was Christum treibet*) (*see* CHRISTOLOGY). Thus, in Lutheran terminology, the Bible is the formal principle while the central doctrine of justification by faith alone is the material principle of the Christian faith.

The Reformation concept of the authority of the Bible is often associated with the slogan *sola scriptura*, "Scripture alone." For the Lutheran reformers and confessions, this has never meant that Scripture is the only authority; rather, it is the supreme, overriding authority. Alongside it and subordinated to it is the authority of the Christian **tradition** to which also the Lutheran confession belongs. Accordingly, the distinction is made between Scripture as the supreme norm (the *norma normans*) that judges all other standards and the authority of the confessions and other forms of tradition as secondary norms subordinated to that of Scripture (the *norma normata*).

The affirmation of biblical authority has remained an essential element of Lutheran **theology** and life. The distinction between Gospel and biblical texts has enabled a great liberty for the historical, critical study of the Bible in which **Lutheranism** — not without internal tensions and controversies — has played a leading role. *See also* BIBLE, INSPIRATION OF. [G.G.]

BIBLE, INSPIRATION OF (Lat *inspirare*, "to breathe in"). Concept of divine assistance to the writers or writing of the biblical texts. The term comes from "All scripture is inspired by God," where 2 Tim 3:16 refers to the Old Testament texts. The New Testament does not generally claim a direct verbal inspiration, but witnesses to the inspiration of persons by the **Holy**

Spirit, among them writers of biblical texts. Early Christian communities employed the concept of verbal inspiration, taken over from Hellenistic-Jewish culture, to contradict the claims of personal inspiration by Gnostic teachers. The early church fathers (*see* PATRISTICS) taught biblical inspiration, but left room for the personal activity of biblical authors. It was only in the late Middle Ages that the concept of verbal inspiration of Scripture gained ground.

Martin Luther and the Lutheran **Reformation** affirmed the inspiration of Scripture, but differentiated between biblical texts according to the degree in which they "convey Christ." Lutheran **Orthodoxy**, however, taught a direct verbal inspiration of the Bible: The Holy Spirit has used the hands of the biblical authors to write each word of Holy Scripture. This concept was to secure the absolute truth, and inerrancy of Scripture, in part also to counter the infallible magisterium of the Roman Catholic Church. The **Word of God** was identified with the words of Scripture. The Enlightenment radically questioned the theory of verbal inspiration and, as a reaction, more open, personal concepts of inspiration were developed. But the **tradition** of verbal inspiration has continued, not so much in Lutheran churches, and has gained new attraction today by offering clear-cut, authoritative answers to all questions. Lutheran churches affirm the inspiration of Holy Scripture, usually interpreted as an implication of the gift of the Holy Spirit to the first Christians and their communities among whom were the authors of the New Testament texts. These texts are marked both by their inspired witness to Jesus Christ and the human condition of their authors. *See also* BIBLE, AUTHORITY OF. [G.G.]

BIBLE, INTERPRETATION OF. The development of biblical interpretation in the **church**. The New Testament continued the tradition of Jewish explanation and teaching of the Scriptures by a new tradition of interpreting the (Old Testament) Scriptures, but now in relation to the confession that "Jesus is the Christ" and undertaken by those who have received the gift (*charisma*) of "teaching" (e.g., Rom 12:7; 1 Cor 4:17). In the early church of the first few centuries, the New Testament itself—being assembled in the **canon of Holy Scripture** and received by the church (*see* RECEPTION)— became the object of interpretation. The **theology** of the church fathers (*see* PATRISTICS) is based on and expressed through biblical interpretation. Important commentaries on biblical books were written (e.g., by Origen and John Chrysostom) with traces of philological interest. Jerome (d. 420) contributed in large measure to the establishment of the authentic Latin text of the Bible in the West, the Vulgate, by revising existing and producing new translations.

During the Middle Ages, the church was mainly concerned with the collection and transmission of patristic exegetical (Gk *exegesis*, "interpretation") texts. Several modes ("senses") of interpreting biblical passages were developed: literal-historical, spiritual, allegorical, moral, and metaphysical or **eschatological**. These modes, especially the allegorical one, served to keep biblical exegesis in line with church **doctrine** (and not the other way around). **Humanism** with its new interest in classical languages and its work on new critical editions (e.g., the New Testament by **Erasmus of Rotterdam** of 1516) provided valuable help for the emphasis on the central role of Holy Scripture in the **Reformation** movement. Similar to **theology** of the early church, but in a new historical and theological context, Reformation theology was essentially biblical interpretation in support of the reinterpretation of doctrine, the reform of the church, and the critique of abuses and false teaching. **Martin Luther**, professor of biblical exegesis, arrived at his decisive Reformation breakthrough by interpreting Paul's Letter to the Romans. The Lutheran reformers regarded Scripture as the "only rule and norm according to which all doctrines and teachers alike must be appraised and judged" (*Formula of Concord*, article 1), but they did not interpret Scripture as a uniform, equally authoritative collection of texts. Their insight that **God's** saving action in Jesus Christ (*see* CHRISTOLOGY) constitutes the center of Scripture in whose light all Scripture has to be explained led to a differentiating view of the canon of Scripture. The reformer's emphasis on the literal and historical sense of Scripture, against the different "senses" of medieval theology, and their principle that Scripture interprets itself, required careful study of biblical language and thinking.

This open approach to the biblical texts was not continued in Lutheran Orthodoxy (*see* ORTHODOXY, LUTHERAN) where many theologians considered Scripture as a closed system of teaching, verbally inspired, free of contradictions, and providing proof texts (*dicta probantia*) for each doctrinal topic. The Enlightenment prepared the ground for a radical change in biblical interpretation: the emergence, initially in German Protestantism, of the historical-critical study of biblical literature in line with general scholarly methods. Historical-critical study in the 19th and 20th centuries (*see*, for example, BULTMANN, RUDOLF) has gone through several stages, according to changing philosophical presuppositions, and has developed a variety of methods: text criticism, literary criticism, form criticism, structuralist analysis, and religion-historical comparison, together with research on early Christianity, Jewish traditions, "historical Jesus," biblical sociology, and so on.

Today, the historical-critical method, in different degrees and forms, is generally accepted in Roman Catholicism and mainstream Protestantism. But there is also a broad recognition that this method must not lose sight of the fundamental dimension of biblical texts as witnesses, inspired by **faith**, which seek to awaken faith. Indeed, there have been in the last seven decades of the 20th century many biblical scholars, including a significant number of Lutherans, who have expanded the understanding of Christian faith and life through their research. [G.G.]

BIBLE, MARTIN LUTHER'S TRANSLATION (1522–1534). During and after the **Reformation**, an unprecedented boom of translations of the Bible set in. This was enabled by (1) the Reformation emphasis on Holy Scripture, (2) advanced printing methods (*see* PRINTING PRESS), and (3) the call of **Humanism** to return to the sources as well as the provision of new, critical editions of the sources. **Martin Luther's** translation of the Bible is part of this context. After the Diet of Worms (*see* WORMS, DIET OF), Luther's protector **Frederick III the Wise** arranged a mock "kidnapping" of Luther on his return trip and hid him for 14 months at Wartburg Castle. There, Luther, using the Greek original edited by **Erasmus of Rotterdam**, translated the New Testament into German, which was first printed in December 1522 with wood carvings by **Lucas Cranach**. After his return from the Wartburg, Luther successively translated from the Hebrew original the main parts of the Old Testament. In 1534 his translation of the whole Bible was published.

Luther had consulted his **Wittenberg** colleagues during his translation work and continued to produce revised editions of his translation in 1535, 1536, 1539, 1540, 1541, and his definitive edition of 1545. He reflected and wrote about his translation methods: to be faithful to the original text and close to the language of the people. The distribution and impact of his Bible was enormous: 87 high German and 19 low German editions of his New Testament were published between 1522 and 1534. Every tenth household in **Protestant** Germany is supposed to have had Luther's New Testament. Translations of the Bible into Danish, Dutch, and Swedish used Luther's text, which also influenced Miles Coverdale's English Bible of 1535.

Luther's translation, its language and terminology, shaped the **faith** and **piety** of the people like no other book. Based on Saxon German, his translation was the decisive contribution to the formation of written high German. His Bible continues to exert a deep influence both on **literature** and popular idiom (e.g., in Luther's rendering of biblical proverbs). The last moderate revision of the "Luther Bible" appeared in 1984. [G.G.]

BIBLE SOCIETIES. Organizations that encourage and promote the translation and distribution of the Bible. The **Reformation**, with its emphasis on the supreme authority of Holy Scripture and on the access of the whole **priesthood of all believers** to the Bible, set in motion a broad movement of Bible translation and distribution. **Pietism** exerted another strong impetus to Bible reading that marked the beginning of organized Bible production, translation, and distribution. In 1710 the von Canstein Bible Institution was founded at Halle. The British and Foreign Bible Society (1804, London) became the model for the great number of Bible societies in nearly all European countries and in North America (American Bible Society, 1816). The work of these societies was closely linked to the missionary movement and its need of translations and inexpensive Bibles or parts of Bibles. The Bible societies are independent organizations, related to the churches, mostly interdenominational, and actively supported by lay people.

The need for coordination and cooperation between the societies led to the foundation of the United Bible Societies (UBS) in 1946 to which 126 national Bible societies or offices are related (1999). The biblical renewal in the Roman Catholic Church, affirmed by the Second Vatican Council, furthered the growth of Catholic Bible societies and ecumenical cooperation with them. Through the work of the Bible societies, parts of the Bible have been translated in 2,212 languages, and the UBS is involved in 685 translation projects (1999). In 1998 20.8 million Bibles and 20.1 million New Testaments were distributed worldwide by Bible societies, together with many more millions of portions of the Bible. *See also* BIBLE, AUTHORITY OF; BIBLE, MARTIN LUTHER'S TRANSLATION; VATICAN COUNCILS I AND II. [G.G.]

BILLING, EINAR (1871–1939). One of the most influential Swedish Lutheran theologian and church leaders in the 20th century. For 20 years Billing was lecturer and professor at Uppsala University (1900–1920) and from 1920 to 1939 bishop of Västeras. His theological work responded to the rise of historical-critical biblical research (*see* BIBLE, INTERPRETATION OF) that he affirmed and used as a positive contribution to the understanding of the **faith**. He originated and developed the idea of an open folk church (cf. his book *The Swedish Folk Church*, 1930) that he based on the concept of the election of all people by the **grace** of **God**. This idea was widely accepted as an expression of the self-understanding of the Swedish church and had a marked influence beyond Billing's lifetime, especially also on the reform of state-church relations (*see* CHURCH AND STATE). Billing contributed significantly to research on **Martin Luther's theology** and on the ethical thinking in primitive Christianity. He was the leading theological spirit in the Young Church Movement that was an important church reform movement up to the middle of the 20th century. Through his theological orientation and methodology and his pupil Gustaf Aulén, he prepared the way for the **Lund School**. [G.G.]

BISHOP (Gk *episcopos*, "overseer"). Ordained minister exercising pastoral leadership and spiritual supervision in a specific geographical area. In the New Testament, the terms *presbyteros* and *episcopos* are still synonymous for people exercising leadership functions. Between the end of the first century and the third century, a generally accepted structure emerges with one bishop as leader of a local church (monarchical episcopacy) and as part of the **apostolic succession** of bishops understood as an effective sign of continuity in the apostolic faith. It was a long way from these local episcopal pastors to the powerful prince-bishops in the late Middle Ages. The Lutheran **Reformation** was prepared to continue the office of bishop in apostolic succession, but in a form and with an understanding that were consistent with Reformation convictions (*see* MINISTRY). The main functions of bishops were to be the same as those of pastors, but bishops might also exercise the special tasks of **ordination**, visitation, and maintaining right teaching. However, during the Reformation the continuation of existing episcopal offices in apostolic succession was only possible in Sweden (with Finland). In Germany, episcopal authority was taken over, as an emergency measure, by **evangelical** princes (*see* SUMMUS EPISCOPUS).

In the 20th century Lutheran churches that did not yet have episcopal offices have introduced them as offices of pastoral and church leadership of a particular church or of a specific area within a church (synods, dioceses, districts, and so on). These offices carry the titles of president, ephorus (in Indonesia), or—increasingly—bishop (and in a few cases also archbishop). Bishops—in a few churches now women as well as men—are usually elected and related to synodical structures (*see* SYNOD). They serve for a limited term or until retirement. Discussion continues within Lutheranism about adequate forms and interpretations of the episcopal ministry and about the possibility, for ecumenical reasons, of accepting the apostolic succession of bishops as a sign of **unity** and continuity within the broader apostolic continuity of the whole **church**. [G.G.]

BONHOEFFER, DIETRICH (1906–1945). Twentieth-century martyr and brilliant theologian. One of the leaders in the **Confessing Church** movement during the period of the Third Reich, Bonhoeffer studied theology at Tübingen and Berlin. After receiving his doctorate in 1930, he studied for a year at the Union Theological Seminary in New York. In protest against the Nazi co-option of the church, Bonhoeffer went to London in 1933, where he pastored two German-speaking congregations. During this time, his **ecumenical** work was more pronounced. He was made an advisory member of the Ecumenical Council for **Life and Work.** In 1935 he was appointed by the Confessing Church to the directorship of the "underground" seminary at Finkenwalde. In 1938 Bonhoeffer was evicted from Berlin. A year later he went to the United States. However, in spite of the lobbying of many at the Union Seminary and elsewhere to stay, in view of the dangerous situation in Germany, he returned a few months later to his homeland with the clear conviction that his vocation of theological leadership was there. He continued his work on his *Ethics*, worked for the Confessing Church, and participated in political resistance. He was arrested on April 5, 1943, after being implicated in an assassination attempt on Hitler. He was imprisoned at Flossenbürg for two years. During this time, he continued to write and preached to his fellow inmates. The Bonhoeffer of these years is most widely known by his *Letters and Papers from Prison*. A few days before the prison camp was liberated by the Allies, he was hanged by the Nazis on April 9, 1945, for his involvement with the attempted assassination of Hitler.

Commemorated on the Lutheran liturgical calendar, Bonhoeffer's life and death exemplify his thought that "religionless Christianity" is the appropriate, indeed the only adequate way of life in a world "come of age." In other words, the lordship of Jesus Christ is to be manifested in everyday life by a free and politically enacted practical conscience that is informed by life in the community of Christ's church. (The Bonhoeffer archives are now housed at the Lutheran Theological Seminary at Philadelphia.) *See also* CHURCH STRUGGLE. [D.H.L.]

BOOK OF CONCORD (1580). The official collection of the Lutheran confessional documents. In the **evangelical** territories, it was soon recognized that so-called **church orders** had to provide a basis and stability for the evolving Lutheran churches in these territories. Such orders should also include doctrinal norms as a binding orientation for the **faith** and teaching of the churches and of their pastors and teachers. Thus, church orders (e.g., the early one of Pomerania in 1535) began to include confessional texts like the *Augsburg Confession*, its *Apology*, **Martin Luther's** *Small Catechism*, and various other texts. In the second half of the 16th century a conscious effort was made to arrive at a common collection of confessional texts in order to strengthen the unity among the Lutheran churches. From 1573 onward endeavors to overcome inner-Lutheran controversies (*see FORMULA OF CONCORD*) and to establish a common body of confessional documents went hand in hand. They resulted in a list of texts with the Bible as the normative authority, followed by the three Ecumenical **Creeds**, the *Augsburg Confession*, its *Apology*, the *Smalcald Articles*, the *Treatise on the Power and Primacy of the Pope*, the *Small* and *Large Catechisms* of Luther, and, after 1577, the *Formula of Concord*. The creeds and the Lutheran confessions were published in 1580 in the form of the *Book of Concord* (*BC*) that was signed by the leaders of the evangelical territories and cities and 8,000 pastors, theologians, and teachers. It thus became the official collection of the Lutheran confessions. A number of Lutheran churches have accepted only some of the confessions assembled in the *BC*, but all subscribe to the *Augsburg Confession* and the *Small Catechism*. *See also* CONFESSIONS, LUTHERAN. [G.G.]

BORA, KATHARINA VON (1499–1552). Wife and supporter of **Martin Luther** and his many activities. Born of a noble family near Leipzig, Bora became a nun in a Cistercian nunnery in Saxony in 1515. As in many other monasteries, the nuns became interested in the teachings and reforms of the Lutheran movement. Just before Easter in 1523 Bora and eight other nuns escaped from the convent and were brought to safety in **Wittenberg**. Luther, who had helped to arrange their escape, married Bora in 1525, after she had indicated to others that she liked him, despite the 16-year age difference.

Their marriage became an exemplary partnership between a self-conscious, energetic, and intelligent wife and the increasingly famous reformer. In their house, a former monastery with over 40 rooms, "Käthe" (Katie) was the authoritative mistress over a large household. It comprised their four surviving children (of six), several foster children, some relatives, student boarders, refugees, visitors from many countries, tutors, and servants, as well as horses and other animals, large gardens, and a brewery in the cellar. Beyond this enormous responsibility, she took interest in the reforming activities of her husband. She often discussed with him and their numerous visitors the events and developments of the **Reformation**. She sustained Martin faithfully in his eccentricities and in periods of illness and depression. He loved her dearly and addressed her as "my dear Lord Katie." Six years after Luther's death, Katharina fled with two of her children from Wittenberg because of the pestilence and died soon afterwards in Torgau on December 20, 1552, as a result of an accident on their flight. *See also* PARSONAGE. [G.G.]

BRENZ, JOHANNES (1499–1570). One of the leading theologians and organizers of the Lutheran **Reformation**. Brenz was born in the imperial city of Weil in southern Germany. As a student at Heidelberg, he met **Martin Luther** in 1518 and was afterwards deeply influenced by Luther's (Augustinian) teaching on **grace**. From 1522 to 1548 Brenz was the **pastor** of Schwäbisch-Hall and introduced the Reformation there, and later in several other cities and territories. He participated in the **Marburg Colloquy** in 1529 and the Diet of Augsburg (*see* AUGSBURG, DIETS OF) in 1530. In 1536 he was asked by his sovereign to introduce the Reformation in Württemberg and in 1550/51 to draw up the *Confessio Virtembergica* for the Council of Trent (*see* TRENT, COUNCIL OF). In 1553 Brenz became chief pastor of the main church at Stuttgart and the leader of the Lutheran church in Württemberg. Together with Duke Christoph, who became his close friend, he worked from 1553 to 1559 towards the reconstitution of Lutheranism in Württemberg after the many setbacks caused by the 1548 **Interim**. He died in Stuttgart.

In discussions among Lutheran theologians and with **Reformed** theologians, Brenz defended Luther's teaching on Christ's undivided human-divine presence in the **Lord's Supper** on the basis of Christ's omnipresence or ubiquity. He was an untiring and able interpreter of Holy Scripture, retained the simple form of the preaching service in the Württemberg church, and relied confidently on God's **justification**. The 517 writings of this immensely active and respected pastor are written in a clear and simple language. After Luther's death Brenz became the leading representative of **Lutheranism**. He has left his mark on **theology**, biblical **faith**, **piety**, and **worship** in Württemberg up to this day. [G.G.]

BRETHREN, LUTHERAN. The Church of the Lutheran Brethren of America (CLBA) is a church body that, since its founding, has remained committed to overseas **mission**. Organized in Milwaukee, Wisconsin, in 1900, it began with a concern that **church discipline** was not exercised according to apostolic usage in the United Norwegian Lutheran Church and the Lutheran Free Church. The CLBA subscribes to the ecumenical **creeds**, the unaltered *Augsburg Confession*, and **Martin Luther's** *Small Catechism*. Its polity is entirely congregational, and communicant membership begins when an individual has experienced awakening and **conversion**. Free prayer and personal testimony are encouraged in worship. For the first 50 years of its existence, more than half of denominational funds were spent on overseas missions. Its "daughter congregations" in Cameroon, Chad, Japan, and Taiwan—which outnumber those in North America by 10 to one—are now organized into separate national churches.

In 1999 there were 123 congregations with 14,000 members in the United States and Canada, concentrated in the upper Midwest, and several educational institutions. [M.O.]

BUCER, MARTIN (1491–1551). Leader in the consolidation of the Lutheran **Reformation**. Born in Schlettstadt in Alsace, Bucer entered the Dominican Order in 1507 and after 1516 studied in Heidelberg. There, in April 1518, he met **Martin Luther** at the Heidelberg Disputation and was convinced by the new theology. He left the order, became a secular priest in 1521, and proclaimed Reformation ideas in many places. In 1524 he became a **pastor** of a congregation at Strasbourg. He helped to reform the orders of worship (*see* WORSHIP, HISTORY AND STRUCTURE) and became the leading personality of the Reformation in Strasbourg and several territories and towns in southern Germany. While drawing a clear line over and against radical reformers (**Anabaptists** and **Spiritualists**), Bucer established friendly contacts with Swiss **Reformed** leaders, including **John Calvin** and **Ulrich Zwingli**. These relationships made him ideally suited to act as mediator in efforts to overcome the Lutheran-Reformed doctrinal differences, especially concerning the understanding of the nature of the **Lord's Supper**.

Together with **Philipp Melanchthon** Bucer prepared the *Wittenberg Concord* of 1536 that formulated the agreement on the Lord's Supper between the Lutherans of the central-northern territories of Germany and of the southern German towns. In 1542/43 Cologne's Archbishop Hermann von Wied invited him to prepare the introduction of the Reformation in his archbishopric, but the emperor prevented this attempt. When Bucer refused to accept the Interim of 1548, Emperor Charles V demanded his removal. The town council of Strasbourg obeyed. Bucer, invited to come to **Wittenberg**, Geneva, or Copenhagen, decided to accept an invitation from England. He became a professor at Cambridge University and was soon influential again by supporting Archbishop Thomas Cranmer's reforming activities, especially by helping to put together the (**Anglican**) *Book of Common Prayer*. This eminent reformer and mediator between different reforming tendencies died in Cambridge. [G.G.]

BUGENHAGEN, JOHANNES (1485–1558). One of the great and efficient organizers of the emerging Lutheran churches in northern Germany and Denmark. Born in Wollin, Pomerania, Bugenhagen studied at Greifswald and was ordained a priest in 1509. It was **Martin Luther**'s *Babylonian Captivity of the Church* (1520) that became decisive for Bugenhagen's theological position. In 1521 he came to **Wittenberg** where Luther and **Philipp Melanchthon** accepted him into their circle. After further studies, he began to lecture in Wittenberg and in 1523 was elected head **pastor** of this town. He became Luther's friend, cooperator, and confessor. Because of his pastoral, practical, and pedagogical gifts, Bugenhagen was often called away from Wittenberg during the years 1528–1532 in order to help to introduce the **Reformation** and reorganize church life in the Hanse towns of Brunswick, Hamburg, and Lübeck. His **church order** for Brunswick (1528) became the model for many others. In 1534/35 he was responsible for visitations in Pomerania, his home area, where he also drew up a new church order.

In 1537/38 Bugenhagen was called by Christian III to introduce the Reformation in Denmark, together with Norway and Schleswig-Holstein. He opened the University of Copenhagen (rector 1538) and lectured there. In 1542–1544 he organized the **evangelical** educational and church system together with the orders of worship (*see* WORSHIP, HISTORY AND STRUCTURE) in northern Germany and defended at the same time the authentic Lutheran teaching against **spiritualist** tendencies. Throughout these years he published biblical commentaries. He preached the sermon at Luther's funeral while Melanchthon preached the sermon at the funeral of this "Reformer of the North." [G.G.]

BULTMANN, RUDOLF (1884–1976). One of the most influential 20th-century theologians. The son of a Lutheran **pastor**, German theologian Rudolf Bultmann in 1921 became a professor of the New Testament at Marburg where he remained until his death. Initially formed by the liberal religion-historical school, Bultmann joined the rejection of theological **Liberalism** after World War I. Related to, but never fully part of the movement of **dialectical theology**, he articulated his critique of Liberalism by affirming **God's** revealing **Word** in the form of the proclaimed **kerygma** of Christ's **cross** and **resurrection** as the decisive saving event. This kerygma is God's Word addressed to humans, calling them to a decision of **faith**.

Bultmann undergirded this interpretation of the biblical message by groundbreaking New Testament research (e.g., *History of the Synoptic Tradition* [1921], *Theology of the New Testament* [1948–1953], and many other publications), but also with the hermeneutical approach (*see* HERMENEUTICS) and the existentialist philosophy of his Marburg colleague Martin Heidegger. This led Bultmann to an "existential interpretation" of the biblical texts both as a witness to God and to the human person (*see* ANTHROPOLOGY). He believed that such interpretation no longer needed to rely on mythological concepts and "historical facts" like the "historical Jesus," including the historicity of his resurrection. In the 1950s this program of existential interpretation and, as its consequence, the method of "demythologizing" created a broad academic discussion and strong protests of more conservative groups and theologians, including many Lutherans. Bultmann himself considered his theological work a contemporary application of basic convictions of the Lutheran **Reformation** such as **justification** by faith alone, the primacy of the **Word of God**, and the continuing significance of the **two kingdoms** concept for Christian **ethics**. Though his more radical theological positions are no longer widely shared, Bultmann's significance for 20th-century theological history is undisputed, and his concern for investigating the possibility of faith under the conditions of modernity remains a central task of **theology**. [G.G.]

BURIAL. The act of transposing a body to its final resting place, and particularly by entombing it in the ground, along with the traditions, rituals, and prayers that surround such an action. Although **Martin Luther** recommended that funerals focus on the proclamation of the **resurrection** in the context of grief, he did not leave any example of an **evangelical** funeral service. Without the controlling hand of Luther as a liturgical writer, however, the different Lutheran churches provided a variety of forms for burial. At first, the burial rite was made up almost entirely of hymns sung by the congregation, at the home of the deceased, at the graveside, and on the way between the two. Soon, however, prayers and preaching were added. In the case of the wealthy and powerful, the **sermon** was often preached not at the burial itself, but at a memorial service held later in the church (Luther's own funeral services were of this character).

Under **Pietism** and **Rationalism**, funeral sermons gave way to eulogies, encomiums to the virtue of the deceased. During the 19th century writers such as **Johann Konrad Wilhelm Löhe** provided a formula that, in its prayers and proclamations, focused once more on the action of **God** in the face of death. These formularies became influential not only in Germany, but also in Africa, Asia, and the Americas. The modern **liturgical movement**, with its emphasis on baptismal and paschal imagery related to death, has shaped most Lutheran burial services printed since 1960. Since this movement has been influenced by and affected most Western churches, there seems to be a growing **ecumenical** convergence, in printed rituals if not in practice.

One controversial issue related to burial has been the practice of cremation. Cremation was unheard of from the time Charlemagne outlawed it (784) until the 17th century. At that point, the practice was urged primarily by those opposed to the church, and for a long time cremation was forbidden by Roman Catholicism and practiced only reluctantly by **Protestants**. Recently, these strictures have eased, and more and more churches have established columbaria or memorial gardens within their precincts for the reception of the ashes of the faithful. [M.O.]

BURSCHE, JULIUS (1862–1942). Polish Lutheran bishop and martyr. Bursche became the **pastor** at the central Trinity Church in Warsaw in 1889 and was the general **superintendent** of the Lutheran church in that region from 1905–1937. During this period, he created several diaconical/social institutions in Warsaw and supported Christian and theological education. He initiated research on the **Reformation** in Poland and succeeded in the establishment of an Evangelical Theological Faculty at the University of Warsaw (1921/22). After 1918 he undertook the reorganization of the Lutheran church in now independent Poland and tried to transform the German-dominated church into a German-Polish church. Nationalistic feelings on both sides and the deteriorating German-Polish political situation stood against these efforts. After the new constitution of the church was accepted in 1936, Bursche was elected **bishop** of the (predominantly Polish-speaking) Evangelical Church of the Augsburg Confession in Poland. At the beginning of World War II, Bishop Bursche was arrested by the Germans and imprisoned in the Oranienburg concentration camp. In February 1942 the SS/Gestapo killed him. [G.G.]

BUXTEHUDE, DIETRICH (1637–1707). Eminent Lutheran church musician and composer. Buxtehude became the organist and *Werkmeister* of the *Marienkirche* in Lübeck in 1668 and served in those positions until his death almost 40 years later. As *Werkmeister*, he was responsible for the finances and physical plant of the 400-year-old church. As organist, he was required to play for morning and afternoon services on Sundays and festivals, as well as at Vespers services the night before. For these services he also had to provide choral music and music to accompany Holy Communion. What brought him international renown, however, were the *Abendmusiken* (Evening Concerts) that he produced following afternoon services five times a year—on the last two Sundays of the **church year** and the second, third, and fourth Sundays of **Advent**. It was these concerts, and especially Buxtehude's compositions and performances as organist that drew the young **Johann Sebastian Bach** to Lübeck to study with the older musician.

About 128 vocal and choral works by Buxtehude survive, all but eight sacred, including arias, **chorale** settings, and **cantatas**. His extant instrumental music includes works for organ, for other keyboard instruments, and for strings. His compositions for organ and voice (particularly his cantatas) are still widely performed. Like his famous student, Buxtehude used Baroque artistry of the highest order to express a lively and popular **piety**. *See also* MUSIC IN THE LUTHERAN CHURCH. [M.O.]

– C –

CALENDAR, LITURGICAL. That complex of **Sundays**, seasons, **festivals**, fasts, appointed lessons, and seasonal practices (whether liturgical or devotional) that are tied to particular times of the year. The 16th-century reformers simplified the liturgical calendar, eliminating from it the commemoration of most nonbiblical saints, and focusing attention on Sunday, rather than such festivals. Similarly, Scripture replaced hagiography as the focus of daily prayer. The calendar became even simpler over the next four centuries, so that in early 19th-century America, communal weekly worship was generally restricted to Sunday mornings and Sunday and Wednesday evenings, and festivals were limited to Christmas, Palm Sunday, Good Friday, Easter, Ascension, and Pentecost. To these historic festivals, however, were often added Harvest Home and Reformation Day. The Lutheran **Awakening** returned many festivals and seasons, with their practices, to the church, and the wider cultural context provided Children's, Mothers, Fathers, and Rally Days as festivals of the church. In the late 20th century the liturgical calendar has become progressively more **ecumenical**, with German churches sharing calendars along with hymnbooks, and several North American churches adopting and elaborating the Revised Common Lectionary with its associated calendar. *See also* CHURCH YEAR; LECTIONARY; PIETY; VESTMENTS. [M.O.]

CALVIN, JOHN (1509–1564). Most significant reformer of the **Presbyterian/Reformed** tradition. Born in Noyon, France, Calvin studied the humanities and law in Paris and Orleans. Influenced by **Humanism** and probably

Lutheran ideas, he seems to have adopted a **Protestant** understanding of **faith** and **church** around 1533/34. The measures against "heretics" in 1535 forced him to flee through Strasbourg to Basel. There, he published in 1536 the first edition of what was to become his major dogmatic work, *Institutes of the Christian Religion.* It was a kind of catechetical instruction and a synopsis of **Reformation** doctrine. This work of a 27-year-old theological autodidact was strongly influenced by writings of **Martin Luther**, but it also showed a remarkable independence of thinking. In the same year during a short stay in Geneva, Calvin was entreated to remain there and support Guillaume Farel, the reformer of that city. In Geneva, Calvin wrote a catechism, followed by his church ordinance *Articles Concerning the Reformation of the Church and the Worship at Geneva,* and a confession of faith (probably written with Farel) that were all printed in 1537. On the basis of his growing influence, he demanded the recognition of the Christian teaching in the civil society as well. Conflicts with the town council forced him and Farel to leave Geneva in 1538. Calvin accepted an invitation of **Martin Bucer** to Strasbourg where he served the French refugee congregation. In 1539 he revised his *Institution* into a book of dogmatic instruction. Three further and considerably expanded editions (1543–1559) made it the most important dogmatic treatise of the Reformation. During this time, he developed together with Bucer his order of worship (*see* WORSHIP, HISTORY AND STRUCTURE).

In 1541 Calvin was called back to Geneva and received with great honors. During that year, he published his **church order** *Ecclesiastical Ordinances* that became the basis of his theocratic system at Geneva and the charter of future **church polity**. The *Ordinances* also made provisions for four offices: **pastors**, presbyters/elders, teachers, and **deacons**, and for a consistory of pastors and elders to supervise strict discipline in church and city. In 1542 he issued his revised order of worship, first worked out with Bucer at Strasbourg. In that same year, his *Catechism* was published in a completely revised form and with a strong emphasis on **God's** law and **church discipline**. With the help of these publications and driven both by a commitment to high ideals and by determination, he introduced with draconian force his theocratic church constitution and ecclesiastical order. Strict moral rules were imposed and secular means of reinforcement and punishment were employed. His agreement with Heinrich Bullinger, **Ulrich Zwingli's** successor at Zürich, on the doctrine of the **Lord's Supper**, formulated in the *Consensus Tigurinus* of 1549, secured the unity of the Reformation of Zürich and Geneva. The confessional character of the Reformed/Presbyterian tradition was thereby established, but the gap with the Lutherans widened.

Calvin's influence through his publications, his correspondence, and hundreds of his pupils at his Geneva Academy (founded in 1559) extended throughout Europe, especially to England (Puritanism), Holland, Scotland, Poland, and Hungary. He shaped the theology, ethos, and polity of the Reformed/Presbyterian churches. The impact of this theologian, who incessantly affirmed God's sovereignty, honor, and glory, was even broader. His presentation of the close relationship between theology and society together with the high estimation of work, vocation, and discipline, and his grounding of the secular state and society in God's will in creation and redemption have all contributed to the emergence of the modern state (*see* CHURCH AND STATE). Calvin was in his theological thinking much closer to the Lutheran tradition than the Zürich reformer Ulrich Zwingli. He established friendly and lasting contacts with **Philipp Melanchthon** and signed the *Augsburg Confession* in both its 1530 and 1540 versions. [G.G.]

CANON OF HOLY SCRIPTURE. List of the biblical texts accepted by the **church** as authoritative. The agreed list or canon of Old Testament writings was established in the second century A.D. and then received by the early church as the source of **God's revelation** and promise of the Christ who was to come. Lists of New Testament writings began to appear in the second century, but the complex process of **reception** of the New Testament canon by the church continued up to the fifth century because of disputes about accepting certain books, among them the Letter to the Hebrews, the Letter of James, and the Revelation of John. At that time, the reception of the canon of the Bible by the (Latin) church was concluded.

The **Reformation** accepted the New Testament canon with its 27 books and the Old Testament canon with its 39 books, but excluded the seven so-called "deuterocanonical" books that were received by the Roman Catholic Church as part of the canon. These seven books are called "apocrypha" by **Protestants** and are sometimes printed in Bibles as an appendix. For **Martin Luther**, the canon was authoritative because of its **apostolicity**, its manifestation of the **consensus** of the church, and primarily because of the fundamental significance and **truth** of its witness to Jesus Christ. This Christological norm (*see* CHRISTOLOGY) led to the internal differentiation within the canon. Not all books and passages were seen as equal in their relation to Christ. Luther distinguished between the most glorious books and those with which he had difficulties, especially James (the famous "epistle of straw"), Hebrews, and Revelation. This differentiated picture of the biblical canon was grounded in Luther's life-long intensive study and translation of Holy Scripture. *See also* BIBLE, AUTHORITY OF; BIBLE, MARTIN LUTHER'S TRANSLATION. [G.G.]

CANON LAW. *See* CHURCH LAW.

CANTATA (Lat *cantare*, "to sing"). A sung composition, longer than an anthem or motet and shorter than an **oratorio** or opera. While it may treat a secular topic and may be voiced for one or more solo voices, it is normally assumed to be a choral treatment of a sacred text, appropriate for use in **worship**. Created during the Renaissance, together with its purely instrumental sibling, the sonata, the cantata is chamber music that is appropriate for a small group in a small room, rather than a massive choir in a huge theater. While Johann Schein, **Heinrich Schütz**, and **Dietrich Buxtehude** all wrote cantatas, the form reached its peak of expression under the hand of **Johann Sebastian Bach**, when it became, after **preaching**, the centerpiece of urban **worship** life.

In Leipzig at the time of Bach, a cantata was performed most Sundays between the reading of the **Gospel** and the recitation of the creed. Often, another accompanied the **communion** of the **congregation**. These works were often based on the *de tempore* **hymn**, and included settings of appropriate Scriptural passages and poetry between settings of the stanzas. The composition and liturgical use of cantatas fell out of favor soon after the time of Bach, and have returned to the concert hall and worship life only in the 20th century. [M.O.]

CARIBBEAN. *See* LATIN AMERICA, LUTHERAN CHURCHES IN.

CATECHESIS/CATECHISM (Gk *katechizein*, "to teach orally"). The process of learning and applying the Christian **faith** to one's life. There is no single context for catechesis: it may form part of **confirmation** ministry, or it may be a preparation for **baptism** as an adult, or it may refer to life-long learning, without a particular goal in sight. A catechism is a written introduction to the basics of the faith, often in question and answer form, that is generally used as the basic text for catechesis. Catechesis had its beginnings in the early church as the process by which candidates for baptism were prepared for initiation. When infant baptism became the norm, this process withered away. **Martin Luther** wrote his *Catechisms* as a way of providing for the growth of children, households, and pastors in the faith. In the generations after Luther, the school dominated catechesis, providing a more intellectual and less practical experience than the reformers had envisioned. In the 19th century this process was supplemented in state churches and replaced in free churches by such voluntary parachurch activities as Sunday church school and youth work, while the Lutheran **Awakening** returned Luther's *Catechisms* to the center of the catechetical preparation of youth. In the 20th century, beginning in **mission** fields and given particular impetus under Communism in the German Democratic Republic, the use of trained lay catechists as mentors as well as instructors made catechesis again a personal learning.

In the mission fields of the late 19th and early 20th centuries the **church** once more had to prepare adults for baptism. This exposure, together with the modern **liturgical movement** gave rise to the renewal of the adult catechumenate. As Europe and America become mission fields, this process incorporates new Christians into the congregation and prepares them to explore and share the faith. It also provides congregations with a missional and catechetical focus for their work and their members with the opportunity to grow in their own faith. *See also CATECHISMS* OF LUTHER; CHRISTIAN EDUCATION; YOUTH. [M.O.]

CATECHISMS OF LUTHER (1529). Two outstanding texts of Christian instruction that eventually became Lutheran confessions. During visits to congregations in 1528 and 1529, **Martin Luther** was shocked by the religious ignorance of church members, laity, as well as pastors. In order to instruct the people in the **faith**, Luther preached three series of **sermons** on the Ten Commandments, Apostles' Creed, Lord's Prayer, **baptism**, and the **Lord's Supper** at **Wittenberg** during 1528–1529. These sermons formed the basis for his short, concise *Small Catechism of Dr. Martin Luther for Ordinary Pastors and Preachers* and his *Large Catechism* (originally *German Catechism*). Luther prepared the two catechisms simultaneously. The *Small Catechism* was first published in 1529 in the form of large posters or charts and then as an illustrated booklet. In addition of the five topics of his sermons, other texts (on confession/absolution, morning and evening prayer, and so on) were included in the *Small Catechism*. Intended for ordinary people, as well as for pastors, it became the most widely distributed text during the **Reformation**. The *Large Catechism*, also printed in 1529, had the basic structure of the *Small Catechism* but was a much longer theological-pastoral text. It was addressed to pastors to help them with the instruction of young people and adults. Luther's catechisms express his lively concern for the religious **education** of members of a church in the process of renewal and reform. The catechisms were included in **church orders** and eventually became part of the corpus of Lutheran confessions, the ***Book of Concord*** of 1580. The *Small Catechism* is, together with the ***Augsburg Confession,*** the most widely accepted Lutheran confession. *See also* CONFESSIONS, LUTHERAN. [G.G.]

CATHOLICITY (Gk *katholikós*, "universal, general, comprehensive, perfect, full"). Attribute of the **church** and of its **faith**. The term appears only once in the New Testament (Acts 4:18), and in a negative meaning, but the idea that the new faith has a universal dimension and is transcending human distinctions and separations is already present. In the early church, the term "catholic" was used as designation of the "catholic epistles" addressed to the whole church and, increasingly, as attribute of the church. The catholic church is coextensive with the whole inhabited world and is truly orthodox in **doctrine**, thereby being the true church as opposed to heretical and schismatic groups. In the Nicene-Constantinopolitan Creed of 381 (*see* CREEDS, ECUMENICAL), "catholic" was received as a basic qualification of the church. Around 350 Cyrill of Jerusalem describes catholicity as a complex concept referring to universal extension, soundness of doctrine, adaptation to the needs of all conditions of people, and moral and spiritual perfection. Today, this understanding is called quantitative (geographical) and qualitative catholicity. In his *Commonitorium*, Vincent of Lerins (d. before 450) states in his famous and simple formula that the catholic church should hold that "which has been believed everywhere, always, and by all."

In the late Middle Ages, a development began toward a "confessional" identification of "catholic" with the Roman Catholic Church, an identification that prevailed through the **Reformation** conflict until the Second Vatican Council (*see* VATICAN COUNCIL II). The Lutheran reformers (and also the Orthodox churches) contested this narrow concept that makes communion with the See of Rome a criterion of catholicity. They affirmed that their churches are part of the one, holy, apostolic, and catholic church through continuity with the faith of the early church. They returned to the broader understanding of catholicity in the early church, enriched by the reference to Holy Scripture: Truly catholic are those who believe that "which is supported by the witness of all time, of all ages, what the prophets and apostles taught, and which does not tolerate factions and heresies" (**Philipp Melanchthon**). In the Lutheran confessions (*see* CONFESSIONS, LUTHERAN), the combination of quantitative and qualitative catholicity, to which the aspect of diversity is added, is expressed in the *Apology of the Augsburg Confession*: The church catholic consists of "people scattered throughout the world who agree in the **Gospel** and have the same Christ, the same **Holy Spirit**, and the same sacraments, whether they have the same human traditions or not" (article 7:10).

In the following centuries of confessional strife, the exclusive claim to catholicity by the Roman Catholic Church led to a narrow, confessional understanding of catholic and the avoidance of the term by the other churches (apart from Anglican "Anglo-Catholics"). The **ecumenical movement** and the Second Vatican Council have liberated the term from its Roman captivity. Vatican II has made it clear that catholicity is broader than the Roman Catholic Church, and the ecumenical movement has recovered and restated the original sense of catholicity with its geographical, temporal, and theological perspectives. Catholicity is a quality that expresses the universal dimension of the church, including the diversity both of contexts and theological and cultural expressions of the faith. Catholicity refers at the same time to the continuity of the church in the fullness of the apostolic faith, to the integrity of the church in **mission**, **witness**, and service to all people, and to the all-inclusive totality of the church's life. The full manifestation of catholicity, however, will only appear in **eschatological** time. [G.G.]

CELIBACY (Lat *caelebs*, "unmarried"). Unmarried state, voluntary abstinence from sexual activity, usually as a characteristic of monastic and clerical life. It took the period between the fourth and the 12th century until clerical celibacy became officially prescribed. Celibacy is affirmed in Lutheranism only where it is an uncompelled divine gift. It is rejected altogether when it is imposed as a requirement toward a more spiritual human life or ministerial vocation. **Philipp Melanchthon** and the reformers rejected celibacy, as per the *Augsburg Confession* and its *Apology* (article 23), because imposed celibacy compromises the divinely intended blessing of **marriage**; correlatively, imposed celibacy opposes a human being's natural state; also correlatively, such an imposition forces a person to sin and is a burden to conscience. Human sexuality, rather, is a good in human life, to be fulfilled in the relationship of marriage. **Martin Luther's** personal exposition of this matter in the *Smalcald Articles* (article 11) is also an argument based as much on **natural law** as on divine **revelation** in Holy Scripture.

Celibacy is a topic within the current intra-Lutheran debate on the possible **ordination** of homosexual persons. Most church policies affirm such ordinations only with the caveat of a vowed celibate lifestyle. With regard to celibacy in general, many individuals and a few Lutheran monastic orders provide evidence that celibacy in Lutheranism may be affirmed and can be cultivated toward an enriching, voluntary, personal as well as communal life. [D.H.L.]

CHARISMATIC MOVEMENT AND RENEWAL. The movement of the middle 20th century that focused congregational life on **sanctification** expressed through the gifts of the **Holy Spirit**, particularly those of tongues and healing. This movement, which has affected almost every denomination and confessional family, seems by the turn of the millennium to become especially powerful and popular among Christians in Africa and South America. While it is similar to the Pentecostal movement, Charismatic Renewal is generally careful not to make of particular spiritual gifts (*charismata*) tests of spiritual maturity. Lutheran charismatics have generally recognized that requiring the gift of *glossalalia* ("speaking in tongues") to prove one is fully baptized—a common requirement among Pentecostals—leads to a division within the community. Since *charismata* are given in order to build up the community rather than to break it apart, such a requirement undermines not only the Lutheran understanding of **baptism**, but also the Pauline understanding of the gifts of the Spirit.

The Charismatic movement shares with **Pietism** a commitment to the importance of emotion and experience in Christian life, an impatience with structures, the use of fervent, intimate small group meetings, and a focus on the relationship between the individual believer and Christ. Unlike Pietism in general, however, it is likely to claim the Spirit, rather than the **Word**, as the person of the **Trinity** at particular work in the world, and to see that Spirit working among and between believers rather than mostly within the individual. [M.O.]

CHEMNITZ, MARTIN (1522–1586). One of the prominent Lutheran reformers. Chemnitz studied at **Wittenberg** in 1545/46. After several years of study and work as librarian in Königsberg, Prussia, he returned in 1554 to Wittenberg where he became closely associated with **Philipp Melanchthon**. In 1566 he was called back to supervise the **Reformation** in Prussia. A year later he was appointed **superintendent** of Braunschweig (1567), and the following year was asked to help to consolidate the Reformation in the duchy of Braunschweig-Wolfenbüttel (1568/69). Chemnitz then began to cooperate especially with **Jakob Andreae** in the work leading up to the *Formula of Concord* (1577) and the *Book of Concord* (1580). He helped to found the University of Helmstedt in 1576 and taught there as professor until 1583/84.

Chemnitz rendered an important and effective contribution to the establishment of the Lutheran Reformation and the struggle towards Lutheran unity. He took a cautious middle path between the **Gnesio-Lutherans** and the **Philippists**. Among his numerous books, his *Examen Concilii Tridentini* (1565–1573) was a careful analysis of the doctrinal decisions of the Council of Trent (*see* TRENT, COUNCIL OF) and found wide and positive attention. [G.G.]

CHOIR. A group of singers providing musical leadership for congregational **worship**. As worship services became more elaborate in Christian history, and as composers set their hand to the composition of settings of the unchangeable texts, trained groups replaced the **congregation** in singing, for instance, the *Sanctus*. **Martin Luther**, in his influential *German Mass*, returned these invariable pieces—the Ordinary—to the congregation in the form of **chorales**. But that is not to say that he outlawed the choirs. Indeed, his *Formula Missae* assumes that the choir will sing the Ordinary. **Johann Walter**, Luther's colleague and musical preceptor, led the way in the establishment of a peculiarly Lutheran use of the choir. His **Kantorei**, a choir of professional musicians, not only performed motets, psalm settings, **passions**, and other music, but also began "alternatim practice," that is, alternating stanzas of **hymns** between congregations and choir, with the choir stanzas sometimes of quite awesome complexity. Under such Baroque masters as **Dietrich Buxtehude** and **Johann Sebastian Bach**, the choir reached a pinnacle in its ability to surround the sermon with an equally expository **cantata**.

During the 19th century this close connection between sermon and choir music became rare. The choir neither led congregational singing nor aided congregational meditation on the lessons. Rather, it performed "special music," rarely connected, except on festivals, to the rest of the service. In mid-20th-century North America this tendency was reversed as chapel choirs at church-related colleges modeled the power of a service integrally connected. This integrity was also encouraged by the rush of choir publications, the establishment of summer music programs, and the revival of the office of cantor as responsible for all congregational song, rather than just that of the choir.

The choir is hardly a feature of European and North American life alone. Indeed, it is a vital part of congregational life throughout Africa, where congregational singing groups compete with one another for clarity of sound, rhythmic invention, and fidelity to the **Gospel**. With a new appreciation for contextual cultural expression, the Gospel is not only sung, but drummed and danced by specially prepared groups in almost every congregation on the continent. *See also* MUSIC IN THE LUTHERAN CHURCH. [M.O.]

CHORALE. A **hymn**, usually from Germany or Scandinavia of the 16th or 17th century. At first intended for unison singing by a **congregation**, it lent itself almost immediately to harmonic and contrapuntal elaboration. It was the chorale, growing from a folk adaptation of the minnesinger tradition, that **Martin Luther** used to return the invariant texts of the Mass to the people. He was himself the first great lyricist of chorales and either by himself or with **Johann Walter** composed the most popular melodies. Some, like *A Mighty Fortress*, were original compositions, but more, like *Savior of the Nations, Come*, and *Christ Jesus Lay in Death's Strong Bands*, were adapted from plainsong. Later, in a practice known as *contrafacta*, the melodies of popular secular songs were replaced by texts appropriate for congregational or meditative singing. Chorales are distinguished from plainsong by their often complicated rhythm and their occasional leaps in melody. They are more rugged, more complicated, and more difficult to sing than the slow-moving Geneva psalm tunes.

By the end of the 16th century composers such as Hans Leo Hassler, Michael Praetorius, and Johann Schein began setting chorales in four-part harmony with more regular rhythm, a practice that eventually all but eliminated the original, unison, rhythmic versions. By the 18th century musical fashions decreed that new, more lyrical tunes be used in **devotion** and music. The existing chorales were still used and in fact enshrined in the *de tempore* system and in the **cantatas**, **oratorios**, and **passions** of **Johann**

Sebastian Bach. It remained for such 20th-century composers as **Hugo Distler** and Jan Bender to recover them in their rugged splendor. [M.O.]

CHRISTIAN EDUCATION. The formation of Christian people in their **faith**. Jesus' own teaching of the disciples, most clearly expressed in the Sermon on the Mount, might be seen as the first example of Christian education, an example the early church was commanded to follow in the Great Commission (cf. Mt 28:19–20). Later generations focused on **catechesis**, the education of those preparing for **baptism**, with continuing education of the baptized concentrating on teaching regarding controverted issues. While the Middle Ages saw an explosion in what might be called graduate studies, the monasteries and monastic tutors also carried on basic education in literacy and the humanities, providing clerks for courts and the developing economic system, an education that was integrated with religious training. **Martin Luther** urged that this system be significantly expanded. While assuming that the curriculum would continue to center on **theology** and the Scriptures, he urged state-sponsored, compulsory education for all boys and girls. In part because of their commitment to preparing **laity** to judge **preaching** and to search the Scriptures, and in part because of their understanding of **vocations**, Lutheran churches have almost universally supported education. In some cases, for instance, in the state churches of Europe and the eastern synods of the United States, this support has led them to encourage and involve themselves in public education. In other cases, for instance, in Africa, Asia, and the Midwestern synods of the United States, this support has led to the establishment of church schools.

Especially in countries where public education is the norm and where the church is excluded from involvement in the schools, Lutherans took part in the Sunday school movement begun in the 18th century, and in the vacation church schools and weekday after-school programs that sprang from that movement. The Sunday school movement involved not only the religious education of children and youth but, especially in the late 19th and early 20th centuries, was also a lay-led movement of adult education. Together with the consistent Lutheran tradition of **confirmation**, the Sunday school was a model of life-long learning that recent efforts, focusing on intergenerational involvement and adult Bible study, have attempted to reestablish. The preparation and support of congregational directors of Christian education, teachers, and **superintendents** has been a constant mission of church related colleges, seminaries, and judicatories. [M.O.]

CHRISTIAN WORLD COMMUNIONS. Worldwide associations of churches belonging to the same confession or tradition. In the 19th century churches belonging to the same tradition began to establish structures and organizations for cooperation, exchange, and furtherance of relationships within their "family." In 1867 the series of Lambeth Conferences of all Anglican bishops was inaugurated, followed by the establishment of the World Alliance of Reformed Churches (1875), the Methodist World Council (1881), the Baptist World Alliance (1905), and others. The youngest among these world communions is the **Lutheran World Federation** (LWF), which was not founded until 1947. These associations or communities were first called "confessional families," but several of them disliked the term. Instead, the term "Christian World Communions" (CWC) has come into common use since about 1980. The CWCs have diverse organizational structures and differ in their self-understanding. However, they have an important feature in common: They are responsible for carrying out the international bilateral dialogues (*see* DIALOGUES, BILATERAL). In order to share their ecumenical experiences and reflect on their place and role in the **ecumenical movement**, the responsible secretaries of the CWCs as well as representatives of the Vatican and the **Orthodox churches** have come together in an annual conference since 1957. Since 1978 their conference has authorized the "Forum on Bilateral Conversations" that has so far held seven meetings. This ecumenical involvement of the CWCs has significantly increased their role and importance in worldwide Christianity. [G.G.]

CHRISTIANSEN, FREDRIK MELIUS (1871–1955). American composer, conductor, and musician. An immigrant from Norway, who studied in America and Germany, Christiansen came to St. Olaf College, Northfield, Minnesota, in 1903 and spent 40 years as chair of the music department. Although at first known primarily as a violinist, he began to focus on choral composition and conducting after studying with the cantor of St. Thomas in Leipzig in 1906–1907. Most of his compositions were of two sorts: arrangements of **chorales**, and settings of poetry and Scripture, reminiscent of Norwegian folk music. Both sorts of compositions were lush, full, melodic, and emotional.

His students included uncounted directors of congregational and collegiate choirs. Most notable among these students were his sons Olaf, who succeeded him in his college post from 1943 until his own retirement in 1968, and Paul, who conducted the Concordia College Choir of Moorhead, Minnesota, for 49 years. Through Fredrik Christiansen's work on *The Lutheran Hymnary* (1913), he helped move many Lutherans of Scandinavian heritage into the use of English with no loss of **piety**. But his main accomplishment was his development of the St. Olaf College Choir, established in 1912, whose tours and alumni defined an ideal choral sound for generations. *See also* MUSIC IN THE LUTHERAN CHURCH. [M.O.]

CHRISTMAS. Feast of the birth of Jesus Christ. Since Christ's **resurrection** was the central festive event for the early **church**, there is evidence for celebrating Christmas (December 25) and Epiphany (January 6) in the West only from the fourth (Roman calendar of 354) century onwards. This pattern of the Western church was continued by the Lutheran churches. Thus, a Christmas season of 12 days (leading to the Twelfth Night) between December 25 and January 6 was established. With its emphasis on a **God** who has come into the midst of human beings, the celebration of the **Incarnation**, of God's becoming human in Jesus Christ, has received major attention in **Lutheranism**. Accordingly, the festive season of Christmas has been celebrated both with deep spiritual **devotion** and with many popular **customs**. As with the whole **Advent** season, the celebration of Christmas ("Christ's Mass") is observed by Lutherans with many glorious **hymns**, great **church music**, and several popular customs including the Christmas tree. In Lutheran churches, Christmas Eve has become a major celebration with large crowds in contrast to the more solemn main **worship** service on Christmas Day [G.G.]

CHRISTOLOGY. The **doctrine** of the personhood of **Jesus Christ**. Christology in the Lutheran tradition is consonant with the whole ecumenical, catholic **tradition**. This is to say that **Lutheranism** also holds within itself all the varieties and extremes of doctrinal proposals relative to the person of Jesus Christ. Steering faithfully between the ruts of ebionitism—which holds that Jesus was but a human servant of **God**—and **docetism**—which holds the opposite, that Jesus was but the *form* of a man—has been as challenging for Lutheran theologians as anyone else.

Martin Luther's own Christology has a variety of emphases, but holds firmly to the classical tradition that Christ was and is of two natures: true God, and true man. What is particularly remarkable about Luther's construal, and all confessional Lutheran theology thereafter, is the claim that in Jesus God was "deep in the flesh" and that what transpired to that flesh had and has direct import for the "divine side" of the experience of God. While this insight was formalized in the Lutheran language of the "communication of attributes" (*communicatio idiomatum*), it emerges from the assembly of other different Lutheran emphases. For example, Luther held that Christ is the "simul"; he is the one divine/human person who unites all contradictions (e.g., God and humanity, time and eternity, righteousness and **sin**). For Luther, Christ is the ontological and metaphysical center in which everything finds its unity.

Secondly, and perhaps more simply, Christ is Lord. In the indulgence controversy, as Luther argued it, it was Christ's very lordship that was at stake, threatened by the whimsical authority of **bishops** and popes (*see* PAPACY). Because Christ is Lord, and Christ has achieved in **justification** the **salvation** of all people, demand for further penance and payment was a direct challenge to the lordship of Christ as well as a bane to the **conscience** of would-be simple believers. Thirdly, Luther mixed and used many different Christological images from the New Testament, **Augustine**, and Bernard of Clairvaux. One sees the titles and images employed freely and abundantly throughout Luther's sermons, exegetical writings, and especially his sacramental theology (*see* SACRAMENTS). That the images could be used in so free a way demonstrates Luther's belief in the significance of Jesus as Lord of all; the use is a practical example of applied high Christology. The distinctiveness of the original Luther insight shines forth especially in the connection of the theology of the **cross** (*theologia crucis*) with the **dogma** of the two natures. In the *Heidelberg Disputation* and in his *Explanations of the Ninety-five Theses*, Luther showed that God chooses to reveal himself in the opposite, particularly in, with, and through that which humanity in its pretensions would never expect: humility, suffering, and death. By becoming so engaged in and with creatures under the condition of sin, without being overwhelmed by sin, God in Jesus thereby has "redeemed me, a lost and condemned creature, delivered me and freed me from all sins, from death, and from the power of the devil" (explanation to article 2, *Small Catechism*).

On the basis of the communication of attributes that unites and redefines both God and humanity in ongoing reciprocity—ongoing because of the fact of Christ's resurrection—second-generation Lutheranism wrote even more trenchantly on God's "depth in the flesh." With the *Formula of Concord*, especially in the argument about real presence with the Sacramentarians, Lutheran Christology's phenomenon of the communication of attributes was given an ongoing present tense; humanity is *still* being created toward the fuller manifestation of the *imago dei* (*see* ANTHROPOLOGY), poignantly so in and through the **Lord's Supper**, and God *too* suffers and enjoys the sins and ecstasies of justified humanity (*see* JUSTIFICATION). Present-day evocations of this perspective in Christology—particularly resonant in the work of Finnish theologians, Eastern Orthodox contributions to **ecumenical theology**, theology on the Trinity (*see* TRINITY, DOGMA OF), and an emerging communion (*koinonia*) ecclesiology—are wholly coherent with the Lutheran tradition, especially with the ways it was spelled out in the work of **Philipp Melanchthon**, **Martin Chemnitz**, and **Johannes Brenz**.

Some theologians have argued that Luther's was a functional Christology, derived from a previous atonement theory. What they do not recognize is that Luther's "high" Christology of the "simul" God-Man is an ontological requirement for whatever **atonement** theory Luther has to succeed. This is clearly the case with Luther's further reflection that Christ is both **sacrament** and model (*sacramentum* and *exemplum*) for humankind. Only because Christ unites in himself the divine and the human, the eternal and the historical, and the suffering and the sublime can Christ then effect the "happy exchange" whereby a sinful humanity is given Christ's crown of glory. Eventually, however, both Lutheran **Orthodoxy** and **Pietism** would borrow from the Calvinist "three office" (*triplex munus*) Christology, wherein Jesus is known from Scripture as priest, prophet, and king. This borrowing would pale somewhat from the original Lutheran insight; it would be paler yet in **Liberalism's** prominent use of the theme. However, when contemporary Christological proposals of representation, by which Jesus is seen to represent fully God to humanity and likewise fully humanity to God *in* Jesus' own person, are rerooted in Luther's high Christology of communion rather than based on Liberalism's view of the *triplex munus*, a Christology of representation may have proclamatory force in a democratic age, as seen in Reformed theologian Douglas John Hall's use of such Lutheran themes. Representation Christology has found depth again in the work of Paul Tillich, mediating Swedish theologians like Anders Nygren and Gustaf Wingren, and in contemporary Finnish theology's accent on deification.

Clearly, Luther and Lutheranism developed new languages to move beyond the Greek categories of substances, accidents, and natures that shaped early Christian confession. Some Lutheran proposals have not endured; a primary Lutheran insight, aided by many images and applications from Luther himself and onward, has abided. Clearly, too, new Christological proposals will rise and fall. Christology is a dynamic enterprise of two reasons: Christ lives and will come again, and intellectual and popular **philosophy** is characterized by ever new predicates. The success of Christological proposals, as ever, will have to do with their ability to be faithful to both the classical witness to the incarnation of God in Jesus Christ and to the peculiar Lutheran insight that God has come "deep into the flesh" for our salvation. [D.H.L.]

CHURCH. (Gk *to kyriakon*, "that which belongs to the Lord"). The community of Christians gathered by the Triune **God** through **Word** and **sacrament**. The early Christian community was convinced, according to the New Testament, that it continued the history of the people of God of the Old Testament, but in a new era of trinitarian and universal dimensions. This continuity was expressed in many ways, for example, by the relationship between the old and the new covenant (Mk 14:24; 1 Cor 11:25) and between promise and fulfillment (Gal 4:4–6; Lk 22:20), and by the salvation historical perspective (*see* SALVATION HISTORY) in which the church presupposes the history of Israel (Heb 1:1ff; Rom 9:6).

The beginnings of the Christian church are today generally seen in the Easter experience of the disciples, confirmed by the sending of the **Holy**

Spirit (Pentecost). The main term for the emerging church is *ekklesia*, which refers both to a local Christian gathering (e.g., Rom 1:7; 16:1; Kol 2:1; 1 Thess 2:14) and to the church in the larger, universal sense (e.g., 1 Cor 2:1; 10:32; Gal 1:13; 1 Thess 2:14; 1 Cor 1:2; 2 Cor 1:1). Among the many images used to characterize the Christian community, the most important ones are Body of Christ (Rom 12; 1 Cor 12) with Christ as its head (Col 1:18); People of God (Heb 4:9; 1 Pet 2:9f.); Temple of the Holy Spirit (1 Cor 6:19); and Koinonia/community (*see* COMMUNION). Diverse gifts of the Holy Spirit (Gk *charismata*) are given to the church (1 Cor 12:4–11), **baptism** and the **eucharist** are celebrated, and ministerial offices begin to emerge (Acts 11:30; 20:17–28; 1 Tim 3:2) together with their responsibility to preserve and hand on the apostolic **faith** (1 Tim 6:20).

The expansion and consolidation of the church during the first centuries led to the general acceptance of the ministerial structure of **bishop** (in **apostolic succession**), presbyter, and **deacon** since the second century and the introduction of the system of parishes since the fourth century. Regional or provincial synods and later the ecumenical councils (*see* COUNCILS, ECUMENICAL) became instruments to safeguard the **unity of the church** and, together with the reception of the **Canon of Holy Scripture** and the use of baptismal **creeds**, to clarify and define official **doctrine**. While the church fathers (*see* PATRISTICS) had considered the church as a community both centered in the bishop and being a mystical, spiritual body of believers, in the medieval church this understanding is absorbed by a concept of the church primarily as a visible, juridical, hierarchical institution. In the High Middle Ages, the church, having its center of authority and power in the pope, claims great spiritual and worldly power. Such a development may have been facilitated by the absence of a systematically developed theological reflection on the nature of the church—a reflection that begins only in the 15th century and then especially in the **Reformation**. There were, however, individual theologians during this period like **Thomas Aquinas** who continued to distinguish between the church as a mystical body and as an institutional, hierarchical society (*societas*).

Martin Luther and other reformers rejected the late medieval image and reality of the church and replaced them with a reform and renewal governed by an understanding of the church as a "creature of the word," a community of believers, a "holy people" under their Lord and Savior Jesus Christ. This community is gathered by the Holy Spirit through the **Gospel** in Word and sacrament as a general **priesthood of all baptized believers,** served by a regularly called and ordained **ministry**. The true church, according to Luther, is hidden in the visible church where it exists along with the false church. But the true church can be recognized with the help of marks such as the **Word of God**, **baptism**, the **Lord's Supper**, the office of the keys (*see* CHURCH DISCIPLINE), **ordination**, prayer to and praise of God, and suffering as a consequence of the **cross**.

In the Lutheran confessions (*see* CONFESSIONS, LUTHERAN), the decisive and much quoted text on the church is article 7 of the *Augsburg Confession*: The church, which will be and remain forever, is an assembly of believers/saints among whom the Gospel is preached in its purity and the sacraments are administered according to Christ's institution. Word and sacrament as the means of the active presence of the Triune God are thus the causal foundation of the existence of the church, the sustaining energy of the life of the church, and the basic condition, when agreed upon—the article continues—of the unity of the church. **Philipp Melanchthon** distinguished in his *Apology of the Augsburg Confession* between the church in the "larger sense" that includes both true Christian and hypocrites and unrepentant sinners, and the church in the "proper sense" of those who truly believe the Gospel. He underlines that the true church is not invisible but is recognizable in the true believers throughout the world and by its marks of the pure teaching of the Gospel and the celebration of the sacraments according to God's Word. It is the Holy Spirit that leads people into the church and is active in and through the church for the **sanctification** of its members. Within the church and through its proclamation, sacraments, and spiritual fellowship, people receive forgiveness of **sins**, **salvation**, and consolation. These affirmations are governed by the center of Reformation thinking: the church is the community of those who are graciously justified by God for Christ's sake. It is a community of persons, a spiritual reality, not constituted by a gathering of like-minded people, but brought together by the Holy Spirit through the Gospel in Word and sacrament.

The later Melanchthon and then Lutheran **Orthodoxy** in the 17th century shifted the emphasis more toward the visible, institutional church, marked by the pure teaching of the Gospel, the use of the sacraments, and obedience to the office of the ministry. The true church became the church with the right doctrine—the Lutheran church, and the false church, the papal church. Lutheran **Pietism** in the 18th century moved away from the orthodox focus on correct doctrine to true personal faith and to the church as a community of converted true believers (also outside the Lutheran church). Since **Enlightenment** and theological **Liberalism** had regarded the church primarily as an association for the cultivation of religious and moral needs, **Neo-Lutheranism** in the 19th century reacted strongly by reemphasizing Lutheran confessional convictions, colored by Lutheran Orthodoxy and Pietism. The church is instituted by Christ mainly as a visible organism in which Word and sacraments are administered by the office of the ministry. The church (of Christ) manifests itself in a number of church bodies or institutions, but in different degrees. This general recognition of the different churches includes the claim, however, that the Lutheran church is the true church because its confessions represent the true faith in full agreement with Holy Scripture.

In the 20th century Lutheran reflection on the church has generally continued the basic lines of Reformation and confessional perspectives. This reflection was forced, however, to reconsider issues like **church and state**, the **mission** of the church through **evangelism** as well as social witness and action, and the relationship between church and society in general and in countries with a state church or folk church tradition in particular. The **ecumenical movement** has helped Lutheran churches to face more concretely the issue of the unity of the church, consider its own worldwide family of Lutheran churches (*see* LUTHERAN WORLD FEDERATION) in an ecclesiological perspective, and become enriched in its own ecclesiological thinking by insights and forms of life of other churches, for example, by viewing the church as a **communion** of faith, life, **witness**, and service. [G.G.]

CHURCH AND SOCIETY or CHURCH IN SOCIETY. A phrase that refers to how Lutheranism understands the divinely intended relationship of the church to the **social order**. While the conjunction "and" has been typical in the phrase; the preposition "in" has recently become the more preferred term. It communicates the conviction that **God** intends the **church** to live from the **Gospel** for the world, while in but not of the world. The distinctions are basic. They summarize that the church is a "new creation" (2 Cor 5:17–18), originated from **Word** and **sacrament**, and active in **love** (*see* ETHICS) for the just relationships and structures of society by mediating conflict and addressing emerging social problems.

In so doing, the church may engage in political advocacy, though without adopting a political or ideological party spirit, in accord with the Lutheran understanding of **two kingdoms**. Working for justice in the social order, then, is a distinct Christian calling (*Augsburg Confession*, article 16) and is the **vocation** of all baptized individuals (*see* PRIESTHOOD OF ALL BELIEVERS) to be exercised according to creative **reason** informed by love. To discharge its duties institutionally and to encourage its individual members, the Lutheran Church in America employs the helpful concept of church as "a community of moral deliberation." *See also* CHURCH AND WORLD. [D.H.L.]

CHURCH AND STATE. The relation of **church** and state. Three general patterns typify the possibilities of church-state relationships, the first of which was the pattern from which the Lutheran **Reformation** broke free; the two subsequent patterns are, arguably, highly influenced by Lutheran theology itself. These patterns are: ruling of the state by the church—known as theocracy; ruling of the church by the state; and legal separation of the two. The immediate background to the Reformation, of course, was basically a theocratic form, wherein spiritual and temporal authority were distinguished, but not separated. The church's spiritual dominion was higher than and included the temporal authority of the princes, as Pope Gelasius I first stated at the end of the fifth century. The distinction without separation was maintained in the Lutheran movement, though more functional authority was given to the temporal state. Spiritual authority, however, was not given over to the state. But, pragmatically, the Reformation advanced and polity was established where there were political friends in high places. For example, because Roman Catholic bishops were not friendly to reforming impulses in Germany, political patrons such as Elector **Frederick the Wise** of Saxony—for **Martin Luther** the model of the pious civil servant—supported Luther and became, de facto, the administrative head of the church in that region; he ratified theological professorships and church **superintendents** (*see SUMMUS EPISCOPUS*).

This model served as a preview of the Religious Peace of Augsburg (1555) (*see* AUGSBURG, PEACE OF), which granted the secular rulers the right to determine the religion (Catholic or Lutheran) of their individual German states or electorates. Thus was set in motion the pattern that states would have purview of the churches. In the Scandinavian countries, this model was (unintentionally) expanded as early as 1530 in Denmark, where King Christian II declared that only **evangelical** Christianity would be allowed. Similar church-state arrangements took hold subsequently in Sweden, Norway, Finland, and Iceland. In a differing pattern, the Reformation took hold in Baltic cities early as well, where the governing oversight was much more local, and similarly in small pockets throughout the rest of Europe by the end of the 16th century.

In all these, though to quite varying degrees, the operation of the church was subject to the administration, at last formally, and financial support of the civil order. Nevertheless, following its own delimitation of episcopal power in article 28 of the *Augsburg Confession* and its *Apology*, as well as in the *Treatise on the Power and Primacy of the Pope*, Lutherans reserved spiritual authority to the church, though it might take a civil magistrate to convene a theological debate to adjudicate orthodoxy.

The fast held distinction between spiritual and temporal power helped to reinforce a legal separation of church and state when Lutheranism was transplanted by immigration and **mission** to other countries, where church life was financed by local voluntary support rather than state taxation. The concept of legal separation includes the possibilities of both friendly and hostile governmental attitudes toward religions or specific churches. In the latter context of **persecution** or discrimination, as in Nazi Germany or communist Central and Eastern Europe, Lutherans have been sustained by **faith** in the ultimacy of spiritual authority. In friendly contexts like the United States, Lutherans have needed to exercise a different caution than that of being taken for granted, as in the European churches. They have needed to guard against the confusion of the church-state separation with a misunderstood (i.e., passive) application of the doctrine of the **two kingdoms**, resulting in social **quietism**. It has been sometimes difficult for Lutherans to live out the mandate for active involvement in the civil order, which the two kingdoms doctrine underscores. This has been especially difficult in a climate in which the church-state separation may be misinterpreted as a divorce of private Christian commitment from public life. [D.H.L.]

CHURCH AND WORLD. Lutheran understanding of their relation. The Lutheran confessions display ambivalence with regard to the term "world" itself. On the one hand, the Lutheran doctrine of **creation** affirms that the natural world is good and displays **God's love**. The laws and authorities that govern the world, too, are established by God, as averred in the doctrine of **two kingdoms** and the Lutheran construal of **natural law**. The **church**, as the body of Christ, thus, lives in and from the world, and Christians embrace the world as the natural theater of God's love and the stage of their **vocation**.

On the other hand, "world" can denote the rebellious quarter of creation that refuses to acknowledge its creator. The world is a place of temptation and **sin**, bringing even Christians to "anger and impatience" (**Martin Luther's** *Large Catechism*, article 3:103). In this respect, the church is Christ's institutional vehicle for **redemption** of the world and the gathering in which Christians are enabled to live for the care of the world without belonging to it. Throughout Christian life, Lutherans perceive that the spiritual and worldly kingdoms each are to be affirmed in their God-created integrity without confusing them together, or by ignoring that each in its creatureliness can be subject to or an agent of sin. In the 20th century one finds this tensive balance most elucidated in the mediating theologies of writers like the Swedish Lutheran theologians Gustaf Wingren and Anders Nygren. *See also* CONFESSIONS, LUTHERAN; ECOLOGY; NATURE; SCIENCE AND CHRISTIANITY. [D.H.L.]

CHURCH DISCIPLINE. Regulations whose purpose is to order the moral and spiritual life of church members. The New Testament witnesses to forms of discipline in the Christian communities for the sake of their communal life and missionary integrity: sinners were privately admonished, then, if unrepentant, publicly, and, finally, expelled (Mt 18:15–18; cf. also 1 Cor 5:1–13; 2 Thess 3:6–13; Tit 3:10–11; and so on). The apostles received the power to bind and loose sinners (Mt 16:19; Jn 20:23), later called the "power of the keys." By the third century this power was exercised by the **bishop**. In the Middle Ages a distinction was made between the sacrament of penance (*see* FORGIVENESS) and ecclesiastical penal law.

Martin Luther wanted the **congregation** to administer church discipline, but in practice it was exercised by the pastors through the office or power of the keys. Luther and the confessions (*see* CONFESSIONS, LUTHERAN) clearly emphasized the pastoral and spiritual nature and practice of discipline. Acts of disciplining people cannot involve a judgement about their **salvation**, but are means to lead them back to **faith** and reestablish spiritual communion. Accordingly, the power of the keys, which could go so far as to exclude people from the **eucharist** until they "mend their ways," the "lesser excommunication," was seen by Luther in the *Smalcald Articles* (part 3, article 4) as one of the five functions of the **Gospel**. The confessions generally see the primary orientation of the power of the keys to pronounce absolution and comfort heart and mind.

Rationalism and **Enlightenment** brought about the disintegration of church discipline in Lutheran churches. Though traces of disciplinary regulations are still included in church constitutions, the dominant tendency today—by far not always practiced—considers pastoral care, proclamation of the Gospel, admission to **sacraments** and pastoral acts, and Christian teaching of faith and morals the most appropriate forms of spiritual and moral discipline. [G.G.]

CHURCH IN SOCIETY. *See* CHURCH AND SOCIETY.

CHURCH LAW. (Gk *kanon*, "rule, measure"). Provisions and laws, also termed "canon law," that regulate the life of a **church** in its historical existence. First traces of ordering church life, **worship**, admission to **sacraments**, behavior of members, and so on are to be found in the New Testament. With the expansion of the church during the first centuries, such rules and structures and soon also decisions of councils (*see* COUNCILS, ECUMENICAL) became part of the law of the church, and later also of imperial law. From the early Middle Ages onwards, codifications and collections of ecclesiastical laws, regulations, and papal decretals were undertaken. In the 16th century the officially approved *Corpus Iuris Canonici* (1580) became the basis for Roman Catholic canon law until 1917. Then it was replaced by the *Codex Iuris Canonici* that was reissued in a revised form in 1983.

The **Reformation** protested against the extension of canon law to secular areas and the burdening of **faith**, life, and consciences of Christians by the domination of canon law. Lutheran **church orders** and later church constitutions avoid legal prescriptions regarding spiritual matters but prefer instruction and admonition. **Church polity** and law ordering external church life in Germany and Scandinavia were part of state law until the 20th century, while churches outside of Europe had to develop their own legal regulations. In contrast to the greater emphasis on the role of church law in the **Reformed/Presbyterian** tradition, Lutherans have tried to keep church law on a secondary, pragmatic level. They regard it as an auxiliary means to assist in the primary task of the proclamation of the **Gospel** and the administration of the sacraments as well as a means to order the institutional life of the **church**. Lutheran churches, along with other churches today, are in danger of exchanging the late medieval church's captivity to canon law with captivity to church bureaucracies and secular management models. The right relation between the spiritual calling of the church and its institutional ordering remains a permanent challenge. [G.G.]

CHURCH MUSIC. The significance and role of music in the church. Behind the **Reformation's** consideration of music stand not only centuries of Christian practice, but millennia of philosophical thought. With Pythagoras's discovery of the mathematical relationships of musical tones, and the similarities to the regularity in the stars, music was seen as basic to **creation**—essential to the cosmic dance that gave visual expression to the music of the spheres. Even older was the notion that music had powerful ethical and psychological effects, that certain melodies and modes not only expressed emotion but also evoked it. Through the work of Boethius and others, these musical ideas held currency through the Middle Ages.

Among the reformers, **Martin Luther**, **Ulrich Zwingli**, and **John Calvin** held exemplary positions on music. Zwingli, probably the best musician of the three, nevertheless could be described as iconoclastic—teaching that music always distracts the Christian from truly spiritual **worship**, and that no form of music should be used in church. This position was modified, after biblical example, into a willingness to allow unaccompanied congregational singing of psalms. Calvin saw music as pedagogical, attracting would-be believers and guiding the immature into deeper connection with **God**. The use of music, however, would eventually be outgrown. While beginning at a position close to Calvin's, Luther, however, later saw music per se as a gift of God, both as a gift to drive away despair, and as a medium for the proclamation of the **Gospel**. Music was not to be outgrown, but delighted in; and this delight included not only congregational singing, but also choral and instrumental music, and even music outside the church with little obvious connection to the Gospel at all.

The theologians of Lutheran **Orthodoxy** honed a theology of music in response to what they considered Calvinist misconceptions. **Jakob Andreae** in particular denied that music itself was an **adiaphoron**, but claimed it as a positive good, going so far as to make it essential to the **Word** and **sacrament**. Other theologians of Orthodoxy and **Pietism**, from Theophilus Grossgebauer in the 17th century to **Samuel Simon Schmucker** in the 19th, dissented from this understanding, teaching that only music associated with an evangelical text was appropriate for worship, for instance. Some pietists went so far as to forbid all but congregational song, although few eliminated **hymns** for a pure reliance on psalms. Most present-day consideration of church music—Lutheran, Reformed, and even Roman Catholic—holds Calvin's understanding as a preconception, that music is to be used to attract worshippers and help them to mature. Recent research into the physiology of music has given scientific support to the ancient teaching of its fundamental connection with the emotions. This discovery has only begun to be explored as a basis for choosing styles of music appropriate for use in church, replacing appeals to tastefulness by other more subjective standards. *See also* HYMN AND HYMNODY, LUTHERAN; HYMNBOOKS, LUTHERAN; MUSIC IN THE LUTHERAN CHURCH. [M.O.]

CHURCH ORDERS. Constitutional documents, established during the **Reformation**, that regulated the life of the emerging Lutheran and **Reformed** churches. When Lutheran churches were recognized in a number of German territories and free cities, the churches needed a constitutional basis for their stability and the preservation of their Reformation understanding of the **Gospel**. Such a basis was also necessary in order to replace traditional **canon law**, liturgies, breviaries, and so on. Requested in most cases by secular authorities, prominent reformers like **Johannes Brenz** (church order of Württemberg 1553 and others), **Martin Bucer** (Strasbourg 1534 and others), **Johannes Bugenhagen** (Braunschweig 1528 [the first church order], Hamburg 1529, Denmark 1537, and others), and **Andreas Osiander** (Brandenburg-Nürnberg 1533 and others) were the authors of numerous church orders. These orders were different in scope, but many of them contained dogmatic instructions and requirements for **pastors** and teachers, confessional texts, orders of **worship**, as well as regulations for **church discipline** and governance, diaconal work, schools, and so on. The church orders, which were also introduced in Reformed churches all over Europe, were crucial for the consolidation of the Reformation. Several of them were issued anew in revised form up to the 19th century, when they were replaced by church constitutions. *See also* CHURCH POLITY; CONFESSIONS, LUTHERAN; DIAKONIA. [G.G.]

CHURCH POLITY (Gk *politeia*, Lat *politia*, "a community, administration of a commonwealth"). Principles and structures for the governance of a **church**. Elements of nascent congregational emphasis and presbyteral and episcopal leadership tasks in the New Testament came together in a structured form in the church of the second century when it generally accepted the threefold pattern of **ministry** of **bishop**, presbyter/**priest**, and **deacon**. The bishops governed the church, first in their own local community, later being in charge of several congregations. At the Council of Nicea in 325 (*see* COUNCILS, ECUMENICAL), the bishops accepted the pattern of dioceses and provinces of the Roman Empire as units for the organization of the church. The system of parishes (*see* CONGREGATION) was introduced in the late fourth century. Bishops of important provincial capitals received special recognition as archbishops (in the West) and metropolitans (in the East). Councils between Nicea 325 and Chalcedon 451 accorded patriarchal status to the churches and bishops of Rome, Constantinople, Alexandria, Antiochia, and Jerusalem. After the division between the Eastern and Western church in 1054, the polity of the church in the West became increasingly concentrated in the hands of the **papacy**, especially after it had consolidated its superiority over councils.

The Lutheran **Reformation** did not aim at establishing a separate church with its own reformed polity. When the break became unavoidable and Lutheran churches had to be organized, a preconceived ideal of church polity was not at hand, contrary to the **Reformed/Presbyterian** tradition with its clearly set out structures of ministry and presbyteral-synodical organs of church governance. Among Lutherans a more pragmatic approach prevailed with the openness to continue existing forms of polity like episcopacy and to create new ones as long as they are understood as being of human law (*iure humano*) and as long as they serve the main task and constitutive marks of the church, the proclamation of the **Gospel**, and the administration of the **sacraments**. Basic were the authority and role of the **congregation** and its ordained **ministry**. **Church orders** were introduced in many Lutheran churches in order to define their confessional stance (*see* CONFESSIONS, LUTHERAN) and to provide dogmatic instruction, orders of **worship**, regulations for **church discipline** and governance, and so on. In Scandinavia, the office of bishop could be continued or was reintroduced during the Reformation. Since this was not possible in central Europe, external church governance was delegated, as a "provisional" measure that lasted for 400 years, to territorial princes and magistrates of free cities (*see SUMMUS EPISCOPUS*). This polity was exercised by state consistories made up by pastors and jurists. In the 19th century the churches began to achieve a growing independence from state governance until they became free after 1918 to develop their own forms of polity.

Today, Lutheran church polity presents itself in a great diversity of forms that are not considered a threat to Lutheran unity. These forms include the basic unit of the congregation, units of several congregations (a deanery, or other designations), dioceses or synods or districts within a larger church, and national churches. The governance and administration of the churches is exercised with the help of congregational councils, synodical assemblies, church councils, consistorial or conciliar bodies, offices of church leadership (presidents and in most cases now bishops), and bishops' conferences as well as other structures and bodies in a variety of combinations and interrelations. [G.G.]

CHURCH STRUGGLE (Ger *Kirchenkampf*). Struggle about true and false **church** during the German Third Reich (1933–1945). The movement of the "German Christians," supported by the Nazi regime, advocated a synthesis between aspects of the nationalistic and racist ideology of the state and (**Protestant**) Christianity. In church elections in 1933, the German Christians gained the majority in the Lutheran, United, and **Reformed** churches. They tried to take over the governing bodies of these churches and form a united national church in line with their leadership principles. This threat provoked the formation of the **Confessing Church** within the different Protestant churches. The groups belonging to the Confessing Church were able to establish themselves in 1934 as the true representation of the German Evangelical Church (a federation of the territorial churches), and adopt as their theological manifesto the ***Barmen Theological Declaration***.

Due to the resistance and clear theological stance of the Confessing Church, the advance of the German Christians was stopped and they lost their initial power. This struggle was predominantly an internal conflict about true and false church. But members of the Confessing Church also became involved in resistance against the state, while the state acted in many instances against the Confessing Church (several martyrs, imprisonments, removal from office, and so on). During World War II, this struggle was taken up by Lutheran and Reformed churches in occupied Denmark, France, Holland, and Norway. In these countries, it also became a patriotic struggle. Despite much courageous witness, the representatives of the Confessing Church felt impelled after World War II to declare in the "Stuttgart Declaration of Guilt" of 1945 that the church had failed to witness more boldly, pray more faithfully, and love more intensely. This declaration opened the door for the full reintegration of the German churches into the **ecumenical movement**. *See also* BERGGRAV, EIVIND; BONHOEFFER, DIETRICH; CHURCH AND STATE. [G.G.]

CHURCH YEAR. The term comes from the 16th century and refers to the annual sequence of the **Sundays**, seasons, and **festivals** of Christian **worship** and spiritual life. The Lutheran **Reformation** maintained the inherited basic structure of the church year, but its late medieval elements were simplified and, where necessary, reshaped in an **evangelical** spirit. The year consists of the six seasons of **Advent**, **Christmas**, **Epiphany**, **Lent**, **Easter**, and **Pentecost** or **Trinity**. The appointed introits, Scripture readings, **hymns**, and **prayers** mark the way through the church year. *See also* SPIRIRITUALITY. [G.G.]

COLONIALISM. *See* MISSION HISTORY.

COMMUNION, HOLY. *See* LORD'S SUPPER.

COMMUNION/KOINONIA (Gk *koinonia*, Lat *communio*, "fellowship, communion, community, participation"). Christian communion/fellowship based on participation in the same divine reality. In Christian terminology "communion" has been used for a long time and with different meanings: The *communio sanctorum* in the Apostles' Creed (*see* CREEDS) was interpreted both as communion of **saints**, that is, the community of living and dead persons who share within the **church** in Christ's **salvation** and in the Holy Spirit's **sanctification**, and as communion in holy things, that is, the sharing in the **sacraments**. Communion is used in connection with the **Lord's Supper**, the Holy Communion, and its interconfessional sharing in open, limited, or reciprocal communion and the refusal of such intercommunion in closed communion (*see* LORD'S SUPPER IN ECUMENICAL DIALOGUE). The sacrament is received on communion days at the communion table or in private communion. The fellowship of all **Anglican** churches describes itself as the Anglican Communion. During recent decades, the term and concept of communion, often together or alternating with its Greek predecessor in the New Testament *koinonia* has steadily moved to the forefront as a term to describe the church and the **unity of the church**. Roman Catholic, Orthodox, and Anglican ecclesiologies have been using the term since the 1960s, which was then taken also into ecumenical dialogue, reflection, and statements. What are the biblical roots of communion/koinonia and the reasons for its new prominence?

In the New Testament, koinonia is understood as a gift of **God** that enables participation and communion with the Trinitarian God (1 Cor 1:9; 2 Cor 13:14; Phil 3:8–11). In the Lord's Supper, the partakers have koinonia with Christ and with one another (1 Cor 10:16–17). The faithful have koinonia in the **Gospel** (Phil 1:5) and in **faith** (Philemon 6). Koinonia constituted in this way is lived out in the sharing of faith, sacraments, **prayer**, and spiritual and material gifts and goods (Acts 2:42–47; 1 Jn 1; Rom 15:26–27; Heb 2:14; 1 Pet 1:4). Developing this biblical material further, the concept of communion/koinonia is seen today as comprehending and integrating the various elements of the understanding and reality of the church: its divine and human character, its interrelated local and universal manifestations, its inclusion of all sorts of persons and contexts, its doxological as well as missionary and social dimension, and its oneness and diversity. Communion/koinonia is able to hold together and interrelate these and other elements in a more inclusive, spiritual, and dynamic manner than traditional terms like fellowship, community, and unity. In ecumenical dialogue, the term is used in the **Faith and Order movement**, bilateral dialogues (*see* DIALOGUES, BILATERAL), and as a term to describe the already achieved full or partial communion between different churches. After years of debate, the **Lutheran World Federation** decided in 1990 to define itself constitutionally and theologically as a "communion of churches," thereby indicating the deeper spiritual and confessional bond that unites its member churches in faith, sacramental fellowship, **witness**, and service. *See also* ECUMENICAL MOVEMENT. [G.G.]

COMMUNION OF SAINTS. *See* CHURCH; COMMUNION/KOINONIA.

COMMUNISM. *See* SOCIALISM.

CONFESSING CHURCH (Ger *Bekennende Kirche*). Self-designation of groups of **laity** and **pastors** in the German Lutheran, United, and **Reformed** churches during the Nazi period from 1933–1945 that rejected and resisted the movement of the "German Christians" and their collaboration with the ideology of the state. The term "Confessing Church" was chosen in order to witness to the commitment, based on Holy Scripture and the confessional writings of the **Reformation**, of confidently confessing the Christian **faith** in response to the false teaching of the German Christians and in defense of the independence of the church over and against state interference. The Confessing Church movement created its own organizational structures, including governing committees, councils, theological seminaries, and especially its "confessing synods." The most famous of the latter was the synod at Barmen in 1934 that formulated and accepted the important *Barmen Theological Declaration*.

The Confessing Church, whose leading members included Karl Barth, **Dietrich Bonhoeffer**, and Martin Niemöller, claimed to be the true representation of the German Evangelical Church (a federation of the territorial churches). It was, indeed, able to considerably restrict the influence of the German Christians, whereas political resistance against the Nazi regime was undertaken only by individual members and small groups of the Confessing Church. Leading members and the theological stance of the Confessing Church very much influenced the rebuilding of church life in postwar Germany as well as the attitudes of the Lutheran and United churches under the Communist regime in East Germany between 1945 and 1989. *See also* CHURCH STRUGGLE. [G.G.]

CONFESSION (Lat *confessio*, "acknowledgment"). The fundamental Christian calling of confessing one's **faith** and confessing one's **sins**. The Old and New Testaments witness to individual and corporate acts both of confession of sin and of confession of faith. Confession of sin was formalized in the early church in the context of confession, repentance, and absolution. It has continued in the church as personal informal confession, corporate liturgical confession, and as part of the sacramental act of private confession and absolution.

Confession of faith, inspired by the **Holy Spirit** and as response to **God's grace**, has continued in Christian history in the form of spontaneous acts of confessing, short confessional texts that have received official status, such as **creeds** or confessional statements, and longer confessional documents, such as the Lutheran confessions that define and express the official teaching, self-understanding, coherence, and mission of a church. In **Protestant** usage, "confession" and "confessional" can also refer to particular church **traditions**, as the Lutheran or **Presbyterian** ones, or to "confessional families" (*see* CHRISTIAN WORLD COMMUNIONS). *See also* CONFESSIONS, LUTHERAN; FORGIVENESS. [G.G.]

CONFESSIONS, LUTHERAN. The authoritative confessional documents officially accepted by the **Lutheran churches**. The confession of **faith** and the confession of **sins** (*see* FORGIVENESS) have been an essential part of Christian faith since its beginning. Those who believe are called to publicly confess their faith with the help of confessional texts. A special type of such texts was developed at the time of the **Reformation** by **Presbyterian/Reformed** and Lutheran churches in the form of **catechisms**, articles of faith, or confessions in order to define and express their self-understanding. In the course of the 16th century the Lutheran confessional writings were officially accepted (*see* RECEPTION) by the Lutheran churches and finally assembled in the *Book of Concord* of 1580: *The Three Chief Symbols* (i.e., the Ecumenical **Creeds**); the *Augsburg Confession* (1530); the *Apology of the Augsburg Confession* (1530/31); the *Smalcald Articles* (1537); the *Treatise on the Power and Primacy of the Pope* (1537); the *Small Catechism* (1529); the *Large Catechism* (1529) (*see* CATECHISMS OF LUTHER); and the *Formula of Concord*. All Lutheran churches have accepted all or some of the confessions in the *Book of Concord*, and in every case the *Augsburg Confession* and the *Small Catechism*.

These confessions helped to preserve the fundamental convictions of faith of the Lutheran Reformation. They served as rallying points for the establishment of Lutheran churches in new lands and worldwide. Today, they are officially recognized by the Lutheran churches and the **Lutheran World Federation**, under the norm of Holy Scripture (*see* BIBLE, AUTHORITY OF), as authoritative criteria and guides for the proclamation, teaching, life, and **ecumenical** involvement of the churches. The confessions are the basis of their unity. More than other churches, the Lutheran churches are marked by the historical and contemporary role and significance of their confessions. But they are also aware that the confessions require new interpretation and application in new historical contexts. [G.G.]

CONFIRMATION. The pastoral and educational **ministry** of the church that is designed to help baptized children identify with the **faith**, life, and mission of the Christian community and that is celebrated in a public rite. In the early church, **baptisms** were generally performed by the **bishop**. When adult catechesis by the bishop became rare in the West, and infant baptisms became the norm, baptism occurred soon after birth and it became impossible for the bishop to take part. To preserve his connection with initiation, a particular part of the service was delayed until, in the normal round of episcopal visitation, the bishop would be present. The part reserved was the prayer for the gifts of the Spirit, together with the laying on of hands and anointing that accompanied that prayer. By the 13th century confirmation was seen as a **sacrament** separate from baptism.

Martin Luther and the confessions (*see* CONFESSIONS, LUTHERAN) denied the sacramental nature of confirmation, holding that it had no biblical warrant and, indeed, insulted baptism by separating the sending of the Spirit from incorporation into the body of Christ. Within the first generation of the **Reformation**, however, the Reformation churches felt the need for some sort of substitute for this rite, and the preparation that accompanied it. Four types of understandings of confirmation appeared among Lutherans soon after the Reformation, and two more appeared a century or two later. Various combinations of these six have characterized confirmation among Lutherans since. These types are: (1) catechetical (didactic, emphasizing the impartation of certain essentials of the faith in order to prepare people to begin receiving Holy Communion); (2) hierarchical (disciplinary, involving a confession of faith and a vow of obedience to the church and its ministers); (3) sacramental (epicletic, completing baptism and conferring a fuller church membership by giving the **Holy Spirit**); (4) traditional (conservative, attempting to hold to ancient use as far as evangelically possible, and not connecting confirmation with first communion); (5) pietistic (subjective, emphasizing the conversion of the confirmand); and (6) rationalist (a rite of passage, marking the entry of the confirmand as an adult into certain national, economic, and cultural groups). Whenever there was a rite of confirmation, it almost always included catechetical preparation, affirmation of belief by the confirmands, and the laying on of hands with intercessory prayer for the Spirit.

Confirmation became problematic when it was seen as the true time of incorporation into the **church**, and when it was seen as the terminus of learning for Christians. These dangers were, indeed, those outlined by Luther himself, but they later became the focus of criticism from the modern **liturgical movement** with its emphasis on baptism and on life-long learning. In the late 20th century worldwide emphasis on confirmation has shifted to its place as an affirmation of baptism, rather than completion of it; to a younger

age for first communion than for confirmation, so that sacramental participation may be a part of a child's growth; and to its inclusion in many transitional points in peoples' lives at which the guidance and gifts of the Spirit
may be prayed for. While the catechesis of adolescents remains important,
the adult catechumenate, leading to baptism rather than confirmation, is becoming more and more central, particularly in **mission** fields such as Europe and North America. [M.O.]

CONGREGATION. Basic unit within Christian churches. In the New Testament the first Christian communities were called *ecclesia*. This term referred both to the local community, gathered around the **Gospel** and the
Lord's Supper, as well as to the **church** in the wider, universal sense.
Within the wider church, the individual congregations, which are the church
in its full sense, are united with one another in a *koinonia* (Gk "communion,
community") of **faith** and **love**. Later parts of the New Testament indicate
the beginnings of a ministerial structure in the different congregations that
developed in the second century into the threefold pattern of **bishop**, presbyter, and **deacon**. The expansion of the church led to a regional (diocesan)
structure headed by a bishop who delegated congregational leadership to the
presbyters. Since the fourth century the parochial/**parish** system, compris-
ing a congregation of people who live in the same geographical area, became the general pattern.

The **Reformation** continued this system, but radically changed its un-
dergirding concept. The congregation no longer represented the lowest level
of a hierarchical order but was given back its essential place and responsibility. **Martin Luther** taught that the congregation has the authority to call
and dismiss pastors and judge their teaching. By translating the biblical *ecclesia* always with *Gemeine* (Ger *Gemeinde*, "congregation"), he may have
contributed to a certain "congregationalism" in Lutheran circles and
churches. However, the Lutheran confessions (*see* CONFESSIONS,
LUTHERAN)—including those written by Luther—clearly consider the
local congregation assembled around **Word** and **sacrament** both as full
manifestation of and integrally linked to the church as a whole.

The parochial system continues today in Germany and Scandinavia,
while on other continents congregations are formed by decisions of their
members. New forms of congregations have appeared for particular groups
of people (students, military, diaconal institutions, and so on) or purposes
(e.g., social engagement of base communities). [G.G.]

CONSCIENCE. The understanding and authority of the conscience in
Lutheranism (*see* ENLIGHTENMENT; ANTHROPOLOGY). Conscience
as an individual's "highest court," even though popularly attributed to **Martin Luther's** declamation of "Here I stand" at the **Diet of Worms**, falsely

characterizes the authentic Lutheran position. At best, the conscience on its own accord is a mode for general knowledge of **God**. Luther goes so far as to say that the conscience in its natural state may mediate a common knowledge that we should worship God and love the neighbor. This is an occasion when Lutherans affirm something close to the **natural law** position of medieval Catholicism. Even as a positive norm with regard to **faith**, conscience never is alone; its accountability formally is always in the context of Scripture (*see* BIBLE, AUTHORITY OF), **tradition**, and the present witness of the **church**. On matters other than **salvation**, as with **free will**, conscience is circumscribed by the qualified natural law mentioned earlier. But generally the conscience is regarded as a risky resource for ethical and religious guidance. As something affected by **original sin**, it must be purified and always brought into keener awareness (*see* LAW AND GOSPEL). When it is made acute by the revelation of divine law, the conscience is cast into anxiety and anguish, for it recognizes then its total inability to meet the law and achieve righteousness.

Luther understood that the conscience was connected with both one's internal and external life, in distinction from the modern **Protestant** psychologism that considers the conscience's arena to be only the solitary individual's internal life. For Luther, the conscience exposes our very life in a world that can become too small for us; the world can afflict and drive us into anguish as much as can the quieter voice of moral law. Conscience may attempt to build its own defenses against the world's threats. It will propose its **virtues**, its **salvation** systems, its substitute for what counts as authentic human being. But the history of conscience notes that it is always fickle. It is never certain about its present situation, and memory can bring past **sins** to haunt. So it was that Luther's keen pastoral understanding of the tenuous character of conscience led him to rediscover that only **justification** in Christ—and Christ *in* the conscience—restores viability to the conscience, bringing it into accord with God and the world. [D.H.L.]

CONSENSUS (Lat *consensus*, "agreement, unanimity, harmony"). Statement of agreement in **faith**. As early as in the New Testament, the diversity between Jewish and Gentile Christians and differences between teachers made it necessary to seek, under the guidance of the **Holy Spirit**, agreements on basic tenets and goals of the new faith. In early church history, consensus was achieved and expressed by creedal statements, the **Canon of Holy Scripture**, the concept of **apostolic succession**, and the decisions of synods and councils (*see* COUNCILS, ECUMENICAL). In the late Middle Ages, the collections of **canon law** and the exercise of papal primacy and infallibility (*see* PAPACY) were means and expressions of consensus. The common faith had to be agreed upon and expressed anew in the face of plurality, division, and **heresies**.

The early development of the Lutheran **Reformation** was marked by the constant struggle for consensus, both about the process and policies of the Lutheran movement and the content of the Christian truth as restated by the reformers. Consensus, under the norm of Holy Scripture (*see* BIBLE, AUTHORITY OF) and inspired by the **Holy Spirit**, became a means of defining doctrinal positions, providing direction for right proclamation, and securing the coherence and unity of the churches. The primary expression of consensus became the Lutheran confessions (*see* CONFESSIONS, LUTHERAN). Their most important text, the *Augsburg Confession*, states at the beginning of its first article: "Our churches teach with great consensus (unanimity)."

Today, diversity within and between churches poses the important task of mutual understanding, exchange, and struggle for the truth, agreement: consensus. Especially in **ecumenical** endeavors, the concept of consensus plays a major role. For Lutherans and some other churches, a theological consensus about fundamental issues of Christian **doctrine** is considered an indispensable presupposition and a basis for forms of the **unity of the church**. [G.G.]

CONSTITUTION. *See* CHURCH ORDERS; CHURCH POLITY.

CONTEXTUAL THEOLOGY. Theology that is attuned to, if not primarily influenced by one's situation, usually with regard to ethnicity, gender, economy, or geography. A product of the **Enlightenment's** "turn to the self," which underscored how one's own person and personal/historical circumstances influence the development and expression of theology, contextual theology seeks to identify more clearly the circumstances from which and for which theology is done. As a 20th-century development, contextual theology broadens the scope of source-awareness beyond the dualism of personal subjectivity and objective **revelation**, and so would guide and include even more than **liberation theology**, **political theology**, **feminist theology**, and so on. Newer expressions of contextual theology are influenced by growing research in sociology, psychology, and other human sciences, as well as the natural sciences (*see* SCIENCE AND CHRISTIANITY).

Of course, no theology would communicate and survive were it not in some degree contextually appropriate. With missiology (*see* MISSION), however, one is faced with the necessity of contextualization in a heightened degree, whether the mission field is local or distant, and it might only be the historian's long reach that can rightly assess how the task was met. Contextual theology was a signal agenda item for **Samuel Simon Schmucker**, for example, as he attempted to adapt Lutheranism to the American scene in the mid-19th century. Those who broke from him and the Gettysburg Seminary judged him to be excessively contextually appropriate. Like all theology that attempts to be both faithful to the past and communicative to the present, contextual theology can be a faith venture. [D.H.L.]

CONVERSION (Lat *conversio*, "turning around"). The radical change of mind and life away from old sinful ways towards a new life with **God** in Christ. In **mission** and evangelization (*see* EVANGELISM), "conversion" is understood as acceptance of the Christian **faith** by a member of another religion or a nonbeliever. The other use of "conversion" as referring to a change in confessional or denominational loyalty is regarded as no longer appropriate in an **ecumenical** era. Today, there is ecumenical agreement that personal conversion is, first of all, a presupposition of faith in God and discipleship of Christ. Such a conversion is described in Holy Scripture as turning to God in Christ, away from the former state of sinful enmity to God, and also as a change of mind and personal orientation toward a life with Christ and according to the values of the **kingdom of God**. Throughout church history there have been famous examples of conversions, and also many different interpretations of this reality.

    Martin Luther and the Lutheran confessions (*see* CONFESSIONS, LUTHERAN) closely link conversion with repentance (*see* FORGIVE-NESS). Contrary to late medieval teaching on human cooperation in the process of repentance and conversion, the Lutheran tradition emphatically underlined that conversion is entirely the work of God. Through the action of the **Holy Spirit**, people are enabled to come to contrition about their sinful existence and to trusting faith in God's forgiveness for Christ's sake (*see* CHRISTOLOGY). Conversion in this sense is a daily, life-long element of Christian existence, not merely a conversion experience on a specific date as described in later **Pietism**. Today, in addition to this basic understanding, the corporate dimension of conversion—conversion of the whole church—and the social-ethical implications of conversion—turning to an alternative Christian lifestyle and to serving those of God's children who are in special need—are also underlined. [G.G.]

COUNCILS, ECUMENICAL (Lat *concilium*, "assembly of the people"). Gathering of representatives of the **church** to discuss and decide matters of **faith** and **church order**. The adjective "ecumenical," that is, representing the whole inhabited world and the whole church, is generally reserved for the first seven councils between Nicea I (325) and Nicea II (787). During the early period of the Christian church, the terms "council" and "**synod**" were used interchangeably. During the second half of the second century regional synods became an important means for the growing church to consider jointly issues of **faith**, **church discipline**, and church unity (*see* UNITY OF THE CHURCH). This "conciliar" method gained special significance in the Roman-Byzantine Empire where it became part of the ecclesiastical as well as the political structure of the empire. The emperors convened all the bishops of the empire to deal with fundamental questions of faith or church order that threatened to divide the church and the empire. The first four ecumenical councils, Nicea I (325), Constantinople I (381), Ephesus (431), and Chalcedon (451), occupy a privileged place for most of Christianity today because of their clarification and formulation of the fundamental Christological and trinitarian dogmas (*see* CHRISTOLOGY; TRINITY, DOCTRINE OF). The three subsequent councils at Constantinople II (553), Constantinople III (680), and Nicea II (787) are recognized by the Orthodox church as also belonging to the seven ecumenical councils of the undivided church. The authority of the councils rested primarily on their faithfulness to the apostolic faith (*see* APOSTOLICITY) and the **reception** of their decisions by the whole church.

At the time of the **Reformation**, **Martin Luther** still hoped that a truly universal council would be able to reform the church. His thinking was in line with the movement of conciliarism in the 14th and 15th centuries, which held that the authority of an ecumenical/general council would overrule that of a pope. But Luther proposed further changes for such a council, especially the participation of competent laity and not only bishops. In 1518 and 1520 Luther appealed for a free, Christian council. In the Leipzig disputation of 1519 he rejected the claim to infallibility of councils—they can and have erred. In his writings about councils, especially also in *On the Councils and the Church* (1539), Luther affirmed again and again that the authority of councils depends on the conformity of their decisions with the **Word of God** in Holy Scripture (*see* BIBLE, AUTHORITY OF). Luther even drafted a statement of basics of **evangelical** belief to be submitted to the council convened by Pope Paul III to meet at Mantua in 1537 (it actually met at Trent, 1545–1563 [*see* TRENT, COUNCIL OF]). The evangelical estates decided against participating in the council and Luther's text became the *Smalcald Articles* of 1537. The great esteem in which the first four councils were held in Lutheranism and the Lutheran confessions (*see* CONFESSIONS, LUTHERAN) has continued in the history of Lutheranism.

After the ninth century particular or general councils have been, in fact, councils of the Roman Catholic Church. The Second Vatican Council (1962–1965) (*see* VATICAN COUNCIL II) affirmed the authority of the pope over the council: the pope convokes a council, presides over it, and confirms its decisions. As a reform council, Vatican II has led to a new appreciation of conciliarity and councils. This also had an effect on the **ecumenical movement** where the concept of conciliarity in the sense of joint deliberation and decision making with the assistance of the **Holy Spirit** has been taken up since the 1960s. The assemblies of the **World Council of Churches** at Uppsala in 1968 and at Nairobi in 1975 expressed the hope that one day a genuinely universal council may once again speak for all Christians who have found their unity in a "conciliar fellowship of churches" (*see* UNITY OF THE CHURCH). [G.G.]

COUNCILS OF CHURCHES. Voluntary associations of churches for the purpose of engaging in common study and action on matters of Christian **unity**, **faith**, and **ethics**, and to undertake programs of joint **witness** and service (*see* DIACONIA). Councils of churches or Christian councils (other designations are also used) have emerged as permanent institutional expressions of the **ecumenical movement**. Mainline **Protestant** churches were the first ones that came together in such voluntary, federative associations. Councils exist on local (e.g., town), regional, and national levels. They respect the full autonomy of their members (churches, **mission** agencies, other church organizations, and so on). Councils go back to early initiatives at the end of the 19th century, and in 1905 the French Protestant Federation became the first one. Three years later, in 1908, the Federal Council of the Churches of Christ in America came into being, and was renamed in 1950 as the National Council of the Churches of Christ in the USA. This organization has by far the most extensive program and the largest staff of all the councils.

The Protestant constituency of the councils has been broadened during the last decades by Orthodox membership and, since the 1970s, by Roman Catholic membership in over 30 national councils. The Roman Catholic Church is also a full member of the Caribbean, Pacific, and Middle East Conference/Council of Churches. Such regional councils of churches are a more recent and very important instrument of ecumenical cooperation: Conference of European Churches (1959), All-Africa Conference of Churches (1963), Pacific Conference of Churches (1966), Christian Conference of Asia (1973), Caribbean Conference of Churches (1973), Middle East Council of Churches (1974), and Latin American Council of Churches (1982). Lutheran churches are generally members of the innumerable local councils, the over 90 national councils, and the seven regional councils. [G.G.]

COUNTER-REFORMATION. This term refers to the reforming initiatives during the 16th and 17th centuries within the **Roman Catholic Church** and its efforts to regain territories that had become fully or partially **Protestant**. Today, the double designation Catholic Reform and Counter-Reformation (first used by Hubert Jedin in 1946) has been widely accepted. Its aim is to indicate the close connection between the reforming efforts within the Catholic church and its reaction against the Protestant challenges and advances. Parallel to the **Reformation** many struggles and diverse activities aimed at the removal of abuses and the renewal of spiritual life (*see* SPIRITUALITY) in the Roman Catholic Church. The Council of Trent (*see*

TRENT, COUNCIL OF) became a major expression of these reforming endeavors, but embodied at the same time the ideals of the Counter-Reformation: the rejection of the Protestant challenges and the recovery of lost ground—spiritually and territorially. The Roman Inquisition (1542), the new Jesuit Order (1540), and Roman Catholic princes became the main instruments of the Counter-Reformation. Sometimes by persuasion and sometimes by violent means—such as war, oppression, persecution, forced conversion, expulsion, and, at best, the discrimination against Protestants—the Habsburg lands of Austria, Bohemia, and Hungary, as well as France (Huguenots), Poland, Bavaria, and the Rhineland—were brought back under Catholic control. Confessional absolutism was the result. Catholic Reform and Counter-Reformation came to an end at the close of the 17th century. [G.G.]

CRANACH, LUCAS (1472–1553). Famous German painter, engraver, and illustrator. Born in Franconia, Cranach became court painter to **Frederick the Wise**, elector of Saxony in 1504, after having studied in Vienna. He prospered as a resident of **Wittenberg**, becoming mayor in 1537. He was particularly gifted as a portraitist, and already by 1510 had painted two Holy Roman emperors. His treatment of female nudes, particularly in mythological settings, was remarkably lifelike, and new to German painting. While living in Wittenberg, Cranach met and befriended **Martin Luther**, and became a convinced Lutheran. An invaluable artistic propagandist for the **evangelical** cause, Cranach painted the most revealing and best known images of the Wittenberg reformers, often including them in altarpieces and other decorations for churches. He was also active as an illustrator, most notably of Bibles. His son of the same name succeeded him as a gifted and well-known painter. *See also* ART; LUTHER IN THE ARTS. [M.O.]

CREATION, LUTHERAN DOCTRINE OF. The creation is the cosmos understood in relation to its origin and sustenance in **God** the Creator. The Lutheran **doctrine** of creation has focused until recently almost wholly on what it means to say that "God is the Creator" or that "God acts." Following the influence of **Thomas Aquinas**, the doctrine of creation has also been treated discretely from the doctrine of **redemption** (*see* CHRISTOLOGY; ATONEMENT).

Recent Lutheran thinking has linked more strongly the doctrine of redemption, and that of **sanctification**, with the doctrine of creation, and this has been done with primary attention to the writings of **Martin Luther**. This thinking holds that all the creation is redeemed and the encounter with God is not just in the human subject. Creation is the theater of God, even the place of God's indwelling, though the ability to identify God therein is unsure. Nevertheless, as Luther says, God is "substantially present everywhere." As Scandinavian Lutheran theologians such as Gustaf Aulén, Regin Prenter, and

Gustaf Wingren have noted, this means that knowledge of God and God's purposes can be drawn from creation, too, though not as conclusively as from God's history in the incarnate Christ. These "mediating theologians" have noted that Luther's own **spirituality** indeed was suffused with a hearty appreciation of creation, and not ascetically sundered from it. God is not to be collapsed or confused with creation, but "nothing can be more truly present and within all creatures than God himself with his power."

Today, this means that a Lutheran doctrine of creation is often trinitarian and panentheistic (i.e., God is in all things), as with the thought of Joseph Sittler and **Wolfhart Pannenberg**. Doctrinal construction also affirms that the sociocommunal, the biophysical, and the geoplanetary are equally the heirs of redemption and the beneficiaries for which Christian **ethics** are to be ecologically responsible. [D.H.L.]

CREEDS (Lat *credo*, "I believe"). A summary statement of Christian belief. The Old and New Testaments both contain short summaries and confessions of **faith**. In the church of the early centuries, such creedal statements were used in **worship**, proclamation, teaching, and especially for the preparation and public confession of candidates for **baptism**. Creeds also served as expressions of the **unity of the church** by confessing the true faith against **heresies**. The Apostles' Creed arose from short trinitarian baptismal confessions of the first centuries. Between the seventh and ninth centuries the creed was received into the liturgy of the Western church. It is still the most widely used creed today. The Nicene-Constantinopolitan or Nicene Creed also follows the classical trinitarian structure. Formulated at the Council of Nicea in 325 (*see* COUNCILS, ECUMENICAL), it was further developed by the Council of Constantinople in 381. It was accepted by the Council of Chalcedon in 451 and then by both the Eastern and Western churches. Thus, the Nicene Creed is an important bond of unity between the Eastern Orthodox and the other Christian traditions. However, the Western addition (beginning in the sixth century) that the **Holy Spirit** proceeds from the Father "and the Son" (the *filioque*) has contributed to the division between East and West.

These two creeds, together with the so-called Athanasian Creed, which emerged most probably in the fifth or sixth century, were accepted into the collection of Lutheran confessions, the ***Book of Concord***, where they occupy a special, first place. This expressed the fundamental conviction of the Lutheran reformers that the emerging Lutheran churches were a part and continuation of the one church of Jesus Christ since the time of the apostles. Since then, the creeds, especially the Apostles' and Nicene Creeds, are an integral element of Lutheran theological tradition and worship life. [G.G.]

CROSS. The central saving significance of the cross of Jesus Christ. In the New Testament, Paul highlights the paradoxical nature of the cross of Jesus

Christ. The ancient instrument of executing a criminal becomes the symbol of Christ's representative suffering and death for the sake of humanity. The "Word of the cross" (1 Cor 1:18), contradicting the wisdom of the world, is the **kerygma**, the decisive message (**Gospel**) of Christ's reconciliation of humans with **God**, mediated by Christ's suffering on the cross (1 Cor 1:18–2:8; 2:2; Gal 6:14; Col 1:20). The theological reflection on the significance of the cross became a central theme of medieval **piety** and **theology** in the West. **Martin Luther** introduced the term "theology of the cross" (*theologia crucis*). It refers to the ways in which knowledge of God is revealed and God's **salvation** is received. Opposed to scholastic speculative theology, the "theology of glory," Luther holds that God's nature is revealed, hidden under its opposite, in the suffering of Christ on the cross. At the same time, the cross is the event of God's critical judgment on the **sin** of the world and God's liberating judgment pronouncing and communicating the unmerited **justification** and salvation of the sinner. For Luther, the cross also implies the shape of life of both the believers and the church.

In Lutheran **Orthodoxy**, the message of the cross became part of the doctrine of the priestly ministry of Christ, while in **Pietism** the call to follow the cross was emphasized. In contemporary theological reflection, the cross is considered as a part of the inner trinitarian reality. This means that the cross is part of God's being, implying that God himself is the "crucified God." In **liberation theology**, following an early Christian understanding, the cross is interpreted as a sign of victory over all powers that stand against God and human beings and as a means of overcoming suffering in unjust and oppressive situations. *See also* CHRISTOLOGY; TRINITY, DOGMA OF. [G.G.]

CRYPTO-CALVINISTS. Pejorative term used against those who were accused of being "hidden" Calvinists and seeking to introduce ideas of the Swiss reformer into Lutheran churches. Beginning with earlier attempts (e.g., **Philipp Melanchthon's** altered *Augsburg Confession* of 1540) and continuing during the doctrinal controversies after the **Interim** (1548), adherents of Melanchthon—also called **Philippists**—and others tried to come to closer Lutheran-**Reformed** relations and even union. Crypto-Calvinists did not accept, among other things, the real presence of Christ in the **Lord's Supper** and the ubiquity of the ascended Christ. They were influential in several German territories (also in Denmark) and especially in Saxony where a Crypto-Calvinist takeover happened in the 1580s that lasted until 1591, when a new elector led the country and church back to a sound **Lutheranism**. *See also* CALVIN, JOHN; CHRISTOLOGY. [G.G.]

CULTURE, LUTHERAN IMPACT ON. The impact of **Lutheranism** on **education**, natural and human sciences, different **art** forms, and social and political life. Throughout church history, a complex interrelation between Christianity and surrounding cultures can be observed. In today's **ecumenical** discourse, the issue of the place and role of cultures in relation to the communication and interpretation of the Christian **faith** has become a major topic (*see* INCULTURATION). The Lutheran church and tradition has been and is part of this general phenomenon. It has assimilated elements of surrounding culture, both positively (like **Humanism** in the 16th century) and negatively (like the uncritical absorption of 19th- and 20th-century liberal optimism in the form of "Culture Protestantism" [Ger *Kulturprotestantismus*]). Lutheranism has occasionally contradicted surrounding culture (at the **Reformation**, in Lutheran **Pietism**, in 20th-century conflicts with Nazism in the German **church struggle**, and with **racism** [apartheid] in southern Africa). Lutheranism has in a considerable measure transformed and shaped surrounding culture. The focus of this entry is on this third point.

The new Reformation emphasis on broad biblical-theological study and reflection and especially the work of **Philipp Melanchthon** led to a radical renewal and expansion of the educational systems in **Protestant** Europe. Many new schools, including the new type of a "humanistic gymnasium" with its study of classical languages, were founded, gifted poor pupils were supported, universities (like that of **Wittenberg**) reformed, and, as a result, a kind of "Lutheran Humanism" has emerged since the 17th century resulting in a class of well-educated people. The emphasis on the education and responsibility of the laity (*see* PRIESTHOOD OF ALL BELIEVERS) prepared people for leading positions in public life, the human and natural sciences, and the arts. An ethos of liberty enabled and stimulated critical thinking in philosophy, like in the **Enlightenment**, and study and research in the universities. Beginning with **Martin Luther**'s linguistically foundational translation of the Bible (*see* BIBLE, MARTIN LUTHER'S TRANSLATION) and other remarkable literary achievements of the Reformation movement in the form of hymns, poems, satirical leaflets, plays, and so on, a strong motivation for literature and poetry has come from the "Church of the Word." The Lutheran influence on the development of vocal and instrumental **church music**, from **Johann Sebastian Bach** up to the present time, is well known. Such influence has been, however, rather weak on the "visible" arts and also on architecture. Because Lutheran congregations simply continued to worship in medieval churches, very few new Lutheran churches were built between the 16th and 18th centuries. The exceptions are some outstanding examples of a simplified "Lutheran baroque" in central and northern Europe (the "Frauenkirche" at Dresden, and churches at Copenhagen, Hamburg, and Stockholm).

The Lutheran concept of the autonomy and liberty—under **God**—of the secular realm (*see* CHURCH AND STATE; CHURCH AND WORLD) has contributed to the emergence of the modern state, including its absolutist and ideological deformations. The pioneering work of Lutherans in social work and their establishing of social institutions during the 19th century (*see* DIACONIA) have strengthened public awareness of the need for social assistance and **justice** at home and, in the 20th century, worldwide. *See also* PARSONAGE, LUTHERAN. [G.G.]

CUSTOMS. Customs related to church life in Lutheran churches. A great number of religious customs or popular customs with a religious meaning or origin enrich the life of Lutheran **congregations**. According to region, there is a great diversity of customs, several are shared with other churches, and many customs have lost their religious significance and have become part of popular culture. The periods of **Advent** and **Christmas** have been especially dear to Lutherans and have provided ground for the creation and observation of customs: the rich tradition of **hymn** singing and **church music**, the Advent wreath as sign of Christ's victory, the Advent calendar with its "windows," candles symbolizing the new light in darkness, the varieties of Advent and Christmas cookies (gingerbread, fruit loaf, and so on) with several spices (originally seven, the holy number), the Christmas tree with glittering decoration and self-made figures and symbols as a reminder of the gold and treasures that the three wise men brought to the Christ Child, the cribs and tableaus within and out front of churches and houses, and the greeting of Christmas morning by hymns and carols blown by trumpets and trombones from church towers.

Lent is a "custom-less" time, but there may be special doughnuts for Shrove Tuesday. **Easter** is greeted by (recently reintroduced) Easter Night Vigils with concluding meals or receptions, while on Easter Day churches are decorated in splendid ways. Pentecost has traditionally been combined with all sorts of congregational celebrations and the decoration of churches with branches from birch trees. Outside the rhythm of the **church year**, additional church festivals have been introduced like Harvest Thanksgiving, Reformation Day (October 31), Day of General Thanksgiving (United States/Canada), and festivals marking the dedication of the church (building). Customs emerged around pastoral acts, such as the use of white robes by confirmands in some countries or, in the 19th century, a special solemn robe worn by women when attending Holy Communion. The rich heritage of customs is believed to help connect the life of **faith** with every day life of people. [G.G.]

– D –

DEACON. *See* DIACONATE.

DEACONESS. *See* DIACONATE.

DÉVAI, MÁTYÁS (originally Mátyás Biró, c.1500–1545). Leading Hungarian reformer. Dévai began study at Cracow in 1523 and joined the Franciscan order in 1526. Already attracted by **Reformation** thinking, he went to **Wittenberg** in 1529 and was in close contact with **Martin Luther**. In 1531 Dévai began his reforming activities in Kosice (now in Slovakia) and in the Hungarian capital Ofen/Buda (today Budapest). Jailed twice during 1531–1534 because of his work as a reformer, he resisted conversion. After 1535 Count Nádasdy protected Dévai who continued his work for the Reformation of church and country in the Danube region as a wandering reformer and preacher as well as rector of a school. He founded a printing shop and wrote a Hungarian elementary grammar. In 1536/37 he again visited Wittenberg. He spent this time mainly with **Philipp Melanchthon**, and also traveled to Nürnberg to see the reformer Veit Dietrich. When the Turks invaded Hungary, Dévai fled in 1541 and found refuge with his friend Melanchthon at Wittenberg and later at Basel. In 1543 he returned to his home country and continued his untiring engagement for the cause of the Reformation. He was a preacher at Miskolc and died as the senior (i.e., **superintendent**) at Debrecen. The "Luther of Hungary," as he was sometimes called, was the most important reformer of his country. [G.G.]

DEVOTION. *See* PIETY.

DEVOTIONAL LITERATURE. Writings of a reflective or edifying nature intended for individual, family, or small group use. These writings would include books of prayers, religious poetry, and meditations, day books, collections of **sermons**, and hymnals. While Lutherans have produced mountains of such material, the genre is ecumenical of its very nature and some of the devotional literature most popular among Lutherans has been written by people from other traditions; Thomas à Kempis's *Imitation of Christ* and the sermons of Charles Spurgeon are perhaps the most common of these "borrowings."

The earliest Lutheran devotional books included **Martin Luther's** *Betbüchlein* (*Prayer Booklet*, 1522) and George Spalatin's collection of the same year. The *Small Catechism*, however, has served Lutherans as a basic text not only for adolescent **catechesis**, but for lifelong devotional use ever since its publication in 1529. The early years of the **Reformation** spawned an immense volume of devotional tracts, aimed at catechesis and at replacing popular Roman Catholic works. The 17th century was the golden age of orthodox devotional literature (*see* OTHODOXY, LUTHERAN). From the crucible of the **Thirty Years' War** came not only the greatest gems of **chorales** (many of which were published as devotional poetry before being set to music), but also the longest lasting of Lutheran devotional prose as well. *True Christianity* (1610), by **Johann Arndt** and several works by **Jo-**

hann Gerhard (his *Fifty Meditations* [1606] and *Schola Pietatis* [1622] foremost among them) began a popularity in the 17th century that has never ended. In the 17th century as well, particularly in Denmark and Sweden, Luther's writings continued to be published for home use, particularly his Postils. For the next two centuries, this collection of sermons would serve a particular need in North America; Lutherans along the frontier would gather in the absence of a **pastor** and a sermon of the Reformer would be read.

The pietists of the 18th century (*see* PIETISM) produced devotional literature in almost incredible volume. Among the works that gained international use were those of **August Hermann Francke** and Philipp Spener, as well as *Toens Speyl* (*Faith's Mirror* [1727]) by Erik Pontoppidan. After the **Enlightenment**, which apparently produced no devotional literature of a lasting quality, the Lutheran **Awakening** of the 19th century brought forth new classics of the genre. Foremost among the authors of this period were C. O. Rosenius in Sweden, **Johann Konrad Wilhelm Löhe** in Germany, **Hans Nielsen Hauge** in Norway, and **Nikolai Frederik Severin Grundtvig** in Denmark. In the 19th century and the early part of the next, Lutherans in North America began making their own contributions to the field, with popular works published by Henry Harms, George Lenski, Alvin Rogness, Joseph A. Seiss, and many others. Lutherans in many parts of the world use the *Daily Texts* published by the Moravians (*see* MORAVIAN CHURCH).

In the category of ephemera, North American Lutherans excelled. Many congregations published seasonal meditations and collections of sermons by their own pastors, for use both as home devotions and as **evangelism** tools. In America and in other countries, the church press, in regular columns and occasional offerings, provides daily devotions and extended meditations. Weekly Sunday school sheets and quarterly devotional pamphlets abound. Technology has also expanded the category of devotional literature, providing not only programs for the radio, television, and compact disc player, but also written and graphic material on the Internet. [M.O.]

DIACONATE. The ministry of deacons and deaconesses. Probably no word has held such a variety of meanings in the church as has the word "deacon." It has referred to a servant; to an ordained minister, but not to the presbyterate; to one preparing to become a **pastor**; to an assistant pastor; to an unordained church worker; and to a member of the **congregation's** governing body. In the early church, deacons were those who, closely associated with the **bishop**, administered the church's financial and charitable affairs; exercised a teaching ministry, particularly in **catechesis**; and carried out liturgical functions that reflected those ministries. By the Middle Ages, the diaconate had become simply a stage in the process of ministerial preparation, the first of three possible **ordinations** one might undergo on one's progress from **laity** to deacon to **priest** to bishop. Women, then, could no longer serve as deacons. Diaconal ministry—focussing on service rather than proclamation—was provided not by deacons but by monastics.

During the **Reformation**, **Martin Luther** recommended the reestablishment of the diaconate with such service as its focus, and sporadically over the next few centuries, the people charged with poor relief, either in church or state, were called deacons. More usually, however, particularly where Lutheranism was not the state church, congregations followed the Reformed practice of electing boards of deacons and elders, where the former were responsible for pastoral and the latter for administrative concerns.

During the Lutheran **Awakening**, rising concern for the economically distressed led to the reestablishment of the diaconate. **Johann Hinrich Wichern** established the first of a series of orphanages run by young men who served as surrogate brothers to the orphans and carried on a range of other service to the poor. These men soon became known as deacons. Similarly and simultaneously, Pastor **Theodor Fliedner** and his wife Friederike established houses of deaconesses, who became teachers, nurses, and social workers. Over the next century, deaconess houses became homes for thousands of unmarried women who, rather than living as a domestic servant or a dependent of their family, were provided training, an important mission, and a supportive community.

Deaconess communities spread across northern Europe, influenced the work of Florence Nightingale in Great Britain, and came, through the work of William Passavant, to North America. Motherhouses connected with the various bodies of Lutherans were established in Philadelphia, Baltimore, Chicago, Omaha, Fort Wayne, Indiana, and Brush, Colorado. **Elisabeth Fedde**, a Norwegian deaconess, established houses and hospitals in Brooklyn and Minneapolis. The deaconess communities provided the church with gifted and dedicated leadership in **education** and social ministry.

In its summary of ecumenical convergences, *Baptism, Eucharist, and Ministry* (1982), the **World Council of Churches** commended the threefold office of bishop, presbyter, and deacon to the church. The hope was that each of these offices would have its own integrity and ministry. Around the world, Roman Catholics, Anglicans, and Methodists have experimented with "permanent deacons," exercising the ministry of service as an end in itself, as opposed to "transitional deacons," who intend to become priests. In 1993 the Evangelical Lutheran Church in America (ELCA) established a roster of diaconal ministers, a shared expression with the Deaconess Community of the diaconate in the ELCA. This roster is distinguished from the presbyterate by its focus on **Word** and service, rather than Word and **sacrament**. Consecrated rather than ordained, deaconesses and diaconal ministers intend to be placed in their service on the margin of church and world. *See also* DIAKONIA; INNER MISSION. [M.O.]

DIAKONIA OR **DIACONIA** (Gk for service or hospitality). Diakonia generally refers to the social service or care that any Christian would daily exercise. It may also refer specifically to the care exercised by those who are ordained or consecrated as deacons or deaconesses. At the time of the **Reformation**, the diaconate had receded substantially as a viable office, though it was given high regard by **John Calvin**. **Martin Luther** thought the office could be useful, were there any examples around to prove so. Indeed, Luther proposed that a reestablishment of the diaconate, especially for the distribution of church aid to the poor, would help free pastors to focus on their particular duties of **Word** and **sacrament** ministry; his suggestions were followed only sporadically, however.

Lutheran use of the term varied subsequent to Luther, referring to the work of an administrator of welfare relief, an "assistant pastor," or lay spiritual leader, as well as general Christian service. Lutherans in North America in the 18th century, like **Henry Melchior Muhlenberg**, employed the term in these ways, including establishing an ordained diaconate to serve, usually for an interim, where ordained pastors were not available. In 19th-century Germany a rebirth of diakonia and the diaconate occurred, in tandem with the rebirth of **Pietism** and its correlative mission movement (*see* MISSION HISTORY), foundings of **hospitals**, and numerous other activities of **social welfare** in the wake of the French Revolution and Napoleonic wars. **Johann Hinrich Wichern**, **Theodor Fliedner**, and Friederike Fliedner, in particular, gave birth to a new form of the diaconate and understanding of diakonia. Wichern founded a network of "brotherhouses" (*Bruderhaus*), beginning in Hamburg, for homeless and vagrant boys, where the older male caregivers came to be called deacons and worked with the poorest of society. The Fliedners did much the same for women and from their influence deaconess societies emerged in Germany and came to the United States as well. **Johann Konrad Wilhelm Löhe** was another example of a German renewer of diakonia, whose work was imported to the United States, later especially to influence the **Lutheran Church-Missouri Synod** form of the deaconess movement.

In America, diakonia was also renewed by William Passavant and **Elisabeth Fedde**. Both were highly influential for the furtherance of the deaconess movement and for the renewal of diakonia throughout the church. Lay male ministry, however, seemed confined to the emerging Missouri Synod forms of ministry, especially parochial school teachers. With the present Evangelical Lutheran Church in America, diakonia is newly emphasized both as a responsibility to be shared by all Christians and as a special ministry served by the lay roster of diaconal ministers charged especially to help bridge **church and world**. *See also* DIACONATE; INNER MISSION. [D.H.L.]

DIALECTICAL THEOLOGY. Major movement in 20th-century **Protestant** theology and church. Rather generally termed, "dialectical theology" was at the center of so-called Protestant "neo-orthodoxy" that to a large degree dominated the theological and church scene between 1920 and 1970. Dialectical theology emerged as a theological response to the crisis of Western culture, society, church, and **theology**, created by the disillusionment of cultural optimism and liberal Protestantism following World War I. Representatives of dialectical theology such as Karl Barth, Friedrich Gogarten, Eduard Thurneysen, **Rudolf Bultmann**, and Emil Brunner, together with other representatives of neo-orthodoxy such as Anders Nygren, Gustaf Aulén, and Reinhold Niebuhr, began in the 1920s to radically criticize and reject the basic tenets of Protestant **Liberalism**: the accommodation of Christianity to modern culture ("culture Protestantism"), religion as human efforts at self-transcendence toward **God**, concepts of the immanence of God and of the inherent goodness of humans, and so on.

Instead, dialectical theology emphasized the radical transcendence and otherness of God, the distance between God and human beings that cannot be bridged by them, the sharp antithesis between the **Word of God** and human reason and culture, and the distinction between **faith** and culture. Only by means of their otherness and their critical challenges can God, faith, and **church** become a saving response to the crisis of the modern world. This is expressed in dialectical thought forms, for example, the "No" of God's critical judgment on human **sin** and his "Yes" of saving **grace**, Christ being "the Lord as Servant" (Barth), the absolute transcendence of God and the self-disclosure of God in Christ, and humans as sinful and yet free. Dialectical theology drew very much on **Reformation** sources and its influence on Lutheran theology was notable. It influenced preaching, the position of the **Confessing Church** in the German **church struggle**, the **ecumenical movement**, and some of its basic concerns have continued to mark theological thinking. [G.G.]

DIALOGUES, BILATERAL. Conversations between two partners. In the first half of the 20th century, bilateral dialogues, which played a major role during the **Reformation**, were revived: Church of England and Scandinavian Lutheran churches (1908 and again after 1930), Anglicans and Old Catholics (1931), and Anglicans and Orthodox (1930/31). The dialogue between Lutheran, United, and **Reformed** churches in Europe from 1955–1973 (*see* LEUENBERG AGREEMENT) was the prelude of a new and intensive phase of bilateral dialogues. This phase was ushered in by the entry of the **Roman Catholic Church** into the **ecumenical movement** after the Second Vatican Council (*see* VATICAN COUNCILS I AND II) and the preference of this church for bilateral dialogues with other worldwide Christian communions (*see* CHRISTIAN WORLD COMMUNIONS,

CWCs). Since the late 1960s there has been a remarkable proliferation of official regional, national, and international bilateral dialogues between the Roman Catholic Church and different Christian World Communions (CWCs), as well as among individual CWCs. The dialogues have led to substantial agreements on such formerly divisive issues as the **sacraments**, the ordained **ministry**, **salvation** and **justification**, and the nature of the **church**.

After the Catholic church, the **Lutheran World Federation** is second in the number of its dialogues (conducting conversations with **Anglicans**, **Baptists**, **Methodists**, **Orthodox**, Reformed, Roman Catholics, and Seventh Day Adventists). Compared to multilateral dialogues, "bilaterals" have the advantage that they are able to focus on specific issues that have been divisive between two church **traditions** and that their results are to be received (*see* RECEPTION) in some form by the two partners involved. The results of these dialogues, thus, hold the chance of transforming relations between the churches (*see* LEUENBERG AGREEMENT and PORVOO COMMON STATEMENT). The bilaterals, in which all major Christian traditions are involved, have become an essential expression of the modern ecumenical movement. [G.G.]

DIALOGUES, MULTILATERAL. *See* FAITH AND ORDER MOVEMENT.

DIASPORA (Gk "a scattering, dispersion"). Term used for the situation of a minority living apart from its home land. The term was first mentioned in the Greek translation of the Old Testament (the Septuagint), referring to the destiny of Jews living "dispersed" outside of Palestine (e.g., Is 11:11ff). The New Testament speaks in a similar way about the diaspora of the Christian congregations outside of Palestine, the exiles of the dispersion (1 Pet 1:1). For centuries, the concept and term "diaspora" was scarcely used. The **Reformation** and **Counter-Reformation** created a new type of diaspora situation: a confessional minority living among (and often suffering under) a different confessional majority. Yet only from the 19th century onwards was the term "diaspora" used for such situations and in connection with **Protestant** and **Roman Catholic** associations specializing in the support of minority churches. Today, many Lutheran churches in Europe and all Lutheran churches in **Latin America** are diaspora churches within a Roman Catholic or **Orthodox** majority. For the pluralistic ecclesiastical situation in North America, the term "diaspora" is rarely used, nor is it applied to the Christian minorities in countries in which another religion forms the majority. In contemporary **theology**, the term is sometimes employed to indicate the basic situation of the **church** and the Christians; living as a minority of strangers dispersed in the world. [G.G.]

DISPLACED PERSONS. *See* REFUGEES.

DISTLER, HUGO (1908–1942). German composer and church musician. While Distler also composed works for the keyboard, it is as a composer and performer of **church music** that he is best known. He was born and studied in Nürnberg before continuing his musical training at Leipzig. He served as a church musician in Lübeck and Stuttgart before coming, in 1940, to Berlin where in 1940 he became professor of composition and organ at the music academy and director of the choir of the (Protestant) cathedral. Always conscious of history, Distler gave contemporary expression to forms and tunes from the **Reformation** and before. The model for his *Spiritual Music for Choir* (*Geistliche Chormusik*) was **Heinrich Schütz**, whose imaginative settings had used both polyphony and counterpoint in providing music for **choirs** in a different, but equally troubled, century. Distler's emotional range included jubilation and delight, but he excelled at expressing the anxiety and transience of life, most particularly in his *Dance of Death* (*Totentanz*). His arrangement of *Ein Lämmlein geht*, the final movement in a projected but uncompleted passion setting, is a sublime expression of confidence in the midst of suffering and sacrifice. Under Nazism, Distler faced greater and greater artistic opposition and competition with the Hitler Youth for the time and attention of his younger singers. Late in 1942 he sent his family away from Berlin for safety. On November 1, 1942, he took his own life, being no longer able to cope with the great political and psychic pressure. Distler's music for choir has found a permanent place in Lutheran church music and beyond. *See also* MUSIC IN THE LUTHERAN CHURCH. [M.O.]

DOCETISM (Gk *dokein*, "to appear, to seem"). Term applied to a view that Jesus Christ only seemed or appeared to be a truly human person. Earliest references to this Christological **heresy** (*see* CHRISTOLOGY) are found in letters of Ignatius of Antiochia (d. after 110) in which he warns **congregations** of heretical teachers according to whom Jesus Christ only appeared to have been born and lived a human life, was crucified, and resurrected. In the New Testament, too, several passages (e.g., 1 Jn 4:2–3; 2 Jn 7) call Christians to confess against "deceivers" that "Jesus Christ has come in the flesh." Docetism was not a school or movement, but a tendency and orientation among Christians who were influenced by the Gnostic devaluation of materiality. Throughout history, docetic tendencies have appeared from time to time. Today, the terms "Gnosticism" and "gnostic" are sometimes used in a broader sense pointing to all tendencies to "spiritualize" in a one-sided way aspects of the Christian **faith**. With its strong emphasis on the humanity of Christ in its doctrines of the **Lord's Supper** and of **salvation** and with its insistence on the transmission of **God's grace** through human words and created elements, the Lutheran tradition is marked by a strong antidocetic spirit. [G.G.]

DOCTRINE. Interpretations of the meaning of the Christian **faith** in the Lutheran **tradition**, though not necessarily meant to be **truth** claims for the whole church, as with **dogma**. Nevertheless, in common use "doctrine" is often used synonymously and confused with dogma, and **dogmatics** may treat doctrine and dogma equally or interchangeably within their various systems. A more precise use of the term, however, would distinguish doctrine from dogma in that the latter has its origins in the ecumenical councils (*see* COUNCILS, ECUMENICAL). Doctrine would refer to that which is normative for particular Christian traditions or denominations, and as such could be considered as "proposals" of dogma to the church catholic, were there ever to be an ecumenical council to consider such. Thus, a doctrine, like that of **justification**, as the foundational doctrine for **Lutheranism's** understanding of the faith, is indeed shared throughout all Christianity, and so may come close to the status of ecumenical dogma, though it may not function in the same way for other traditions as it does for Lutherans. However, the doctrine of the immaculate conception (*see* MARY) or papal infallibility (*see* PAPACY) have no function whatsoever in the Lutheran tradition and would have no place in Lutheran dogmatics. One finds a confused use of the term throughout Lutheran history, nevertheless, and it might be only systematic theologians, among which **Martin Luther** himself was not identified, who would wish for more exactness. [D.H.L.]

DOGMA. Normative or authoritative interpretation of the meaning of Christian **faith**. The Lutheran affirmation of the authority of dogma is based on the understanding that the heart of dogma is Jesus Christ himself. Thus, dogma is universally normative as the right interpretation of the **Gospel**. While the church in its ecumenical councils (*see* COUNCILS, ECUMENICAL) has defined dogma, dogma is not authoritative simply because the **church** says so, but because (and if) dogma conveys the truth of the Gospel. **Martin Luther**, for example, was expressly opposed to dogma that was not derived from the **Word of God**, materially construed, and Holy Scripture, formally construed.

Modern historical consciousness has eroded the binding authority of dogma. **Adolf von Harnack's** emphasis on the historical contextualization of dogma has been perceived by Lutherans too much to compromise their **truth** claims. In response, existential theologians like Emil Brunner or Paul Tillich, both of the 20th century, may be argued to have existentially privatized the truth claims of dogma. More recently, Edmund Schlink has acknowledged the historical situatedness of dogmatic claims, but argued that they nevertheless are expressions of the Christian community's witness to what **God** has revealed. **Wolfhart Pannenberg**, a student of Schlink, has argued that dogma expresses the apostolic witness to the **revelation** in history of Jesus Christ. He further notes that dogmas are not, however, complete in themselves—which was the notion that the tradition of Harnack criticized—but are provisional truth claims that point to and will only be completed in the eschatological consummation of history (*see* ESCHATOLOGY). Thus dogma may be subject to reformation and is authoritative, whatever its expression, insofar as it above all conveys Jesus Christ, is derived from Scripture, and is oriented to the final lordship of Christ. The latter criterion of Christ's lordship includes within it the concepts of continuity and **catholicity**, so that Lutherans do not argue toward the future with easy abandonment of the past. *See also* DOCTRINE; DOGMATICS. [D.H.L.]

DOGMATICS. The critical theological interpretation of Church **dogma** and **doctrine** in view of contemporary popular and intellectual culture. Such interpretation is done within and in faithfulness to the **church** for the sake of its **mission** to the world. As a discipline, dogmatics is necessarily governed more by creedal core principles than is the wider known exercise of systematic theology. Lutheran dogmatics, consequently, is normed by such characteristically Lutheran formal and material principles as the Bible, the sovereignty of Christ, and the doctrine of **justification** by **grace** through **faith**, as well as by **catholicity**, **apostolicity**, and so on.

The first example of Lutheran dogmatics was the *Loci Communes* of **Philipp Melanchthon** in 1521. Lutheran dogmatics became more confessionally self-conscious with the hardening of the **Reformation** and **Counter-Reformation** divisions. While the Reformed movement grew into severalfold self-definitions in the likes of the *Heidelberg Catechism* (1563) or the *Westminster Confession* (1647), the Lutheran parallel developed as Lutheran **Orthodoxy**. Its leader was **Martin Chemnitz**, whose major dogmatic work was the *Loci Theologici*, an interpretation of Melanchthon's treatise, published in 1591. Lutheran Orthodoxy was specially characterized by a concern to correlate central Lutheran principles again with the medieval period's Aristotelian emphases on **reason** and **natural law**, so to cast the Lutheran principles in the form of true propositions of doctrine, immune to destruction by syllogism. This concern for propositional truthfulness waned, however, in the face of the **Enlightenment** (*see also* KANT, IMMANUEL), which cast **theology** as a moral or practical discourse, rather than as a category open and subject to formal scientific reason. The weighty objectivity and aridity of Lutheran Orthodoxy happened to collude, too, with the Enlightenment's circumscription of reason; together they drove theology into the mode of **Pietism**, emphasizing the subjective and experiential side of faith.

Dogmatics, subsequently, was practiced generally in one of three major modes: as the exposition of the viability of faith deriving from the subjective apprehension within the church community, as signaled by Friedrich Schleiermacher; as the metaphysical exposition of the actualization of Spirit in history, as begun in the philosophy of **Georg Wilhelm Friedrich Hegel**; and finally as distinctly antimetaphysical iterations for appropriate and historically generated practical moral life, begun by Kant and particularly developed in the work of Albrecht Ritschl. It was Ritschl's influence that characterized much of Lutheran dogmatics from the latter period of the 19th century into the early 20th century. Such **Liberalism** gave way in the crisis of World War I to the neo-orthodox theology of **Reformed** theologians Karl Barth and Emil Brunner, and the existentially influenced dogmatics of Paul Tillich, who drew heavily also on Hegel's idealism.

A return in dogmatics to the Christocentricity of **Martin Luther** marked, then, the theology of Swedish theologians Gustaf Aulén and Anders Nygren (*see* LUND SCHOOL). Other theologians began primarily to draw on so-called process philosophy to develop process theology and ecology-sensitive theologies. Others used language philosophy to develop new "narrative" or "language game" understandings of internal church/theology discourse, of which the work of Hans Frei and George Lindbeck are examples. Hegel's influence is renewed in the work of **Wolfhart Pannenberg**. Only recently flowering are proposals for more comprehensive dogmatic systems that take into account recent pioneering work in **liberation** and **feminist theology** from a variety of cultural settings. In all these Lutheran dogmaticians, one discerns the attempt to synthesize the best of previous intellectual criticism and develop new, pertinent theological insight, while remaining true to the ancient and Reformation witness of the Lutheran tradition. They exemplify rigorous and creative dogmatic proposals even as they echo also the increasing pluralism of popular and intellectual cultures. [D.H.L.]

– E –

EASTER. Feast of the **resurrection** of Jesus Christ. Very early in Christian history, the remembrance of Jesus' death and the celebration of his resurrection assumed fundamental significance in the Christian church. **Lutheranism** has continued this tradition by especially highlighting the central role of the **cross** of Jesus and his representative suffering, death, and resurrection as the enabling basis of the **justification** and **salvation** of all who believe in him. Accordingly, Easter is, together with Christmas, the most important feast in the **Lutheran church**. Many congregations have reintroduced the Easter Vigil, and various popular customs are associated with the feast.

It took a while until disputes over the proper date for Easter were settled. That there are different dates for Easter in the Western and Eastern tradition of Christianity is seen today as an ecumenical and social problem (the dates of holidays in some countries). In 325 the Council of Nicea decided to set

March 21 as the spring equinox and fix Easter on the Sunday after the first full moon after the equinox. Because **Christmas** has a fixed date and Easter a movable one, an early date of Easter necessitates shortening the weeks of **Epiphany** while a late date requires a reduction of the weeks of **Pentecost**. Today, ecumenical efforts are being undertaken to arrive at a common and fixed date of Easter. Holy Week, the week leading up to Easter, came into use in Rome in the fifth or sixth century. Maundy Thursday became linked to the institution of the **eucharist**, Good Friday remembered the crucifixion, and toward the end of Saturday the Easter Vigil began. [G.G.]

ECCLESIOLOGY. *See* CHURCH.

ECOLOGY. Lutheran understanding of and ethical practice (*see* ETHICS) toward the natural environment. A renewal of concern for the health of the natural world in Lutheran circles has proceeded along the lines of growth of ecological consciousness in the **ecumenical** and secular arenas. **Martin Luther's** thought, in particular, is recognized anew as a rich resource for an ethic of ecology. For example, Luther repeatedly wrote of a deep human kinship with all creatures. Further, following **Augustine**, Luther affirmed **God's** sacramental-like relationship "in, with, and under" all creaturely things. Indeed, Luther had, one might say, an expansive notion of antidocetism, holding that though God's ways are masked epistemologically to human beings, God nevertheless is always present in bodily ways; thus Luther asserted, "Nothing can be more truly present and within all creatures than God himself with his power" (*Adoration of the Sacrament*). The 1997 **Lutheran World Federation** statement on "In Christ—Called to Witness for the Care of Creation" (Assembly of the Lutheran World Federation) adopted at its global assembly in Hong Kong, reflects this theocentric and incarnational basis for ecological ethics.

The theological moorings for an emerging ethics of respect for ecology have been identified in the contemporary writings, especially, of H. Paul Santmire and echoed in **Wolfhart Pannenberg,** Larry Rasmussen (*Earth Community, Earth Ethics*, 1996) and Dieter Hessel (*Theology for Earth Community, A Field Guide*, 1996). The moorings will not themselves be connected, however, nor will a more unified Lutheran perspective on ecology be achieved, until the theological **doctrines** of **creation**, **redemption**, and **eschatology**, including the Lutheran subtheme of **two kingdoms**, are themselves less discrete and more enmeshed. *See also* STEWARDSHIP. [D.H.L.]

ECUMENICAL MOVEMENT (Gk *oikoumene*, "inhabited world"). A Christian movement aiming at overcoming the divisions among the churches and to manifest their unity. From the time of the New Testament, church history has been marked by efforts to preserve or restore the **unity of the church**. The second half of the 19th century saw the beginning of broader and more intensive efforts towards Christian unity. They prepared the way for the first World Missionary Conference at Edinburgh in 1910. It was the first representative gathering in modern history of a large section of (i.e., **Anglican** and **Protestant**) Christianity. The conference is generally considered the beginning of the modern ecumenical movement. Its impact led to the formation of the **Faith and Order** (1910) and **Life and Work movements** (1920) and of the **International Missionary Council** (IMC, 1921). In 1920 an encyclical letter of the Ecumenical Patriarch (of Constantinople) opened the way for the participation of the Eastern Orthodox churches in the ecumenical movement. The **Roman Catholic Church** refused to participate because it saw the unity of the church already realized within itself. Faith and Order and Life and Work united in 1948 to form the **World Council of Churches** (WCC). In 1961 the IMC joined the WCC, which continues the tasks of these three movements. The Second Vatican Council (*see* VATICAN COUNCIL II) marked a reversal of the position of the Catholic church and enabled its entry into the ecumenical movement, especially in the form of bilateral dialogues (*see* DIALOGUES, BILATERAL).

Lutheran churches, theologians, and church leaders have participated in the ecumenical movement since 1910. The most outstanding and influential Lutheran ecumenical pioneer has been Archbishop **Nathan Söderblom** of Sweden. However, during the first few decades of the ecumenical movement (1910–1948), Lutherans have taken a rather cautious and reluctant attitude against the ecumenical optimism of liberal or pietistic Protestants and have rejected the Anglican insistence on making a particular form of ministry (the historic episcopate, *see* BISHOP) a condition of Christian unity. According to the Lutheran emphasis on theological clarification and agreement on fundamental matters of **faith** as a necessary presupposition for steps towards closer ecclesiastical relationships (*see* CONSENSUS), Lutheran ecumenical involvement has been particularly strong in theological dialogues (in Faith and Order and bilateral conversations). But in recent decades, Lutheran churches have also supported many other ecumenical activities, especially programs of aid for **refugees**, and of **emergency and development aid**. The majority of the Lutheran churches consider themselves an integral and active partner in the ecumenical movement on the international, national, and local level.

The ecumenical movement has helped churches to overcome centuries of division, enmity, isolation, and competition. It has enabled churches to establish manifold contacts, develop better mutual understanding, undertake dialogue on theological and moral issues, enter into forms of cooperation and of joint missionary and social witness, and agree on different forms of official church relationships ranging from eucharistic hospitality to united churches. The ecumenical movement has radically changed the relationships within Christianity and can thus be seen as the most important element of 20th-century church history. [G.G.]

ECUMENICAL THEOLOGY. Theological research and reflection on the multiple aspects of the **ecumenical movement** as well as theological reflection undertaken in an ecumenical perspective. The modern ecumenical movement has led to a new theological discipline: ecumenical theology. The term has two different meanings: (1) Directly related to the ecumenical movement, ecumenical theology refers to an analytical and prospective enterprise. It studies and evaluates the history and achievements of the ecumenical movement, seeks to clarify its methodologies and main tasks, and envisages the goals of the ecumenical search for Christian unity. Ecumenical theology communicates the results of its work to theological students and the ecumenical community and represents a broad field of research and study in many theological seminaries and faculties, ecumenical institutes, and study centers. (2) In a broader sense, ecumenical theology refers to theological study and research that transcends the traditional boundaries of confessional or denominational theologies. For Lutherans (and others), it is a mode of theological reflection that affirms its own confessional or denominational **tradition** and seeks to broaden and enrich this tradition by integrating into the theological thinking both the insights of other Christian traditions and the results of ecumenical study and dialogue. *See also* DIALOGUES, BILATERAL; FAITH AND ORDER MOVEMENT; THEOLOGY; UNITY OF THE CHURCH. [G.G.]

ECUMENISM. *See* ECUMENICAL MOVEMENT; UNITY OF THE CHURCH; WORLD COUNCIL OF CHURCHES.

EDUCATION. The impact of **Lutheranism** on education. It is no surprise that a movement that had a university as its cradle would carry secular education at its heart as it developed. Education has been an important part of Lutheranism, not only in congregational education regarding the **faith**, but more general schooling. **Martin Luther** urged the German nobility to establish schools in which boys and girls might be prepared, in basic literacy, for the responsibilities of **work** and **family** life. But it was **Philipp Melanchthon**, the preceptor of Germany, who made Lutheranism's most enduring contribution to education. A gifted teacher and amazing polymath himself, he gave lectures for over 40 years to classes as large as 800, leaving a legacy of personal connection with teachers and professionals across Europe. He established the German school system with its three tiers (elementary, gymnasium, and university) that has spread around the world. Not only did he reorganize **Wittenberg** University after the troubles of the early 1520s, making it the leading school in Germany, but he also oversaw the reorganizations of Frankfurt/Oder, Heidelberg, Leipzig, Rostock, and Tübingen, and the establishment of universities at Marburg, Königsberg, and Jena. Lutheran **Orthodoxy** and **Rationalism** built upon and renewed these foundations, but it was **Pietism** and the Lutheran **Awakening**, with their interest in **youth** and formation, and their predisposition to founding institutions, that truly advanced them.

In the younger churches, Lutheran dedication to learning combined with a desire for indigenous clergy to establish schools from elementary to graduate. The **Lutheran Church-Missouri Synod** system, which has always been a priority of that body, is an unusually complete one. Colleges related to Lutheran churches are found in **Africa**, **Asia**, and **Latin America**, and Lutherans have established church-related elementary and high schools almost everywhere in the world where they have **congregations** or **mission** outposts. *See also* CHRISTIAN EDUCATION. [M.O.]

ELERT, WERNER (1885–1954). Systematic theologian and leader in the 20th-century renewal of Luther studies. Elert was educated in **theology**, philosophy, history, jurisprudence, and psychology at the universities of Breslau, Erlangen, and Leipzig. He served as a field chaplain during World War I, as well as a **pastor** in Seefeld, before becoming director of a Lutheran free church seminary in Breslau in 1919. In 1923 he was called to a professorial position in historical theology at Erlangen, where he also taught systematic theology from 1932 onward.

Elert made the "Erlangen School" world famous as a center for **Neo-Lutheranism**, while he was regarded as one of the most original and comprehensive of Lutheran thinkers in the first half of the 20th century. Though critical of Lutheran **dogmatics** and dogmaticians, including **Philipp Melanchthon**, he considered his vocation to be an extension of Lutheranism's dialectical opposition between **law and Gospel** (contrary to Karl Barth). This dialectic also applied to **ethics** and commended Lutheranism as the most fruitful theological frame for all **faith** and life, as he argued the case in his magisterial, two-volume work, *The Structure of Lutheranism* (*Morphologie des Luthertums* [1931–1932]). He also wrote in the areas of **Christology**, sacramentology, church history, and other topics in systematic theology.

Elert's sense of an organic, yet differentiated relation between **church and state**, informed by his interpretation of **Martin Luther's two kingdoms** theory, however, led to a certain affinity with ideas of national socialism about "folk," nation, and the Jewish danger. He considered the *Barmen Theological Declaration* (*see also* CHURCH STRUGGLE) to be a repetition of **Reformation** period antinomianism, contravening the rightful authority of the state. However, as dean of the theological faculty from 1935–1943, he worked diligently to keep his faculty at Erlangen free of interference by the state. With regard to the church itself, he remained a strong advocate of Lutheran confessionalism and **mission** until he died on November 21, 1954. [D.H.L.]

ELISABETH OF BRAUNSCHWEIG-CALENBERG (1510–1558). Ruler who helped to introduce the **Reformation** in her country. In 1525 Elisabeth married the duke of Braunschweig-Calenberg in northern Germany. In the following years, she developed an interest in the **evangelical** faith and in 1538 the Landgrave of Hesse sent her, at her request, an evangelical preacher, Antonius Corvinus. Her husband, a Roman Catholic, loved her very much, and did nothing to hinder her reforming activities. Deeply impressed by Corvinus's proclamation, Elisabeth began to confess her evangelical faith openly and to receive communion in both kinds (*see* LORD'S SUPPER). Representing a new Renaissance-type of women in authority, she became determined to use all means at her disposal, including political ones, to further the Reformation movement. She even used the education and marriage of her children to support the reform of the church in accordance with the **Word of God**.

After the death of her husband, Elisabeth ruled the Braunschweig-Calenberg territory for five years until her son could take over. During this period she employed her extraordinary energy for the furtherance of the evangelical cause. She invited more evangelical preachers to come, and Corvinus provided her with a hymnbook and a **church order**. Together with him she was instrumental in moving her country towards the Lutheran Reformation. After the defeat of the **Smalcald League** in 1547 and because of efforts to reestablish the Catholic religion in her country as a result of the **Interim** of 1548, Elisabeth was exiled for a time, but finally experienced the consolidation of Lutheranism after the **Religious Peace of Augsburg** in 1555. Probably no other woman has been as influential in furthering the Reformation. [G.G.]

EMERGENCY AND DEVELOPMENT AID. The involvement of Lutheran churches in international aid. Among the largest nongovernmental organizations involved in emergency and development aid are the Christian churches. They implement this service either individually through their proper aid agencies, such as the Roman Catholic Church; corporately through their **Christian World Communions**, the **World Council of Churches**, and other common instruments; or through a large number of independent, voluntary Christian aid organizations. Lutheran churches play a significant part in this work because of the material resources and state support of several of them. For them, this international aid work is closely connected with their own coming together as a confessional family. A major role in this movement through cooperation to unity was played by the **National Lutheran Council** in the United States after 1918 with its substantial aid programs and its influence on the formation of the **Lutheran World Convention** (LWC) in 1923. The LWC began soon afterwards to support suffering Lutherans in the Soviet Union, and at the end of World War II mounted a massive aid program for millions of **refugees**, displaced persons, and the hungry in Europe and some parts of Asia.

After 1947 this work was continued by the **Lutheran World Federation** (LWF) and many national Lutheran aid agencies. From the 1960s onwards most programs and projects moved to the Southern Hemisphere. Through its Commission on World Service, the LWF has assisted in broad repatriation and resettlement programs for refugees in Africa, in reconstruction of devastated areas in war-torn Liberia and Croatia (in former Yugoslavia), as well as help to victims of natural disasters in Asia, and funding health care projects in Latin America. Some $105 million were spent in 1999 on these projects that were complemented by several hundred smaller development projects, for example, in the areas of rural and community development, primary health care, reforestation, potable water supply, and land and water conservation. [G.G.]

EMIGRATION. The role of emigration, of people leaving their home country, within Lutheran history. Emigration for confessional reasons began for Lutherans at the time of the **Reformation**. The peace settlement of Augsburg in 1555 (*see* AUGSBURG, RELIGIOUS PEACE OF) included the provision that people who did not belong to or convert to the legally established religion (either adherents of the *Augsburg Confession* or Roman Catholics) in their particular territory had to emigrate. The **Counter-Reformation** forced Lutherans (e.g., in Salzburg, Austria) to emigrate to countries where they were welcomed. The Lutheran-Reformed Prussian Union (*see* UNION) in 1817 led to the emigration of Lutheran groups to Australia (*see* AUSTRALIA, LUTHERANS IN) and North America.

Of much larger dimensions was the emigration of German people since the 12th century and in different waves to eastern Europe, especially to the Baltic countries, Russia, and the Habsburg lands. These emigrants either became Lutherans during the Reformation (as in Transylvania) or came already as Lutherans. An even larger emigration of Lutherans from Europe to North and South America began in the 17th century and reached its climax in the second part of the 19th century. Millions of Lutherans settled on these two continents and a much smaller number in Australia and southern Africa. The large movements of **refugees** after World War II again brought many Lutheran emigrants to North and South America and to Australia. *See also* LUTHERAN CHURCHES OF THE WORLD. [G.G.]

ENLIGHTENMENT. The development of ideas that generally characterize the intellectual climate of 18th-century Europe, though the term originally was the translation of the German *Aufklärung*. Those who subscribed to

Enlightenment **philosophy** distrusted the received authorities of **tradition** and **revelation**, preferring instead the autonomy of **reason** and the primacy of the self's experience. While these latter two categories did not necessarily cohere in Enlightenment philosophy, they nevertheless outlined a "turn to the self" as authoritative, whether through reason, experience, or both.

From such norms, the **church** was significantly challenged, particularly where it insisted upon sustaining its supernaturalist dogmatics. David Hume's empirical inductive philosophy, both accepted and qualified by **Immanuel Kant's** outline of reason's transcendental grounds, led theologically to a rigorous revisioning of Christian **theology** primarily as a subject of **Rationalism** and the individual moral life (*see* ETHICS; LIBERALISM). Especially salutary for theology in this time of the Enlightenment's critical spirit were the rise of biblical criticism and modern science (*see* SCIENCE AND CHRISTIANITY), both of which evidenced a wholly positive and authoritative regard for the category of history. Friedrich Schleiermacher's reception of Enlightenment principles enabled his redefinition of dogmatic theology as an historical science, centered in the experience of the church. **Georg Wilhelm Friedrich Hegel**, however, took theology in a polar opposite direction by subsuming it under universal philosophical dialectical principles. With Kant, these two giants deeply influenced almost all subsequent theology up until the rejection of metaphysics in works by the Lutherans Albrecht Ritschl, Martin Kähler, and Adolf Schlatter. These modern theologians, nevertheless, continued to uphold the Enlightenment's high valuation of the individual human being and the irresistibility of human progress. [D.H.L.]

ENTHUSIASM/SCHWÄRMEREI. *See* SPIRITUALISM.

ENVIRONMENT. *See* ECOLOGY.

EPIPHANY. *See* CHRISTMAS.

ERASMUS OF ROTTERDAM (1469–1536). Most eminent Christian humanist scholar, writer, and theologian. Erasmus grew up in Holland and developed early on a lively interest in Latin and Greek antiquity. He was ordained a priest in 1492 and from then on lived for shorter or longer periods in Holland, Paris, several times in England, Italy, Belgium, Basel (1521–1529), then Freiburg im Breisgau (1529–1535), and back in Basel where he died in 1536. He was a European citizen far ahead of his time. He taught Greek and was a professor of divinity at Cambridge for a few years, and because of his growing reputation, he was offered important positions. He refused, however, never holding a firm position for a long period. Encouraged by humanists in England (John Colet and Thomas More), Erasmus deepened his knowledge of antiquity, learned Greek, researched in Italian libraries, collected manuscripts, and acquainted himself with biblical philology and exegesis. The humanist of antique literature became a biblical and patristic humanist: He prepared a new Latin translation of the Bible and published the first Greek edition of the New Testament (with grammatical and exegetical notes) in 1516, which he revised several times and which became the standard text for generations (*see* BIBLE, TRANSLATIONS). The other large project that occupied him until his death was the editing as well as supervising the editing of texts of the church fathers, for example, Jerome (1516), Cyprian (1520), and others.

Erasmus also excelled as a theologian. Among his writings, the *Handbook of a Christian Soldier* (*Enchiridion militis Christiani*) of 1503 (reprinted at least 20 times), became one of the most influential humanist works in Europe in the early decades of the 16th century. Marked by a morally informed **piety**, his ideal was a dynamic, Scripture-based **faith** active in **love**. He was inspired by the vision of the education of humanity in a process leading from flesh to spirit, imperfection to perfection, and sinner to saint. Such a process should receive its impetus from the spiritual law of Christ and the history of **salvation**, and it should go beyond the restoration of individual human nature by **grace** and extend to a Christian formation of public life and a Christian permeation of the orders of the world.

In witty, sarcastical texts, Erasmus criticized the corruption and abuses of his church. He disliked metaphysical speculation and scholastic dogmatism (*see* MEDIEVAL CHURCH AND THEOLOGY). With his writings, his deep desire for a reform of the church based on a return to the Bible and the church of the first centuries, and especially his editions of biblical and patristic texts, helped to prepare the advance of the **Reformation**. However, he remained loyal to his church, cautiously seeking to stay with the stability of tradition. In his *Diatribe on Free Will* (*De libero arbitrio diatribe*) of 1524 (*see* FREE WILL), he defended the freedom of the will in salvation. This provoked **Martin Luther's** famous and sharp reaction in which he confidently denied the freedom of the will in matters pertaining to salvation: *The Bondage of the Will* (*De servo arbitrio*) of 1525. This signaled Erasmus's break with Luther and the Reformation. Ironically, Erasmus was also criticized by conservative forces in his own church and after his death his writings were forbidden several times. Nevertheless, the thinking of the scholarly, wise, peace-loving, and tolerant humanist had an influence on such reformers as **Ulrich Zwingli** and **Philipp Melanchthon,** continuing far beyond the 16th century. *See also* HUMANISM. [G.G.]

ESCHATOLOGY. The subject matter that includes all things related to "last things" and to life beyond death, including heaven and hell, final judgement, the second coming of the Christ, and with him the **Kingdom of God** in its fullness and **resurrection.** But eschatology is also more than these. It also includes Christian life, which is directly guided and inspired by the eschatologically oriented lights of **faith** and **hope**. A specifically "Lutheran" understanding of eschatology, of course, presumes much significant ecumenical (*see* ECUMENICAL THEOLOGY) research and classical **dogma** and **doctrine**. The resurgence of interest in New Testament eschatology emerges from **Albert Schweitzer's** ground-breaking insights as to the apocalyptic self-understanding of Jesus. In the 20th century Norman Perrin and Joachim Jeremias, two prominent New Testament exegetes, have parlayed Schweitzer's perspectives into the argument that Jesus himself actually deepened the expectations and themes of eschatology in the manner of his teaching and self-understanding. He did so in a confrontative manner, however, by presenting those who heard him with occasions of crisis in which they must decide for or against him. In following Jesus as the bringer of the Kingdom of God, Paul the Apostle also represented an eschatological outlook that lived wholly from the future that Christ promised and that was centered in Christ's person, the presence of the risen Christ himself (*see* RESURRECTION).

Martin Luther inherited and followed the same eschatological perspective, and so also was not given to the enthusiastic fantasy (*see* SPIRITU-ALISTS) of millennialists like Joachim de Fiore or **Thomas Müntzer**. Nevertheless, under the influence of **Pietism** and anti-**Enlightenment** sentiment, eschatology assumed a timbre of other-worldliness in the 18th and 19th centuries. With **Liberalism**, theology tried to overcome these extremes by treating eschatology as a moral category. Albrecht Ritschl, for example, claimed—in some error—that Luther understood eschatology as the spiritual and ethical rule *over* the world from which Christians are freed. Eschatology, therefore, became the horizon in which human beings could and would achieve inexorable moral progress.

When eschatology, with most New Testament language, appeared no longer able to withstand the modernist challenges to its moral or supernatural framings, **Rudolf Bultmann** and Charles H. Dodd brought an individualistic existentialist (*see* PHILOSOPHY) interpretation to Scripture that allowed the reader to discover his or her own meaning in the eschatological symbols. The evident inadequacy of the existentialist approach in answering clear cosmological questions presented by the eschatological and apocalyptic texts, however, invited new research in such questions as a Hebrew understanding of time and eternity. Oscar Cullmann, for one, discerned a biblical view of time and history that led to the idea of a **salvation history** "above" natural history, open to the eyes of faith. While this aspect of his work was much debated, Cullmann did present a helpful distinction between realized and imminent eschatology. This double-sidedness to the whole matter of eschatology helped subsequent **theology** to accent both eschatology's entry into history and its abiding transcendence. Thus,

Wolfhart Pannenberg could proceed to lay the foundations for a theology of history (*see* HISTORY, THEOLOGY OF) that was deeply related to the causal agency of the eschatological dimension of existence.

The placement of eschatology into the setting of history bore exceptional new theological fruit. Because history need no longer be accepted as an extrapolation from the past tense and was seen afresh as enabled by the transcending and coming future of **God**, history was newly the place for theological proactivity fueled by faith and hope; thus the newer genres of **political theology**, **liberation theology**, and other varieties of **contextual theology**. Eschatology's relatedness to all that theology comprehends, including physical reality, has also driven toward the recognition that **ethics** can and must no longer be humanocentric, but must become an eschatologically sensitive ethics for a viable cosmos. *See also* CREATION; SCIENCE AND CHRISTIANITY. [D.H.L.]

ETHICS. Basic Christian reflection and orientation on moral life and action. Despite the great diversity of ethical concepts and their justification and application in Christian history, several foundational motives and perspectives of Christian ethics, as compared to philosophical ethics, clearly show forth in Holy Scripture. The Old Testament contains clear ethical directives and admonitions, for example, in the Decalogue (Ex 20:3–17) or in the critical ethical proclamation of the prophets (cf. especially Amos). It is decisive, however, that the Old Testament grounds ethics in the will of **God** and in what God has done as creator and redeemer. This fundamental concept of ethics as a response of **faith** based on the prior saving action of God is continued and is further developed in the New Testament. Jesus' proclamation of the near presence of the **Kingdom of God** confronts people with God's liberating but also committing will. Jesus radicalizes Jewish law by challenging the mind and motive behind behavior (e.g., Mt 5:17–48). He elementarizes Christian morals in the framework of the overriding commandment to love God and neighbor (Mt 22:35–40). Paul explicates the gift of **justification** with its ethical consequences in terms of the relationship between the gift of **salvation** and the moral task, and between indicative and imperative (Gal 5:25; 1 Cor 5:7; Phil 2:12; Rom 6). Jewish and Hellenistic paraenesis (moral instruction) is taken up and reformulated as Christian responsibility within existing social structures (cf. the so-called household tables, Col 3:18–4:1). The "new obedience" of the Christians is related to God's salvific action in Christ as its center (*see* CHRISTOLOGY). It is a response to this action by following Christ (Synoptics), and is the fruit of the **Holy Spirit** (Rom 8:1–4; Gal 5:22–23).

The development of Christian ethics in history has been shaped by its biblical foundations, rejection—or reception—of philosophical moral teachings, formation of **canon law** and **church discipline**, penitential practice (*see* FORGIVENESS), contexts of changing societies, **secularization**, and so on. In the church of the first few centuries, individual morality in the sense of Christian perfection, morality, ethos, and ecclesiastical ordering of the conduct of life were important distinctive marks of Christianity in a pagan context. In medieval scholastic theology, ethics became systematized in connection with **dogmatics**. Basic concepts emerge such as **virtue**, the bonum (good), divine order and eternal law that agree with human **reason**, a **natural law** interpretation of reality with ethics deduced from it, and the development of norms for moral behavior. Fundamental here is the connection between moral direction and ecclesial mediation of **salvation** through the practice of penitence and **confession**.

Martin Luther and the Lutheran **Reformation** transpose ethics into a new theological framework: the ethical issue of a good, God pleasing life is intrinsically connected with the issue of the assurance of salvation. Contrary to late medieval penitential practice, the assurance of salvation is grounded in the prevenient justifying **grace** of God that liberates, enables, and commits sinful human beings to live a moral life in **love** toward God and neighbor. Ethics are, thus, grounded in and qualified by faith and the relation to God, and are reconstituted through justification by faith and through grace alone. On this foundation, Luther and the Lutheran confessions (*see* CONFESSIONS, LUTHERAN) speak of the new liberty of justified sinners to live a responsible life in the ordinary conditions of daily life. Christians do this by their life and **vocation** within the three estates of family and profession, the church, and government. The confessions consider secular government and established rule and laws as instituted by God for the sake of good order. Through them, God reigns indirectly through persons in authority and by the use of law (*see* TWO KINGDOMS).

The moral life of Christians is to be guided by the Decalogue and exercised by the use of human reason as well as through love as the instrument of God's love. Princes and other leaders are to serve God by serving their subjects. In all these secular activities, Christians are to be seen as coworkers with God in his preserving and sustaining work for **creation** and humanity. Lutheran Orthodoxy (*see* ORTHODOXY, LUTHERAN) considered ethics, also in its form of casuistry, as one aspect of the dogmatic system. In **Pietism**, ethics were seen mainly in terms of the morality of the individual person, a tendency pushed to the extreme in **Enlightenment** thinking where ethics were located in the self-sufficiency of autonomous human reason or **conscience**. **Søren Aabye Kierkegaard, Neo-Lutheranism**, and, in the 20th century, **dialectical theology** moved ethics back into a theological framework. Here, the moral life of individuals and communities was reflected upon in the perspective of sinful human rebellion and the critical transcendence of God's command that was then related and applied, for example, by **Dietrich Bonhoeffer**, to life in God's created orders such as labor, **marriage**, government, and church.

Today, ethical reflection in Lutheran churches, as in other churches, is concerned with specific contemporary moral issues such as social **justice**, **peace**, conflict resolution, marriage and **family**, birth control, social security, **ecology**, and other topics. Lutherans participate at the same time in the discussion about the role of general ethical norms or rules in relation to moral decisions in specific situations or problems. Here the concept of "middle axioms," first developed in **ecumenical** social thought, seems to gain significance and acceptance again. It refers to a middle course between universal principles of social ethics and particular informed empirical judgments and actions. New emphasis is also placed on the importance of the Christian community and the use of its Holy Scriptures as place and instrument of moral formation, guidance, and orientation. *See also* CHURCH AND STATE; CHURCH AND WORLD; LIBERATION THEOLOGY; POLITICAL THEOLOGY. [G.G.]

ETHNICITY (Gk *ethnos*, "a nation, a people"). The role of particular peoples and their ethnic and cultural identity in Christian history. The history of the Old Testament People of God began with God's election of a particular people (Deut 7:6). This particularity, however, was transcended by the vision of the prophets and psalms that included "all the nations" (e.g., Is 2:2; Ps 86:9). This universalization of God's election was realized in the early Christian communities. Their mission took the **Gospel** of Jesus Christ to both Jews and Gentiles, inviting all people to the Church of Christ, which transcends all ethnic boundaries because in Christ "there is neither Jew nor Greek . . . for all are one in Christ" (Gal 3:27). Accordingly, the succeeding early church was not structured on an ethnic or national but territorial basis.

The **Roman Catholic Church** has always emphasized its universal character, but has come to a more positive acceptance of its multinational character only in the second half of the 20th century. In contrast, the Orthodox churches have always recognized their diverse national and cultural identities within one communion. In **diaspora** situations, however, this has led to an unfortunate parallel presence of distinct Orthodox jurisdictions in the same country based on ethnic origin. Lutheran churches, too, were influenced during their history in the expressions of their **faith** and **piety** by the diverse ethnic and cultural contexts of Europe. In North America, this led to the formation of ethnic—Danish, German, Norwegian, Swedish, and so on—Lutheran churches that in a longer process of unification during the 19th and 20th centuries became churches in which ethnic backgrounds are still felt and are appreciated, but are no longer dominant elements. Also in central eastern Europe, Lutheran churches were, and some still are, organized along ethnic lines, as are churches on other continents. At a time when ethnic conflicts lead to "ethnic cleansings," churches are among those who struggle against ethnic intolerance and aggression, pleading for a peaceful life together of different ethnic groups in community. [G.G.]

EUCHARIST. *See* LORD'S SUPPER.

EUROPE, LUTHERAN CHURCHES IN. The Lutheran reform movement originated in Germany. Facilitated by the new print media (*see* PRINTING PRESS), the studies of future Lutheran leaders in **Wittenberg**, and responding to an enormous pressure for reform in many parts of Europe, the burgeoning Lutheran movement spread very soon (after 1520) to other European countries: to the Habsburg territories in the central and southeast, to Scandinavia in the north, to the Spanish Netherlands and, later, to parts of France in the west. This broad movement was stopped and partly pushed back by the **Counter-Reformation** of the 16th and 17th centuries (especially Austria and Hungary). During the 19th century and again after World War II, millions of Lutherans left Europe to emigrate to North and South America and Australia (*see* EMIGRATION). Today, Lutheranism remains the third largest confessional group in Europe (after Roman Catholicism and Eastern Orthodoxy). On a world level, European Lutherans still represent, with over 37 million members (1999), the majority of the world's more than 61 million Lutherans.

In Germany, the homeland of Lutheranism, the formation and consolidation of Lutheran churches in territories and free cities that were open to the **Reformation** began after the **Diet of Augsburg** in 1530, when Lutheran princes and city councils signed their *Augsburg Confession*. Twenty-five years later, Lutheranism was recognized by imperial law at the **Religious Peace of Augsburg** in 1555, as one of the two religions of the empire. With the collection of the Lutheran confessional writings in the *Book of Concord* of 1580, development toward a common Lutheran confessional identity came to a conclusion. Today, there are 10 Lutheran territorial churches in several regions of Germany, as well as United churches (Lutheran and **Reformed**) and two small Reformed churches in other regions. All these churches live side by side with the (equally strong) **Roman Catholic Church** and some very small Free churches. In 1998 there were 14 million members of the Lutheran churches in Germany (and many Lutherans in the United churches). Germany remains the country with the world's largest Lutheran population.

In northern Europe, the Lutheran Reformation was introduced in all countries—Denmark, along with Iceland and Norway, Sweden along with Finland—by decisions of kings, parliaments, and church synods in ongoing processes from the 1530s into the 17th century. The structure of **bishops** in **apostolic succession** was preserved in Sweden/Finland. All the Lutheran churches became state churches, but during the second half of the 20th century they have reached a large degree of independence. In all these countries, over 85 percent of the population are members of Lutheran churches. With 7.5 million members the Church of Sweden is the largest individual Lutheran church in the world. It is followed by the Evangelical Lutheran Church of Finland (4.6 million), the Evangelical Lutheran Church in Denmark (4.5 million), the Church of Norway (3.8 million), and the Evangelical Lutheran Church of Iceland (244,000). By way of Germany and Scandinavia, Lutheranism reached the Baltic region where the majority of the population in Estonia and Latvia became Lutheran. Today, in the postcommunist situation of rebuilding church life, there are 400,000 to 500,000 Lutherans in these two countries as well as a small Lutheran church in predominantly Roman Catholic Lithuania.

Lutheranism in central southeast Europe had reached large portions of the population during the Reformation, but was then reduced by the state-supported Counter-Reformation to minority and **diaspora** churches in countries with Roman Catholic or Orthodox majorities. The Lutheran presence was reduced again by the waves of **refugees** and displaced/expelled persons during and after World War II. Of about six million Lutherans living in central and eastern Europe in 1917, only 1.2 million remain today. The larger Lutheran churches are in Hungary (430,000), Austria (337,000), Slovakia (329,000), and the Russian Federation with the Commonwealth of Independent States (about 265,000). Here, in the former Soviet Union, Stalin resettled large groups of ethnic Germans in the Asian parts of the union. Without **pastors**, these people preserved their Christian tradition in a remarkable history of Christian faithfulness. In the late 1980s they began to form **congregations** again that have now established the Evangelical Lutheran Church in Russia and Other States. Geographically, it is the largest Lutheran church in the world. Smaller Lutheran churches exist in Croatia, the Czech Republic, Romania, Slovenia, and Yugoslavia.

In western Europe, two Lutheran churches have existed since the time of the Reformation in France: the Church of the Augsburg Confession of Alsace and Lorraine (210,000) and the Evangelical Lutheran Church of France in Paris and Montbeliard (40,000). There are smaller Lutheran churches in Great Britain, Netherlands, Italy, and Switzerland. [G.G.]

EVANGELICAL (Gk *euangélion*, "good news"; Gk *euangelikós*, "according to the **Gospel**" or "related to the Gospel"). Designation of the early reformers, their supporters, and their understanding of the **faith**. The term has been used since the second century, but received prominence in the **Reformation**, especially through **Martin Luther**. For him, the evangelical faith was marked by insights and teachings drawn from the Gospel. The term was then applied as a name for the Reformation movement, the self-identification of its adherents, and for the territories and churches that had joined the Reformation. Since that time, the term has become the general designation of Lutheran and **Reformed** Christians and churches in Europe in distinction to **Roman Catholics** or **Orthodox**. It is still used with this understanding, but it has also become part of the names of churches: Evangelical Lutheran Church in America, of Finland, in Tanzania, and so on. Since the 18th century "evangelical" has also been used in a more specific sense for pietistic and "low church" movements and is in common use today, referring to evangelical movements and groups of a more conservative biblical and theological orientation. [G.G.]

EVANGELISM (Gk *euangelizo*, "the telling of the **Gospel**—the Good News"). It is difficult to distinguish evangelism from **mission** and **witness**, and indeed the three have often been used synonymously. Contemporary usage, however, seems to have settled on: "mission" as both the wider term for the fundamental function for the church and for the narrower meaning of proclamation to those who have never heard the Gospel before; "witness" as the means by which that proclamation happens; and "evangelism" as proclamation to those who have already heard the Gospel, but need to be called back to faithfulness or to be led to greater maturity in the **faith**. In this sense, evangelism, as well as mission, has been a mark of the church from its beginning. Christ's teaching of the disciples in general and his reincorporation of Peter after his denial are both examples of this, as are the admonitions of Paul and other New Testament writers to their already established communities. The mendicant orders served as the main evangelizing tools of the Middle Ages.

While **Martin Luther** has been accused of ignoring the concept of mission, there is little doubt that in his preaching, teaching, and writing, he was a firm advocate of and practitioner of evangelism. His catechetical work (*see* CATECHISMS OF LUTHER), hymnwriting, and emphasis on **law and Gospel** were aimed not only at nurturing the faith of those firmly in the community, but also at "reconverting" those he called "Christian Turks"—nominal Christians. This effort slackened to a degree during Lutheran Orthodoxy (*see* ORTHODOXY, LUTHERAN) that denied the continuing force of the Great Commission (cf. Mt 28:19–20) and too often identified right living with affirmation of formulations. Continuing conversion and growth, however, was a hallmark of **Pietism**, and much of the effort of that movement was directed at applying the Gospel to those who had heard and turned away from it. The missionary ventures of Pietism and the Lutheran Awakening (*see* AWAKENING, LUTHERAN) were directed not only toward non-Christians, but to the scattered, uncared for Christians in such places as the (American) frontier and rapidly growing cities as well (*see* HOME MISSIONS).

At the end of the 20th century efforts were made to prepare both individual evangelists and evangelizing communities for outreach to neighbors, whether those neighbors had heard the Gospel before or not. Those efforts ranged from training and supporting women evangelists in India to various programs connecting Bible study with training for witness in North America. They included rethinking the tasks of **worship** and **preaching** with an eye to attracting and involving those whose connection with the community was tenuous at best. [M.O.]

EVIL. The power that is in fundamental contradiction to the will of **God**. Christianity—as well as other religions and philosophies—has continuously struggled with the question of the nature and especially the origin of evil. Both the Old and New Testaments witness to the reality of evil not only as something negative and destructive in the life of people but also, and primarily, as a transhuman power, the evil one, and evil forces and spirits that are opposed to God (e.g., Lk 7:11; Mt 4:1–11; 5:37; 6:13). This power and these evil forces are to be resisted by overcoming evil with good (Rom 12:21), and they are overcome in the process of **salvation history** beginning with **creation** and continuing through **salvation** by Christ's victory over **sin** and death (1 Jn 3:8) until the completion of God's **creation** in the new heaven and earth (*see* ESCHATOLOGY).

Augustine (354–430) considered the nature and origin of evil, the absence of good, the "most difficult question." Since his time, **theology** has struggled with the question whether God has also created evil (his own enemy), whether the evil one, the devil, was among God's created angels, but became apostate and an enemy of God, whether evil originated from the liberty of the human person to sin, or whether evil has its origin outside of God's creation (which would imply that God has not created all things). The Lutheran confessions clearly reject the idea that God is the source or creator of sin and evil. It is not God's will that evil things happen. Rather, sin and evil are caused by the perverted will of the devil and of all ungodly people. Contemporary theology has no difficulties in describing evil in terms of physical, natural, metaphysical, moral, and socially caused evil. Yet, when it comes to the question of the origin or final cause of evil and the justification of God's goodness in the face of the reality of evil in nature and human lives (the issue of "theodicy"), Lutheran and other theologians admit to having no final answers. It is, however, clear that Christians are called to resist and combat evil in its multiple forms in the confidence of God's final victory. [G.G.]

– F –

FAITH (Lat *fides* and Gk *pistis*). Faith means believing or trusting, and includes both cognitive and affective giving of one's self to another authority. The Lutheran understanding, particularly, of faith in **God** is that it is a gift solely from God. As **Martin Luther** wrote in the *Small Catechism* (*see* CATECHISMS OF LUTHER), one cannot come to believe in God with one's own **reason** or will, but can only do so once the **Holy Spirit** has called and illumined the new believer. Thus, faith and the unilateral divine act of **justification** of the ungodly by God's **grace** on the merit of Christ (*see* ATONEMENT) belong together. Because faith is a gift, Lutheran teaching also emphasizes that faith comes "from outside" ourselves (*extra nos*), and this (given the aural-oral culture of the **Reformation**) "by hearing" (*ex auditu*). Furthermore, when one believes, or has faith, one "has God." Of course, *which* god may be at question here. Luther's definition of faith as "to trust and believe from the heart" is equal, psychologically, to "having a god," as Luther himself explicates in the *Large Catechism*. Faith "by hearing" is one criterion by which Lutheranism would ensure that the object of one's faith is not merely subjectively imagined. Faith's connection with the witness of the Bible, the **Canon of Holy Scripture** as witness to the **Word of God**, and the external **promise** of the **Gospel**—summarized in the slogans *sola fide*, *sola gratia*, *solus Christus*—finally ensures that it is the God and Father of Jesus Christ to which Christian faith attests and in which Christian faith lives.

The assurance (*certitudo*) of faith, while—to be sure—encompassing substantive matters of knowledge, was understood in a new way by the reformers more as faith's comfort for a troubled **conscience**. That justifying faith liberated the believer from anxiety about his or her **salvation**, comforted the conscience with the promise of the Gospel, and liberated the believer for selfless service to the neighbor (*see* ETHICS) was proof for the reformers that their theology was correct. As **Philipp Melanchthon** summarizes in the *Apology of the Augsburg Confession* (4), "This faith is no idle knowledge, nor can it exist with mortal sin; but it is a work of the Holy Spirit, that frees us from death, comforting and quickening terrified minds."

Such faith is not simply irrational or arational. While reason of its own cannot bring one to faith—or, with **Søren Aabye Kierkegaard** and others, might provide the prelude from which an arational "leap" of faith is made necessary—Luther and the reformers believed that faith could and should press reason for more understanding, as well as pressing reason to communicate as coherently and cogently as possible the mystery of faith. Thus, Lutherans have carried forward another traditional distinction of faith as that with which one believes/trusts (*fides qua creditur*) and the stated faith which one believes (*fides quae creditur*), as stated in **creeds**, confessions, **catechisms**, and so forth. History shows, however, that an overemphasis on either the *qua* or the *quae* can shift the practice of faith perhaps too much toward subjective **Pietism**, in the former case, or a more rigid orthodoxy, even **fundamentalism**, in the latter case. Lutheranism struggles to keep the *qua*—the act of faith—as a basis for the *quae*—the content of faith—while insisting that the objective presence of God is the only viable ground for the former; always the two sides must be related in a more holistic understanding of faith.

Dialectical theology has given modern **Lutheranism** the helpful reminder that faith lives only because of its object, which is a useful paraphrase of Lutheranism's slogan that faith is a gift from God. Though not a dialectical theologian, properly speaking, Paul Tillich is among the most influential of contemporary theologians who has captured the subjective and objective referential character of faith when he defines it as "ultimate concern." Lived from this complex, faith finally desires to confess itself (*see* EVANGELISM) and to be active in **love** (*see* ETHICS and WORK), thus never is apart from reason or works, though founded on neither. [D.H.L.]

FAITH AND ORDER MOVEMENT. A movement within the broader **ecumenical movement** that aims at manifesting the visible unity of the Christian churches. The Faith and Order movement, together with the **Life and Work movement** and the **International Missionary Council**, shaped the first phase of the **ecumenical movement** between 1910 and 1948. This movement began in 1910 when a commission of the Protestant Episcopal Church in the United States of America was charged to prepare a world conference for the study and discussion of questions of "Faith and Order" as a first step toward unity. A theological movement was born that became international and interconfessional in 1920 and held its first World Conference on Faith and Order in 1927 at Lausanne, Switzerland. Here, and in the decades that followed, the main controversial issues that have divided the churches—like **baptism**, the **Lord's Supper**, ordained **ministry**, the **church**—have been and still are on the agenda of Faith and Order.

In 1948 Faith and Order and Life and Work joined to form the **World Council of Churches** (WCC). Within this broader structure, the Commission on Faith and Order with its 120 members continues its theological work for the **unity of the church**. Since the **Roman Catholic Church** and other nonmember churches of the WCC are officially represented on this commission, it is the most representative theological forum in the world. With its world conferences (the so far last one took place in 1993 at Santiago de Compostela), consultations, studies, and publications, Faith and Order has rendered a significant contribution to theological understanding and agreement between churches as presuppositions for closer relationships. Its *Baptism, Eucharist, and Ministry* document (1982), for example, has become the most widely distributed and discussed text in the history of the ecumenical movement. Because of the theological emphasis of Faith and Order, quite a number of Lutheran churches are among the most active supporters of this branch of the ecumenical movement—which has become much broader than the WCC itself, for example, in the form of bilateral dialogues (*see* DIALOGUES, BILATERAL). [G.G.]

FAMILY. This fundamental unit of society is extremely and increasingly difficult to define. The word may refer to a "household" made up of people related by blood, **marriage**, or agreement living together, perhaps with employees and servants as well. A "nuclear family" is generally thought of as parent(s) and children dwelling together. An "extended family" is made up of people related by a certain closeness of blood or marriage, whether or not they live together. Recently, the phrases "family of origin" (one's birth parents and siblings), "family of choice" (especially close friends), and "blended family" (spouses living with children from previous marriages) have been added. While none of these structures is new—blended families were common in earlier generations because of mortality in child-birth rather than divorce—neither can any of them claim exclusive title to the name "family." For the sake of convenience, the first definition will be taken as the basic one.

Martin Luther continued the long-established respect for the family as a basic order of **creation**. Not only did he find marriage and parenthood to be a vocation equal to that of monasticism, but he also set family, together with the ministry of the **Word** and government as the basic building blocks of human society. Indeed, he used the fourth commandment (to honor father and mother) to base secular government on the model of the family. He further established the family as a basic locus for **evangelism**, writing his *Small Catechism* (*see* CATECHISMS OF LUTHER) for the use of heads of household in inculcating **faith** and **piety** in their charges—children and servants. This task continued to be taught through all the varieties of Lutheranism, bringing with it a flood of devotional material to be used for family devotions or, as it became known in the United States, the "home altar." It seems to have been only in the late 20th century that the practice of family prayer has become the rarity rather than the norm. In the late 20th century, however, the centrifugal forces separating family members from one another (including into different interest groups and even worship services in the **church**) caused a reaction in the church to provide opportunities to strengthen the family. Multigenerational experiences, classes in parental education, enlistment of the family in **catechesis**, and a new stream of **devotional literature** have resulted from the efforts of the church to strengthen the family, however it may be constituted or defined. [M.O.]

FASCISM. *See* CHURCH STRUGGLE.

FEDDE, ELISABETH (1850–1921). Pioneer Lutheran deaconess in North America. Born at Egersund in Norway, Fedde grew up in the spirit of the pietistic Haugian movement (*see* HAUGE, HANS NIELSEN) in Norway. In 1873 she joined the motherhouse of the new deaconess order (*see* DIA-

CONATE) in Oslo. After completing her training as a nurse and several years of work in northern Norway, she accepted an invitation to help Norwegian immigrants in New York. She arrived in New York in 1883 and with the support of Norwegian **pastors** of that city she organized the Voluntary Relief Society for the Sick and the Poor. She began to train assistants and in 1885 opened a small **hospital** in Brooklyn, New York. The society was renamed Norwegian Relief Society and in 1892 the society built a larger hospital. In the same year, the society became the Norwegian Lutheran Deaconess Home and Hospital and today is the Lutheran Medical Center.

In 1888 Fedde moved to Minneapolis, Minnesota, to spend two years setting up a deaconess home there. When she returned to Brooklyn, she directed the further development of her institutions that were open to people from different national and religious backgrounds. After 13 years of intensive work during which she started and developed a system of social service and medical care for the Scandinavian American community, this energetic, resourceful, and creative deaconess returned to Norway in 1896. There she married and lived the last 25 years of her life on a farm. [G.G.]

FEDERATION (Lat *foedus*, "covenant," "alliance," "bond"). In church contexts: A structured relationship between churches that maintains their separate identities. Federations of churches are a product of the modern **ecumenical movement**. They were established when churches agreed to enter with one another into an organizational structure and common bond that allowed them to collaborate in specific areas, for example, in social work, common studies, joint statements and representations on public issues, while at the same time maintaining their full autonomy. Federations are formed by different denominations on local, regional, national, continental, and international levels, especially in the form of **councils of churches** (one of the first being the Federal Council of the Churches of Christ in America [1908], and the largest being the **World Council of Churches**) or conferences of churches like the All-Africa Conference of Churches.

Churches belonging to the same confessional family, too, have come together in worldwide federal organizations, today called **Christian World Communions**. Among them is the **Lutheran World Federation** that combines in its self-understanding and constitution the theological claim of being a **communion** of churches with the organizational provision of being a federation of autonomous churches. Today, many do not share the view that a federation of churches is an adequate, sufficient expression of the **unity of the church**. Rather, federal relations between churches are seen as a meaningful and practical framework for relationships between churches that are very different in their **doctrine** and structure or that are dispersed over a large geographical area (e.g., continent) and, in other situations, as a provisional, intermediate form of Christian togetherness on the way to fuller unity. [G.G.]

FELLOWSHIP. *See* COMMUNION.

FEMINISM. Movement to overcome all forms of discrimination against women and establish gender equality in all areas of society, culture, and **church**. The first phase of the feminist movement during the late 19th and early 20th centuries aimed at the full participation of women in the institutions of society and in political life. The movement originated in North America, as did the second phase of feminism that began in the late 1960s and has since become active in western Europe, Australia, and in small groups on other continents. Feminism started as and still is a movement of mainly white, middle-class, academically trained women. Yet, without becoming a mass movement, it had a remarkable impact on social and political life and awareness. The movement is highly diverse and increasingly marked by internal controversies between liberal, radical, socialist, mystical-spiritualist, and other feminist positions. A common concern of all groups is to overcome patriarchy (male domination in all areas of life), sexism (the unjust treatment of women on the basis of their sex), and androcentrism (the normative character of male perspectives on human reality). Feminism seeks to establish the identity of women as autonomous, independent subjects in full equality with men. It considers itself to be a liberation movement.

In the **Roman Catholic Church** and mainline **Protestant** churches, feminism became an influential movement in North America and, to a lesser degree, in western Europe, Australia, and among some Western-educated women in Africa, Asia, and Latin America. The movement challenged, first of all, male-dominated structures of the churches. It demanded full inclusion of women in decision-making bodies and different **ministries** of the churches as well as equal opportunities for women in the institutions of the church and in the responsibilities and tasks of church life. In this respect, much was achieved during the last few decades of the 20th century. Since its initial international conference, *Sexism in the 1970s*, and its large study project, *The Community of Women and Men in the Church* (1974–1981), the **World Council of Churches** has been a major force on raising the awareness of women's issues in the churches. The **Lutheran World Federation** has helped churches in Africa, Asia, and Latin America to train women for leadership positions, to include them in theological education, and to enhance the role of women in all areas of the life of the church.

Theological research and reflection from a feminist perspective (*see* FEMINIST THEOLOGY) has assumed an important role in North America where it has received much more institutional support (e.g., chairs of feminist theology) than in Europe and other parts of the world. Different sociocultural contexts and theological emphases have led African American women theologians to call their thought "womanist," while Hispanic women theologians prefer to call their theology "mujerista." While there is as yet no recognizably "Lutheran" school of feminist theology, Lutherans in North America and western Europe, in accordance with their general theological stance, have taken a "middle position" concerning feminist theology. There is resistance against the more radical and, what many consider ideological, expressions of feminist theology. But there is in many parts of **Lutheranism** considerable openness for the critical as well as constructive rereading of Christian and especially Lutheran history by women theologians, while feminist analysis constructively influences academic and practical arenas of Lutheran life. *See also* BORA, KATHARINA VON; BRAUNSCHWEIG, ELISABETH VON; FEDDE, ELISABETH; GRUMBACH, ARGULA VON; KUGLER, ANNA SARAH; ORDINATION OF WOMEN; PAULSSEN, BERTHA; SIEVEKING, AMALIE WILHELMINE; WASA, ANNA; WOMEN IN THE CHURCH; ZELL, KATHARINA. [G.G.]

FEMINIST THEOLOGY. As with all further predications of **contextual theology**, feminist theology conducts critical and constructive reflection from the primacy of female identity, historical awareness, and experience. In doing so, it challenges basic gender-based assumptions of personal identity, the nature of **God**, and human behavior. Though as diverse as the feminist movement as a whole, feminist theological reflection has created a critical awareness of the marginalization and "making invisible" of women in much of Christian history and theology. Recognition of this has led to a rereading of Christian history by employing a hermeneutic of "suspicion" and of discovery (*see* HERMENEUTICS). Biblical, historical, and theological studies from a feminist perspective have uncovered early instances of inclusive Christian communities, the presence and role of outstanding women in Christian history, and have challenged one-sided male-oriented interpretations of Christian theology. Current feminist theology analyzes the influences of theoretical horizons, including the abstractions of denominational identities.

Because feminist theology refutes the totalizing tendencies of theory per se, especially as theory has reflected masculine domination, some would consider a Lutheran-feminist or feminist-Lutheran theology, at least in the first generation of feminist reflection, as something of a self-contradiction and would prefer to speak of feminist theology in the context of the Lutheran tradition. *See also* FEMINISM. [D.H.L.]

FESTIVALS OF THE CHURCH YEAR. Festivals, commemorations, and other special occasions during the **church year**. The three initial major festivals of the church year in the early church—**Easter**, **Pentecost**, and **Epiphany**—to which three additional festivals have been added since the fourth century—**Christmas**, Good Friday, and Ascension Day—have always been surrounded by many other festivals, commemorations, and saints' days. The Lutheran reformers tried to reduce the number of these feasts and have kept only those for whom Scriptural reference could be found (*see* BIBLE, AUTHORITY OF). But beginning in 1667 they also added the festival of the **Reformation** on October 31 (or the Sunday preceding it) to commemorate **Martin Luther's** publication of his *Ninety-five Theses* in **Wittenberg** on October 31, 1517. Many Lutheran churches have introduced liturgical orders for Harvest Thanksgiving, Day of Penance and Prayer (Ger *Buss-und Bettag*), Day of General Thanksgiving (United States/Canada), and Festival of the Dedication of the Church. Some churches have reestablished a rather extensive calendar of commemorating outstanding Christians past and present. Lutheran churches participate in **ecumenical** observances of the Week of Prayer for Christian Unity (January 18–25 or at Pentecost) and the World Day of Prayer (first Friday of March), as well as a number of **Sundays** focusing on other specific concerns. [G.G.]

FLACIUS ILLYRICUS, MATTHIAS (1520–1575). Leader of the **Gnesio-Lutheran** party of second-generation Lutheranism. Born near Trieste, in what is now Croatia, Flacius matriculated at the University of **Wittenberg** in 1541 and was appointed as a professor of Hebrew in 1544. His **theology** was characterized by a subtle assimilation of **Martin Luther's** thought with Aristotelianism, evident the most publicly in his argument that human beings have no **free will** whatsoever and have lost the image of God (*imago dei*). "Flacianism" was pronounced as heresy in article 1 of the *Formula of Concord*. The objective otherness of **God's** gracious initiative was a hallmark concept in Flacius's thought that identified him as a leader against any perceived compromise of the **Gospel** to other authorities. For example, when **Philipp Melanchthon** espoused a conciliatory policy during the Augsburg **Interim**, Flacius urged total resistance, naming the occasion a "situation of confession" (*see STATUS CONFESSIONIS*). Subsequently (in 1549), Flacius moved to Magdeburg. There he rallied public opinion against the Interim and motivated the elector, Moritz of Saxony, to attack Charles V, who was once an ally. This Princes' Revolt overturned the conclusion of the Smalcald War and led to the 1555 **Religious Peace of Augsburg** and **religious freedom** for **Reformation** territories. Thus Flacius's theological convictions led toward the formation of political policy. Regarding other contributions by Flacius, contemporary philosopher Hans Georg Gadamer regards Flacius as the father of **hermeneutics**. Flacius is also noted for his organizing of the *Magdeburg Centuries* (1559ff), a collection of primary historical documents, thereby establishing the academic discipline of church history.

Flacius's zealous defense of what he considered pure Lutheran **doctrine** and his harsh attacks against all who did not share such a position, especially the **Philippists**, led to his dismissal from the university. Between 1557 and 1575 he lived, until dismissed again, in Regensburg, Antwerp, Strasbourg, and Frankfurt. He died in Frankfurt am Main on March 11, 1575, just a few days prior to another scheduled banishment. [D.H.L.]

FLIEDNER, THEODOR (1800–1864). Founder of the **deaconess** movement and women's diaconical work. Influenced by revivalist ideas and discovering a renewed biblical theology, Fliedner served as the **pastor** in Kaiserswerth, Germany, from 1821–1849. During this period, he established a veritable empire of deaconess and diaconic (*see* DIAKONIA) institutions. Among them he established a home for discharged female prisoners in 1833 and the first nursery school in Germany at Düsseldorf in 1836. In the same year, Fliedner founded the modern deaconess movement when, together with friends, he organized the Rhenish-Westphalian Deaconess Society that was based on a hospital that also served as a training center for nurses/deaconesses. Fliedner's wife Friederike became the headmistress of the first deaconess mother house later that year. An orphanage for girls was opened in 1842. In 1844 a deaconess house was established at Dresden, and at Duisburg a school for male parish workers (later deacon's seminary). A seminary for women teachers was created in 1847.

In 1849 Fliedner went to Pittsburgh, Pennsylvania, with four deaconesses from the motherhouse at Kaiserswerth to establish a motherhouse there. Other institutions outside Germany followed: first a hospital and training school for nurses at Jerusalem (1851) and soon after, similar institutions and vocational schools at Constantinople, Beirut, Bucharest, Florence, Smyrna, and Alexandria. Between 1849 and 1857 Fliedner spent half of his time traveling to oversee the wide network of deaconess motherhouses (26) and the many social and educational institutions. His most famous disciple was Florence Nightingale (1850/51). With his unceasing activity Fliedner responded to the needs of the time and provided thousands of women with responsible activity. He revived the New Testament deaconate and gave it the form of a permanent community of **faith** and service. [G.G.]

FORGIVENESS. Forgiveness of **sins** is at the center of the message of the Christian **Gospel**. Acts of forgiveness authoritatively declared and effectively communicated through the **means of grace** (Word and sacrament) are a constitutive element of the biblical witness and of the **tradition** of the Christian faith. Forgiveness effects **reconciliation** of estranged humanity with **God** on account of Christ's mediation; forgiveness liberates people from the burden of their guilt and their sinful self-centeredness; and forgiveness is essential for the restoration of broken human relations. In the early church, forgiveness of sins was formalized in the framework of **confession**, repentance, and absolution. Anglo-Irish monks introduced a private and pastoral form of confession that became the rule after the sixth century and developed into the sacrament of penance. After the Fourth Lateran Council in 1215, penance became an obligatory sacrament (at least once a year), necessary for **salvation**, at which the enumeration of all sins was required. **Thomas Aquinas** clarified this sacrament by defining its matter (*materia*) as contrition, confession, and satisfaction of the penitent, while its form (*forma*) was the absolution pronounced by the priest. Thomas's teaching was made official church teaching by the Council of Florence in 1439 and then by the Council of Trent (*see* TRENT, COUNCIL OF).

The Lutheran **Reformation** affirmed the tradition of the church, agreeing that even subsequent to **baptism** confession of sin, repentance, and forgiveness of sin through absolution were essential for the life of Christians. But **Martin Luther** and the Lutheran confessions (*see* CONFESSIONS, LUTHERAN) rejected the late medieval formalized system of penance with its emphasis on human efforts and cooperation, coercion, full enumeration of sins, and the inhuman burden of performing meritorious works of satisfaction. Luther stated in the first of his *Ninety-five Theses* (1517) that "the entire life of believers to be one of repentance." He and the confessions insisted on the continuation of corporate and especially private confession and absolution. In contrast to the medieval system, however, they focused on these two aspects of penitence: contrition as a result of the proclamation of the law and **faith** in the **Gospel** and absolution where God's free gift of grace and effective declaration of forgiveness for the sake of Christ are received. This gift of forgiveness and reconciliation—**justification**—is communicated by the **Holy Spirit** through Word and sacrament. Thus, forgiveness of sin was understood in relation to confession and absolution as the pastoral application of the central doctrines of **law and Gospel** and of justification by faith alone. While **Philipp Melanchthon** counts penance (confession and absolution) among the sacraments in the *Augsburg Confession* (articles 9–13), Luther links repentance with the life-long significance of baptism. He emphasizes absolution as the liberating and justifying **Word of God** and praises the wonderful and comforting reality of confession and forgiveness of sins, which is declared in absolution and to which one should gladly run more than a hundred miles (*Large Catechism*).

In recent decades, Lutheran churches have begun to rediscover the pastoral significance of forgiveness of sins in the context of corporate and especially in individual confession of sins. This includes a realization of the holistic and social dimension of forgiveness: God's effective forgiveness of sins constitutes a new reality in which human lives can be healed, reconciled, come to peace with themselves, and are led to renewed relationships with others. *See also* RECONCILIATION; SACRAMENTS. [G.G.]

FORMULA OF CONCORD (*FC*) (1577). A confessional text that settled inner-Lutheran controversies in the 16th century. Since the middle of the 16th century differences among Lutheran theologians concerning the interpretation of central issues of **Reformation** theology had led to bitter theological battles about **law and Gospel, adiaphora**, the relation between **salvation** and **good works**, Christ's real presence in the **Lord's Supper**, (human) **free will, original sin**, and so on. After 1555 efforts were undertaken to settle these controversies between **Gnesio-Lutherans, Philippists**, and **Crypto-Calvinists** by a binding exposition of the *Augsburg Confession*. The **evangelical** princes and cities supported these efforts in order to overcome disunity in Lutheran territories and to safeguard the settlement of the **Religious Peace of Augsburg** of 1555. During the 1570s several theological statements were drafted, discussed, and revised by Lutheran theologians, and then formulated in the *Torgau Book* of 1576. A summary of this book, the *Epitome*, became the first part of the *FC*, and a revised version of the *Torgau Book*, the *Bergen Book* of 1577, became the second part, the *Solid Declaration*, of the *FC*. Between 1578 and 1580 the *FC* was accepted by 86 territories and free cities and included in the *Book of Concord* of 1580. The *FC* understands and presents itself as an exposition of the **faith** of the *Augsburg Confession* and reflects serious theological struggles about the right understanding of the **truth** of the Christian faith. It has preserved inner-Lutheran unity, and its highly doctrinal style and language marks the transition to Lutheran Orthodoxy (*see* ORTHODOXY, LUTHERAN). [G.G.]

FRANCKE, AUGUST HERMANN (1663–1727). Influential Lutheran pietistic theologian and a leader in pedagogical and social reform. In 1669, two years after a personal **conversion** experience, the Leipzig professor of oriental languages became the leader of a pietistic revival (*see* PIETISM) among students and citizens of Leipzig. He was dismissed from the university. In 1691 the new university of Halle appointed him professor of oriental languages. There, Francke established a student city of worldwide reputation. It began in 1695 with a school for the poor, followed by several other schools (including a first one for girls), a training institution for teachers, an orphanage, workshops, a library, a printing shop, and so on. Over 3,000 pupils and students lived on the "campus." In 1698 Francke was also appointed professor of theology. He introduced educational reforms aiming at a closer connection between theory and praxis (his students had to teach in the schools and the pupils had to learn a craft). He proposed social reforms to the state. Francke combined his pietistic orientation with solid biblical studies and thus created his particular form of (Halle) Pietism.

Ecumenical relations with many countries and churches were developed and students from these countries flocked to Halle. Francke became a pioneer of foreign **mission** work (Danish-Halle Mission), especially in India (*see* MISSION HISTORY). He and his son Gotthilf August sent their students as preachers and teachers to serve Lutheran churches in many countries, including the early congregations in Pennsylvania (*see* HENRY MELCHIOR MUHLENBERG). Over half a million of August Francke's **sermons** and pamphlets were printed. The work of this social, educational, **ecumenical**, and missionary pioneer and reformer is continued by the Francke Foundation (*Franckesche Stiftungen*) up to the present day. *See also* EDUCATION. [G.G.]

FREDERICK III THE WISE, ELECTOR OF SAXONY (1463–1525). Frederick was **Martin Luther's** sovereign and protector. He became elector in 1486 and was generally regarded as a learned, wise, just, pious, and conscientious ruler. Being highly respected beyond the boundaries of his territory, he was able, though being a convinced Catholic, to protect his **Wittenberg** professor Luther. Frederick had founded the university in 1502, and used his great diplomatic skills to secure Luther's trials in Germany (Augsburg 1518 and Worms 1521) and not in Rome. He devised the plan to bring Luther to Wartburg Castle after he was banned at Worms. His support of Luther came out of a sincere respect for the convictions of others and a sense of appreciation of his increasingly famous professor—whom he probably never met in person. On his deathbed, he received **Holy Communion** in both kinds, and Luther preached the **sermon** at his funeral. In a sense, Frederick made the origins of the Lutheran **Reformation** at Wittenberg possible. [G.G.]

FREE CHURCHES, LUTHERAN. Churches that have separated themselves from established Lutheran and United churches. If churches that maintain themselves and conduct their activities without close ties to governments and state financial support are considered "free churches," then all Lutheran churches outside of Europe and several of them in Europe are "free churches." In a more specific and historical sense, however, those churches are considered "free churches" that separated themselves from established **Anglican**, **Lutheran**, and **Reformed** churches in Europe. In the case of Lutheran free churches, this happened in the 19th century when groups and **congregations** with a strong confessional consciousness (*see* CONFESSIONS, LUTHERAN) protested against the state-decreed **unions** of Lutherans and Reformed in Prussia (1817) and several other German territories and were allowed, after some time, to form their own church bodies. Thus emerged a number of Lutheran free churches in Germany. Most of them united in 1972, 1976, and 1991 to form the Independent Evangelical Lutheran Church with 40,000 members (1999). In Scandinavian countries, small groups formed free churches during the 19th century in protest against what they regarded as liberal tendencies in their established state or folk churches. These churches are tiny, with the exception of the Evangelical Lutheran Free Church of Norway (1877), which has 21,000 members and is an associated member church of the **Lutheran World Federation** since 1997. The different Lutheran free churches are generally closely related in confessional stance and relationship to the **Lutheran Church-Missouri Synod** and the **International Lutheran Council**. [G.G.]

FREE WILL. The **Reformation** debate about the role of the human will in the process of **faith** and **salvation**. The Lutheran Reformation saw itself confronted with the ideas of representatives of late medieval nominalism like William of Ockham (c.1285–1347) and Gabriel Biel (c.1410–1495) who taught that **original sin** had not destroyed the ability of the human will to turn to **God** and earn **grace** "by doing one's best." For **Martin Luther**, this was a negation of the sole activity of God in leading a person to faith, **justification**, and a new life in Christ through grace and by faith alone. All depends on God's undeserved and unconditional gift. In this process, the will has no positive role to play because, since the fall, the will is under the domination of **sin**. Solely through the justification of the sinner by God the human will is brought under the rule of God and is able, led by the Holy Spirit, to do what is good and obey God's commandments.

This conflict found a special literary expression in the controversy between Luther and **Erasmus of Rotterdam**. The humanist scholar had moved towards a nominalist position and wrote in his *Disquisition on Free Will* (*De libero arbitrio* [1524]) against Luther that the free will has been "wounded through sin," but it can still enable people to "apply themselves to or turn away from that which leads unto eternal salvation." Luther responded in his *The Bondage of the Will* (*De servo arbitrio* [1525]) and sternly affirmed that "man has no free will, but is captive, servant, and bondslave, either to the will of God or to the will of the devil." Before **baptism** and justification, the will is not free, it cannot change itself. Luther did not exclude, however, the reality of free will in everyday choices. The Lutheran confessions (*see* CONFESSIONS, LUTHERAN) underline that the human will can make choices in the civil realm, but not concerning the relationship of a person to God. The will is captive to sin. But after a person has been baptized and lives a Christian life of faith and renewal in Christ, this Christian has a "liberated will" that is able to do good and delights in God's law. [G.G.]

FRY, FRANKLIN CLARK (1900–1968). Fry was one of the most outstanding church leaders in the United States ("Mister Lutheran") (*see* NORTH AMERICA, LUTHERAN CHURCHES IN) as well as a remarkable and highly respected Lutheran ecumenist. Born in Bethlehem, Pennsylvania, he served, after ordination in 1925, for 19 years as a parish **pastor**. In 1944 he was elected president of the United Lutheran Church in America. Committed to Lutheran **unity** and to the **ecumenical movement**, he was actively involved in the foundation of the **Lutheran World Federation** (LWF) in 1947, the **World Council of Churches** (WCC) in 1948, and the restructured National Council of the Churches of Christ in the USA in 1950. When four Lutheran churches merged in 1962 to form the Lutheran Church in America, Fry was elected its president. In the WCC, he was moderator of the Central and Executive Committees from 1954 until 1968 where his moderatorship was generally admired (and feared). From 1957–1963 he was president of the LWF and a member of its Executive Committee until his death in 1968. His remarkable career, with its great national and international responsibilities, was accompanied by a personal concern and support for suffering people all over the world. [G.G.]

FUNDAMENTALISM. A mode of **faith** expression, born out of the early 20th century with the publication in America of a tract series called *The Fundamentals* (1905–1913), which holds that certain 19th- and 20th-century conservative beliefs, like the imminent end of the world and eminence of **free will** have their authority and basis anchored in a literalistic and inerrant reading of the Bible. While some contemporary Lutherans may in this respect happen also to be fundamentalists, Lutheranism per se is not fundamentalistic. The Lutheran understanding of Scripture's authority was originally quite differentiated. While **Martin Luther** accepted with other **Protestants** the authority of Scripture, he differed by holding that Scripture's authority was based upon its communication of the **Gospel** as **promise**. With Lutheran **Orthodoxy**, authority of Scripture came to be identified with the inspired text as the verbatim **Word of God**, though first generation Lutheran Orthodox dogmaticians (*see* DOGMATICS) attempted to maintain some nuance.

Thus, by the beginning of the third generation of Lutheranism, the **Canon of Holy Scripture** was understood by many as closed and rigid. The original reforming **Protestant** insight that the Word of God was the living voice of the Gospel for every generation and people to hear anew, especially in the word of **preaching** and the "visible word" of **sacraments**, was reduced to the understanding that the Word of God was but its written form. This provided the ground for eventual claims that doctrines, which were themselves once flexible for interpretation, like **atonement** theory or **eschatology**, could now be interpreted only in a narrow fashion. These were the themes that would provide the content to contemporary fundamentalism in a number of Christian communities. *See also* BIBLE, AUTHORITY OF; BIBLE, INSPIRATION. [D.H.L.]

– G –

GERHARD, JOHANN (1582–1637). The most important representative of Lutheran Orthodoxy (*see* ORTHODOXY, LUTHERAN). Born in Quedlinburg, Germany, Gerhard was appointed the **superintendent** in Heldburg (1606) and the general superintendent in Coburg (1615) where he prepared a new **church order** for the duchy. In 1616 he became a professor of theology in Jena and remained at this university, despite dozens of offers, until his death. In addition to his academic work, he was widely consulted, participated in theological discussions, and entertained a massive correspondence. With his enormous literary output of exegetical, systematic, apologetical, and devotional works, he is believed to have presented the most thorough exposition of classical Lutheran **theology** in the 17th century.

Most famous among his writings were the nine-volume **dogmatics** *Loci theologici* (1610–1622). Influenced by the Aristotelian philosophy and metaphysics of the schools, the different topics (*loci*) of his dogmatics are presented in a strict systematic and historical manner with their biblical basis, patristic (*see* PATRISTICS) and Lutheran background, dogmatic exposition, apologetical distinction over and against especially **Roman Catholicism** and Calvinism, and their application (*usus*) to Christian life and **piety**. His *Loci*, introduced by a foundational affirmation of the inspired and infallible norm of Holy Scripture (*see* BIBLE, AUTHORITY OF), were intended to serve the purity of Lutheran teaching. The *Loci* and other works like his four-volume apologetics *Confessio Catholica* (1634–1637) or the much translated contemplations *Meditationes sacrae* (1610) remained in people's studies far beyond Gerhard's lifetime. This gentle, generous, knowledgeable professor was at his time the most influential Lutheran theologian in Europe. [G.G.]

GERHARD, PAUL (1607–1676). Important German hymnwriter, **pastor**, and theologian. Born near **Wittenberg**, his studies in that university appear to have been interrupted by the **Thirty Years' War**, since he was in his mid-thirties when he left it. He served as a tutor in the family of his future wife and as the pastor in Mittenwalde, outside of Berlin. In 1657 he was called to be the pastor of St. Nicholas's Church in Berlin, where he served until 1669. Firmly convinced of the anti-Calvinistic tenets of the *Formula of Concord*, he refused to sign a pledge to refrain from polemics in the pulpit, and was deposed from his office. Reluctant to return to Prussian territory because it would require silence in the face of what he considered false **doctrine**, he lived in poverty for several years before obtaining a call to a Saxon congregation described as "a rough and unsympathetic people" in 1669. Gerhard's personal life was as difficult as his professional life: four of his five children died in infancy, and Gerhard's wife died bearing the last. Gerhard's portrait in Lübben bears the inscription, "A theologian sifted in Satan's sieve."

From the first, Gerhard's **hymn** texts and poetry combine orthodox formulation (*see* ORTHODOXY, LUTHERAN) with fervent emotion, without the sentimentality or showmanship so common among his Baroque contemporaries. Attention to biblical themes and imagery, the centrality of human sinfulness and the **atonement**, and the evident, heartfelt gratitude of a rescued soul mark Gerhard as a forebear of **Pietism**. It is, then, no surprise that **John Wesley** would find his hymns so well suited to his own **piety** that he would translate them into English and introduce them to the people called **Methodists**.

Gerhard's first hymns were published in the third edition of his *Praxis Pietatis Melica*, edited by his friend Johann Crüger, who composed some of the best known tunes for Gerhard's texts. Eventually, Gerhard wrote over 130 hymns in German and at least 14 in Latin, including "O Sacred Head Now Wounded" and "Now All the Woods Are Sleeping." [M.O.]

GLÜCK, ERNST (1652–1705). Lutheran educator and translator in Latvia and Russia. Born near Halle in Germany, Glück studied theology and later ancient languages. After his **ordination** in 1673 he went to Livonia and served several Latvian congregations there. He also was appointed the district **superintendent** at Marienburg. He learned Latvian and Estonian and translated the Bible into Latvian. The New Testament came out in 1685 and the Old Testament in 1688; the whole Bible was printed in 1694.

Glück's special concern was the **education** of ordinary people. He assisted in the efforts of the Swedish government (at that time Sweden ruled the country) by creating schools, establishing three teachers' training colleges, and publishing school books. He translated the *Small Catechism* of **Martin Luther** (*see* CATECHISMS OF LUTHER) into Latvian. In the Nordic War between Russia and Sweden, Glück became a Russian prisoner in 1702 and was taken to Russia. Released in 1703, he remained there, founded a grammar school at Moscow, and became its headmaster. He translated the Slavonic Bible into Russian and wrote a number of books for schools. [G.G.]

GNESIO-LUTHERANS (Gk *gnesios*, "genuine" or "pure"). Pejorative term applied to those who regarded themselves as the genuine successors of **Martin Luther** (and called themselves "Lutherans"). During the inner-Lutheran theological controversies between the **Interim** (1548) and the *Formula of Concord* (1577), a group of faithful, but also combative, sometimes violent and overly polemical conservative adherents of Luther fought for the preservation of Luther's heritage against all compromises. Leading figures were Nikolaus von Amsdorf and **Matthias Illyricus Flacius**. The centers were Magdeburg and later the University of Jena (founded 1588). In the *Formula of Concord*, the more extreme positions of the Gnesio-Lutherans were rejected, but in many individual points their protest against the **Philippists** and **Crypto-Calvinists** have had a lasting effect. [G.G.]

GOD. *See* TRINITY, DOGMA OF.

GÓMEZ, MEDARDO ERNESTO (1945–). **Bishop** of the Salvadoran Lutheran Synod. Gómez was born in San Miguel. From an early age he had wanted to become a **priest**, but because his parents were not married in the Roman Catholic Church, he was refused entrance to seminary. Invited by David Fernández—who himself would become a Lutheran **pastor** and was assassinated in 1984—to become a Lutheran, Gómez joined the Lutheran church in 1964. In 1966 he attended the Augsburg Lutheran Seminary in Mexico City, from which he graduated in 1970. He received a graduate degree, too, from Francisco Gavidia University in San Salvador in 1982 as well as numerous honorary degrees and recognitions from institutions throughout the world. He was consecrated as the first bishop of the Salvadoran Lutheran Synod in 1986.

Gómez is seen globally as a stalwart pastor who stood by the poor and ensured the survival of the Lutheran witness through the tumultuous years of the Salvadoran civil war. His visible solidarity with the Salvadoran majority, clear voice against oppression, and facile mixture of **liberation theology** with institutional administration made him both a model of faithfulness and the target of many death threats. Gómez's work has been a model of politically savvy contextual leadership (*see* CONTEXTUAL THEOLOGY) throughout the churches of the **Lutheran World Federation**. Once a candidate for the Nobel Peace Prize, he has been recognized ecumenically as a colleague of and heir to the regard for martyred Roman Catholic bishop Oscar Romero. Of his writings that have been translated, two primary ones are *Fire Against Fire: Christian Ministry Face-to-Face with Persecution* (1990) and *And the Word Became History: Messages Forged in the Fires of Central American Conflict* (1992). [D.H.L.]

GOOD WORKS. Key term for the Lutheran **Reformation** in the clarification of the **evangelical** understanding of **faith**. The Lutheran confessions (*see* CONFESSIONS, LUTHERAN), the writings of **Martin Luther** and **Philipp Melanchthon**, and also the *Formula of Concord* (article 4) describe the relationship between faith and good works in a twofold way: First, negatively, good works stand for human religious efforts that are considered in late medieval theology and practice as contributing to receiving **God's** gift of **justification**, **forgiveness** of sins, and **salvation**. Together with faith, good works merit this gracious response of God. This position, which has fine differentiations not always noted, is vehemently rejected by the reformers as the abominable **heresy** of the medieval church by which the saving work of God in Jesus Christ is negated or obscured. Rather, this saving work, God's justification of the sinner for Christ's sake, is received through **grace** alone and by faith alone, gratuitously, without any human contribution, without good works. The much quoted biblical basis for this reaction are the Pauline letters, especially Romans.

Second, positively, after having achieved clarity at this point, the other statement is made: Good works are a necessary and natural consequence and fruit of the faith, renewal, and forgiveness of a person justified by God by faith alone. Such works are commanded by God and done with the help of the Holy Spirit. They are an expression of the "new obedience" and of a grateful heart. Without them, faith would not be right and would not endure. Good works are not necessary for salvation, but because God wills them, they are an essential element in the life of people reconciled to God. Yet again and again it is repeated that such works do not merit favor before God. Furthermore, such works are no longer seen as acts of piety and charity, but rather as acts of Christian love and faithful obedience to God's commands in the secular day-to-day life of Christians. The careful balance between faith and good works has occupied Lutheran thinking up to the present. *See also* ETHICS; FREE WILL. [G.G.]

GOSPEL. In the literal sense, Gospel means good news (Gk *euangelion*), the announcement of **salvation** in Christ (e.g., Rom 15:19; Gal 1:7). In the literary sense, Gospel is a narrative genre, and refers to one of the four narratives of the New Testament—Mark, Matthew, Luke, and John—that give a narrative theological perspective on the life and significance of Jesus of Nazareth (*see* CHRISTOLOGY). Gospel is a central concept in Lutheran theological use where the term refers simultaneously to the whole activity of **God** in Jesus Christ and the free gift of salvation, including **faith** itself, to humankind, which by its own lights could never gain such bliss. In varying contexts, the communication of the Gospel as a liberating and consoling message is and must be appropriately predicated, but its substance is ever the same: that God saves humanity and all **creation** through the divine gift of **grace** in Christ alone, and that even the faith, which in **repentance** grasps this gift, is an occasion of God's grace. This is the substantive core of what **Lutheranism** intends in the term "Gospel." In formal terms, it is phrased in the grammar of the doctrine of **justification**. [D.H.L.]

GOVERNMENT. *See* CHURCH AND STATE.

GRACE (Gk *charis*, Lat *gratia*, "favor, kindness, benevolence"). The unconditional favor and loving action of **God** in Jesus Christ extended to sinful humanity for its **salvation**. The Old Testament uses various terms to describe the favor, love, kindness, and devotion of God to his people, especially in the covenant. In the New Testament the majority of the 550 uses of "grace" are in Paul's letters. For his proclamation of **justification** and salvation, the concept of grace is central and essential. It refers to God's unconditional loving concern for sinners who are justified by his grace through the redemption that is in Jesus Christ (Rom 3:24). Grace is closely connected with God's love shown in Christ's saving death and **resurrection** for the sake of **reconciliation** and the reestablishment of **communion** of people with God (Rom 5:1–11). Thus, in the grace of Jesus Christ (2 Cor 13:14) the power of God's grace over **sin** has been manifested. Grace has also overcome the way of the law (Rom 3:21f.; Gal 5:2). Within the realm of grace in which believers stand (Rom 5:2) and from which they can fall away (Gal 5:4), grace becomes concrete in manifold gifts of grace (Gk *charismata*) (1 Cor 12:4–11; Rom 12:6–8). Grace is an unmerited gift (Rom 3:24) and universal in scope (Rom 4:16: 5:15).

During the first centuries, the Greek fathers of the church emphasized an understanding of grace as the working of the Triune God in **salvation history** for the divinization of believers. In the West, it was **Augustine** who shaped the doctrine of grace for later generations in such a way that since the sixth century it was received (*see* RECEPTION) by the church as its official teaching. Augustine taught the total dependency of sinful human beings on God's grace in Jesus Christ and that, accordingly, the absolute initiative in the process of salvation belongs to the grace of God. Through the action of God's grace people are made righteous before God.

Between the 12th and the 16th centuries the connection between human effort and God's efficacious grace in the process of salvation was differently interpreted in the various scholastic schools that developed sophisticated systems of the functions and roles of grace (e.g., the prevenient, infused, inhering, justifying, and the subsequent or cooperating grace). The so-called Franciscan school in High Scholasticism of the 13th century considered the way of salvation as a process of human efforts by "doing one's best" (*facere quod in se est*) that would merit God's grace and justification. In contrast to this position, **Thomas Aquinas** again affirmed the absolute primacy of grace. For him, grace is an infused, inner *habitus* in humans. Through the virtues infused by grace, Christians are internally changed and spontaneously do what is good, freely fulfilling the law. Justification is realized in this way without claiming any merit before God. Scholastic teaching from the 14th to the 16th centuries was marked by theologians who stressed the meritorious role of human efforts in securing grace (e.g., William of Ockham [c.1285–1349], and Gabriel Biel [c.1410–1495]), as well as by the Augustinian school of Gregory of Rimini (c.1300–1358) that reappropriated the teaching of Augustine.

Martin Luther reacted sharply against the late medieval concepts of grace cooperating with human **free will** and **good works**, or grace as being merited by such human efforts. In line with his rediscovery of the focus of Pauline theology and, consequently, in the framework of his Christocentrism and teaching on justification, Luther stressed the absolute sovereignty of God's grace that comes to human beings from the outside and is independent of any precondition or human merit. Grace, thus, is a free gift, clearly communicating God's favor, forgiveness, reconciliation, salvation, and justification of sinners for Christ's sake and in Christ. Justification is given to believers by grace alone (*sola gratia*). Luther's emphasis on and praise of God's unmerited grace, mediated through the **means of grace**—**Word** and **sacrament**—is echoed in the Lutheran confessions (*see* CONFESSIONS, LUTHERAN) that teach justification by grace alone and affirm, for example, in the *Formula of Concord*, the sole efficacy of grace, apart from the human will and effort. Lutheran **Orthodoxy** returned to a differentiation between different actions of grace (vocation, enlightenment, justification, rebirth, and sanctification) within an inner process of being saved (*see* ORDER OF SALVATION). The Council of Trent (*see* TRENT, COUNCIL OF) responded to the **Reformation** by teaching the necessity of a special grace that awakens and supports human endeavors as preparation for justification. This grace is not only the favor of God but also a new reality in humans infused by the Holy Spirit.

In Lutheran **Pietism** in the 18th century a fresh effort is noticeable to connect grace and justification with experience, **piety**, and sanctification. In the 20th century, after numerous idealistic or moralistic misinterpretations by various theologians of grace as a human faculty, the great Reformed theologian Karl Barth brought grace back to the center of the Christian faith by highlighting the triumph of grace, while Lutheran **Dietrich Bonhoeffer** warned against a "cheap grace" when it is too easily promised without repentance and obedience. In **ecumenical** dialogue, there is far-reaching agreement on the unconditional character and clear priority of divine grace as God's loving and liberating action to which human will and religious activity are subordinated. It is held that grace is a transforming power for the whole existence of people, and that grace is God's saving and transforming action not only in relation to individuals but also in relation to the Christian community as a whole and to its service for the wider human community. [G.G.]

GRUMBACH, ARGULA VON (c.1492–1568). One of the most remarkable Lutheran women at the time of the **Reformation**. Born in Bavaria, she was educated—being an orphan—at the Munich court. As a younger and well-instructed woman, she seems to have become interested in Reformation ideas. In 1523 she said of herself that she had read all that **Martin Luther** had published in the German language. She corresponded with Luther and other leading reformers. In order to defend young magister Arsacius See-hofer who was accused of strong Lutheran sympathies, she sent and published in 1523 letters to the duke of Bavaria and Seehofer's University of Ingolstadt. They received a lot of publicity. In one letter she defended not only Seehofer, but also Luther and **Philipp Melanchthon** as well as her right as a woman not to remain silent when no man would or could speak. In another letter, addressed to the duke and magistrates, she admonished them not to misuse their **authority** received from **God**. In 1530 she seems to have met Luther at Coburg Castle.

Despite her privileged position as the wife of a ruler of a small territory, Grumbach suffered, even from her own family, for her public stance in favor of Reformation ideals. About her later life little is known. During the years when she administered her territory after the death of her second husband, she remained faithful to her Lutheran convictions in a strictly Catholic country. Even at the age of 70 she may have been in prison at Straubing for a short while in 1563 for providing the people in her territory with literature supporting the Reformation. Luther called this courageous and strong woman "a unique instrument of Christ." [G.G.]

GRUNDTVIG, NIKOLAI FREDERIK SEVERIN (1783–1872). Eminent Danish theologian, philosopher, educator, and hymnwriter. The son of a Lutheran **pastor**, Grundtvig's early life was spent studying, retelling, and imitating the poetry of Norse mythology that gave, he believed, the peculiar ethos to the Danish people. From 1805–1808 he served as a tutor in a landed family, from 1808–1811 he taught at a high school at Copenhagen, and in 1811 he returned home to serve as his father's assistant. His **ordination sermon** was, however, so scathing a denunciation of the rationalism of the Danish clergy that he was reprimanded by the ministerium. Because of his orthodox Lutheran views, it was not until 1821 that he was called to a **parish**. He served several **congregations**, interrupted by periods when he had to survive as a freelance writer. From 1848–1858 he was a member of parliament.

While beginning with a strong commitment to the centrality of Scripture, Grundtvig moved to a position in which he placed the living voice of Christ—present above all in the **Apostles' Creed** and the **sacraments**—above even the written **Word** of the Bible. His ideas emphasized the relationship between the people ("folk") and the **church**, and between the human and the Christian. His followers remained a part of the Danish church and, in the New World, formed the American Evangelical Lutheran Church that became part of the Lutheran Church in America in 1962.

Grundtvig left, however, two legacies of which even his theological adversaries approved. The first was his body of hymnody, now through translation available ecumenically and worldwide—"Built on a Rock" is probably his best known. The second was his system of "folk high schools," which began in Denmark, but quickly spread across the borders. Up to this day there exists a Christian and popular movement in Denmark called "Grundvigianism." [M.O.]

GUSTAVUS II ADOLPHUS (1594–1632). King of Sweden and Lutheran statesman. The grandson of Gustavus Vasa who had introduced the **Reformation** in Sweden, Gustavus Adolphus became king of Sweden in 1611. After consolidating his kingdom in several wars, the young king decided in 1630 to confront the forces of the **Counter-Reformation** with his own army. Political pressures and his ambitious determination to pursue his interests and those of a mighty Sweden motivated his involvement in the **Thirty Years' War**, but he was also moved by the compelling moral force of his deep Lutheran faith. With several victories in 1631 and 1632, he helped to restore the freedom of the **Protestant** churches in southern and southwestern Germany. In the battle of Lützen, in which he was victorious, he was mortally wounded and died on the battlefield. Gustavus Adolphus is widely remembered today as a defender of the Reformation heritage. [G.G.]

GUTENBERG, JOHANNES. *See* PRINTING PRESS.

– H –

HAMMARSKJÖLD, DAG (1905–1961). Famous international Lutheran layman. The son of the prime minister of Sweden, Dag Hjalmar Agne Carl Hammarskjöld followed his father into public life. Hammarskjöld studied law and economics at the universities of Uppsala and Stockholm. He taught political economics at the University of Stockholm from 1933–1936 and then served as a civil servant in the Swedish government. In 1953 Hammarskjöld was elected to a five-year term as the secretary general of the United Nations; in 1957 he was unanimously elected to a second term.

Hammarskjöld's diplomatic activity as secretary general was prodigious, while he nevertheless attempted to avoid the spotlights on his center stage role, opting instead for quieter and personal diplomacy. His work included handling the end of the Korean War, conflict in the Middle East, and the Suez Canal crisis. With the independence of the Belgian Congo in 1960, civil war erupted. On a mission to negotiate a cease-fire between United Nations troops and the Katanga forces of President Moise Tschombe, Hammarskjöld was killed in a plane crash near Ndola, in what is now Zambia.

Hammarskjöld's public life was not that only of a career politician, as the posthumous publication of his book, *Markings* (1964), would show. With this deeply **devotional** book's publication, people saw for a first time a public person whose life was profoundly reflective, spiritual, and quite self-consciously Christian. *Markings* records how his understanding of his **faith** led him into public life and guided his practice of diplomacy. As Hammarskjöld himself wrote, in and from his own activity of service to humanity he would learn more about the character of **God**. Without saying so in "large letters," Hammarskjöld's life is an example of the Lutheran attitude to secular **professions**, the relation of **church and state**, and even the doctrine of **two kingdoms**. [D.H.L.]

HARNACK, KARL GUSTAF ADOLF VON (1851–1930). One of the most significant historical theologians of the modern period. Born in Dorpat (today Tartu in Estonia) to Theodosius Harnack, a confessional Lutheran theologian influential in the Baltic states, Adolf von Harnack was educated at Dorpat and Leipzig, and from 1876 on was a professor in Leipzig, Giessen, Marburg, and Berlin. He was both a student of Albrecht Ritschl and a teacher of Karl Barth. Harnack exemplified the modern liberal (*see* LIBERALISM) spirit, of stressing the ethical character of Christianity, so typical then of "the Berlin school." In addition to his academic positions, he was a leading figure in **Protestant** organizations and was appointed first president of the Kaiser-Wilhelm-Gesellschaft, the famous society for the advancement of human and natural sciences.

Harnack started a critical edition of early Greek Christian literature (*see* PATRISTICS) and published studies about all periods of church history as well as publications on social and political subjects. He is best known for the thesis that the Hellenization of Christianity into codified **dogma** detracted from its true, primitive message of God's fatherhood and Jesus' revelation of faithful, ethical life. Important texts of his include the three-volume *The History of Dogma* (1885–1889), *The Apostolic Creed* (1901), and especially *The Essence of Christianity* (1900). Also, in 1876 he cofounded, with Emil Schürer, the important journal *Theologische Literaturzeitung*. [D.H.L.]

HAUGE, HANS NIELSEN (1771–1824). Norwegian Lutheran lay preacher and revival movement leader. Coming from a peasant family, Hauge read religious authors, including **Martin Luther**, already during his youth. In a religious experience in 1796, he sensed a call from **God** to move out and evangelize his "sleeping" fellow Christians. By boat and on foot he traversed the country during 1797–1804 and addressed gatherings of people. He emphasized **conversion**, obedience, and **sanctification**. In his *Testament to his Friends* (1821), he warned against separation and urged loyalty to the national (Lutheran) church. He gathered a large following that led to several short arrests because the law forbade itinerant lay preaching. When he started some business enterprises and helped his friends to found firms and factories in efforts to improve living conditions, merchants joined church and state authorities in their attitude against Hauge. He was again accused of transgressing the Conventicle Act and put into prison from 1804 to 1811. In 1813 and 1814 he was sentenced once again but came away with only a fine. A broken man, he settled on a farm and corresponded with his followers.

In his last years Hauge's unique significance was slowly recognized and even high-standing clergymen visited him. After 1796 he wrote a number of books that had a wide circulation. He had probably a deeper impact on church life in Norway than any other person. Through the **emigration** of Norwegian peasants to North America, the Haugian revival movement crossed the Atlantic Ocean and became a strong force among the emerging Norwegian Lutheran churches in the United States. One of them carried his name: Hauge's Norwegian Evangelical Lutheran Synod in America (1875/76) that later united with other Lutheran churches. [G.G.]

HEALTH AND HEALING. The Lutheran churches' involvement in health care. Healing people was an integral part of Jesus' earthly ministry. In his teaching and actions, physical and spiritual health were intimately interrelated. Jesus sent his disciples to preach the **kingdom** and heal the sick (Lk 9:1–2). Since then, service to the sick and needy has been an important element of the ministry of the Christian **church. Martin Luther** emphasized the responsibility of the extended family, civil authorities, and the churches to care for the sick. Luther knew, "where the soul is healed, the body has benefited also." Lutheran **Pietism** in the 18th century strongly promoted the Christian healing ministry, which led, in the second part of the 19th century, to the **Inner Mission** movement in several European countries, the social work of pioneers such as **Johann Hinrich Wichern**, **Theodor Fliedner**, and **Amalie Sieveking**, as well as the establishment of the ministries of deacons and deaconesses (*see* DIACONATE). A growing number of **hospitals**, institutions for handicapped people, rehabilitation centers, and other health care facilities were created, often outside official church structures. Lutheran **mission societies** regarded it as a main task to create primary health centers and hospitals in Africa and Asia.

Today, Lutheran health care institutions, often supported by the state, seek to complement public health services by a more personal and holistic approach. Two groundbreaking joint consultations in 1964 and 1968 of the **Lutheran World Federation** and the **World Council of Churches** also promoted such approaches. They underlined not only the social, economic, spiritual, and psychological causes of diseases, but also the political ones: The greatest cause of disease in the world is poverty. Accordingly, in many situations social change and primary health care must go hand in hand. In present discussion of the churches' role in a comprehensive health care system, many emphasize the holistic and spiritual dimension of healing, underlining that psychosomatic causes of disease should be addressed and healing is best assisted by life within a forgiving and accepting community that lives in harmony with **God** and neighbor. [G.G.]

HEGEL, GEORG WILHELM FRIEDRICH (1770–1831). Renowned and influential philosopher for part of the 19th century and the whole of the 20th century. Hegel was born in Stuttgart and educated in Tübingen. He taught philosophy in Jena, Heidelberg, and Berlin (from 1818) until his death. His **philosophy** deeply influenced Lutheran **theology** up until the present day. Hegel's philosophy is the foundation of modern dialectical thought—that historical reality is constituted as the synthesis of thesis and antithesis. Primary texts with which one should work fully to understand Hegel's thought (no small task) include the early theological writings (1793–1800), *Phenomenology of Mind* (1807), *Science of Logic* (1812–1816), *Principles of the Philosophy of Law* (1821), *Lectures on the Philosophy of History* (1822–1823), and the monumental *Philosophy of Religion* (1821).

Hegel's thought contributed immensely to the new sense of historicism and evolutionary development of modernism. In political theory it elided with economic analysis to support Marxism, on the left, and—when assumed to be a description of an inexorable process of history—it could support fascist ideology, on the right. In theology, Hegel's thought first leaned towards a rather sterile redescription of **God's** ways with history. When voiced from the pulpit, this elicited the loud objections of philosophers such as **Søren Aabye Kierkegaard** against life explained as "historical system." But a rediscovery of Hegel, "apart" from the "Hegelians" who followed him, has recently underscored for theology the relational character of reality. This has heartily influenced the thought of Karl Barth, **Wolfhart Pannenberg**, and others who have led toward a reflowering of contemporary trinitarian theology. Hegel's philosophy, too, has contributed to a renewal of "Christian metaphysics" in contemporary thought; where once, as with Albrecht Ritschl, Lutheran theology refrained from claims as to the nature of reality, Hegel's thought figures into a contemporary reclamation of theological metaphysics. *See also* ANTHROPOLOGY; CREATION; SCIENCE AND CHRISTIANITY. [D.H.L.]

HEIM, KARL (1874–1958). Leading Lutheran systematic theologian and pioneer of dialogue between **theology** and natural sciences. Heim studied theology at Tübingen, to which he returned as a professor of theology in 1920, after teaching in Halle and Münster. Heim's theology was a rare combination of Württemberg evangelical piety (*see* PIETISM), interest in natural science (*see* SCIENCE AND CHRISTIANITY), and interest in Asian religions and in **mission**. In 1929 he participated in the World Mission Conference at Jerusalem.

Heim believed that the task of theology was primarily apologetical. Sound theology should bring a person to the point of making an informed decision either in favor of skepticism or **faith** in Christ. The apologetical aim of theology thus implied for Heim a coherent worldview in which Christian faith could and should coexist with all intellectual pursuit. Indeed, his systematic structuring of theology anticipated a dominant contemporary view in theology informed by science that **God** unifies all the dimensions and contingencies of the physical universe. Furthermore, for Heim, God's definitive **revelation** is in Christ; therein the biblical message relates to the physical, historical, and existential reality of human existence. Representative of his numerous works, in English translation, are *The Idea of the Universe in the Coming Time* (1904), *God Transcendent* (1936), and *Christian Faith and Natural Science* (1953). These titles belong to his multivolume systematic theology entitled *Protestant Belief and Modern Thought: Outlines of a Christian View of Life* (1931ff). [D.H.L.]

HEIN, CARL CHRISTIAN (1868–1937). American Lutheran **pastor** and church executive. Born in Wiesbaden, Germany, Hein came to America at the age of five, and graduated from the Capitol University and Seminary in Columbus. Following service as a parish pastor in Wisconsin, Michigan, and Ohio, he was elected president of the Joint Synod of Ohio in 1920. He served in that office until the creation of the American Lutheran Church (ALC) in 1930, and served as the president of the ALC from its formation until 1936. He was instrumental in organizing the **Lutheran World Convention**, and active at its early meetings.

In 1925 Hein convened the Minneapolis Colloquy, attended by representatives of the Joint Ohio Synod, the Norwegian Lutheran Church, and the Iowa and Buffalo Synods, to clarify the basis of the fellowship shared by the four churches. The basis included theological and confessional agreement, and joint statements on secret societies and fellowship with non-Lutherans. Over the opposition of the Iowa Synod, Hein's position on the inspiration (*see* BIBLE, INSPIRATION OF) was adopted: the Scriptures "as a whole and in all their parts, [are] the divinely inspired, revealed, and inerrant Word of God" (*see* BIBLE, AUTHORITY OF). Over a decade later, when the three German-heritage synods had merged to form the American Lutheran Church, Hein urged this formulation on inspiration as the basis for agreement with the United Lutheran Church in America (ULCA). It was rejected by the ULCA, but remained part of the confession of faith in the ALC's constitution until the formation of the Evangelical Lutheran Church in America in 1988. *See also* NORTH AMERICA, LUTHERAN CHURCHES IN. [M.O.]

HERDER, JOHANN GOTTFRIED (1744–1803). Eminent Lutheran theologian, philosopher, and poet. Herder was born in Mohrungen, East Prussia. He grew to become a well-known German Lutheran churchman and poet whose lyrics would be set to music by composers like Ludwig van Beethoven, Johannes Brahms, Richard Strauss, and Carl Maria von Weber. At Königsberg, Herder studied under **Immanuel Kant**. At Hamburg, he conversed with Hermann Samuel Reimarus, a famous critic of Christianity. On a visit to Strasbourg, he began a life-long and often tense acquaintance with Johann Wolfgang von Goethe. In Reimarus and Goethe we may see the markers of Herder's eventual antipathy to the intellectual sterility of **Enlightenment** rationalism and moralism.

Herder had been the chief **pastor** in Bückeburg when Goethe convinced him in 1776 to assume the general **superintendent** position at Weimar, a cultural center in Germany. There, he became an influential proponent of both classicism and romanticism. An early exponent of the new historical consciousness, Herder stressed the dynamism and revelatory character of the historical process, as well as the historical particularity (positiveness) of individuals, cultures, and historical epochs. He taught that language and religion are the intimate, connected, expressions of experience-centered **piety**. They were, indeed, the deepest aspects of one's humanity, which were most readily evoked by the most communicative of all the arts, **music** (though he deplored pietistic **hymnody**).

Herder's thought was an attempt to reunite mind with nature, **reason** with **revelation**, and the individual with society. This philosophical synthesis, which emphasized the experiential character of religion and was informed by a sensibility for the unity of the universe, was expressed in his powerful preaching and highly respected pastoral leadership. Music and poetry were integral to Herder's unifying vision. When he died, this translator of George Frederic Handel's *Messiah* into German was celebrated as the president of the high consistory at Weimar and the leader of the renaissance in **church music**. [D.H.L.]

HERESY (Gk *hairesis*, "choice, preference," and from there "sect, party"). Teaching that contradicts or rejects officially established norms of Christian **faith**. Out of the concern of the religious community to preserve its sound **tradition** and its fellowship in **unity** and **truth**, the reality and term of heresy emerged in late Old Testament Judaism and in the New Testament (e.g., 1 Cor 11:18f.; Gal 5:20; 2 Pet 2:1; 1 Tim 6:3–5). For the church fathers (*see* PATRISTICS), "heresy" became a standard term when the distinction between right faith and heresy occupied much of the **theology** of the church during the second until fifth centuries. The criterion for this distinction was the apostolic **tradition** and the rule of faith (*regula fidei*). The institutions that declared a teaching to be a heresy were synods and councils (*see* COUNCILS, ECUMENICAL), in the Middle Ages the papal office (*see* PAPACY), and after 1231 also the Inquisition. To be declared heretical implied excommunication.

The Lutheran **Reformation** affirmed the commitment to Holy Scripture as criterion for right **doctrine** (*see* BIBLE, AUTHORITY OF). Those who were seen to contradict this criterion, such as the **Anabaptists** and **Spiritualists**, were regarded as heretics. **Martin Luther** emphasized that heresy, as a spiritual matter, should be combated only by the Word. But he agreed that the secular arm might act against heretics when they threaten the foundations of public order. In **Lutheranism** today, the **Word of God** as witnessed in Holy Scripture and affirmed in the confessions (*see* CONFESSIONS, LUTHERAN) is considered the basic criterion of right teaching. If **pastors** contradict this criterion—and thereby their **ordination** vows—in their proclamation and teaching, they can be removed from office. The concept of heresy is employed today primarily by conservative church bodies, but also by liberal theologians and activist groups in their denunciation of "moral heresies" (like **racism** or support of oppressive regimes). [G.G.]

HERMENEUTICS (Gk *hermeneuein*, "to interpret, to translate"). The theory and art of interpreting (biblical) texts. While hermeneutics is a relatively new term and a scholarly reflected concept, its concerns are old. The New Testament knows already about the need to understand the **faith** and give an account of it (1 Pet 3:15). There is an awareness of the preconditions and criteria that determine the interpretation of biblical texts (1 Cor 2:6–16; 15:1–11; 2 Tim 3:14–17). There is no completely free, unconditioned interpretation. In the early church, interpretation of the Bible (*see* BIBLE, INTERPRETATION OF) was undertaken within the framework of the rule of faith, while in the Middle Ages the theory of a fourfold sense of Scripture (literal, allegorical, moral, and eschatological) was developed. **Thomas Aquinas** emphasized the literal sense of biblical interpretation as well as the decisive hermeneutical **authority** of the **church**. The Lutheran **Reformation** unequivocally reaffirmed the normative character of Holy Scripture (*see* BIBLE, AUTHORITY OF), and, as a consequence, gave extraordinary importance to scriptural interpretation. Lutheranism considered the center of Scripture, the **Gospel** or Jesus Christ, to be the hermeneutical orientation for such interpretation.

With the emergence of the historical-critical interpretation of the Bible, the 19th and 20th centuries became the arena for intensive hermeneutical reflection (which went far beyond biblical interpretation). The decisive hermeneutical approach works with the relationship between text, context, and interpreter (e.g., Wilhelm Dilthey [1833–1911]). Martin Heidegger (1889–1976) was highly influential in outlining the "hermeneutical circle" in which the interpreter with his or her preunderstanding is always part of a process of interpretation in which the preunderstanding is changed by new understanding. Hans-Georg Gadamer (1900–) had an even greater influence on modern **theology**. For him, understanding of texts happens by situating them in an interplay between their context of historical effective tradition and the interpreter's own context of present tradition. This process leads to a "fusion of horizons" in which new understanding becomes possible.

Efforts in modern theology to turn hermeneutics into a kind of fundamental theology in which **salvation** is understood as a "language event" or "word event" have been balanced by a broader perspective in which the church is understood as a "locus of hermeneutics," and as a "hermeneutical community" seeking to understand Scripture in interaction with **worship**, **ethics**, and the understanding of the church. Lutherans agree with this approach, adding the central message of the Gospel as basic hermeneutical perspective and the witness of the Lutheran confessions (*see* CONFESSIONS, LUTHERAN) as guide for the interpretation and understanding of Scripture. *See also* BULTMANN, RUDOLF. [G.G.]

HISTORY, THEOLOGY OF. Theological understanding of history. Christianity is a historical religion. It emerged in and interacted with history, became itself history, and has shaped world history. As an historical reality, Christianity is not only a subject of history, but is also an object of historical investigation of its origins, sources, history, and ideas, as well as its interaction with secular history. This close interrelation between Christianity and history is the theme of the theological interpretation of history that began in the Old Testament where such events of historical significance as the exodus out of Egypt or the exile of the People of Israel were interpreted in terms of **God's** judging and saving intervention in history. The New Testament interprets God's coming into the world in the incarnation and destiny of Jesus (*see* CHRISTOLOGY) as the decisive historical action of God for the **salvation** of humanity and the subsequent course of history towards its fulfillment.

Augustine was the first one who formulated a theological concept of history that remained influential for centuries. He viewed history as a process moving from **creation** to its triumphant conclusion in judgment and salvation (*see* ESCHATOLOGY). This process, however, is marked by the duality between the two dominions, the dominion of all those who love God above all things and those who love themselves. Among concepts of history during the Middle Ages, two were especially influential. Joachim of Fiore (c.1130–1202) proposed for the first time in medieval historical consciousness a prophetic view of progress in the course of history with his idea of a sequence of the age of the Father (Old Testament) to the age of the Son and, in the present, soon to be followed by the age of the **Holy Spirit**. Medieval reform movements, on the other hand, developed a concept of history that considered the present time as one of decadence, marked by the domination of the pope (*see* PAPACY), the decay of the **church**, and the perversion of pure **faith** and **doctrine**.

This concept of decadence was taken up by the **Reformation** that also continued in a modified form the biblical-Augustinian view of history with its beginning in creation, center, and climax in Christ, and its end time in the present, moving toward its final judgment and fulfillment. **Martin Luther**, drawing on his conflictual Reformation experiences, restated Augustine's dualism. For him it is now the official church that is dominated by anti-Christ while the community of God's faithful witnesses is represented by the minority of the true, often persecuted Christians. Luther also saw the omnipresent power of God present and active in the events of the world. Not that this was easily discernable, because God is hidden in world history. But God makes the historical actions of humans the instruments of his sovereign rule. Thus, faith can recognize in historical events God's judgment and **grace**.

The **Enlightenment** went on to develop, now in the framework of the dominance of **reason**, a vision of the unity, meaning, and goal of history (e.g., **Georg Wilhelm Friedrich Hegel**, and later on Karl Marx), while thinkers of the 19th and 20th centuries have become skeptical of such coherent systems of universal explanation of the course and goal of history. Theologians, among them prominent Lutherans such as **Wolfhart Pannenberg**, continue today to reflect on the integral relationship between **salvation history** and world history. Different **theologies** of history seek to discern the traces of God's action in history, for example, in movements of liberation and transformation (*see* LIBERATION THEOLOGY), the impact of church history on world history, and vice versa. Such theological reflection tries to uphold a vision of history in time and space, its beginning and end, and its inclusion of all peoples and creation that can provide people with a sense of God's leading history to its eschatological goal and fulfillment. [G.G.]

HOLINESS. The holy is that which is separate from **creation**, different in kind and not simply in degree. Biblically, holiness is the very nature of **God**, who alone is called "the Holy One." While the term occurs rarely in the New Testament, its occurrences are important (the Lord's Prayer, for instance) and the concept of holiness is presupposed in the authors' understanding of God. By extension, people and things that are closely connected with the Holy One might be termed holy themselves. Thus, there are holy people (through whose call, life, and proclamation God is transparently active), holy places (where God has acted in particularly clear ways), and holy things (whose use links them with the **Word** or **worship** of God). But the holiness of these is derivative, not intrinsic.

While **Martin Luther** preserved the notion of holiness as otherness—including in his **theology** the understanding that in the context of **sin**, holiness is experienced as wrath—holiness in common parlance came to have a more limited, anthropocentric meaning. Holiness has always had an ethical dimension (*see* ETHICS); God is not only the source of all being, and ontologically superior to all other beings, but also thereby the source of all good, and ethically superior to creation as well. Thus those who are closely associated with the Holy One are expected to exhibit a high morality in turn. But under Lutheran **Orthodoxy, Pietism**, and **Rationalism**, this aspect of the holy life became paramount—holiness, particularly as applied to humans, became synonymous with moral perfection. The writings of Rudolf Otto at the beginning of the 20th century began the return of the concept of the holy to its biblical breadth. Otto, working from the history of religion **tradition**, reaffirmed the holy as the entirely Other that, when breaking into the world, is both magnetic and terrifying. Otto's insight affected not only the **liturgical movement**, but also neo-orthodox theology, with its concentration on God as wholly other. [M.O.]

HOLL, KARL (1866–1926). Influential Lutheran scholar. Oscillating between Berlin and Tübingen as a student and lecturer, Holl was appointed professor in 1900 before going on, finally, to the University of Berlin in 1906, where he was a colleague of **Adolf von Harnack**. Holl's scholarly work was wide ranging and profound. A **patristic** scholar, he edited several texts for the Prussian Academy. Holl's place in **Lutheranism** is the most pronounced in this century, however, because of his pioneering leadership in **Luther research**, and signaled by the publication of his book *Luther* in 1921.

Holl's theological mind was not altogether consistent over his life, however. Ordained as a Lutheran **pastor** in 1888, he had been steeped in Tübingen's and Berlin's theological **Liberalism**. With the outbreak of World War I, influenced by Karl Barth's *Letter to the Romans,* and having come closer to the Lutheran confessionalism of colleague Reinhold Seeberg, Holl finally adopted systematic theological positions that were not so close to those implied in the liberalism of Harnack and others. Particularly with his doctrine of **God**, Holl stood in sharp contrast to the idealistic Liberalism of the 19th century, explicating his understanding of God through the centrality of Jesus, interpreted through Paul and **Martin Luther**, rather than through religious psychology or human experience. Yet it was not only as a "Luther researcher" that Holl found possibilities for contemporary theological syntheses; he was also indebted to **John Calvin** and distanced himself particularly from Luther's political **ethics**, given their possibilities for co-option by German nationalism (*see* TWO KINGDOMS). Those directly influenced by Holl, who came to be recognized as members of the "Holl School," became influential in their own right. In them and beyond into contemporary Luther research, Karl Holl exemplifies how comprehensive historical understanding and firm personal identity are necessary groundwork for the construction of fruitful and trenchant confessional systematic **theology**. [D.H.L.]

HOLY SPIRIT. The third person of the **Trinity**, present and active in creating and sustaining **faith** in individuals and in the **church**. The Old Testament presents the spirit of **God** as God's creative power and wisdom (e.g., Gen 1:2; Ps 104:30; Isa 40:13). The witness of the New Testament to the Holy Spirit (Gk *pneuma*, "pneumatology" being the theological reflection on the Holy Spirit) is rich and diverse. Here, Jesus and the Holy Spirit are closely related. The Spirit acts through Jesus' ministry (Mt 12:28; Lk 4:18f.), while the departing Jesus, according to the **Gospel** of John, sends the Spirit, the "paraclete" (Jn 14:16f., 26; 20:22). In Paul we find a Spirit-**Christology** that speaks of the *pneuma* of the *kyrios* (2 Cor 3:17; Gal 4:6), and of Christ as well as the Spirit being in believers (Rom 8:9ff) and/or of believers being in Christ as well as in the Spirit (Rom 8:1.9–10). The Spirit is the creative power of God in believers that leads them to life (Rom 8:9), to faith in Christ as Lord (1Cor 12:3), to calling God Father (Rom 8:14–17), to proclaiming **salvation** in Jesus (Acts 8:29), and to leading a responsible Christian life in **love** (2 Tim 1:7; Tit 3:5) and with the fruits of the Spirit (Gal 5:22–23). The Holy Spirit gathers the Christian community and builds it up through the various spiritual gifts (Gk *charismata*) and the **sacraments** (Acts 2; Rom 12:4–8;1 Cor 12:12–13; 14:1–5). First trinitarian (*see* TRINITY, DOGMA OF) formulas appear: Matthew 28:19; 2 Corinthians 13:13; and Romans 8:26ff.

This trinitarian framework of the Holy Spirit was clarified and made part of the **dogma** of the church only after a longer period during which the clarification of the Christological dogma was given priority. It was in 381 that the Council of Constantinople through its Nicene-Constantinopolitan Creed (or Nicene Creed) affirmed the equal divinity, lordship, and glory of the Spirit with the Father and the Son. Beginning with the sixth century, the church in the West added to the formulation in the Nicene Creed that the Holy Spirit "proceeds from the Father" the words "and the Son" (the famous *filioque*). This addition has contributed to the division between East and West. **Augustine** reflected on the Holy Spirit in the framework of his trinitarian **doctrine** and particularly in his explication of the Nicene Creed. Medieval **theology**, including **mysticism** with its strong Christological orientation, did not focus on the doctrine of the Holy Spirit. Such neglect was reversed by the **Reformation**. **Martin Luther** emphasized and praised the role of the Holy Spirit as the creator of faith and new life by imparting the "alien righteousness" of Christ in **justification** and **sanctification**. The Lutheran Reformation accepted the trinitarian dogma of the church and integrated it into the Lutheran confessions (see CONFESSIONS, LUTHERAN). They contain a remarkably strong and consistent testimony, often forgotten or ignored in Lutheran history, to the presence and work of the Holy Spirit. The Spirit of God in Jesus Christ is always active in and with the **means of grace**, bound to the **Word of God** in its proclamation and to the **sacraments**—an insistence directed against the **Spiritualists** and others who claim to receive direct inspiration by the Holy Spirit. The Holy Spirit creates faith and hope in individuals and leads them to Christ and a right relationship with God. The Spirit sanctifies believers, preserves them in their faith, and inspires love for God and neighbor. The Spirit gathers, enlivens, and enlightens each Christian community and the whole Christian church on earth. The church is thus the "creature" of the Holy Spirit, who is at work in the church and through the church as an instrument.

Lutheran **Orthodoxy** reintroduced the concept of the verbal inspiration of Holy Scripture by the Holy Spirit (*see* BIBLE, INSPIRATION OF) and taught the role of the Spirit in communicating and receiving salvation in the process of the **order of salvation**. **Pietism** underlined the role of the Spirit in religious experience, **piety**, regeneration, sanctification, and in creating the new existence of the Christian. The theological heritage of the **Enlightenment**, **Rationalism**, and **Liberalism** has "spiritualized" as well as marginalized the awareness and understanding of the role and reality of the Holy Spirit in personal and ecclesiastical life. A Lutheran aversion, since the time of the Reformation, against all forms of "enthusiasm" may also have contributed to a certain "Spirit forgetfulness." With the renewal of Reformation theology in the 20th century, and influenced by the **ecumenical movement** and the strong witness to the Holy Spirit in the Eastern and Oriental Orthodox tradition, Lutheran theology and church today are affirming once again the creative, inspiring, guiding, and transforming work of the Holy Spirit in individuals, Christian communities, and the universal church of Jesus Christ. [G.G.]

HOME MISSIONS. The organized effort to establish **congregations** in one's own country, mostly to serve those already identified as Lutherans. Because of the press of immigration and domestic migration, home missions has been a major effort of the Lutheran churches in North America. It may be distinguished from overseas or foreign **missions**, but also from **Inner Mission**, which targets social service and improvement.

Home missions in North America began with **Henry Melchior Muhlenberg** and the Ministerium of Pennsylvania, whose polity was aimed at organizing and establishing congregations to serve those, mostly Germans, who had emigrated to the continent. From that point on, almost all Lutheran synods struggled to collect and serve recent immigrants. Usually this struggle was focused among those of the same ethnic or language group as the majority of the synod, but there were significant exceptions, particularly in missions aimed at Jewish, Native American, and African American populations. When immigration peaked and began to recede in the early years of the 20th century, home missions concentrated on establishing congregations in new neighborhoods and suburbs, to which members of established congregations had moved. During both world wars, defense plants led to new housing patterns, to which the churches responded. This pressure, together with the relief efforts and military chaplaincy, led to previously unheard-of cooperation among Lutheran bodies, a cooperation that continued after the end of the wars. Until the 1970s, the members of the **National Lutheran Council** and the Lutheran Council in the United States of America planned home missions strategy together, avoiding the establishment of competing congregations in new neighborhoods. In the late 20th century, home missions focused on the areas in the United States with growing populations, gathering self-identified Lutherans, but also reaching out to the unchurched. *See also* NORTH AMERICA, LUTHERAN CHURCHES IN. [M.O.]

HOPE. *See* ESCHATOLOGY.

HOSPITALS. Lutheran involvement in establishing hospitals. The link between religion and houses of healing is a long and strong one. The early Christian church's diaconal ministry (*see* DIAKONIA) included care of the sick among its essential tasks. The rise of monasteries, together with the need to lodge and care for those who went on pilgrimages and crusades, shaped hospitals in the Middle Ages. In fact, it gave them their present name, from the order of Knights Hospitalers. In the **Reformation**, **Martin Luther** urged government to accept oversight of this sort of health care, although most was provided by family members and fraternities. It was not until the rise of **Pietism** in the 17th century that Lutherans established institutions for health care. During the 19th century there was an explosion of social ministry institutions established by Lutherans, especially from the **Inner Mission** movement in Denmark, Sweden, and Germany. **Johann Hinrich Wichern** and **Theodor Fliedner**, in reestablishing the **diaconate**, established hospitals as prime places of service for deacons and deaconesses. William Alfred Passavant transplanted this effort to North America, and included hospitals among the large number of institutions he established. **Elisabeth Fedde**, the Norwegian deaconess, established hospitals in Brooklyn and Minneapolis.

Throughout the 19th and 20th centuries permanent hospitals and primary as well as emergency health services were major parts of **mission** outreach in Africa and Asia. The Augusta Victoria Hospital in Jerusalem deserves particular attention for its continuous service to the poor, and particularly to Arabs, through the changing conditions of the 20th century. While health care in the developed world is increasingly in the hands of government or corporations, the church's institutional care for the sick continues in church-related hospitals in many places, especially in the Southern Hemisphere.

Everywhere the church exists there are also church-related hospice programs for those often ignored by health providers: the terminally ill, those with particularly feared communicable diseases, and the poor. *See also* HEALTH AND HEALING. [M.O.]

HUMANISM. Term coined by German scholars in the 19th century for an educational and cultural movement in the broader context of the Renaissance. This movement began in the 14th century in Italy and focused on the rediscovery of Greek and Latin antiquity. Humanism was of particular significance for efforts towards reform in the Catholic church (*see* COUNTER-REFORMATION) and for the **Reformation**. The slogan of the humanists *Ad fontes*, "to the sources," led to a recovery of classical, biblical, and **patristic** texts in their original versions and new scholarly editions, together with grammars and dictionaries. This was considered by Christian humanists a presupposition for the renewal of **theology, piety**, and morality. Most humanists did not share Lutheran or **Reformed** doctrinal positions. But they provided the texts, philological tools, methods of discourse, rhetorical styles, and the emphasis on formal **education** that became indispensable ingredients of the work of the reformers.

Among Lutheran reformers, **Philipp Melanchthon** was most strongly influenced by humanist classical learning, irenic spirit, and emphasis on secondary and theological education. He inaugurated a system of "humanistic" high schools in Germany. **Martin Bucer** and the Strasbourg Reformation were inspired by humanist ideals. **Johannes Bugenhagen** began as a classical scholar. And **Martin Luther** himself used humanist textual/philological groundwork and shared humanist enthusiasm for classics. He supported the important humanist studies at his University of **Wittenberg**. Some interpreters speak of a kind of "Lutheran Humanism" that stimulated literary production and was marked by humanist education and outlooks. It formed a culture of the educated classes in Lutheran Europe into the 17th century and continued in later intellectual movements. [G.G.]

HUMAN RIGHTS. Rights pertaining to all human beings by virtue of their humanity. The **Reformation** emphasis on the dignity of each individual and first steps towards religious tolerance (*see* AUGSBURG, RELIGIOUS PEACE OF), together with the tradition of natural law, helped to prepare the way for the formulation of human rights. This development began in the 17th and 18th centuries. The English *Bill of Rights* of 1689, the *Virginia Declaration of Rights* of 1776, the *Declaration of Independence* of the United States of 1776 and its *Constitution* of 1789 together with its amendments of 1790, and the French *Declaration of the Rights of Man* of 1789 contained important statements on the innate and inalienable rights of all persons. The first provisions for human rights and civil liberties were introduced into national constitutions in the 19th century. The 20th century saw the internationalization and an enormous expansion of human rights.

The United Nations' *Universal Declaration of Human Rights* of 1948 takes the inherent dignity and the equal and inalienable rights of all persons as the foundation of freedom, **justice**, and **peace** of the world. International and regional human rights conventions have continuously enlarged the scope of human rights beyond the four basic groups of civil, political, and social rights: the inviolability of the individual person, by which life, privacy, home, and property are protected; freedom of thought, conscience, religion, opinion, expression, association, and movement; the equality of all persons and exclusion of discrimination; and participation in public life and in decisions affecting society. Additional rights were introduced in the areas of employment and working conditions, **education**, health care, and social security, while the new nations in the Third World demanded rights of self-determination and development.

Because human rights originated in **enlightenment** thinking, the Christian churches for a long time rejected or ignored the concept of human rights. A change in the position of the **Roman Catholic Church** came with the encyclicals *Rerum Novarum* (1891) and especially *Pacem in Terris* (1963), which affirmed a broad range of human rights. Today, the *Pastoral Constitution on the Church in the Modern World* (1965) of the Second Vatican Council (*see* VATICAN COUNCIL II) provides the basis of Catholic teaching on human rights. The **ecumenical movement** led the other churches to an awareness of and commitment to human rights. This involvement began with the participation of the **World Council of Churches**, represented by a leading Lutheran staff member, Frederick Nolde, in the drafting of the *Universal Declaration of Human Rights* from 1946–1948 and has continued through numerous statements and programs on human rights, their advocacy in concrete situations, and the support of learning processes in the churches. More recently, the need to deal with the root causes of human rights abuses has been emphasized. The **Lutheran World Federation** has significantly contributed to the ecumenical involvement with human rights through human rights studies and statements of its assemblies from the one at Evian in 1970 to the one at Hong Kong in 1997. Christian support of human rights is generally based on the belief in the dignity and equality of all human beings as created in the image of **God** and accepted, for Jesus Christ's sake, as children of God. *See also* RELIGIOUS LIBERTY. [G.G.]

HYMN AND HYMNODY, LUTHERAN. A hymn is a strophic text set to music, intended to be sung by the assembly at Christian **worship** to give voice to its **faith**. Hymns have been a favored form of expression among Lutherans from the beginning of the **Reformation**. **Martin Luther** wrote hymns that mobilized support for martyrs to the cause of the Reformation and for the Holy Roman Empire in its defensive effort against the Turks. He also composed hymns explaining the parts of the catechism, which were used for centuries. Most importantly, however, in his immensely influential *Deutsche Messe* (*German Mass*), he included hymn paraphrases of the ordinary of the mass—Kyrie, Gloria, Creed, and Sanctus—and returned these invariable portions of the service to the **congregation**. Luther was, indeed, so good a hymnwriter and so central a figure, that no German successor grew in his shadow for almost a full century. It was not until the crucible of the **Thirty Years' War** brought forth expressions of confidence and trust tried by incredible suffering, that new lyrical poets and composers added to the corpus of German Lutheran hymnody. This flowering of the **chorale** provided the backbone for several centuries of congregational song and artistic expression. Unlike the work of Luther, these chorales did not eliminate other expressions. **Pietism** produced a plethora of hymns, particularly for the use of families and small groups, which extended the tendency of chorales to focus on heart-felt faith, confidence in suffering, and a unity of the soul with Christ. The 19th and early 20th centuries saw many efforts to express the basic themes of Reformation faith in new forms.

The hymns of Luther became the basis for a national hymnody almost everywhere **Lutheranism** was planted. In Slovakia, **Jur Tranovsky** provided a corpus of liturgical and occasional hymnody that sufficed for the church's need for more than three centuries. In Scandinavia, the work of **Olavus Petri** and **Laurentius Petri** and other early reformers, together with translations of German hymns, lasted until the 19th century. The Lutheran **Awakening**, however, included more contemporary and local artistic expressions in congregational song. In Denmark, **Nikolai Frederik Severin Grundtvig** is perhaps the best known of the cadre of authors and composers who, for inspiration, looked to folk tradition. In Sweden in particular, Carolina Sandell Berg and others married folk traditions to the new American Gospel style.

In North America, immigrant communities retained their native hymnody as long as they retained their native language. Poor translations and sociological factors, however, meant that once they began to worship in English, Lutherans reflected the dominant anglophone hymnody. East Coast Lutherans, for instance, lost almost all connection with German chorales in the early 19th century, regaining them only when Catherine Winkworth's translations introduced them to the English-speaking world. Until the late 20th century English-speaking Lutherans, like their neighbors, sang Isaac Watts and Charles Wesley texts to Lowell Mason tunes, and few American Lutherans wrote new hymns.

That changed dramatically with the worldwide hymn explosion, beginning in the 1960s. Lutherans on all continents began writing new hymns. In America, Lutherans reclaimed their heritage in translation and participated in the renewal of the "classic hymn" as well as in the folk revival that began on college campuses in the 1960s and continued through the "contemporary worship" movement later in the century. Increasingly, European and American Lutherans have included in their hymnody hymns of their sister churches in Africa, Asia, and Latin America. *See also* HYMNBOOKS, LUTHERAN. [M.O.]

HYMNBOOKS, LUTHERAN. Collections of hymns. Such collections, with or without tunes, have been for centuries not only a basic **worship** resource for Lutherans, but also a basic source of private, family, and small group devotional life (*see* DEVOTIONAL LITERATURE). In Germany, the first Lutheran hymnbook was *Etliche christlich Lieder* (1524), whose eight hymns included four by **Martin Luther**. Luther himself edited several editions of *Geistliche Lieder*, beginning in 1529, which was used for a century in most of Germany, and formed the basis for many other regionally popular hymnals. In the early 1640s Johann Crueger collected over 1,000 **chorales** and published them in the *Praxis Pietatis Melica*. The great hymnal of **Pietism** was Johannes Anastasius Freylinghausen's *Geistreiches Gesangbuch* (1704). A monument of the Lutheran **Awakening** was Albert Knapp's *Evangelischer Lieder-Schatz* (1837), a collection of 3,590 hymns, to which 250 more were added in a supplement four years later. With the publication of Friedrich Spitta's *Elsaesser Gesangbuch* (1899), it became clear that there was a central corpus of German hymns, and work began on the collection of a common hymnal for Germany. In 1949 the *Evangelische Kirchengesangbuch* fulfilled this desire. It was replaced in the 1990s by the new *Evangelisches Gesangbuch* that includes a larger number of recently composed and international hymns.

The first important hymnbook in Denmark (with Norway) was *Den Danske Salmebog* (1569), which included 268 hymns. The 1573 edition of this work was dominant for the next century. Beginning in 1699 *Kingo's Salmebog* was the most popular until the rise of **Nikolai Frederik Severin Grundtvig**, whose works were included in the 1911 *Salmebog för Kirke og Hjem*. In 1953 this work was replaced by *Den Danske Salmebog*. There was no generally accepted Norwegian hymnbook until 1861, which remained the standard until the publication of the *Norsk Salme Bok* in 1984/85. The first Swedish hymnal was *Swenska Songer eller Wissor*, edited by **Olavus Petri** in 1526. In 1543 a four-century series of hymnbooks began, each bearing the name *Den Svenska Psalmeboken*. A new edition was prepared in 1937, including not only 19th-century Swedish contributions, but also those of Christians from around the world. All Scandinavian Lutheran churches published new hymnbooks in the 1980s and 1990s.

There has never been a common hymnal used by all North American Lutherans (*see* NORTH AMERICA, LUTHERAN CHURCHES IN). Most immigrants brought their own hymnbooks with them, to the enrichment and confusion of the worship life of the churches. Not until 1786 did American Lutherans prepare a common hymnal, the *Erbauliche Lieder Sammlungen* with an introduction by **Henry Melchior Muhlenberg**. This was followed by several German hymnals of the General Synod, and finally replaced by the General Council's *Kirchenbuch* (1877), a product of the Lutheran Awakening that eliminated most of the popular hymns of Pietism. English-language hymnals were published by several synods in different parts of the United States during the 19th and early 20th centuries. In 1958 the churches that would later make up the Lutheran Church in America and the American Lutheran Church cooperated on the *Service Book and Hymnal*. The **Lutheran Church-Missouri Synod** (LC–MS), at the urging of **Carl Ferdinand Wilhelm Walther**, published the *Kirchengesangbuch* in 1847, with revisions regularly made until the final edition in 1917. Its English hymnals included the *Evangelical Lutheran Hymnbook* (1885) and *The Lutheran Hymnal* (1940). At the invitation of the LC–MS, the American Lutheran Church and the Lutheran Church in America cooperated on the production of a new hymnal. When it was printed in 1978 as the *Lutheran Book of Worship*, the LC–MS decided not to participate in its production, but rather to release its own *Lutheran Worship*.

Lutheran churches throughout the world have developed their own hymnbooks that generally include a common core of Lutheran hymns from the 16th to the 19th centuries as well as old and new hymns from their own tradition. The rich heritage of hymns is a particular characteristic of Lutheranism. *See also* HYMN AND HYMNODY. [M.O.]

– I –

IDEALISM. The philosophical-metaphysical view that reality is composed by mind. With regard to the creative mind, however, idealism may be either subjective or objective. Subjective idealism holds that reality is created by the human mind. Objective idealism is external and transcendent to the human; in other words, **God**. Whatever its declension, while idealism shares with naturalism and empiricism the conviction that reality is indeed "real," it contrasts with these Western bases of materialism and secularism because idealism maintains that the meaning and origin of the real lies beyond them in one causal agency. Most "popular" idealism is of the subjective sort, with intellectual moorings in the philosophies of George Berkeley, Johannes Gottlieb Fichte, and Gottfried Wilhelm Leibniz. Contemporary **philosophy** and **theology** generally dismisses subjective idealism as inescapably pluralistic and solipsistic. Nevertheless, it reappears in current theories of theological cosmology, based upon insights of quantum physics (*see* SCIENCE AND CHRISTIANITY).

Objective idealism, however, has significantly influenced Lutheran theology, though in different ways toward different ends. **Georg Wilhelm Friedrich Hegel's** system implied a monistic, impersonal idealism, wherein the mind was equivalent to the grand processes of history. In consequence of this view, theology would usually be the activity of symbol interpretation, as exemplified in the work of Paul Tillich. It would also lead to the contemporary reflowering of theologies of the **Trinity**, representative as the **doctrine** is of God's originating of complex relationality. **Immanuel Kant's** idealism, however, which greatly influenced Lutheran theology in another direction, was understood as personalistic. Though God could not be known by critical **reason**, in Kant's view, God was understood by practical reason as the personal cause of meaning behind every event. In consequence of this influence, certain Lutheran theologies would be more directly referential to God's acts in history (*see* HISTORY, THEOLOGY OF). Lutheran theologies so affected would also become more ethically mindful, if—oddly, in comparison to the Hegelian influences—also quasi-deist and uninterested in trinitarian thinking (cf. Albrecht Ritschl, highly influenced by Kant's critical idealism). A synthesis of these divergent objective idealisms with effective methodologies garnered from the empirical sciences is high on the agenda for future constructive Lutheran theologies. [D.H.L.]

INCARNATION. *See* CHRISTOLOGY.

INCULTURATION. Task to make Christianity truly at home in each culture. Inculturation is similar in meaning to indigenization or contextualization (*see* THEOLOGY, CONTEXTUAL) and is different from enculturation (becoming part of a culture) or acculturation (interaction of cultures). Inculturation has been used since the 1970s but refers to a reality that is as old as Christianity: the inescapable interrelation between **faith** and **culture**. The entry of Jesus into this world was an **incarnation**—that is the key term for the concept of inculturation—into a particular historical, religious, and social context. His message and the first communities of his followers were shaped by this culture and transformed it. The debate of the Apostle Paul with the Jewish Christians led to the liberation of the faith from the captivity to a particular culture and its inculturation into Greek, Roman, Germanic, Slavic, Anglo-Saxon, and other cultures. However, since the late Middle Ages the tendency to export Christianity in its Western cultural forms prevailed.

With the growing **ecumenical** awareness in the 20th century and the independence of nations and indigenization of churches in Africa and Asia, the task of inculturation of the Christian faith has been reasserted both by the

Second Vatican Council (*see* VATICAN COUNCIL II) and the **World Council of Churches** (WCC). The last World Conference on Mission and Evangelism of the WCC in 1996 had as its theme *Called to One Hope: The Gospel in Diverse Cultures*. The complex relationship between faith and culture raises these problem areas, among others, that need constant clarification: How can the universality of the Christian faith be preserved together with the particularity of its forms of expression in diverse cultural contexts? How can a genuine inculturation be achieved in which the elements of culture become vehicles of expressing the Christian faith and the life of the **church**, while at the same time the Christian faith challenges and transforms those elements of a culture that contradict or distort the message of the Gospel (like **racism**, discrimination of **women**, syncretism, and so on)? [G.G.]

INNER MISSION. Christian social and evangelistic (*see* EVANGELISM) activity within particular countries. The 19th century witnessed not only the rapid expansion of **Protestant** foreign **mission** work, but also a new concern for mission work at home (therefore the term "Inner Mission" in contrast to "outer" or "foreign" mission). In an "Appeal to the German Nation" in 1849, the Lutheran pastor **Johann Hinrich Wichern**, generally regarded as the initiator of the movement of Inner Mission, defined Inner Mission as including evangelization and social work for the spiritual and material rescue of the de-Christianized masses in emerging industrial societies. Such mission should be independent of the established churches and of the state, in order to achieve a re-Christianization of the population. Wichern used the term "Inner Mission" (Ger *Innere Mission*) since 1843.

The movement found many enthusiastic supporters and soon spread to other European countries. Social **institutions** (**hospitals**, orphanages, hostels, training schools, and so on) and evangelistic groups were founded in ever growing numbers, and an impressive network of social and evangelistic work emerged (e.g., in 1939 the Inner Mission organizations in Germany alone employed 70,000 people in over 7,000 institutions). Because social work increasingly received priority over evangelistic work, the tradition and institutions of Inner Mission are today carried on by the diaconic work and institutions of Lutheran and other Protestant churches. *See also* DIAKONIA; HOME MISSION. [G.G.]

INSPIRATION OF THE BIBLE. *See* BIBLE, INSPIRATION OF.

INSTITUTION (Lat *instituere* and *institutio*, "act of creating, setting up, instituting" and "what has been created, instituted"). The institutional aspect of Christianity. There is wide agreement today about the ambivalent character of the term "institution." Sociological definitions of institution refer to organizations that shape, sustain, and express social life in established structural, legal, and more or less permanent forms: state, school, judicial system, military, labor unions, churches, and so on. In theological debate, after a period characterized by an "anti-institutional affect" in church and society, today a critical acceptance of the need for institutional structures of human social existence has taken place. However, the provisional nature of institutions, their accountability, and the need to change them, is underscored. Earlier confrontational antitheses between a charismatic and juridical church structure, or between event and institution, basic communities and institutional church, and charisma and office, have been overcome, especially in **ecumenical** dialogue, by holding together both aspects in mutual correction.

The Lutheran **Reformation**, on the one hand, took a positive attitude to institutions such as church or state, partly provoked by spiritualist, anti-institutional Reformation movements. On the other hand, Lutherans severely criticized or even rejected ecclesiastical institutions wherever they were seen as dominating or obscuring **God's** free **grace**. In line with an understanding of institution in the sense of an act of divine institution, an interpretation rooted in earlier Latin **canon law**, **Martin Luther** and the Lutheran confessions (*see* CONFESSIONS, LUTHERAN) considered the concept of God's institution as essential for a right understanding of the **Gospel**, the **Word of God**, the **sacraments**, the **church**, and the **ministry**. In a secondary sense, also civil government and other public orders were regarded as instituted by God for the sake of good order, peace, and preservation of life in a fallen world. [G.G.]

INSTITUTIONS. Organizational and institutional forms of church activity. It was not self-evident that the **church** would establish institutions beyond the assembly of worshipers (whether **congregation** or monastery) and the confederation of those assemblies (in diocese or monastic order). In fact, most institutions, like **hospitals**, seem to have begun as outgrowths of those establishments. Still today, even though they are organically separate, they remain tied to a **congregation**, district, synod, or other judicatory. Institutions, in a bewildering variety, have been established to meet needs of benevolence or **mission**.

Among the types of institutions related to the **Lutheran churches of the world** are: educational foundations (such as parochial schools, boarding schools, choir schools, Bible schools, colleges and universities, theological seminaries, and training institutions for social and youth workers as well as church musicians and parish assistants, research and study centers); services for the aging (residential units, adult day care, and respite care); health services (hospitals, home health care and hospice, and visiting nurses associations); relief (provision of food and other basic services and disaster relief); services for immigrants (immigration and refugee services, certain adoption services, and settlement houses); services for youth (camps, programs for adjudicated youth, adoption services, and orphanages); chaplaincy and counseling services (military, prison, college/university, and hospital chaplaincies, and pastoral counseling centers); **evangelism** (programming for radio, television, and other mass media, training centers, and institutes for ministry in particular situations); orders (**deaconess** communities, monastic establishments, and retreat centers); and media (newspapers, journals, radio, and television stations). [M.O.]

INTERCOMMUNION. Participation of Christians in the **Lord's Supper** of a **church** that is not united or in full **communion** with their own church. For the New Testament, the church of the first few centuries, and in church history until modern times the principle was clear: eucharistic **fellowship**/communion is identical with church fellowship. The **eucharist** is a central expression of the **unity** of a church. Thus, there can be no eucharistic sharing between separated churches and their members. This principle is, on the whole, still held by the **Roman Catholic** and the **Orthodox** churches. **Anglican** and Lutheran churches, too, affirm this principle but have moved to a more open practice under the influence of the modern **ecumenical movement**. It was in the first few decades of this movement since 1910 that the basic and continuing ecumenical issue concerning eucharistic fellowship and with it the term "intercommunion" emerged: Is intercommunion only legitimate and meaningful in the form of eucharistic communion at the end of the process toward Christian unity and as an expression and seal of that unity? Or does the ecumenical process of better mutual understanding and forms of closer relationships between churches and Christians allow for regular or at least occasional sharing in the eucharist by Christians of different churches? Is, therefore, intercommunion legitimate and meaningful as a stage and encouragement on the way, expressing the already achieved partial communion between different churches?

Today, the term "intercommunion" is increasingly replaced by expressions like "eucharistic hospitality" (usually for the declared readiness of a church to welcome baptized members of other churches at its eucharists), and "eucharistic sharing" or "eucharistic fellowship/communion" (usually for an agreement between two or more churches about mutual participation of members—and ordained ministers—in each other's eucharists). Such agreements are either part of a more comprehensive declaration of church fellowship (e.g., the **Leuenberg Agreement** [1973] or the *Porvoo Common Statement* [1992]), or such agreements are directly related to eucharistic sharing (e.g., the agreement on Interim Sharing of the Eucharistic between Lutherans and Episcopalians in the United States [1982]), or limited to pastoral necessities (e.g., between the Roman Catholic Church and the Syrian Orthodox Church [1984]).

In the second half of the 20th century most non-Catholic and non-Orthodox churches have either officially declared (e.g., declaration of the

World Alliance of Reformed Churches in 1954 or the Lutheran Churches in Germany in 1975), or in their general practice exercised eucharistic hospitality (sometimes under certain conditions, such as the nonavailability of worship services for visitors in their own church) and have allowed their members to participate in the Lord's Supper of other churches. The Roman Catholic Church has made provisions for eucharistic hospitality in exceptional cases of pastoral necessity or emergency. There is growing pressure and hope among many church members and theologians that the Roman Catholic Church and other churches authorize forms of eucharistic sharing for people who live in mixed marriages or participate in ecumenical groups and at ecumenical events, and also more generally as a provisional sign and celebration of the degree of Christian unity that has been achieved in the course of the 20th century. *See also* LORD'S SUPPER IN ECUMENICAL DIALOGUE. [G.G.]

INTER-CONFESSIONAL RESEARCH, LUTHERAN FOUNDATION FOR. Foundation established by the assembly of the **Lutheran World Federation** (LWF) at Helsinki in 1963. The purpose of the foundation is to further the **ecumenical** thinking and involvement of both the Lutheran churches and the LWF. In 1965 the foundation set up the Institute for Ecumenical Research at Strasbourg, France. Several research professors, assistants, and support staff carry out the work of the institute, which is guided by a board of trustees. Work is undertaken in four main areas: ecumenical research on specific projects; theological support of and staff participation in the **bilateral dialogues** and other ecumenical activities of the LWF; communication and interpretation of ecumenical developments and achievements through annual seminars at Strasbourg, publications, and lectures; and ecumenical consultations in different countries. The institute works in close cooperation with the LWF and has become a valuable resource and instrument for its ecumenical tasks. *See also* ECUMENICAL MOVEMENT. [G.G.]

INTERIM (Augsburg and Leipzig, 1548). Provisional settlement of Lutheran-Roman Catholic disputes *between* (i.e., interim) the Diet of Augsburg (1548) and the conclusion of the Council of Trent. The victory of Emperor Charles V in the Smalcald War (1546/47) enabled him to impose the imperial decree of the Augsburg Interim (1548) on the Lutheran estates. The doctrinal articles of the Interim moved towards a convergence with Lutheran positions while Catholic ceremonies should be reintroduced as far as possible. The Interim was not accepted by the Roman Catholic estates and was rejected by strict Lutherans. Charles V enforced the Interim by military power in Württemberg while other territories tried to postpone or partially avoid its implementation. In Saxony, a particular form of the Interim was worked out, the Leipzig Interim of 1548. It tried to preserve **evangelical** teachings but demanded the reintroduction of Catholic ceremonies. These Roman Catholic ceremonies were considered by **Philipp Melanchthon** and his followers **"adiaphora"** (i.e., nonessential) and therefore acceptable. The **Gnesio-Lutherans** rejected this interpretation and the controversy about adiaphora was launched. The two Interims came to an end with the Peace of Passau in 1552. *See also* AUGSBURG, DIETS OF; TRENT, COUNCIL OF. [G.G.]

INTERNATIONAL AFFAIRS. The involvement of the ecumenical community of churches in issues of international order, relations, cooperation, law, and institutions, as well as in international efforts to promote **peace**, resolution of conflicts, and sustainable social and economic development. The emergence at the turn of the 20th century of new awareness of an interdependent world had a deep impact on the early development of the **ecumenical movement** during the same period. Parallel to the creation of an international agency of the nations in the form of the League of Nations in 1919, the emerging ecumenical movement enabled the churches for the first time in history to consider and exercise their responsibility in an international perspective. The World Alliance for Promoting International Friendship through the Churches (1919) and the movement of **Life and Work** with its first World Conference at Stockholm in 1925 were the initial instruments of **Protestant** and **Orthodox** churches to address issues of international order and relations. This involvement was reinforced after 1948 by the **World Council of Churches** (WCC) and especially by its Commission of the Churches on International Affairs that was established in 1946. During the period of the "cold war" after 1945, and the emergence of new independent states in Africa and Asia in the 1960s, peaceful coexistence and socioeconomic development in the Southern Hemisphere were major concerns of the WCC.

The **Roman Catholic Church** entered the scene of international order and affairs with the new orientations developed at the Second Vatican Council (*see* VATICAN COUNCIL II) and the Encyclicals *Pacem in Terris* (1962) and *Populorum Progressio* (1967). After the assembly of the WCC at Uppsala in 1968, changes in the world situation led to new ecumenical concerns in international affairs: **human rights**, **racism**, the international role of science and technology, disarmament, pressure for a new world economic order, people's participation in economic development, and so on. In order to integrate several of these issues in a coherent perspective, the program on *Justice, Peace and the Integrity of Creation* was launched by the WCC after 1983. In the framework of this program, the concerns for the care and responsible use of the world's natural resources became a major theme of involvement of the WCC and many churches.

Toward the end of the 20th century growing national, ethnic, and religious tensions and conflicts in many parts of the world forced the ecumenical community to give high priority to efforts of conflict resolution, mediation, and reconciliation, and overcoming violence. The 1999 assembly of the WCC at Harare, Zimbabwe, highlighted the international debt crisis as a major topic for ecumenical involvement. The active involvement of the **Lutheran World Federation** in international affairs during the last decades of the 20th century focused on human rights, racism (apartheid in southern Africa), support of peace processes (especially in the Middle East and Central America), and programs of community development as well as international **emergency and development aid**. *See also* ETHICS; RESPONSIBLE SOCIETY. [G. G.]

INTERNATIONAL LUTHERAN COUNCIL (ILC). Association of conservative Lutheran churches. Formed in 1993 as a council of church bodies, the ILC has 26 participating churches on all continents. Most of them are related to the **Lutheran Church-Missouri Synod**, which is by far the largest and most influential church in the ILC with its constituency of about 2.6 million members. The ILC seeks to strengthen confessional Lutheran **theology** and practice in its member churches as well as closer relations between them. The council, which has a very loose organizational structure, meets every two years. Encounters between the ILC and the **Lutheran World Federation** have not led to regular relations so far. [G.G.]

INTERNATIONAL MISSIONARY COUNCIL (IMC). **Mission** organization within the broader **ecumenical movement** that furthered cooperation, coordination, and consultation among **Protestant** mission agencies. The IMC, together with the movements on **Faith and Order** and **Life and Work**, shaped the first phase of the ecumenical movement between 1910 and 1948. The World Missionary Conference at Edinburgh in 1910 was the first international church conference in modern times and is therefore regarded as the beginning of the contemporary ecumenical movement. Excitement about this new venture in worldwide Christian relations led to the formation of the IMC in 1921. The initial leaders and supporters of the IMC were people who were deeply convinced of the urgency of the Christian missionary task in the world as well as the need to implement this task no longer in competition but rather in relationship. Members of the IMC were National Christian Councils, councils of Protestant missionary agencies, and **councils of churches** in Africa, Asia, and Latin America.

The IMC has continued the *International Review of Missions*, founded previously in 1912, and has organized a series of important world missionary conferences (the first took place at Jerusalem in 1928). With these initiatives and its global network of coordinated activities, common studies, and consultations, the council has rendered a crucial contribution to the consolidation and ecumenical orientation of the fellowship between Western mission agencies and younger churches in the Southern Hemisphere, as well as to the furtherance of the ecumenical movement. Thus, for many it was only logical that the IMC was integrated with the **World Council of Churches** in 1961 where its tasks are continued by the Commission on World Mission and Evangelism. [G.G.]

INTERRELIGIOUS DIALOGUE. Conversations and encounters between Christians and representatives of other world **religions**. From the time of the Old and New Testaments, the history of Christianity has also been a history of relationships, for the most part defensive and conflictual, with other religions. A major concern during the first Christian centuries was to defend the purity of the Christian **faith** against the danger of permeation by elements of other religions. A more open attitude to other religions was favored by representatives of the **Enlightenment**, while the relationship between Christian **mission** and other religions has become a prominent area of discussion at the (Christian) world missionary conferences since 1910 (see INTERNATIONAL MISSIONARY COUNCIL). They have struggled with the task of holding together the claim to the **uniqueness of Christ** and Christianity and a more open and considerate approach to other living faiths. The earlier missionary movement believed that the world religions were retreating, but the middle of the 20th century saw their renaissance. This new development together with the increased mobility of people has led to the growing presence of other religions in many countries with a Christian history. There are now more Muslims living in France than **Protestants**. Members of different religions have become neighbors in a smaller world.

Attempts have been undertaken to positively consider other religions in a Christian perspective, for example, with the concepts of a universal or cosmic Christ (see CHRISTOLOGY), a particular (Christian) and general history of salvation (see SALVATION HISTORY), the salvific work of Christ in the **church**, and the activity of the **Holy Spirit** in the world. Other theologians reject such attempts as negating the uniqueness of Christ or as subtle forms of spiritual colonization. The new religious pluralism, as well as an increasing number of religious-ethnic conflicts in the present world have led to the recognition of the urgency of improving relations between the different religions. Interreligious dialogue is considered the most appropriate method for furthering this goal. Such dialogue was initiated by the **World Council of Churches** (WCC) in the late 1960s, and a first multifaith dialogue was held in 1970 between Buddhists, Hindus, Moslems, and Christians. This activity of the WCC has been continued by many further dialogue meetings, studies, and statements on interreligious relations. In 1979 the WCC published *Guidelines on Dialogue with People of Living Faiths*

and Ideologies. In 1965 the Second Vatican Council (*see* VATICAN COUN-
CIL II) had already accepted its *Declaration on the Relation of the Church
to Non-Christian Religions* that affirmed a new and more open understanding of other religions. In 1984 the **Lutheran World Federation** began with
a program on Theological Perspectives on Other Faiths. Many churches and
ecumenical bodies are engaged in similar dialogue efforts.

However, Christians differ in their theological perspectives on other
faiths. Such differences reach from the widely held conviction that dialogue should always include authentic **witness** to one's own Christian faith
to more daring and explorative concepts like the conviction that dialogue
is a common pilgrimage toward a fuller understanding of the **truth**, or the
belief that the Trinitarian God (*see* TRINITY, DOGMA OF) is also present
and active in other religions. But there is general agreement that efforts towards better mutual understanding and respect between religions and,
where possible, cooperation in social issues are an absolute necessity in
view of the future of humanity and, therefore, a major task for the churches
in the new millennium. [G.G.]

– J –

JESUS CHRIST. *See* CHRISTOLOGY.

JEWISH-LUTHERAN DIALOGUE. Official conversation by theological
and pastoral representatives of Lutheran churches on the churches' behalf
and similar representatives on behalf of Judaism. Numerous occasions for
theological conversation and/or joint programmatic efforts (e.g., to address
efforts affecting civic life and public policy) on disparate topics have been
celebrated in the latter half of the 20th century. However, there has been no
official international or American Jewish-Lutheran dialogue of a sustained
sort comparable to other Lutheran **ecumenical** dialogues, characterized by
appointed representatives who would work together on a theme or several
themes for many years. Two significant international conferences, sponsored by the **Lutheran World Federation** and the International Jewish
Committee on Interreligious Consultation, have been held. The first met in
Copenhagen in 1981 and considered Jewish and Christian teachings on the
nature of humankind (theological **anthropology**). The second, a group of 12
Jewish and 15 Lutheran participants, met in Stockholm from July 11–13,
1983, under the theme *Luther, Lutheranism, and the Jews*, the outcome of
which was a mutual commitment to respect and nonproselytizing of each
other, combat of all forms of racial and religious prejudice, and commitment
to a new age of global peace and justice making. American Lutheran com-

mitment to Jewish-Lutheran dialogue has been formally signified in the establishing of a desk for Jewish-Lutheran concerns in the offices of the Evangelical Lutheran Church in America, Lutheran participation in the National Workshop on Christian-Jewish Relations, and support for the Commission on the Church and the Jewish People of the **World Council of Churches** and the Lutheran European Commission on the Church and the Jewish People. *See also* JEWISH-LUTHERAN RELATIONS. [D.H.L.]

JEWISH-LUTHERAN RELATIONS. Relationships between Lutheran churches and formal representatives of Jewish communities and agencies. The history of relations between Lutherans and Jews is not a wholly positive one, though contemporary Lutherans have taken great steps to distance themselves from the anti-Semitism of their tradition and **Martin Luther**. Today, Lutherans increasingly advocate a nonsupersessionist stance in **theology**—that is, Lutherans more and more do not suggest that Christianity "replaces" or "fulfills" Judaism. Furthermore, Lutherans provide leadership for interfaith public policy issues, particularly with the Jewish community, as expressed in local and national activity of the Unites States National Conference of Christians and Jews, **ecumenical** conferences, and institutes for Jewish and Christian studies.

The reformers were both inheritors of medieval anti-Semitic opinions and pioneers in Renaissance Christian **Humanism** that brought closer and more appreciated contact between Jewish and Christian scholars. This is exemplified especially by Lutheran theological interest in learning and teaching Hebrew and conducting primary exegesis in the Hebrew Scriptures. Christian humanists, such as Johann Reuchlin and **Andreas Osiander**, spoke out for the fundamental humanitarian, political, and civil rights of Jews and rejected forceful efforts at their **conversion**. These arguments eventually won the support of civil leaders like Emperor Maximilian and **Frederick the Wise, elector of Saxony**.

Luther himself has a mixed record on the subject. He reflected the intolerance of medieval Catholicism as well as a more charitable humanistic attitude. His commentaries on the New Testament books do not treat their Jewish figures positively. Yet, with regard to his contemporary Jewish public, Luther advocated that they be treated with mandated Christian **love**, as he wrote in *The Magnificat* (1521) and *That Jesus Christ Was Born a Jew* (1523). This civil concern became ensconced in much public policy thereafter, and must be understood, too, by its correlation with Luther's exercise of the **two kingdoms** doctrine. Nevertheless, in later years Luther was keenly disappointed by the Jewish community's unresponsiveness to the **evangelical** movement; he had thought that when presented with a reformed case for the **Gospel** they would convert. Their own use of print technology for proselytism further exacerbated his disappointment, expressed in vehemently intemperate language in several writings, chiefly the tract *Concerning the Jews and Their Lies* (1543). In these later publications, Luther wildly diverged from the charitable stance he had maintained in his younger life, advocating repression of Jewish teaching and worship, even their expulsion from Germany. While civil authorities did not take such recommendations to heart in Luther's day, the use by fascist propagandists in the 20th century of Luther's position as a precedent for Nazi policy can only be regarded as horrific and antithetical to any authentic Lutheran **ethics**.

Contemporary Lutheranism has publicly distanced itself from Luther's unfortunate legacy in many ways. Memorials to the Holocaust are found throughout Germany, signaling a more positive course for Jewish-Lutheran relations. The **Lutheran World Federation**, speaking for the global communion, and the Evangelical Lutheran Church in America have spoken in words that now conclude a public multimedia presentation on anti-Semitism and the Holocaust at the Holocaust Museum in Washington, D.C. These words clearly reject Luther's position, deplore any use of Luther's words to support anti-Semitism, express **repentance**, and commit Lutherans to positive relationships with the Jewish community. Though some Lutherans still affirm **evangelism** efforts directed specifically at the Jews (*see* JEWISH MISSIONS), one discerns increasing rapprochement among Jews and Lutherans. Exemplary efforts include renewed biblical exegesis that benefits from Jewish insight; increasing appropriation of a two covenants theory, expressed earlier in this century in the correspondence of Eugen Rosenstock-Huessy and Franz Rosenzweig and later in the biblical theology of Krister Stendahl; the work of historian Harold H. Ditmanson and many others in the advancement of formal dialogue; and nonsupersessionist platforms of younger Lutheran theologians. In practical life, one discerns a flowering of positive local relationships in many countries among clergy and **congregations**, as with community liturgical observances of Yom Ha Shoa and various civic observances. Efforts at jointly influencing public policy are undertaken in many contexts. *See also* JEWISH-LUTHERAN DIALOGUE. [D.H.L.]

JEWISH MISSIONS. Christian **mission** to the Jewish people. The contemporary Lutheran attitude toward the question of whether Jews should be proselytized is mixed between traditional supersessionism (that the new covenant of Christianity supersedes or even replaces the "old" covenant of Judaism) and the revised notion that Jews should remain Jews. **Martin Luther**'s convictions were of the former type. His surprise at their lack of receptivity to the **Gospel**, as well as their use of print technology for commending their own tradition, fed his latter and unfortunate anti-Semitic expressions. All of this underscores Luther's "traditional view" that the Jewish covenant was incomplete and had given way to a "new" Christian covenant.

Today, the attitude of those Lutherans who belong to the **Lutheran World Federation** (LWF) is mixed, but tends towards a revised concept and is expressed primarily in four documents. The LWF *Løgumkloster Report* (produced in 1964 and affirmed by the Fifth Assembly of the LWF in Evian in 1970), suggested, in carefully nuanced **theology**, that the Lutheran category of **law and Gospel** might not apply in stereotypical fashion to the Jewish people as representatives of legalism. Rather, the Pauline dialectic might apply to a sect within the Judaism of the first century. The report also calls for Christians to engage in conversation with the Jewish people, particularly with the aim toward mutual understanding and discovery of commonalities.

The concerns of the *Løgumkloster Report* were broadened and its "revisionism" extended in the LWF *Neuendettelsau Report* of 1973. This report urged that Christians care for and promote friendly relationships with their Jewish neighbors, making common cause with them whenever and wherever possible. The *Oslo Report* of 1975 suggests that Christians do not abandon the singular centrality of Christ (*see* CHRISTOLOGY) for **salvation**, but rather encourage at the same time mutual respect among the traditions, Christian humility, solidarity with the Jewish people, the elimination of anti-Semitism, and advocacy for **reconciliation** in the Middle East. Finally, traditional and revisionist attitudes balance each other out in the *Bossey Report* of 1982. It speaks of Judaism's self-understanding as a "radiation of God's presence in the world" and of Christian vocations as "sent forth to proclaim the Gospel in word and deed." Again, encouraging mutual respect on a moral level, the document presents mixed self-understanding among Lutherans on the theological level, consistent with Lutheranism's recent history.

Similar guidance is provided for Lutherans in the United States on a local level with *Some Observations and Guidelines for Conversations between Lutherans and Jews* (Lutheran Council in the United States, 1971), and *The American Lutheran Church and the Jewish Community* (American Lutheran Church, 1974). More intentional **evangelism** to and among Jews is affirmed, however, in three traditionalist documents of the **Lutheran Church-Missouri Synod**: *To Share Gospel with Jews* (1977), *To Encourage Evangelism among the Jews* (1977), and *A Statement of Jewish-Lutheran Concerns* (1978).

Mixed attitudes about Christian mission to the Jewish people still characterize Lutherans. One notes, though, that the increasingly pluralistic character of popular culture affects relationships between Jewish people and Lutherans at both local practical and ecclesial theological levels, such that supersessionism is no longer an altogether welcome term in many Lutheran venues. [D.H.L.]

JONAS, JUSTUS (1493–1555). Reformer and close collaborator of **Martin Luther**. Jonas studied law at Erfurt and **Wittenberg**, was ordained a **priest**, and in 1518 became a professor of law at Erfurt. Influenced by **Humanism**, in 1519 he visited **Erasmus of Rotterdam** who aroused his theological interests. In 1521 Jonas became a professor of **canon law** at Wittenberg, joined Luther there, and became his friend and collaborator. In 1521 Jonas received his doctor of theology and served as the dean of the theological faculty from 1523–1533. During this period at Wittenberg, Jonas worked for the **Reformation** in Electoral Saxony and Meissen and helped to draft **church orders**, for example, for Albertine Saxony in 1539 (he was after all also a jurist). He participated in the **Marburg Colloquy** of 1529 and the Diet of Augsburg in 1530 (*see* AUGSBURG CONFESSION).

In 1541 Jonas came to Halle and began his intensive work for the Reformation of the church there. He provided a church order for the city in 1543 and reformed its forms of worship. In 1544 he was appointed the **pastor** and **superintendent** of Halle. After the Smalcald War of 1546/47 (*see* SMALCALD LEAGUE) difficult years began for Jonas. He was exiled from Halle in 1546 but was allowed to return in 1548 without assuming his former positions. In 1546 Jonas accompanied Luther on his last journey, stood at Luther's deathbed, and preached the funeral sermon at Eisleben. During the controversies connected with the **Interim** (*see also* ADIAPHORA) he moved toward a strict Lutheran position. After work as the pastor in Coburg (from 1550) and Regensburg (from 1552) he became, finally, the superintendent at Eisfeld in 1553 where he died in 1555. Jonas was important as a reformer but also as the translator of 35 writings of Luther and **Philipp Melanchthon** into German or into Latin, including Luther's *The Bondage of the Will* and Melanchthon's *Apology of the Augsburg Confession*. [G.G.]

JUDAISM AND CHRISTIANITY. *See* JEWISH-LUTHERAN DIALOGUE.

JUDGMENT, LAST. *See* ESCHATOLOGY.

JUSTICE. *See* ETHICS.

JUSTIFICATION (Lat *iustificatio*, "to justify"). Central Lutheran **doctrine** referring to **God's** reckoning or making sinful persons just or righteous. The juridical imagery of describing God's saving work is already used in the Old Testament where reference is made to God's just and saving judgment (Isa 50:7–9; 51:5–8; Ps 71:19; 89:16). But also the suffering servant of God is confessed as one who "shall make many righteous" (Isa 53:11). In the New Testament the concept and language is at the center of especially Paul's theology. His own life has been marked by the experience of received justification (Phil 3:4–11), and this theme runs through all of his letters. Particularly, the Letter to the Romans can be understood as one comprehensive message of God's justification in Christ for the **salvation** of the whole world. The foundation of God's gift of justification of sinful human beings by God's **grace** through **faith** is Jesus' sacrificial death and resurrection for us (Rom 3:23–25; 4:25; 1 Cor 1:30; Gal 2:20). Christ's justification is imputed to all who recognize themselves as ungodly and trust in God, their faith is reckoned as righteousness (Rom 4:5). The "righteousness of God is revealed through faith to faith" (Rom 1:16–17). Such faith in Christ alone and not works of the law grants justification (Rom 3:21–31; Gal 2:16). Justification is forgiveness of **sins** (Rom 3:23–25; 5:12–21) and **reconciliation** to and peace with God (2 Cor 5:18–21; Rom 5:1). The new being of the justified and sanctified Christian is received by faith and in **baptism** and is lived by those who are in Christ and in the **Holy Spirit** (1 Cor 6:11; Rom 6:1ff; 8:1–2; 9–11). It is the beginning of a life of righteousness from God, guided by the Holy Spirit in **sanctification** and **love** of others, and moving toward eternal life (Phil 3:7–16; Gal 5:6.16–25; Rom 6:19–23).

The New Testament also uses other terms and concepts to describe the saving work of God in Christ, such as **redemption**, reconciliation, salvation, and liberation. In the early church and in the Middle Ages, the concept of justification was reflected upon in the framework of the doctrine of grace. Here it was **Augustine** who shaped the doctrine of grace in such a way that it was received by the **church** as its official teaching. Augustine affirmed that God's grace in Jesus Christ is an unconditional divine gift that transforms people and makes them righteous before God. The absolute initiative in this process belongs to God. The connection between human effort and God's grace in the process of justification, indicated in a careful way by Augustine, became a major theme in the different schools in **Scholasticism** and led to more extreme understandings when, for example, the *via moderna* wing of scholastic theology in the 14th and 15th centuries taught that human beings are by themselves able to act in a God-pleasing way and thereby merit justification before God by their **good works**.

It was this kind of teaching and its even more simplistic popular use against which the **Reformation** reacted. The message and concept of justification was freed from the preoccupation with the question of how human nature could be transformed and assisted by divine grace in a process of divine-human interaction and cooperation toward justification. Instead, it was affirmed that human beings, because of their sinful condition, were completely unable to cooperate with God and merit their salvation. They are utterly dependent on God's unmerited saving and justifying grace grounded in Christ's **cross** and **resurrection** for them. In an existential struggle about the right understanding of God's righteousness and the achievement of his own righteousness before God, **Martin Luther** came to the liberating recognition of God's free, unmerited gift of justification, received by sinners by faith alone and by grace alone. Christ's "alien righteousness," grounded in his representative suffering on the cross and his resurrection, is imputed (i.e., granted) to believers and makes them worthy of God's reconciling and justifying judgment. This message and teaching is the central explication of the **Gospel** and, at the same time, the "first and chief article" of faith and the "ruler and judge over all other Christian doctrines."

Luther's teaching on justification was taken over by other reformers and found its place in the Lutheran confessions (*see* CONFESSIONS, LUTHERAN). The affirmations in the confessions underline that the teaching on justification is based on Holy Scripture and the **tradition** of the church; that the sole saving activity is with the Triune God; that justification has a personal and pastoral (consolation of heart and mind) aim; that as a free, unmerited gift it has its center in Christ's saving suffering and resurrection; that justification is communicated to faith, awakened by the Holy Spirit, through **Word** and **sacrament**; that human beings are justified by faith alone and through God's grace alone; that justification is both a declaring or reckoning righteous (e.g., forensic understanding) and a making righteous (effective understanding); that the church is the community in which justification is communicated and received; that the justified ones are at the same time sinners (*simul justus et peccator*) and are in need of renewal and sanctification; and that good works and a Christian life in obedience to God's will are a necessary consequence of the gift of justification.

Through the centuries following the Reformation, the message and doctrine of justification by faith alone and through grace alone has been a constant *cantus firmus* of Lutheran faith and **theology** in the midst of changing theological epochs and schools. Today, some Lutherans argue that the conceptual framework and language of justification no longer speak to modern minds. But most Lutheran theologians emphasize that the message of justification, under the condition that it is translated into contemporary language and thought forms and explicated in relation to modern life experiences, is very well able to liberate people from false religious and secular captivities and lead them to a richer life in confidence to God and service to others.

The doctrine of justification has been the main theological cause of the dramatic Reformation controversies and the ensuing division of the church in the West. From the 16th until the 20th centuries this doctrine has been seen as a major element of the continuing division between the Reformation churches and the **Roman Catholic Church**. Thus it was only logical that this doctrine became an important theme of the **Lutheran-Roman Catholic Dialogue**, ongoing at both international and national levels, since 1970. This dialogue has led to the recognition "that a consensus in basic truths of the doctrine of justification exists between Lutherans and Catholics" and that the mutual condemnations of the 16th century concerning the doctrine of justification that were expressed in the Lutheran confessions and by the Council of Trent (*see* TRENT, COUNCIL OF) no longer apply today. This conclusion comes from the *Joint Declaration on the Doctrine of Justification* that was prepared in 1997 by representatives of the **Lutheran World Federation** (LWF) and the (Vatican) Pontifical Council for Promoting Christian Unity and that was signed by representatives of the LWF and the Roman Catholic Church on October 31, 1999, at Augsburg, Germany. This historic achievement and event has not only opened the way for strengthening closer Lutheran-Roman Catholic relations, but has also brought the doctrine of justification back to the attention of many people together with the need to explain it to 21st-century Christians. [G.G.]

JUST WAR. Theories justifying just war and just violence. The Roman Catholic version of just war theory, inherited from the ethical formulations of **Thomas Aquinas**, has often been noted in the Lutheran tradition, though notably revised. The Roman Catholic concept lists proportionality of time and power spent in the wage of war, neighborly concern, self-defense, and failure of diplomacy among other caveats as permissive of state-conducted war. Generally, basic elements of just war theory are just cause, just end, just means, last resort, and legitimate authority. **Lutheranism** has recast the issue in terms of general violence allowable under the conditions of **two kingdoms** theory. Individual violent resistance—particularly understood as **faith** active in **love**—is justified, Lutheranism has argued, so to protect the self, one's household, and the neighbor. Along the same principles, when writ large, political violent resistance is justified when legitimate government conducts it, and Christian are free to participate in a just war. **Martin Luther** also argued that unless the Christian is a political ruler, responsible for the defense and well-being of those in his or her charge, the Christian is generally to suffer political violence rather than to resist it with force; that is, until the violence affects the Christian's neighbor, at which point the Christian is obligated to step in with a violent exercise of defense, if necessary.

Lutherans have subsequently argued that Luther's exhortation to accept political violence personally can make sense only if one holds central the sovereignty of **God** and the reality of Christian **liberty**. Use of the maxim also implies a contemporary application of the theology of the **cross**. Yet, the argument is not wholly shared. In a medieval world wherein the reigns or kingdoms of God were thought to be ontologically separate, the call to suffer for a "higher" cause might be reasonable. In the contemporary theological scene, where **eschatology** means that God's sovereignty is not so divisible, **political theology** argues the ineluctable connection between care for the neighbor and appropriate care for the self, whether individually or corporately understood. This may well invoke Reinhold Niebuhr's "Christian realism" that violence is inescapable, and so must be employed in the most judicious and justice-achieving of ways. This is in line with the 20th-century debate in the **ecumenical movement** about "just revolution" and about the appropriateness of the just war theory in view of the use of military violence as a means of settling political-ethnic conflicts. Yet again, a significant number of Lutherans (and other Christians) receive both Luther's injunction toward personal suffering and Christ's teaching to turn the cheek as clear commands for nonviolent resistance. Whether just war, just violence, or just revolution, there is no Lutheran unanimity in theory or practice, but for the common recognition that in the face of nuclear war, even the very threat is immoral. *See also* ETHICS; PACIFISM; PEACE; REVOLUTION; SUFFERING. [D.H.L.]

– K –

KANT, IMMANUEL (1724–1804). Highly influential German philosopher and professor of logic at the University of Königsberg. A Lutheran with a background in **Pietism,** Kant's **philosophy** strongly influenced **Lutheranism** and Protestantism. His "critical idealism" definitively shaped the **Enlightenment** and its modernist legacy of **Liberalism**. Kant set out to "remove reason from faith so to save faith." As stated in his *Critique of Pure Reason* (1781), he sought to set out the transcendental grounds for knowledge that could be entirely deductive and permanent. In so doing, he reversed the traditional metaphysical assumptions by arguing that the understanding (*Verstand*) prescribed the lawfulness of nature; that is, lawfulness, and so deductibility, was brought to nature by the mind.

What cannot be established on such grounds of pure **reason**, however, are the practical verities of aesthetics, **ethics**, and religious **faith**. Kant believed that the individual **conscience**, discerned in a practical and inductive way, required further lawful structures to make sense of it. Thus the sense of duty requires a greater horizon of freedom, and then the greater sense of immortality, the ground of which is **God**. These arguments were primarily set forth in his *Critique of Practical Reason* and *Religion within the Limits of Reason Alone*. These parameters for religion, finally, implied for Kant no need for the category of the mystical or for a personal savior. His religious expression came to be deistic and the rightly, virtuously, religious person was the one who recognized duties as divinely authored. It is perhaps ironic that the philosopher's desire to save religion immensely influenced both liberal and fundamentalistic trajectories in Christianity that gave more prominence to human ability and will than to a personal God who created them. In that respect, Kant's legacy was at root quite "non-Lutheran," though so influential for much Lutheran **theology**, particularly that which turned against metaphysics and would emphasize practical life, as in the work of Albrecht Ritschl in the 19th century and Gerhard Ebeling, a leader in the **Luther Renaissance** of the 20th century. [D.H.L.]

KANTOREI. A professional or semiprofessional **choir** officially connected with a church, court, university, or city. The most famous Lutheran kantorei was that of **Martin Luther's** musical colleague, Johann Walter, in Torgau, which functioned almost as a commune, with Walter the cantor as housefather. His mixture of training, discipline, and oversight was so attractive that Luther sent his son Hans to Torgau for his education. At some times and places, the kantorei often became simply hired singers. Occasionally, however, they were also extensions of the pastoral **ministry** of the **church**, providing not only musical leadership for the **congregation**, but also home visitation of the sick and grieving (*see* BURIAL). Even today church choirs in Germany and some other countries are quite often called "kantorei."

The closest North American equivalent to this group would be the paid soloists who often served as the nucleus for choirs at city churches in the early 20th century. While the kantorei is rare today outside of some college and university choirs, the office of the leader, the cantor, has been renewed as the leader of the song, not of the select choir alone, but of the whole congregation. *See also* MUSIC IN THE LUTHERAN CHURCH. [M.O.]

KARLSTADT, ANDREAS BODENSTEIN VON (1486–1541). One of the most influential leaders of the Radical Reformation. While **Martin Luther** was in hiding at the Wartburg Castle (1521/22), Karlstadt emerged as a primary leader for reforms in **Wittenberg**. He hoped to realize his desire for theological and juridical synthesis by making of Wittenberg an example of a genuine "Christian city." With his order for the mass and his desire for biblical guidance for both church and social life, Karlstadt inaugurated a campaign of radical reform. With this as the backdrop, Luther returned to Wittenberg in 1522, reassumed leadership, and, with the help of other reformers, effectively marginalized Karlstadt as an extremist. Karlstadt was restricted to teaching. In 1523 he was working on a spiritualistic **doctrine** (*see* SPIRITUALISTS) of **revelation** and his theology of the **sacraments**, which represented a profound break with the Lutheran position. Ministering at a **parish** in Orlamünde, Thuringia, he was able for a brief time to see to the establishment of an egalitarian iconoclastic religious community that practiced an evangelical mass, spoken **confession**, fasting, relief for the poor, and abolished infant **baptism**. Karlstadt was exiled from Saxony in 1524. In southwestern Germany he became acquainted with numerous **Anabaptists.** Several tracts were printed at Basel repudiating the Lutheran doctrine of the **Lord's Supper**. In 1530 Karlstadt finally settled in Zürich with the help of **Ulrich Zwingli**, and in 1534 became a professor of the Old Testament at the University of Basel and the **pastor** of St. Peter's church. There, he carried on his work in **theology**, writing on how **sanctification** as the proper and necessary flowering of initial **justification** would manifest itself in deep **spirituality** and vigorous social concern.

Karlstadt's attacks on infant baptism and the Lord's Supper and images affected the whole of the **Reformation**. Perhaps ironically, Karlstadt's emphasis on a mystical **piety** and the necessity of personal regeneration deeply influenced a later generation of Lutheran pietists (*see* PIETISM), whose own tradition of devotion positively marks many Lutherans to the present day. [D.H.L.]

KERYGMA (Gk *keryssein*, "proclaiming publicly," *kerygma*, "proclamation, public announcement"). The content of the central Christian message of **salvation** as well as its proclamation. In the New Testament, the term "kerygma" is used for the summary message of salvation (1 Cor 2:2; Rom 16:25–27), in terms of content and communication. There are a number of kerygmatic formulas, referring to the saving nature of Christ's life, ministry, death, resurrection, and final return (e.g., 1 Cor 1:18ff; 15:3–5; Acts 10:36–43). The crucified one is interpreted and proclaimed as the end of the law and the beginning of new life for all who have been reconciled with **God** in Christ.

The term and concept of kerygma have received programmatic significance in modern **theology**, especially through the work of **Rudolf Bultmann**. For him and his followers, it is the kerygmatic Christ, the proclaimed Christ, the Christ-message (and not the "historical Christ") that serves as an approach to understanding the significance of Christ and as a proclamation that calls for an existential human decision of **faith**. Today, the danger of a kerygma theology becoming rather abstract is recognized and the "historical Jesus" again receives attention, as does the understanding of the Christian message (kerygma) in the framework of the relationship between **Word** and faith and history (or experience) and **revelation**. *See also* CHRISTOLOGY. [G.G.]

KEYS, OFFICE OF THE. The power to forgive or retain **sins**, delivered to the **church** by Christ (Mt 18:18). The exercise of such power was part of the life of the Christian community from its beginnings. The declaration of **forgiveness** came to be understood as representing not simply a judicial sentence, but as **salvation** and life itself. Therefore, the office of the keys, in the course of church history soon to be limited to ordained ministers, is not simply absolution declared after **confession**, but also includes every way in which the church bears the ministry of Christ: **preaching**, teaching, celebrating the **sacraments**, and carrying on the conversation and consolation of the faithful.

The *Augsburg Confession* (*CA*) is at pains to outline the power of this office and its limitation. On the one hand, the announcement of forgiveness, since it is done in the name of Jesus and by his command, is absolutely dependable. Such absolution needs no further confirmation nor may it be overruled by any other authority. On the other hand, the office of the keys may not be used to confuse this absolution, or the repentance that precedes it, with human ceremonies or conditions. This confusion, the *CA* charges, was the practice of the Church of Rome in its abuses from simony to indulgences. Lutherans have generally restricted the public use of the office of the keys—for instance, declaring absolutions and blessings in church services—to **pastors**. There has been some controversy about whether this restriction is part of the definition of **ordination** and the call or simply a voluntary delegation of authority from the **congregation** to its minister. [M.O.]

KIBIRA, JOSIA M. (1925–1988). The first representative of Lutheranism in the so-called Third World to become president of the **Lutheran World Federation** (LWF). Kibira was born near Bukoba in Tanzania. After work as a teacher at a high school, he studied for the ministry in Germany (Bethel), was ordained in 1960, and undertook further studies in Hamburg, Germany, and Boston, Massachusetts. In 1964 he was elected bishop of the Northwestern Diocese of the Evangelical Lutheran Church in Tanzania. He was consecrated by his predecessor, teacher, and spiritual father, the Swedish missiologist Bengt Sundkler. In 1961 Kibira became a member of the **Faith and Order** Commission of the **World Council of Churches** (WCC) and in 1968 a member of the Central Committee of the WCC. In 1970 he was elected chair of the Commission on Church Cooperation of the LWF, and in 1977 the Sixth Assembly of the LWF at Dar es Salaam elected him the sixth president of the LWF (until 1984).

During the early period of independence of African nations and churches, Kibira became an increasingly active and respected spokesperson for the religious and social concerns of his continent. He was a forceful advocate for selfhood and self-confidence of the African churches. Interpreting **Martin Luther** as a preacher and **pastor**, Kibira combined earlier revivalist **piety**, consciousness of the richness of African culture and church life, and commitment to theological study, **mission**, and social **justice**. Through his remarkable personal witness, he had a decisive influence on the growth of the Lutheran churches towards a truly worldwide **communion**. [G.G.]

KIERKEGAARD, SØREN AABYE (1813–1855). Eminent Lutheran philosopher. Kierkegaard was born in Copenhagen. He is known as a father of existentialism, though recognition of this did not come until well after his death. His relatively brief life was marked instead by loneliness, melancholy, and enervating production of writings of theological, psychological, and literary genius. These include *Either-Or* (1843), *Fear and Trembling* (1843), *The Concept of Dread* (1844), *Philosophical Fragments* (1844), *Concluding Unscientific Postscript* (1846), and *Sickness Unto Death* (1849). As is evident in his *Training in Christianity*, Kierkegaard was deeply dissatisfied with the dry life of the state church, which also was deeply affected by **idealism** to the point that even the preaching was but the opaque exposition of the thought of **Georg Wilhelm Friedrich Hegel**. Kierkegaard's primary message was that the aesthetic and reflective life was insufficient for attaining authenticity; that on the basis of **reason** one finally must make one's own decision or irrational "leap" of **faith** to believe in Jesus Christ as the God-Man for one's self. But this was no sterile choice; Kierkegaard pushed here for the union of passion with reason as definitive for Christian character. The life of faith was to be experienced, and would be fraught with risk, something that a strictly philosophical or esthetical description of Christian faith could never communicate; instead, the imagination had to be sparked, and faith would have to be evoked by ways other than through intellect.

Kierkegaard's last—and perhaps definitive—battles with the state church left him with few sympathizers. Only a priest and Kierkegaard's brother were present at his burial; his gravesite itself was long unmarked. With late 19th-century forms of **Pietism**, however, and especially with the flowering of existentialism in the 20th century and—perhaps remarkably—the language theory of Ludwig Wittgenstein, as well as contemporary postmodern literary and philosophical theory, Kierkegaard's memory and influence is maintained by innumerable admirers. [D.H.L.]

KINGDOM OF GOD. God's present and ultimate rule over all people and nations. In contemporary theological terminology there is a certain preference for the term "reign" of God since it expresses in a more dynamic and relational way the sovereignty and rule of God than the more static "kingdom" of God. The metaphor and concept has its roots in the Old Testament where it expresses in a diversity of modes and shades God's present sovereignty and lordship over Israel's life and all the nations, as well as the expectation and **promise** of God's ultimate reign with **salvation** and peace (e.g., Ps 145; Is 11; Dan 7). This vision is often expressed in theocratic perspectives where the secular kingdoms participate in God's rule. In the New Testament, the kingdom or reign of God is a major theme in the Gospels where it occupies a central place in the proclamation, actions, and parables of Jesus. Jesus announces and enacts the beginning, presence, and final fulfillment of God's reign in the form of healing, **forgiveness, reconciliation**, salvation, **grace**, defeat of evil powers, norm of behavior, and also judgement. God's gift of the kingdom, already present in Christ and yet to come in its fullness, requires **repentance**, belief, and a response of faithful life in **love** and **justice**. (Some examples of the 150 occurrences of kingdom/reign of God are: Mk 1:14–15; 4:3–9; Mt 6:33; 11:4–5; 20:1–16; Lk 4:43; 17:21).

While in patristic theology (*see* PATRISTICS) the future themes of the relation between the reign of God and the **church** or between the kingdom of God and secular kingdoms are already announced, **Augustine** continues to emphasize the other-worldliness of God's kingdom and relates it to the church triumphant. In later medieval **theology**, the kingdom of God is often identified with the historical church or closely related to a messianic vision of the Roman Empire (13th century). Spiritualistic interpretations also appear that anticipate later social utopias. **Martin Luther** and the Lutheran confessions (*see* CONFESSIONS, LUTHERAN) reject such ecclesiological, political, and spiritualist identifications with the kingdom of God and stress its distinctiveness. Indeed, God's kingdom has to be distinguished from a political kingdom and is opposed to the devil's kingdom. The kingdom or reign of God is a spiritual reality. It presupposes acceptance of God's unmerited love. It consists of trusting **faith** in God and of Christ's **redemption** and deliverance of the faithful from the power of evil so that God may rule over them as a king of righteousness, blessed life, and salvation, granting them the beginning of eternal life. It is both present and eschatological. "God's kingdom comes to us in two ways: first, it comes here, in time, through the **Word** and faith, and secondly, in eternity, it comes through the final revelation" (*Large Catechism*). The kingdom is received in faith, a faith that becomes active in love in daily life and relationships.

Lutheran **Pietism** (as well as the **mission** movement one century later) has been motivated in missionary zeal by the idea of mission as work for the coming kingdom of God, while the **Enlightenment** has seen in the metaphor of the kingdom a moral impulse for progress toward eternal peace. Theology in the 20th century restated, in the Social Gospel movement in North America, earlier concepts by relating the kingdom of God to social reality as an inspiration toward human progress in social, economic, and political life. In the second part of the 20th century and in reaction to this and to other forms of liberal interpretation, Lutherans and many others once again affirm the kingdom or reign of God as a transcendent reality to be brought about by God alone and not by human efforts. The reign of God is also conceived as the critical challenge to all totalitarian human institutions and claims. It is the fundament and goal of Christian hope and, especially in **liberation theology**, the goal of historical and saving liberation of all people in need. A foretaste of God's final reign is experienced through anticipation in the church when, by the **Holy Spirit**, people receive God's salvation in Christ to be shared with all people. [G.G.]

KNUBEL, FREDERICK HERMAN (1870–1945). American **pastor** and church leader. A graduate of the General Synod's institutions in Gettysburg and of the University of Leipzig, Knubel returned to his native New York City to found the Church of the Atonement in 1896. In 1918 he was elected the first president of the United Lutheran Church in America (ULCA). Knubel was a representative of the General Synod's metropolitan wing — pastors of city congregations who ministered to immigrants and the educated. He guided the ULCA in its early years, including the aftermath of World War I, and through the exuberant 1920s and the Great Depression. By 1944 it was clear that Knubel's health was failing, and that he was not equal to the tasks demanded by the wartime and postwartime world. A group of younger pastors, including Knubel's own son, reluctantly engineered his defeat for reelection, and the succession of **Franklin Clark Fry**, the second and last president of the ULCA.

Knubel played an important role in the **ecumenical movement** and imbued the ULCA with its commitment to **ecumenism** and social activity. Active in the American Bible Society and the American Tract Society, he was one of the founders of the **National Lutheran Council** (in 1918) and one of the first leaders of the **Lutheran World Convention**. Together with the ULCA's dominant theologian, Henry Eyster Jacobs, Knubel outlined an irenic approach to cooperation with non-Lutheran churches. Later, together with Jacobs's son Charles, he offered an understanding of Scriptural inspiration that did not include the attention to inerrancy demanded by the Ohio Synod and others. *See also* BIBLE, INSPIRATION OF; HEIN, CARL CHRISTIAN; NORTH AMERICA, LUTHERAN CHURCHES IN. [M.O.]

KOINONIA. *See* COMMUNION.

KOSSUTH, LAJOS (1802–1894). Hungarian Lutheran patriot and national leader. Educated as a jurist, Kossuth became an editor of the newspaper *Pesti Hirlap* (1841) and transformed it into the first political newspaper of Hungary. In 1847 he was elected to the Diet as leader of the liberals. Kossuth played a decisive role in the bloodless revolution of 1848 that gave Hungary a large degree of independence from Austria. In April 1849 he was acclaimed as the governor/president of the country. Some months later Austrian troops occupied Hungary and he fled to Turkey. From there in 1851 he went to the United States and in 1852 returned to Europe. He remained there in exile (mainly in Italy), despite the offer of amnesty, until his death in Turin. While in exile, Kossuth, who was a brilliant and highly knowledgeable speaker, continued to draw attention to the cause of Hungary's national independence. He is remembered as a leader in the struggle for national independence, the emancipation of the peasantry, and civil rights. Kossuth was a committed Lutheran layman who in 1848 achieved legal equality for the Christian churches in Hungary, published numerous articles on religious issues in his newspaper, and served faithfully as the lay president (*inspector*) of the church council of his village. [G.G.]

KRAUTH, CHARLES PORTERFIELD (1823–1883). Leading Lutheran theologian and church leader in the United States. After graduating from the Lutheran Theological Seminary at Gettysburg, Krauth served congregations in Maryland, Pennsylvania, and Virginia from 1841–1861. He was a professor of systematic theology at the new Lutheran seminary in Philadelphia from 1864–1883. In reaction to the more liberal tendencies in the 19th-century "American Lutheranism" movement, Krauth became a prominent defender of traditional Lutheran **doctrine** and practice. He insisted on the unfailing adherence to the distinctive and fundamental Lutheran theological convictions and authoritative texts (*see* CONFESSIONS, LUTHERAN) and opposed all attempts at modernizing the **faith** and interconfessional **union**. He advocated his ideas through many writings and his periodicals *Lutheran and Missionary* (editor 1861–1867) and *Lutheran Church Review* (1882).

Dissatisfied with the growing liberal influences within the General Synod (*see* SCHMUCKER, SAMUEL SIMON) in which several Lutheran synods had come together, Krauth assisted in founding the theological seminary (Mt. Airy) at Philadelphia in 1864 and became its first professor of theology. He played a leading role in the formation of the General Council of the Evangelical Lutheran Church in 1867 for which he composed the principles on **faith** and **church polity**. Both institutions served to preserve and strengthen a confessional **Lutheranism**. Their life and theological profile were to a large degree shaped by Krauth's scholarship, teaching, and intellectual and ecclesiastical leadership. His most well-known publication was the collection of writings *The Conservative Reformation and its Theology* (1871). [G.G.]

KUGLER, ANNA SARAH (1856–1930). Lutheran pioneer woman missionary. A native of Pennsylvania, Kugler studied at the Women's Medical College of Pennsylvania (Philadelphia) and graduated in 1879. After work in a hospital, she applied in 1882 to serve as a medical missionary in India. The **mission** board of the General Synod of the Evangelical Lutheran Church rejected this particular application. Instead, she was assigned to evangelistic work among women and children in India. She arrived there in 1883 and persisted in her commitment to work as a missionary doctor. In 1884 she treated several hundred women in her home and in their homes. She visited villages and rented houses as dispensaries. By 1855 she had reached her goal: She was appointed by the Lutheran Women's Missionary Convention a medical missionary, the only woman doctor in Madras state. In 1893 she inaugurated a women's dispensary. In 1897 a hospital was erected at Guntur with exemplary facilities: maternity and children's wards, a chapel, and a nurses' home. Kugler was both founder and supervising doctor of the institution that was later named Kugler Hospital in her honor. In a typical Lutheran manner, she saw in competent medical practice an effective **witness** to the **love** of Christ. Hundreds of Indian nurses and assistants received their training from her. Kugler was the first Lutheran woman medical missionary in India and one of the first American women to become a leading physician. She successfully integrated in an exemplary way medical work and Christian **faith**. She died in her hospital in 1930. [G.G.]

– L –

LAITY. The role and place of lay people in the **church**. The word *laikos* (layperson) does not occur in the New Testament or the Septuagint, and when *laos* (people) does occur, it does not distinguish members from leadership. Thus, it is not until Clement of Rome (late first century) and later writers that "laity" emerges as a group distinguished from the **ministry**. From this time forward, most consideration given to the laity seems to focus on guarding the tasks most closely associated with the ordained ministry from lay leadership. **Preaching** and public teaching by the laity were forbidden by the Quinisext Council of 692. The unordained were forbidden to preside at the **Lord's Supper** or, except in emergencies, at **baptism**. The participation of laity in election of their **bishops** was severely curtailed. In the West, medieval theologians guarded these practices with the notion of **ordination** as bestowing a certain indelible character, changing the ordinand in substance. This understanding of a higher spiritual status of the ordained was rejected by **Martin Luther** and the other reformers. By affirming the general **priesthood of all believers**, Luther restored equal dignity to the laity and provided the laity with responsibilities and leadership in the church. While underlining the responsibility of all people for the proclamation of the **Gospel**, both corporately and individually, Lutherans guarded against the self-appointed prophecy of the **Enthusiasts** by requiring that no one teach or preach without "being rightly called" (**Augsburg Confession**, article 16).

In Lutheran **Pietism**, the converted and believing individual, leading a Christian life, became the ideal. As a consequence, the laity received new importance in the missionary, evangelistic, and social work of the church (*see* MISSION; EVANGELISM; INNER MISSION). The followers of **Hans Nielsen Hauge**, for example, have established a long tradition of lay preaching and presiding. Particularly in mission fields, evangelists, lay readers, and catechists have regularly served as preachers. In most Lutheran churches, the **congregation's** affairs, including the call of **pastors**, are administered by lay members of the congregation.

It is unfortunate, however, that so much attention has been paid to the boundaries between laity and clergy, since most of the ministry of the laity occurs outside of the walls of the church. The **Reformation** affirmation of the priesthood of all believers, of course, has little to do with offices and functions in the church, and much more to do with the day-to-day proclamation and intercession (*see* PRAYER) that is the right and responsibility of all the baptized. The **witness** of the **people of God**, offered in service and conversation, forms the backbone of this ministry. This witness is combined with the **vocation** of Christians to share in God's continuing creation in the context of home, occupation, and state. These tasks require the assurance of **forgiveness**, reliance on the gifts of the **Holy Spirit**, theological acumen, the support of a community, and constant prayer, so that the life of the laity is one of continual preparation and revivification. Both the modern **ecumenical movement** and the Second Vatican Council (*see* VATICAN COUNCIL II) have reaffirmed the important place of the laity in the church and daily Christian witness; and in ecumenical dialogue the functions and responsibilities of the ordained ministry are generally described as being closely related to the ministries of the whole people of God. [M.O.]

LARGE CATECHISM. See CATECHISMS OF LUTHER.

LATIN AMERICA, LUTHERAN CHURCHES IN. The origins of Lutheranism in Latin America reach back to the first influx of immigrants during the 18th and 19th centuries. The oldest **congregations** were founded by Lutherans from Amsterdam/Holland in 1741 in Surinam and in 1743 in Guyana. Beginning in 1824 larger groups of German Lutheran settlers came to Brazil and after 1840 to Argentina and Chile. After World War I and especially World War II, new waves of immigrants came to Latin America that now included Lutherans from Estonia, Hungary, Latvia, and Slovakia and ethnic Germans from Eastern Europe (*see* EMIGRATION). **Mission** work among indigenous peoples, carried out by North American missions and churches, began in 1899 in Puerto Rico, in 1908 in Argentina, and later in Brazil, Bolivia, Columbia, and Mexico.

After World War II, the **Lutheran World Federation** assisted in the consolidation of the smaller Lutheran groups. They now form churches that represent a tiny minority in most Latin American countries. The exceptions among the 1.1 million Lutherans in Latin America are Brazil (Evangelical Church of the Lutheran Confession in Brazil with 700,000 members, and the Evangelical Lutheran Church of Brazil with 215,000 members) and Argentina with 97,000 members of the Lutheran and United churches. The

Lutheran churches in Latin America seek to respond through their **witness** and service to the great social, economic, and political problems of their countries. They endeavor to improve relationships with the dominant **Roman Catholic Church**, and they insist that their voice be heard within world Lutheranism.

There has never been Lutheran **mission** work in the Caribbean. The 10,000 Lutherans who live in that region, predominantly in Puerto Rico, belong to the Evangelical Lutheran Church in America and to the **Lutheran Church-Missouri Synod**. [G.G.]

LAW AND GOSPEL. Important criterion of Lutheran proclamation and teaching. In the framework of the reaction of the Lutheran **Reformation** against the late medieval penitential system (*see* FORGIVENESS), the distinction between law and **Gospel** became an important element of the theology of **Martin Luther**, his co-reformers, and the Lutheran confessions (*see* CONFESSIONS, LUTHERAN). The presupposition is that Holy Scripture or the **Word of God** comes to us in the twofold form of law and Gospel. The relationship between the two is not presented as a separate doctrinal topic but as framework and criterion for dealing with several aspects of Christian **faith** and life. The law, in the form of biblical commandments, has to be proclaimed in order that people, regarding themselves in the mirror of the law, recognize their inability to present themselves as righteous before **God** and, therefore, acknowledge their sinfulness and need of forgiveness. The Gospel as the joyful message of God's **grace** and **justification** in Jesus Christ must be proclaimed in order to liberate people from their captivity to **sin**. Accordingly, the principle of law and Gospel is applied as a hermeneutical tool for interpreting Scripture (*see* BIBLE, INTERPRETATION OF) and for proclaiming both God's will and God's forgiveness.

During the 16th century the concept of the three "uses" or functions of the law emerged in Lutheran **theology**. There was much agreement on the first function or use, the "civil use," referring to the fact that every society requires a set of laws to order and protect its life. The second function or use of the law, its "theological" or "spiritual use," refers to the function of the law to lead to the recognition of one's own sinfulness. The third function or use of the law, simply called the "third use," refers to the law as a necessary guide and orientation for the life of Christians. Christians are called to perform **good works** and exercise Christian **love** as a consequence of their justification, but not under pressure from the law. Considerable debate in the 16th and following centuries focused on the place and role of the law and its commandments in the Christian life (*see* ETHICS). There were Lutheran theologians who did not consider the preaching of the law necessary for leading people to **repentance** but held that this could be done by the Gospel alone. Others saw no reason for the proclamation of the law for the Christian life because this was against the new liberty of the forgiven ones. In responding to such forms of "antinomianism," the Lutheran confessions insisted on proclaiming, distinguishing, and holding together law and Gospel. But clearly the Gospel received overriding priority.

The continuing significance of applying the principle of law and Gospel is seen by the Lutheran churches as a means of avoiding distortions of the Christian faith and proclamation. Such a distortion happens where the essence of being Christian is based primarily on a set of ethical, practical, and structural norms and forms of Christian and church life—on the law, in other words—as a kind of self-justification. Such distortion also happens where the essence of being Christian is based on an understanding of the Gospel in the sense of an elevated and isolated **spirituality** that ignores God's commandments in the service of others. Holding fast to the right understanding of law and Gospel and keeping their proper balance continues to be part of the art, often neglected, of Lutheran teaching and proclamation. [G.G.]

LECTIONARY. The system of readings from Scripture for use at particular days and occasions in the **church year** or, less commonly, the book in which those lessons are printed in order. Pre-Christian Jewish practice was to assign certain books to certain festivals, and a continuous reading for Sabbaths. This usage was apparently adopted by the early **church**, so that many of our earliest witnesses to the Gospels are preserved lectionary books. In the eighth century Alcuin constructed a single Western lectionary for **Sundays** from the variety of systems prevalent in his day. This lectionary was basically the one used by Lutherans, along with **Anglicans** and **Roman Catholics**, until the late 20th century, although the practices of continuous readings (recommended by **Martin Luther** for daily services) and lessons chosen freely were widely practiced.

In the 19th century the lectionary was widely criticized for its narrow selection of biblical texts and lack of coherence between the lessons. Both Germany and Scandinavia attempted to reform the lectionary by prescribing preaching texts in addition to the set lessons. Experimentation went on worldwide. Wide-ranging lectionary reform, however, had to wait for the Roman Missal, ordered by the Second Vatican Council (*see* VATICAN COUNCIL II). This missal established a three-year lectionary. Along with most other **Protestant** denominations on the continent, North American Lutherans adapted this lectionary for their own use in the service books of the late 1970s. The Evangelical Lutheran Church in America cooperated with other English-speaking Protestant and Anglican bodies in the production of a Revised Common Lectionary (adopted in 1992) that included a wider range of readings from the Hebrew scriptures, more feminine images for **God** and the believer, and an improved use of the psalter. European

Lutheran bodies have not adopted the three-year lectionary and continue to use the historic one-year series, often with Old Testament lessons added. [M.O.]

LENT. Period in the **church year** leading up to **Easter**. The Council of Nicea (325) mentions for the first time Lent as a period of 40 days of fasting in preparation for Easter (since the seventh century the beginning of Lent was advanced to Ash Wednesday). In many Lutheran churches, the **Sundays** during this Lenten season are called by the first word of their respective Latin Introitus (with the exception of Palm/Passion Sunday): *Invocavit*, *Reminiscere*, *Oculi*, *Laetare*, and *Judica*. Many Lutheran **church orders** of the 16th century retained the observation of the Lenten fast, and Lutherans have observed this season with a serene, earnest attitude. Special days of eucharistic **communion** were set aside on Maundy Thursday and Good Friday. Today, Lutherans seek to revive forms of fasting as a spiritual preparation for Easter and as a sign of solidarity with those in need. [G.G.]

LEUENBERG AGREEMENT (1973). Agreement declaring church fellowship between Lutheran, Reformed, and United churches in Europe. After several attempts to form a united **evangelical** movement had failed at the time of the **Reformation**, a new effort at **reconciliation** was made in the framework of the modern **ecumenical movement**. In the second half of the 20th century Lutheran-Reformed conversations in France, Germany, and Holland set the stage for conversations on the European level. Three phases of Lutheran-Reformed dialogues—1955–1960, 1964–1967, and 1969–1973—led to the Leuenberg Agreement (or Concord) of 1973 (since Leuenberg is a conference center near Basel, Switzerland). This agreement consists of a statement on the common understanding of the gospel; an affirmation that the mutual doctrinal condemnations at the time of the Reformation no longer apply (*see* ANATHEMA); and a declaration of full church fellowship (*see* UNITY OF THE CHURCH) between the churches that subscribe to the Leuenberg Agreement. The agreement does not change the confessional and organizational structure of the churches, but it does allow the churches to live in close fellowship with one another. Over 85 churches in Europe and four in Argentina have so far subscribed to the agreement, which represents an important historical and ecumenical achievement in the 20th century. *See also* LUTHERAN-REFORMED DIALOGUE. [G.G.]

LEX ORANDI, LEX CREDENDI (Lat "law of praying, law of believing"). The relationship between Christian **worship** and **doctrine**. The formula *lex orandi, lex credendi* emerged in the fifth century and may have originally meant that the **church's** liturgy must govern what is taught in the church. While many of the biblical texts have grown out of worship settings and the Bible itself emerged from and is still used in the contexts of worship, succeeding developments have led to a differentiation between the language and forms of worship and the language and forms of teaching and doctrine. Today, *lex orandi, lex credendi* is interpreted as indicating the close interrelation of worship and doctrine as well as the insight that in history there have been instances when liturgical practice has shaped what has been formulated as **dogma**, doctrine, catechetical, and theological instruction, and that there have been instances when structures and texts of worship have been defined by doctrinal definitions.

This latter position was taken by the **Reformation**, which rejected or reformed late medieval orders of worship by using as criterion either the text of Holy Scripture in the **Reformed** tradition or the priority of the clear proclamation of God's **Gospel** in the Lutheran tradition. Consequently, **Martin Luther** and his co-reformers dedicated much energy to the reform of worship, and the consolidation of Lutheran churches in different countries was always accompanied and marked by the elaboration and introduction of new liturgical service books. Thus, the priority of doctrine over worship was balanced by an awareness of the doctrinal (and catechetical) significance of worship. Today, such a balance is missing in those Lutheran **congregations** where there is still the old-fashioned liberal tendency to use worship services in a one-sided way as an educational or social action instrument instead of being an occasion of praise, proclamation, and **prayer**. [G.G.]

LIBERALISM. A theological movement with roots in the mid-19th century, influenced in general by the **Enlightenment** and the experiential emphases of the age of Romanticism, and in particular by the work of **Immanuel Kant**, **Georg Wilhelm Friedrich Hegel**, Friedrich Schleiermacher, **Karl Adolf von Harnack**, Albrecht Ritschl, and others. Liberalism can be characterized generally in its preference for history over metaphysics and for human goodness and potential (with the inevitability of social progress) over **sin** (*see* ANTHROPOLOGY). Liberal **Christology** emphasizes Jesus more as a moral example than as **God** incarnate, and holds that an appropriate picture of the historical Jesus might be found in a deeply historically minded critical inquiry of the New Testament (*see* SCHWEITZER, ALBERT). Furthermore, Liberalism contributes both to biblicism and **Pietism** by its understanding of **faith** as trust more than as acceptance of a body of creeds and assertions (Lat *fides qua creditur*, "the act of believing" versus *fides quae creditur*, "the content of what is believed").

On the background of the terrible impact of World War I, Liberalism was rejected by the movement of **dialectical theology**, led by the great Reformed theologian Karl Barth. Many of the Lutherans who joined this movement reacted to Liberalism by emphasizing an inner **spirituality** of God's eternal truths and a history "above" history (**salvation history** —

Heilsgeschichte—meant to save and recast the metaphysical concerns of pre-19th-century theology) in which God, not human beings, is the subject and primary causal agent. This school began with the work of **Rudolf Bultmann** and Paul Tillich, and ended with the metaphysically consequential reaffirmation of history per se by Lutheran theologians such as Carl Braaten, Robert Jenson, Tuomo Mannermaa, and **Wolfhart Pannenberg** (*see* ESCHATOLOGY), among many others, who, though critically conservative of the whole Lutheran tradition, are not quite so regarded today among most Lutherans. The further irony is that what does pass today for conservative theology has imbibed deeply from the 19th-century wells of Liberalism. [D.H.L.]

LIBERATION THEOLOGY. Theological reflection that proceeds from the experience of those, originally in Central and South America, who are poor and marginalized by capitalist and oligarchical politics. The central themes of liberation theology are these: that **God** has decisively made a preferential option for the poor, that the **people of God** are to image this option, and that praxis on behalf of the poor, therefore, precedes theological reflection, which in turn is to provide the symbolic value to, motivation for, and historical articulation of such praxis. With regard to schools or styles of theology, liberation theology is a direct consequence of **political theology**. Its historical situation begins with the poor in Latin America, and was first given theological expression in the work of Dom Helder Camara, Gustavo Gutierrez, Jon Sobrino, Juan Luis Segundo, José Miguez Bonino, and Leonardo Boff, among many others. As a primary mode of theological reflection that is always predicated by local political circumstances, liberation theology has grown to inform and characterize **feminist theology**, black theology, and African and Asian theologies. Wider frames of **theology** influenced by liberation praxis/theory include ecotheology and a liberation theology of world religions.

The distinctly Lutheran contribution to liberation theology is the argument that **justification** is necessarily linked to **justice**, as proposed by Latin American Lutheran theologians and discussed by a conference of younger Lutheran theologians sponsored by the **Lutheran World Federation** at Wittenberg, Germany, on October 31, 1998. Original proponents for this include theologians Walter Altmann and Wanda Deifeldt, both of Brazil, and an exemplar of solidarity with the oppressed in El Salvador, Bishop **Medardo Gomez**. Liberation theology puts into effect Karl Marx's thesis (against Ludwig Feuerbach) that the point of **philosophy** is to change the world, not simply to interpret it, and that it provides the horizon of theological self-understanding for a political enactment of Christian ethical life. [D.H.L.]

LIBERTY. The category by which Lutherans address the topics of **free will** and the Christian life. While the **Enlightenment** ideal of human dignity, based in part on a healthy doctrine of **creation**, is not gainsaid in **Lutheranism**, the supposition that human beings are capable of deciding upon and constructing wholly their own relationship to **God** is the primary target attacked by the **doctrine** of **justification**, as well as by a thoroughly theocentric application of the doctrine of God. In his debates with **Erasmus of Rotterdam** and others, epitomized in his treatise *The Bondage of the Will* (1525), **Martin Luther** underscored that human finitude exacerbated by **original sin** (*see* ANTHROPOLOGY) makes impossible any human state of neutrality toward God or ability to ask anything of God. The **Reformation** summary position was that humans are free in everything except anything concerning their eternal **salvation**. All claims that humans can decide *for* God, the confessions (*see* CONFESSIONS, LUTHERAN) say, are illusory, and where such decisions are thought to be made, the confessions hold that this is in fact the activity of the **Holy Spirit**, working through the proclaimed **Word of God** and through the **sacraments**.

A "liberated will" is bestowed on the Christian, however, in terms of the Christian's liberation from **sin**; those who are baptized "now have a liberated will" (*Formula of Concord*, article 2:67). They are freed, too, from the shadows of their own guilt and anxieties at having had to—they wrongly supposed—atone for their own **sins**. This is the marvelous liberty of which Luther writes in *The Freedom of a Christian* (1520). But this freedom *from* sin and the convicting power of the law (*see* LAW AND GOSPEL) entails for the Christian a freedom *for* sin, which is a new kind of servitude on behalf of the neighbor (*see* VOCATION). Lutheran **theology** recognizes that liberty is the full and joyful exercise of a role within its natural orderings; like a horse, as Luther said, that with the right rider can now gallop full out in a proper direction, thus fulfilling its nature. Like the dialectical relation of law to **Gospel**, the liberty of the justified life in Christ expresses in a form of nature God's intents of blessing and creaturely joy. [D.H.L.]

LIFE AND WORK MOVEMENT. Movement within the broader **ecumenical movement** that furthers joint study and action on social-ethical issues. The Life and Work movement, together with the **Faith and Order movement** and the **International Missionary Council**, shaped the first phase of the ecumenical movement between 1910 and 1948. The impact of World War I and the enormous social, economic, political (Bolshevism in Russia, and Fascism in Italy and Germany), and moral issues after the war led to plans for a conference that would enable the Christian churches to develop a common response to the problems of the time. It was especially the deep social and ecumenical commitment and unceasing energy of Lutheran archbishop **Nathan Söderblom** of Sweden that made the Universal Christian Conference on Life and Work possible. The conference took place at Stockholm in 1925 and signaled the beginning of ecumenical studies and conferences on social and political issues.

In 1948 Life and Work joined Faith and Order to form the **World Council of Churches** (WCC). Within this broader structure, the main concerns of the former Life and Work became the larger part of the structure and programs of the WCC. They included: the basic issues of the relationship of **church** and society and many specific issues such as **religious liberty**, the role of science and technology, **human rights**, social and economic **justice**, **international affairs**, **peace**, care of **creation**, **racism**, and so on. Work on these issues has been done through world conferences, consultations, studies, public statements, advocacy, practical cooperation in support of minorities and popular movements, **emergency and development aid**, involvement in conflict resolution, and so on. This broad spectrum of activity that extends far beyond the WCC has been supported by Lutheran churches, who have been reluctant on the more radical sociopolitical positions and more supportive of human rights and aid programs. *See also* CHURCH AND WORLD; ETHICS; SCIENCE AND CHRISTIANITY. [G.G.]

LILJE, HANNS (1899–1977). One of the major "international Lutherans" of the 20th century. Born at Hannover, Germany, Lilje received his **ecumenical** training in Christian student work where he was vice president of the World Student Christian Federation from 1932–1935. From 1935–1945 he was the general-secretary of the **Lutheran World Convention**, the predecessor organization of the **Lutheran World Federation** (LWF). It was logical that Lilje would be among the founders of the LWF in 1947. From 1952–1957 he was president of the LWF and from 1947–1970 a member of its Executive Committee. Before this time, during the rule of the Nazi party, he was actively involved in the work and leadership of the **Confessing Church** (*see* CHURCH STRUGGLE). Because of his contacts with people participating in the plot against Hitler, Lilje was sent, by the High Court, to prison where American soldiers liberated him in 1945.

Lilje was elected **bishop** of the Evangelical Lutheran Church of Hannover in 1947. He participated in the foundation of the **World Council of Churches** (WCC) in 1948, became a member of its Central Committee that same year, and was elected as one of its four presidents from 1968–1975. Inspired by a solid knowledge of **Martin Luther's** life and work, and active in efforts to build bridges between the Christian church and the political and public life of contemporary society (*see* CHURCH AND WORLD), Lilje exercised a formative influence on the course of his Lutheran church in Germany, the Lutheran church worldwide, and on the ecumenical involvement of the Lutheran churches in the postwar period. [G.G.]

LITERATURE. The relationship between literature and **Lutheranism**. Christianity and literature are related in two major ways. First, Christianity itself is a part of literature, in the sense that the Bible, Christianity's foundational document, is literature that employs and creates many linguistic styles and literary forms. Along with the Bible, the history of Christian **theology** and of the Christian **church** find their articulation and communication in literary forms up to this day. Second, Christianity has had an impact on literature in a wider sense. Both ways, often closely interrelated, are manifest in the Lutheran **Reformation**. With his translation of the Bible, itself a masterwork of literature, **Martin Luther** created the literary German language (*see* BIBLE, MARTIN LUTHER'S TRANSLATION). Through the style and language of his translation, he deeply influenced German and north European literature as well as everyday language (such as specific terms, proverbs, sayings, and allusions). Luther's writings, **sermons**, tracts, **chorales**, and poems, as well as other literary products at the time of the Reformation (such as the famous satirical leaflets, religious dramas, and mystical poetry) constitute a rich and influential literary heritage.

This literary heritage was continued during the period of Lutheran **Orthodoxy** by the writing of hundreds of **hymns** of deep poetic beauty, and by the rich literary productivity of Lutherans during the **Enlightenment** period by such poets as Christian Fürchtegott Gellert, Friedrich Gottlieb Kloppstock, and the general **superintendent** of Weimar, **Johann Gottfried Herder**, the father of German Romanticism. The literary excellence and theological originality of **Søren Aabye Kierkegaard** and **Nikolai Federik Severin Grundtvig** had a far-reaching influence on literature in Europe and North America in the 19th and 20th centuries. Lutheran history and especially certain Lutheran religious concepts can be found in modern poetry, autobiographies, and the mostly indirect or implicit religious references in modern literature. *See also* CULTURE, LUTHERAN IMPACT ON; LUTHER IN THE ARTS. [G.G.]

LITURGICAL MOVEMENT. The stream of 20th-century church life that aimed at the renewal of congregational **worship**. This movement found its most potent expression in the liturgical decrees of the Second Vatican Council (*see* VATICAN COUNCIL II), even so, it affected all of the groups of the Western church. While the liturgical movement is primarily centered on accessible language, the biblical roots and center of worship, and the connection between worship and the rest of human life, it has its 19th-century roots in the various Romantic revivals of **patristics**, ritual, and **art** such as the Oxford and Cambridge movements in England. The Lutheran **Awakening** was particularly influential, since it hearkened back to the early years of the **Reformation**. Thus, it held high the reformers' efforts in crafting worship in the vernacular, and returning active participation to the **congregation**.

The Roman Catholic *Motu Proprio* of 1903 on the place of **church music** in nurturing the congregation's more active participation in worship is generally acknowledged to be the opening of the modern liturgical movement. While the next 40 years saw this movement led by monastics such as Lambert Bauduin, Odo Casel, and Gregory Dix, its attention was focused on popular appeal rather than a specialized academic or ascetic audience. With the aid of conferences and journals, the movement influenced **priests**, **laity**, and members of other churches.

The influence of the liturgical movement became obvious and solidified in 1963 when *The Constitution on the Sacred Liturgy* was the first document adopted by the Second Vatican Council. At a stroke, vernacular became the normal language for the mass, the altar was moved from the east wall to a central location, the laity were encouraged to exercise liturgical leadership, and corporate services aimed to replace the exclusive focus on private devotion that had been dominant since the late Middle Ages. Soon, the **calendar** was revised to give centrality to **Sundays**, rather than saint days and, by a three-year **lectionary**, to greatly increase the biblical writings heard by the congregation. This reform soon affected all the Western churches, including those in Africa and Asia, where the Church of South India was a worldwide leader in **ecumenical** liturgical convergence.

The fundamental principles of the modern liturgical movement include the centrality and importance of **baptism** for Christian life; the goal of an active, knowledgeable assembly, led by the presider and other ministers; the importance of biblical proclamation, and therefore of exegesis and **preaching**; and worship crafted to reflect its context within the traditional shape of the Western rite. *See also* LITURGICAL RENEWAL. [M.O.]

LITURGICAL RENEWAL. The recovery of Lutheran principles of **worship** and their incarnation in the life of Lutheran **congregations**. The liturgical renewal had its origin in the Lutheran **Awakening** and has continued through Lutheran involvement in the modern **liturgical movement**. One of the goals of the Awakening was the return to the worship practices of the first generation of the **Reformation**. While this work was colored by the archaism and aestheticism of its Romantic origin, its aim, largely achieved, was to give 19th-century expression to the 16th-century ideals of Lutheran worship. Thus, along with much that was anachronistic and picayune, it reintroduced congregational responses, sacramental centrality, and a focus on incarnational **revelation** to much of the **Lutheran church**.

These emphases were lifted up in the 20th century by the liturgical movement, along with a renewed sense of the centrality of Scripture (*see* BIBLE, AUTHORITY OF) and **baptism** for the Christian **church**. Thus, participation in this **ecumenical movement** was natural for Lutherans. Until the 1960s much of the work of liturgical renewal, both in Europe and the United

States, was carried on by voluntary societies of interested individuals. Afterwards, in the aftermath of the Second Vatican Council (*see* VATICAN COUNCIL II), the work of experimentation and trial was carried out mainly by denominational executives and youth workers. In Germany, the excitement and high level of participation in the large church gatherings (*Kirchentage*) contrasted with what many saw as the sterility of parochial worship. In the United States, the *Lutheran Book of Worship* and *Lutheran Worship* (*see* HYMNBOOKS, LUTHERAN) were the first official fruits of the modern liturgical movement. The trial liturgies and introductory materials for these service books, and the discussion of official practice statements related to **sacraments** and worship spread the principles of liturgical renewal more widely among laity than had ever before been the case.

Until the 1980s much of the **music** and most of the orders of service of the Lutheran churches in **Africa**, **Asia**, and **Latin America** were simply transplanted and translated from the home country of the missionaries. With the new emphasis, however, on indigenization and contextualization (*see* INCULTURALIZATION), the younger churches broke forth in an explosion of **hymnody** and church practice. At the end of the century, the **Lutheran World Federation** launched a decade-long, multivolume study on the relationship of **culture** and liturgy to help churches to learn from each other's experiences and experimentation about the cultural, countercultural, and transcultural aspects of worship. This effort, with its emphases on **evangelism** and formation, may be the next frontier of liturgical renewal. [M.O.]

LITURGY. *See* WORSHIP.

LOCAL CHURCH. *See* CONGREGATION; CHURCH.

LÖHE, JOHANN KONRAD WILHELM (1808–1872). German **pastor**, important theologian of **Neo-Lutheranism**, devotional and liturgical writer, and organizer of missionary and social ministry ventures. Coming under the influence of the Lutheran **Awakening** during his days as a student at Erlangen, Löhe was passionately committed to the Lutheran confessions (*see* CONFESSIONS, LUTHERAN), from which he derived his very high view of the **church** and the ordained **ministry**. He became the pastor of the church at Neuendettelsau in 1837, and remained there until his death. When he came to this Franconian village, it was isolated and impoverished. At his death, it was a world-renowned center for missionary activity, the home of a renewed **diaconate**, with associated **Inner Mission** institutions, and a producer of devotional and liturgical writings that affected Lutherans around the world. This transformation was due to his ability not only as an organizer and author, but also as a pastor, preacher, and counselor.

In 1841 Löhe dispatched a group of Franconians to form a community in Michigan. This group, which settled in Frankenmuth, was only the first of

several he sent, along with an almost unending stream of advice and uncounted pastors and teachers to care for German emigrants (also in Canada,
Australia, and Brazil). In North America, many of his followers gathered together in the Iowa Synod, which continued his attitudes toward confessions,
church, and ministry. Some others, however, including the Frankenmuth
colony, eventually rejected his high view of **ordination** and joined together
with other groups to found the **Lutheran Church-Missouri Synod**. Together
with other theologians, Löhe offered a return to the liturgical practices of the
early **Reformation**. He appears to have coined the image of **preaching** and
the **Lord's Supper** as the equally important "twin peaks" of Lutheran **worship**. In North America, the *Common Service* both echoed and relied upon his
Lutheran order of worship and American church life was more subtly affected by his *Three Books about the Church* (1845/1908). [M.O.]

LORD'S SUPPER. Together with the proclamation of the **Gospel** and **baptism**, the foundational sacramental celebration of the Christian **church**. The
New Testament contains four accounts of Jesus' institution of the eucharist:
Mk 14:22–25; Mt 26:26–29; Lk 22:15–20; 1 Cor 11:23–26. These accounts
have a historical basis, but also reflect elements of the liturgical practice of
early Christian communities. The last meal of Jesus was part of the tradition
of other meals Jesus shared with his disciples, tax collectors, and sinners.
But it assumed a new significance by the presence and promise of the one
who gives his life for many, and thereby creates life-giving **communion**
with himself and a community of mutual service among those who participate. As a remembrance (*anamnesis*) of Jesus' death and an anticipation of
his coming again (1 Cor 11:26), the Lord's Supper soon became a central element of emerging forms of Christian **worship** and was known by different
names: Lord's Supper (1 Cor 11:20), the breaking of the bread (1 Cor 10:16;
Acts 2:46; 20:7.11). At the turn to the second century, the introductory
prayer formula of the meal (Heb *beraka*, "blessing," Gk *eucharistia*,
"thanksgiving," [cf. 1 Cor 11:24]) became the designation of the whole
sacramental action: the eucharist. During the second century, the final separation of the sacramental meal from an ordinary meal occurred. The eucharist became the Christological (*see* CHRISTOLOGY) basis for the interpretation of the death of Jesus as offering his life for many and, thus, as
representative **atonement** for the sins of humans. This offering of Jesus was
at the same time seen as constitutive of the community of the church.
Through sharing in the gifts of Jesus' body and blood, the church becomes
the Body of Christ (1 Cor 10:16–17).

During the first centuries, the eucharist was not at the center of major
doctrinal conflicts, and it did not become the theme of an evolving eucharistic **dogma**. In the course of this period, the basic structure of the celebration of the Lord's Supper was already developed, **bishops** (or **priests**)

came to be celebrant, and **Sunday** became the regular day to assemble for the eucharist. The term "mass" (Lat *missa*) for the eucharist came into general use since the fifth century. The church fathers taught a close relation between the eucharistic elements of bread and wine with Christ's body and blood by holding closely together symbol (*figura*) or sign (*signum*) and symbolized/signified reality. When this close connection was no longer understood, the relation between the sacramental elements/signs and the signified reality of Christ's body and blood became a hotly debated issue from the ninth to the 11th century. The debate ended with the victory of eucharistic realism and even the affirmation of a change within the elements. This change was called transubstantiation from the 13th century on, and found its classical definition in **Thomas Aquinas**: The substance or essence (*substantia*) of bread and wine are transformed—transubstantiated—into the substances of Christ's body and blood, while the outward appearance (*accidens*) of bread and wine remains. The Fourth Lateran Council in 1215 declared transubstantiation part of the faith of the church.

A related line of doctrinal development in the late Middle Ages led to an exaltation of the sacrificial aspect of the mass. It was often understood as a bloodless repetition, a reenactment of Christ's **sacrifice** on the cross, offered by the priest as a propitiatory sacrifice for the remission of the **sins** of the living and also of the dead. This practice and other developments in the understanding and practice of the mass led to a multiplication of private votive masses, a radical decline of participation in the public mass, devotion to the reserved and displayed sacrament (processions), and distribution of the sacrament to the **laity** only in one kind, the bread (from the 13th century). These developments in eucharistic theology and practice were criticized by many scholastic theologians, but were eventually affirmed in more moderate formulations by the Council of Trent (*see* TRENT, COUNCIL OF).

Martin Luther rejected late medieval theology and practice at no other point so vehemently as in the case of the mass. While sternly insisting on the real presence of Christ in the sacrament as essential for the certainty of **salvation**, he rejected the theory of transubstantiation, the sacrifice of the mass, and the distribution of the sacrament in only one kind because they all contradicted Christ's institution and **promise**. He restated eucharistic doctrine by highlighting the unmerited divine gift of this Gospel sacrament full of **grace**, its communal nature, the need to receive it frequently, the fundamental role of the words of institution as Christ's institution, command, and promise, the importance of the response of **faith**, and the pastoral nature of Holy Communion. Luther renewed the traditional eucharistic liturgy by introducing the vernacular, enabling participation of the congregation, and—in following Christ's example—reintroducing the distribution in both kinds, bread and wine, to the laity.

With this position, however, Luther also came into conflict with the Swiss reformer **Ulrich Zwingli**. Zwingli argued that Christ, risen to the right hand of God, cannot be in many places at the same time, and that the words of institution "this *is* my body" have to be understood—as so often in the Bible—metaphorically: "is" meaning "signifies." Luther replied to Zwingli in 1527 with the publication of *That These Words of Christ "This Is My Body" Still Stand Firm against the Fanatics*. The attempt of Luther and Zwingli at the **Marburg Colloquy** in 1529 to overcome their difference failed, and the division between Lutheran and **Reformed** churches that had begun already before the middle of the 16th century, was to a large degree a consequence of this disagreement about Holy Communion.

The Lutheran confessions (*see* CONFESSIONS, LUTHERAN) teach that together with the proclamation of the Gospel and the sacrament of baptism, the Lord's Supper is the fundamental **means of grace** through which the Triune God offers to all people salvation, **forgiveness** of sin, and all the blessings of a new life in communion with Christ. Holy Communion thus belongs to the existential center of Christian life and of the worship of the Christian community. Essential for this sacrament and its understanding are Christ's constitutive words of institution; the assurance that Christ through his own words and in the power of the **Holy Spirit** makes himself truly present in, with, and under the bread and wine; that faith, understood as trust and confidence, is necessary for a blessed reception of the gracious gifts of the sacrament; and that the Lord's Supper is a communal meal that is foundational for the existence, life, and mission of the church.

In recent **ecumenical** dialogues, Lutherans have broadened this understanding of the eucharist by including and also rediscovering the aspects of thanksgiving and praise for God's work in **creation** and history, the significance of the invocation of the Holy Spirit (*epiclesis*), and the social-ethical implications of the eucharist. These dialogues have made it possible to overcome, despite remaining theological differences, the Lutheran-Reformed division over the Lord's Supper (*see* LEUENBERG AGREEMENT; LUTHERAN-REFORMED DIALOGUE). The dialogues have also led to far-reaching agreements and convergences about the eucharist between Lutherans and Roman Catholics (*see* LUTHERAN-ROMAN CATHOLIC DIALOGUE). *See also* LORD'S SUPPER IN ECUMENICAL DIALOGUE; SACRAMENTS. [G.G.]

LORD'S SUPPER IN ECUMENICAL DIALOGUE. The central significance of ecumenical dialogue about the **Lord's Supper** for Christian **unity**. During the first decades of the 20th century, participants in meetings of the **Faith and Order movement** soon identified the Lord's Supper as one of the main issues for their work. They knew that the separation between churches has usually been marked both by divisive differences in the understanding of the eucharist and the breakup of community at the Lord's Table. Correspondingly, a **reconciliation** or reunion of hitherto separated churches presupposed overcoming differences in the understanding of the eucharist (as well as other doctrines) and such reunion would only be finalized and celebrated by reestablishing eucharistic fellowship. Thus, since the 1920s until the end of the century, the Lord's Supper has been a major topic in multilateral dialogues of Faith and Order and bilateral dialogues between **Christian World Communions**.

These dialogues have led to agreements and convergences on such controversial aspects of eucharistic doctrine as the real presence of Christ in the sacramental action and the sacrificial nature of the sacrament (*see* SACRIFICE). Such agreements have been formulated in documents such as Faith and Order's *Baptism, Eucharist, and Ministry* (1982), the international Lutheran-Roman Catholic report *The Eucharist* (1978), and several other texts. Together with agreements on other issues, the growing common understanding, despite remaining differences of theological interpretation, of the basic meaning of the Lord's Supper has contributed to eucharistic fellowship as part of full **communion** between churches, based on such documents as the ***Porvoo Common Statement*** and the **Leuenberg Agreement**. Eucharistic hospitality is practiced between most **Protestant** churches, often under certain conditions, while the **Roman Catholic** and **Orthodox** churches hold that eucharistic fellowship (apart from exceptions in cases of pastoral necessity) is only possible when full unity has been reached. Thus, the dialogue must continue. *See also* DIALOGUES, BILATERAL. [G.G.]

LOVE. Fundamental expression of the relationship between **God** and human beings. The Old Testament describes God's election of the People of Israel and their covenant relationship in terms of God's faithful love to the people (Deut 6:5; Isa 54:5). The New Testament highlights the boundless love of God that has come into the world in Jesus Christ, the beloved Son of God, whose incarnation, life, **cross**, and **resurrection** manifested God's love to his people (e.g., Jn 3:16: 15:13; Rom 5:8: 8:39). God is love (1 Jn 4:8–10). This love is the source and impulse of the twofold command for Christians: to love God and their neighbors (Mt 22:34–40). God's love is the basis of mutual love of Christians (Jn 13:34) and of the fellowship of love by which the members of the Body of Christ are bound together (1 Cor 12–13). The love poured out into human hearts through the **Holy Spirit** (Rom 5:5) is to be passed on, even to enemies (Mt 5:43–48) and without conditions (Rom 15:1–3; Phil 2:4). This selfless, free, pure love of others is termed in the New Testament *agape* in contrast to *eros*, the sensual, erotic form of love. *Agape and Eros* (1930) was a widely read and influential book of the Swedish Lutheran theologian and **bishop** Anders Nygren.

Augustine did not see such a sharp contrast between *eros* and *agape*. If human desire is directed toward God, whose love dwells in us, it is true love (Lat *caritas*). If human desire is directed to earthly things, it becomes a false love in the form of *cupiditas*. **Scholasticism** understood **faith** informed by love (*fides caritate formata*) as one of the conditions for **justification**, while sublime forms of mystical love of God were developed in high medieval **mysticism** (e.g., Bernhard of Clairvaux, 1090–1153) and—centuries later— in a Protestant shape in **Pietism**. **Martin Luther** saw in forms of self-love and even in attempts to love God by one's own human efforts, a futile and sinful attempt of self-realization and self-justification. Rather, love has its origin in God as creator and reconciler, in God's love for sinners in Jesus Christ. This love is offered to the sinner who is called to accept it in faith. God's love fills faith with confidence and the freedom to love others. This is the foundation of a new **ethics** that is realized by communicating Christ's love by means of the free and selfless love of others.

For **Georg Wilhelm Friedrich Hegel**, the intention of God's love is the humane and moral national state, while the church as a social-moral institution of love has the continuing task of being on the side of those who are "most close to infinite pain." In Pietism, God's love and Christian love were among the most powerful motives of **mission** and social involvement. Today, Hegel's concept of the social dimension of love is expressed in a new historical context and in new forms, underlining that God's love is to be communicated especially to the poor, suffering, and oppressed. God's love is experienced in **forgiveness** and liberation to a new life, but this love must also be handed on in solidarity and struggle for **justice**. Lutheran theologians share these perspectives, but they also emphasize an ethics of reasoned action informed by love. [G.G.]

LUND SCHOOL. An internationally recognized group of Lutheran theologians in the Swedish University of Lund. The Swedish theologian and **bishop Einar Billing** prepared the way for this school with his emphasis on scientific methodology in theological work, the role of history, and research on **Martin Luther**. These emphases were taken up by his pupil Gustaf Aulén (1879–1977). During the 1920s and 1930s, but with an impact beyond this period, the so-called Lund School became an internationally prestigious group of theological scholars. It was marked by its integration of scientific methods into **theology**, the use of "motif research," the emphasis on the concept of the history of ideas in systematic theology, contacts with Anglo-Saxon **philosophy**, and intensive study of Luther's theology. Between 1924 and 1933 Anders Nygren (1890–1978) and Aulén were the main representatives of this school.

Nygren was professor at Lund and then bishop of this diocese. From 1947–1952 he was the first president of the **Lutheran World Federation** that was founded in Lund in 1947. Aulén was professor at Lund and then bishop of Strängnäs. With books like *Christus Victor* (1931) he contributed magnificently to the creation of a systematic theology in Sweden with its distinct profile. A third important Lundensian theologian was Yngve Brillioth (1891–1959). He was professor at Lund, bishop of Växjö, archbishop of Uppsala, and moderator of the **Faith and Order** Commission of the **World Council of Churches**. In connection with his special interest in Anglicanism (*The Anglican Revival* [1925]) he promoted the role of the Swedish church as a "bridge church" between the confessions. A younger representative, Ragnar Bring (1895–1990), continued the tradition of the Lundensian School into the 1960s. [G.G.]

LUTHER, MARTIN (1483–1546). The most prominent and formative leader of the **Reformation** movement that led to the establishment of Lutheran churches all over Europe (*see also* LUTHER'S THEOLOGY). Luther was born on November 10, 1483, at Eisleben in Saxony. From 1501–1505 he studied at Erfurt, and in 1505 he joined the Augustinian order in that city. In 1507 he was ordained a **priest** and in 1512 he graduated as Doctor of Theology. In 1510/11 he traveled to Rome, and after his return was sent by his superior and esteemed teacher Johann von Staupitz to **Wittenberg** to teach there as a professor of biblical interpretation. He began his teaching career with lectures on the Psalms and the Letter to the Romans. Theological reflection and existential struggle about his relationship to a righteous **God** led him to his Reformation breakthrough between 1514 and 1518. There is much debate among scholars about a more precise date of this breakthrough, even though all agree that it happened in the framework of a longer process between 1513 and 1520 in the course of which Luther worked out his Reformation position. This position was biblically grounded in the recognition that the righteousness of God is not a condemning righteousness of a wrathful, distant God, but a gracious, forgiving righteousness of a loving God who is near to us in Jesus Christ. Luther understood this righteousness as being revealed and communicated by the **Gospel**. He believed that sinful people are justified by God, made right with God for Christ's sake through **grace** alone and by **faith** alone, that is, without the condition of human-divine cooperation in **good works** and merits earned thereby.

This understanding of **justification** signaled the mounting conflict with the dominant late medieval scholastic (nominalist) theology. The conflict achieved ecclesial dimensions with the publication in 1517 of Luther's *Ninety-five Theses* against the late medieval penitential system (indulgences). With the help of the improved **printing press**, Luther's ideas became quickly and widely known, and as a result he himself came into serious conflict with his church authorities. When he refused to retract, a process against him was initiated in Rome. In 1520 Luther burned the papal bull announcing his ban. In the same year, he published his three major Reformation writings: *The Babylonian Captivity of the Church*, denouncing the Roman sacramental teaching and practice; *Appeal to the Christian Nobility of the German Nation*, calling upon secular authorities to support the reform of the church; and *The Freedom of a Christian*, defining the Christian life, justified through grace and by faith alone.

Called to appear before the Diet of Worms in 1521(*see* WORMS, DIET OF), Luther refused again to retract and, as a result, was banned together with his followers. Protected by his sovereign, **Frederick the Wise**, he found refuge at Wartburg Castle where he translated the New Testament (*see* BIBLE, MARTIN LUTHER'S TRANSLATION). This translation was not only of great religious and Reformation significance but it also established the modern German language. In 1522 he returned to Wittenberg and brought an end to the radical reforms in that city. He was involved in the reordering of church life and reform of **worship**. In addition to his conflicts with the Catholic church, he strongly and repeatedly criticized the theological and political views of radical reformers (e.g. the **Peasants' War**), **Ulrich Zwingli's** teaching on the **Lord's Supper,** and the teaching of **Erasmus of Rotterdam** on **free will**. Dismayed by his experiences during visitations to **congregations** of the lack of knowledge concerning the basics of Christian faith and life, his special concern was the **Christian education** of church people, **laity** as well as **pastors**. For this purpose, he wrote his *Small* and *Large Catechisms* in 1529 (*see* CATECHISMS OF LUTHER). As a kind of theological testament, Luther wrote what came soon to be called the *Smalcald Articles* in 1537. They and the *Catechisms* were received (*see* RECEPTION) by the churches as confessions of the church (*see* CONFESSIONS, LUTHERAN). While he was not primarily an organizer, his broad and lasting impact came from his extraordinary ability to combine creative and deep theological reflection with its down-to-earth pastoral and practical communication. Supported and cared for by his wife, **Katharina von Bora**, whom he married in 1525, his ideas and commitments were spread by an enormous publication activity (*see* LUTHER'S WORKS) and were carried to many European lands by his numerous pupils. Luther died on February 18, 1546, at Eisleben.

Luther considered himself an interpreter of Holy Scripture and a preacher of the **Word of God**. He restored to the lay people, both humble and of high estate, their dignity as mature and coresponsible members of the **church** and of civil society. He preached and taught the gracious justification of sinners and, thus, the liberation and consolation of burdened hearts and consciences. God's precious Gospel, communicated by the **Holy Spirit** through **Word** and **sacrament**, was praised by him incessantly as the center and fountain of Christian life and of the existence of the church. Gifted by an imaginative mastery of language, Luther wrote poems, **hymns**, and prayers of great poetic quality that were part of his rich literary output. Luther insisted on preserving inherited theological and ecclesiastical traditions wherever they expressed or served the Gospel, and he affirmed the necessity and dignity of secular institutions and vocations as instruments of God's sustaining purpose for humanity and **creation**. Through his diverse activities, Luther shaped the **piety**, the pastoral and theological orientation, and the cultural and social ethos of **Lutheranism**. Luther and his ideas have often been misrepresented and misused, but again and again rediscovered as a source of Lutheran identity in changing times and in very diverse contexts of worldwide Lutheranism (*see* LUTHER AS SEEN BY OTHERS). In recent decades Luther has received increasing attention by other Christian traditions. The highly competent Roman Catholic **Luther research** has especially led to a new appreciation of Luther as a "teacher of the church" beyond his Lutheran tribe. *See also* LUTHER IN THE ARTS; LUTHER RENAISSANCE. [G.G.]

LUTHERAN CHURCH. *See* INTRODUCTION.

LUTHERAN CHURCHES OF THE WORLD. *See* INTRODUCTION.

LUTHERAN CHURCH-MISSOURI SYNOD (LC–MS). At the end of the 20th century, the second largest and historically among the most theologically conservative of Lutheran bodies in the United States. The LC–MS was founded in 1847 by three groups of recent German immigrants. The first and largest group, led from Saxony by Martin Stephan, had settled in Perry County, Missouri, in 1839. After Stephan had been accused of episcopal ambitions and ethical indiscretions, he was replaced as leader by **Carl Ferdinand Wilhelm Walther**. The second group were Franconians sent to Michigan by **Johann Konrad Wilhelm Löhe** as immigrant communes and missionaries to the Chippewa. The third were the followers of Friedrich Wyneken, whose open letters back to Germany bewailed the conditions of German emigrants and the theological positions of American synods. From the start, the German Evangelical Lutheran Synod of Missouri, Ohio, and Other States was opposed to the unionism (*see* UNION) that had caused its members to flee Germany, and gathered under the banner of subscription to the ***Book of Concord*** as the pure and unadulterated explanation and presentation of the **Word of God**. Reacting against Stephan's authoritarianism and Löhe's high view of the **church** and **ordination**, the synod was proposed as a purely advisory body, with no authority over **congregations**.

The establishment and support of a parochial school has been an important ministry in many Missouri Synod congregations. Especially from the Civil War until World War I, they also served to preserve German language and culture, although the large number of African American members of the synod shows that this cultural emphasis was not entirely exclusive. Parochial elementary schools and cooperative high schools were soon joined by a nation-wide network of colleges to provide a formidable preparation for the body's seminaries. The number of members who attained great success in academia and society bear witness to the excellence of this system.

Under the forceful theological leadership of Walther, the synod held that **fellowship** between churches could only be based on complete theological agreement (*see* CONSENSUS). This position limited, but did not eliminate the synod's involvement in Lutheran cooperation. The LC–MS refused to join the General Council (*see* NORTH AMERICA, LUTHERAN CHURCHES IN), and in 1872, together with the Ohio, Wisconsin, Norwegian, and other synods, it founded the Synodical Conference. This body, however, was soon torn apart by the **predestination** controversy, in which Missouri took the position exactly opposite the Ohio Synod. The experience of cooperation in times of war and other emergencies, however, led to closer and closer connections. In the 1960s the LC–MS entered into altar and pulpit fellowship with the American Lutheran Church (ALC) and joined the Lutheran Council in the USA. These relationships came to an end with the **ordination of women** by the ALC, the establishment of the Evangelical Lutheran Church in America, and the internal controversies within the LC–MS of the 1970s.

These controversies included a struggle between conservative forces, led by Jacob A. O. Preuss, and moderate forces, led by John Tietjen. When, in 1972, Tietjen was deposed as president of Concordia Seminary, and most students and faculty resigned to form Christ Seminary in Exile, the synod was split by the largest and most painful schism of its history, when about 100,000 members left to form the Association of Evangelical Lutheran Churches. Since that time, the Lutheran Church-Missouri Synod has continued its historical commitment to the inerrancy of Scripture and the Lutheran confessions (*see* CONFESSIONS, LUTHERAN). It has also committed itself publicly and institutionally to church growth and to opposition to abortion. In 1999 the LC–MS had 2.6 million members. It is related through the **International Lutheran Council** to a number of small Lutheran churches in other parts of the world. [M.O.]

LUTHERAN FOUNDATION FOR INTER-CONFESSIONAL RE-SEARCH. *See* INTER-CONFESSIONAL RESEARCH.

LUTHERAN-ANGLICAN RELATIONS AND DIALOGUE. Relations and official conversations between Anglican and Lutheran churches. Newer studies have affirmed the many affinities—theological, spiritual, and social—between the **Reformation** on the European Continent and in England despite the differences in the implementation of reforms. At an early stage of the Reformation period, there were numerous direct contacts between the Lutheran movement and the emerging Church of England, the mother church of the Anglican Communion. Future leaders of the Church of England studied the works of **Martin Luther** during the 1520s. The translation of the English Bible by William Tyndale, begun in 1523 and completed by Miles Coverdale in 1535, was influenced by Luther's translation and terminology. Several Lutheran **church orders** were used for the compilation of the first (**Anglican**) *Book of Common Prayer* in 1549. A first dialogue between Anglican and Lutheran theologians, including Robert Barnes, Martin Luther, and **Philipp Melanchthon**, took place at **Wittenberg** in 1536 and agreed upon the *Wittenberg Articles* based on the *Augsburg Confession*. The articles continued to have an influence throughout a series of English articles of faith leading up to the *Articles of Religion* of 1571 ("Thirty-nine Articles"). However, these contacts between 1520 and 1550 gave way to separate theological and ecclesiastical developments that, over the centuries, created considerable differences between the Anglican and Lutheran traditions, reinforced by different political, cultural, and intellectual developments in England and on the European continent from the 17th to the 20th centuries.

The **ecumenical movement** in the 20th century, as well as increased exchange, liturgical revival, independence of former **mission** churches in Africa and Asia, recognition of common missionary and social tasks in countries where Anglicans and Lutherans live side by side, and the growing acknowledgment of many theological affinities led to a renewal of Anglican-Lutheran relations in the 20th century and a remarkable movement toward closer **fellowship** at the end of that century. Formal Lutheran-Anglican dialogues began in 1908 with conversations between the Church of England and the (Lutheran) Church of Sweden and, after 1930, with the other Scandinavian and Baltic Lutheran churches. Inaugurating the recent phase of dialogue was the Episcopal-Lutheran dialogue in the United States from 1969–1991. It led in 1982 to an agreement on Interim Eucharistic Sharing, and its recommendation for full **communion** between the Evangelical Lutheran Church in America and the Episcopal Church (including Lutheran acceptance of the historic succession of **bishops**) was approved by the Episcopalians in 1997 and by the Lutherans in 1999. This represents a remarkable ecumenical achievement.

A first round of Anglican-Lutheran International Conversations in 1970–1972, authorized by the Lambeth Conference (of all Anglican bishops) and the **Lutheran World Federation**, is continued by a new Anglican-Lutheran International Commission since 1986. The international dialogue has provided a stimulus for Anglican-Lutheran conversations in several regions and countries: Australia 1972–1984 and renewed after 1988; Europe 1980–1982; Africa, where consultation since 1992 led, in 1999, to the proposal to establish a Pan-African Anglican-Lutheran Commission; Canada, aiming at full communion in 2001; France, since 1994; Church of England and Lutheran, United, and Reformed churches in Germany, resulting in the 1988 *Meissen Common Statement* for eucharistic sharing and closer contacts; and, finally, the dialogue between the Anglican churches of Great Britain and Ireland and the Nordic and Baltic Lutheran churches that, on the basis of the *Porvoo Common Statement* of 1992, established full communion in 1996 between the four Anglican and six of the eight participating Lutheran churches. This significant achievement and the worldwide growth in Anglican-Lutheran fellowship in general is one of the outstanding features of Lutheran history in the 20th century. *See also* DIALOGUES, BILATERAL. [G.G.]

LUTHERAN-BAPTIST RELATIONS AND DIALOGUE. Relations and official conversations between Lutheran and Baptist churches. Modern Baptist churches have their origin in the 17th century, in the radical separatist movement in England that advocated separation from the state church, the Church of England, because it could not be purified according to the ideals of the separatists. In addition to their emphasis on strict separation of **church and state**, **religious freedom**, and a voluntary, congregationalist concept of the **church**, the separatists also came to reject infant **baptism** as contrary to Holy Scripture. In 1608 a whole refugee-congregation from England was rebaptized in Holland as believers, and in 1611 the first Baptist church was established in England.

Though not direct descendants of the **Anabaptists** of the 16th century, Baptists generally consider themselves spiritual descendants of the Anabaptists. At this point their relationship with the Lutheran tradition becomes relevant. **Martin Luther** and the Lutheran confessions (*see* CONFESSIONS, LUTHERAN) strongly criticized the Anabaptist movement because of its rejection of infant baptism and of the participation by Christians in public functions and responsibilities, and its claim to direct inspiration by the **Holy Spirit**. The *Formula of Concord* states: "We reject and condemn the erroneous and heretical teaching of the Anabaptists which cannot be suffered or tolerated in the churches or in the body politic or in domestic society" (article 12). Persecution and discrimination of Anabaptists by secular authorities were the consequence. Accordingly, Lutherans and the direct or spiritual descendants of the Anabaptists lived for centuries under the cloud—generally ignored by Lutherans—of their painful **Reformation** heritage. But there were also other deep differences between them, especially concerning the Baptist refusal of infant baptism and the practice of many Baptist churches, up to the present day, to baptize a second time converts to Baptist churches, a practice that other churches generally regard as rebaptism.

The new situation in the 20th century created by the **ecumenical movement** and the Baptist concern that the Lutheran condemnations of the Anabaptists in the 16th century be reconsidered led to first contacts between the Baptist World Alliance (founded in 1905) and the **Lutheran World Federation** in 1975. Plans for a Baptist-Lutheran dialogue were developed and a Baptist-Lutheran Joint Commission, appointed by the two world bodies, met from 1986–1989. Its final report was able to describe common ground in the areas of **authority**, baptism, and the **church**, but also noted continuing deeper differences, among them the still unresolved issue of different understandings of the relationship between baptism and **faith** and its consequences for baptismal practice. The report stated that Lutherans should mention in connection with their confessions that the condemnations of the Reformation era no longer apply in Lutheran-Baptist relations today. Among national Baptist-Lutheran dialogues, one took place in the United States from 1979–1981 and two in the two German states where the issue of the condemnations as part of German history was more urgently felt. In the Federal Republic of Germany, a dialogue was held from 1980–1981 and in the German Democratic Republic from 1982–1983. The dialogues and other encounters have helped to reestablish Baptist-Lutheran relations in many places, as well as creating better mutual understanding and respect. *See also* DIALOGUES, BILATERAL. [G.G.]

LUTHERANISM. *See* INTRODUCTION.

LUTHERAN-METHODIST RELATIONS AND DIALOGUE. Relations and official conversations between Lutheran and Methodist churches. The Lutheran and Methodist traditions have very different origins. Lutheranism emerged through the process of the **Reformation** in the 16th century, considering itself as the reformed and renewed **church** of Jesus Christ in continuity with the church since the time of the apostles. Its identity was shaped by its distinction from the late medieval Roman Catholic Church, the Radical, and in part also **Reformed** traditions and by its positive restatement of the biblical **faith** in the Lutheran confessions (*see* CONFESSIONS, LUTHERAN). Methodism, too, originated as a reform movement, but two hundred years later, in the 18th century, and within the completely different and much less controversial context of **Anglicanism**. It was shaped by movements of awakening and renewal within the Church of England, by the evangelistic impulse to spread scriptural Christianity to all people, by its reaction against the developing unbelief of the **Enlightenment** era, and by its social concerns in the wake of massive human problems created by industrialization and urbanization.

Charles Wesley, the great hymnwriter (over 6,000 hymns), and **John Wesley**, the organizer and theologian, formed early Methodism spiritually and structurally. Like the Lutheran movement they did not want to create a new church but developments both in the Methodist movement and in the Church of England led to the emergence of independent Methodist churches from the late 18th century onwards. By means of migration and very active missionary outreach, Methodism moved beyond England to North America, Africa, Asia, Australia, and Latin America. Returning migrants from North America brought Methodism to Continental Europe where small Methodist churches were formed as Free Churches in predominantly Lutheran or Roman Catholic lands. The Wesley brothers were influenced by writings of **Martin Luther**—his preface to Paul's Letter to the Romans made a deep impact on John—and by Lutheran and Moravian (*see* MORAVIAN CHURCH) **Pietism**. This explains close similarities between Lutheran and Methodist teaching on the authority of Holy Scripture (*see* BIBLE, AUTHORITY OF), **justification**, the **church**, and the **means of grace**.

Methodists and Lutherans have lived side by side in many countries, but on the whole there have been no closer contacts and relationships. A breakthrough in furthering Lutheran-Methodist relationships came with new encounters within the **ecumenical movement** and mainly by the initiation of international bilateral conversations between the **Lutheran World Federation** and the Methodist World Council from 1977/79 until 1984. Despite remaining differences, basic agreements on important **doctrines** allowed the proposal that the participating churches take steps to declare and establish pulpit and altar **fellowship**. Such a step was taken in Germany after the conclusion of a Lutheran-Methodist dialogue in the Federal Republic of Germany in 1980–1982 and 1985, when pulpit and altar fellowship between the two churches was declared in 1986/87. The report enabling such a step was also accepted by the United and **Reformed** churches in the Federal Republic and in 1990 by the churches in the German Democratic Republic. A similar decision has been taken in Norway in 1996. In the United States, the Evangelical Lutheran Church in America is in dialogue with two Methodist churches, the African Methodist Episcopal Church (since 1992) and the United Methodist Church (third round since 1999). In other countries, too, Lutherans and Methodists have greatly improved their relationships. *See also* DIALOGUES, BILATERAL. [G.G.]

LUTHERAN-ORTHODOX RELATIONS AND DIALOGUE. Relations and official conversations between Lutheran and Orthodox churches. The Lutheran **Reformation** seemed to entertain a rather positive picture of the Eastern Orthodox tradition. **Martin Luther** expressed interest in that tradition and the Lutheran confessions (*see* CONFESSIONS, LUTHERAN) regarded the Orthodox churches somehow as allies because of their strong biblical and **patristic** emphasis and their rejection of the **papacy**. **Philipp Melanchthon** tried to establish contacts with the Orthodox by his attempt in

1559 to send a letter and a Greek translation of the *Augsburg Confession* to the Ecumenical Patriarch at Constantinople. Some time later, between 1573 and 1581, Patriarch Jeremiah II and several Lutheran theologians at Tübingen exchanged letters on controversial theological topics, such as invocation of **saints**, monasticism, **tradition**, **faith** and **good works**, **sacraments**, and the procession of the **Holy Spirit** (from the Father, or from the Father *and* the Son, the *filioque*). In the patriarch's last letter the Lutherans are described as heretics, and the attempt came to a close. After the 16th century there have been occasional Lutheran-Orthodox encounters in countries where they lived side by side, such as in Finland, Romania, and Russia.

It took the **ecumenical movement** and the growing Orthodox **diaspora** in western Europe and North and South America to bring Lutherans and Orthodox into closer contact. Theological exchange and study at each other's theological institutions, encounters at ecumenical meetings, and Lutheran support of Orthodox institutions and migrant communities led to better mutual knowledge and appreciation. A number of national and regional dialogues have sought to grasp something of each other's different modes of thinking and to discover the common ground of faith behind these different spiritual worlds. The first official dialogue was initiated in 1959 between the Evangelical Church in Germany (Ger *Evangelische Kirche in Deutschland* [EKD]), the federation of Lutheran, United, and **Reformed** churches of that country, and the Russian Orthodox Church—a dialogue also inspired by efforts at German-Russian reconciliation. The dialogue has been most productive in its output of theological papers and reports. Ten years later, in 1969, the EKD began a dialogue with the Ecumenical Patriarchate (until 1994), and again 10 years later, in 1979, the EKD began a dialogue with the Romanian Orthodox Church (until 1991). During the period of the (political) division of Germany, the Lutheran and United churches in the German Democratic Republic were engaged in a dialogue with the Russian Orthodox Church (1974–1990) and the Bulgarian Orthodox Church (1978–1992). The dialogue between the Evangelical Lutheran Church of Finland with the Russian Orthodox Church from 1970 to 1992 is of particular importance because of the presence of an autonomous Orthodox Church in Finland and the attempts to include results of Finnish **Luther research** in this dialogue. Other national Lutheran-Orthodox dialogues were conducted in the United States from 1967–1969 and then from 1983–1989, followed by a third round since 1994; in Finland from 1989–1993; and in Sweden where there are also conversations with Oriental Orthodox churches.

From 1978–1980 a Lutheran dialogue team, appointed by the **Lutheran World Federation**, and an Orthodox dialogue team representing all autonomous Orthodox churches, prepared in separate meetings an international dialogue. The first meeting of the international Lutheran-Orthodox

Joint Commission took place in 1981. Up to now, the commission has agreed on statements on *Divine Revelation* (1985), *Scripture and Tradition* (1987), and *The Canon and the Inspiration of Holy Scriptures* (1989). The dialogue continues, and it has, together with other encounters and efforts, significantly contributed to the nurturing of Lutheran-Orthodox relations in several parts of the world and enriched Lutheran theological thinking and spiritual life. *See also* DIALOGUES, BILATERAL. [G.G.]

LUTHERAN-REFORMED RELATIONS AND DIALOGUE. Relations and official conversations between Lutheran and Reformed/Presbyterian churches. Of the four major **Reformation** movements—**Anglican**, Lutheran, Radical, and Reformed—the Lutheran and Reformed ones were most closely related during the first decades of the Reformation. Geographical proximity in central Europe and theological affinities in such fundamental concerns as the preeminence of the **Gospel**, the authority of Scripture (*see* BIBLE, AUTHORITY OF), and the central significance of **justification**, created an awareness of being part of a common reforming movement despite obvious differences. These differences, especially between **Martin Luther** and **Ulrich Zwingli,** which focused on the understanding of the **Lord's Supper** and its Christological presuppositions (*see* CHRISTOLOGY), led to growing estrangement between these two wings of the Reformation. Several attempts to preserve or reestablish the unity of the Reformation movement failed, the most famous encounter being the Marburg Colloquy of 1529. The initial estrangement between the Lutheran and Reformed traditions further increased by their separate developments and in each taking root in some parts of Europe where the other partner was not present, the Reformed, for example, in parts of France and in Scotland, the Lutherans, for example, in Scandinavia. Still, an awareness of common Reformation roots continued in many places in Europe where friendly relations, including eucharistic hospitality, were entertained during post-Reformation centuries. Such an awareness also marked certain immigrant groups in America in the 19th century who formed a joint association in 1841 and about one hundred years later the Evangelical and Reformed Church, now part of the United Church of Christ.

But 19th-century **Neo-Lutheranism** with its emphasis on Lutheran identity in distinction from the Reformed tradition and the reaction of Lutheran groups to the imposed Prussian Union of 1817 (*see* UNION) increased among many people a sense of Lutheran-Reformed separation, especially in North America. In other parts of the world, Lutheran and Presbyterian **mission** churches became independent churches in the 1960s without the historical consciousness of common origins in 16th-century Europe and, accordingly, without closer mutual relations. In the 20th century, the **ecumenical movement** and increased contacts brought Lutheran and Reformed/Presbyterian churches closer together again. In Europe, a dialogue between the Lutheran, United, and Reformed churches led to the **Leuenberg Agreement** of 1973 that serves now as the basis of full church fellowship (without merger) between most Reformation churches in Europe. A similar step toward establishing full **communion** was undertaken in 1997 by the Evangelical Lutheran Church in America and the Presbyterian Church (U.S.A.), the United Church of Christ, and the Reformed Church in America. An international dialogue sponsored by the **Lutheran World Federation** and the World Alliance of Reformed Churches took place from 1970–1975 and from 1985–1988. It is now being continued by a Lutheran-Reformed International Working Group, and cooperation between the two world bodies has increased. Outside Europe and North America, Lutheran-Reformed relations have also developed in the Netherlands and Indonesia. *See also* DIALOGUES, BILATERAL. [G.G.]

LUTHERAN-ROMAN CATHOLIC DIALOGUE. The theological dialogue between the **Lutheran World Federation** (LWF) and the Roman Catholic Church as well as dialogues on national level. In light of the tragic historical heritage of the **Reformation**, many Lutherans consider overcoming the division between the Lutheran and Roman Catholic Churches a primary responsibility (*see* ROMAN CATHOLIC CHURCH AND LUTHERANISM). Accordingly, the first bilateral initiative of the LWF was with the Roman Catholic Church in the form of the Roman Catholic-Lutheran Working Group in 1965 and 1966, which prepared an official dialogue between the LWF and the Catholic church. The Joint Lutheran-Roman Catholic Study Commission on "The Gospel and the Church" (1967–1971) was a first experiment in **bilateral dialogue** methodology. The wide range of topics covered in its report, commonly called the *Malta Report* (1972), served as an assurance that such a dialogue would be fruitful and served as a basis for further conversations.

A second Roman Catholic-Lutheran Joint Commission, meeting from 1973 to 1984, produced a whole series of reports that received considerable attention because of their far-reaching agreements and convergences: *The Eucharist* (1980); *Ways to Community* (1981); *All under One Christ* (1980), on the occasion of the 450th anniversary of the *Augsburg Confession*; *The Ministry, the Church* (1982); *Martin Luther—Witness to Jesus Christ* (1982), as a common appreciation on the 500th anniversary of **Martin Luther's** birth; and *Facing Unity: Models, Forms and Phases of Catholic-Lutheran Church Fellowship* (1985). A third Lutheran-Roman Catholic Joint Commission met from 1986–1993 and published the report *Church and Justification: Understanding the Church in the Light of the Doctrine of Justification* (1994). The fourth Lutheran-Roman Catholic Commission on Unity began in 1995 its work on the **apostolicity** of the **church**. The international

Catholic-Lutheran dialogue has probably been the most productive of all bilateral dialogues and has greatly contributed to an appreciation of each other's theological traditions and a growing exchange between them.

The impact of the international Lutheran-Roman Catholic dialogue was reinforced by two important national dialogues. The most intensive one has been conducted in the United States from 1965 onwards and is still going on (in 2001). Here, Lutherans and Catholics have addressed issues, often accompanied by special studies, like the **eucharist**, the **ministry**, the role and place of **Mary**, Scripture and **tradition**, and the most difficult issue, namely **papacy**, in their reports on *Papal Primacy and the Universal Church* (1974) and *Teaching Authority and Infallibility in the Church* (1980). The carefully prepared text on *Justification by Faith* (1985) seeks to help overcome the deep Reformation split over this fundamental issue. In Germany, the Ecumenical Working Group of **Protestant** (i.e., mostly Lutheran) and Catholic Theologians, whose unofficial and daring origins go back to 1945, has published, among other texts, *The Condemnations of the Reformation Era—Do They Still Divide?* (1990). The dialogue between the United Evangelical Lutheran Church of Germany and the Roman Catholic Bishop's Conference of Germany from 1976–1983 published a comprehensive report on *Church Fellowship in Word and Sacrament* in 1984. Lutheran-Roman Catholic dialogues are also conducted in Argentina, Australia, Brazil, Norway, and Sweden. Collectively, they are a sign and instrument of growing Lutheran-Catholic **fellowship**.

This growth in fellowship will be further encouraged and sustained by the *Joint Declaration on the Doctrine of Justification* (1999). This text was formulated by a Lutheran-Roman Catholic Working Group on the basis of the results of the international dialogue and the dialogues in Germany and in the United States. It has been accepted by the great majority of the member churches of the LWF and by the Roman Catholic Church and was signed in a festive worship on Reformation Day, October 31, 1999, at Augsburg, Germany. So far, this represents the most significant step forward in Lutheran-Catholic relations. [G.G.]

LUTHERAN UNION MOVEMENT. Movement of individual Lutheran churches to form united Lutheran churches. The most outstanding historical example of this movement is in North America. Here, over 20 Lutheran churches in the early 19th century, defined by both ethnic background and regional location, undertook the first steps towards closer affiliation in the General Synod of 1820 and the General Council of 1867. In the 20th century, after a series of smaller mergers, several Lutheran churches united to form the American Lutheran Church in 1960 and the Lutheran Church in America in 1962. These two and the Association of Evangelical Lutheran Churches (1976), created in 1987 the Evangelical Lutheran Church in

America. A similar process took place in Canada. In the United States, the more conservative Lutheran churches came together in the **Lutheran Church-Missouri Synod** (1847–1947) and the Evangelical Lutheran Wisconsin Synod (1917).

Eight of the 10 Lutheran churches in Germany founded the United Evangelical Lutheran Church if Germany in 1948. A similar community of (organizationally independent) Lutheran churches is the United Evangelical Lutheran Church in India (1975) with 10 member churches. The two Lutheran churches in Australia united in 1966 to form the Lutheran Church of Australia. In former mission areas, churches that had been related to different foreign **mission societies** came together and formed federations of Lutheran churches or founded united churches, for example, in Madagascar (1950), New Guinea (1957), Cameroon (1960), and Tanzania (1963).

On the world level, movement toward Lutheran **unity** began with the activities of the General Evangelical Lutheran Conference (founded in Germany in 1868 and soon becoming more international) and the **National Lutheran Council** in the United States (1919). Both sent out invitations to the first **Lutheran World Convention** at Eisenach in 1923. After the following two conventions in 1929 and 1935 the **Lutheran World Federation** was founded in 1947. [G.G.]

LUTHERAN WORLD CONVENTION (LWC). First worldwide organizational structure of Lutheran churches. The Lutheran churches were the last grouping of churches with the same confession and **tradition** to establish a worldwide structure. The impetus for such a step came from the **National Lutheran Council** in the United States. In 1923 the 144 representatives of Lutheran churches in 22 countries assembled at Eisenach, Germany, to found the Lutheran World Convention. There, the **unity** of world **Lutheranism** was affirmed on the basis of the common confession (*see* CONFESSIONS, LUTHERAN). Theological and **ecumenical** questions were discussed, forms of cooperation (**diaspora, mission,** support of small churches, and so on) were initiated, and an Executive Committee was formed. The second Lutheran World Convention took place in 1929 at Copenhagen and the third one in 1935 at Paris. After World War II the LWC participated in massive aid programs for suffering people in Europe (*see* EMERGENCY AND DEVELOPMENT AID). This experience of solidarity and emerging closer relations among Lutheran churches led, in 1946, to the decision of the Executive Committee of the LWC to transform the LWC into the **Lutheran World Federation.** [G.G.]

LUTHERAN WORLD FEDERATION (LWF). The worldwide organization and **communion** of Lutheran churches. The **Lutheran World Convention** (LWC), founded in 1923, had strengthened the awareness of fellowship among the Lutheran churches. In 1946 the Executive Committee of the LWC decided to transform this body into a Lutheran World Federation. One year later (1947) in Lund, Sweden, the 184 delegates of 49 Lutheran churches established the Lutheran World Federation, the youngest among the **Christian World Communions**. The delegates at the assembly in Lund accepted the constitution of the LWF. In its "doctrinal basis," the constitution refers to Holy Scripture as the decisive norm and to the three Ecumenical **Creeds** and the Lutheran confessions (*see* CONFESSIONS, LUTHERAN), especially the *Augsburg Confession* and **Martin Luther's** *Small Catechism*, as pure expositions of the **Word of God**. While the constitution cautiously described the "nature" of the LWF as a "free association of Lutheran churches," the revised constitution of 1990 defined the LWF as a "communion of churches which confess the Triune **God**, agree in the proclamation of the Word of God and are united in pulpit and altar fellowship."

This change of self-understanding is due to the growing awareness of being part of a worldwide communion of churches, an awareness enabled by the LWF through interchurch relationships, mutual sharing and solidarity, **bilateral dialogues**, and other ecumenical activities (also supported by the LWF–related **Lutheran Foundation for Inter-Confessional Research**). The LWF also engages in common studies, joint involvement in social issues (like apartheid, **human rights**, and the role of **women**), support of educational and **mission** work, communication activities, and important programs of **emergency and development aid**. These widespread activities (including several hundred development, mission, and communication projects and programs) are carried out by the staff of the LWF in its headquarters in Geneva, Switzerland, which houses the general-secretariat and the Departments for Theology and Studies, World Service, and Mission and Development.

The highest decision-making body of the LWF is its assembly, held normally every six years: Lund 1947; Hannover 1952; Minneapolis 1957; Helsinki 1963; Evian 1970; Dar es Salaam 1977; Budapest 1984; Curitiba 1990; and Hong Kong 1997. Between assemblies, the LWF is governed by a council that meets annually. In 1999 the LWF had 128 member churches in 69 countries representing over 59 million of the world's 63 million Lutherans. The work of the LWF is widely appreciated by the Lutheran churches and also by governmental and international development and aid agencies. Through its bilateral ecumenical dialogues with other worldwide communions, including the **Roman Catholic Church**, the LWF has contributed significantly to the overcoming of divisions within Christianity, thereby assuming an important ecumenical role. [G.G.]

LUTHER AS SEEN BY OTHERS. The portrayal of **Martin Luther** by secular authors. The complex personality of Luther and the impact of his work have attracted a wealth of interpretations of his person and thinking throughout the centuries. These interpretations reflect more the cultural, social, and political spirit of a particular time and author than that of the genuine Luther. Modern **Luther research** is seeking to liberate the true Luther from the Luther of tradition, misunderstanding, and misrepresentation, while being conscious that the Luther of contemporary investigation will still be only an approximation to the original.

During the 16th and 17th centuries, Luther was generally highly esteemed in the **Protestant** world, while the **Roman Catholic** world was marked from the beginning and far into the 20th century by the extremely negative depiction of the reformer in a first Luther biography by Johannes Cochläus (1479–1552) in which Luther was condemned as **antichrist**. This opened up a tradition that considered Luther as the destroyer of the unity of Western Christendom, a traitor of the true **faith**, and a morally inferior creature. In the **Enlightenment** period of the 18th century, Luther was greeted as the great liberator from the **papacy**, ecclesiastical power, the yoke of **tradition**, and the bondage of **conscience**. But he was also criticized as being as irrational as his Roman opponents (Voltaire) or, though having opened the way to **reason** and humanity, not having gone far enough (Frederick the Great). In the context of the 18th-and 19th-century Romantic movement, Luther was praised as an artistic, literary genius (Friedrich Nietzsche), molder of a beautiful language (Heinrich Heine), and the great revolutionary hero of history (Thomas Carlyle), who was at the root of a process that led to a free and democratic America.

Quite contrary to this last American evaluation, Luther was co-opted by German nationalism in the 19th century as the German hero and representative of the German national spirit and temperament. This one-sided portrayal was followed by another one-sided one in the 20th century, presented by a few historians and writers during and after World War II: Luther as initiating a development of authoritarian ideology and slavish obedience that finally led to Adolf Hitler's Nazism. Marxism, on the other hand, developed its own image of Luther as an early bourgeois revolutionary (Friedrich Engels) who initiated a revolutionary movement, but did not recognize and accept its inherent social consequences. Finally, the complex personality of Luther became a fertile ground for Freudian psychoanalytical investigation, most well known by Erik H. Erikson's reflections on Luther's childhood experiences, traits of his character, and his lifelong illness and periods of depression.

Contrary to all these highly diverse portrayals of Luther, there has been a constant and general appreciation by many great personalities of Luther's contribution to the renewal of the German language and to literature in general, to music and the **arts**, **education**, **marriage**, and the moral life. Luther belongs to the most commented on and written about personalities in history. *See also* LUTHER IN THE ARTS. [G.G.]

LUTHER IN THE ARTS. The portrayal of **Martin Luther** in the different art forms. The great reformer was also an accomplished writer, poet, and musician, and he became the object of the arts in a grand way: from statues in town squares to small pictures in village churches, from grandiose altar paintings in large churches to commemorative postal stamps. It is claimed that Luther is one of the most frequently portrayed personalities of world history. The "Luther Hall" at **Wittenberg** alone has collected over 2,400 portraits of Luther. Well known (and valuable) is the series of Luther portraits made by his friend **Lucas Cranach** and Cranach's son from 1520 throughout his life, and thereafter copied in Cranach's workshop. Cranach also created the famous altar paintings at Weimar and Wittenberg that show Luther with his colleagues, as well as a famous portrait of Luther's wife, **Katharina von Bora**. Luther's portraits by Cranach and many others were used as "propaganda weapons" on leaflets and brochures during the **Reformation** battles, as were caricatures of Luther by his opponents.

Other famous artists like Hans Baldung Grien, Albrecht Altdorfer, Hans Holbein, and in our time Lovis Corinth and Ernst Barlach, portrayed Luther. These artists, together with hundreds of lesser known or unknown ones, portrayed Luther in paintings, copper etchings, wood carvings, medallions, metal plates, clay tiles, stained glass windows, tapestries, in innumerable sculptures and on monuments in stone, marble, and bronze. Even in his own time, these portrayals of Luther began to reflect certain images imposed on his personality that became typical from the 17th until 19th centuries: hero, rebel, Knight St. George, church father, teacher of the nation, the mighty protesting **Protestant**. Recent portrayals of Luther are more sober again. The reformer has also been a frequent subject of many authors in **literature** and drama, from Hans Sachs (1523) to August Strindberg (1915) and John Osborn (1963), and in documentary films. [G.G.]

LUTHER RENAISSANCE. General term for a 20th-century movement of intensive studies on **Martin Luther's theology** and its relevance. The late 19th century saw a broader "back to Luther" movement in **Protestant** Europe, initiated by liberal theologians such as Albrecht Ritschl (1822–1889). This led in the 20th century to a rapidly expanding number of studies on Luther that sought to spell out the relevance of his thinking for the modern world. Aided by the progress of the new critical Weimar Edition of Luther's works, these studies were based on an examination of the sources and intended to show Luther's significance for European intellectual history as the one who helped to usher in modernity (against Ernst Troeltsch's thesis of 1911/12 that Luther and **Lutheranism** had been still essentially medieval).

The most outstanding pioneer of Luther studies in the context of the Luther renaissance was **Karl Holl** who broke, like many others, with **Liberalism** under the impact of World War I. His school of Luther studies, together with other Luther scholars, and despite their questionable national-political views, brought Luther back to the center of serious theological and historical enquiry. A similar and highly important school of **Luther research** developed in Sweden, represented by theologians of the **Lund School** such as Anders Nygren, Ragnar Bring, and Gustaf Aulén. They used "motive research" as methodology to understand Luther's theology. Also in North America a dawn of Luther studies began during the first decades of the 20th century. The movement of **dialectical theology** contributed to the new interest in Luther by its return to fundamental **Reformation** convictions, as did the beginnings of a change in **Roman Catholic** interpretations of the Reformation and of Luther, inaugurated by Joseph Lortz's influential *Reformation in Germany* (1939, English translation 1968). The studies in this wider framework of the Luther renaissance were continued with new methods and orientations by the broad process of Luther research in the second part of the 20th century. *See also* LUTHER'S WORKS. [G.G.]

LUTHER RESEARCH. Scholarly investigation of the life, work, and impact of **Martin Luther**. There has been ongoing research related to Luther throughout the centuries since his death. Motivated by their specific presuppositions and interests, the 19th-century movements of Romanticism, **Liberalism**, **Neo-Lutheranism**, and nationalism saw a remarkable resurgence of studies on (their image of) Luther. This interest continued with new methods and postliberal orientations in the 20th century within the broader framework of the **Luther Renaissance**. The new phase of Luther research since the 1920s, led (especially after 1950) to an ever increasing number of studies on the date of Luther's personal **Reformation** discovery or breakthrough, on practically all major themes of his theology from his concept of **God** to his social **ethics**, on Luther as interpreter of Holy Scripture, and on the relation of his **theology** to late medieval theology, nominalism, Renaissance, mysticism, **Augustine**, **Humanism**, and the radical Reformation. Several new biographies of Luther and comprehensive surveys of his life and theology have appeared.

Contemporary Luther research is marked, after a period of highly polemical **Roman Catholic** works on Luther's person and work, by a considerable number of significant and positive contributions by Roman Catholic scholars, and by works of secular historians. Luther research is international and is underlined by the series of International Congresses on Luther Research held, since 1956, every five or six years under the auspices of the **Lutheran World Federation**. The international Luther bibliography (published in the *Lutherjahrbuch* since 1957) listing each year several hundred (and occasionally over one thousand) titles, is only one indication of the extent and importance of Luther research today. [G.G.]

LUTHER ROSE. The seal internationally recognized as a central symbol of **Martin Luther** and Lutherans, chosen by Luther himself, and explained in a letter of July 8, 1530, to Lazarus Spengler. At the center is a black cross, presenting the suffering Christ underwent and that Christians continue to undergo. This cross is set within a red heart, showing that **faith** grasps this crucified Savior, and that the **cross** does not destroy, but keeps the believer alive. The heart itself is set within a white rose, symbolizing the joy of the redeemed. This joy is also reflected, joined by hope, in the blue background. The whole is surrounded by a gold ring, which symbolizes heaven. [M.O.]

LUTHER SOCIETIES. Associations whose goal is to further the knowledge of **Martin Luther** and his **theology** as well as to support Lutheran **diaspora** churches. The second half of the 19th century saw the foundation of numerous Luther-associations. One type of association was concerned with the erection of monuments of the reformer. The other type, influenced by the **Awakening** and **Neo-Lutheranism**, tried to assist Lutheran emigrants in North and South America and in Australia, as well as Lutheran diaspora churches in eastern Europe. These aid associations united in 1932 to form the Martin Luther Federation (Ger *Martin-Luther-Bund*) that today is a major German support organization of Lutheran churches in Eastern Europe and in Brazil.

A more scholarly purpose is pursued by the Luther Association in Germany (Ger *Luther Gesellschaft*), founded in 1918, and by the Luther-Agricola-Association in Finland, founded in 1841. These associations seek to disseminate the results of research on Luther and the **Reformation** and Lutheran systematic studies through publications and conferences. *See also* AGRICOLA, MIKAEL; LUTHER IN THE ARTS; LUTHER RESEARCH. [G.G.]

LUTHER'S THEOLOGY. Nature and main aspects of **Martin Luther's** theology. The Lutheran **Reformation** was led by Luther and by several other reformers, even though he was its most important and influential personality, mainly because of the depth and convincing power of his theological thinking. Luther expressed his **theology** through a great diversity of forms: **sermons**, lectures, disputations, pamphlets, letters, appeals, public utterances, catechisms, articles of **faith**, **hymns**, and, of course, theological treatises. He was a biblical and contextual theologian in the service of the **church**. His theological reflections were based on Scriptural interpretation, related to his own personal struggle of faith, developed in critique and controversy both against late medieval **Scholasticism** and church and the radical reformers. His theological work was oriented toward serving the faith of the people and of the church. The nature of his theology explains why Luther has not left us with a systematic and comprehensive summary of his theology. Rather, his theology reflects developments and differing emphases according to changing contexts. Thus, Luther has provided work for generations of Luther scholars and publishing houses (*see* LUTHER RESEARCH).

Theological influences that helped shaped the thinking of the young professor of biblical interpretation (since 1512) include the tradition of his own Augustinian Order, most prominently **Augustine** himself, as well as German **mysticism**, **Humanism** with its new tools for biblical study, and Luther's own biblical studies in preparation for his lectures. These influences contributed to his "Reformation breakthrough" in his existential struggle with the late medieval practice of penance in search of a gracious **God**. This breakthrough occurred in a process of reflection and clarification between 1515 and 1518 (scholars propose either 1515/16 or 1517/18), and it consisted in the recognition of God's **justification** of the sinner by **grace** alone and by **faith** alone. Accordingly, Luther later declared (1532) the center of his theology to be the human person under the judgment of **sin** and the justifying God and Savior. This emphasis on justification and **salvation** was provoked by the late medieval sacramental system against which Luther reacted and which led to a certain preoccupation with the third article of the creed, that is, the issues of faith, salvation, **sacraments**, church, and the Christian life. This also shaped Luther's theology as a pastoral theology, always related to the salvation, consolation, and new life of people. The norm of his theology is Holy Scripture as the authoritative witness to the **Word of God** or the **Gospel**. Here, Luther makes a distinction between the text of Scripture, the book, and its center, the Gospel. The supreme authority of Scripture is combined with the appeal to **tradition** (e.g., the church fathers) and the right use of **reason**, as long as these secondary authorities do not contradict Scripture.

Anthropology. There is the basic conviction that human religious efforts, reason, and especially the human will are not able to contribute to justification or cooperate with divine grace. In matters of salvation, the human will is in bondage to sin, which Luther affirmed against **Erasmus of Rotterdam**. And sin, inherited since the Fall and primarily understood as revolt against God or "failure to fear, **love**, and trust in God above all things," remains a permanent human condition in the life of the baptized, though its domination has been overcome through Christ.

Christian Life. In their daily life, Christians practice the implications of their justification by being free people, liberated from the burden of trying to secure or contribute to their salvation, and also liberated to serve God and their neighbors. Continually strengthened in their faith through Word, sacrament, and prayer, Christians are called and enabled to do true **good works** in love to their neighbors and as cooperators in God's sustaining work for **creation** and humanity. In this service, they are guided by God's commandments (the so-called "third use" of the law). They live out their lives in the three "estates" to which they are assigned by God: **marriage** and occupation, government and public life, and the **ministry** of the church. In these areas Christians live their calling or vocation received from God.

Christology. Foundational for Luther's theology is **Christology** with the focus on the cross of Christ as the event of Christ's redemptive, justifying work for the liberation of believers from their captivity to sin and their restoration to the favor of and **communion** with God. The union of the divine and human natures in Christ is the presupposition for **redemption**. Only by being human could Christ achieve satisfaction for sin and victory over death for all of humanity, and only by his being divine could God achieve this in and through him. The same Christ, in the act of justification, imputes not only his righteousness to the believer, but becomes so united with the believer that sin and forgiveness are exchanged between Christ and believer.

Church. For Luther, the church is primarily an assembly, a community of believers, a holy Christian people, gathered together and sanctified by the Holy Spirit, and nourished and sustained by God's Word and sacrament. The church of true believers, the true church is hidden in and with the visible church, always being in conflict with the false church. The marks of the true church are the Word of God, baptism, the Lord's Supper, the **office of the keys**, ordination, **worship** and **prayer**, and suffering in following the cross.

Church and World. The church is related to the world and to secular authority by the lives of Christians living in both realms and, above all, by the two reigns of God (or the **two kingdoms**). God governs the world spiritually through the proclamation of the Gospel within the church, and secularly through the use of the law of God for peace and good order (the so-called "first use" or "political use" of the law) by secular authorities. Their authority, too, is established by God, and Christians should serve in public offices and **vocations** and obey those who govern them, except when they hinder proclamation or force Christians to transgress God's law. Christians should not seek to abolish evil conditions by force (a much debated position of Luther in the late 20th century).

Faith. The sinful person receives and accepts justification and forgiveness by faith. Faith is understood not as a human initiative, but as a gift of God through the Holy Spirit. It consists not primarily in a formal act of believing certain things, but is confident trust in God's goodness and love, making one's own the gift of new and eternal life because the justified believers still remain exposed to sin, they are both righteous and sinful (*simul iustus et peccator*).

Holy Spirit. A fundamental role in Luther's theology is attributed, finally, to the Holy Spirit. The Spirit, the third person of the Trinity, has been sent at **Pentecost** and is sent ever anew through the means of grace into the heart of believers. The Spirit causes, preserves, increases, and strengthens the faith of the justified ones. The Spirit, which calls, gathers, enlightens, and sanctifies the church, is the vital power of the life and **mission** of the church.

Justification. Luther's personal experience and theological rediscovery, on the basis of Romans 1:16–17 and other biblical passages, of God's justification of the sinner by grace through faith in Christ, gratuitously and without any meritorious works of the believer, became for him and the Lutheran movement the center or "the first and chief article" of faith, the fundamental content and criterion of faith. The Gospel's promise of God's gift of justification for Christ's sake is **forgiveness** of sins, **reconciliation** with God, and a new life with Christ and in loving service to the neighbor. This gift of righteousness is communicated to sinners by the **Holy Spirit** who is active through the proclaimed Word of God and the celebrated **sacraments**, thereby creating the faith that receives God's gracious gift. This understanding of justification, of putting people right with God, with themselves, and with their neighbors implies for Luther a number of related issues.

Law and Gospel. This gift is offered through the Word of God, and this Word is understood as presenting both God's **law and Gospel**. Each one must be preached and clearly distinguished. The right distinction becomes for Luther the structural framework of his theology. God's Word as law reveals the sinful state of people and calls them to **repentance** and openness to the Gospel (the so-called "second use" of the law, while its "first use" relates to the ordering of public life and its "third use" serves to guide Christian life). God's Word as Gospel conveys to those who have turned to God the forgiving, consoling, and transforming gift of God's love and grace. God's Word as Gospel is an active Word, which effects what it says. It is communicated through proclamation and sacrament. These external means, the **means of grace**, underline that God's salvation comes from outside (*extra nos*) as a gift. God has chosen, Luther underlines, to act through such outward means in order that grace and salvation can be grasped also by the senses, and not by direct (and uncertain) inspiration as **Anabaptists** and **Spiritualists** claimed.

Ordained Ministry. Word and sacrament, the means of grace, are served by a called and ordained **ministry**, that is instituted by God. The **congregation** or church has the responsibility to call **pastors**. An episcopal leadership of the church, including **ordination** of pastors by **bishops**, would be possible according to human right and if bishops were serving the Gospel. Against the late medieval teaching on the superiority of the clergy, Luther highlighted the **priesthood of all baptized believers** in serving each other spiritually and carrying out, when in a position of secular authority, the reform of the church.

Sacraments. Luther accepted **baptism** and the **Lord's Supper** as the two sacraments that correspond to the three constitutive marks of a sacrament, namely a word of promise, a visible sign, and a divine mandate or institution. As a washing of regeneration in the Holy Spirit, baptism effects forgiveness, delivers from death and the devil, and grants salvation. As entry into a new life with Christ, baptism is of permanent significance for the life of the baptized, and infants should not be excluded from Christ's promise of **redemption**. Luther understood the former sacrament of penance as being substituted by walking in the new life received in baptism. He put great weight on the role of **confession** and **absolution**.

Luther's doctrine of the Lord's Supper continued the traditional emphasis on the real presence of the body and blood of Christ in the sacrament, but rejected its philosophical explanation in the theory of transubstantiation as "subtle sophistry." Luther's own teaching was further developed during the controversy with **Ulrich Zwingli's** teaching on the symbolical presence of Christ, a teaching that contributed to the split between the Lutheran and **Reformed/Presbyterian** movements. Luther insisted on the literal meaning of Christ's words of institution "this is my body" and so on, because their reliability and efficacy were crucial for his pastoral concern. Through these words, Christ makes himself present, the whole Christ, body and blood, human and divine. The presence of Christ's human nature under the elements is promised and made possible on account of the union of the human and divine natures in the person of Christ. From there, it follows that the properties of the human nature participate in the properties of the divine nature (and vice versa, the *communicatio idiomatum*). Accordingly, the human nature, too, can be present everywhere, and it is this same nature that has received salvation at the **cross**. This salvation is now communicated through the presence of Christ in the supper. It is this decisive pastoral interest that marks the insistence on the real presence.

Trinity. A presupposition and basis of all of Luther's theology is the classical trinitarian **dogma** of the church. He affirms this dogma and underlines the awesome majesty of the almighty God, hidden as the *deus absconditus* and revealed as the *deus revelatus* in Jesus Christ, a near God who turns to humans in fatherly love and care. In his ***Large Catechism***, Luther describes, full of wonder and in a comprehensive vision, God as creator and giver of the abundant wealth and diversity of earthly and eternal gifts, and of all the necessities of personal and communal life. Life and the whole creation are sustained by God for which work he uses the cooperation of human beings. At the same time, Luther sharply criticizes the misuse of the gifts of creation for human greed and pride.

Luther's theology continues much of the theology of the Christian church, a theology that has been developed and clarified throughout the centuries. However, Luther restates this theology in a new historical situation of Christianity and with new insights and perspectives that have been, together with the confessions, of formative significance for the **Lutheran church** up to the present. There are other aspects of Luther's theology, for example, his terrible statements about the Jews or about the peasants during the **Peasants' War** that are marked by time-bound limited and wrong perspectives. He was not an infallible Lutheran church father. However, he was and is a teacher of the church, and is increasingly being recognized as such even beyond the boundaries of his own church. *See also* BIBLE, AUTHORITY OF; CONFESSIONS, LUTHERAN; FORGIVENESS; FREE WILL; JEWISH-LUTHERAN RELATIONS; LUTHER, MARTIN; LUTHER RESEARCH; LUTHER'S WORKS; TRINITY, DOGMA OF. [G.G.]

LUTHER'S WORKS. The collected editions of **Martin Luther's** writings. During his lifetime, collections of Luther's writings were already being published, the first one in 1518 at Basel. A first, more comprehensive edition of 12 German and seven Latin works appeared in 1539 and 1559 at **Wittenberg**. It became the basis for further editions. One of them was published at Jena in 1555. After the devastation of the **Thirty Years' War** new editions appeared, one of them at Altenburg from 1661–1664. It provided the basis for a Leipzig edition of 22 volumes published from 1729–1740, followed by the so-called Walch edition (Johann Gerhard Walch) at Halle from 1740–1753 with 24 volumes. From 1880–1910 a revised and expanded edition of the Walch collection was published in St. Louis, Missouri. A reprint came out in 1986/87. In the meantime, the most complete edition so far was published at Erlangen. Its German series (1826–1857) consisted of 67 volumes and the Latin series (1829–1886) of 35 volumes.

A new stage arrived when a **pastor** and collector of books Joachim Friedrich Karl Knaake (1835–1905) started *D. Martin Luther's Werke. Kritische Gesamtausgabe*, published at Weimar (the "Weimarana"). This private initiative became one of the monumental editing enterprises of our time. From the first volume in 1883 up to the present, numerous prominent Reformation and Luther scholars have contributed to this enterprise. The edition has reached more than 100 volumes, while supplements, revisions, and a voluminous index are still in the process of being published.

Collected works of Luther in English were published at London in 1826, Newmarket, Virginia, from 1827–1869, Minneapolis from 1903–1910, and Philadelphia from 1915–1932. The most recent and comprehensive edition in English are *Luther's Works* with 55 volumes, published at St. Louis and

Philadelphia from 1955–1986. Smaller and larger collections of Luther's works have come out in all European countries with a Lutheran presence, but more recently also in Italian, Portuguese (Brazil), Japanese, and Korean. [G.G.]

– M –

MAGISTERIUM. *See* TEACHING AUTHORITY.

MAJOR, GEORG (1502–1574). A member of the original circle of reformer theologians surrounding **Martin Luther** and **Philipp Melanchthon**, and after Luther's death a leading figure in the **Philippist** group. Major was a preacher in the **Wittenberg** Castle Church (1537) and a professor of theology at the University of Wittenberg (1545). His involvement in the formulation of the Leipzig **Interim** after the Smalcald War led him into a controversy, from which he could never be freed and was named after him, the Majoristic controversy. He had argued in 1551 with his friend and colleague, **Nikolaus von Amsdorf**, that "good works are necessary for salvation." However, Major did not teach that **good works** merited **salvation**. He argued against Amsdorf and others, that good works were everything that the Christian does, including the activity itself, empowered by the **Holy Spirit**, of trusting the **Gospel**. Furthermore, Major understood that salvation referred to the entire Christian life, and not just to the initiating event into Christian life. The foil against which Major argued was the false idea that the Lutheran position on salvation and its ethical consequences (*see* Ethics) was entirely passive, as if the will played no role at all. Major's nuanced position, nevertheless, was lost on his own followers, and his misunderstood phrase that "good works are necessary for salvation" was rejected by the reformers in article 4 of the *Formula of Concord*.

After a brief period of civil service in Merseburg and a term as a church **superintendent**, Major returned again to Wittenberg, leading the Wittenberg faculty from 1560 after the deaths of **Johannes Bugenhagen** and Melanchthon. He published textbooks on the psalms, the catechism, and some humanist literature. He edited volumes of Luther's works, presented an early Lutheran concept of the verbal **inspiration** of Scripture, and wrote a tract against the anti-Trinitarian Samosatenes (1569) that summarized the church's teaching on the **Trinity** from Genesis through his own time. Compromised by his lack of theological subtlety, Major nevertheless demonstrated faithful stewardship of the emerging public institutional character of the **Reformation**. [D.H.L.]

MANIKAM, RAJAH BUSHANAM (1897–1969). Indian Lutheran and ecumenical leader. Coming from a Tamil-Telugu as well as Anglican-Lutheran family, Manikam received his doctorate from Columbia University and his Bachelor of Divinity from the Lutheran Theological Seminary at Philadelphia. He was a college teacher in Andhra for eight years and joined the National Christian Council of India in 1937. There, his responsibilities included church-mission relations, ecumenical work, and higher **education**. Predestined by his international experience, he was appointed joint East Asia secretary of the **International Missionary Council** and the **World Council of Churches** in 1950. In 1956 he became the fourth **bishop** of the Tamil Evangelical Lutheran Church in Tranquebar. He was instrumental in creating the East Asia Christian Conference in 1957. He rendered significant contributions to ecumenical thought in Asia through his books *Christianity and the Asian Revolution* (1954) and *The Church in South East Asia* (with W. T. Thomas, 1956). In 1954 he was made president of the Federation of Lutheran Churches in India and as an experienced representative of the "younger churches" in **Asia** and **Africa** he became a key figure in the growth of the **Lutheran World Federation**. [G.G.]

MARBURG, COLLOQUY OF (1529). Conference called to seek **unity** between Lutherans and Zwinglians. Philip of Hesse convened this conference of leading Lutheran and Zwinglian theologians in 1529 at his castle at Marburg. For political and religious reasons he hoped that the conference would lead to agreements between the two wings of the **Reformation**. **Martin Luther**, **Philipp Melanchthon**, **Johannes Brenz**, and other Lutheran reformers debated issues with **Ulrich Zwingli**, Heinricht Bullinger, Johannes Oecolampadius, and other leading **Reformed** theologians. **Martin Bucer** acted as mediator between the two groups. Luther drafted a concluding statement that stated points of agreement in 14 articles (there are doubts whether there really was a full agreement). However, in the 15th article a remaining decisive difference concerning (Luther's insistence on) the bodily presence of Christ in the **Lord's Supper** had to be admitted. This signified the failure of the colloquy and the beginning of a growing Lutheran-Reformed division within the Reformation movement. [G.G.]

MARRIAGE. According to Lutheran **doctrine**, it is a covenant of fidelity, a life-long commitment of one man and one woman in a personal and sexual union. Since this institution has been held to be an order of **creation**, it is no surprise that marriage existed before and exists outside the **church**. The church, however, has usually been involved in interpreting and supporting it, not only because marriage is a basic biblical metaphor for the relationship between **God** and the chosen people, but also because marriage creates the **family**, the basic unit of society, and the essential locus of Christian formation. During the Middle Ages, the church, which had earlier simply blessed marriages, replaced the state as the guardian of legality, establishing appropriate degrees of consanguinity and safeguarding freedom of consent. This guardianship was made possible by the concept of the sacramentality of marriage. Instead of considering marriage a **sacrament**, reflection within **Lutheranism** has seen marriage as a **vocation**—an institution into which God calls Christians to live out their **baptism** for their own good and the good of others. Lutherans have generally echoed the rest of the church in seeing three reasons for the institution of marriage: mutual growth and affection of the spouses; the procreation and rearing of children; and the restraint of lust and fornication. Within these strictures, and because of its exclusive, indissoluble nature, marriage also serves as a reflection of the relationship between Christ and the church. That is, it is in intention an institution where opposites meet and create new life, where **forgiveness** overpowers **sin** and disappointment, where **sacrifice** is freely offered and gratefully received, and where clear-sighted knowledge does not eliminate heartfelt love.

The wedding service, which formally initiates the institution of marriage, has always reflected these images. It is also the rite of the church that seems best suited to include practices of the wider **culture**. **Martin Luther** himself, in his *Little Wedding Book* of 1529, balanced late medieval practice with **Johannes Bugenhagen's** recent, reformed rite. Luther's order included three parts: the public announcement of the couple's intention (banns); the betrothal at the church door; and the blessing of the marriage at the altar, occurring the day following the betrothal. This order has dominated the practice in Germany, even after the mid-19th century, when civil marriage became obligatory, and the church ceremony simply confirmed the state's. In the English-speaking world, the (**Anglican**) *Book of Common Prayer* became the norm for all wedding services, including those of Lutherans. Indeed, **Henry Melchior Muhlenberg's** sons not only used the Anglican form for English services, but translated it into German and bound that translation into their handwritten *Agende*. Surrounding these official forms have been folk practices of feasting and festivity, and almost everywhere humans have sealed and celebrated the new family with a community meal.

While continuing to affirm the life-long character of marriage, Lutheran (and other) churches have accepted the reality of a breakdown of marriage and have responded to this situation by increased marriage counseling and **ministry** to divorced people. *See also* ETHICS. [M.O.]

MARY. The mother of Jesus Christ. The classic distinction that Christians may venerate the **saints**, but worship only **God** is particularly applicable in the case of Mary. **Martin Luther** argued vehemently against asserting

Mary was a co-redemptrix with Christ of humanity, but retained an admiration and pious devotion toward her. He retained, for instance, the devotional use of the *Ave Maria*, acclaimed Mary as a model of humble willingness to serve, and used the *Magnificat* as a central text for his **theology** of the **cross**. He saw Mary, further, as an important example of unmerited **grace**, since chosen not for her virtue or worthiness, but simply chosen. The confessions (*see* CONFESSIONS, LUTHERAN) also treat Mary with respect. While denying that she is to be addressed as an intercessor, they grant that she prays for the **church**. She is given her traditional titles: not only blessed and virgin, but *Theotokos* and even "ever-virgin."

With the increasing anti-Roman polemic of the next few centuries, and particularly given Rome's definition of various Marian **doctrines** that seemed to elevate Mary above humanity, Lutherans became more and more reluctant even to venerate the Virgin. Few churches and communities were named in her honor, and the festivals associated with her were rarely observed. When considered, she was used didactically or romantically as a model woman, mother, or peasant. During the Lutheran **Awakening** and **Neo-Lutheranism**, however, **Johann Konrad Wilhelm Löhe** and others began to pay attention to her liturgically. North American Lutherans now include several festivals associated with Mary on their calendars—not only her name day (August 15), but also the Annunciation and Presentation of our Lord and the Visitation. **Feminist** and Womanist theologies, together with **ecumenical** conversations, have led to a reconsideration of her character and a renewed sense of her place (particularly in the Gospels of Luke and John) as a model for the believer and a type of the church. [M.O.]

MEANS OF GRACE. The modes, according to Lutheran teaching, by which God's **promise** of **forgiveness** and new life are communicated. The phrase refers primarily and materially to the preached **Word of God** and the **sacraments** of **baptism** and the **Lord's Supper**. The rite of **confession** and absolution (*see* FORGIVENESS) may also be listed as a sacrament. Some argue that it is a mode of the preached Word. Either way, it serves, too, as a means—or vehicle—of **grace**. The terminology of "means of grace" also intends to assert that **God** does not work without tangible modes for communicating the divine free gifts of **justification** and **salvation**, though these modes are never reducible simply to purely human **traditions**. [D.H.L.]

MEDIEVAL CHURCH AND THEOLOGY. The historical and theological background and framework of the **Reformation**. The Lutheran movement and its **theology** can only be brought into sharper focus when one can define the background to which it responded. Often understood under the general term of Scholasticism—which aimed at a better understanding of revealed

truth through intellectual reasoning—medieval theology was actually a mix of **Augustine's** theology, mystical theology (*see* MYSTICISM), and the emerging "Thomism" of **Thomas Aquinas**, significantly inspired by the rediscovery of Aristotle. Medieval theology was also much informed by nominalism—a theory of knowledge that denied the reality of so-called universal concepts—of William of Occam, Gabriel Biel, and others. In addition to this pluralism of formal theologies was a pluralism of church authorities, though the Western church had recently (1415) been reunified under one pope (*see* PAPACY). General church councils (*see* COUNCILS, ECUMENICAL) could be called, at least in theory, when one desired to appeal a decision to another authority other than the pope or emperor. Also, one could find spiritual **authority** and teaching from many monasteries due to the flourishing of **monasticism**. And **priests** were in abundance. Ill-educated men entered the "lower-level" priesthood in large numbers, often only to say masses for remuneration; in some areas there would be one priest for every 10 citizens.

Behind this proliferation of ecclesial authorities and pluralism of theological outlooks, however, was one popular theology of penitential **piety**. The practice in all areas of life of penitential piety (*see* FORGIVENESS) required a person to be as full and honest in accounting for one's **sins** as possible, and then to atone for them on one's own, usually by performing a variety of religious works like alms-giving, buying indulgences, or taking pilgrimages, all to lessen one's time in purgatory and hasten one's entry into heaven. Here, medieval theology provided its formal rationale called the "medieval synthesis": do that which is in you (*facere quod in se est*) and God shall provide the rest in **grace** through Christ. This presupposed that a sinful person had both the essential good and the **free will** to perform a genuinely righteous work. However, from the Lutheran perspective, certainty of **salvation** was thus left in abeyance. A believer caught in this system would not be freed of the burdened **conscience**. The **promise** of the **Gospel** was left in doubt; indeed, the proper priority of Gospel over the law and Gospel (*see* LAW AND GOSPEL) was reversed. The Lutheran concern for pastoral care was compounded by the evident diminution of the sovereignty of God. In this medieval synthesis scheme of "works righteousness," the very gift itself of **justification** by God through Christ appeared to be compromised by **pelagianism** or **synergism**, at best, and God's sovereignty seemingly dishonored.

As since rediscovered, the scholasticism of Thomas Aquinas, affirmed in the Council of Trent (*see* TRENT, COUNCIL OF) ostensibly over and against Lutherans and other **Protestants**, was not the theological bearer of the previously mentioned medieval outlook. It was particularly the support of nominalism for penitential piety, mixed with a yet to be accepted new papal authority, that painted the backdrop for **Lutheranism's** theological and ecclesial emergence. Nevertheless, the Lutheran Reformation has received the **faith** of the **church** through the ages in conversation with the medieval church and theology. Accordingly, there has not been a radical break with **tradition**, though received **doctrines** and thought-forms have been recast in a Reformation perspective. This means, too, that Lutheranism rejected late medieval theology and practice only where they were seen to contradict the fundamental criteria of the Reformation. [D.H.L.]

MELANCHTHON, PHILIPP (1497–1560). Together with **Martin Luther** the leading theological mind of the Lutheran **Reformation**. Melanchthon was born on February 16, 1497, in the small town of Bretten in southwest Germany. At the age of 12 he entered the University of Heidelberg. From 1512–1518 he studied at Tübingen where he graduated as Master of Arts when he was 15, and in 1518, when he was 21, he was called to teach Greek at **Wittenberg**. There, he also became increasingly involved in theological studies, but he was too modest to aspire to a Doctor of Theology. He became Luther's colleague, friend, and collaborator for 27 years until Luther's death. They remained loyal to each other despite certain theological differences (e.g., on **free will**) and an obvious difference in temperament between the eruptive, combative Luther and the humane, irenic Melanchthon.

Deeply influenced by Luther's thinking as well as by **Humanism**, Melanchthon became convinced of the gift of **God's** free **grace** and the authority of Holy Scripture (*see* BIBLE, AUTHORITY OF), and began to develop his comprehensive understanding of Reformation **faith**. His numerous theological and organizational gifts enabled him to work as a competent and leading reformer of the school and university system in the Lutheran territories (*see* EDUCATION). He traveled widely to advise territories and cities in matters of reform of church, school, and university, and his influence extended far beyond Germany. His sharp and precise thinking helped him to write instructions for church visitations, statutes for universities and faculties, the first **evangelical** dogmatics, his *Loci communes* of 1521 (later called *Loci theologici*) and 25 revised editions afterwards with translations into Croatian, Dutch, French, and Italian. The themes of **sin**, law, and **grace**, taken from the Letter to the Romans, served as the organizing principle of this work, which he later expanded by including the doctrine of God (*see* TRINITY, DOGMA OF) and **Christology**. Most significantly and influential for the future course of **Lutheranism** was the fact that he formulated three of the six Lutheran confessional documents (*see* CONFESSIONS, LUTHERAN): the *Augsburg Confession* of 1530, the *Apology of the Augsburg Confession* of 1530/31, and the *Treatise on the Power and Primacy of the Pope* of 1537. A large number of other writings, including interpretations of Aristotle, witnessed to his great literary and scholarly abilities.

Melanchthon's enormous correspondence, the frequent demands to consult or write an expert opinion, his indispensable role in church-political negotiations and conversations with both **Roman Catholics** and **Reformed** (e.g., he wrote the *Wittenberg Concord* of 1536)—all these were part of his important role and influence as a reformer. After Luther's death, Melanchthon was regarded as the theological leader of the Lutheran movement. He was not able, however, to reconcile and hold together the different tendencies in Lutheran theological thinking. He himself, and later his followers, often called **Philippists**, became part of frequent, and sometimes quite wild, theological conflicts. Stricter Lutherans accused Melanchthon of being too "soft" both concerning the **Interim** (Augsburg and Leipzig) with its attempt to reintroduce certain external matters that led to conflict over the issue of **adiaphora** and concerning certain Calvinistic/Reformed positions. Melanchthon highlighted basic Reformation concepts such as **justification** by faith and grace alone and the distinction between **law and Gospel**. His historic significance consists in his role as an ecclesiastical and educational reformer who tried to keep a balance between **revelation** and **reason**, and philosophical/humanist learning and theology. During his later years, he took a firm stand against **Counter-Reformation** attacks. He died on April 19, 1560, at Wittenberg and was buried beside Luther in Wittenberg's Castle Church. [G.G.]

METHODISM. *See* LUTHERAN-METHODIST RELATIONS AND DIALOGUE.

MIDDLE EAST, LUTHERAN PRESENCE IN THE. Out of approximately 12 million Christians in the Middle East, Lutherans in Israel, Jordan, and Palestine form a tiny minority. There are a few thousand members in the Evangelical Lutheran Church in Jordan (organized in 1959), several foreign-language **congregations** in Beirut, Cairo, Istanbul, Jerusalem, and Teheran, and some small groups in Israel. German **deaconesses** came to Jerusalem in 1851 to establish an orphanage and hospital. They set up similar institutions in Constantinople (1852), Smyrna (1854), Alexandria (1857), and Beirut (1860). The (Lutheran) Redeemer Church was built in the Old City of Jerusalem in 1898 and the Auguste Victoria Foundation (today the Auguste Victoria Hospital) in 1911. Schools and vocational training centers were founded in Palestine, Jordan, and Lebanon.

After the proclamation of the State of Israel in 1948, the **Lutheran World Federation** (LWF) was responsible for the largest part of aid and support work among the 500,000 Palestinian refugees for decades. Today, the LWF and foreign Lutheran churches continue to support a considerable social and educational activity and the Israeli-Palestinian **peace** process in this region. [G.G.]

MILLENNIUM (Lat *mille*, "thousand," and *annus*, "year). According to Revelation 19 and 20, the period of 1,000 years between the binding and release (for a short period) of Satan, during which Christ and the **saints** will rule on earth. The lack of specificity in biblical texts did not prevent Christians from trying to predict the end times, mostly using passages from Daniel and Revelation. From the dispensationalism (the sequence of three ages) of Joachim of Fiore (d. 1202), the late Middle Ages inherited and passed on this speculation in a variety of religious and political dresses.

One such teaching is condemned in the ***Augsburg Confession***, the opinion that saints will establish an earthly kingdom before the **resurrection** from the dead. This is not simply theological conjecture: radical reformers of society were eager to identify their own work with this kingdom and to "annihilate all the godless." This understanding of the millennium (including identifying the godless to be annihilated) gained popular currency in the United States in the period between the Revolution and the Civil War—the new nation's manifest destiny was to establish the millennium, the *novus ordo seclorum*, toward which humanity was progressing. It is no surprise, then, that the issue of chiliasm, the belief that Christ will return to earth for a 1,000-year reign, was one of the "Four Points," that is, the touchstones by which Midwestern Lutherans measured the eastern, more Americanized, synods (*see* NORTH AMERICA, LUTHERAN CHURCHES IN). [M.O.]

MINISTERIAL FORMATION. *See* THEOLOGICAL SCHOOLS.

MINISTRY (Lat *ministerium*, "service," *minister*, "servant"). Different forms of service exercised in the **church** by ordained ministers as well as by lay people. Today, Lutheran churches, together with other churches, underline the calling of all church members to different forms of Christian ministry in their everyday life or in church activities, in a variety of full-time compensated or voluntary lay ministries (e.g., musicians, catechists/teachers, deacons and deaconesses, social and youth workers, and members of councils and synods), or in ordained ministries of deacons (in some churches), **pastors/priests**, and **bishops**. This entry will deal primarily with the ordained ministry, that is, persons called, ordained, and sent to work as pastors or in other ministries in the church. (For other forms of ministry, *see* PRIESTHOOD OF ALL BELIEVERS; DIACONATE; LAITY.)

The fundamental understanding of ministry and ministers as service and servants is clearly present in the New Testament. Such service is enabled by the manifold gifts of the **Holy Spirit** (Gk *charismata*) for the upbuilding of the Christian communities. Later, New Testament texts witness to the emergence of specific ministries like those of apostle, prophet, teacher, evangelist, presbyter, *episkopos*, and deacon. Forms of **ordination** seem to appear, and the general purpose of all ministries was to proclaim the **Gospel** of

Jesus Christ, maintain and hand on the apostolic **faith**, and serve the Christian communities and their mission. But there was not as yet a uniform and institutionalized pattern of ministries. The development of such a pattern began at the end of the first century and continued through the two following centuries, leading to the threefold structure of ordained ministry — bishops, priests, and deacons — as the generally accepted pattern in the church. This pattern had its center in the bishops whose ministry was regarded as constitutive for the church and who were part of the **apostolic succession** that was seen as a defense against **heresies**, a safeguard of church **unity**, and a guarantee of continuity in the right faith. Part of this concept is the rule that only bishops are authorized to consecrate bishops and ordain pastors.

Augustine (354–430) was one of the first to view ordination as a **sacrament** that imparts a special character, later called "indelible character" (*character indelebilis*). Beginning with the sixth century, the office of priest became predominantly sacral and liturgical in its exercise, equipped with sacramental power both to effect the change in the eucharistic elements and, according to later developments, "to offer the **sacrifice** in the church for the living and the dead" (Council of Florence, 1439). This elevated status, reinforced by the general requirement of clerical **celibacy** (First Lateran Council, 1123), led to the distinction between clergy and laity as two classes or orders. During the High Middle Ages, the power and privileges of bishops were massively enlarged, together with the increase of papal superiority and supremacy — both ecclesiastical and secular (*see* PAPACY).

Martin Luther, and the **Reformation** in general, brought the latent yearning for reform to a breakthrough that turned the late medieval system and practice of ordained ministry upside down. Bishops and priests who were seen as mediators of **salvation** were replaced by ministers who served the Gospel and the people by administering the **means of grace**. The elevated status of clergy over laity was replaced by the emphasis on the dignity and calling of the priesthood of all believers. Rejected were enforced celibacy of the clergy, the intertwining of spiritual and secular power in the office of bishops, and the papal claims to absolute power by divine right. Other aspects of the ministerial tradition of the church were continued in a renewed, reformed manner by the Lutheran confessions (*see* CONFESSIONS, LUTHERAN) in their teaching, and the Lutheran churches in their practice. The ordained ministry was seen as essential for the church because of its being a servant (*minister*) of Word and Sacrament and thus an instrument of the saving work of the Triune **God**. For this purpose, God had instituted and commanded the office (Ger *Amt*) of the ministry that, accordingly, is not just a practical arrangement in order to delegate to some persons functions that are basically common to all. The church calls and ordains people into the ministry that has been given by God: to proclaim the

Gospel, celebrate the sacraments, exercise the **office of the keys** in absolving those who repent and excommunicating those who refuse to repent, care pastorally for people and instruct them in the faith, and lead the **worship** of the community. Ordination is regarded as necessary for the exercise of the public ministry that is basically one ministry, but may be exercised by different ministries like those of pastors and bishops. The confessions are open to the continuation of the office of bishop in apostolic succession if bishops are ready to serve the Gospel and ordain **evangelical** pastors. Because the bishops (in Germany) were unwilling to do this, the confessions put the blame on them for the break in the line of the apostolic succession at the time of the Reformation.

During the following centuries, there has been great freedom in the Lutheran churches concerning structures and interpretations of ordained ministry as long as its basic tasks of proclaiming the Gospel and administering the sacraments were maintained. The most persistent difference in interpretation among Lutherans is that between the understanding of ordained ministry either as instituted by God (or Christ) or as delegated by the community to exercise in its name certain functions. Today, there is renewed insistence on the essential pastoral functions of the ordained ministry, its exercise in new forms in response to the needs of modern societies, and its close interrelation with the ministries and gifts of all members of the church. Current ecumenical dialogues (*see* DIALOGUES, BILATERAL), especially with **Anglican**, **Roman Catholic**, and **Orthodox** churches challenge Lutherans to reconsider their concepts of ordained ministry and face seriously the issue of apostolic succession of bishops in a form that is consistent with Lutheran teaching. [G.G.]

MINOR OFFICES. Services of public **worship** supplementary to the main service of the assembly. The Minor Offices include, but are not limited to, the **prayer** services tied to particular times of the day: Matins, Vespers, and Compline, and the lesser hours of Terce, Sext, and None (appointed for midmorning, noon, and midafternoon, respectively). The three greater offices are generally the same in structure: opening sentences, followed by psalms, a lesson with response, a Gospel Canticle (the *Benedictus* for Matins, the *Magnificat* for Vespers, the *Nunc Dimittis* for Compline), and ending with prayers and a benediction. All three also include an office **hymn**. The structure of the lesser offices is similar, but simpler. Minor offices unrelated to parts of the day include three forms of prayer that may be used as separate services: the Litany, a lengthy series of petitions; Responsive Prayer, or Suffrages, made up of the Lord's Prayer and the **Apostles' Creed**, preces, and a series of collects; and the Bidding Prayer in which an assisting minister bids the **congregation** to pray for a cause and silent prayer is offered, concluding with a collect (prayer).

While not intended as preaching offices, the Lutheran emphasis on proclamation made **sermons** a normal part of morning and evening prayer, the two most common offices. The daily services fell into disuse until certain sections of the Lutheran **Awakening** revived them for parochial, private, and communal use. The forms were reintroduced in North America along with the Common Service, where it was common for the **Sunday** evening service to take the form of Vespers, and not unusual for one of several Sunday morning services to be Matins. Many service books of Lutheran churches included these services. [M.O.]

MISSION (Lat *missio*, from *mittere*, "to send"). The sending (mission) of the whole church to bring the whole **Gospel** of **God's salvation** in Jesus Christ to the whole world. This understanding of mission expresses an integral and fundamental aspect of the nature of the Christian **church**. The New Testament clearly witnesses that the history of the first Christian communities was mission and that their **theology** was mission theology—otherwise the life, message, and destiny of Jesus would have been restricted to a Jewish sect in Palestine. The words and actions of Jesus and the post-**Easter** proclamation of Jesus and about him were inspired by a missionary impulse to transcend ethnic, cultural, and geographic borders. Jesus Christ was seen as being sent by God, and his followers were sent to participate in his messianic mission to the nations. The mandate of this mission is expressed in the classical "Great Commission" (Mt 28:19), where the risen Christ, with the Gospel promise to be with them, sends his disciples as missionaries to the nations. In the work and teaching of the Apostle Paul, this commission becomes a communication of the Gospel in the framework of the universal history marked both by the **kingdom of God** and world history (*see* HISTORY, THEOLOGY OF).

The movement of God's mission (*missio Dei*) in Christ and in the power of the **Holy Spirit** has been conceived in modern concepts of mission as the trinitarian mission of the whole church with the participation of all its members, a mission with the whole Gospel with all its spiritual and social dimensions, and a mission to the whole world of all peoples and situations. A concept of mission like this one was not strange to **Martin Luther**. Not at all has he ignored the dimension of mission, as he was criticized by some 19th-century missiologists who applied in an unhistorical manner their own criteria of foreign mission activity. Newer studies (e.g., by **Werner Elert)** have uncovered the profound missionary structure of Luther's thinking. It was his burning desire that the justifying and liberating **grace** of God is transmitted to all people. And this, not because of the supremacy of the Christian faith over non-Christian religiosity and morality, but because he believed that all people, Christians and non-Christians, are in need of the Gospel. The church is the instrument of this mission, but not its goal, and all its members are called by their **baptism** to participate in mission by their daily witness (*see* PRIESTHOOD OF ALL BELIEVERS).

In the 19th and first half of the 20th centuries mission was understood by Lutherans and other churches primarily as the task of missionaries to proclaim the good news in foreign lands, convert the "heathen," and gather Christian communities. With the independence of nations and churches in **Africa**, **Asia**, and other parts of the world during the second half of the 20th century, concepts and forms of mission were radically challenged and then changed or modified in the **Roman Catholic Church** and in other mainline churches, including Lutheran ones. These churches seem to agree that the understanding of Christian mission must be a world mission ("mission on six continents"), rather than a "Western" one; that there are no longer "sending" and "receiving" churches but churches that are sharing in God's mission; that the missionary task is holistic, in that it includes soul and body, salvation and well-being, and the individual and the community; that the missionary proclamation of the Gospel must respect and involve the cultural context of its addressees (*see* INCULTURATION); and that mission has to be seen in relation to dialogue with other religions (*see* INTERRELIGIOUS DIALOGUE).

Conflicts have arisen where in recent decades this broader concept of mission has been further extended to also include social-political action, or where "mission" has become such a general and vague term in liberal **Protestant** jargon that it can refer to all and everything that the churches and their institutions are doing. This stands in stark contrast to the understanding and practice of mission of Evangelical and Pentecostal churches and movements with their focus on the Gospel and **conversion**. These churches and movements represent today by far the largest sector of non-Roman Catholic traditional missionary activity. However, the last years of the 20th century also saw in the Catholic, **Anglican**, Lutheran, and several other churches, a return to a more specific understanding of mission. This renewed understanding preserves the broader perspectives mentioned earlier. But it considers again, as its center, the contextual proclamation of the transforming power of the Gospel among peoples and cultures where it is not known or where it is no longer known. This understanding is closely related to the frequently used term "evangelization" (*see* EVANGELISM). *See also* MISSION COOPERATION, LUTHERAN; MISSION HISTORY, LUTHERAN; MISSION SOCIETIES, LUTHERAN. [G.G.]

MISSION COOPERATION, LUTHERAN. Cooperation of Lutheran foreign mission organizations began in the 19th century. When several **mission societies** and mission boards undertook missionary work in the same country, cooperation and coordination became necessary. Joint mission committees or federations of Lutheran churches were formed in **Africa** and **Asia**.

Common mission support of individual churches is being undertaken today (e.g., in Tanzania, West Africa, Madagascar, Ethiopia, Japan, or in Papua New Guinea where a joint mission staff has been working since 1948). Occasionally, one mission society/board has taken over the work of another one, for example in 1865, when the German Hermannsburg Mission continued American mission work in India because of the Civil War in America. This mutuality became crucial when, during World Wars I and II, the Lutheran Foreign Mission Conference (1919) of the **National Lutheran Council** in the United States, and individual Lutheran mission boards in the United States, Canada, Australia, and Sweden continued the work of "orphaned missions" of German churches and also, during World War II, of Danish, Finnish, and Norwegian mission societies

In 1923 the first meeting of the **Lutheran World Convention** identified "foreign missions" as one of the priorities of international Lutheran cooperation, and since 1949 the Commission on World Mission of the **Lutheran World Federation** (LWF), today the Department for Mission and Development of the LWF, has served as an instrument of worldwide cooperation, sharing of information, and common reflection in the area of Lutheran missionary responsibility. *See also* MISSION; MISSION HISTORY, LUTHERAN. [G.G.]

MISSION HISTORY, LUTHERAN. Main developments of Lutheran missionary activity among non-Christians and post-Christians. The history of Lutheran **mission** began with the mission of Jesus Christ into the world and the mission of his followers with the **Gospel** to their Jewish neighbors in Palestine and, after **Easter** and **Pentecost**, to all peoples. This missionary movement in the perspective of **salvation history** as well as world history, ambivalent in its failures and glory, was affirmed by the **Reformation**. Recent studies have shown that **Martin Luther's theology** and that of the confessions (*see* CONFESSIONS, LUTHERAN) was in its basic orientation a missionary one. However, the enormous tasks of consolidating Lutheran churches and coping with inner-Lutheran controversies, as well as with the pressures of the **Counter-Reformation** did not leave the emerging Lutheran churches any room or energy to engage in mission to non-Christians. Things were not much different during the time of Lutheran **Orthodoxy** in the 17th century, though there was at that time already a considerable tradition of **Roman Catholic** mission and of **Reformed** and Puritan missionary activities in Holland and England. Lutherans were missionary latecomers. However, there were exceptions: As early as in 1559 King Gustavus I Vasa of Sweden (1496–1560) sent pastors north, to work among the Laps. In the 1640s Swedish Lutheran colonists in North America supported a missionary among the Delaware Indians. And Lutheran layman Baron Justinian Welz (1621–1668) appealed forcefully—but unsuccessfully—to the Lutheran churches and estates in Germany to take on their missionary responsibility and create missionary organizations for work overseas.

The dream of this prophet of Lutheran mission later came true, in the context and under the impact of **Pietism** in the 18th century. The epoch of continuous Lutheran mission activity began when King Frederick IV of Denmark (1671–1730) started the Danish Mission. **August Hermann Francke** in Halle supported this initiative, so that it became the Danish-Halle Mission in 1706. In the same year, Francke's pupils **Bartholomäus Ziegenbalg** and Heinrich Plütschau were sent to India. This initiative became exemplary, because Ziegenbalg envisioned a culturally indigenous **church** with its own collaborators, its own missionary commitment, as well as being open to encounters with Hinduism and Islam. Ziegenbalg's work in Tranquebar had far-reaching influence on the Moravian Mission begun in 1732, Lutheran missionary work among the Laps in Northern Norway and Sweden, and among the Eskimos of Greenland (the "Apostle of the North" Hans Egede, 1686–1758), as well as the emerging Methodist mission of Charles Wesley and **John Wesley**. This period saw the foundation of Anglican missionary societies in England (the Society for Promoting Christian Knowledge and the Society for the Propagation of the Gospel) and of the Baptist Missionary Society (1792) by another important missionary pioneer, William Carey (1761–1834), as well as the great missionary and ecumenical visions of Jonathan Edwards (1703–1758) in the context of North American revivalism and congregationalism.

These and other developments prepared the explosion of missionary enthusiasm and activity of the 19th century that received its impulses and strength from the different forms of Christian **awakening** and revivalism. Great Britain and North America took the lead and **Protestant** continental Europe followed. During that time, numerous mission organizations were founded. Many of them were interdenominational, such as the London Missionary Society (1795) and the Basel Mission (1815) . But the joint influence of awakening and **Neo-Lutheranism** also led to the formation of a great number of voluntary Lutheran **mission societies** in Europe. In North America, efforts to reach the new immigrants had priority, but increasingly Lutheran churches (synods) began to make mission their own responsibility (mission boards). These European and North American organizations sent a large number of missionaries to work in **Africa** (especially in Tanganyika, southern Africa, and Madagascar), **Asia** (especially in India, China, and New Guinea), and, to a much lesser degree, to **Latin America**. In **Australia**, Lutheran mission among Aborigines began in 1866, and in New Guinea Australian Lutherans have participated in mission work since 1886.

Among the several thousand Lutheran missionaries was an increasing number of **women**. In several countries they soon outnumbered men in missionary work. Either as wives of missionaries or, after having established their own mission societies as single persons, these women worked with dedication and vision in educational, medical, and evangelistic projects (e.g., *see* KUGLER, ANNA SARAH). Probably the first of the many women's missionary societies was the Women's Oriental Mission, established at Berlin in 1842. Another particular aspect of Lutheran mission work was the distinction between "home mission" and "foreign mission" in North America. The task of home mission was to reach the masses of immigrants who came to America in the 19th century. In Germany and Scandinavia, a similar distinction was made between "**Inner Mission**" and "foreign mission." Here, Inner Mission referred to evangelistic activities and increasingly to different forms of social and diaconal work and institutions (*see* DIACONIA; FEDDE, ELISABETH; SIEVEKING, ANNA AMALIA; WICHERN, HEINRICH).

The intensive Lutheran missionary activity continued into the first half of the 20th century. It was affected, however, by the two world wars. They had a strong impact especially on Lutheran missions because German and, during World War II, also Danish, Finnish, and Norwegian mission work was not possible. These "orphaned missions" had to be taken over by other Lutheran missions (*see* MISSION COOPERATION, LUTHERAN). Another crucial event for the missions was the Chinese revolution that, after 1949, brought an end to the extremely strong Lutheran (and other) missionary engagement there. Even more radical were the changes in the second half of the 20th century. The former mission churches became autonomous, and indigenous church leaders took over. The Western Lutheran (and other) mission societies and missions boards as well as the churches themselves were forced to redefine and reorganize their relations with the "younger churches." The number of mission personnel declined drastically (while the personnel of Evangelical and Pentecostal missions continues to grow rapidly) and new forms of partnership, exchange, and support had to be developed, especially in the context of the **Lutheran World Federation** and the new concept of a communion of Lutheran churches.

Today, the ambiguous connection of much foreign mission work with Western colonialism is recognized, as is the sacrificial commitment of missionaries and their research on indigenous languages and cultures as well as the contribution of missions to **education** and **health** care and, in more recent years, to social and economic development of the younger nations in the Southern Hemisphere. The "children of the mission" are today the fastest growing Lutheran churches in the world. [G.G.]

MISSION SOCIETIES, LUTHERAN. Voluntary societies for foreign **mission** work. Such societies are supported by committed groups and individuals within the churches, but they are not part of official church structures. This mission society pattern began in Lutheran churches in Europe with the Danish-Halle Mission in 1706 and blossomed in the missionary awakening of the 19th century and into the 20th century. Many Lutheran mission societies were founded: the Dresden (1836) and later Leipzig Mission (1848); the Hermannsburg (1849), Neuendettelsau (1841/1849), and Breklum (1876) Missions; and the Danish (1821), Finnish (1859), Norwegian (1842), and Icelandic (1929) Mission Societies. The Church of Sweden Mission (1874) was the only mission that was an integral part of the **church**. In addition, many smaller mission societies were founded that were of a more conservative orientation or concentrated on a particular need (e.g., mission to the blind) or on a particular region (e.g., Santal Mission). In Scandinavia alone, over 80 mission societies exist. Lutherans in France and Holland also created their own societies.

In North America (*see* NORTH AMERICA, LUTHERAN CHURCHES IN), the Foreign Mission Society of the Evangelical German Churches in the United States (1837) became the General Synod-related Foreign Missionary Society of the Evangelical Lutheran Church in the United States in 1841. The Central Missionary Society, formed in 1836 by the Ministerium of Pennsylvania, served the General Council. They were the forerunners of similar organizations, including the Women's Foreign Missionary Society of the General Synod (1879). However, the general pattern became the integration of home and foreign mission work into the general structure of the churches under the supervision of mission boards. After World War II this pattern was also adopted by the German Lutheran churches in order to underline the integral relationship between church and mission. *See also* MISSION HISTORY, LUTHERAN. [G.G.]

MONASTICISM. The movement to establish rules of eremitic or community life focused on **prayer**, contemplation, and purity. Originating in Egypt during the third century, the movement spread quickly. By the Middle Ages, monasticism was the dominant factor in the life of the **church** and, through its ownership of property, in the life of Western **culture** as well. Western monasticism received its classic expression in the Rule of St. Benedict (529) that tied monks to particular houses and established hours of prayers, welcome for visitors, and an avowed life of poverty, chastity, and obedience. Monasticism rendered a lasting contribution to art, architecture, and learning. Faced with new social conditions, Francis of Assisi (c.1181–1226) began a different model of monasticism, founding an order of wandering mendicants dedicated to living out as closely as possible the dictates of the Sermon on the Mount. From this model sprang the Franciscans, Dominicans, and Augustinians; all of these orders, becoming wealthy from donations, eventually focused on ministries of preaching and teaching.

The abuses of monasticism—worldly monks violating their vows and cheating the poor—were widely criticized in the late Middle Ages. Lutheran criticism of monasticism, however, concentrated on its very heart. While condemning such abuses as involuntary vows (particularly by women), **Martin Luther** and the confessions (*see* CONFESSIONS, LUTHERAN) reject even more fervently the claims of monasticism to superior Christian status. The notion that monastics constitute the ideal of the Christian life—celibate, contemplative, and removed from worldly concerns—was replaced on the one hand with the concept of Christian **vocation** and on the other with the demand that all Christians attend to the ethical implications of the **Gospel**. Generally speaking, monasteries were dispersed in **Protestant** lands, although monasticism as a voluntary institution never entirely died out among Lutherans (*see* ORDERS/COMMUNITIES, RELIGIOUS). [M.O.]

MORAVIAN CHURCH. Christian Denomination that is historically and spiritually closely connected with **Lutheranism**. "Moravian Church" is the English name of the Unitas Fratrum, the Unity of the Brethren/United Brethren, sometimes also called Renewed Moravian Brethren. The origins of this denomination reach back to the 15th-century pre-**Reformation** reform movements in Bohemia and Moravia (present-day Czech Republic). One of these movements, the Unity of the Brethren, established itself beginning in 1467 as an independent Christian community, accepting Holy Scripture as the only authority for its **faith** and life. In 1628 the **Counter-Reformation** drove the flourishing church underground or into exile. In Poland, the outstanding teacher and writer Jan Amos Comenius (1592–1670) was the leader of the exiles. In 1722 a group of Brethren emigrated to Saxony and formed a community at Herrnhut under the leadership of Count Nikolaus von Zinzendorf (1700–1760), a Lutheran layman deeply influenced by **Pietism**. Under the influence of Pietism and the writings of Comenius, the community developed into a revival of the Unitas Fratrum and celebrated its birthday in 1727. Though initially considered by Zinzendorf as a particular churchly community within the established Lutheran church of Saxony, the growing missionary zeal of the community led to the introduction of their own ministries of presbyter and deacon along with the transfer of the episcopate of the old Moravian Brethren by Moravian bishop Daniel Ernst Jablonski (1660–1741) of Berlin to one of the first missionaries of the Herrnhuters and to Zinzendorf himself (1737).

Moravian missionary (*see* MISSION) activity in **Africa**, **Asia**, the **Caribbean**, and **North** and **South America** led to the establishment of Moravian churches that today form the 18 autonomous provinces of the worldwide Unitas Fratrum. The great majority of the over 500,000 Moravians live on these continents while in Europe their number has remained very small. Involved in **ecumenical** cooperation and active in social, educational, and missionary work, the Moravian church has consistently emphasized a Christ-centered faith (*see* CHRISTOLOGY) and the importance of a Christian life according to biblical precepts, while at the same time attributing less significance to formal doctrinal systems and confessional commitments. However, in line with its renewed origins at Herrnhut, a closeness to Lutheran thinking has continued. In 1748 the General Synod of the Moravians accepted the *Augsburg Confession* as a pure statement of biblical **truth**. **Martin Luther's** *Small Catechism* is often used. In Lutheran parts of Europe, especially Germany, many Moravians are also members of Lutheran churches. The Moravian Church in South Africa (over 100,000 members) is a member of the **Lutheran World Federation**. Bilateral conversations (*see* DIALOGUES, BILATERAL) between the Evangelical Lutheran Church in America and the two Provinces of the Moravian Church in America led in 1999 to the declaration of full **communion** (*see* UNITY OF THE CHURCH) between the two churches. [G.G.]

MOREHEAD, JOHN ALFRED (1867–1936). American Lutheran theologian and prominent pioneer of worldwide Lutheran **fellowship**. Morehead grew up in Virginia, graduated from the Lutheran Seminary at Philadelphia, and was ordained in 1892. After serving several **congregations** in Virginia, he became professor and president at Southern Lutheran Seminary in Columbia, South Carolina, from 1898–1903. From 1903–1919 he was president of Roanoke College. Morehead's important international career started in 1919 when he began serving in Europe as relief commissioner of the **National Lutheran Council** (NLC), continuing until 1923. During this period he chaired the Council's European Commission. He was executive director of the NLC from 1923–1930. His experiences and close contacts in Europe made him a tireless promoter of wider Lutheran **fellowship**. As early as 1919 he proposed the formation of a **Lutheran World Convention** (LWC) that was organized at First Assembly at Eisenach in 1923. Morehead became chairman of the Executive/Continuation Committee of the LWC and presided over its assemblies at Copenhagen in 1929 and Paris in 1935. His organizing skills and his commitment both to confessional **Lutheranism** and to helping people in need won him high respect both in church and secular circles, at home, and abroad. He personified and promoted the growing awareness among Lutherans of being a worldwide fellowship. [G.G.]

MUHLENBERG (MÜHLENBERG), HENRY MELCHIOR (1711–1787). First organizer and "patriarch" of the **Lutheran church** in America. Born in Einbeck near Hannover, Germany, Muhlenberg was ordained to the Lutheran **ministry** in 1739. In 1742 people at the Francke Foundation in Halle (*see* FRANCKE, AUGUST HERMANN) convinced him to travel to

Pennsylvania and to serve the German settlers there. He became pastor of three **congregations** in the Philadelphia vicinity and served them from 1742–1779. He was confronted with a still very provisional and often chaotic church situation in the colonies. His congregations served as the solid basis for an incredibly intensive and enduring travel activity in Pennsylvania and beyond, as far as Georgia. Muhlenberg served scattered settlers with the **Word of God** and the **sacraments**, reorganized existing and organized new congregations, settled conflicts, and supported and advised people in all kinds of practical matters. All this was possible thanks to a strong body, a warm and mildly pietistic personality, a strong biblical and confessional **faith**, good biblical and theological scholarship, and an extraordinary organizational talent.

In 1745 Muhlenberg was joined by three helpers from Halle, and in 1748, in view of the growing number of congregations, he convened the first gathering of the Evangelical Lutheran Ministerium of Pennsylvania at Philadelphia. The ministerium, together with its new authority to ordain **pastors**, represented the beginning of organized Lutheran church life in America. In addition to his congregational work, Muhlenberg helped to prepare a common **liturgy** in 1746, was the main compiler of the first **hymnbook** of the ministerium (1786), and his model constitution (*see* CHURCH POLITY) was accepted by the congregations in 1761. All this contributed to the **unity**, independence, and coherence of the young church. His unceasing activity, spiritual authority, and vision of a new church in a new land made Muhlenberg the founder and patriarch of the Lutheran church in America. *See also* NORTH AMERICA, LUTHERAN CHURCHES IN. [G.G.]

MUNK, KAJ (1898–1944). Danish Lutheran **pastor**, writer, patriot, and martyr. Adopted as an orphan by the Munk family, Kaj Munk studied theology and was ordained in 1924. He became a pastor of a small village **congregation** near the North Sea and served there for 20 years until his death. His writings made this simple village pastor within a short time the most discussed personality in Danish cultural life and one of the best known writers in Scandinavia. His plays renewed the Danish dramatic scene, and they often exhibited a fascination with strong personalities whose failures and weaknesses were radically unmasked in the light of a stronger one, Jesus Christ. During World War II and the German occupation of Denmark, Munk's patriotic articles and **sermons** were printed and distributed illegally and helped to strengthen the resistance movement. The Nazis saw in him a dangerous enemy. They arrested him on January 4, 1944, and had him shot the next day. His death was regarded as national martyrdom and became of decisive significance for Denmark's freedom struggle. [G.G.]

MÜNTZER, THOMAS (c.1490–1525). One of the leaders of the radical **Reformation**. Müntzer was born in Stolberg, Germany, and studied theology in Leipzig and Frankfurt on the Oder. He was well versed in Greek, Hebrew, and the Church Fathers (*see* PATRISTICS). It is likely that he met **Martin Luther** at a disputation in Leipzig in 1519, and it appears that Luther recommended Müntzer to become the main preacher at Zwickau. At Zwickau, however, Müntzer was influenced by the zealous mysticism of the so-called Zwickau Prophets, a pneumatological group (*see* SPIRITUALISTS) that taught the priority of one's own "inner light." Thus inspired, Müntzer's preaching became subversive and often attacked both the Catholic and emerging **evangelical** positions, which also marked him as an early leader of **Anabaptists**.

After he was banned from Zwickau, Müntzer moved on to organize German vernacular services in Allstedt, antedating Luther's own *German Mass* by several years. There, he also founded a society of "people of faithful obedience to God," comprised especially of the working poor. The more he was attacked for his radical beliefs, the more overtly political he became, such as by advocating a radical theocracy. A lightning rod in the Lutheran conflict with enthusiasm/spiritualism, he attacked Luther, as well as the Lutheran positions on infant **baptism** and the interpretation of the **Canon of Holy Scripture**, and preached **revolution**. Müntzer's **theology**, indeed, gave priority to individual human **free will** and was given toward a literal and apocalyptic style of biblical interpretation. Thus, he believed that radical obedience to Jesus' commands would help to usher in the end times (*see* ESCHATOLOGY).

Under threat of arrest, Müntzer fled to Mülhausen in 1524. When expelled from there, he assumed leadership in the **Peasants' War**. On May 15, 1525, his army was obliterated by the armies of the princes at Frankenhausen, and he was captured. He was tortured until he recanted his faith, then beheaded. [D.H.L.]

MUSIC IN THE LUTHERAN CHURCH. As part of its incarnational focus, **Lutheranism** has generally affirmed that the material is capable of bearing the spiritual, and therefore the **arts**, and music primary among them, have been valued as part of the church's liturgical, devotional, and kerygmatic life. Because its **doctrine** of the **Word** does not restrict the **church** to practices specifically affirmed in the New Testament, Lutherans have been free to use instrumental music, even without an associated text. Thus, Lutheranism has been rich soil for the composition and performance of musical works. It has given a home and an outlet for geniuses, from **Heinrich Schütz** to **Hugo Distler** and **Johann Sebastian Bach**. More importantly, it has nourished thousands of composers and performers and millions of purely amateur singers, players, and listeners, providing an aesthetic **spirituality** that has valued not only the beauty of **holiness**, but the holiness of beauty.

During the first generation of the **Reformation**, following the lead of **Martin Luther** and **Johann Walter**, Lutherans made the **congregation** active participants in the service by returning to them the ordinary of the mass, set to **chorales**. The **kantorei** and the **organ** were given responsibilities as well, in alternation with the whole assembly. **Hymns** filled liturgical needs and reflected on the events, ecclesial, political, and military of the day. After 1600 instruments, including the organ, were more often used to undergird singing, and to provide music unassociated with any text or hymn. The *de tempore* system provided a weekly hymn for use in church, home, and school, giving a kernel of texts, often theologically profound, that became second nature to the congregations, and that eventually became the subject of chorale preludes and **cantatas**. The sufferings endured during the **Thirty Years' War**, and the **pietist** emphasis on small group worship led to a hymnody of peculiar warmth, and to home devotions centering on singing and playing these hymns—while Germany was a central source of this music, Sweden and Slovakia as well as other countries provided their own, of particular depth and beauty.

In America during the 19th century, church music often changed with the language of **worship**. Lowell Mason and the Gospel hymn tradition, rather than translations of immigrant hymns, were most popular in English-speaking homes and Sunday schools, many of which had their own bands and orchestras. This style of music, in fact, spread back to the immigrants' homelands and, through **mission societies**, into the younger churches. The **liturgical movement** of the mid-20th century, with its desire for refining the peculiar gifts of each **tradition**, brought new attention to chorales, alternation practice, and *de tempore* hymnody. At the end of the 20th century attention seems to be focused particularly on the appropriation of the music of a church's **culture**. This appropriation may take the form, in North America, of "contemporary services," with music provided by a band of musicians in a folk, rock, jazz, gospel, or country style. In **Africa** and **Asia**, it includes the use of indigenous instruments and chants. In **Latin America**, it includes the use of complex rhythms and newly composed texts that often reflect **liberation theologies**. Church music is a critical laboratory for figuring out how faithful worship may and must be cultural, cross-cultural, countercultural, and transcultural. [M.O.]

MYSTICAL UNION. The relationship established between Christ and the believer through **justification**, initiated and deepened in the **sacraments** and the whole of Christian **vocation**. **Martin Luther** wrote of this relation as a "happy exchange," whereby Christ freely and graciously gives believers his eternal life and assumes their **sin,** guilt, and punishment (*see* ATONEMENT). The soul that clings to the **promises** of **God**, Luther said, becomes "so closely united with them and altogether absorbed by them" that it shares in all their power and is "saturated and intoxicated by them"

(*The Freedom of a Christian*). Luther also wrote of this relation in terms of the communion of a bride and groom, in which the righteousness and life of the groom (i.e., Christ) are so larger and weightier than the bride's (i.e., the human being) sin and death that the latter are swallowed up and transmuted into their opposites by the former. Furthermore, what God imparts in this union are not merely metaphorical references; they make a difference in actual **anthropology**, as the believer is literally given the Christological qualities of priesthood and kingship in addition to innocence and inheritance of eternal life. Christian life, denoted in the term of mystical union, fully shares in Christ's life.

Mystical union has had, apart from this specific understanding in Lutheran **theology**, a history in which its emotive or psychological aspects were more accented than the anthropological or cognitive aspects described earlier, particularly in times and places where **Pietism** or an emphasis upon charismatic gifts and the presence of the **Holy Spirit** was more ascendant. Where and when **faith** as cognitive belief and subjective trust are in equal emphases—as with instances of **prayer** and sensitive **liturgy**—"mystical union" is as apt a doxological descriptive as there ever rightly has been in Lutheran tradition. [D.H.L.]

MYSTICISM. The effort to attain unity with the Divine, and the attempt to communicate this experience. This approach to **theology** is not limited to Christianity—it is not only shared with the Eastern **religions** and their offshoots, but also with Judaism (particularly the Kabbalah), and Islam. In the late Middle Ages, particularly in Germany, mysticism functioned as a practical protest against the arid dialecticism of **Scholasticism**. Tired of making sharper and sharper distinctions, seemingly without end, the mystics affirmed the fundamental unity of all things in **God**. These mystics included Hildegard of Bingen, Elizabeth of Hungary, and Mechthild of Magdeburg, who outlined a "theology of the heart."

Martin Luther's relationship with mysticism is a complicated one. He was critical of mysticism seen as a ladder to heaven—humans earned **salvation** no more by asceticism than by any other activity—and he had harsh words for the *Schwärmer* (enthusiasts) who used the language of mysticism to eliminate reliance on the external **Word** (*see* SPIRITUALISM; MEANS OF GRACE). Heavily influenced by such mystics as Bernhard of Clairvaux and Johannes Tauler, he published the *Theologia Deutsch*, that masterpiece of the Brethren of the Common Life. Throughout the history of Lutheran **devotional literature**, themes of mysticism continue to appear. Writer after writer, from **Johann Gerhard** and **Paul Gerhard** to **Johann Arndt** and **Søren Aabye Kierkegaard**, affirm the importance of inwardly appropriating the means of grace and the **order of salvation** and the use of the image of Christ as bridegroom of the soul, which implies intimate unity as its consummation.

Many, however, especially during the **Enlightenment** and 20th-century neo-orthodoxy, have rejected any notion of mysticism as incompatible with **Lutheranism**. Mysticism has been accused of sanctifying political quietism and theological heterodoxy. It has, it is said, denied the pervasiveness of **sin**, the necessity of **grace**, and the centrality of Word and **sacrament**. Against this chorus, Bengt Hoffman proved the positive influence of mysticism on Luther and the confessions (*see* CONFESSIONS, LUTHERAN). The recent work of Finnish Luther scholars, with their focus on the connection between Luther's (and Lutheran) theology and the Eastern Orthodox notion of *theosis* (deification), promises to show Mysticism in an even more favorable light. [M.O.]

– N –

NATIONAL LUTHERAN COUNCIL (NLC). The NLC was the most important American inter-Lutheran organization in the 20th century and played a decisive role in the formation of world **Lutheranism**. Organized in 1918 by eight Lutheran churches that merged between 1960 and 1963 to form the American Lutheran Church (ALC) and Lutheran Church in America (LCA) (*see* NORTH AMERICA, LUTHERAN CHURCHES IN), the NLC developed joint Lutheran work within the United States (**home mission** in industrial centers, work with Lutheran students in non-Lutheran colleges and universities, publications, and so on). After the upheavals of World War I, its major task became relief work for European Lutherans. Its World Service Program assisted Lutheran churches in over 20 countries in Europe, Africa, and Asia. World War II challenged the NLC to engage in even broader activity. It helped to care for "orphaned" missions where missionaries had been interned during the war (*see* MISSION, HISTORY). Through Lutheran World Relief, set up in 1945 together with the **Lutheran Church-Missouri Synod**, an extensive relief program was undertaken for people distressed by war and postwar conditions. In 1950 another joint NLC–Missouri Synod agency was formed: the Lutheran Immigration Service that helped to resettle **refugees** and migrants (*see* EMIGRATION). With an annual budget in the 1960s of over $5 million, the NLC furthered joint activities within the United States and abroad.

The international involvement of the NLC was influential in forming the **Lutheran World Convention** in 1923 and the **Lutheran World Federation** in 1947 in which the NLC became the U.S. National Committee. The NLC was phased out when the ALC, LCA, and the Missouri Synod formed the Lutheran Council in the United States in 1967. In 1987 the Lutheran Council was dissolved and a remarkable period of Lutheran cooperation in the United States and internationally came to an end. [G.G.]

NATURAL LAW. The collection of basic moral principles, common to **God's** design of the **creation**. This classically **Roman Catholic** understanding is often shared by Lutherans, though the understanding of natural law's relation to "revealed" law is not. Lutherans usually access natural law indirectly, preferring to speak first of a distinction between the "order of creation" (*ordo creatio*) (*see* CREATION, DOCTRINE OF) and the "**order of salvation**" (*ordo salutis*). Also, Lutherans would first discuss the role of **conscience** as the mode of aligning natural law to specific ethical questions. Like its critical appreciation of conscience, though, Lutheranism recognizes that the **Enlightenment** regard of practical **reason**, which supports the classical view of natural law, is impaired because of **original sin**. Natural law therefore—while it indeed exists as a structure or principle in creation expressive of the divine purpose of **love**—is not easily discerned. It is certainly neither discernible as an independent objective principle, nor as part of a clear design in nature, nor as even a commonly held subjective conviction. Natural law is recognized, though, where in varying contexts and circumstances there is correspondence between God's revealed law—as with the Decalogue, the Sermon on the Mount, and the great "**love**" commandment—and human traditions and structures.

One may conclude that the natural law is recognized only through the lens of Christian discipleship. Therefore, and apart from a Christian perspective, while it may be natural, a principle may at best be regarded not as "law," but as a presumption, open to the critique and ambiguity of reason from many directions. Thus, in **Lutheranism**, whatever would be recognized as natural law is always subject to the revealed law of Scripture, and the two modes are never entertained as if on equal footing. Natural law cannot lead to saving **faith**, and Lutheranism tends to argue that only saving faith can even discern natural law. [D.H.L.]

NATURE. The created world (*see* CREATION). **Lutheranism** also uses the term in a secondary, technical sense with regard to the humanity and divinity of Christ (*see* CHRISTOLOGY); in a tertiary technical sense with regard to **sin** and theological **anthropology**. Here we treat only the first and most general sense.

With most of Christianity, Lutherans have not been averse to regarding nature as the place of God's **revelation**, often using the phrase of "The two books of revelation [The Book of Scripture and the Book of Nature]." On the one hand, Lutherans qualify the use by emphasizing that **God** is present but hidden in nature and explicitly revealed in the proclamation of the **Word** and in the **sacraments**. Furthermore, God's **revelation** of himself in the sacraments may enable Christian vision to discern the presence of God more clearly in nature, but never with certainty, and never in such a way that nature should be considered pantheistically as equal to God. Also, the

theology of the **cross** holds that God's self-revelation occurs in the opposite: wherever there is **suffering** and injustice, thus assuring that God is present with and cares for the victims of sin and **evil**.

On the other hand, Lutherans and **Martin Luther** aver to nature as a treasure to be cherished in its own right (*see* ECOLOGY) and as both direct reference and metaphor for how God relates caringly to the world. Luther's lectures on Genesis, his use of images in nature to elucidate his theology of the sacraments, his practical teaching in the *Small* and *Large Catechism* (*see* CATECHISMS OF LUTHER), along with many other instances, evince a very positive regard for nature and mandate for its stewardship that Lutherans have—in the main—long held. This positive regard also explains, in part, why Lutherans have been concerned to have a positive theological estimation of the relationship between **Christianity and Science**. *See also* CHURCH AND WORLD; NATURAL LAW; TWO KINGDOMS. [D.H.L.]

NEO-LUTHERANISM. Confessional renewal movement in Lutheran churches in the 19th century. The term "Neo-Lutheranism" refers to the third significant and formative period in the history of **Lutheranism**, after the Lutheran **Reformation** in the 16th century and the period of so-called Lutheran Orthodoxy (*see* ORTHODOXY, LUTHERAN) from the late 16th century far into the 18th century. Several factors and developments led to the emergence of Neo-Lutheranism (also called "confessional Lutheranism"). First, **awakenings** in several Lutheran areas of Germany in the first decades of the 19th century revolted against the influence of **Enlightenment**-inspired **Rationalism** in **church** and **theology** and advocated a renewal of church life. Accepting a stronger confessional orientation, many of the awakened groups joined Neo-Lutheranism. Second, theological circles returned to the fundamental convictions of the Lutheran Reformation as a result of their reaction against the primacy of **reason** in Rationalism and its critique of the authority of Holy Scripture (*see* BIBLE, AUTHORITY OF) as well as its negation of the confessions (*see* CONFESSIONS, LUTHERAN). Third, the Prussian **Union** of 1817 that united Lutherans and the **Reformed** in the Prussian territories by royal decree, stirred up Lutheran self-consciousness in these territories and beyond. And, fourth, the celebrations of the 300th anniversary of both the Reformation in 1817 (**Martin Luther**'s *Ninety-five Theses*) and the *Augsburg Confession* in 1830 sparked off the movement of renewed study of **Luther's theology**, of rediscovery of the confessions, and of church renewal.

The Lutheran **pastor** Claus Harms (1778–1855) was one of the first who formulated in his *Ninety-five Theses* of 1817 the concern and goals of the new movement. Soon, the theological faculty at Erlangen University (Adolf von Harless, Johann Christian Konrad von Hofmann, Theodosius Harnack, Johann Wilhelm Friedrich Höfling, Gottfried Thomasius, and others) provided the emerging movement with theological-scholarly support and was joined by the faculties of Leipzig, Rostock, and Dorpat (today Tartu in Estonia) with theological leaders like Franz Delitsch, Ernst Sartorius, and others. The small Bavarian town of Neuendettelsau became another kind of center for Neo-Lutheranism where Pastor **Johann Konrad Wilhelm Löhe** worked for a renewal of church life by revitalizing **worship, sacraments**, and **piety**. He also initiated diaconal (*see* DIAKONIA) and **mission** work and furthered relations with and support of Lutherans in North America. Similar centers were created in Breklum and Hermannsburg. The movement found broad support among theologians (e.g., August Vilmar and Ludwig Harms), pastors and **laity** in different parts of Germany, the Baltic region, Denmark, and Sweden (where it prepared the High Church Movement). In North America, Neo-Lutheranism was "imported" by the great waves of migrants in the middle of the 19th century and reinforced efforts there towards a stronger Lutheran confessional profile (*see* NORTH AMERICA, LUTHERAN CHURCHES IN; KRAUTH, CHARLES PORTERFIELD). A more direct influence in North America was exercised by Löhe and the pastors he sent to America, and especially—though modified by a biblicism and congregationalism alien to Neo-Lutheranism—by **Carl Ferdinand Wilhelm Walther** and his founding of the **Lutheran Church-Missouri Synod**.

Neo-Lutheranism was marked by theological differences between individuals and groups. Nevertheless, its main theological emphases and orientations can be indicated as emphasis on and commitment to (1) the objectivity and reality of **revelation** as witnessed normatively by Holy Scripture (*see* BIBLE, AUTHORITY OF); (2) the Lutheran confessions as authoritative orientation for **faith** and life, grounded in the conviction that the confessions represent the true and organic continuation (an idea of Romanticism) of the development of Christian **doctrine** since the first centuries; (3) the central significance of the **Word of God** and the sacraments, especially the **Lord's Supper**; (4) the fundamental role of the church and its worship as the community of believers (against the individualism of Rationalism) or even as the organ and means of **God's** saving action; and (5) the importance of the ordained **ministry** in close connection with the **priesthood of all believers**, or as related to a conservative constitutional view of the church, or expressed in episcopal leadership structures of the church in contrast to the existing church government by secular authority (*see* CHURCH POLITY).

Despite its concern to recover and preserve the Lutheran heritage, confessional Lutheranism represented not simply a repristination of the past. Though conservative in character, it nevertheless addressed new questions, furthered theological research, and integrated influences of its intellectual context represented by Romanticism and idealism (Friedrich Wilhelm

Joseph Schelling and **Georg Wilhelm Friedrich Hegel**). Subsequent to transconfessional Rationalism and **Pietism** in church and theology, Neo-Lutheranism has revived the confessional identity (the title "Evangelical-Lutheran Church" was introduced); contributed to the renewal of the church in worship, piety, diaconal work, mission, and churchly orientation of academic theology; and broadened ecclesial consciousness and thereby initiated efforts toward closer Lutheran relationships within countries and between them (e.g., Germany and North America) that finally led to the formation of the **Lutheran World Convention** in 1923 and the **Lutheran World Federation** in 1947. [G.G.]

NEW TESTAMENT CANON. *See* CANON OF HOLY SCRIPTURE.

NICENE CREED. *See* CREEDS.

NINETY-FIVE THESES. **Martin Luther's** call for debate that marked the beginning of the Lutheran **Reformation**. Influenced by his biblical insights and his struggle towards a correct understanding of **sin**, **repentance**, and **forgiveness** (the sacrament of penance), in 1517 Luther wrote 95 theses entitled *Disputation on the Power and Efficacy of Indulgences*. In the theses, he criticized the late medieval practice to grant indulgences, that is, remission or shortening of temporal punishment, on earth or in purgatory, due to sins already forgiven. Such indulgences were granted in response to religious works or payments.

Against this system, the basic **Reformation** thrust on daily repentance together with **faith** in God's unconditional **promise** of forgiveness is announced. It is generally believed that on October 31, 1517, Luther nailed his theses to the door of the Castle Church at **Wittenberg**, since the door served as "notice board" of the university. Since 1962 a book by Catholic theologian Erwin Iserloh has kindled a lively debate among Reformation historians about whether Luther actually published his theses with a hammer in his hand and on that specific date (some believe now that it was later in November 1517). The singular significance of the theses became apparent when they, though being intended as an invitation to a scholarly debate, were immediately copied, printed, and within weeks distributed all over Germany. Suddenly and overwhelmingly, Luther's theses became a major impetus for the Reformation movement. In remembrance of this event, many Lutheran churches observe October 31 or the following Sunday as Reformation Day. [G.G.]

NOMMENSEN, INGWER LUDWIG (1834–1918). Known as the "Apostle of the Bataks." After graduating from the seminary of the Rhenisch Mission Society in Germany, which had its basis in the United churches, Nommensen went in 1861 to Sumatra, Indonesia (then the Netherland's East

Indies). As a missionary of the society, he worked among the Toba Batak people. After the **baptism** of the first converts in 1865, he began to build up Christian groups rooted in their village communities, thereby preserving their social structures. This was facilitated by the cooperation of tribal chiefs. In order to provide stability, structure, and growth for the emerging Christian community, Nommensen drafted rules of the church and an order of **worship** (1866) and later a constitution (1881). He established schools, **hospitals**, and a theological seminary. In 1875 he began training teachers/preachers, and in 1882, **pastors**. After the first three pastors had been ordained in 1885, he moved on and worked in the Lake Toba region and in 1893 extended the work to the Simalungun Bataks.

For 56 years, from 1862–1918, Nommensen was the leading missionary among the Bataks. He translated **Martin Luther's** *Small Catechism* (1874), the New Testament (1878), and Old Testament stories into Batak. This warm-hearted missionary, who was respectful of indigenous customs and structures, was highly regarded and honored because of his effective missionary methods and his personal commitment to his missionary calling. In1881 he became ephorus (leader) of the Rhenish Batak Mission (church), and when he died the Batak church had 180,000 members in over 500 **congregations**. From this church, several churches have developed that are all members of the **Lutheran World Federation** today. *See also* ASIA, LUTHERAN CHURCHES IN; MISSION; MISSION HISTORY. [G.G.]

NON-CHRISTIAN RELIGIONS. The Christian understanding of and relationship with other religions. Both the Old and New Testaments describe how the People of Israel and the early Christian communities struggled to maintain their identity of **faith** and life over and against other religious traditions. This critical attitude to other religions, combined with the claim to absolute **truth** of the **revelation** and **salvation** of **God** in Jesus Christ (*see* UNIQUENESS OF CHRIST) is a continuing mark of much of Christian thinking up to the present. However, even during the lifetimes of the church fathers (*see* PATRISTICS) there have been attempts to see in other religions seeds of divine presence. **Thomas Aquinas** believed a natural **revelation** to be operative in other religions, and at the time of the **Reformation** there were people who believed that non-Christians were predisposed in some way toward a fuller knowledge of the Christian God.

Martin Luther could admit positive elements in other religions, but in general has considered them as vain efforts at self-justification and producing one's own salvation. In the 20th century a similar position of radical criticism was taken by the great Reformed theologian Karl Barth and, following him, by the Lutheran **Dietrich Bonhoeffer**. For them, the revelation of God in Christ is radically opposed to all religion, whether in the form of traditional religions or general religious attitudes. Today, new contexts of religious pluralism have led mainline Christianity to affirm **religious liberty** and the need for **interreligious dialogue** and respect. Some theologians seek to develop more inclusive relations with other religions by holding that they are part of God's work of **creation** and preservation, or that non-Christians can be saved through Christ who is present among them but not known to them (Karl Rahner). Some hold that the **Holy Spirit** is active in other religions. Lutherans are generally reluctant to follow such speculations, but have come to a recognition of positive elements in other religions and join other churches in efforts towards interreligious dialogue and understanding. [G.G.]

NORTH AMERICA, LUTHERAN CHURCHES IN. Unavoidably, the story of Lutherans in North America is primarily the story of immigration, maintenance, and **unity**. Until the establishment of the Evangelical Lutheran Church in Canada in 1986 and the Lutheran Church-Canada in 1988, almost all of the general bodies mentioned in this entry included **congregations** in both the United States and Canada.

Colonial Period (1630–1780). The first Lutheran church on the continent was established in New Sweden (now Delaware) before 1640. Congregations, formed at the mouth of the Delaware River near Philadelphia, were served by Swedish mission **pastors** even after the control of the colony was lost. New Netherland included Dutch Lutherans who, despite the opposition of the colony, received pastors from the Lutheran church in Amsterdam. The **church polity** of Amsterdam, as one of the few Lutheran free (not state) churches, determined American Lutheran polity until the mid-19th century. Lutherans exiled from Salzburg, Austria, arrived in Georgia in 1734. Germans emigrated to New York and Pennsylvania before 1700, and settled in the Shenandoah Valley from Maryland through Virginia to the Carolinas. These groups established scattered congregations, several of whom combined in 1742 to call **Henry Melchior Muhlenberg** through the **pietist** institutions in Halle. He furnished leadership to Lutheran congregations scattered from Nova Scotia to Georgia, and established the first lasting Lutheran church body on the continent, the Ministerium of Pennsylvania. It provided communication, polity, a competent clergy, a shared **liturgy**, and financial support to Lutherans following its establishment in 1748.

Federal (1780–1838). After the Revolution, immigration from northern Europe slowed considerably. The Ministerium of Pennsylvania spun off daughter synods in New York, North Carolina, and Ohio. Particularly along the seaboard, the rationalist bent of the new nation (and of the European universities) was reflected in a declining loyalty to the confessions (*see* CONFESSIONS, LUTHERAN), while on the frontier the Tennessee and Ohio Synods were established as particularly orthodox Lutheran bodies. In the early 1820s the General Synod was formed. At first encompassing only synods in the south and central Pennsylvania, the General Synod went on to include the largest synods in the East. With its combined resources and under the active leadership of **Samuel Simon Schmucker**, it was active in the benevolent endeavors of the federalist period, including missionary work, the establishment of Sunday schools, Bible and tract societies, and temperance and sabbatarian movements. While the body was silent on the divisive issue, Schmucker himself was a fervent opponent of slavery.

Awakening (1838–1880). The middle third of the 19th century saw an explosion in immigration from central and northern Europe. Some of this immigration was organized, such as the colonists sent by **Johann Konrad Wilhelm Löhe**, the Saxons under the leadership of **Carl Ferdinand Wilhelm Walther** (*see* LUTHERAN CHURCH-MISSOURI SYNOD), or the Prussians who established the Buffalo Synod. Norwegians began to settle in Illinois and Wisconsin before 1840 and, by 1870, had founded synods whose theological and practical positions reflected those in the Church of Norway. Swedes and Danes gathered together in the Augustana Synod. Many of these bodies, especially those who had emigrated to escape the Prussian **Union**, were ardent confessionalists. They were outraged by the unionism of the General Synod, and particularly by the proposal, made by Schmucker in the *Definite Synodical Platform* (1855), that a recension of the *Augsburg Confession* be made, adapting Lutheran teaching to the American theological scene. This proposal, in fact, was rejected by the members of the General Synod, where native-born and immigrant confessionalism was on the rise. During the Civil War, the southern synods left the General Synod to form the General Synod of the South. In 1864 the more confessionalist synods left the General Synod, led by the Ministerium of Pennsylvania, to form the General Council, which proposed cooperation based on subscription to the Unaltered Augsburg Confession. This basis was insufficient for most Midwestern bodies, although the Augustana Synod did join, and the Iowa Synod remained a close associate of the General Council. In 1872 six synods, including Missouri, Ohio, the Norwegian, and Wisconsin, formed the Synodical Conference as a strongly confessionalist cooperative body. The Synodical Conference was shaken, however, beginning in 1880 by the **Predestination** Controversy that pitted the Norwegian and Ohio Synods against Missouri. In 1882 the former left the association.

Gilded Age (1880–1920). Old controversies colored the beginning of this period. The General Council continued to struggle with the issue of pulpit and altar **fellowship**; the Predestination Controversy raged on well into the 20th century; and language controversies, from the establishment of English-language services to the propriety of non-English-language parochial schools, divided many congregations. While established bodies continued to grow, immigration of Lutherans began in this period from some new areas: the Icelandic Synod was formed in 1885, the Finnish Suomi Synod in 1890, and the Slovak Synod in 1902. World War I and the 400th anniversary of the Reformation provided the occasion for Lutherans to work together on matters related to chaplaincy, home missions, war relief efforts, and shared history. Out of these occasions came the formation of the American Lutheran Publicity Bureau, the Norwegian Lutheran Church in 1917, the reunion of the General Synod, the United Synod of the South, and the General Council (without the Augustana Synod) into the United Lutheran Church in America in 1918, and the **National Lutheran Council** in 1918.

Midcentury (1920–1970). Dislocations caused by the turbulent twenties, the Great Depression, and World War II made conditions ripe for Lutherans to cooperate on measures related to **ministry** and **mission**. Mergers continued in this period as the American Lutheran Church was formed in 1930 by the Iowa, Ohio, and Buffalo Synods. In 1960 this body joined with a Danish and two Norwegian synods to form The American Lutheran Church. In 1958 the Augustana Synod and the United Lutheran Church in America joined with a Finnish and a Danish body to form the Lutheran Church in America. With these mergers, the National Lutheran Council was reduced to two members, and in 1966 it went out of existence, to be replaced by the Lutheran Council in the United States of America, in which the Lutheran Church-Missouri held membership as well. The Canadian Lutheran Council, representing the Canadian sections of the National Lutheran Council, was formed in 1952 and transformed in 1966 into the Lutheran Council in Canada, including the Lutheran Church-Missouri Synod (LC–MS).

Fin de siècle (1970–). In the early 1970s the LC–MS suffered through a controversy related to **authority** and biblical interpretation that culminated in the formation of the Association of Evangelical Lutheran Churches in 1976.This body declared its intention to have a decade of life, during which it would bring about the merger of the American Lutheran Church and the Lutheran Church in America. In 1986 the Canadian sections of these churches formed the Evangelical Lutheran Church in Canada, and two years later the churches in the United States formed the Evangelical Lutheran Church in America (ELCA). Also in 1988 the Lutheran Church-Canada became autonomous from the LC–MS. In 1999 the ELCA had 5,178,000 baptized members; the LC–MS had about 2,600,000; and the Wisconsin Evangelical Lutheran Synod had about 413,000. The Evangelical Lutheran Church in Canada had 196,000 baptized members and the Lutheran Church-Canada had 79,800. Eight smaller bodies in the United States totaled about 133,000 baptized members, and there were seven more with baptized membership of fewer than 1,000. [M.O.]

– O –

OIKOUMENE. *See* ECUMENISM.

OLD TESTAMENT CANON. *See* CANON OF HOLY SCRIPTURE.

ORATORIO. A musical composition for vocal soloists, chorus, and orchestra distinguished by the religious character and length of its libretto and the absence of scenery, costumes, or staging in performances. Settings of passion histories, masses, and requiems are generally considered as being distinct from oratorios. Growing from the liturgical dramas of the Middle Ages, the oratorio began its distinctive life as a popular outreach tool of the **Counter-Reformation** in Italy. **Heinrich Schütz**, however, introduced the form to German **Protestants** in the mid-17th century with his **Easter** and **Christmas** oratorios. Many German composers tried their hands at the oratorio over the next century, but generally preferred to write **cantatas**. George Frederic Handel, however, became the 18th-century master of the oratorio. When the operas he preferred to write became unpopular and, furthermore, when the theaters were closed during **Lent**, he turned his hand to oratorios, and most famously to the *Messiah* (1742). The form has never since lost popularity, and its most famous practitioners have included Joseph Haydn (*The Creation* and *The Seasons*), Ludwig van Beethoven (*Christ on the Mount of Olives*), and Felix Mendelssohn-Bartholdy (*Elijah* and *St. Paul*). But other composers—from Richard Wagner to Igor Stravinsky and beyond—have written oratorios in their own styles. While rarely performed in church, and even more rarely as part of a church service, the arias and choruses from these works have been mainstays of **church music** for centuries. [M.O.]

ORDASS, LAJOS (1901–1978). Hungarian Lutheran **bishop** and defender of the freedom of the church. After German troops occupied Hungary in March 1944, the Budapest pastor Lajos Ordass (Wolf was his original ethnic German family name) helped Jews to escape and protected politically persecuted people in his parsonage. After World War II, Ordass was elected one of the four bishops of the Hungarian Lutheran Church in September 1945. Soon he became the leading spokesman of his church in relations to **ecumenical** partners abroad and to the Hungarian government. In 1948 the government, which had been progressively taken over by communists, demanded a change of leadership of the church, as well as unambiguous support of the new communist regime and the "voluntary" transfer of the many church schools to the state (*see* SOCIALISM). Ordass refused. His clear rejection of state interference in church affairs led to his arrest (*see* CHURCH AND STATE). He refused to resign from his office as bishop, and was condemned to two years in prison for "currency fraud." In 1950 a special church court dismissed him, under pressure from the government, from his office as bishop. In May 1950 he was released from prison.

During the political changes in 1956, Ordass was rehabilitated by state and church courts and reinstated as bishop in October 1956. With the return to power of the communists, the state deposed him again in October 1958 and forced him into retirement and isolation. His many ecumenical contacts—he was vice president of the Executive Committee of the Lutheran World Federation (1947–1952 and 1957–1963) and a member of the Central Committee of the World Council of Churches (1948–1954)—made his courageous stance for the freedom of the church internationally known. In 1990 the state rehabilitated the late Bishop Ordass and in 1995 a disciplinary court of the church followed suit. [G.G.]

ORDER OF SALVATION (Lat *ordo salutis*). The design or scheme by which **God** intends and achieves the **salvation** of the world. The language of "order of salvation" was initially intended to describe the one act of God in the terms of the **Holy Spirit** that wrought **justification** for humankind. Thus, **Philipp Melanchthon** spoke of the Spirit's working of knowledge, assent, and trust (*notitia, assensus,* and *fiducia*) in the believer. Subsequent orthodox Lutheran theologians such as **Johannes Brenz**, **Martin Chemnitz**, and others further defined the theologic of Melanchthon's trifold description in terms like call, illumination, **conversion**, regeneration, **mystical union**, and renovation. The shift from understanding the theo-logic as a description of the one objective act of God to a prescription for how a would-be believer "should" subjectively and progressively appropriate salvation is too easily made, however. Such a shift transpired under the pressure of **Pietism** represented in **August Hermann Francke** and the "turn to the subject" in the philosophy of the **Enlightenment**, as well as in the fusing of justification and **sanctification** in New England Puritanism, greatly influencing **Lutheranism** on the American scene. The result was an understanding of the order of salvation as a series of works that must be performed by the human subject, which could compromise the centrality of justification by God's **grace** through **faith** because of Christ, according to original Lutheranism. [D.H.L.]

ORDERS/COMMUNITIES, RELIGIOUS. Monastic orders and organized religious communities, especially in **Lutheranism**. If an order may be defined as a group of people who are bound by a common practice or rule and some expression of solidarity (ranging from mutual intercessory **prayer** to scheduled mutual discipline), there have been orders in the **church** from its very beginning. Certainly the descriptions of the church in the Acts present that body as being such a community, sharing goods in common and meeting for stated prayer, fellowship, and cooperative care. Monastic orders became the dominant pattern in the Middle Ages, and often presented their rule or vows as a higher calling than that fulfilled by Christians outside those orders. But such orders were not the only ones in existence and, when monasticism fell from favor in **Protestant** lands, many of these orders remained in existence. The Brethren of the Common Life, which was the fountainhead of the Rhineland mystics, and the Unitas Fratrum, which was transformed into the **Moravian Church** in the 18th century, were only two of these communities.

From the 18th century on orders (in the wider sense) were established in Lutheranism, usually around common interests or characteristics. Perhaps the most common were **mission societies** beginning in the 18th century. While they were not the only supporters, missions often formed the basis for **women's** organizations, whose support of missionaries in prayer and finance may include them within the definition of missions. In the 18th and early 19th century a number of utopian and mystical communities sprang up from Lutheran roots, both in Europe and the United States. The reestablished **diaconate**, especially with its large communities of deaconesses, composed itself as a nonmonastic order. The early 20th century saw a number of organizations established for people of different ages or circumstances—youth, students, and **pastors** most especially. **Dietrich Bonhoeffer's** *Life Together* outlines the rule of a covenanted community at the seminary of the **Confessing Church**. In the late 20th century many pastors and lay people bonded together in communities with an ordered spiritual life and around particular concerns and interests, such as preaching, counseling, **evangelism**, **peace**, and racial harmony. Finally, monasticism never entirely disappeared from Lutheranism and the late 20th century saw not only Lutheran interest and participation in the ecumenical community of Taizé, but also Lutheran monastic communities in Europe and the United States following the Augustinian, Franciscan, or Benedictine rule. *See also* MONASTICISM. [M.O.]

ORDINATION (Lat *ordinatio*, "ordering"). The action of setting a person apart to the ministry of **Word** and **sacrament**. In the second century, ordination became a general practice in the **church**, and **Augustine** was among the first who termed it a sacrament. While other churches have used this term for the entry into the orders of the episcopate (*see* BISHOP), presbyterate (*see* PRIEST), and the **diaconate**, Lutherans have generally reserved it for the presbyterate (*see* MINISTRY). Of all **Martin Luther's** liturgical work, his ordination service (1539) was the last to be composed and the least connected with medieval antecedents. Its structure has dominated Lutheran ordination services ever since: examination of and prayer for the candidate; hymn—usually *Veni sancte spiritus*; prayer; lessons; admonition; laying on of hands with the Lord's Prayer; exposition of the Lord's Prayer related to the **ministry**; biblical address; and benediction. In different times and places, this service has been adorned by pomp and symbolism or marked by simplicity, and its content has reflected different theological emphases, but it has rarely changed in outline.

Certain elements have been almost universal in Lutheran ordination services. Almost all include reference to the dual necessities of certification by the church and call by a **congregation**. Almost all refer to certain important tasks of the **pastor**: teaching, preaching, administration of the sacraments, pastoral care, **evangelism**, and service as a moral example. Most have included confessional subscription (*see* CONFESSIONS, LUTHERAN), and many have included promises of obedience to ecclesial authorities. Few services claim that ordination confers the gifts or abilities necessary to the office of the pastor, although all pray for the fitness of the candidate to the task. In most Lutheran churches, ordination is administered by a bishop. Ordination is understood as involving a calling, blessing, and mission (sending). It is seen as an unrepeatable, life-long commitment, grounded in the assurance of **God's** faithful guidance and support. [M.O.]

ORDINATION OF WOMEN. The **ordination** of women to the **ministry** of **pastor** and **bishop**. Until the mid-20th century Lutherans discussed the issue of the ordination of women only occasionally. While the New Testament describes women acting as apostles, functioning as **deacons**, hosting house churches, and being indistinguishable under the **Gospel** to men, these factors were no more compelling to Lutherans than the examples of other churches, particularly in the holiness and Pentecostal traditions. Before 1950 women had regularly taught, provided **pastoral care** and leadership, especially in supporting **missions**, and, on occasion, preached, but they had never been considered candidates for ordination. This circumstance changed first in Europe, where after 1950 most churches accepted the ordination of women, following the earlier examples of the Lutherans in the Netherlands (1920) and in Alsace-Lorraine (1929). In North America, while Lutheran women had functioned as preachers, none were ordained before 1970. In that year two of the three largest Lutheran bodies changed their constitutions to permit the practice. Almost immediately, the American Lutheran Church ordained Barbara Anderson and the Lutheran Church in America ordained Elizabeth Platz. By the end of the century, there were over 2,000 women pastors in the Evangelical Lutheran Church in America. Neither the **Lutheran Church-Missouri Synod** nor the Wisconsin Evangelical Lutheran Synod ordain women. While several Lutheran churches in **Africa**, **Asia**, and **Latin America** ordain women, the practice is far from universal.

Together with **ecumenical** concerns, arguments against the practice of the ordination of women focused mostly on Scripture, and particularly on the New Testament strictures against women speaking in church. Theologians and debaters set these commands against Jesus' own treatment of women and Paul's insight that, under the Gospel, there is no more male or female. Thirty years after the ordination of women in North America and some other countries, however, opposition remains. It has been difficult for women to be accepted as pastors. But presiding, preaching, teaching, and theological reflection by ordained women has changed the **church** significantly. Issues such as domestic violence, hunger, and care for children are now higher on the church's agenda than they might otherwise have been. It is also true that collaborative rather than hierarchical leadership, the simultaneous holding of a variety of perspectives, and the use of a wider variety of biblical and historical images for **God** are now expected, if not universally practiced. While many of these changes are cultural and might have occurred otherwise, the presence of ordained women in the church has been an important change agent. *See also* WOMEN IN THE CHURCH. [M.O.]

ORGAN/ORGAN MUSIC. The role of the organ in Lutheran **worship**. Since the organ produces sound in the same way humans do—by blowing air through a pipe—it is particularly well suited to encouraging congregational singing. Nonetheless, its use in worship has not been universal. The Eastern churches have never used organs in worship, and **Reformed** churches have often forbidden them. Because of Lutheranism's attitude toward **creation**, incarnation, and the **arts**, it began to foster organ music.

Until the mid-17th century the organ was usually an active solo participant in worship, rather than an accompaniment. Alternation practice was used; that is, the **congregation** or **choir** would sing verses in unison without accompaniment, alternating with the organ playing verses in polyphonic settings. Not only **hymns** were treated in this fashion; such liturgical chants as the Introit and Kyrie at Mass and the Magnificat at Vespers were arranged for alternation. This practice led to the composition of organ chorales—settings of hymn tunes and chants. When the organ became primarily an accompaniment for singing, these compositions were generally replaced by more straightforward settings for such use, as well as by more imaginative chorale preludes, to be used as introductions. To these pieces were added such voluntary music as fugues, preludes, and toccatas.

Small, portable organs played a significant role in home devotions and missionary activity even before the electronic age. The first Lutheran **ordination** in North America was accompanied by an organ, and the instrument has been used to attract attention as well as to encourage song in many other **mission** fields. At the end of the 20th century, even with the attention given electronic keyboards and recorded music, more organ concerts are being performed and more pipe organs are being built for worship spaces (and concert halls) than ever before. *See also* MUSIC IN THE LUTHERAN CHURCH; WORSHIP AND THE ARTS. [M.O.]

ORIGINAL SIN. The sinfulness of humanity caused by the **sin** of the first human beings. The story of Adam and Eve's disobedience is narrated (Gen 3) as the beginning of a history of increasing human sinfulness up to the Tower of Babel (Gen 4–11). This story is taken up by Paul (Rom 5:12–21). Here, the history of sin that began with Adam and is continued by the sin of all is contrasted with the **grace** of **justification** that has entered the world through Jesus Christ. In the framework of his foundational teaching on sin, **Augustine** held that the whole human race sinned in Adam and that thereby sin has become such a universal destiny and power that humans are "not able not to sin." But in **baptism** people are freed from original sin and only a tendency towards sin (concupiscence) remains. For **Thomas Aquinas**, original sin is the ontological loss of original righteousness that is remitted by justifying grace in baptism. The Council of Trent (*see* TRENT, COUN-CIL OF) dogmatized the full remission of original sin in baptism. The con-cupiscence that remains after baptism is a tendency toward sin but no longer original sin.

It was at this last point that the Lutheran **Reformation** contradicted late medieval **theology**. The overpowering reality of the sinfulness of humanity in its self-centered turning away from **God** and its resulting sinful acts is seen as the manifestation of original sin that has come through Adam to hu-manity and continues to be present and active also after baptism. Humans are not able to free themselves from their distorted relationship with God. The extreme position of **Matthias Illyricus Flacius**, who taught that origi-nal sin has become the substance of human nature, was rejected by the Lutheran confessions (*see* CONFESSIONS, LUTHERAN), which under-lined that those who are born again through baptism and the **Holy Spirit** are freed from the bondage of original sin. Today, original sin, understood not primarily as biological heritage, is seen as pointing towards the universal power of evil in a world estranged from God and called to receive God's lib-eration from that power in order to overcome it by **faith**, **love** and action. [G.G.]

ORTHODOX CHURCHES. *See* LUTHERAN-ORTHODOX RELATIONS AND DIALOGUE.

ORTHODOXY, LUTHERAN (Gk *orthodoxia*, from *orthos*, "right," and *doxa*, "glory" or "opinion/belief," thus: "right belief"). Post-**Reformation** period of Lutheran **theology** and **church**. The time immediately following the formative events and developments of the Reformation was marked by innerconfessional consolidation that took the form of Reformed Orthodoxy, Roman Catholic **Counter-Reformation**, and Lutheran Orthodoxy. The term was used from the end of the 16th century, and referred to the self-confidence of Lutheran theologians in clearly holding the authentic **truths**

of the Christian **faith**. Polemics against the "Calvinists" and "Papists"—and their polemics against the Lutherans—blossomed. The beginnings of Lutheran Orthodoxy are usually seen either in 1555 (*see* AUGSBURG, RELIGIOUS PEACE OF) or in the inner-Lutheran controversies and their settlement by the *Formula of Concord* in 1577. The most important phase of Lutheran Orthodoxy ("High Orthodoxy") covers most of the 17th century, while late Orthodoxy extends far into the 18th century when it is progressively replaced by **Pietism** and theological thinking influenced by the **Enlightenment**.

In order to undergird the claim of the **Lutheran church** to be a true manifestation of the church of Jesus Christ, Lutheran Orthodoxy initiated a highly systematic and differentiated scholarly exposition of Christian—and Lutheran—**doctrine** in the form of exegetical, dogmatic, polemical, and apologetical treatises (often all in one). As a methodological tool for this task, the earlier loci-method (Lat *loci*, "places," here "headings," and "topics") in which individual topics of Christian teaching were presented in sequence was changed to be more coherent, systematic, and logical-analytical. Ironically, this reintroduced the high medieval neo-Aristotelian scholastic method (*see* MEDIEVAL CHURCH AND THEOLOGY) just a hundred years after its violent rejection by the reformers. An important feature and implication of this methodology, and of the theological orientation of Lutheran Orthodoxy, was to systematize (and "canonize") the unsystematic writings of **Martin Luther** and the confessions (*see* CONFESSIONS, LUTHERAN) to prove their full accord with Holy Scripture. Traditional Lutheran emphasis on Scripture as normative for the understanding of God's living Word and **Gospel** (*see* BIBLE, AUTHORITY OF) was further "fortified" by introducing something that had been foreign to the Lutheran Reformation and the confessions: a **doctrine** of Holy Scripture that was moved to the top of the system. This doctrine included the concept of verbal inspiration (*see* BIBLE, INSPIRATION OF) in the sense that the biblical texts had been written by the prophets and apostles under the inspiration and direction of the **Holy Spirit**. Thus, the **Word of God** became identical with the written Word of the Bible.

An important place in the dogmatic system was accorded to the doctrine of the person of Christ (*see* CHRISTOLOGY), as foundation for the doctrine of **salvation**, the **order of salvation** (*ordo salutis*), Word and sacrament as **means of grace**, and the **mystical union** with Christ (*unio mystica*). **Justification** by faith alone, however, the center and criterion for the reformers and confessions, was now integrated into the system as one topic in the sequence of the order of salvation or in the section on the appropriation of **grace** and faith. Scripture and **tradition**, including Luther, the confessions, and also the church of the first centuries, provided the basis and orientation, often in the form of proof-texts, by which the "fundamental articles" (another new concept) of the faith were presented in scholarly reflected and clearly argued and articulated formulations and propositions.

The diverse forces of Lutheran Orthodoxy quite naturally found their main centers in the theological faculties of universities that thereby gained new significance as places of churchly teaching (*see* TEACHING AUTHORITY). Prominent among orthodox university faculties were: Helmstedt, Jena, Leipzig, Rostock, and **Wittenberg**. Outstanding representatives of Lutheran Orthodoxy were **Johann Gerhard** (1582–1637), Georg Calixt (1586–1656), Abraham Calov (1612–1686), and Johann Andreas Quenstedt (1617–1688). Lutheran Orthodoxy was not only a major movement in Germany, but also in Scandinavia. In Denmark, Orthodoxy became victorious in the late 16th century. In Finland, rather strict forms of Orthodoxy were upheld by the **bishops** in the 17th century. During the same period, Orthodoxy reigned in Norway and produced a remarkable level of scholarship among **pastors**. In Sweden, the Aristotelian scholasticism of Orthodoxy was introduced by students returning from German universities up until 1624, when the new University of Uppsala began to develop a more independent theology for the country.

Often criticized as a period of arid, conservative, polemical, and abstract theologizing, Lutheran Orthodoxy is considered today in a more balanced way. Though there were these more negative aspects, there was also a lively, engaged, remarkable theological reflection and learned scholarship that firmly confessed the fundaments of faith. At the same time, a profound and confident life of faith is encountered during a period that experienced the horror and devastation of the **Thirty Years' War** and, during the Baroque period, a flourishing of **hymns**, **devotional literature**, poetry, architecture, and great church **music** (**Johann Sebastian Bach**, **Heinrich Schütz**, and others). Certain aspects of Lutheran Orthodoxy were influential into the 19th century and across the waters to North America (*see* KRAUTH, CHARLES PORTERFIELD; WALTHER, CARL FERDINAND WILHELM). Lutheran Orthodoxy has bequeathed to the continuing history of **Lutheranism** the gifts of theological precision, aspects of Lutheran identity, and the task to respond to new situations and contexts with new methods and ways of thinking. [G.G.]

OSIANDER, ANDREAS (c.1496–1552). Eminent Lutheran theologian and reformer in Nürnberg. Osiander is known for his significant publications, theological and humanistic leadership, as well as the controversy of interpretation regarding the doctrine of **justification** that was named after him (Osiandrianism). His argument that one was saved by the infusion of the divine nature of Christ into the believer held implications for **Christology**

and **atonement** theory that were finally decided to be unacceptable by second generation Lutheran reformers and rejected in the *Formula of Concord*. Ordained in 1520, Osiander taught Hebrew at the Nürnberg Augustinian monastery and began preaching at the parish church of Saint Lorenz in 1522. He represented the **evangelical** movement in Nürnberg before the city council in 1523 that resulted in the official acceptance of the **Reformation** in that city. Osiander participated in the **Marburg Colloquy** of 1529, the **Augsburg Diet** in 1530, the Smalcald Conference in 1537, and more.

In 1548 Osiander left for Königsberg, where he became the city's sole **pastor** and a university professor, which is where the Osiander controversy begins. Osiander taught that a person was justified by the indwelling of the divine nature of Christ. This argument, as Osiander's detractors saw, tempted a heretical Christology by separating the two natures of Christ and prioritizing divine nature at human nature's expense. However, Osiander's abiding and positive concern regarding justification was that a singularly forensic (juridical and external) understanding of justification did not fully represent **Martin Luther's** theology. Osiander also anticipated contemporary criticism of atonement theory by observing that the linking of the **doctrine** of justification primarily with Anselm of Canterbury's doctrine of satisfaction was too narrow and did not express the fullness of Luther's thinking on the atonement. His concerns are enjoying new appreciation in **ecumenical** theological conversation on the subjects of atonement and justification, especially between Lutheran and Eastern Orthodox Christians, and are led by distinctive **Luther research** in Finland. [D.H.L.]

– P –

PACIFISM. Attitude of nonviolence against others, including refusal of military service. This position, based on moral and religious grounds and expressed in a variety of forms, has been justified by Christians with reference to Jesus who blessed the peacemakers (Mt 5:9; also Mt 5:39) and his general nonviolent attitude. In the early church, many Christians refused military service and propagated a pacifist stance (e.g., Origin and Tertullian), while others served in the Roman army. When Christianity became the official religion of the Roman Empire, and with the emergence of the **just war** concept in the fourth and fifth centuries, pacifism receded and was continued by small groups or outstanding individuals like Francis of Assisi. At the time of the **Reformation**, radical reforming movements rejected military service. They were the predecessors of today's "Peace Churches" (Mennonites, Quakers, Church of the Brethren, and so on) and of 20th-century

Christian peace groups and movements. Pacifism had a broad following between the two world wars until it waned with the advent of fascism. A new wave of pacifism since the late 1970s was represented by the movement against the threat of nuclear weapons.

Martin Luther and the Lutheran confessions (*see* CONFESSIONS, LUTHERAN) argued against the withdrawal of Christians from public responsibilities, including service in an army and in war. Since then Lutheran churches have generally accepted military service and the use of force as unavoidable, though ambiguous actions in the conditions of a fallen, sinful world. Today, they insist on the possibility of conscientious objection, support peaceful means of conflict resolution, and respect the **witness** of pacifists as a reminder of the Christian ideal which is so sadly contradicted by reality. There exists an **ecumenical** consensus in rejecting war as a means of settling conflicts, but also a recognition that an absolute pacifism is not always a viable means to cope with the many ethnic, nationalist, religious, and social-political conflicts that burden humanity at the end of the 20th century. *See also* PEACE. [G.G.]

PANNENBERG, WOLFHART (1928–). Eminent German Lutheran theologian. Having been a student of Karl Barth in Basel in 1950, Pannenberg moved to Heidelberg where he completed his doctoral studies with a focus on the doctrine of **revelation**. He first taught in Wuppertal, then Mainz, and finally became a professor of systematic theology in 1968 in the Protestant Faculty of Theology at the University of Munich.

Pannenberg's work covers the entire **dogmatic** corpus, but has especially illumined the doctrine of revelation, **Christology**, **resurrection**, the theology of history (*see* HISTORY, THEOLOGY OF), **eschatology**, the **church**, **science and Christianity**, **anthropology**, **ethics**, and **ecumenism**. Pannenberg's position is unique in that he argues for the historicity of Christ's resurrection by linking a Hegelian (*see* HEGEL, GEORG WILHELM FRIEDRICH) philosophy of history to eschatology and an apocalyptic **hermeneutic**. This he undergirds with a metaphysics that gives a priority of causal agency to **God** as the power of the future. Pannenberg's full vision is laid out in his three-volume *Systematic Theology* (translated into English in 1991ff). His work throughout bears the character of apologia, arguing for the **truth** of Christian belief before an intellectual astute agnosticism, and in so doing, as Pannenberg himself avows, proposes what appears to be a "liberal" **ecclesiology** with a "conservative" emphasis upon **doctrine**. Pannenberg has significantly contributed to the theological work of the **Faith and Order** Commission of the **World Council of Churches** and to the achievements of the **Lutheran-Roman Catholic Dialogue**. He is regarded as one of the leading Lutheran theologians in the present, and the influence of his thinking clearly extends beyond the boundaries of his Lutheran church. [D.H.L.]

PAPACY. The office of the bishop of Rome, spiritual head of the **Roman Catholic Church**, and its understanding and exercise. From the third century onwards the prestige of the church of Rome and the special **authority** of its bishop were increasingly seen as preeminent for the **church** in the West. In the high Middle Ages, this development had led to a situation in which the popes, as "vicars of Christ," had assumed unlimited religious and secular power. It was this system against which the **Reformation** protested. Accordingly, the Lutheran attitude toward the papacy and popes has often been characterized according to the polemical language of the 16th century. At this time, the pope was even labeled as the **"antichrist"** because of the perception that his office was more authoritative than the **Gospel** itself. Correlatively, antagonists to the papacy thought that it opposed the Gospel of **justification** by **grace** through **faith** through the imposition of a system that burdened individual consciences and withheld the comfort of **salvation**. This was the critical stance of the Lutheran confessions (*see* CONFESSIONS, LUTHERAN).

The confessional and theological position regarding the papacy, however, is so polemical only in the event that any ministry would subvert the **Gospel**. Indeed, the confessional position even allows a positive regard for the papacy. Articles 28 of both the *Augsburg Confession* (*CA*) and its *Apology*, article 4 of **Martin Luther's** *Smalcald Articles*, and **Philipp Melanchthon's** *Treatise on the Power and the Primacy of the Pope*, all affirm the possibility of papal oversight of the church as a human tradition for the sake of the **unity of the church**. The pope, as with all **bishops** and **priests** (*see* APOSTOLICITY and APOSTOLIC SUCCESSION), however, is constrained to "preach the Gospel, forgive sins, judge **doctrine** and condemn doctrine that is contrary to the Gospel, and exclude from the Christian community the ungodly," all according not to some divine right, nor human power, but by "God's **Word** alone" (*CA*, article 28). Such authority derived under and by God's Word is circumscribed as a strictly ecclesiastical authority; Lutherans do not recognize any authority for affairs of state to be exercised by bishops or the papacy as such. Ecclesiastical authority, however and again, is not by divine right per se. It exercises the ministry of the Gospel in and not over the church in common with all believers.

Official **Lutheran–Roman Catholic dialogue** from 1970–1978 on papal primacy and infallibility in the United States has led to the conclusion that if the papal office were constructed and exercised clearly in subordination and service to the Gospel, did not subvert Christian freedom, and allowed for self-governance in the Lutheran **communion**, Lutherans could increasingly affirm the need for a ministry serving the unity of the whole church and work toward deeper **reconciliation** of the two communions. The international church agreement between the Vatican and the **Lutheran World**

Federation on the foundational import of the doctrine of justification (*Joint Declaration on the Doctrine of Justification*, 1999) may provide promise of such reconciliation. However, among other evidences, the continued practice of indulgences in Roman Catholicism and the perception by many Lutherans that the papal office is not exercised in a way sympathetic to conciliarism makes further visible reform necessary before anything like a papal office could be acceptable to most contemporary Lutherans. [D.H.L.]

PARISH (Gk *paroikia*, "an ecclesiastical district"). This word may refer to the members of a **congregation,** or it may refer to the neighborhood in which a church is located, and to all the residents of that neighborhood. In the fourth century "parish," according to this second meaning, became the basic public and ecclesiastical administrative district in the Roman Empire. Today, the two meanings are closely connected in European established churches and in Roman Catholicism. They are, however, widely different in cultures where church membership is entirely voluntary. Thus, in North America, the number of members who live within walking distance of their church building might be negligible, and the overlap between a congregation's membership and its neighborhood very slight. In the 1970s the concept of parish as place was emphasized as a way to encourage outreach beyond the membership of a congregation into changed neighborhoods. Congregations, even those made up almost entirely of commuting members, were urged to address the needs of their parish, and to reflect its **culture** in its **worship**. In many Lutheran churches in the world, the parish continues as basic unit of the structure of a church body and is normally governed by a parish council. [M.O.]

PAROUSIA. *See* ESCHATOLOGY.

PARSONAGE, LUTHERAN. The influence of Lutheran **pastors'** families on cultural, social, and political life. The **Reformation** created a new social entity: the families of married pastors that soon became the center of congregational life. The Lutheran emphasis on theological study, **education**, **music**, and **literature**, and on the general improvement of the conditions of human life found a special expression in the spiritual and intellectual atmosphere in pastors' families in their house, the parsonage. Beginning with the model, often idealized, of **Martin Luther's** family and household at **Wittenberg** (*see* BORA, KATHARINA VON) until well into the 20th century, the parsonage has frequently been the home of a well-educated, artistically and socially interested **family** within a Christian-bourgeois milieu. This family was regarded as a model of Christian **piety** and lifestyle, and often overburdened by high expectations. It had, especially in rural settings, a considerable influence in promoting new developments in **health** care, support of the poor, general education, gardening, music in the family, and so on. The wives of pastors played a crucial role in making parsonages into such places, and they furthered social work, the education of other women and their entry into professional activities.

All this provided the fertile ground for an impressive number—far out of proportion with the factual percentage of pastors within the educated classes—of highly educated and motivated children of pastor's families who became major figures in public life, universities, and the arts. Only a handful can be mentioned: the poet Gotthold Ephraim Lessing, the philosopher Friedrich Nietzsche, the educator Friedrich Fröbel, the composer Michael Praetorius, the North American politicians Frederick Augustus Conrad Muhlenberg and John Peter Gabriel Muhlenberg (*see* MUHLEN-BERG, HENRY MELCHIOR), and the contemporary Swedish filmmaker Ingmar Bergmann. *See also* CULTURE, LUTHERAN IMPACT ON. [G.G.]

PASSION MUSIC. A musical setting of Christ's **passion** history according to one of the four Evangelists. In the Middle Ages, these four were spread over Holy Week—Matthew on Palm Sunday, Mark on Tuesday, Luke on Thursday, and John on Friday—and the chanting of the texts led naturally to plainsong Passions. In these settings, the words of the evangelist, the crowd, and Jesus were chanted to different pitches and speeds. The development of polyphony led to settings in this style. At first only the crowd, then only certain characters were given polyphonic treatment, leaving at least the evangelist chanted by a soloist. During the **Reformation**, this form was adapted to include vernacular texts—**Johann Walter's** St. Matthew's Passion was used in Nürnberg for over 250 years. Simultaneously, Lutheran composers such as Leonard Lechner wrote completely polyphonic Passions. In the next century, baroque composers elaborated the form to include more complex instrumentation and the interpolation of **chorales** (the three Passions by **Heinrich Schütz** are the best representatives of this 17th-century style). The 18th century saw the interpolations preserved, but the **Gospel** readings were replaced by paraphrases, that is until **Johann Sebastian Bach** returned to the older style in his St. John and St. Matthew Passions. Generally, the composers of the 19th and 20th centuries treated the subject of Jesus' Passion with **oratorios** (based, for instance, on the "Last Words of Christ") rather than Passion music strictly so called. The most popular example of such an oratorio is *Jesus Christ, Superstar*, by Andrew Lloyd Webber and Tim Rice. Such 20th-century composers as **Hugo Distler** and Ernst Pepping, however, have composed Passion settings as well. [M.O.]

PASSION OF CHRIST. *See* CHRISTOLOGY.

PASTOR (Lat for "shepherd"). Title of ordained ministers of **Word** and **sacrament** in Lutheran (and other) churches. The title "pastor" appeared in the New Testament (e.g., Eph 4:11). In the course of church history, it has come to refer in a broad sense to spiritual oversight and responsibility over a **congregation** or a church body (diocese, and so on). Ordained ministers, whether the leader (presbyter) of a local congregation, a **bishop**, or even the pope (*see* PAPACY) use the term "pastor" to indicate their "pastoral" ministry. In addition to this general usage, in the Lutheran tradition "pastor" has become the title of the minister of a local congregation or **parish** (in German a female pastor is a *Pastorin*). The title "pastor" was adopted in many Lutheran churches because it suggests another understanding of ministry than the traditional title **priest** (which was, however, continued by the Scandinavian Lutheran churches) or the German title *Pfarrer* (Lat *parochus*, "the leader of a parish") that reflected a certain superior, if not authoritarian understanding of ministry.

In addition to the understanding of their functions, role, and **ordination**, one aspect that marked the status of Lutheran pastors (and their families, *see* PARSONAGE) was the emphasis on their academic theological training. This gave them an elevated position in many societies. Already in 1535 the ordination of Lutheran pastors in Germany was made dependent on a successful theological examination that became increasingly more difficult. In modern societies, at least in the West, the special status of pastors has disappeared. The public recognition and respect of a pastor depends on his or her credibility, human qualities, and spiritual authority. *See also* MINISTRY. [G.G.]

PASTORAL CARE. Care of souls and personal assistance. In the early days of the **church**, pastoral care was primarily the responsibility of the **bishop** whose counseling, of course, took place within the care of **deacons**, widows, and ordinary Christians for one another. During the Middle Ages, parish clergy were expected to provide such care, often through the confessional. **Martin Luther** himself began the practice of Lutheran pastoral care, not only in his direct care for the sick and troubled, but also in his correspondence, collected in "Letters of Spiritual Counsel." He established certain themes that pervade Lutheran practice to the present, such as the expectation of involvement of **pastors** in their parishioners' personal and family life, the practical application in specific circumstances of such theological themes as **law and Gospel** and the **two kingdoms**, and the involvement of **prayer** and the **sacraments** in pastoral conversation. In his own **ordination** service, and in those that Lutherans composed over the centuries, the responsibility of clergy for pastoral care in preparing individuals to receive the **sacraments**, to be married or confirmed, and at times of crisis, most especially death, is universally highlighted.

Every sort of **Lutheranism** has attended to *Seelsorge*, the care of souls. Lutheran **Orthodoxy**, for instance, with its concern for the **order of salvation**, lifted up the notion of the pastor as guide on that path. **Pietism** has perhaps given it the most careful consideration, going so far, in its Halle manifestation (*see* FRANCKE, AUGUST HERMANN), as foreshadowing Freudianism by outlining a form of "soul analysis" that checked for spiritual dryness, before seeking and applying joy or consolation. The Lutheranism, particularly in the United States, has followed the general **Protestant** progression in understanding the task of pastoral care. At first, pastoral care was generally seen as a way of driving the soul to self-despair and **conversion**, which often led to the more communal and manipulative practice of revivalism. By about 1900 this understanding gave way to a search for adjustment and mental health, often leaving little distinction between pastoral care and psychological counseling. The late 20th century saw a return to respect for **spirituality**, the sacraments, and the faith community in pastoral care. While training in pastoral care has almost always been a part of preparation for **ordination**, Clinical Pastoral Education in the United States set this training in actual situations—usually in **hospitals** or other institutions. Lutherans were among the leaders in establishing this program. [M.O.]

PATRISTICS. Study and use of the theology of the "fathers of the **church**." The term is to be distinguished from "patrology," which refers to the literary and historical study of the works of the church fathers. The period of the church fathers, the great theologians of the early church, whose teaching was recognized by the church as orthodox, covers the first seven centuries—in the Eastern tradition, the first eight centuries. While the **Orthodox church** had always preserved a high esteem of the fathers of the church alongside the **authority** of Holy Scripture and as an alternative to the authority of the pope (*see* PAPACY), in the West a renewed interest in patristics came only with the Renaissance and the **Reformation**. New editions of the church fathers were produced, and the reformers, with their good knowledge of the writings of the fathers, referred to them quite frequently. The many references to and quotations from patristic sources in the Lutheran confessions (*see* CONFESSIONS, LUTHERAN) served to underline the continuity, **catholicity**, and **apostolicity** of Lutheran teaching. Lutherans were the first to use the term *theologia patristica* in the late 17th century (*see* ORTHODOXY, LUTHERAN); and it was in the writings of the Lutheran **Johann Gerhard** that the term "patrology" first appeared. In **Neo-Lutheranism**, the Lutheran confessions were considered to be the true continuation of the teaching of the fathers of the church.

Today, the study and knowledge of the **theology** of the church fathers has become an essential element of theological dialogue and mutual understanding within the **ecumenical movement**. Common roots are rediscovered in the contributions of the church fathers to the formation of the **Canon of Holy Scripture**, the development of **creeds** and fundamental Christian **doctrines**, and the articulation of theological and spiritual insights that have shaped the history of theology up to our time. [G.G.]

PAULSSEN, BERTHA (1891–1973). German and American social worker, sociologist, and teacher. Having completed university studies in mathematics, science, philosophy, psychology, and education, Paulssen received her doctorate from the University of Leipzig in 1917, and remained in that institution as a librarian and assistant. After two years, she began her career as a social worker, working with young women in Frankfurt, the Lutheran **Inner Mission** in northern Germany, and establishing Women's Auxiliaries in the Lutheran churches in eastern Germany. In the early 1920s she introduced modern methods of care and management to the youth services in Hamburg, and began her career as a teacher in social psychology. When Adolf Hitler came to power, she left Germany for the United States in 1936, and began settlement work in New York City. Over the next few years, she worked at several social ministry institutions while teaching at the Philadelphia Deaconess Motherhouse and at Wagner, Gettysburg, and Muhlenberg Colleges.

In 1946 Paulssen became the first full-time professor of Christian sociology and psychology and the first tenured woman at an American Lutheran seminary, serving at the Gettysburg Seminary until her retirement in 1963. There, she trained a generation of **pastors** and lay people who became leaders in social ministry, communications, and pastoral counseling. Because of her infectious vision and commitment, it is to no small degree that, 25 years after her death, the network of social ministry organizations related to the Lutheran churches in North America was the largest such web on the continent. [M.O.]

PEACE. The Christian and ecumenical witness to peace. The Old Testament term "*shalom*" has become a key concept in modern Christian reflection and action concerning peace on earth. *Shalom* points not only to an absence or reduction of conflict, but also in a more basic and comprehensive way to wholeness, peace with **justice**, righteousness, and the good order **God** desires for humanity, all of which God will accomplish in its fullness in eschatological (*see* ESCHATOLOGY), messianic time (e.g., Lev 26:3–13; Ezek 37:26; Is 2:2–4; Mic 4:11ff; Ps 72). Both in his person and in his message, Jesus Christ brings God's peace (Jn 14:27; Jn 16:33). Peace on earth is proclaimed at Jesus' birth (Lk 2:14); he blesses the peacemakers (Mt 5:9); in him people are reconciled and a new humanity is created whose peace he is (Eph 2:13–18); he pleads for peace (Rom 12:18).

This strong biblical peace **witness** has inspired Christians and churches throughout history in their words and actions. **Martin Luther** declared that it is a special human responsibility to preserve peace on earth as the supreme good, even if this may involve the use of force. Groups belonging to the radical **Reformation** went further and practiced a strict **pacifism** that has become a mark of today's "peace churches": Mennonites, Friends (Quakers), Brethren, Amish, and other groups.

But in Christian history, there has also been much involvement of churches in wars, blessing of weapons, and support of aggressive or racist nationalism that led to war. It took the shock of two world wars in the 20th century, and peace efforts during the early stages of the **ecumenical movement** (e.g., by Archbishop **Nathan Söderblom** of Sweden) to begin to change this history and get involved in a widespread and active Christian concern for peace. Particularly during the period of the "cold war" after 1945 with its arms race between East and West and the threat of nuclear war, the peace studies, statements, consultations, and encounters enabled by the **World Council of Churches** and also by the Second Vatican Council (VATICAN COUNCIL II) have provided a strong stimulus for numerous Christian peace groups and movements. Many Lutheran churches as well as the **Lutheran World Federation** (LWF) have supported these initiatives. In addition to more general peace statements and studies, the LWF became especially active during the 1980s and 1990s assisting in the Israeli-Palestinian peace process and helping to negotiate peace agreements in Central America. In support of these and similar activities, the LWF has established a Peace Fund.

Despite differences between and within churches and the ecumenical movement concerning the continued relevance of the **just war** concept, pacifism, use of military force, and methods to be employed for national and international security, churches today generally agree that an active commitment to the cause of peace among nations and groups within nations is an essential part of the Christian **mission**, that the furtherance of **human rights** and social and economic justice is a necessary condition of peace, that the churches have an important task of mediation and reconciliation in situations of conflict, and that churches should support both peace education among their members and the strengthening of international peacekeeping institutions and measures. *See also* VIOLENCE AND NONVIOLENCE. [G.G.]

PEASANTS' WAR (1524–1525). A revolt of German, Swiss, and Austrian peasants against their ecclesiastical and secular lords. The deteriorating social and economic situation of peasants in central Europe created by increased rents, dues, taxes, and tithes, and by serfdom led to growing suffering and unrest among peasants. They reacted, finally, in a series of more or less well-organized violent revolts during 1524/25 in Alsace, Frankonia, the Palatinate, Swabia, Thuringia, and parts of Austria and Switzerland. Leaders and participants in these revolts had also been inspired and motivated by **evangelical** preaching, including **Martin Luther's**, about the **liberty** of Christians, the right of believing communities to elect their own **pastors**, the dignity of the common people in the sight of **God**, social **justice**, and the critique of ecclesiastical and secular authorities. This provided the ideological basis for their struggle. Several preachers joined the rebellious peasants, **Thomas Müntzer** being the most prominent one. In the *Ten Articles* of the Swabian peasants, the social reforms that they demanded were legitimized by references to the **Word of God** in the Bible.

Luther, who had admonished peasants as well as princes not to use violence, protested against this use of the Word of God for social-political ends (*see* ETHICS). He protested even more vehemently when the peasant's revolution began. After the peasants were brutally defeated by the princes' armies, Luther and some other reformers like **Johannes Brenz** pleaded with the princes to deal leniently with the defeated peasants and to alleviate their social situation. To a certain degree this happened, not least out of the self-interest of the princes. The Peasants' War revealed the potential social and political implications of the **Reformation** as well as the difficulty of Lutherans in coping theologically and politically with these implications. [G.G.]

PELAGIANISM. The fourth-century **heresy** that attributed to humans a natural ability to obey **God's** will and achieve **salvation**. **Augustine** held that this possibility was wholly negated by **original sin** and that humans could be saved only by God apart from human works. The heresy was repeatedly condemned (*see* ANATHEMA) and the condemnation's interpretation repeatedly extended, so that the Council of Orange (529) declared that even the desire for **faith** was itself a gracious gift of God.

Reformation-era Lutheran **theology** was a coalescence of many preceding critiques against claims that "God does not withhold his grace from those who do that which is in them" (*facere quod in se est*). "Mainstream" medieval Catholicism, as well as early reformers, thought this nominalist view was a fatal compromise yet again of the Pauline-Augustinian view of divine sovereignty and **grace**, as over and against the bondage of the sinful human will. But the reformers leveled their anti-Pelagian sights at Catholicism, too, perceiving that its advocacy of a processive view of **justification**, completed by the Christian's cooperation and righteous work, was semi-Pelagian at best (*see* SYNERGISM). Against this Catholic attitude, reaffirmed by the Council of Trent (*see* TRENT, COUNCIL OF), the reformers argued for the complete sufficiency and adequacy of justification by grace through faith apart from works, achieved already and attributed to a sinful humanity on the merit of Christ alone. Justification, for the Lutherans, in other words, was an unmerited free gift by imputation of Christ's "alien righteousness."

Medieval Catholicism was not the only target for Pelagianist claims. Indeed, the radical reformers—with their advocacy of believer's **baptism**, **free will**, voluntary **church**, and personal acts of **sanctification**—were more often the cause for anti-Pelagian suspicions. **Martin Luther** often attacked **Anabaptist** claims, himself declaring that the Anabaptists taught a new form of justification by works. [D.H.L.]

PENANCE AND RECONCILIATION. *See* FORGIVENESS.

PENTECOST. Feast of the outpouring of the **Holy Spirit**. The celebration of the outpouring of the Holy Spirit upon the disciples (Acts 2:1) 50 days after the **resurrection** of Christ is the foundation event of the feast of Pentecost ("fiftieth"). In Christian history, Pentecost is considered the "birthday" of the **church**, and for Lutherans this feast highlights the essential role of the Holy Spirit, active through **Word** and **sacrament**, in creating **faith** and gathering the church. First evidence of the observance of Pentecost comes from the third century (Tertullian), more clearly from the fourth century (Eusebius), and then again from the sixth century. Preceding Pentecost is Ascension Day, the 40th day after the resurrection (Acts 1:3). This "Holy Thursday" has been observed since the end of the fourth century. The **Sunday** following Pentecost is Trinity Sunday or the festival of the Holy **Trinity**. In 1343 the general observance of this feast was ordered throughout the Western church. Trinity Sunday marks the end of the first half of the **church year**. For the second half of the year, the Trinity Season, Lutherans, **Anglicans**, and others have continued the tradition to number the subsequent Sundays "after Trinity." Roman Catholics number these Sundays "after Pentecost," a custom that was also adopted by Lutheran churches in North America and Scandinavia. [G.G.]

PEOPLE OF GOD. *See* CHURCH.

PERSECUTION. Discrimination and persecution of Christians. From the beginning, the first Christian communities experienced persecution by Jewish and civil authorities (Acts 6:8–8:1; 12:3). Up until 313, when Christianity became the state religion under Constantine, Christians were persecuted sporadically by the Roman state, and numerous martyrs and confessors were held in high esteem by the **church**. Throughout the Middle Ages, often with the help of the state, Christians themselves began to persecute other Christians considered to be heretics. Again and again they also participated in the persecution of Jews in different parts of Europe. During the **Reformation**, alternate efforts were undertaken to either suppress the Reformation (e.g., the St. Bartholomew's night in 1572 in France when about 20,000 Huguenots were killed) or to regain lost ground during the **Counter-Reformation** when Protestants in Austria (Salzburgers), Hungary, and the Czech and Slovak lands were persecuted. Sadly, even Lutherans and the **Reformed** churches had the state persecute members of radical Reformation movements.

The most comprehensive and powerful attack on Christianity was undertaken by totalitarian regimes in the 20th century. The Nazi regime in Germany and in its occupied countries (1939–1945) persecuted Christians who resisted the regime (e.g., martyrs such as **Dietrich Bonhoeffer**, **Julius Bursche**, and **Kaj Munk**) and discriminated against Christians in general. An even more terrible persecution of Christians was organized by the state in the Soviet Union with several thousand martyrs among bishops, priests, monastics, and uncounted lay people. Albania and China saw similar forms of persecution, while in other communist states the life of the church was severely limited and many Christians were victims of various forms of discrimination. Lutherans were among those who experienced the different forms of persecution in Germany (in Nazi and later Communist East Germany), the Soviet Union (the ethnic German minority of some two millions), the Baltic countries, and in other countries. *See also* CONFESSING CHURCH. [G.G.]

PERSON. *See* ANTHROPOLOGY.

PETRI, LAURENTIUS (1499–1573). First Lutheran archbishop of Sweden. Petri studied in **Wittenberg** and was influenced by **Martin Luther** and the ideals of the **Reformation**. After his return to Sweden he worked as a schoolmaster at Uppsala. In 1531 he was elected first Lutheran archbishop of Uppsala and occupied this position for 42 years. When he was consecrated **bishop**, the historic episcopate was preserved because the Roman Catholic bishop of Västerås, Petrus Magni, was the consecrator (*see* APOSTOLIC SUCCESSION). He directed, supported by his brother **Olaus Petri**, the process of the Reformation and of ecclesiastical reconstruction in Sweden and Finland (which belonged at that time to Sweden). Though he was close to the king, a tension arose when King Gustavus I Wasa tried to establish full state control over the church and abolish the episcopate.

Laurentius Petri helped significantly to produce the Swedish Bible translation, the so-called *Gustav-Wasa-Bible* of 1541 and the Swedish **hymnbook** of 1567. The Swedish **church order** (draft 1561), which regulated the life of the church, was almost entirely his work. It could not be introduced immediately because of the strong Calvinistic tendencies of King Eric XIV. The great moment came when, under the newly appointed King John III, Petri could present his church order for adoption in 1571. *See also* APOSTOLIC SUCCESSION. [G.G.]

PETRI, OLAUS (1493–1552). The most important reformer in Sweden. Olaus Petri (brother of **Laurentius Petri**) came to **Wittenberg** in 1516 where he studied with **Martin Luther**. He returned to Sweden in 1518/19 and began to proclaim the new teachings of the **Reformation**. Sent in 1524 by King Gustavus I Wasa to Stockholm as town clerk, he continued to work for the introduction of the Reformation there. In 1531 he was appointed chancellor of the Kingdom of Sweden (until 1533). In this position, he supported the implementation of the Reformation, which had been officially accepted in 1527. However, when the king wanted to abolish the office of **bishop** in order to introduce direct state governance of the church, Petri protested. Because of this stance and other differences with the king he was accused of high treason in 1539/40. He was condemned to death, but finally pardoned against payment—by the citizenship of Stockholm—of a high fine.

In 1543 Petri became senior **pastor** of Stockholm and served in this position until his death. Between 1525 and 1531 he wrote, translated, and published a number of catechetical, pastoral, and liturgical texts that became influential for the further course of the Swedish reformation: 1525/26 a first translation of the New Testament into Swedish, 1526 a small **hymnal** in Swedish that was expanded in 1530 and again in 1536, 1526 a devotional and prayer book in an **evangelical** spirit, 1528 a kind of pastoral theology for **evangelical** preachers, and 1529 the Swedish **worship** agenda to be followed in 1531 by the order of the Swedish mass that transformed this service into a Lutheran one. These and other texts became foundational for the course of the Swedish Reformation and the emerging shape of the Swedish church. [G.G.]

PHILIPPISTS. Pejorative term applied by **Gnesio-Lutherans** to adherents of **Philipp Melanchthon**. The term and the group to which it refers have their roots—like the two other polemical designations **Crypto-Calvinists** and Gnesio-Lutherans—in the intra-Lutheran doctrinal controversies after the **Interim** (1548). The Philippists (also called Crypto-Calvinists but not in all cases identical with them) followed the more open position of Melanchthon towards both the **Roman Catholic** and the **Reformed** traditions as well as **Humanism**. When the doctrinal controversies were settled by the *Formula of Concord* (1577), the Philippists lost their influence. Some of them were still around in the 17th century. [G.G.]

PHILOSOPHY. The role of philosophy in the Lutheran **tradition**. Philosophy has always been important as a servant of **theology** in **Lutheranism**, though it has also since **Martin Luther** been strongly criticized when it exceeds its appropriate function. In the *Heidelberg Disputation* (1518) and several succeeding tracts (e.g., *The Babylonian Captivity of the Church* [1520], and *The Bondage of the Will* [1525]), Luther condemned philosophy—with all use of **reason**—when philosophy and reason would extrapolate from human thought and experience in the pretension that something could be said authoritatively about the nature and ways of **God**. Such efforts amounted to a misdirected "theology of glory"—never a positive phrase in Luther's view—while the only correct understanding of God was from where reason could not discern God, namely in the revelational theology of the **cross** of Jesus Christ.

The Lutheran emphasis on **revelation** informing reason does not entirely discount reason or philosophy, however, and philosophy has served significantly in the framing of Lutheran theological systems over the centuries. After Luther's and **Philipp Melanchthon's** delimitation of philosophy (cf. Luther's *Small Catechism*, Creed, article 3; Melanchthon's *Apology of the Augsburg Confession*, article 4), one may discern at least four general ways in which philosophy is used. First, philosophy may be used as a tool to define the current dominant intellectual horizon in which theology is to function. Existentialist philosophy, inherited in its Christian form from **Søren Aabye Kierkegaard**, distinctly informed the theologies of **Rudolf Bultmann** and Paul Tillich, who in turn highly influenced other modern theologies of the **Word**. The process philosophy of Alfred North Whitehead has similarly influenced contemporary **feminist theology** and many other postmodern theological proposals, much as in earlier generations Aristotelian categories had continued to inform Lutheran scholasticism and other versions of Protestant **Orthodoxy**.

The **Enlightenment**, however, legitimated philosophy apart from theology and established normativity of philosophy more on its own terms, especially through the work of **Immanuel Kant**. At that point, theology either had to be nonphilosophically argued, as with Orthodoxy or later fundamentalism, or was co-opted by philosophy; thus, a second mode for philosophy in Lutheranism, whereby philosophy normatively explicates Christian doctrine. **Georg Wilhelm Friedrich Hegel's** idealistic (*see* IDEALISM) transmutation of traditional doctrinal claims, or even certain applications of the already mentioned existentialist or process theologies, may serve as examples of philosophers doing theology *as* philosophical theology, not theology as traditionally used within the **church** by the norm of Holy Scripture (*see* BIBLE, AUTHORITY OF).

More toward the limited role, again, philosophy has been explicitly used in Lutheran theology to explore the distinctly philosophical questions that theology engenders. For example, the speech-act and intentionalist philosophy of John Searle or the language philosophy of Ludwig Wittgenstein have served to clarify questions raised by Gerhard Ebeling's theology of the **Word** and George Lindbeck's proposal for narrative theology. This use of philosophy, when even broader, would liken to a fourth style, where philosophy functions as translation between theology and cultures of apparently incommensurate paradigms of understanding, as between theology and science (*see* SCIENCE AND CHRISTIANITY). This has been perhaps philosophy's most vigorous employment over all the Christian centuries. Within Lutheranism itself, philosophy provides the language to present, commend, or defend the **faith** before an unbelieving audience: philosophy as apology. [D.H.L.]

PIETISM. Wide-ranging, diverse spiritual movement that began in the 17th century and continues through the present, and that has focussed on the regeneration or **conversion** of the believer, and on living, active, heartfelt **faith**. While drawing on medieval **mysticism**, **John Calvin**, **Anabaptists**, and other sources, Pietism seems to have begun in **Lutheranism** as a reaction to Lutheran **Orthodoxy**, and spread through the **Reformed** churches and **Roman Catholicism**. Pietism has obvious parallels with Anglican Puritanism, and was a major influence on **John Wesley**. While it is difficult to generalize Pietism, it seems to be **ecumenical**, emotional, lay-focused, and interested in **institutions** only if they are voluntary associations. It opposed Orthodoxy for its overattention to the will and the intellect, seeing it as encouraging a barren and arid assent rather than a living faith. Later, Pietism opposed its own child, **Enlightenment** rationalism, for its overattention to **reason**, seeing it as setting skepticism above faith.

　Johann Arndt and Philipp Spener (1635–1705) are generally acknowledged as the grandfather and father of Pietism, respectively. Spener gave the movement its characteristic form—the small group (conventicle or church-within-a-church) that would guide the believer through the **order of salvation**, with particular attention paid to illumination, **conversion**, and regeneration. The most influential sort of Pietism within Lutheranism during the 17th and 18th centuries was Halle Pietism, founded by **August Hermann Francke**. Francke saw the life of a Christian as begun with a "breakthrough" of conversion, marked by sorrowful **repentance**, that begins a lifetime of increasing intimacy with Jesus. Francke's understanding of the Christian life was influential on its own, but received most of its power from its institutional expression. Under the leadership of Francke, his son, their wives, and their colleagues at the university, Halle became the center of an immense Christian endeavor that included establishing schools, an orphanage, a publication house, and a foreign **mission society**. Through these institutions, their products, and their imitators, Halle Pietism spread not only across Europe, but to India (*see* ZIEGNEBALG, BATHOLOMAEUS) and North America, where **Henry Melchior Muhlenberg** and his fellow graduates of the institutions gave order to the Lutheran churches. Under the leadership of Count Nikolaus Ludwig von Zinzendorf, a graduate and opponent of Halle, the pre-Reformation Bohemian Unitas Fratrum were reorganized into the **Moravian church**, which linked Halle Pietism with mystical **spirituality** and the basic teachings of **Martin Luther**.

　Pietism's concentration on an active faith rather than on doctrinal formulations led to its ecumenical bent—Lutheran pietists cooperated with and welcomed other **Protestants**, even Roman Catholics and skeptics, who shared their warmth of devotion. This ecumenism, together with the pietists' demand for a converted clergy, and the natural tendency of conventicles to condescend to and even separate from the wider **church**, led to a rather tenuous relationship between Pietism and the state churches. In fact, in most such states conventicles were prohibited by law. This proscription did not prevent Pietism from spreading. In Sweden, Halle Pietism attracted many aristocrats and clergy, while Moravianism was extremely popular among commoners. Norway and Denmark were shaped in the early 18th century by missionary ventures to the Lapps and Greenland and by the devotional writings of Erik Pontoppidan.

Pietism has shaped Christianity in many ways. Modern methods of Bible study, spiritual formation, psychological autobiography, lay ministry, **evangelism**, **stewardship**, and social ministry all hearken back to that movement. It had its besetting weaknesses: rejection of the world and **creation**; an overeagerness to reject form, **doctrine**, and **tradition** prima facie as empty show; its desire to achieve quietism and perfectionism. Its popularity and influence sprang, however, from its ability to shape lives in accord with its central metaphor: the marriage of Christ and the soul. [M.O.]

PIETY. One's inner, personal attitude toward **God**, or the practices that spring from that attitude. Piety includes such **devotional** practices as **prayer** and meditation, regular **worship** and study, as well as ways of living as the intentional **stewardship** of one's political, economic, or social power. These practices both depend upon and help shape the believer's fundamental, often unreflected upon attitude toward God. The root and useful meaning of "piety" and "pious" is that of an honest and respectful affection. Indeed, the story of Christian piety is one of a constant quest for honesty, for expressions that reflect the heartfelt devotion of the believer and are not simply the adopted formulations of an earlier day. Thus, according to its own lights, Lutheran **Orthodoxy** rejected the rude and rugged expressions of the Reformers, **Pietism** rejected the overprecise lip-service of Orthodoxy, the **Enlightenment** rejected the otherworldly self-righteousness of Pietism, the **Awakening** rejected the arid Rationalism of the Enlightenment, **Liberalism** rejected the self-centered Romanticism of the Awakening, and so on, each searching for an honest expression of its own **faith** in its own day. Of its nature, then, piety will reflect the culture and worldview in which it is set.

From the theological presuppositions of **Lutheranism**, piety will almost unavoidably be Christocentric (*see* CHRISTOLOGY)—incarnational and shaped by the **theology** of the **cross**. It will be shaped as well by Lutheranism's own cultural heritage—for instance, almost all Lutheran piety gives great importance to **hymnody** and hymn singing. But if it is going to be as honest as it intends, Lutheran piety must also be adapted to the **culture** in which it finds itself. Thus, for instance, piety among Lutherans in **Asia** and **Africa** has paid considerable attention to the place of ancestors, while that among African American Lutherans centers much more upon themes of liberation than that among white Americans. [M.O.]

POLITICAL THEOLOGY. A **contextual theology** movement of the 20th century that intended to serve as critique and correction of a writer's political situation, drawing from explicitly political as well as biblical and classical theological sources. This genre chronologically preceded and was a direct influence on **liberation theology**. It was shaped especially by the German theologians Jürgen Moltmann and Johann Baptist Metz. Political theology, however, has not assumed a specifically Lutheran character, except perhaps in the work of several Latin American theologians, certain adaptations of the thought of **Dietrich Bonhoeffer** that critique culture, and selected social statements of national churches. Insofar as the theological themes of **eschatology** and the renewed sense of **God's** action in history are interpreted afresh and together, as in the thought of Carl Braaten or **Wolfhart Pannenberg**, one will find suggestions for **ethics** that have clear political resonance. In general, however, when political interpretation is wrested from the category of God's sovereignty and eschatology is reduced to a political agenda for the **church**, Lutherans would warn against a coming new tyranny to replace the perceived old one. The integral Lutheran position is that Christians are not to be driven fundamentally by ideology, though the use of political, economic, and social analysis may well fund good theological reflection. Rather, impelled by the good news and new reality of **justification**, the church will be appropriately political, whatever the strategies, when it lives in the **faith** that the **Kingdom of God** will come in God's good time and when it inspires Christians, in the meantime, to care for each other, for **justice** and **peace** in the world, and for **creation**. *See also* CHURCH AND WORLD; SOCIAL SCIENCES. [D.H.L.]

PORVOO COMMON STATEMENT (1992). Agreement between **Anglican** and Lutheran churches in northern Europe on full church fellowship. From 1989–1992 a bilateral dialogue was conducted by the four Anglican churches of Great Britain and Ireland and the eight Nordic and Baltic Lutheran churches. The conversations led to agreement on the fundamental elements of the **faith** and arrived also at a common understanding of the controversial issue of **bishops** in **apostolic succession**. In the concluding *Porvoo Common Statement* of 1992 (Porvoo is the town in Finland where the statement was finalized), mutual recognition and acceptance of the participating churches is expressed and full **communion** between them is declared. This new relationship would include full sacramental fellowship, exchange of **ministries**, common **witness** in present-day Europe, joint **congregations** in foreign lands, and many other forms of exchange and cooperation. The four Anglican churches and six (Estonia, Finland, Iceland,

Lithuania, Norway, and Sweden) of the eight Lutheran churches have accepted the statement and celebrated the agreement in 1996. It does not change the confessional identity of the churches, but it does bring the majority of Christians in northern Europe into this form of Christian unity. Many regard the statement as one of the few most important ecumenical events in the last decade of the 20th century. *See also* DIALOGUES, BILATERAL; ECUMENICAL MOVEMENT; LUTHERAN-ANGLICAN RELATIONS AND DIALOGUE; UNITY OF THE CHURCH. [G.G.]

PRAYER. Prayer is, most generally, a human's or humans' conscious relationship with **God**; more specifically, conversation with God; most specifically, that part of the conversation that is primarily human speaking, as opposed to meditation, which is primarily human listening. The wider definitions of prayer imply that God is able and willing to listen and to respond, meaning, that God is personally present and responsive to the one praying. Prayer certainly includes both personal and corporate expressions, and may include such nonverbal practices as "centering" and fasting, and acts of benevolence. Spoken prayer has traditionally included the categories of adoration, **confession**, petition, praise, and thanksgiving. Prayer is both taught (in the Lord's Prayer) and enjoined (e.g., in thanksgiving and for civil authorities) in the New Testament. While the scholastics tended to limit prayer to petition, mystical, spiritual, and devotional writers of the later Middle Ages included its other aspects, and linked it closely with meditation and contemplation. In his own writings on prayer, including his extensive recommendations in correspondence, **Martin Luther** was part of this more inclusive movement. Rather than focusing on the literary quality of a prayer, he advised that its sincerity and fidelity were more important, but recommended that one constantly rely most on the **promise** of God to hear and respond. In most of his suggested forms for personal prayer, he began with confession of **sin**, a recommendation that he shared with both **Augustine** and with Ignatius of Loyola, but with few writers in the later Middle Ages. In his adaptation of the *lectio divina* (meditative reading of Scripture), he recommended beginning every session with prayer, asking that all competing voices, of expectation or familiarity, as well as of misleading reason or will, be silenced before the **Word of God**.

This practice was continued and expanded under both Lutheran **Orthodoxy** and **Pietism**. For most orthodox theologians, prayer was the irreplaceable first step in **theology**, which gave the theologian humility and guarded the theologian's **faith**. Personal and small group prayer, usually spontaneous, and always directed to the life situation of the prayers, has been a central mark of Pietism in almost all of its incarnations, but among the followers of **Hans Nielsen Hauge** perhaps most of all. Contemporary practices of prayer among Lutherans have included a return to lay-led prayer in **worship** services and small groups, the adoption of Eastern Orthodox and monastic practices in prayer forms, inclusion of prayers from and for worldwide Christianity, greater attention to prayers for healing, and a renewed interest in meditation and meditative prayer. *See also* SPIRITUALITY. [M.O.]

PREACHING. The public proclamation of the **Word of God**. Jesus' **sermon** in Luke 4 is part of a tradition of preaching in synagogues, and the New Testament goes on to give many examples of kerygmatic (*see* KERYGMA), exhortative, and evangelistic sermons. Many of the church fathers (*see* PATRISTICS) were known best as preachers, and the **Reformation** was preceded by a revival of popular preaching, led by the mendicant **orders**. This preaching, however, differed from that of the early church by being separated from the mass. The Lutheran Reformation, however, made preaching integral to the weekly service of the **Lord's Supper**, while encouraging sermons at daily services as well. Thus, Lutheran preaching was shaped by its juxtaposition with the **sacrament**, based on biblical texts (the historic **lectionary** on **Sundays** and **festivals**, *lectio continua* on weekdays) or on the **catechism. Martin Luther's** model of preaching, made familiar by his best-selling postils (collections of sermons), was influential, but finally inimitable. It was **Philipp Melanchthon** who first systematized Lutheran preaching, using the study of rhetoric of which he was a master, and making it less conversational than rhetorical, less occasional than doctrinal, and less devotional than intellectual.

Later strains of **Lutheranism** mirrored their characteristics in their styles of preaching. Lutheran **Orthodoxy**, with its interest in polemics, doctrinal purity, and Scholastic categories, returned to late medieval models and often turned the sermon into an attack on Rome or Calvinism, or into a learned lecture on **dogma**. Because of the length of the sermon—normally an hour—preachers' powers of imagination were often strained. As such, published sermons and the use of texts chosen from the catechism or **hymns** were common. **Pietism**—with its **ecumenical** dimension and interest in emotion and in individual rebirth and **sanctification**—was eager to use the models of other Christians, rather than using **doctrine** in its preaching. Sermons were addressed not to the community, but to individuals, calling them to **repentance** and new life. The ideal pietist sermon would include reference to all the stages of the **order of salvation**, and proclaim the law to the unrepentant and the **Gospel** to the awakened, as well as offer guidance to the regenerate (*see* LAW AND GOSPEL). It is easy to caricature the preaching of the **Enlightenment** as well crafted but vacuous, and focusing on morality and self-improvement rather than on doctrine or **piety** (for instance, sermons encouraging clean barns were preached from the Nativity texts). But preaching during this period did, in fact, reflect its context, with the spirit of the age fascinated by the proofs of **God** in nature and human progress. The sermons of the **Awakening**, like the much broader Romantic movement, combined the strengths of Orthodoxy and Pietism. This combination occurred in individual sermons, such as by providing heartfelt explications of doctrines. In North America, Lutherans were split between those whose pietistic heritage led them to sermons that were very similar to the revivalistic methods of their **Protestant** neighbors and those whose neoconfessionalism led them to prefer **catechesis** to revivalism. Worldwide, the 19th century was the heyday of the star preacher—the ecclesial version of the Romantic cult of the hero—whose **congregations** became tourist destinations and whose published sermons became devotional classics.

It is almost impossible to generalize about the present state of Lutheran preaching. The **liturgical movement** has assured that preaching remains tied to the **sacraments** and to a more generous **lectionary**. **Feminism, liberation theologies**, and the waves of biblical interpretation—the historical-critical method, canonical analysis, deconstruction, and so on—have all had their formative impact. The use of technology, especially changes in communication media, and the importance of narrative have shaped preaching, but what its future shape will be is not yet clear. [M.O.]

PREDESTINATION. God's foreordaining of people as justified. More precisely, in Lutheran vocabulary, predestination describes the grammar of **justification** when its acting subject is the electing **God**. Predestination is thus the logical description of the gracious activity of God in Christ, who alone and unconditionally wills **salvation**. As a descriptive grammar that is only about God the subject and promise maker, the concept of predestination in **Lutheranism** differs radically from so-called double predestination: that God from the beginning decides every individual's future of salvation or condemnation. If the Lutheran conceptuality resembles anything of such in **Reformed** theology, it is only in terms of single-predestination, and this is meant to be a consoling address to the one who already believes. The Lutheran language of predestination, then, is above all the explication of the **Gospel** for the faithful, not a third party description of God's ways to the uninitiated or merely speculatively interested. According to the *Formula of Concord*, Solid Declaration, article 11, predestination is "the counsel, decision and determination of God in Christ Jesus, who is the real 'book of life,' as it is revealed to us through the **Word**."

While some detours of speculation were followed in the age of Lutheran **Orthodoxy**, perhaps ironically, Reformed theologian Karl Barth helped Lutherans to recapture their original insight in the 20th century with his emphasis on the electing God. Lutherans and Calvinists alike have converged in their understandings of predestination language as focusing on God's sole saving activity and have called for abandonment of double-predestination vocabulary. Theologians who emphasize **eschatology**, like **Wolfhart Pannenberg**, have begun to accent the future causal sense of predestination: that God destines humankind from the future, not the past, so that humankind might share even now in just that future. Further theological reflection may rightly conclude that "God alone wills salvation" also entails that "God alone wills all." Understood thus, predestination again is a deepening of the meaning of God's sovereignty for the faithful. [D.H.L.]

PRESBYTERIAN CHURCHES. *See* LUTHERAN-REFORMED RELATIONS AND DIALOGUE.

PRIEST (Gk *presbyteros*, "elder"). Term for clergy in some churches. In the New Testament, the terms "priest" or "priesthood" are not used in relation to what later became the ordained **ministry**. Only Jesus is called the (new) high priest (Heb 4:14ff), and the Christians together are called a holy or royal priesthood or priests (e.g., 1 Pet 2:5.9.; Rev 1:6). In the early church, since the third century, the term "priest" became the designation of the ordained minister who presided at the **eucharist**. This connection between priest and eucharist as the memorial and celebration of the **sacrifice** of Christ was further developed in the Middle Ages toward a sacerdotal understanding and practice of the priestly office. It was against this understanding and its popular practice that the **Reformation** reacted. The concept of a sacrificing priest at the altar, mediating between **God** and the faithful, and elevated above the **laity** was rejected. In Lutheran circles, the term "priest" was occasionally used, especially in the Pauline sense of a "priestly service of the Gospel of God" (Rom 15:16) and in the concept of the **priesthood of all believers**. The Lutheran churches in Scandinavia have retained the term priest as a designation for **pastors**. The Second Vatican Council has redefined the understanding of the office of priest by emphasizing its tasks of **preaching** and **pastoral care**, in addition to its sacramental function. *See also* VATICAN COUNCIL II. [G.G.]

PRIESTHOOD OF ALL BELIEVERS. The common and equal status, dignity, and calling of all baptized believers before **God** and one another. **Martin Luther** reaffirmed this biblical (e.g., 1 Pet 2:4–10) and **patristic** understanding in his new **Reformation** context. He and his co-reformers wanted to liberate the **laity** from their imposed inferior and subordinate status over and against the elevated superior sacramental status of the clergy. Against this position, Luther held that all Christians have been consecrated priests by their **baptism** and, through the gift of justifying **faith**, have been given equal spiritual dignity, power, and direct access to God. Their priestly calling is exercised in their priestly standing before God in intercession for others, their being priests to their neighbors in **pastoral care** and declaration of **forgiveness**, their **witness** to the **Gospel** through their words and lives, and their full participation in the governance of the **church**. People in all walks of life, and especially those in high places, are called to live their lives as a living **sacrifice** before God and to exercise their common priesthood in **family**, profession, and society. All members of the universal priesthood have, in principle, access to the public, ordained **ministry**. But for those who exercise this ministry, which has been instituted by God, a regular call and **ordination** by the church (and God) are necessary.

The full implications of this concept of common priesthood, one of the significant historical achievements of the Reformation, were seldom realized in Lutheran history and in that of other traditions. **Pietism** with its emphasis on the calling of each individual Christian to prayer and loving witness and its many voluntary lay activities in mission and social work (*see* DIAKCONIA; INNER MISSION) revitalized this concept. Today, Lutheran and other churches (e.g., the **Roman Catholic Church** at the **Second Vatican Council**) seek to give more adequate expression to the universal priesthood of all baptized believers in their teaching, structures, and life. [G.G.]

PRINTING PRESS. The importance of the development of the printing press for the spread of the **Reformation**. Johannes Gutenberg (c.1400–1460) perfected the invention of printing around 1450–1455 at Mainz and Strasbourg. The beginning of the Reformation coincided with the further development of printing between 1520 and 1540 and the rapid increase of printing shops in Germany and then all over Europe. The relative freedom of printing in many places allowed for the dissemination of the works of the reformers. **Martin Luther**'s writings like the *Ninety-five Theses* and many Reformation leaflets and tracts reached all parts of Europe in an incredibly short time. A "pamphlet war" raged in Germany between 1520 and 1525 helping to spread Luther's name everywhere. The larger works of the reformers were printed within a short time and reprinted in many cities—there existed no copyright at that time. As a result of this explosion of Reformation printing activity, the small town of **Wittenberg** rose to fifth place among centers of printing in Germany. Since the majority of people were illiterate, the printed Word explaining the **faith** supported oral proclamation and communication. Thus, the printed Word received new authority, and through its educational activity, **Protestantism** promoted the ability of people to read it. [G.G.]

PROFESSIONS, SECULAR. Lutheran understanding of secular professions, meaning nonchurch **work** or **vocation**. In the popular and intellectual climate at the time of the **Reformation**, secular professions were thought to be less dignified and less meriting of divine affirmation, if at all, than churchly professions. Against the medieval concept that divinely affirmed vocation (Ger *Beruf*) pertained only to monasticism, **Martin Luther** and the reformers were clear that daily work and service to the neighbor were the primary places where **God** intends vocations to be fulfilled. In this, Lutherans saw vocation as related both to the doctrine of **justification** and to the doctrine of the **two kingdoms**. The "holy" life does not consist in special religious performances or removal from the world, but in entry into the world, especially that the neighbor and society might be served. Thus, Luther would speak to his barber that God would have him do his best at barbering, and that the housecleaner or mother washing diapers were splendid examples of people fulfilling God's call, not because work per se is holy, but because it served others.

The Lutheran understanding of vocation, in other words, holds at its core the ethical criterion of **love**. It was not merely an affirmation originally of feudalistic economics, but served then as it serves now as a fundamental vision for how one may discern one's own secular vocation as a divine call. This understanding of vocation, then, ties personal vocation with the social good. Furthermore, the believer may be assured, on the basis of justification, that God affirms the believer's free use of **reason** in the service of **love** within secular professions. Finally, the believer need not be concerned that his or her profession is a "proof" of God's justification (as would seem to be the case with the **Reformed** connection between work and **predestination**), but is the way Christian witness is made during the "interim" of earthly life. [D.H.L.]

PROMISE (Lat *promissio*). The central role of **God's** promise in Lutheran **theology**. The Bible is a book of promises in the sense of the announcement of the saving purposes and intentions of God. Promises in the Old Testament relate to the promised land, prosperity, liberation from slavery in Egypt, and exile in Babylon. In the New Testament, the hermeneutical approach (*see* HERMENEUTICS) of promise and fulfillment serves to interpret the relationship between the Old and New Testament: Christ is the fulfillment of Old Testament promises. Many of the New Testament texts are formulated in the style of Christ's promises (e.g., Mt 16:18; 28:20; Jn 16:13), and generally as the promise of God's gift of **salvation**, **grace**, new life, **resurrection**, **kingdom of God**, and a new heaven and earth (*see* ESCHATOLOGY).

In **Martin Luther**'s theology and the Lutheran confessions (*see* CONFESSIONS, LUTHERAN), promise (*promissio*) receives a central place and significance. Promise does not refer to something to be expected in the future, but to something promised by God and Christ in the past, offered and received here and now, and to be fulfilled in the future. God's and Christ's promises are **forgiveness** of **sins**, grace, and salvation, and thus identical with the **Gospel**. The promise is the Gospel, the Gospel is proclaimed as promise. Accordingly, promise (Gospel) and law (*see* LAW AND GOSPEL) are considered the two parts of God's **Word**. **Faith** consists of assent to and acceptance of the promises of God. These promises are communicated by Word and **sacrament**. For **Philipp Melanchthon**, sacraments are defined by a promise of grace (*promissio gratiae*) and a divine command/mandate. A person who believes in and relies on the promises of Christ receives **justification** and salvation. The interrelation of God's promise and human faith is fundamental for providing the firm basis of Christian life in an uncertain world. [G.G.]

PROTESTANT. General designation for the **Reformation** movements in the 16th century and their adherents today. The Diet of Speyer in 1526 had decided that each territory in the German empire was free to decide about its religious allegiance according to the decision of its ruler. But three years later the Diet of Speyer in 1529 rescinded with a majority vote of the papal party the unanimous action of 1526. Against this vote, six evangelical princes and 14 imperial cities used the legal means of *protestatio* in order to object to the decision of the majority. Since then, others frequently called them the protesting estates or the protesting ones. Their own designation in the 16th century was not "protestant" but **evangelical** or "those related in religion" or "adherents of the *Augsburg Confession.*" Only after 1700 was the term "protestant" used as self-designation; and decades later the term "Protestantism" followed suit. A legal term had become a confessional one.

In England and France, the term "protestant" was employed to indicate the contrast and objection to the **Roman Catholic Church**. In the 18th-century **Enlightenment**, the term became programmatic. It was understood as referring to the critical and constructive emancipatory potential of Reformation insights for the self-understanding of evangelical Christianity. Today, the term is used in a more general sense in the English and French-speaking world for non-Roman Catholic and non-Orthodox Christians, while in Germany and some other countries the terms "Reformation churches" and "evangelical" are preferred. Despite attempts to give the term "protestant" a positive meaning by reference to the usage of *protestari*, "to witness," **Anglicans** and Lutherans—but also the great **Reformed** theologian Karl Barth—are reluctant to use the term because of its negative connotations. [G.G.]

PROVIDENCE, DIVINE (Gk *pronoia*, Lat *providentia* from *providere*, "to provide"). **God's** continuing creative, sustaining, and governing involvement with **creation**. Reinterpreting Hellenistic-Jewish concepts in the framework of biblical references, the Greek church fathers (*see* PATRISTICS) developed the notion of divine providence: God the creator maintains his creation through the divine **Word**, the *logos*, and leads it toward its fulfillment. In the West, **Augustine** (354–430) became formative with his distinction between the personal, individual dimension of God's providence by which humans are enabled to move from unbelief to **faith** (his own personal experience), and the universal dimension of God's providence by which world history as a whole, including evil, is brought to the goal of God's kingdom (*see* KINGDOM OF GOD).

Martin Luther emphasized God's personal relationship to the world as continuing creative and sustaining action in history that also involves the relatively independent participation and cooperation of human beings. Lutheran Orthodoxy (*see* ORTHODOXY, LUTHERAN) employed the classical scholastic distinction between God's sustaining action in creation and history (*conservatio*), God's cooperative and accompanying involvement in the processes of world and history (*concursus*), and God's governance of the world (*gubernatio*). The main concern of the Christian **doctrine** of providence has been, and is, to affirm the ongoing, creative relation of God to creation: God's creation is not left to itself, to autonomous mechanisms, or to other powers and forces. God remains actively and positively involved in creation and history, leading them both to divine consummation. According to Lutheran doctrine, it is God's saving and liberating purpose, revealed in Jesus Christ, that endows God's providence with redemptive (*see* REDEMPTION) significance and power in the face of the evil and **sin** that threaten God's good creation. [G.G.]

– Q –

QUIETISM. In its most ecumenically familiar sense, this term refers to an international type of **Pietism** of the 17th and 18th centuries that saw rest in **God** as possible only given complete passivity of the human will. While influential in **Roman Catholic mysticism**, and in some **Reformed**, **Methodist**, and Quaker circles, it was generally rejected as making benevolence and virtue irrelevant to the Christian life.

The term is also used to characterize Lutheran **ethics** as requiring separation from political or social activity. Ernst Troeltsch developed this accusation most clearly, accusing **Martin Luther** of having separated personal from social ethics so completely as to leave the individual free from any responsibility for the latter. The notion of **two kingdoms** (*see also* CHURCH AND WORLD) was seen as nurturing complete obedience to political **authority**. Since this notion taught that the state was as much the locus of God's activity as was the **church**, it was seen as implying as well that the state was beyond the church's, indeed beyond the Christian's criticism or opposition. During and after World War II, observers such as Dean William Inge and William Shirer blamed German servility to Nazi atrocities on the quietism inspired by Luther and Lutheran **theology**. Without trying to deny partial Lutheran culpability for national socialism, one must note that this explanation fails to account for the efforts of the **Confessing Church** in Germany (*see* CHURCH STRUGGLE) and of such Lutheran theologians and leaders as **Eivind Berggrav** in Norway and **Kaj Munk** in Denmark. While the record of political leadership exercised by Lutherans in North America has been spotty, sociological factors seem to be more important motivators than theological ones. And quietism has hardly characterized the Lutheran church's leadership in Namibia and South Africa at the close of the colonial and apartheid period, and in East Germany at the end of socialist totalitarianism. [M.O.]

– R –

RACISM. Issue of primary importance for the **ecumenical** community and the **Lutheran World Federation** (LWF) in the struggle against all forms of discrimination on the basis of race, color, or ethnic origin (*see* ETHNICITY). In the 20th century racism has become a major public and international concern. The many forms of racism include state, political-ideological, economic, public opinion, and everyday prejudicial racism. Christian churches have been both accomplices in forms of racism as well as critics of racism. A strong ecumenical impetus for rejecting racism began with the first World Missionary Conference at Edinburgh in 1910 and was continued by succeeding world conferences organized by the **International Missionary Council**. The **World Council of Churches** (WCC) took up the struggle after 1948. The Second Assembly in 1954 declared that "any form of segregation based on race, color or ethnic origin is contrary to the gospel and is incompatible with the Christian doctrine of man and with the nature of the Church of Christ."

In 1970 the WCC launched the Program to Combat Racism, one of the most well-known and discussed activities of the WCC. Through its support of the struggle of South African churches and the mobilization of public opinion in Europe and North America, the program has contributed significantly to the end of state apartheid in southern Africa. Because of the strong Lutheran presence in southern Africa, the apartheid issue also aroused growing attention in the LWF. This led to the much debated statement of the LWF assembly in Dar es Salaam in 1977 "that the situation in Southern Africa constitutes a *status confessionis*" (*see STATUS CONFESSIONIS*) and declared the rejection of apartheid a matter of **faith** and Lutheran confessional **unity**. In following up this resolution, two white churches in southern Africa were suspended from LWF membership. They were readmitted in 1991 after they had clearly changed their position. But structural and popular racism continues in many places and the churches are challenged to implement their conviction that racism is **sin**. [G.G.]

RATIONALISM. A philosophical genre after the **Enlightenment** centered on the autonomy and ultimate authority of **reason**. The genre and "age" of Rationalism are indebted philosophically above all to the work of Gottfried Wilhelm Leibniz (1646–1716). He held that the moral and natural worlds are perfect because they are created by a perfect deity that, necessarily, created the best of all possible worlds. The space-time world that most perceive is a benign, natural illusion. Evil is, nevertheless, a historical reality that serves a divine purpose in allowing yet more good to arise and flourish. All that is, in other words, is in accord with God's lawful and perfect will, and history, therefore, is to be met with unqualified optimism. In such an order of positive historical progress, the rationalist figure of Jesus is a teacher of moral enlightenment and model for human behavior. Not an incarnation of the divine who does not interfere with the worldly processes so once perfectly initiated, Jesus is a teacher of the eternal **truths** of reasonable religion. Rationalist **Christology**, therefore, verges on ebionitism, the Christological heresy that believed Jesus was but a human servant of God.

Needless to say, Rationalism's efforts to affirm the goodness of an impersonal god who was uninvolved with current worldly affairs hardly cohered with traditional Lutheran **theology**. In the face of Rationalism's dulling of **faith**, theology's response was more emphatically pietistic (*see* PIETISM), or orthodox (*see* ORTHODOXY), or even fideistic (anti-intellectual). In so behaving, theology perhaps inadvertently proved the post-Enlightenment point: that traditional Christian faith was intellectually irrelevant. It would take Friedrich Schleiermacher's (1768–1834) address to cultured despisers and **Georg Wilhelm Friedrich Hegel's** philosophy of religion to begin to turn the tide. [D.H.L.]

REASON (Lat *ratio*). The intellectual ability of humans to think, in contrast to their sensory forms of experience and perception. The Christian church has inherited this or similar definitions of reason from antiquity, and throughout the history of Christianity the relationship between **faith** and reason has been a constant theme of **theology**. While patristic theology (*see* PATRISTICS) consciously employed human reason in its apologetical efforts to defend the faith, scholastic theology was concerned with developing and showing forth the coherence between the different propositions of Christian teaching as well as their harmony with principles of rational perception. In the framework of the concepts of **natural law** and natural **revelation**, reason could even have a constitutive function of perceiving elements of **God's** revelation and moral prescription. The Lutheran

Reformation and **Martin Luther** rejected such a dominant role of reason in matters of faith, though Luther's understanding of the role and significance of reason was more complex. His important insight was that reason does not represent an objective, autonomous human faculty; rather, it is always dependent on the person who uses reason and on the purposes for which reason is used. Thus, reason can be used for very different ends and, from this perspective, Luther can call it "the devil's whore." In matters of faith, reason is indeed "blind," it cannot lead to a knowledge of God. In the secular realm, however, reason is of the highest authority and is necessary for the proper ordering of life in the world. Between these two signposts, Luther is able to attribute a positive role to reason for theological reflection. Despite its limits and when enlightened and renewed by faith, reason may have an authority, under Scripture, for decisions of faith.

Lutheran **Orthodoxy** systematized this differentiated approach by distinguishing between the reason (*ratio*) of the natural person and the renewed reason (*ratio renata*) of the believer. The **Enlightenment** programmatically elevated reason to being a supreme authority, even in matters of religion. Meanwhile, philosophers such as **Immanuel Kant** and **Georg Wilhelm Friedrich Hegel** still tried to include in their concept of reason the idea of God and of God's Spirit directing history. Today, Lutheran theology, in new intellectual contexts but also with a certain liberty over and against different philosophical concepts of reason that are *en vogue*, continues to affirm the indispensable place and role of reason in the pursuit of theological research and for theological reflection. Systematic and coherent theological interpretation of God's **Word** and its significance for contemporary humanity cannot be appropriately undertaken without the careful consideration of reason in its limits and possibilities as a contributing factor to Christian understanding and as a necessary tool in theological work. [G.G.]

RECEPTION (Lat *recipere*, *receptio*, "to receive," "to accept"). A relatively new term within Christianity referring to the reception of or acceptance of **doctrines**, confessions, decisions, and forms of practice (e.g., liturgies) into the life and teaching of a **church** or group of churches. Throughout church history such processes of reception have been a basic structure of Christian **faith** and life. There was the reception of the biblical **Gospel** by the first Christian communities and the reception of the decisions of the councils by the early church, and today there is the task faced by the churches to receive and accept new interpretations of the **faith** (e.g., the role and purpose of the Second Vatican Council). At the time of the **Reformation**, the emerging Lutheran churches received and integrated the faith of the church—in the form of the **creeds**, the **theology** of the church fathers (*see* PATRISTICS), and so on—into their confessional basis (*see* CONFESSIONS, LUTHERAN). Their own confessional texts, written for a specific purpose, were received and thereby given official status via inclusion in **church orders**, decisions of the **Smalcald League**, and acceptance into the *Book of Concord*. Lutheran churches outside Germany received the Lutheran confessions by means of decisions of rulers, parliaments, and church assemblies. Today, Lutheran churches face the challenge, together with other churches, to receive the results of ecumenical dialogues into their teaching, life, and relationships with other churches. *See also* COUNCILS, ECUMENICAL; DIALOGUES, BILATERAL; VATICAN COUNCIL II. [G.G.]

RECONCILIATION. Overcoming division and enmity. In addition to its classical understanding in the framework of **atonement** and **forgiveness**, the term is used today in Lutheran (and other) ecumenical and social ethical thinking in two respects. First, the ecumenical goal has been defined in Lutheran statements as "unity in reconciled diversity" (*see* UNITY OF THE CHURCH). This concept implies reconciliation between churches by overcoming their dividing differences so that they become legitimate and acceptable and, thus, reconciled diversities. Second, confronted with many contemporary ethnic, social, political, and religious conflicts, Christians and churches consider it as one of their major social-ethical tasks today to work towards reconciliation between those who are opposed to each other. Such efforts for reconciliation are grounded in Christ's reconciliation of human beings with **God** and with one another (*see* CHRISTOLOGY). It involves committed and competent social, political, and psychological mediation between opposing groups and an alleviation of the root causes of conflicts. *See also* ETHICS. [G.G.]

REDEMPTION (Lat *redemptio* from *redimere/redemere*, "to buy back, redeem, deliver, release"). The deliverance or liberation of the believer from the bondage to **sin** and evil powers. In the Bible, redemption is presented as one interpretation of **God's** saving work for humanity, and is closely related to the concepts of **atonement**, **reconciliation**, **salvation**, and **justification**. In the Old Testament, the idea of redemption refers to buying back a person from slavery and the deliverance of Israel from captivity in Egypt and exile in Babylon. In the New Testament, Jesus Christ's vicarious death, his shedding of blood for others, and his **resurrection** as victory over all evil powers is the way of redemption, of liberating people from the bondage to sin and death and leading them back into a reconciled relationship with God (Rom 3:24f.; Eph 1:7.14; Gal 3:13; Col 1:14; Heb 1:1–4; Mk 14:24). Redemption through Christ effects a change of allegiance, a liberation from bondage to acceptance into the freedom of the children of God. The Latin church fathers emphasized the first aspect of expiation and liberation, while the Greek church fathers focused more on the second aspect, the restoration of **communion** with God.

Medieval concepts of redemption were dominated by Anselm of Canterbury's (1033–1109) legal and rigorous theory of satisfaction: only the divine-human Christ was able to render satisfaction to God for the offense and unfaithfulness of human sin. This theory was modified by **Thomas Aquinas**. He presented redemption as Christ's free gift for all those who are united with him, a gift merited by Christ's obedient **love**, manifested in his redemptive incarnation, life, suffering, death, and resurrection. The Lutheran **Reformation** rejected medieval concepts of satisfaction and, similarly to Thomas, understood redemption in the sense of Christ's representative and substitutional role in relation to sinful humanity. **Martin Luther** taught that in suffering and dying, Christ who is free from sin, has borne divine punishment on behalf of all sinners while the sinners, in a "happy exchange," share in Christ's **righteousness** and thereby receive **forgiveness** of sin and are justified by God without any merit on their side. Today, the interpretation of God's saving work in terms of redemption emphasizes the liberating character of redemption in the sense of deliverance from all forms of human (and cosmic) bondage and estrangement. Redemption, thus understood, is a basic concept in **liberation theology** and **political theology**. In other theological circles, the anthropological (*see* ANTHROPOLOGY) and Christological emphasis of redemption concepts is complemented by a more trinitarian (all three divine persons are involved in redemptive activity), an **ecclesiological** (not only individuals but also the Christian community receives God's liberating redemption), and an **eschatological** (redemption is the anticipation of God's final victory and fulfillment) understanding. *See also* CHRISTOLOGY. [G.G.]

REFORMATION. Epoch of European history during the 16th century marked by several movements pursuing the reform of the late medieval **church**. The term "Reformation" was first used by Latin authors and then by the church fathers (*see* PATROLOGY) for efforts to improve and renew moral and political conditions (e.g., Seneca, d. 65) and the Christian life. **Martin Luther** seldom used the term. Since the 17th century in Lutheran historiography Reformation was primarily seen as the Lutheran reformation movement, and in the 18th century the term was used for the first time to refer to an epoch of European history. Today, most Reformation scholars underline that there were several Reformation movements with different geographical centers and leading personalities as well as distinctive features, aims, and social-political and cultural impacts.

Prominent among these movements was the Lutheran one. In many ways related was the Zwinglian-Calvinist Reformed movement (*see* ZWINGLI, ULRICH; CALVIN, JOHN), which led to the introduction of the Reformation in Swiss cantons (Zürich 1522–1525, Basel 1529, Geneva 1536) and which spread from there to parts of Germany, France (1529 first evangelical national synod), Scotland (1560 *Confessio Scotica*), parts of Transylvania, The Netherlands (second half of the 16th century), and to some other areas. The Reformation in England followed its own political course towards establishing a national church free from Rome (1534), while the theological orientation of the English reformers was strongly influenced first by Lutheran (the first *Book of Common Prayer*, 1549) and then by Reformed ideas. The radical Reformation movements, represented mainly by the **Anabaptists** and **Spiritualists**, originated in several cases within the "mainline" Reformation movements, but moved toward a much more radical position concerning church reform, **doctrine**, **church-state** relationships, and Christian life. Beginning in the 1520s the "Radical Reformation" gained followers all over central Europe. They were often persecuted and remained small in numbers.

What made these movements part of a broader historical epoch was their basic religious motivation and orientation, their common goal of reforming the church of their time, and their several common or similar characteristics. These included the notion of the ultimate authority of Holy Scripture (*see* BIBLE, AUTHORITY OF), appreciation of the **faith** and life of the early church, reforms of **worship** and spiritual life (*see* SPIRITUALITY), primacy of the proclamation of the **Gospel**, reduction of the number of **sacraments**, reintroduction of clerical **marriage**, dissolution of monasteries, influence of **Humanism**, abolition of the secular power of the church, rejection of the **papacy**, reform of the structure of the church, restoration of the dignity and role of the **laity**, emphasis on **education** and service to the poor and sick. Within the framework of these elements, there were, naturally, considerable differences between the various Reformation movements.

Marxist historians, especially in the former German Democratic Republic, have interpreted the Reformation as part of the early bourgeois revolution leading to the transition from feudalism to capitalism, but these historians have also come to acknowledge the primary religious character of the Reformation. Other historians have underlined the significant role of the cities, especially the imperial free cities, for the expansion of the Reformation. It is, however, also recognized that the reforming movements found many supporters in rural areas, and there is general acknowledgment that without the active support of the **evangelical** estates in the empire and of the rulers and/or parliaments in Scandinavia, England, Scotland, and Switzerland, the Reformation would not have succeeded.

Several reform movements in the medieval church preceded the Reformation. They aimed at a renewal of monastic and spiritual life, criticized the claims and power of the **papacy**, and pleaded for reforms of church life and **theology** (e.g., John Wycliffe, who was also influential for the Hussites in Bohemia/Moravia during the 14th and early 15th centuries). **Mysticism** and

Humanism were spiritual and intellectual reform movements, while estates in the empire as well as peasants and burghers pressed for political and social reforms. But it required a more determined and theological profound reforming energy and appeal to turn these widespread yearnings for change and reform into a veritable Reformation. This was the work of Luther and his co-reformers and of Calvin and Zwingli together with their co-reformers.

Indeed, the Reformation inaugurated by these leaders had such far-reaching consequences that it could be likened to a revolution. Clerical rule over many territories was abolished and the papal hierarchical and canonical system was removed. A large part of the possessions of the church was expropriated, scholastic theology and late medieval forms of **piety** were replaced by the new emphases of reformation theology and church life. **Education** was reformed and schools, **hospitals**, and care for the poor were established. Clerical dominance in many areas of public life was abolished and a new **Protestant culture** emerged.

The Lutheran Reformation had its main center at the university of **Wittenberg** and its leading personality was Luther (*see* LUTHER'S THEOLOGY). But the new movement spread rapidly to other places in Germany and to other parts of Europe, while Luther was soon joined by other reformers such as **Philipp Melanchthon, Nikolaus von Amsdorf, Johannes Bugenhagen, Martin Bucer, Johannes Brenz, Justus Jonas, Urbanus Rhegius**, and many others. In a dynamic historical process marked by **evangelical** preaching, the effective use of the improved print media (*see* PRINTING PRESS), reforms of **worship**, bible translations, study by future leaders at Wittenberg, and support by reform-minded princes and city councils, the Lutheran Reformation was accepted in several German territories and free cities. It was officially introduced in all the Scandinavian and Baltic countries. In central and southeastern Europe, Lutheranism found a broad echo in Hungary (which included present-day Slovakia), Austria, parts of Poland, and other regions. However, the Lutheran presence in these same countries and regions was reduced to a minority by the **Counter-Reformation**. The Lutheran Reformation established its own identity by accepting its confessions (*see* CONFESSIONS, LUTHERAN) and **church orders,** through legal recognition as one of the two religions in the empire (*see* AUGSBURG, RELIGIOUS PEACE OF) in 1555, and by receiving institutional expression in a considerable number of Lutheran churches.

Today, the Lutheran Reformation is considered not only an important event in the past. It is valued as an essential point of reference for present-day Christian faith and life, and as a necessary reminder that the church at all times is called to reform itself in accordance with **God's** will and in response to the challenges of new times and situations. *See also* EUROPE, LUTHERAN CHURCHES IN; LUTHERAN CHURCHES OF THE WORLD. [G.G.]

REFORMED. *See* LUTHERAN-REFORMED RELATIONS AND DIALOGUE.

REFUGEES. Persons who had to leave their home countries. The 20th century has been called the "century of the refugees." Under the impact of oppressive political regimes in the Soviet Union and Nazi Germany, refugee movements entered the world scene in the 1920s and 1930s, reaching their climax with over 13 million refugees and displaced persons after World War II. Dramatic new waves of refugees emerged from the 1960s onwards, now mainly in the Southern Hemisphere. Natural disasters, wars between and within nations, ethnic conflicts, political oppression, droughts, and other situations forced people to flee their home countries or become displaced within their own countries. Over 70 percent of the more than 15 million refugees at the end of the 20th century were women and children, and most of the refugees were in the poorer nations of the world.

The international community reacted to this situation in 1951 by the creation of the Office of the United Nations High Commissioner for Refugees (UNHCR) and numerous governmental and nongovernmental aid organizations. Among the latter, churches and ecumenical organizations play a major role. The first operational agency of the new **Lutheran World Federation** (LWF) in 1947 was its Service to Refugees that helped tens of thousands of refugees and displaced persons in Europe through material support, assistance in resettlement and local reintegration, and pastoral care. During the following decades, the LWF has developed extensive programs to aid refugees and internally displaced persons through emergency assistance, resettlement, repatriation, and rehabilitation of living conditions, as well as encouragement of refugee self-sufficiency. In many situations, this work in **Africa**, **Asia**, **Latin America**, the **Middle East**, and former Yugoslavia is done in cooperation with **ecumenical** and **Roman Catholic** agencies and with funds provided by the UNHCR and governments. Together with others, the LWF seeks to address the root causes of refugee movements and to advocate in favor of the rights of refugees. In 1999 the LWF had supported about 500,000 refugees in camps and repatriation projects. [G.G.]

REGENSBURG (RATISBON), COLLOQUY OF. Colloquy that continued the **Worms Colloquy** between Lutheran and **Roman Catholic** theologians. Three representatives from each side met in April 1541, in Regensburg, Germany, in a further attempt to restore religious **unity** in Germany. The leaders at the colloquy were, as in Worms, John Eck and **Philipp Melanchthon**. The papal legate, Cardinal Gasparo Contarini, also played a major role. The discussions were based on the so-called *Regensburg Book* that had been prepared in secret negotiations by a small Lutheran-Catholic group (including **Martin Bucer**). Agreement was reached on the first four of the 23 articles of this book, related to the understanding of **sin**. Though a partial agreement on **justification** was also achieved, the colloquy came to no positive conclusion because agreement on other doctrinal issues was not achieved. Regensburg saw the last important effort to reach a doctrinal accord between Lutherans and Roman Catholics. A later similar and equally unsuccessful conference at Regensburg in 1546 was merely a postscript to the various efforts to seek understanding and unity in the midst of bitter **Reformation** controversies and conflicts. [G.G.]

RELIGIONS. *See* NON-CHRISTIAN RELIGIONS.

RELIGIOUS COMMUNITIES. *See* ORDERS AND COMMUNITIES.

RELIGIOUS LIBERTY. The **human right** to choose, confess, and practice individually or as a group a religion, as well as to adhere to no religious belief. Religious liberty is a relatively modern concept. It was completely absent during the period when Christianity became the official religion of the Roman Empire in 380, and when **church and state** together were responsible for maintaining religious conformity and unity. This unity was challenged by the **Reformation** that claimed freedom for the **Gospel** and the formation of **evangelical** churches. **Martin Luther** insisted on the right of **conscience** to follow the **truth** even against the established church. Luther was against coercion in matters of **faith**, but he—and even more so **John Calvin**—was not at all pleading for religious tolerance by state and church. This concern was left to small groups of the radical Reformation that suffered under church-supported state repression.

In a process extending from **Humanism**, **Enlightenment**, and **Pietism**, to increasing **secularization**, the concept of religious liberty informed the development of modern legislation and was reluctantly accepted by the churches. After the first steps towards a limited religious liberty in England and Holland in the 17th century and an already far-reaching provision of religious liberty in the constitution of Brandenburg-Prussia, since 1640, the *Virginia Declaration of Rights* (1776) for the first time declared religious liberty an inherent birthright of all people. The French *Declaration of Human and Civil Rights* (1789) and the First Amendment of the Constitution of the United States (1791) followed. Since then, religious liberty has become part of the fundamental rights in all democratic constitutions and international **human rights** conventions.

The **ecumenical movement** has helped the churches to accept and affirm the notion of religious liberty both in the sense of intra-Christian and interreligious liberty. The **World Council of Churches** (WCC) has been actively involved in the drafting of the United Nation's *Universal Declaration of Human Rights* (1948) with its affirmation of religious liberty. Since then, the WCC and the **Lutheran World Federation** have actively supported the notion and application of religious liberty as a fundamental human right and a contribution to international **peace** and order. The **Roman Catholic Church** has radically changed its previously negative attitude to religious liberty at the Second Vatican Council (*see* VATICAN COUNCIL II) with its *Declaration on Religious Freedom* (1965). At the end of the 20th century religious liberty is threatened in new ways by growing religious fundamentalism and aggressive nationalism in several countries, legally sanctioned domination of majority religions, conflicts between authoritarian governments, and involvement of Christian and other religious groups in political and social issues of **justice**, among other factors. Religious liberty remains a pressing issue for worldwide Christianity and the international community of nations. *See also* NON-CHRISTIAN RELIGIONS. [G.G.]

RENAISSANCE. *See* HUMANISM.

REPENTANCE. *See* FORGIVENESS.

RESPONSIBILITY. *See* ETHICS.

RESPONSIBLE SOCIETY. Ecumenical social-ethical concept. The concept of responsible society found broad acceptance in 20th-century ecumenical reflections on the criterion and goal of the churches' common involvement in social-political issues. Highlighted at the First Assembly of the **World Council of Churches** (WCC) at Amsterdam in 1948, the concept of responsible society referred to the responsibility of people and nations to serve **justice** and public order. Amsterdam underlined this responsibility both to **God** and to the people by those who wield political **authority** and economic power. In such a society with a mixed economy and adequate social services, all citizens are guaranteed freedom, and both individuals and the state aspire to social and economic justice. The idea of responsible society was developed in the 1950s and 1960s as a criterion by which to judge existing **social orders** and as a guide for establishing social-political goals. After 1968 the social-ethical reflection in the WCC moved beyond the notion of responsible society to various concepts of national and global social and economic justice in order to accommodate the current global realities of newly independent and developing nations, the growing disparity between the rich and poor nations, and the emergence of popular and liberation movements with their pressure for social change.

Because of its roots in biblical and **Reformation** thinking, together with the heritage of the **Enlightenment**, Lutherans have generally welcomed the concept of responsible society. They believe that its basic orientations, when adapted to changed social and international conditions, are still viable criteria for personal as well as for public ethical standards and guidelines for action. *See also* ETHICS; INTERNATIONAL AFFAIRS. [G.G.]

RESURRECTION. Lutheran understanding of the resurrection of Jesus Christ and of the body. **Martin Luther** and the vast majority of the **tradition** following him had little varying opinion as to the reality and meaning of the resurrection of Jesus Christ (*see* CHRISTOLOGY), and of the promised resurrection to life eternal with God (*see* TRINITY, DOGMA OF) of all those who have **faith** in Christ. Dissensus began to emerge with the **Enlightenment** and its concomitant challenges to the authority of the Bible and the **church**. The dissensus has grown with the increase of secularity and the weaker relation between the **church and world**, particularly mirrored in the conflictual relation of **science and Christianity** that grew out of the late 19th century.

In sum, and in general Lutheran understanding, the resurrection of Jesus Christ, with his crucifixion (*see* CROSS), is seen as the proof of Jesus' messiahship, the divine confirmation of his office as king of the **Kingdom of God** that he preached. Furthermore, **Easter** was an eschatological (*see* ESCHATOLOGY) event that inaugurated the coming kingdom. The resurrection also belongs to the historicity of Jesus; without it, the historical meaning of Jesus as the prophet-priest-king for all people would not be discerned at all. And this historicity of the resurrection, for the dominant number of Lutherans, is affirmed as a basis for faith, rather than seen from faith. Finally, the resurrection of Jesus Christ has consequences for **anthropology**. Because it belongs to Jesus' humanity, all those whose humanity is fulfilled in Christ find that humanity is eschatologically qualified. That is, God adds eschatological fulfillment to the definition of humanity itself. Thus, **hope**— in addition to **faith** and **love**—is a fundamental quality of authentic human being and finds its end in life after death.

The synthetic statement just read can only be constructed after having traveled the recent 20th-century course of Lutheran theological interpretation regarding the resurrection. In the earlier part of the century, **Rudolf Bultmann** was a leading influence in response to the secularism and modernism that threatened to deny any credibility to the biblical witness. Bultmann answered that an existentialist (*see* PHILOSOPHY) use of the category of myth was necessary to save such symbols as the resurrection from abandon as historically and scientifically meaningless concepts. In a somewhat similar fashion, Paul Tillich also employed an existentialist perspective to argue that the resurrection was a symbol that pointed to the transcending **truth** of the divine-human relation, a paradox that was otherwise—outside of symbolic force—inexplicable. **Paul Althaus**, a leader in the **Luther Renaissance**, argued that the resurrection was an historical event that was incapable of historical verification. In this he brought to the fore the eschatological and apocalyptic character of the resurrection while still maintaining its historical veracity. Gustaf Aulén, however, as with his whole Christology, interpreted the resurrection in a thoroughgoing apocalyptic fashion, ending slightly closer to Bultmann than to Althaus. Finally, **Wolfhart Pannenberg** represents a distancing from Althaus and existentialism. He argues that the resurrection was an apocalyptic event in history that is logically capable of being verified with historiographical tools, though it cannot be fully understood by finite human minds. Pannenberg is also primarily responsible for recognizing the eschatological character and meaning of the resurrection that was stated earlier.

With the eschatological predicate in mind, faithful Christians may come to recognize that our promised resurrection constitutes neither a denial of death nor its mirror image of refuge in immortality. As a resurrection of the body and not merely a "spiritual" occasion, our resurrection will be an entry into dynamic communion with the living God. And because resurrection is a **promise** of God (*see* JUSTIFICATION), it is also a release and command into the freedom of dynamic communion with the creaturely neighbor in the present tense. [D.H.L.]

REVELATION (Lat *revelatio*, "uncovering, unveiling"). Event and process of God's self-disclosure in history. In general usage "revelation" may refer to the event of revealing (*revelatio*) as well as to that which is revealed (*revelata*). The Old Testament narrates many instances of **God's** disclosing of divine realities and purposes, for example, the revelation of God's name (Gen 17; Ex 3:14). The aim of revelation is not the communication of knowledge, inaccessible to human **reason**, but rather the enabling of **communion** with God. The same applies to the many references in the New Testament to God's revealing actions. Here, the Old Testament is presented as the book of such actions in history (Rom 1:1ff; Heb 11). Other texts refer to the hidden God (Rom 16:25–26; 1 Tim 6:16) disclosing himself in the world through the **Word** that has become flesh in Jesus Christ (1 Jn 1:1–4; Col 1:25–27; 1 Tim 3:16). God's coming to humanity (Emmanuel) and Jesus' revealing of God's presence and will (Mt 1:21.23; Jn 17; Acts 4:12; Heb 1:1–4) and the revelation given in Jesus Christ (Jn 1:18; Acts 13:16–41) are of decisive importance. God's righteousness is revealed through the **Gospel** (Rom 1:17; 3:21). This and all God's revealing action is given for the purpose of human **salvation**.

In the early church, references to divine revelation were part of the defense of the Christian **faith** against **heresies** and other beliefs. In the Middle Ages, in line with the scholastic interest in philosophical speculation, the relation between reason and revelation became a major concern. It was affirmed that natural reason is capable of recognizing in the created order the existence of God, but that the **truth** transcending such reason comes to us through revelation, while the human spirit is elevated to a vision of what is revealed. **Martin Luther** and the Lutheran confessions (*see* CONFESSIONS,

LUTHERAN) were not interested in such speculations, nor, besides affirming that God encounters us as the revealed one in Jesus Christ alone, did they pay much attention to the concept of revelation. Rather, it was God's **promise** of salvation—and not revelation—that correlates to **faith**. In Lutheran **Orthodoxy**, the concept of revelation appears as part of the introduction to **dogmatics** together with the distinction between natural and revealed revelation and the relation between reason and revelation. In the **Enlightenment** tradition, the notion of revelation is increasingly reinterpreted in terms of the achievements of human reason and is, finally, relegated to the study of the history of religion.

In 20th-century **dialectical theology**, revelation again became an important part of theological reflection. Highly influential was the **Reformed** theologian Karl Barth (1886–1968) who taught that the Trinitarian God is the subject of revelation and that Jesus Christ, the **Word of God**, is the only way of receiving and appropriating God's revelation. As a consequence, the *Barmen Theological Declaration* (1934) of the **Confessing Church** in the German **church struggle** declared that besides Jesus Christ as the Word of God there exists no other source of revelation, neither in nature (race or blood) nor in history (a *Führer*). Today, the **salvation historical** dimension of revelation from **creation** through reconciliation to fulfillment as well as the interrelation between revelation and world history (*see* HISTORY, THEOLOGY OF) are studied. In **liberation theology** and **political theology**, the discernment of God's will and action in concrete social situations is undertaken in an effort to understand God's revealed saving and liberating purpose in history and for all people. [G.G.]

REVOLUTION. The rapid and usually violent overthrow of the established political order. Revolution is an activity rarely connected with the **Lutheran church**. And yet, as a movement led by a person under the ban of the empire, and supported by princes who thereby were in revolt against their overlord, the **Lutheranism** of the 16th century had to deal with the theology of revolution. **Martin Luther** himself began by teaching that a tyrant, like the plague, needed to be suffered as a judgment from a benevolent if sometimes inexplicable **God**. By 1530, however, the doctrine of "lesser magistrates," originating in southern Germany had gained sway in **Wittenberg**. This doctrine held that God ordained each level of the political order and that, in order to protect those placed in their care, underlings were bound to revolt against tyrannical superiors. Over the next several centuries, this understanding was overshadowed in Lutheranism by the **two kingdoms** ethic, which seemed to require obedience to established authority, no matter how unjust it might be. This attitude led to some great discomfort at revolutionary moments, when it was not entirely clear what authority was established. **Henry Melchior Muhlenberg**, for instance, seems to have kept silent during the American

Revolution. Other Lutherans, including Muhlenberg's own sons, became leaders in the revolutionary struggle.

In the 20th century as well, Lutherans have participated in liberation movements, both violent and nonviolent, beginning with resistance in occupied countries and in Germany itself to the Nazi regime. Lutherans took part in and supported the end of colonialism in **Africa**, and most particularly the struggle to free Namibia from South African control. **Latin American** churches have undergone **persecution** for caring for those who have fought against unjust systems (*see* GOMEZ, MEDARDO). Lutheran Christians were actively involved in the peaceful revolution that led to an end of communist domination of eastern Europe, particularly in East Germany. *See also* LIBERATION THEOLOGY; SOCIALISM; QUIETISM. [M.O.]

RHEGIUS, URBANUS (1489–1541; German name: Urban Rieger or König). Influential German Lutheran reformer. Urbanus Rhegius was born near Lindau in southern Germany. He studied the liberal arts and **theology** and in 1520 received a doctorate in theology from the University of Basel. A humanist (*see* HUMANISM) and concerned with the reform of the clergy, he was ordained a **priest** in 1519, and in 1520 became cathedral preacher in Augsburg. Two years later, he was removed from this position because of his Lutheran views, but in 1523 Augsburg's town council invited him to return. He remained in the city as a Lutheran **pastor** until 1530. He was in contact with **Martin Luther** and **Ulrich Zwingli,** but later criticized Zwingli as well as the **Anabaptists** and **Spiritualists**. In 1530 Rhegius attended the Diet of Augsburg as a member of the Lutheran group (*see* AUGSBURG CONFESSION). In the same year, he was invited by Duke Ernst of Lüneburg to consolidate the **Reformation** in the duchy of Lüneburg in northern Germany and was appointed **superintendent** of the church in that territory. He helped to reform the monasteries and was engaged in the education of the clergy for whom he wrote a widely read handbook on preaching and teaching in 1535/36. It was reprinted many times. In addition, he helped to formulate the *Wittenberg Concord* of 1536 (agreement on Christ's real presence in the **Lord's Supper** between **evangelical** theologians from southern Germany and Lutheran theologians in **Wittenberg**), wrote **church orders** for the towns of Hannover and Lüneburg, and assisted in the Reformation of other German towns. In 1537 he attended the meeting of the **Smalcald League** where he signed Luther's *Smalcald Articles*. Rhegius held the basic Lutheran theological convictions and insisted on their continuity with the teaching of the church fathers (*see* PATRISTICS). Characterized by Luther as the **bishop** of Lower Saxony, he was a theological, pastoral, and practical reformer. [G.G.]

RIGHTEOUSNESS. *See* JUSTIFICATION.

ROMAN CATHOLIC CHURCH AND LUTHERANISM. The development of relationships between the Roman Catholic Church and the Lutheran churches. The title "Roman Catholic Church" presupposes two historical developments: the emergence of the notion of "catholic" (*see* CATHOLICITY) and its reception (*see* RECEPTION) into the Nicene-Constantinopolitan Creed of 381 (*see* CREEDS, ECUMENICAL), and the growing preeminence of the local church of Rome and its **bishop** among the other local churches during the first five centuries. From an early period, these two developments combined and shaped the character of the Western church: its profession of catholicity and its commitment to the priority of the Church of Rome and its bishop. With the further development of the **papacy** and the accumulation of ecclesiastical and secular power in the high medieval papacy, the exclusive claim to represent the true, catholic **church** was more and more linked to the Roman center of the church.

This claim was rejected by the different **Reformation** movements. The Lutheran reformers and confessions (*see* CONFESSIONS, LUTHERAN) affirmed the catholicity of the emerging Lutheran churches as well as that of the Eastern Orthodox Church and even that of the Roman church in so far as in that church the **Gospel**, the true **sacraments**, and faithful Christians are present. The late medieval church was thereby denied its claim to be the only and exclusive representation of the church of Jesus Christ. The late medieval church became now, indeed, the *Roman* Catholic Church alongside the different Reformation churches. Accordingly, the profession of faith of the Council of Trent (*see* TRENT, COUNCIL OF) speaks in 1564 of the "holy Roman Church" (*sancta Romana Ecclesia*) or "holy catholic and apostolic Roman Church." The Rome-centeredness of the late medieval church, its *Romanitas*, became now the distinguishing and constitutive element of its ecclesial and confessional self-understanding.

At the Diet of Augsburg in 1530, the **evangelical** party avoided in its *Augsburg Confession* harsh polemics against Rome in the hope that a solution of the Reformation controversy was still possible. Once the efforts to preserve the **unity of the church** failed, the Lutheran confessions after 1530 employed highly critical language and even condemnations (*see* ANATHEMA) over and against what they regarded as Roman **heresies**. In turn, the Roman response to the Reformation, the Council of Trent, rejected and condemned what it regarded as Lutheran heresies. But already decades before, the beginning of division was signaled by **Martin Luther's** condemnation by pope and emperor in 1521, and the tone of ensuing controversies was set when the Edict of Worms (*see* WORMS, DIET OF) called Luther "a wicked demon in the form of man," while Luther repeatedly called the pope "Antichrist" and gave him, the hierarchy, and the whole Roman church a great variety of bitter names from his rich vocabulary. When the religious peace settlement in 1555 (*see* AUGSBURG, RELIGIOUS PEACE OF) and other processes made the split between Rome and the Lutheran churches a definite and permanent one, centuries of Lutheran-Roman Catholic controversy followed with far-reaching implications not only for **theology** and church life, but also for political, social, and intellectual developments in Europe.

The **Counter-Reformation** reduced flourishing Lutheran churches in the Habsburg lands to small **diaspora** groups until toleration in 1781 gave them some breathing space. Political and religious motives mingled in the **Thirty Years' War** (1618–1648). Catholic minorities in Lutheran countries were discriminated against into the 19th century. Forms of mutual discrimination by the respective majorities (e.g., regarding leading positions in public life or education) continued not only in some European countries, but also in Latin America, until the middle of the 20th century. This was accompanied by mutual isolation, ignorance, and misrepresentation, as well as by popular prejudices. Theologically, a time of controversy and confrontational apologetics began in the late 16th century and continued into the 20th century. This led to an increasingly stern apologetical-defensive position of the Roman Catholic Church in order to undergird its claim to be the only true church. This church, interpreted primarily in a hierarchical, juridical sense, had its center as well as its head in the person of the pope whose immediate primatial power over the church and, under certain conditions, infallible judgement in matters of faith and morals finally became official **dogma** at the First Vatican Council in 1869–1870 (*see* VATICAN COUNCILS I AND II). But there were also Lutheran voices that claimed, especially in the context of **Neo-Lutheranism** in the 19th century, that the Lutheran church alone represented the true church of Jesus Christ. Lutherans generally considered the Roman Church as heretical.

However, throughout the centuries since the Reformation there have been individuals in both churches, ordained and lay, who searched and hoped for a rapprochement between Roman Catholics and Lutherans. Their efforts and dreams have come true in the 20th century. The ground for this was prepared by new theological developments in the Roman Catholic Church since the late 19th century, 20th-century Roman Catholic **Luther research**, the **ecumenical movement,** and the Second Vatican Council. This council with its theological changes and practical reforms of historical significance enabled, among other things, the church's participation in the ecumenical movement. The Lutheran churches recognized the extraordinary importance of the council that opened up a new era of Lutheran-Roman Catholic relations, and they saw in the furtherance of these relations their historically imposed priority. Through the creation of the **Lutheran Foundation for Inter-Confessional Research** in 1963, and the **Lutheran-Roman Catholic dialogue** with its remarkable agreements and convergences so far, including the 1999 agreement on **justification**, and through theological exchange, as well as the achievements of Roman Catholic Luther research, cooperation, and many other forms of growing relationships, the healing of the Reformation division is making significant progress. [G.G.]

RUOTSALAINEN, PAAVO (1777–1852). Finnish Lutheran lay preacher and leader of a revival movement. This poor peasant, who never learned to write (he dictated), became the central figure of a form of Finnish **Pietism** and perhaps the most remarkable layman in the history of the Finnish church. Intensive study of the Bible led him to a deep Christ-centered **faith** by which he experienced anew daily God's forgiving **grace** in Christ Jesus. Reacting critically against what he believed were all the manifestations of a superficial, formal Christianity, he set out to inspire in people a living faith and to improve their social condition. Being an effective preacher, Ruotsalainen spoke to small and large groups in farmhouses and outdoors. Gifted with a lively natural intellect, spiritual insight, and knowledge of human nature, he acted as a spiritual counselor to many people, and dictated letters to high authorities on spiritual and social issues. He became the leader and coordinator of a revival movement in the broader context of the secular national revival in mid-19th-century Finland. He traveled all over the country gathering a strong following among the rural population, and also among **pastors**. The work of this "prophet of the wilderness" is continued in revival and pietistic movements in Finland up to the present. [G.G.]

– S –

SACRAMENTARIANS. Term applied to those who believe—according to the judgment of Lutheran reformers—in the external sign (*sacramentum*) but not the inner reality (*res*) of the **sacraments**. **Martin Luther** and the Lutheran confessions (*see* CONFESSIONS, LUTHERAN), such as the *Formula of Concord*, article 8, applied the term to the Swiss reformer **Ulrich Zwingli** and others who denied the real bodily presence of Christ in the **Lord's Supper**. Later, the term was also used for those who, on the contrary, emphasized the importance of the sacraments. [G.G.]

SACRAMENTS (Lat *sacramentum*, "oath"). Outward means and rituals through which **God** is active in the **church**. **Augustine** (354–430) was one of the first to propose a theory and terminology of sacraments: Sacraments are visible signs of an invisible, divine reality. Constitutive of a sacrament is the **Word** (of God) and the outward element. Hence his famous definition: "The word comes to the element and it becomes a sacrament." **Martin Luther** liked this definition and quotes it in his *Smalcald Articles* and his *Large Catechism*. The efficacy of the sacramental action is underlined by Peter Lombard (c.1100–1160) who adds the notion of "cause" to the medieval sacramental constituents of form (*forma*, referring to the signifying words) and matter (*materia*, referring to the elements). Thus: A sacrament is a visible sign of an invisible **grace** of God and causes what it signifies (*efficit quod figurat*).

Thomas Aquinas taught that sacraments are necessary for **faith** and **salvation**. He affirmed the concept of *ex opere operato*, "by the work performed," according to which the efficacy and validity of a sacrament depend on the right performance of the sacramental rite itself, understood as an action of Christ, and not on the quality or merit of the celebrant or recipient. This concept, originally destined to secure the objectivity of the sacramental action, was later often misinterpreted and misused as a kind of automatism independent of God's action and the faithful response of the recipients. Accordingly, the *opus operatum* was vehemently attacked by the Lutheran confessions (*see* CONFESSIONS, LUTHERAN). The Council of Florence (1438–1445) in 1439 decreed the first authoritative teaching on the sacraments: There are seven sacraments—baptism, confirmation, eucharist, penance, extreme unction, orders (ordination), and marriage—and the essential elements of a sacrament are its matter (the elements), its form (like the words of institution), and the intention (of the minister to do what the church does).

Luther denounced the "Babylonian captivity" of the sacraments in late medieval Catholicism. He considered only **baptism** and the **Lord's Supper** as sacraments and emphasized the nature of sacraments as **Gospel**, as gifts of God's **grace** for believing people, as external signs that have God's institution and **promise**. Luther and the Lutheran **Reformation** held sacraments in high esteem and criticized strongly what they considered a devaluation of the sacraments by Swiss Reformer **Ulrich Zwingli** and others. The Lutheran reformers did not proceed from a formally defined concept and number of sacraments, but rather from the inherited main sacraments: baptism and the Lord's Supper and, according to **Philipp Melanchthon**, possibly also penance (**confession** and absolution) and **ordination**.

In addition to accepting Augustine's previously mentioned definition, the Lutheran confessions consider two things as essential for a sacrament: an institution/mandate of God, and a divine promise of grace. Sacraments are effective signs and means of God's grace and through them **forgiveness** and communion with Christ are given. They require **faith** in order for the promise to be realized. The proclaimed Word of God and the sacraments are two equally valid means of God's saving action—a Reformation emphasis that is today helping to overcome a certain tradition in **Roman Catholicism** that elevates the sacraments above the proclaimed Word of God and an opposite tendency in **Protestantism** to underestimate the sacraments over and against the Word of God. The number of sacraments, too, seems to be no longer an ecumenical problem. It is recognized that the number is dependent on the definition of "sacrament." [G.G.]

SACRIFICE (Lat *sacrificium*, from *sacer*, "holy, sacred," and *facere*, "to make"). An offering made in order to establish or repair a bond between the divine and human. Sacrifice in its many forms is present in all cultures and religions. In the Old Testament, sacrifices play a major role in connection with the covenant and for the purpose of **atonement**, **prayer**, praise, thanksgiving, and so on (e.g., Ex 24:3–8; Gen 8:20–22). Prophetic criticism is directed against a superficial and routine practice of sacrifices (Jer 7:21–23; Hos 6:4–6; Amos 5:21–25). The New Testament proclaims the end of traditional forms of sacrifice in the unique, once-for-all sacrifice of Jesus on the **cross** for the **sins** of the world. Jesus is both the new high priest and the one, true sacrificial lamb (cf. Hebrews; Jn 1:29–36; 1 Cor 5:7; Eph 5:2; Rev 5:6). Sacrificial language is also used in relation to the **eucharist** (cf. Mt 26:28 and par), and to describe the graceful self-offering of Christians to God in service, praise, and love (Rom 12:1; Heb 13:15; 1 Pet 2:4–10).

The connection between Christ's sacrifice and the **Lord's Supper** reached an extreme form in the late Middle Ages. The eucharist was frequently understood as a bloodless repetition of Christ's sacrifice on the cross, to be offered by the priest in the mass as a propitiatory sacrifice for the remission of sins. With less extreme formulations, the understanding of the eucharist as representing Christ's sacrifice was decreed as **dogma** by Trent in 1562 (*see* TRENT, COUNCIL OF). The Lutheran **Reformation** rejected this understanding, removed sacrificial language from the liturgies, and emphasized the once-for-all character of Christ's sacrificial death as essential for its doctrine of **justification**. The Lutheran confessions (*see* CONFESSIONS, LUTHERAN) speak, in line with the biblical witness, about a "sacrifice of praise" or "spiritual sacrifice" of Christians in gratitude for the **forgiveness** and blessing they have received. The language of the self-offering of Christ and of the self-offering of Christians in praise of God and service to others is preferred by contemporary Lutherans over and against the language of "sacrifice." [G.G.]

SAINTS. Persons considered holy or especially close to **God**. By the late Middle Ages, the place of saints in the Western church was clearly distinguished from the place of ordinary Christians. Saints were those believers whose **faith** and behavior were so evidently exemplary that they were supposed to have compiled merit above and beyond that which they themselves needed to be justified. This merit was available, then, to be used by lesser Christians for their own **salvation**. Saints were considered valuable intercessors with God, an understanding that in **mission** fields allowed for the transfer of devotions from pre-Christian worship of gods to Christian veneration of saints.

The **Reformation's** concentration on **justification** through faith made this conception of saints untenable, and **Protestants** generally returned the Word to its New Testament and creedal use, describing all the baptized. The *Augsburg Confession* and the *Smalcald Articles* reject the invocation of saints as intercessors and the cult of saints in general. Even the use of the term as a title was severely restricted, limited to people mentioned in the New Testament. This rule was only sporadically followed, however, and such popular figures as Francis, Lucy, Olaf, and Augustine continue to be designated "saint." The concept of saint among Lutherans, however, has been far from arid. Beginning with **Martin Luther's** pamphlet on *The Blessed Sacrament*, the "communion of saints" has provided an important connection between the **Lord's Supper** and social **ethics**. The invocation of the saints, turned horizontal, became the conversation and consolation of the faithful. The festival of All Saints, now commemorating all dead believers, has become an important tool in **pastoral care** of the grieving. Nor have Lutherans entirely eliminated the category of exemplary believer. Although not given the title of saints, the gifts and examples of those people who have entries in this encyclopedia have given them an authority in the **Lutheran church** that long outlived them. [M.O.]

SALVATION (Lat *salvatio*, from *salvare*, "to save"). A comprehensive term referring to all that **God** has done for humanity through Jesus Christ. Salvation points in an inclusive way to God's saving, justifying, reconciling, restoring, perfecting, and healing activity by which human beings are liberated from their predicament. They are thereby brought back to their original destiny of living in a right relationship with God, with one another, and with **creation**. They receive wholeness of life, consolation and healing, and hope of eternal life.

Examples of such liberating and saving action of God are in the Old Testament, such as the exodus event (Ex 12–18), the gift and blessing of the promised land (Gen 12:1–3; Dtn 26:1ff), and the prophetic expectation of a salvation-filled future (Ez 37:1ff; Isa 54:9ff). In the New Testament, salvation is closely related to the **Kingdom of God**, life, **righteousness**, freedom, and **reconciliation**. Salvation in the sense of being saved from some enslaving or threatening reality has its center in the Christological **kerygma** (*see* CHRISTOLOGY): Jesus' work is a struggle against demonic powers (Lk 11:20) and a victory over them in his **cross** and **resurrection** by which human beings are liberated from their captivity (Gal 2:20; 5:1). This salvation is proclaimed (Mt 1:21; Acts 4:12), leading to **reconciliation** and restored **communion** with God (Rom 5:1.10; 2 Cor 5:17–19). It is God's saving will that all people come to know and love God and thus receive salvation (1 Tim 2:4; 2 Pet 3:9). This liberating and restoring work of God through Christ is for the whole human person (the healings of Jesus, e.g., Mk 5:34) and the whole creation (Rom 8:19–23). Though the history of salvation is fulfilled with the coming of Jesus Christ in the fullness of time (Gal 4:4–5; Eph 1:10), the Triune God's saving work will find its perfection in the eschatological future (Rom 8:24; 1 Pet 1:5). The Christian community with its proclamation and **sacraments** is the arena of the experience of salvation that should find its daily expression in new human behavior (Gal 5:1.16–26).

In the early church, salvation was understood as victory over death, liberation from the finiteness of human existence, and, on this basis, as "deification" (Gk *theosis*), that is, transformation by the **Holy Spirit** into an acknowledgment and vision of God and communion with God. The different interpretations of salvation during the Middle Ages saw salvation founded in the vicarious satisfaction for **sin** of Jesus Christ or as liberation from the realm of sin and death to a life filled by **grace** and thus enabled to do God's will and contribute to one's acceptance by God. **Martin Luther** and the Lutheran **Reformation** radically reversed this relationship between salvation and human action. Salvation is now understood as received from outside of us. It comes from God alone without human merits or cooperation. It is grounded in Christ's cross and **resurrection** for all people. Salvation is the action of the Triune God by which people are saved, liberated from captivity to the domination of sin, expressed in the "incurvation" into themselves and their ensuing estrangement from God. For Luther, Jesus Christ is our savior and salvation. Salvation becomes effective in the lives of individuals and in the Christian community as **justification**, the free gift of saving grace, leading to a new life in communion with God in Christ, a life that is guided by the Holy Spirit in **sanctification** and service to the neighbor.

Lutheran Orthodoxy (*see* ORTHODOXY, LUTHERAN) systematized salvation in the form of an **order of salvation** by which the salvation of sinful human beings is accomplished in a process including call to **faith**, illumination by the Holy Spirit, **conversion**, sanctification, and **mystical union** with the Triune God. **Pietism** considered conversion as experience of salvation and emphasized the realization of the assurance of salvation in the practice of **piety** and, later, diaconic and missionary involvement. The rationalistic and ethical interpretation of salvation during the period of the **Enlightenment** was continued in new forms in theological **Liberalism** into the 20th century. This development met, after World War I, with the strong criticism and rejection of **dialectical theology**, which connected theology back to its Christological foundations and to its critical instance of the **Word of God**. Today, Lutheran **theology** participates in a general trend that seeks to restate the traditional understanding of salvation in a broader perspective. Such restatement aims at a holistic concept of salvation that should include the social-ethical implications of salvation (e.g., the relationship between liberation from the bondage to sin and liberation from sinful social conditions), the personal dimension of salvation and the healing of the whole person, and finally the communal perspective of salvation: salvation is not an egoistic possession, rather, it is to be shared within the **church** both as a community of salvation and as a saving, healing community. [G.G.]

SALVATION HISTORY (Ger *Heilsgeschichte*). The history of **God's** revelatory and salvific purpose, and its relation to world history. The term "salvation history" emerged in 19th-century German **theology** under the influence of **Georg Wilhelm Friedrich Hegel's** elevating history as primary category of interpretation. Lutheran theologian Johann Christian Konrad von Hofmann (1810–1877) and the Erlangen School, to which he belonged, made the concept of salvation history prominent as a means to interpret the history of God's **revelation** and **salvation** in progressive historical stages from **creation** to the fulfillment of history in the final **Kingdom of God**. Up till now, such a concept is based on the biblical witness of the different stages of God's history with his people from creation to exodus to covenant, and leading to the prophetic vision of a new covenant; on the sequence from the Old to the New Testament interpreted as promise and fulfillment; on Jesus Christ as the center of time; on the sequence between the old and the new eon; and so on. The different New Testament writers structure their writings in such perspectives of salvation history.

In contemporary efforts to recover the dimension of history in theology, the concept of salvation history was revived in the second half of the 20th century, especially in the writings of two Lutherans. Oscar Cullmann (1902–1998) conceived "salvation as history," moving to its center of time, Christ, and from him to the **church** and the final Kingdom. **Wolfhart Pannenberg** has been influential in his efforts to overcome the separation between salvation history and world history by mediating revelation with universal history and stressing the wholeness and finality of all history whose final consummation is anticipated in Jesus Christ. In **ecumenical** theology, too, the concept of salvation history is considered as an appropriate way to describe and celebrate God's creative and transforming presence in this world and history, a presence that already now points to the full revelation of God's reign. *See also* HISTORY, THEOLOGY OF. [G.G.]

SANCTIFICATION. The process of being set apart or "made holy." Sanctification is understood by **Lutheranism** as the Christian life that begins with **baptism** and is always a return to or remembrance of baptism. In article 6 of the *Augsburg Confession*, though the word is not used, sanctification is the life of new obedience made possible only by the gift of **justification** in

Christ. Thus, sanctification is not simply a process in which the Christian can engage on the basis of one's own human ability. Sanctification presumes justification, and the two are a dynamic unity such that the life of **good works** is always based on **God's grace**, not human compulsion. The Christian life, in other words, is one into which the justified believer freely enters in **love** and gratitude, aided by the Holy Spirit. Thus, discipline belongs to the Christian life, and includes faithful **worship**, **prayer**, study, **confession**, reception of the **Lord's Supper**, ascetic practices like fasting and contemplative retreat, and service to the neighbor and world (*see* DIAKONIA; TWO KINGDOMS). **Suffering**, too, when it comes as the unsought but necessary consequence of faithful life, is a characteristic of sanctification.

Finally, however, sanctification is never complete in this life and believers cannot rest assured on the basis of their own definitions or experiences of sanctification. A life of subjective ecstasy "in the Spirit" cannot be one's basis for **faith** either, as the reformers argued against the enthusiasts (*see* SPIRITUALISM). Furthermore, one must avoid the temptation to turn healthy **piety** into moralistic legalism, as has sometimes happened in Lutheran practice. While good works naturally issue from the justified life and Christian character is indeed distinctive, God's eschatological (*see* ESCHATOLOGY) Word of justification is the Christian's only basis for confidence. For these reasons, one sees in Lutheran theological systems a relative de-emphasis of the term "sanctification" in favor of "Christian life," and in more favor yet of maintaining the centrality of **salvation** as God's work. [D.H.L.]

SCHMUCKER, SAMUEL SIMON (1799–1873). American Lutheran leader and ecumenical pioneer. Schmucker graduated from Princeton Seminary in 1820. After serving as a **pastor** in Virginia, he helped to found the first Lutheran seminary in North America at Gettysburg, Pennsylvania, in 1826 and Gettysburg College in 1832. He became the first professor at the seminary and taught there from 1826–1864. By 1820 Schmucker was involved in the formation of the General Synod, a first attempt to bring together the scattered Lutheran synods in North America (NORTH AMERICA, LUTHERAN CHURCHES IN). Because of his theological competence, deep personal **piety**, and outstanding gifts as a church leader, he soon became the leading figure of the General Synod that was for him also a means of adapting Lutheran life and thinking to their new American context (*see* INCULTURATION). This movement towards an "American Lutheranism" was marked by a more liberal interpretation of the Lutheran doctrinal heritage, which went as far as Schmucker's revision of some articles—because of their "errors"—of the *Augsburg Confession*. These attempts aroused controversy and were confronted by the renaissance of a stronger Lutheran confessional consciousness (*see* KRAUTH, CHARLES PORTERFIELD). Schmucker lost much of his support and resigned from the seminary in 1864. He died nine years later in Gettysburg.

Part of Schmucker's abilities as an organizer and a promoter of Lutheran **unity** and renewal was his broader ecumenical vision. With his *Fraternal Appeal to the American People* of 1838, he proposed for the first time the model of a **federation** of churches assembled together for cooperation and spiritual fellowship (*see* UNITY OF THE CHURCH). This model was implemented when the Federal Council of the Churches of Christ in America was founded in 1905. Schmucker's lasting significance is that he was one of the first who called Lutheran synods, and the American churches in general, from division to unity. [G.G.]

SCHOLASTICISM. *See* MEDIEVAL CHURCH AND THEOLOGY.

SCHÜTZ, HEINRICH (1585–1672). Outstanding German composer and church musician. Son of a tavern-keeper, whose musical abilities were early recognized, Schütz studied under a student of **Johann Walter**. He was given a stipend to study in Venice for two years where he became a favorite student of Giovanni Gabrieli. Returning to Germany, he became the organist of the electoral chapel in Dresden. In 1625 his wife died (he never married again, and outlived their two daughters), and as "a comforter in sadness" he composed settings to the complete psalter, translated metrically by Cornelius Becker. Faced with the death of many colleagues and friends, and the advent of the **Thirty Years' War**, Schütz was permitted to return to Venice for a year to study the latest developments in music. While his time there coincided with that of Claudio Monteverdi, and while Schütz's later work shows the influence of that composer, there is no evidence that the two ever met.

Upon his return to Dresden, devastated by war and then by the Black Death, Schütz took on the responsibility for leading the redevelopment of church music in northern Europe. He composed for and directed **choirs** and orchestral ensembles of smaller and smaller sizes, as resources became less and less abundant; often, he paid the musicians out of his own pocket. He conducted choirs around central Germany and took important offices in Copenhagen. His students, while never equaling his genius, brought Lutheran **church music** to standards that surpassed those from before the war. He directed that his funeral **sermon** be preached not on his life or example, but on the place of music in the service of **God**. Separating the two proved to be impossible for the preacher, whose oration has been an inspiration for centuries of church musicians. Schütz was perhaps the most famous German composer of his century, equidistant from **Martin Luther** and **Johann Sebastian Bach**, and able to transplant the fruits of the Venetian school to Northern Europe. *See also* MUSIC IN THE LUTHERAN CHURCH. [M.O.]

SCHWEITZER, ALBERT (1875–1965). Leading Lutheran theologian, musician, and missionary. A man of remarkable gifts and dedication, Albert Schweitzer was born in Kaysersberg, Upper Alsace. He studied at the University of Strasbourg, where he received his doctorate in 1889, his Licentiate in Theology in 1900, and his Doctorate of Medicine in 1912. Schweitzer also studied at Paris and at Berlin under **Adolf von Harnack**; thus, his formal credentials for fame were as a biblical scholar, theologian, philosopher, and medical missionary, as well as church musician. An accomplished musicologist, he published an edition of the works of **Johann Sebastian Bach** (1912ff) and wrote a formidable book about Bach (1905/8). Early in his career, in 1899, Schweitzer served as an assistant **pastor** and taught New Testament at Strasbourg. His research on the historical Jesus culminated in his groundbreaking work in 1906, *The Quest of the Historical Jesus*, which stressed the eschatological/apocalyptic character of Jesus' thought and milieu, thus bringing to a close previous attempts "purely" to define Jesus in historical terms that did not accommodate **eschatology**. The key mark of Jesus' character that Schweitzer brought to the fore, as he saw it, was Jesus' self-dedication unto **suffering** for others so as to inaugurate the coming of the **Kingdom of God**.

In 1913 Schweitzer left Europe to serve as a missionary, mostly as a surgeon, for the Paris Missionary Society at Lambarene, Gabon. He supported most of his work as director of the hospital there with the earnings of his own numerous publications and his **organ** recitals in Europe. As a consequence of his ethical interpretation of the Christian **faith**, he was outspoken against development of nuclear weapons and supported the international peace movement. He lived his whole life under his principle of "reverence for life," which he understood to be demanded by both the Scriptures and the natural world. In 1952 Schweitzer received the Nobel Peace Prize, remaining in Africa until his death. [D.H.L.]

SCIENCE AND CHRISTIANITY. Their relationship from the perspective of Lutheran **theology** and practice. Though the relationship between science and Christianity is thought in popular American culture (influenced mightily by 19th-century fundamentalism) to be a negative one, it is actually the case since the beginning of **Lutheranism** that Lutherans have held high and positive regard for the natural sciences. This is continuous, too, with Western Christianity since **Augustine**, reinformed in **Thomas Aquinas**, who observed that **nature** was not and could not be opposed to **revelation** (*see* CHURCH AND WORLD; NATURAL LAW). As Timothy Wengert recently observed, **Philipp Melanchthon** held in his own person passion and gifts for both theology and science, "a kind of **Albert Schweitzer** of his day," maintaining that scientists could be faithful and expert in their own work and still faithful to their Christian calling (*see* VOCATION). **Andreas**

Osiander was another early Lutheran theologian who gave explicit support to the sciences; he was a personal friend to and advocate for Nicolaus Copernicus, having written a preface of support for Copernicus's controversial theory on the heliocentric solar system. Lutheran theology in general, particularly on the basis of its positive doctrine of **creation**, saw (and still sees) that natural science is a worthy endeavor that should inform responsible Christian reflection.

While, to be sure, there have been times in Lutheran history when the positive mutual regard was not held—such as with some strains of **Pietism** that were anti-intellectual and with 18th- and 19th-century forms of Lutheran **Orthodoxy** that were distinctly supernaturalist and anti-**Enlightenment**—Lutherans especially in the late 20th century have been at the vanguard of renewed rapprochement between theology and science. Since Albert Einstein, many Lutheran theologians have been intrigued with envisioning how theological reference could transcend **Rudolf Bultmann's** existentialist delimitations of theological language. Pioneer Lutherans include the German **Karl Heim**, whose work was highly influenced by the new physics, and American Joseph Sittler, who led Lutheranism toward both a renewed ecological consciousness and a winsome theological conjunction of **justification** and nature. While many Lutherans under the influence of Karl Barth have been interested, at best, in a complementary relationship of the sciences and theology, an increasing number of theologians are interested in how the disciplines can be mutually informing. This means for them that theology must be newly apologetic, applying insights from current science to commend the **faith** to the contemporary cultured despiser of religion. It also means that science should be shown to illumine theology in such a way that confessional believers might see new and appropriate meanings of their faith disclosed for them. In other words, while use of the sciences, as in the work of **Wolfhart Pannenberg**, Ted Peters, or Philip Hefner, might commend something of the reality of **God's** existence to the agnostic, it might also illumine believers who may harbor some fear of neo-Darwinian evolutionary theory's or cybernetics' effect on **anthropology**, or of Einstein's relativity theories' bearing on **eschatology**, with new and deep meanings of sacramentology and **ecclesiology**, for example, by the help of those very scientific theories. This, indeed, is the current agenda of many constructive theologians.

The positive relationship of science and theology is beginning to have an effect for the scientific enterprise itself. Already, it has been the case that scientists have asked, on the basis of their research, questions that theretofore had been the purview of theologians. The scientific establishment is taking more to heart now, though slowly, theoretical and—especially—ethical agendas of theology. Lutherans in the Unites States have led interdisciplinary research groups to set the ethical and spiritual criteriology for appropriate application of technologies derived from the Human Genome Project. Creative Lutheran presence and insight has been lent to information theory and robotics/cybernetics research. Conversely, again, virtually every specific domain of the sciences has directly influenced constructive theological writing in, arguably, the most ecumenical (*see* ECUMENICAL THEOLOGY) of endeavors; the new rapprochement has been enabled by truly international and multichurch involvement, as well as by significant infusions of money from secular foundations devoted to the new interrelationship. With such support, in the past decade the field has grown from a nascent genre into a grand web of academic and popular conversation. The need, nevertheless, is still to popularize and expand the field so that it readily informs both theological education curricula and congregational adult **catechesis**. [D.H.L.]

SECULARIZATION (Lat *saeculum*, "age, era, generation, period of time"). The term originally referred in the 16th century to the transfer or takeover of ecclesiastical property by the state. Today, secularization is understood as a process in which the **authority**, influence, and role of organized religion in public life retreats and reality (society, culture, and so on) is no longer interpreted in religious terms in the thinking and lives of people. Distinguished from the historical process of secularization is "secularism" as an ideology of a conscious nonreligious or antireligious approach to individual and social life, which affirms a secular **Humanism**. Some scholars see the beginnings of secularization already in the Bible (e.g., the de-deification of nature), while generally the **Reformation** is regarded as exercising a major impetus on the process of secularization by breaking up the powerful unity of the late medieval church, and abolishing, especially in the Lutheran Reformation, clerical and ecclesiastical domination of many areas of life. Other contributing factors to the secularization process have been **Humanism**, the **Enlightenment**, **Liberalism**, and the ascendancy of the scientific and technological culture.

During the 1950s and 1960s several theologians tried to adapt Christian **theology** to secularization, embracing **Dietrich Bonhoeffer's** acceptance of a world and humanity "come of age" and his proposal that Christ should confront the world in its secular strength. Today, secularization in the West has lost much of its convincing power because confidence in natural human goodness and unlimited progress has been undermined by historical and social developments. Furthermore, a revival of **religion** in a wide variety of forms is presently contradicting earlier prognostics of a "religion-less" age. On the other hand, the Christian **church** and theology are increasingly confronted by an ongoing practical secularization in the West in terms of the attitudes and lifestyles of many people. [G.G.]

SERMON. *See* PREACHING.

SIEVEKING, AMALIE WILHELMINE (1794–1859). German Lutheran pioneer of the emancipation of women through Christian social work (*see* WOMEN IN THE CHURCH). Sieveking was born to a patrician family at Hamburg. She became an orphan and had a very difficult youth. Inspired by Thomas à Kempis and the pietist leader **August Hermann Francke**, as a young woman she turned to the Bible and studied it intensively. She developed a concern for the poor and a desire to provide possibilities of employment for women. In 1813 she opened her first school with six girls. In 1832 she founded the Women's Society for the Care of the Poor and Needy, which enabled women to engage in social work. She inspired the establishment of similar societies in other cities and founded several institutions. Sieveking declined offers of leadership positions in **deaconess** and **hospital** work. She saw her calling rather in opening up new ways for women to develop their own professional activity by providing them with work in the service of others and teaching them to take initiatives. Inspired by her Christian **faith**, she advocated the "emancipation of women" (her own words) in her annual reports, in other writings, and through her active commitment. *See also* DIACONATE; DIAKONIA. [G.G.]

SILBERMANN, GOTTFRIED (1683–1753). Famous Lutheran **organ** builder. Gottfried Silbermann was a member of a family of German organ builders and instrument makers. His older brother, Andreas Silbermann (1678–1734), moved from their home base in Saxony to Strasbourg where he and his son Johann Andreas Silbermann (1712–1783) became famous organ builders in that city and in France. Gottfried stayed for several years with his brother Andreas at Strasbourg and learned the art of organ building from him, working for some time as his partner. He built several organs in Strasbourg and in the surrounding area. In 1710 he returned to Saxony. He built many organs in that region, including organs for the Frauenkirche, the Catholic Court Church (Hofkirche) at Dresden, and the cathedral at Freiberg, Saxony.

Gottfried Silbermann also built clavicords and the first pianos in Germany. Three were built by him for Frederick the Great at Potsdam, and he presented two to **Johann Sebastian Bach** with whom he was acquainted. Bach praised the profound bass and the brilliant, silvery quality of the upper voices of the Silbermann organs—a characteristic mark for which he is famous up to this day. A perfectionist, Silbermann produced only high quality. He was a genial craftsman and artist and has, in his way, contributed to the great musical tradition of the **Lutheran church**. [G.G.]

SIMUL JUSTUS ET PECCATOR. *See* JUSTIFICATION.

SIN. Condition of human existence in estrangement from **God** and resulting in acts of wrongdoing. In contrast to moralistic misinterpretations in Christian history and popular opinion, sin is understood in the Bible primarily as a break and distortion of human relationships with God. While sin in the Old Testament is seen in acts directed against God, in breaking the covenant with God or putting oneself in the place of God, the New Testament, especially Paul, considers sin as a power that has taken hold of human beings and marks their existence. Sinful acts, then, are the consequence of the reign of sin in human beings. This state of sinfulness is only recognized and overcome through God's **salvation** and **justification** for Christ's sake. The new being in Christ leads to the **good works** of the justified ones. **Augustine** (354–430) has shaped the theological understanding of sin in a permanent manner by insisting both on the responsibility for sin by human free choice (against Manichaeism) and the corruption of humans by the universal destiny and power of **original sin** (against **Pelagianism**). The nature of sin consists in turning away from God and focus on oneself, leading to self-love and concupiscence. **Thomas Aquinas** further developed the understanding of sin in the context of his teaching on virtues and his **anthropology**. He and other medieval theologians introduced the differentiation between mortal sins, which deserve eternal damnation, and venial sins, which do not exclude from **grace**.

Martin Luther and the Lutheran confessions (*see* CONFESSIONS, LUTHERAN) conceive of sin in the perspective of justification by **faith** alone: Only in this spiritual and not simply anthropological framework can sin be recognized in its true reality. As such, sin is not only a series of wrong deeds, but also—following Augustine—fundamental estrangement from God, unbelief, rejection of the first commandment. Sinful people are turned into themselves (*incurvatio*), with pride and concupiscence in the sense of the wrong orientation of the heart away from God. As with Paul, sin is seen primarily as sinfulness, an overpowering reality that has taken hold of the whole person so that **free will** (choosing God or sin) is excluded (against both **Scholasticism** and **Humanism**, especially **Erasmus of Rotterdam**). Thus, sinful acts are a consequence of the prior reality of human sinfulness. Human beings are and remain sinful. But the domination of sin is overcome through God's liberating grace in Jesus Christ, and sinful acts are forgiven through God's justification of sinners.

Today, sin is generally understood by Lutherans as life-negating power and evil actions. They are rooted in human estrangement from God and neighbor, and in the desire to be like God and to fabricate one's own salvation. Beyond individual sinfulness, forms of structural or social sin are increasingly being recognized, where people become both perpetrators and victims of inhuman structures of injustice, discrimination, oppression, and exploitation. These structural forms of sin represent a powerful negation of God's good **creation** and purpose. However, where people accept God's liberation from the domination of sin and live accordingly, the evil power of sinfulness in the world can be overcome. [G.G.]

SLAVERY. Lutheran attitudes to slavery. The first generations of the **Reformation** had little contact with slavery. When the condition appears in **Martin Luther's** writings, for instance, it is usually spiritualized into a metaphor for bondage to **sin**. When he treated it ethically or exegetically, however, slavery was not a state to be escaped, but a situation in which to serve. This **quietism** did not prevent later opposition to slavery by Lutherans; in 1792 Lutheran Denmark became the first colonial power to outlaw the slave trade in its possessions.

With few exceptions, Lutherans in **North America** were not vigorous in working for the abolition of slavery. The Salzburgers, upon settling in Georgia in the 18th century, at first opposed the system, but within a decade adopted it. **Henry Melchior Muhlenberg** was outraged by slavery, but did not work for its end. Until the Civil War, Lutheran synods were silent on the matter with two exceptions. The Frankean Synod of upstate New York excluded from membership any tavern-keeper or slave holder. The Augustana Synod criticized slavery in the 1850s in its journal and synodical motions. Individual Lutherans, most notably **Samuel Simon Schmucker**, were vocal and active in opposition to slavery. But the General Synod South went so far as to declare at its constituting convention that slavery had Scriptural warrant and was, in fact, a positive force.

Slavery and practices similar to it continued. In the 19th century Swedish missionaries, excluded from Ethiopia, purchased Onesimos Nesib at the slave market, freed, trained, baptized him, and sent him back home where he founded the (Lutheran) Mekane Jesus Church (*see* AFRICA, LUTHERAN CHURCHES IN). Lutheran churches have cooperated with other religious groups, as well as agencies of the League of Nations and later the United Nations, in working against forms of slavery (including forced prostitution), particularly in southern Africa and eastern Asia. [M.O.]

SMALCALD ARTICLES (1537). **Martin Luther's** theological testament that became a Lutheran confession (*see* CONFESSIONS, LUTHERAN). In 1536 Pope Paul III called a general council to meet in 1537 at Mantua (the council actually opened at 1545 at Trent [*see* TRENT, COUNCIL OF]). Since there was some expectation on the **evangelical** side to be able to participate in the council, Luther was asked by his sovereign, Elector John Frederic of Saxony, to write a theological statement that could be submitted to the council. The statement was to contain articles of faith in which agreement existed; articles in which the specific Lutheran position had to be upheld; and articles in which concessions had to be made for the sake of religious peace. Luther's articles, which he wrote within a few days, were presented to the assembly of the **Smalcald League** in 1537. They were not accepted by the representatives of the evangelical estates, but they were signed by many of the clergy present at Smalcald. The *Smalcald Articles*, as they were later called (beginning in 1553), were printed in 1538 and included in territorial **church orders** since the 1550s. They became part of the *Book of Concord* of 1580, the definitive collection of Lutheran confessions. The *Smalcald Articles*, written, according to Luther's own words, as his final theological witness and testament, centered on the "first and chief article" of **God's** gracious **justification** of the sinner for Christ's sake. [G.G.]

SMALCALD LEAGUE. Political-religious alliance of **evangelical** territories and cities during the **Reformation**. After the recess of the Diet of Augsburg in 1530 (*see* AUGSBURG, DIETS OF), which demanded a return to the faith and practice of the **Roman Catholic Church**, **evangelical** territories and cities formed a defense alliance against the threat to their freedom in December 1530 in Schmalkalden, Thuringia. By 1537, 35 states and cities—both Lutheran and Zwinglian—had joined the league. Besides its military function, it exercised a church-political one as well. **Martin Luther's** *Smalcald Articles* were originally drafted for a meeting of the league in 1537. At that same meeting, **Philipp Melanchthon's** *Treatise on the Power and Primacy of the Pope* was accepted by the league. For 16 years the league served as a shield protecting the emerging Lutheran and Reformed churches. Internal dissension led to its military defeat and dissolution in the Smalcald War of 1546/47. [G.G.]

SMALL CATECHISM. See CATECHISMS OF LUTHER.

SOCIAL ACTION. *See* ETHICS.

SOCIAL ETHICS. *See* ETHICS.

SOCIALISM. Social theories and systems that aim at more justice and equality for all people. The term "socialism" came to be used in the first half of the 19th century for a position of critique of social conditions of the working class created by the Industrial Revolution. Socialists were demanding steps toward social **justice** and changes and material equality, including redistribution of private property and limitation of private economic power. In the 20th century the theory of socialism became a forceful political reality in the form of social-democratic parties and was influential in trade unions. Socialism found its most radical ideological expression in Marxism and its powerful political implementation in communist takeovers of Russia and, after World War II, in the satellite countries of the Soviet Union in Central and Eastern Europe as well as in communist regimes in China, North Korea, and Cuba. Other and less oppressive forms of socialism were introduced in countries of Africa and Asia. Socialist and social-democratic movements and parties gained political power through democratic-parliamentary means in several European countries and in other parts of the world. In these countries, socialism aimed at forms of a democratic welfare state and a social market economy with a strong "social net."

Since the 19th century a considerable number of Christians have accepted socialist ideals as having a clear affinity to Christian social beliefs. The first Christian socialist movement emerged in France and then, since the middle of the century, in England. Similar movements followed in the 20th century. They saw in socialism a viable alternative to the system and spirit of capitalism. There were also attempts to overcome the traditionally sharp antagonism between Christianity and the Marxist form of socialism. Accordingly, in the latter half of the 20th century encounters of a Christian-Marxist dialogue took place in some countries in Eastern and Western Europe, while certain socioeconomic Marxist analyses were also taken over by **liberation theology**. In countries with totalitarian socialist-communist regimes, churches in some of these countries were persecuted (*see* PERSECUTION) and in all of these countries were discriminated against. In some socialist-communist countries, such as Czechoslovakia, the German Democratic Republic, Hungary, Poland, and Yugoslavia, the churches, including several Lutheran ones, became places of passive resistance, carriers of the cultural heritage rejected or ignored by the ruling regime, places of free discussion about a socialism with a more democratic and humane face, and centers of peaceful change that contributed to the demise of the totalitarian "real existing socialism" in 1989. Today, the **Roman Catholic Church** and mainline **Protestant** churches continue to reject forms of totalitarian socialism and refrain from advocating a particular social-political system. But these churches show some openness to certain socialist ideals when confronted by negative social, political, and ecological consequences of an unchecked capitalist market economy. [G.G.]

SOCIAL ORDER. Christian perspectives on structures of society. The issue of social order is discussed in the Lutheran "theology of order." It has its roots in **Reformation** teaching on orders or estates that provide human social life with an ordering framework. The Lutheran concept, based on medieval theories of **natural law**, refers to the three estates of **marriage** and occupation, government, **church** and its **ministry**. It is also presented as government, state, marriage, family, property, public service, economy, and so on that all belong to the good orders that **God** has given as a means to sustain the world and to provide space for the proclamation of the **Gospel**. With the exception of the church, these orders belong to God's secular reign (*see* TWO KINGDOMS). After the **Enlightenment** had turned the idea of social order around as something not given but to be created by human **reason**, **Neo-Lutheranism** until the mid-20th century restated the theology of order. **Paul Althaus**, **Werner Elert**, Helmut Thielicke (1908–1986), and others taught that certain basic social realities such as state, marriage, work, and property are given as normative mandates that should orient social **ethics**. These orders, instituted by God, can be recognized by reason. In a similar vein, **Dietrich Bonhoeffer** spoke of the divine mandates of work, marriage, government, and church. Contemporary Lutheran social-ethical thinking acknowledges the limitations of theologies of order and looks to the biblical witness for ethical orientation and to the orders of this world for indications for moral behavior.

Modern **ecumenical** reflection on social order began with the acknowledgment of the reality of "disorder" of society and international relations (First Assembly of the **World Council of Churches** 1948 at Amsterdam). Since then, concepts such as **responsible society** and the search for just, participatory, and sustainable social ordering, a new international economic order, and a responsible ecological order have been orientation marks of ecumenical discussion on social order. [G.G.]

SOCIAL SCIENCES. Their use in Lutheran **theology**. The disparate disciplines of psychology, sociology, demography, and other "soft" sciences have all come to bear in differing ways on the resources and practices of theology and **ministry**. Until roughly the period of **Liberalism** just following the **Enlightenment,** Scripture and **tradition,** with their attendant **dogma** and **doctrine,** were assumed to be sufficient resources for the doing of theology. But with the so-called "turn to the self" came the recognition, especially with renewed emphasis on **anthropology**, that social, psychological, and other larger contextual (*see* CONTEXTUAL THEOLOGY) predicates needed to be taken into account for the **Gospel** to be interpreted and proclaimed appropriately (*see* HERMENEUTICS). In the first half of the 20th century, particularly in American theological education, the social sciences became more and more an integral part of the curriculum. This was signaled in **Lutheranism** by the appointment after World War II of **Bertha Paulssen**, a German sociologist and psychologist, to the faculty of the Lutheran Theological Seminary at Gettysburg. Paulssen was both the first sociologist and first tenured woman faculty member on a Lutheran seminary campus in the United States.

The import of the social sciences for the theological curriculum is both theoretical and practical. They are increasingly important in historical and biblical studies, to the point even that theologians complain that the history of ideas and the theological values themselves that guided church theology are becoming overwhelmed by social science and its current preference for statistical analysis. Nevertheless, especially with systematic and biblical theology, the insights of the social sciences have illumined large, new questions for ongoing research, as, for example, the role that the guilds in late first-century Mediterranean life played in the rhetoric of the (New Testament) letters of Peter. Social sciences, including economics, play a very important role in the understanding of **culture** and persons for which ministry must be done, and is exercised in as personal a skill as clinical **pastoral care** or as large a concern as relevant strategies for **evangelism**. *See also* SCIENCE AND CHRISTIANITY. [D.H.L.]

SOCIAL WELFARE. Christian social work. The New Testament gives abundant evidence that the **church** has been involved in social welfare ventures from its beginning, and the **patristic** writings show that this care for the hungry, the homeless, the sick, travelers, orphans, widows, and prisoners continued throughout the early generations of the church. By the Middle Ages, this care had been institutionalized with the establishment of **hospitals**, schools, hospices, and orders dedicated to caring for the sick and protecting pilgrims. Much of this care was provided by the monastic orders (*see* MONASTICISM), but institutions established by royalty and by such **bishops** as Nicholas of Cusa also provided some assistance. In the **Reformation**, the emptying of the monasteries simultaneously depleted the number of caregivers and increased the number of the indigent. Thus, the reformers and their princes were forced to address the shared problem of social welfare. Both **Martin Luther** and **Johannes Bugenhagen** encouraged the establishment of "community chests," made up of voluntary contributions to help the poor. The **Wittenberg** example, in which this fund was administered by a commission composed of the mayor, the **pastor**, and three councilmen, became almost universal in Lutheran towns and cities.

Not until the 18th century was any other mode of social service attempted. Then Halle **Pietism** provided a model for social ministry organizations that spread over northern Europe and North America. A century later, out of the ferment that produced the revolutions of 1848 and the *Communist Manifesto*, came the **Inner Mission** movement. This movement, led by **Johann Hinrich Wichern**, led to a new web of social ministry organizations, separate from the official church and from the state, but drawing on the **Gospel** and Scriptural imperatives for their work. It was this movement that, in settlement houses and other institutions, addressed the terrible urban effects of the Industrial Revolution. Joined with **Amalie Wilhelmine Sieveking**, **Theodor Fliedner**, and the renewed **diaconate**, and such rural activists as Johann Oberlin and **Johann Konard Wilhelm Löhe**, the Inner Mission movement became the diaconal hallmark of the Lutheran **Awakening**, and its institutions still remain busy around the world. In the period following World War II, Lutheran social ministry was significantly affected by the various political systems in which the church found itself. In Eastern Europe, Lutheran churches were excluded, except in the German Democratic Republic, from the state's provision of social service under **communism**; after the fall of those regimes, the churches struggled to reestablish and support those **ministries**. In the United States and other mixed economies, particularly after the Great Society programs of the 1960s, churches and church agencies received significant amounts of government funds, but only for specific, limited uses. In **Africa** and **Asia**, Lutheran churches had to deal with governments whose policies toward their social ministry veered from active support to confiscation.

While Lutheran churches have an admirable record of providing direct care to those who are suffering, Lutheran **theology** has been reluctant to address deeper systemic change. Less because of **quietism** than because of a sense of the pervasiveness of **sin**, **Lutheranism** has not generally joined in such theological movements as the Social Gospel or **liberation theology**. The proliferation of officially approved social statements, of legislative advocacy movements, and of organizations (such as Bread for the World) dedicated to societal change may mean that a new social-political awareness is emerging in Lutheran theology. [M.O.]

SÖDERBLOM, NATHAN (1866–1931). Swedish archbishop and **ecumenical** pioneer. Söderblom, born in Trönö, Sweden, grew up in a **parsonage** and became involved in Christian youth and student movements. After his theological studies, he became the **pastor** of the Swedish Lutheran congregation in Paris from 1894–1901. During these years he received his doctorate from the Sorbonne University. From 1901–1914 he taught, with growing international recognition, history and philosophy of religion at Uppsala University and also in Leipzig from 1912–1914. From 1914–1931 he served as archbishop of the (Lutheran) Church of Sweden. A deep commitment marked his life and active involvement in social-ethical as well as doctrinal-ecumenical efforts. He envisioned an ecumenical council of churches as a first ecumenical organization of Anglican, Protestant, and Orthodox churches. He initiated the movement on **Life and Work** and presided over its first World Conference in 1925 at Stockholm. Söderblom created an awareness of common Christian responsibility for global human life in **peace**, freedom, and justice (*see* ETHICS). He was also active in the parallel movement in **Faith and Order** and was one of the leaders at its first World Conference in 1927 at Lausanne, Switzerland. There, he acted as the moderator of its important section on the **unity of the church**. In recognition of his active and continuous commitment to the furtherance of international peace since World War I, Archbishop Söderblom received the Nobel Peace Prize in 1930. [G.G.]

SPIRITUALISTS. Pejorative term applied to groups within the radical **Reformation**. Dissatisfied with the **Protestant** Reformation, which they regarded as full of compromises, a number of reformers (many with a Lutheran background) propagated a more radical reform of the **church** during the first decades of the Reformation. This movement of diverse personalities with differing positions (often called *Schwärmer*, "enthusiasts") included **Andreas Bodenstein von Karlstadt**, **Thomas Müntzer**, Sebastian Franck, Hans Denck, Kaspar Schwenckfeld, and Valentin Weigel. They continued and heightened the trajectory of late medieval impulses towards individualism, interior subjective experience, and in general a spiritualization of Christian **faith**. Accordingly, the Spiritualists claimed a direct **revelation** of and inspiration by the **Holy Spirit**. They emphasized the inner Word over and against the outer Word, a subjective awareness of **salvation**, and an invisible **fellowship** of reborn individuals illuminated and instructed by the inner Word and led to a true, living faith. On the basis of a dualistic view of spirit and matter, they rejected or devalued formal **dogma**, the visible **church** and its outward rites and ceremonies, **Word** and **sacrament** as **means of grace**, as well as **ordination** and **ministry**.

The Spiritualists formed no religious organization, but the influence of their ideas, including religious tolerance, among urban populations was broader than their relatively small numbers. Certain Spiritualist motives continued in late 17th-century **Pietism** and later in liberal subjective expressions of faith. The Lutheran Reformation vehemently rejected the general orientation and individual tenets of the Spiritualists. *See also* ANABAPTISTS. [G.G.]

SPIRITUALITY. There is no clear definition of "spirituality." One that captures the holistic, personal, questing nature of the term is "that relationship which aims at being central to every aspect of a person's life." **Piety** is then the external expression of this relationship, and devotions are those practices that nurture it and that serve its aim. For Christians, of course, this relationship is that with the Triune God (*see* TRINITY, DOGMA OF), and the quality expressing this relationship consists of **prayer**, meditation on the **Word of God**, openness for the guidance of the **Holy Spirit**, use of **hymns** and other forms of Christian **art**, struggle to discern the will of **God**, and conversation with sisters and brothers in the **faith**. Beliefs about the Triune God will determine the shape of the relationship to God. A distinctly Lutheran understanding of God will lead to some distinguishing marks of Lutheran spirituality. The notion of the externality of the Word, for instance, will lead Lutherans to reject **mysticism**, understood as the search of the innate divine spark for God. (Thus the "quest for God" is nuanced so that Word and Spirit are always companions and guides along the road, never goals themselves for the lonely soul.) The centrality of the incarnation for Lutherans (*see*

CHRISTOLOGY) will lead to a spirituality that never seeks to grow beyond the **sacraments** or seeks to set spirit against matter. Thus, in almost every party of **Lutheranism**, spiritual leaders have been writers of **hymns**, that quintessential Lutheran marriage of **creation** and faith. The pervasiveness of **sin** and the constant necessity of repentance (*see* FORGIVENESS) will lead to a consistent modesty about the possibility of perfection.

As in **social ethics**, Lutheran spirituality might be classified under Reinhold Niebuhr's category of "Christ and Culture in Paradox." This classification does not mean that there have never been Lutheran spiritual writers who have set **grace** against **nature**, or who have identified faith in God with that in **culture**. However, it seems that Lutheran spirituality has been characterized generally by conflict and paradox, but also by consolation of heart and mind. It constantly follows **Martin Luther's** dictum that "Prayer, meditation, and trial make the theologian." Lutheran spiritual writers, from Luther himself to **Johann Arndt**, **Søren Aabye Kierkegaard**, **Dietrich Bonhoeffer**, and **Dag Hammarskjöld**, display this pattern. *See also* DEVOTIONAL LITERATURE; HOLINESS; PIETISM. [M.O.]

STATE. *See* CHURCH AND STATE.

STATUS CONFESSIONIS. A situation in which the **church** is called upon to confess its **faith** and in which, in fact, its very practice will be a **confession** of faith. Generally, this is a crisis in which an external authority—political, social, or ecclesiastical—attempts to require or forbid a particular **adiaphoron** or free practice. According to article 10 of the ***Formula of Concord*** (*FC*), in time of **persecution**, when a clear-cut confession of faith is demanded of Lutherans, they should not yield to the persecutors in such indifferent things (i.e., adiaphora). Or, as **Matthias Illyricus Flacius** put it more succinctly, "In a time of confession, there are no adiaphora." The *FC* resolved the adiaphoristic controversy when, under the Leipzig **Interim**, **Philipp Melanchthon** and others were willing to bow to the emperor's (Roman Catholic) liturgical demands in order to avoid persecution. Other theologians argued that in such a case, to compromise by adopting even such free and indeed trivial matters as **vestments** implied that were necessary to **salvation**. Thus, the church was impelled to take a confessional stance and to refuse to adopt what the external authorities required.

During the 20th century it was recognized that the church was placed in *statu confessionis* at least twice more. The German **Confessing Church** under national socialism (*see* CHURCH STRUGGLE) opposed the government's requirements as a violation of this confessional standard. Later, a worldwide movement was mobilized against the apartheid in southern Africa. The **Lutheran World Federation** at its assembly at Dar es Salaam in 1977 declared this situation to constitute a *status confessionis*, which left the church no choice but to confess its faith, by action or inaction. [M.O.]

STEWARDSHIP. The biblical image of a steward is a famous one. The trustee who manages the property on behalf of its owner is a common character in Jesus' parables. This concept was used as a metaphor for leadership in the **church** as early as 1 Corinthians and occurs as well in Ephesians and 1 Peter. It would seem to be a natural metaphor for humanity's care for **creation** or the church's care for the **Gospel**, but it was used little until 17th century America. Puritan "success preachers" used the term to describe the practice of charitable giving, praised as a virtue in itself and a wise business practice. The concept began its modern use, however, in North America in the decades before the Civil War. **Mission societies** used the image of a steward—a caretaker of another's property who is bound to use the property as the owner would—to raise funds for overseas **evangelism**. Used by such organizations as the Young Men's Christian Association, stewardship became a central image encouraging the financial support of other **institutions** and **ministries**, and finally of **congregations** as well.

Meanwhile, the equivalent term in German, *Haushalterschaft*, also became important in church life, referring less to financial support than to home visitation for **pastoral care** and evangelism as well as to responsible participation of the **laity** in all areas of church work. After 1950 stewardship became a primary emphasis of the **Lutheran World Federation**, not least through its church workers' exchange program, and acquired particular importance in Asia and Africa. In recent years, there have been regular attempts to widen the concept, to affirm that Christians are stewards of many more gifts and powers than money. This concept has also been applied to humanity's care for creation, thereby providing one of many theological perspectives on the **ecology**. [M.O.]

SUFFERING. The experience of pain and alienation in the **creation**, in the human being, and between the creation, humans, and **God**. **Lutheranism** treats the issue of suffering by addressing three general questions: Why is there suffering and what end, if any, does it serve? Does God suffer? Is suffering necessarily a part of a specifically Christian vocation? We treat the questions respectively.

The first—and most asked—question of suffering, especially vis à vis the existence of a benevolent **God**, is called the question of theodicy (concerning the righteousness or goodness of God). With regard to human **evil**, the consequences of human **sin**, Lutheranism has held, with **Augustine** and most of the Christian **tradition**, that such suffering is subsequent to the misuse of human freedom (*see* LIBERTY). With regard to radical or "natural" evil, Lutheran **Orthodoxy** has answered by speaking of God's "alien" work, using the opposite to achieve a salutary end. This and its corollaries of the principle of plenitude (what could be should be, so that goodness is ever the greater) or the principle of contrast (that the opposite is necessary if the good is to be appreciated), or an educative principle (that God "sends" evil to aid in growth), or even a principle of theonomy (that *whatever* God ordains is right), are finally refused by basic Lutheran convictions. Those convictions are that God intends blessing in the creation, in the covenant, and in Christ; and that God does not "do" all particular things. Metaphysical dualism—that evil is all the responsibility of Satan—has never been an acceptable answer either. A general—and not necessarily emotionally satisfying—answer to the question of theodicy, then, posits freedom as more than a moral category, but indeed an ontological constituent in the natural world. This means that the natural world is neutral with regard to human affairs. Furthermore, for the world to remain neutral as a place for human freedom to be exercised means that God in so creating this structure has also limited the ways by which God might act within the natural order. "Natural suffering," then, would appear to be a tragic necessity in a created order that is yet under construction (*creatio continua*), within which the experience of blessing is to be celebrated in its own right and as a down payment in **faith** on what is more to come. At least this is what a majority of theologians in the **Reformation** tradition had to say on this matter.

God's self-limitation and **promise** to be intimately present with all creation already implies, in response to the second question, that God has also chosen a temporal path of suffering within the divine eternal life. The Lutheran theology of the **cross**, poignantly outlined in **Martin Luther's** *Heidelberg Disputation* (1518), makes this point surprisingly clear. Contemporary Lutheran **feminist theology**, as in the work of Dorothee Sölle, restates the point. That God suffers has long been iterated particularly in Lutheran **Christology**, which holds that what human **nature** suffers is indeed and fully communicated to the divine nature (*communicatio idiomatum*). This logic is held to such a degree that Luther could say, with clear trinitarian assumptions (*see* TRINITY, DOGMA OF), that God the Father suffered the death of the Son, indeed that God died on the cross. God's suffering, of course, is also the necessary and full consequence of God's **love** for the world.

Finally, inasmuch as the Christian is called to be Christ and to love the neighbor and world (*see* VOCATION), the Christian is bound to suffer on behalf of the neighbor and world. This is, as well, a consequence of Christian liberty. That the Christian is freed from concern about his or her eternal relationship with God by the Gospel of **justification** in Jesus Christ means that the Christian is thus duty bound to care for the neighbor (*see* DIAKONIA; JUST WAR), thereby exercising the agency of God that the whole creation might flourish even more in anticipation of the coming of the **Kingdom of God**. [D.H.L.]

SUMMUS EPISCOPUS (Lat "supreme bishop"). Term used in relation to German princes who took over the governance of Lutheran churches during the **Reformation**. The Lutheran Reformation was prepared to continue the office of **bishop** for its churches, but in a form and with an understanding that were consistent with Reformation convictions (*see* MINISTRY). Since bishops in Germany, with few exceptions, refused to join the Reformation movement, **Martin Luther** and his co-reformers saw no other solution than to entrust the **evangelical** territorial princes and magistrates of free cities with the consolidation and governance of the emerging Lutheran churches. This solution with the help of "emergency bishops" (Ger *Notbischöfe*) was understood as a provisional measure, and those entrusted with this responsibility were regarded as the most eminent lay members of the church (*see* PRIESTHOOD OF ALL BELIEVERS) and not, in the first place, as the incumbents of secular power.

The **Religious Peace of Augsburg** of 1555 finally settled the establishment of church governance by princes, who became the *summus episcopus* of their territory and thereby the legal successor of the former bishops. The ecclesiastical authority of the princes was restricted, however, to external church governance (*episcopus in externis*)—they neither preached nor administered the **sacraments**—and the organization of visitations. In most cases, the princes and magistrates delegated their authority to consistories of theologians and jurists who administered the **church**, whereas spiritual leadership and, increasingly, visitation of **congregations** and **pastors** were delegated to **superintendents**. This system of church governance in Germany, later continued by United churches and modified in the 19th century by granting more independence to the churches, came to an end in 1918. *See also* CHURCH POLITY. [G.G.]

SUNDAY. The basic structure of the **church year** is given by the Sunday. The early Christians changed their weekly festive day from the seventh day of the week, the Sabbath (Saturday), to the first day, Sunday (Acts 20:7), to mark the day on which Christ rose. Christian communities gathered on this day around the **Lord's Supper** to celebrate with joy and thanksgiving Christ's **resurrection**, his victory over death. Accordingly, Sunday was called *dies dominica*, "Lord's Day" (Rev 1:10), by the end of the first century. The early church gave two other days of the week special significance: Wednesday and Friday became days of fasting in memory of the betrayal of Christ and of his crucifixion and death. Today, Sunday remains the main occasion for Christian **worship** despite changes in social and economic life that have taken away much of the former religious significance of this "day of rest" and celebration. [G.G.]

SUPERINTENDENT (Lat "overseer"). A pastor who exercises middle-level leadership of a district within a Lutheran (or other) church body. The title was first used in 1527 in Electoral Saxony for **pastors** appointed as spiritual overseers (especially for visitations) of an ecclesiastical district. Other Lutheran churches also introduced this office and title, and it is still used in Germany and several other European countries for **parish** pastors who exercise pastoral and administrative leadership in a smaller ecclesiastical area (e.g., with 12 **congregations**). Other titles used for the same office are *Dekan* (Ger for "dean," southern Germany), *Inspecteur* (France), *Propst* (Ger for "provost," northern Germany), and *Senior* (central and southeastern Europe). During the **Reformation** period, this title was also used for a short time for **bishops** in Scandinavian countries. A *Landessuperintendent* in the Lutheran Church of Hannover exercises episcopal functions in a larger ecclesiastical region. There are similar offices in other larger Lutheran churches. [G.G.]

SYNERGISM (Lat *synergismos*, "a working together"). The claim that the human will could cooperate with divine **grace** to achieve **salvation**. Also known as semi-Pelagianism (*see* PELAGIANISM), this medieval Catholic position took on new features when (Lutheran) **Philippists** were accused by **Gnesio-Lutherans** of readopting this position in the synergistic controversy of the late 1550s. The Philippists had developed their arguments—intended to promote virtuous lifestyles—on the basis of **Philipp Melanchthon's** own writing in which he distinguished the will of reborn Christians from the enslaved will prior to initial **conversion**. Melanchthon was concerned that Gnesio-Lutheran caricatures of **ethics** led too much toward a concept of **predestination** that rendered humans, even Christians, wholly passive in their lives subsequent to **conversion**. This argument could rationalize moral laxity.

The Gnesio-Lutheran leaders such as **Nikolaus von Amsdorf** and **Matthias Illyricus Flacius** pushed forward a published condemnation of errors, including those of "the synergists," that Valentin Strigel, one of the Philippists, refused to sign. Strigel was then imprisoned, until an inconclusive debate (August 2–8, 1560) was held between Flacius and Strigel in Weimar. Johann Friedrich, duke of Ernestine Saxony, recognized that the disputants were talking past each other and ended the debate. He restored Strigel to his teaching position and finally exiled Flacius.

The framers of the *Formula of Concord* finally "resolved" the issue, however, by reinstating confusion. In article 2 they condemned anything of Melanchthon's or subsequent statements about the postconversion ability of the will as synergistic. In article 3, however, the Gnesio-Lutheran camp ironically affirmed Strigel's position, stating that the human will was "not idle in the daily exercise of repentance, but cooperates in all the works that the Holy Spirit does through us." To the degree that such language was codified in a Lutheran confession, one might say that the Synergists won their point. *See also* CONFESSIONS, LUTHERAN. [D.H.L.]

SYNOD (Gk *synodos*, "together on the way," "a meeting"). An authoritative assembly of church representatives to deal with **doctrine**, organization, and practice. During the first few Christian centuries, the terms "synod" and "council" were interchangeable (*see* COUNCILS, ECUMENICAL). With the emergence of the ecumenical councils of the Roman-Byzantine Empire, the term "synod" was often reserved for representative meetings of a smaller geographical area of the **church**. At the time of the **Reformation**, synodical structures of church government were introduced by the **Reformed/Presbyterian** churches and have become a major characteristic of this church tradition. The French (Reformed) church order of 1559 prescribed three synodical levels: local consistories, provincial synods, and the general synod of the whole church.

The Lutheran churches in Germany introduced synodical structures as their highest decision-making body, together with the office of **bishop**, only after 1918 when church government by secular authorities was abolished. In North America, beginning with the last decades of the 18th century, synodical meetings of **pastors** and increasingly with **laity** were also organized. These meetings led to the establishment of church bodies themselves called "synods" (*see* NORTH AMERICA, LUTHERAN CHURCHES IN). During the 20th century most Lutheran churches in the world have introduced synodical structures (with various names such as "assembly," "council," and so on, besides "synod" or "general synod"). They are composed of ordained and lay representatives, have decision-making authority, and are differently related to other expressions of church leadership such as **bishops**, bishops' conferences, church councils, and so on.

After the Second Vatican Council (*see* VATICAN COUNCIL II), the **Roman Catholic Church** introduced the (consultative) Synod of Bishops and diocesan synods. The **Orthodox churches** have the Holy Synod of the bishops of an autocephalous church. Most other churches have developed their own forms of synodical government. *See also* CHURCH POLITY. [G.G.]

– T –

TAUSEN, HANS (1494–1561). Leader of the Lutheran reform movement in Denmark. Tausen was won over for the Lutheran **Reformation** while he was studying under **Martin Luther** in **Wittenberg** (1523/24). He began to preach Reformation **doctrine** to large crowds at Viborg (1525) and then also in Copenhagen. King Frederik I made him the royal chaplain in 1526 and protected him, allowing him to continue preaching at Viborg. After the Diet of Odense in 1526, when **Lutheranism** and Catholicism were granted equal rights, the king called Tausen to Copenhagen. There, the Lutherans under his leadership presented a statement with 43 articles of their faith at the 1530 Diet of Copenhagen. Tausen was the main author of this *Confessio Hafniensis* (*Hafnia* is the old Latin name of Copenhagen). In 1533, after the death of Frederik I, the Catholics tried to regain control and ordered Tausen to leave Copenhagen. The citizens rose to his defense and would have nearly killed the Roman Catholic **bishop** had not Tausen protected him. After the formal introduction of the Reformation in 1536 (under King Christian III), Tausen was asked to continue preaching in Copenhagen and to lecture at the university. In 1542 he became the bishop of Ribe. He wrote about the Gospels and Epistles, translated the Pentateuch into Danish, helped to work out a Danish agenda/order of worship (*see* WORSHIP, HISTORY AND STRUCTURE) and a Latin **church order**, established schools, and thus was instrumental in the reordering of worship and **faith** of the Danish people. [G.G.]

TEACHING AUTHORITY. Authority in the **church** to clarify, express, and guard the **faith** of the **church**. Teaching the Christian faith with authority was integral to the proclamation of Jesus and the activity of the apostles. The expansion of the early church and the threat of false teachers and sects required an institutionalization of teaching authority. It was lodged in the office of **bishops** with their claim to **apostolic succession** and was exercised with the help of the **Canon of Holy Scripture**, doctrinal decisions of synods and councils (*see* COUNCILS, ECUMENICAL), **creeds,** liturgical orders, and the personal authority of the church fathers (*see* PATRISTICS). During the Middle Ages, teaching authority in the church, the *magisterium*, became more and more concentrated in the bishops, that is, in (episcopal) synods and councils, and finally and primarily in the **papacy** after its victory in the conflict between papal and conciliar authority.

Martin Luther challenged the teaching authority of his church by his appeal to the superior authority of Holy Scripture (*see* BIBLE, AUTHORITY OF) and its decisive **witness** to the **Gospel** of Jesus Christ. Under this norm, teaching authority was to be exercised through the **means of grace**—**Word** and **sacrament**—and the **ministry** serving these means. The Lutheran confessions (*see* CONFESSIONS, LUTHERAN), through their **reception** by the churches and their inclusion into various **church orders**, assumed authority by stating and guarding the faith of the church, by rejecting false teaching (*see* ANATHEMA), and by resolving inner-Lutheran theological controversies. **Laity** and **congregations** were given the right to judge **doc-**

trine. Theological faculties became, especially at the time of Lutheran Orthodoxy (*see* ORTHODOXY, LUTHERAN), a part of the Lutheran *magisterium*. Today, teaching authority in Lutheran churches is exercised by their ordained ministers, theological teachers, and by the cooperation of ordained and lay members in—mostly synodical (*see* SYNOD)—organs of church leadership. *See also* AUTHORITY. [G.G.]

TECHNOLOGY. The practical applications of scientific research. **Lutheranism** regards technology, like any exercise of **reason**, positively insofar as technology's end is the good of the neighbor; and like any idol or ideology, technology is to be criticized when it would serve its own or harmful ends. In any event, Lutheran theologians recognize, since **Karl Heim** and before, that they must better understand the new technologies themselves, as well as their promises and dangers.

Moreover, Lutheran theologians recognize anew that the overarching paradigm or worldview today in the West is at base scientific/technological, and so calls for a renewed sophistication in both theological understanding and evangelical outreach. The use of computers and telecommunications demonstrates how churches recognize the need to communicate the **Gospel** more effectively and contextually. Leading ethical analysis of matters like the Human Genome Project and cloning evidences how Lutherans would seek to provide guidelines for use of technology, particularly where the applications, in league with unchecked capitalistic interests, would submerge cultural differences, degrade the environment, or deny people and countries basic rights of access to food, **health** care, and sustainable economies.

Lutheran theologians are active and lead in such discussions in number beyond their denominational due. This is likely because of Lutheranism's positive regard for the **creation** and humanity's role as "created cocreators" in **God's** ongoing creativity (*see* PROVIDENCE, DIVINE); the positive—though qualified—regard for **reason** itself; and the Christian injunction to do whatever possible in Christ's name for the advancement of the good on behalf of the neighbor. *See also* CHURCH AND SOCIETY; ETHICS; SCIENCE AND CHRISTIANITY. [D.H.L.]

TEMPTATION (Lat *tentatio*). The test of **faith** through enticement to **evil**, **sin**, and unbelief. The Bible has been called a "book of temptations" because in its first book it narrates the temptation of the first humans (Gen 3) and in its last book it announces the hour of trial that is coming on the whole world (Rev 3:10). In between, there are deep and worrying temptation stories of Abraham (Gen 22) and Job (Book of Job), the temptation of Jesus himself by the devil in the desert (Mt 4:1–11), and in his desperation on the **cross** (Mk 15:34). The Old and New Testaments tell of many instances where the faith of people is tempted by way of enticement to sin, evil, unbelief, pride, despair, and so on. Temptation is part of the history of **God** with humanity as a deadly serious struggle about eternal **salvation** or eternal death, leading to the **prayer** that asks not to be led into temptation (Mt 6:13). Temptation is caused by Satan, the world, and the flesh, and also by God as a test of faith.

Martin Luther is regarded as the one who has deepened in an extraordinary way the understanding of temptation as a spiritual reality. On the basis of his personal spiritual struggles, he has used the German term *Anfechtung* (trial, affliction, tribulation, or distress that are caused by doubt, anxiety, or uncertainty—there exists no exact English equivalent) to circumscribe a temptation and testing that threatens the believer in his or her innermost relation with God. In his quest to find a gracious God, Luther experienced anxiety and frustration despite all his religious efforts to make himself acceptable to God and receive consolation of heart and mind. Later, he considered such *Anfechtung* to be caused by the law that leads to hatred against God because it cannot be fulfilled. Temptation is caused by sin and the mighty tempter, the devil. On its deepest level, *Anfechtung* or temptation is the experience of the absent or hidden God. But through insistent faith, prayer, and life in community, the tempted person will be called back into God's arms. Thus the flight from God becomes a flight to God. This concept of *Anfechtung* is seen today, under different terms, as a general psychosomatic experience of the "homeless mind" of many persons. [G.G.]

THEOLOGICAL SCHOOLS. Lutheran institutions for the training of **pastors** and other church workers. **Martin Luther**, **Philipp Melanchthon**, and several other Lutheran reformers were university professors. They applied their intensive biblical, historical, and theological scholarship to the cause of the **Reformation**. The results of their studies were widely published in many publications as were Bible translations, reforms of **worship**, **church orders**, and above all confessional documents (*see* CONFESSIONS, LUTHERAN). Consequently, the universities in Lutheran countries, reformed in their curricula and methods at the time of the Reformation, became important centers for the training of future Lutheran leaders in Europe. The University of **Wittenberg** played a leading role. Since that time, the emphasis on thorough theological study has been a mark of the **education** of future Lutheran pastors.

Until today, the majority of Lutheran pastors in western Europe and, since the political changes of 1989/90, in Estonia, Hungary, Latvia, Poland, and Slovakia, receive their theological training at theological faculties of state universities. Generally, five years of academic study are followed by one or two years of practical training. Among the older and important theological faculties with a strong Lutheran tradition are Copenhagen, Dorpat/Tartu (Estonia), Erlangen, Halle, Heidelberg, Jena, Königsberg, Leipzig,

Lund, Rostock, Tübingen, Turku (Finland), Uppsala, and Wittenberg. Today, there are also a few theological seminaries in Europe supported by Lutheran churches.

After Lutheran migrants had brought their **faith** and **church** to North and South America and Australia (*see* NORTH AMERICA, LUTHERAN CHURCHES IN; LATIN AMERICA, LUTHERAN CHURCHES IN; AUSTRALIA, LUTHERANS IN), it took quite some time until the emerging Lutheran church bodies were able to set up their own theological seminaries, a break with their European tradition required by the separation of **church and state**. The first Lutheran seminary in North America was the Lutheran Theological Seminary at Gettysburg, Pennsylvania, founded in 1826, which was followed by a considerable number of Lutheran seminaries in different parts of the country. Their comparatively short academic program of three years may be complemented by postgraduate studies. The first seminary in Latin America was Seminario Concordia in São Leopoldo, Brazil, founded in 1907. The much larger theological faculty of the Evangelical Church of the Lutheran Confession in Brazil at São Leopoldo was founded in 1940. The two Lutheran seminaries in Adelaide, Australia, later to be united, were founded in 1895 and 1904.

Theological training of future pastors and evangelists in Africa and Asia began in many countries long before the Lutheran churches received their independence (*see* AFRICA, LUTHERAN CHURCHES IN; ASIA, LUTHERAN CHURCHES IN). Accordingly, in Africa, the first seminaries were founded in present-day Namibia (1866) and Madagascar (1871). Other seminaries followed in South Africa, Tanzania, and since 1950 in several other countries. The origins of the training of Lutheran pastors in Asia can be traced back to the arrival of **Bartholomäus Ziegenbalg** at Tranquebar in India in 1706, followed by a first seminary in Indonesia in 1883. The majority of seminaries on these two continents were founded in the 20th century. While theological training in the past was shaped by simplified European and North American standards and traditions, the seminaries in Africa and Asia today seek to provide theological preparation for **ministry** that combines the transmission of the Lutheran heritage with a training that is relevant to the cultural, religious, and social contexts in which the future pastors are going to serve.

The most recent Lutheran theological seminary to date was inaugurated in 1998 near St. Petersburg by the Evangelical Lutheran Church in Russia and Other States. Together with its older sister seminaries and faculties, it seeks to continue the Lutheran **tradition** of solid theological training of pastors in the new situations and conditions of the 21st century. [G.G.]

THEOLOGY (Gk *theo-logia*, "God-talk"). The task of the Christian **church** to clarify, interpret, and communicate its **faith** in an understandable manner and relate it to the challenges of a particular time and place. The **revelation** of **God** in Jesus Christ (*see* CHRISTOLOGY) through the **Holy Spirit** is neither identical with nor captive to its theological expositions. However, this revelation comes to us, since biblical times, in no other form than in the form of revelation, normatively witnessed to by biblical texts and professed in **doctrines** and confessions, but also clarified, expressed, and communicated through methods and means of theological reflection and interpretation. Such interpretation of the **truth** is integral to the Christian faith and is always shaped by the respective confessional, historical, and cultural context.

Accordingly, there is also a Lutheran theology. Its specific characteristics are, first, that it is a theology for which the **Word of God** as witnessed to in Holy Scripture is normative (*see* BIBLE, AUTHORITY OF) and for which the **tradition** of the faith (i.e., the handing on and content of the faith), expressed especially by the dogmatic decisions of the first centuries (*see* CREEDS) and in the Lutheran confessions (*see* CONFESSIONS, LUTHERAN) of the 16th century, is authoritative. Second, it is a theology done by people who are informed by the history, life, and faith tradition of the **Lutheran church**. Third, it is a theology that both mirrors and, when necessary, contradicts the spirit and **culture** of a given time. Fourth, it is a theology that has occupied and still occupies a highly important, but often also controversial, place in the life and the self-understanding of **Lutheranism**. Fifth, it is a theology that claims to be a scholarly discipline using all the available scholarly tools and methodologies for its biblical, historical, systematic, practical, and other studies among the human sciences. Sixth, it is a theology that sees its final purpose in the clarification and elucidation of the **Gospel** message in Word and **sacrament** for the church in its **mission** to the world. *See also* LUTHER'S THEOLOGY. [G.G.]

THIRTY YEARS' WAR (1618–1648). A chain of conflicts between **Protestant** and **Roman Catholic** powers in central Europe. It began as a religious controversy but was soon dominated by political goals. During the first period (1618–1623), Protestants of Bohemia revolted against their Catholic Habsburg ruler and in 1619 deposed Ferdinand II, king of Bohemia. They chose as their king Frederick V, the Protestant elector of the Palatinate. The Protestant forces were defeated near Prague in 1620 and the **Counter-Reformation** was implemented by force. The second period (1625–1629) began when Christian IV of Denmark assumed the role of defender of the (**evangelical**) faith, but he also wanted to protect and expand his German possessions. The Catholic armies drove him out of Germany and nearly into the Baltic Sea. The third period (1630–1635) was marked by the entry of **Gustavus II Adolphus** into the conflicts. He won several battles that saved **Lutheranism** in parts of Germany. The fourth period (1635–1648) no longer had any religious ingredients. Germany became the theater—and wasteland—of the struggle for supremacy between Bourbon France (together with Sweden) and Habsburg Austria-Spain. The war came to an end with the Peace of Westphalia in 1648, and with it the Holy Roman Empire in its traditional form also came to an end. A group of sovereign European states with equal rights emerged. The center of power was transferred from the emperor to the estates of the empire. [G.G.]

THOMAS AQUINAS (c.1225–1274). One of the great theologians of the Christian **church**. Thomas was born in Italy. While studying at Naples from 1240–1244, he joined the Dominican Order. From 1245–1248 he studied at Paris under Albertus Magnus and followed him to Cologne to continue his studies there (1248–1251/2). In 1525 Thomas returned to Paris and lectured there until 1259. Between 1259 and 1268 he taught in Italy, returned to Paris for a second teaching period from 1268/9–1272, and then taught again in Italy until his death in 1274. Thomas produced an enormous body of writings, including biblical commentaries, commentaries on Aristotle's works, studies on a number of debated theological questions, and especially his *Summa theologiae* (or *theologica* [1266–1273]). Thomas, in whom great intellectual energy and deep spirituality were combined, was canonized in 1323 and made a "Doctor of the Church" in 1567.

Though he was not immediately accepted by the church as its leading theologian, Thomas's philosophical-theological method as well as his teachings on **God**, **grace**, **justification**, **sacraments**, **salvation** in Christ, and so on, became an influential synthesis of medieval **theology**. Thomism, a widely diverse school of thought, sought to continue the teaching of Thomas in new historical situations and with new theological expositions. Thomism was highly influential in the 16th and 17th centuries and continued into the 20th century. **Martin Luther** had a fairly good knowledge of Thomas and respected him as an eminent theologian. Nevertheless, Luther in his frequent references to Thomas was rather critical of him and considered him as "the source and foundation of all **heresy**, all error and the obliteration of the **Gospel**" (1524). Modern scholars have concluded that this judgment was influenced more by Scholasticism at the time of Luther (with its distortions of Thomas's teaching) than by the true ideas of Thomas himself. These ideas reveal, though arrived at by a philosophical methodology that was rejected by Luther, many similarities with Luther's theology. *See also* MEDIEVAL CHURCH AND THEOLOGY. [G.G.]

TORLÁKSSON, GUDBRANDUR (1541–1627). **Bishop** who consolidated the Lutheran **Reformation** in Iceland. An earlier promoter of the Reformation in Iceland, Gissur Einarsson (c. 1508–1548), had become the first Lutheran bishop of Skálholt in 1540/42. He had begun to introduce the

Reformation but was not able to complete his reforming work because of his early death. Gudbrandur Torláksson, who was ordained as the bishop of Hólar in 1571 and served there for 56 years, continued Einarsson's efforts. This long period enabled the widely educated bishop to utilize his extraordinary talents to firmly establish **Lutheranism** in Iceland. He did this mainly by means of an intensive publishing activity for the support of general and Christian **education**. His printing shop published 90 different books. In 1584 he published the Icelandic Bible *Gudbrandsbiblia* to which he contributed some translations. The Bible, as so often, was of great importance for the national and church language. Torláksson also published **catechisms**, **prayers**, **sermons**, a new **hymnbook** (1589), and the first service book with orders for **worship** (1594). He introduced **confirmation** with instruction by **Martin Luther's** *Small Catechism*. All of his activity aimed at a general awakening of **evangelical faith** and morals and the preservation of the national language and **culture**. [G.G.]

TRADITION. The act or process of handing on (Lat *traditio*) something, as well as the content of what is handed on (Lat *traditum*). Over and against earlier narrow and often negative concepts of "tradition," today it is generally recognized that tradition is an essential element of all life and, thus, also of religion. The reality of tradition in these two meanings can be observed in the Bible and throughout church history. **God's revelation** and **Gospel** in Jesus Christ, authoritatively witnessed to by Holy Scripture (*see* BIBLE, AUTHORITY OF) and clarified, defined, confessed, and handed on by the **church** in **doctrines**, **creeds**, and other afffirmations of faith, together constitute the Tradition (capital T) or the apostolic tradition. The theological interpretations of this primary tradition and the forms, institutions, and structures of ecclesiastical life are expressed and handed on in the form of ecclesial and confessional traditions.

The **Reformation** rejected the multiplication, preponderance, and dominance of authoritative ecclesial traditions (**canon law**, hierarchical structures, imposed regulations, and so on) and established the single normative and critical authority of Holy Scripture for the faith and life of the church (*see* BIBLE, AUTHORITY OF). However, the Lutheran confessions (*see* CONFESSIONS, LUTHERAN) also accept, under the criterion of Scripture, the apostolic tradition in the form of the dogmatic decisions of the first centuries, writings of the church fathers (*see* PATRISTICS), and decisions of the early councils (*see* COUNCILS, ECUMENICAL) as confirmation of their own confessional position and its continuity since apostolic times. Church traditions (e.g., liturgical forms, orders of ministry, and religious customs) are continued with an **evangelical** interpretation and insofar as they do not contradict or obscure God's free **grace**. To keep a proper balance between loyalty to the fundamental apostolic tradition and critical liberty over and against ecclesial traditions still remains a crucial task for Lutheran (and other) churches.

The term "tradition" is also used to refer to a confessional family with its history, fundamental doctrines and ethical positions, ethos and identity, and forms of worship and spiritual life, such as the "Lutheran tradition." [G.G.]

TRANOVSKY, JUR (JURAJ) (1592–1637). Czech, Polish, and Slovak Lutheran churchman and hymnwriter. Born in Teschen, Silesia, Tranovsky studied at **Wittenberg**, and in 1611 began a teaching career in Prague. In 1616 he became a Lutheran **pastor** in Moravia where he translated the *Augsburg Confession* into Czech (1620). Exiled in 1620 by the **Counter-Reformation** he returned to Silesia and held several pastoral positions there. In 1631 he moved to Slovakia and became pastor in Liptovský Svätý Mikuláš. Together with other exiled Lutherans, who also had come to Slovakia, Tranovsky helped to strengthen the **Reformation** in Slovakia. They were supported in this work by Reformation writings, the Bible, and a collection of **hymns** that they had brought with them. During this last period of his active life, Tranovsky wrote a collection of **prayers** for the home and church (1635) and put together a collection of hymns, *Cithara Sanctorum*, "Harp of the Saints." Popularly called *Tranoscius* (1536), it contained 412 hymns, including about 90 of his own (*see* HYMNBOOKS, LUTHERAN). Since then *Tranoscius* has had 150 editions. These works preserved the Czech Lutheran liturgical heritage and hymnology and gave Lutherans in Slovakia the spiritual resources that helped them to survive under religious oppression. The orthodox Lutheran (*see* ORTHODOXY, LUTHERAN) Tranovsky is still remembered in Bohemia, Silesia, Poland, and Slovakia as the one who "inculturated" Lutheranism in this western Slavic region (*see* INCULTURATION). [G.G.]

TREATISE ON THE POWER AND PRIMACY OF THE POPE (1537). One of the Lutheran confessions. Since the issue of the **papacy** had not been included in the *Augsburg Confession* (*CA*), in order not to endanger the negotiations at the **Diet of Augsburg** in 1530, an official statement on this topic was requested during the meeting of the **Smalcald League** in 1537. Accordingly, **Philipp Melanchthon** was asked to write the *Treatise on the Power and Primacy of the Pope*, and his text was immediately accepted by the Smalcald meeting as a confession of faith. The text formulates the strong **Reformation** critique of the late medieval understanding and practice of the papal office and of the great secular power and unlimited jurisdiction of the **bishops**. It was included in the collection of Lutheran confessions, the *Book of Concord* of 1580. *See also* CONFESSIONS, LUTHERAN. [G.G.]

TRENT, COUNCIL OF. The council that responded to the **Reformation** and shaped the Catholic church up to the 20th century. In 1536 Pope Paul III

(1534–1549) convoked a council to Mantua in 1537. After several postponements the council came together at Trent in 1545 and met in three convocations: 1545–1548, 1551–1552, and 1562–1563. The Lutheran estates and theologians, originally favorable to a General Council (cf. **Martin Luther**'s appeals in 1518 and 1520 and the original intention of the *Smalcald Articles* of 1537), rejected the council. However, **Philipp Melanchthon** and others were prepared to attend and defend their teaching. The Council of Trent responded to the challenges of the Reformation concerning **doctrine** and in so doing restated Roman Catholic teaching. Despite a certain rapprochement to Lutheran positions, Roman Catholic teaching was stated in a way that made the split irrevocable: Scripture and **tradition** as two sources of **revelation**, elimination of **original sin** by **baptism**, **justification** by grace together with human cooperation, seven **sacraments**, **sacrifice** of the mass, as well as other issues. Trent also responded to the **Protestant** challenges concerning abuses and deformations in church life and to the widespread pressure within the Roman Catholic Church for reforms. Accordingly, a number of reform measures were promulgated and gradually implemented after the council, but not in all parts of the church.

After a period of controversy and radical change, Trent led to a renewal and doctrinal cohesiveness in the Roman Catholic Church, but also transformed this church into another confessional church. The council strengthened the Counter-Reformation and the polarization with the Lutherans, and it shaped the Roman Catholic Church for the succeeding centuries. During the last decades of the 20th century Lutherans and Catholics began to come a long way towards overcoming the chasm that had divided them since Trent. *See also* COUNTER-REFORMATION; LUTHERAN-ROMAN CATHOLIC DIALOGUE. [G.G.]

TRINITY. The identity of **God** as Father, Son (*see* CHRISTOLOGY), and **Holy Spirit**. The **dogma** of the Trinity has been assumed as foundational throughout **Lutheranism's** existence. Explicit consideration of Lutheran doctrine in light of the assumption, however, has not been carried through until the 20th century, as has been the case with most ecumenical **Protestant** theology. However, only with recent **Luther research** has come the recognition that **Martin Luther's** Augustinian and Thomistic (*see* MEDIEVAL CHURCH AND THEOLOGY) heritage was basically unquestioned on the point of the dogma of the Trinity; here, the Lutheran confessions (*see* CONFESSIONS, LUTHERAN) claim no new insights.

Nor need they have done so, given that the very existence and identity of God, as well as the dogma itself, was rarely questioned until the **Enlightenment**. But under the critical gaze of enlightened, liberal **Rationalism** (*see* LIBERALISM), as well as the apparent irrelevance of trinitarian dogma to practical life—given the heightened esoteric and formulaic character of most trinitarian thinking that was conducted—the dogma came to be popularly regarded as dissolute and quaint. The situation called for a renewal of trinitarian thinking in the 20th century, and this came mostly from Roman Catholic and Reformed quarters. In other words, under the influence of **ecumenical theology** today, Lutheranism has revisited its trinitarian claims and has begun to significantly rehearse its doctrine in its light. The basic characteristics of contemporary Lutheran trinitarian theology follow, with some allusion to their impact upon other doctrinal/theological reconstruction.

First, the dogma of the Trinity concerns the identity of God. Because the dogma is a compact expression of Scripture's witness to God active in history, "who" God is precedes discussion on God's existence and nature. "Father, Son, and Holy Spirit" language, then, synthesizes—as well as gives proper signification to—the whole narrative of God's ways with **creation**. This narrative begins with Holy Scripture; is focused in the life, death, and **resurrection** of Jesus Christ; extends through the apostolic age (*see* APOSTOLICITY) with focus on the Holy Spirit and the early history of the **church**; and continues "beyond" the Scriptural witness through the current life of the church until the last days (*see* ESCHATOLOGY).

There is a dialectical principle implied by the Christian narrative, too, which subverts much of the Western theological trajectory regarding language about the Trinity. Inasmuch as the Scriptural witness is to God's activity in history—often called God's economy—that history reveals a three foldedness (or plurality) to God's identity in history. Thus, as **Wolfhart Pannenberg** and Eberhard Jüngel write, among other significant Lutheran theologians of the 20th century, God's identity as one must be understood in the light of the communitarian "three," rather than the three somehow derived from God's unity. In other words, the Trinity is to be understood dialectically (*see* GEORG WILHELM FRIEDRICH HEGEL; IDEALISM); trinitarian identifications denote God as communal and simple, as well as transcendent and immanent, simultaneously. Classic philosophical abstraction about the oneness of God, or even an emphasis upon God's simple unity prior to God's threefoldedness, leads one to regard God as immune to change and to time. These are the dire consequences of much of the Western tradition's preference for God's unity before Trinity, and so of the popular irrelevance of the dogma.

In other words, and secondly, the dogma of the Trinity is a complex of expressions, even a meta-dogma, that is concerned with no one **doctrine** (e.g., the doctrine of **justification**), but rather with the whole set of Christian claims. All Christian doctrine must be informed by and recur to the Trinity if such doctrine is authentically Christian. Thus, justification or **atonement**, for example, cannot end with an individual's being right with a solitary God, but with a whole community and ecology, if God is indeed the communitarian and transcendent ground and goal of all life. Or, to pose another example of the dogma's normativity, a **church** cannot be merely a voluntary organization of individuals; rather, it must be—in light of its trinitarian frame—a local realization of a holistic, catholic, body of Christ. Even the human person must be understood as a person-in-relation, a being-in-communion (*see* ANTHROPOLOGY), or, exclusive of relationality or communality, achieves no personhood whatever. Such are suggestive trajectories when theology is grounded thoroughly in the overarching dogma of the Trinity.

This leads to a third and final point: that the dogma of the Trinity functions as a metaphysical principle. It accounts for diversity while maintaining the unity and coherence of the cosmos. It solves, so to speak, the problem of the "one and the many" by revealing that the "many" are already grounded in and constitute together a holistic "one." Thus, as Colin Gunton observes, the common and contradictory options for interpreting the Trinity are revealed to be against the dogma altogether. A hegemonous notion of unity (suggested by classical, nontrinitarian theism) can only be totalitarian; and a simplistic notion of diversity (based on mere tritheism) can only be incoherent chaos. But where diversity relationally constitutes community through the reciprocity of selfless and self-giving **love**, and where love wholly grounds the community, one discovers the **truth** and beauty of life in the Trinity, of life biblically known as the image of God (*imago dei*) itself. [D.H.L.]

TRUTH (Lat *veritas*). The Christian understanding of truth. In biblical and Christian thinking, as opposed to Greek thinking, the response to Pilate's famous question "What is truth?" (Jn 18:38) is no longer formulated in speculative theories and rational definitions. According to the biblical witness, truth is a person and an event: Jesus Christ (Jn 14:6–7). In his life, ministry, and destiny, the truth of **God** is revealed, which is God's **love** as **grace** and **salvation** for all humanity (Jn 1:17; 3:16). This truth is not known by virtue of human reasoning, but truth reveals itself in its self-evidence (*see* REVELATION), it happens and takes hold of all who have been understood by the truth (1 Cor 13:12), who are led by the **Holy Spirit** into the truth (Jn 16:13). The divine and saving truth is addressed through the **Word of God** and perceived only by those who believe in Christ and follow him (Jn 3:21). They recognize the truth only partially (1 Cor 13:9), they have it in "earthen vessels" (2 Cor 4:7), yet they are made free by the truth (Jn 8:31ff) because the divine truth is experienced in God's justifying action in Jesus Christ.

This personal and dynamic understanding of the truth had to be handed on and guarded against **heresy**, that is, untruth. Accordingly, a process of formulating and protecting the truth by means of "right teaching," doctrinal statements, and creedal formulations began already in biblical times. God's truth also became truth about God. This development reaches its climax in the great medieval theological-philosophical systems. For **Thomas Aquinas**, truth, in a famous formula, is the adequate correspondence or agreement between a thing/reality and its cognitive perception (*veritas est adaequatio rei et intellectus*). **Martin Luther** and the Lutheran confessions (*see* CONFESSION, LUTHERAN), however, restated truth in its biblical meaning: the eternal and infinite truth is Christ himself, or truth is God revealed in his saving action for all people in Jesus Christ and through the Holy Spirit. This truth is present in and communicated by the Word of God in proclamation and the **sacraments.** It has to be confessed and taught, it must not be denied. It is witnessed to by the Lutheran confessions and the **church**, the pillar of truth, which cannot be without the truth because it is God's gracious salvation of human beings in Jesus Christ.

Whereas most Christian theologians still continue to see their task in interpreting and communicating the Christian truth with the help of scientific-scholarly methods, the analysis and working out of methodologies and theories about clarifying and defining truth has become a major field of study in some circles. Many Lutheran theologians seek to combine the affirmation of the inherited personal and dynamic understanding of truth with their contemporary task of explicating this truth in a methodologically clear and coherent manner and to speak the truth in a credible and trustworthy way. [G.G.]

TWO KINGDOMS. The concept that **God** instituted two modes or realms of divine rule through spiritual and secular authorities. Known also as the theory of the two swords, two regiments (*regimen*), or the two reigns (*regnum*), the latter increasingly is the more preferred English terminology. **Martin Luther** appropriated the theory from **Augustine**, but diverged from Augustine's in that Luther saw the kingdom of the left (the left hand of God), the secular kingdom, positively as established by God. God was seen to exercise his rule through secular authorities to maintain civil order. The function of governing authorities was to punish evildoers, to uphold **justice**, and to protect the people. The authority of the kingdom of the right (hand of God), however, as strictly spiritual authority, was not to be confused with that of the secular order. The spiritual reign of God was exercised in the enhancement of **faith** through the preaching of the **Gospel** and the faithful administration of the **sacraments** in the **church**. It was not a civil order over which spiritual authority was exercised, but the hearts and consciences of believing Christians.

Luther first reflected on the distinction between spiritual and secular **authority** in his sermons of October 1522 and in his 1523 tract, *Concerning Secular Government, How It Is to Be Obeyed.* In that tract, Luther argued that secular authority was legitimate on theological grounds (based on Rom 13:1–7 and 1 Pet 2:13–14). Secular government, however, does tend to exhibit a tendency towards totalitarianism and, because of **original sin**, can be perverted to the kingdom of the devil (*regnum diaboli*). One tendency toward totalitarianism is the state's attempt to control matters of faith and ultimacy, a clear attempt to overreach, at which point Luther argued in the

1530s that Christians may resist verbally, though not with force. It should be recalled, though, that Luther's regard for the civil order was largely positive, based on his high respect for the beneficent and pious ruler, **Frederick the Wise**, whom Luther regarded as a model of civil service. Meanwhile, Luther's low regard of churchly intrusion into secular matters was based on his experience of the overreaching hegemony of the **papacy**. Luther's trials and ultimate impatience with the latter found correction and happiness in the former.

The **doctrine** of the two kingdoms does not imply an ontological distinction between the kingdoms of the left and the right. Nor is it a mandate that Christians must function differently in the two realms. Rather, the doctrine could be understood as an ethico-hermeneutical lens by which the believing Christian should interpret **culture** and act accordingly. As Luther argued, Christians belong to both realms, while unbelievers belong only in the secular realm. Christians are subject *both* to secular and spiritual law, and are subject to the former especially for the salutary sake of the neighbor. It would be an error, though, for the Christian to use spiritual authority in the civil realm, as that spiritual activity of God is not recognized by the *civitas* per se. The Christian is to be involved in the secular or civil realm, however, precisely because the Christian sees God at work therein through the means of **love** active through **reason**.

This mandate for the Christian to participate in both realms, yet distinguishing them, distances the Lutheran position from those of the radical reformers (like **Thomas Müntzer**) who would fuse church and state under a literal reading of the Sermon on the Mount, and from those (like early **Anabaptists**) who, for **piety's** sake based their position on a different reading of the Sermon on the Mount, would wholly remove themselves from public life. **Lutheranism** refuses both the confusion of the two reigns and the sheer separation of them. Such a careful positioning clearly does not allow the abetting of fascism, as was blamed of Lutheranism in post–World War II Germany; nor does it cohere with or allow an absolute separation of **church and state** for Lutherans living in the United States, as is falsely claimed today. Both realms are under God and are the arena of responsible Christian and ecclesial life and action. One also sees in Luther's position a dependence upon the Aristotelian and medieval concept of the three estates: the *ecclesia*, *oeconomia*, and *politia* (see CHURCH AND WORLD). Church and **family** life were established by God as components of **creation** and civil government was a necessary addition after the fall to curtail evil. **Philipp Melanchthon** argued similarly, although he based more explicitly the foundation for civil authority on **natural law**, and he codified the basic Lutheran understanding then in articles 16 and 28 of the *Augsburg Confession* and its *Apology*. [D.H.L.]

TWO NATURES OF CHRIST. *See* CHRISTOLOGY.

– U –

UBIQUITY. *See* LORD'S SUPPER; CHRISTOLOGY.

UNION. One of the main concepts of the **unity of the church**. Throughout church history there have been attempts to unite separated churches by merging so that they form a united church. Such efforts may aim at a transconfessional union of churches belonging to different Christian **traditions**, like the Church of South India in which the **Anglican, Methodist**, and United (**Presbyterian** and Congregationalist) churches of that region came together in 1947. Less complicated (and not so ecumenically significant) are unions of churches belonging to the same confession, for example, the history of intra-Lutheran unions in North America leading to the formation of the Evangelical Lutheran Church in America in 1987. Lutherans have also been involved in a few transconfessional unions. During the 19th century the princes and their governments of several German territories decreed a union between Lutherans and **Reformed**. The most well known is the Prussian Union of 1817 that was conceived as an administrative union by allowing **pastors** and **congregations** to retain their confessional allegiance and liturgy. When after some time pressures for more uniformity were felt, conservative Lutheran groups either emigrated to North America and Australia or formed in Prussia and other united territories (small) Lutheran **free churches**. Another union that included Lutherans was the United Church of Christ in Japan, formed in 1941 by a decision of the government. In this instance, Lutherans left this union after World War II.

Under the impact of the **ecumenical movement** of the 20th century, transconfessional church union negotiations and unions became a major expression of church unity. The Church of South India became the symbol of this new effort. About 20 united churches have been formed since then. The only one that Lutherans have joined is the Church of Pakistan (1970). Lutheran churches have been reluctant to participate in church union negotiations and unions because they wish to preserve their confessional heritage while seeking unity with other churches through forms of full **communion**—a generally growing ecumenical tendency. [G.G.]

UNIQUENESS OF CHRIST. The confession of Jesus Christ as Son of **God** and as the only and universal savior of the world. The New Testament witnesses to the unique relationship of Jesus to God and attributes to Jesus a singular significance for the **salvation** of people in and through him (Acts 4:12), who is confessed to be the Lord (Rom 10:8–13). All things are made through him and for him (Jn 1:1–3. 14; I Cor 8:6; Col 1:15–20; Heb 1:1–3), and all authority has been given to him (Mt 28:18–19). The confession of the early Christian communities to God's work of salvation and **redemption** through the **incarnation**, life, crucifixion, and **resurrection** of the Son of God has been the basis for the missionary zeal of the early church. It has remained a constitutive element of Christian **faith** and life throughout the centuries.

Martin Luther and the **Reformation** as a whole have reemphasized the unique saving significance of Christ. "Christ alone" is the mediator between God and humanity. By being both human and divine, Christ alone is able to reconcile sinful humanity with God. In the new context of the missionary movement and of growing religious pluralism in the 20th century, earlier forms of arrogant or aggressive presentation of the uniqueness of Christ have been discarded by most churches. Out of a bad conscience about the past and with a desire to not devalue other **religions**, some **Roman Catholic** and liberal **Protestant** theologians have recently given up the concept of the uniqueness of Christ by proposing that all religions are equally true and salvific in nature. Others have judged this position as contradicting Holy Scripture as well as the claims to uniqueness of other religions. The ecumenical community as a whole has continued, for example, at World Missionary Conferences and the assemblies of the **World Council of Churches**, to affirm the unique saving significance of Jesus Christ. It has affirmed this in the context both of the calling of Christianity in world history today and of dialogue with and respect of other religions. *See also* CHRISTOLOGY; ECUMENICAL MOVEMENT; INTERRELIGIOUS DIALOGUE; NON-CHRISTIAN RELIGIONS. [G.G.]

UNITY OF THE CHURCH. One of the attributes of the Christian church. Not only key texts (like 1 Cor 12, Eph 4:4–6, or Jn 17:21–23), but also the whole New Testament witness refers to the unity of the emerging Christian communities. Individually and together they manifest the one **church**, the one Body of Christ. Their unity of **faith**, **sacraments**, community, **worship**, and **mission** is given in the one **baptism** and in the communion of the one body and blood of Christ in the **Lord's Supper**. The unity of the church is ultimately grounded in the unity of the one, Trinitarian God (*see* TRINITY, DOGMA OF) and should reflect that unity. Unity must comprehend diversity of spiritual gifts and human conditions, while discord and division have to be overcome. The New Testament also refers to the reality that this unity was often threatened within and between the communities and that apostles like Paul were constantly struggling to preserve or reestablish unity.

To maintain unity in faith and life became an even more pressing task for the expanding church of the first centuries. Several instruments to serve the unity of the church were introduced: the **Canon of Holy Scripture** to provide the common normative texts, the office of **bishops** in **apostolic succession** to serve and safeguard apostolic continuity and unity of the churches, the meeting of bishops in regional councils or synods to express unity between churches, the formulation of baptismal **creeds** and confessions as expressions of the fundamentals of the common faith, the growing importance of the church of Rome and its bishop as a place of appeal in doctrinal and other controversies, and especially, beginning in the fourth century, the great councils of the whole church (*see* COUNCILS, ECUMENICAL) that played a decisive role in the preservation of the unity of the church during the first eight centuries.

After the division between the Western Catholic Church and the Eastern **Orthodox Church** in 1054, the Orthodox churches have based their unity in faith and sacraments on the concept and practice of conciliarity between the different local churches. This conciliarity is expressed in sacramental **communion**, councils, synodical meetings, mutual visits and contacts, other bishops' participation in the consecration of a bishop, and in numerous other ways. In the West, the **Roman Catholic Church** has continued to maintain and manifest its unity by means of general councils, but during the High Middle Ages it made the **papacy** into the center and guardian of its unity. With the Second Vatican Council (*see* VATICAN COUNCIL II) and its entry into the **ecumenical movement**, the Roman Catholic Church has opened up its traditional identification of the unity of the church with itself and has participated in ecumenical reflections on the foundations and forms of Christian unity.

The basic aim of the Lutheran **Reformation** has been to renew the late medieval church while at the same time preserving its unity. This concern for the unity of the church is repeatedly expressed in the Lutheran confessions (*see* CONFESSIONS, LUTHERAN). They plead for a unity based on agreement in the proclamation of the **Gospel** and celebration of the sacraments under the norm of Holy Scripture (*see* BIBLE, AUTHORITY OF) and in continuity with the faith of the church since the time of the apostles. Church unity does not, however, require uniformity of ecclesiastical traditions, structures of **church polity**, ceremonies, and so on. This concentration on **consensus** in faith has also marked the position and involvement of Lutheran churches in the modern ecumenical movement. Such consensus or agreement in faith should enable a relationship that traditionally has been called by Lutherans "pulpit and altar fellowship," which is considered as church unity in its full sense, but does not necessarily include a merger of separated churches in order to form a united church.

Other forms of church unity have been considered in the ecumenical movement: a spiritual or invisible unity grounded in mutual belief in Christ, **prayer**, **witness**, and cooperation; a **federation** of churches for the purpose of social cooperation and witness; a corporate union of churches that form one united church but preserve, as groups within such a church, their specific liturgical, spiritual, theological, and juridical characteristics; the comprehensive organic unity that would enable churches from different Christian **traditions** to merge with one another and form united churches (as in Australia, Canada, Great Britain, Jamaica, southern and northern India, and so on). At its assembly at Canberra in 1991, the **World Council of Churches** reformulated earlier descriptions of church unity (assemblies at New Delhi 1961 and Nairobi 1975). Canberra introduced the concept of "koinonia"—communion—in order to interpret the goal of all ecumenical efforts in a more dynamic and open manner than the traditional term "unity" was able to do. According to this new concept, the unity of the church should take the form of a koinonia based on and expressed by the common confession of the apostolic faith, a shared sacramental life, mutual recognition and **reconciliation** of members and ministries, and a common mission in witnessing to the Gospel and serving all creation.

These basic elements of koinonia/communion are also integral to the concepts of "unity in reconciled diversity" and "full communion" that explicitly recognize the continuing significance of—reconciled—confessional traditions. These concepts have received a certain preference in the ecumenical efforts of the **Lutheran World Federation** and Lutheran churches (and increasingly among other churches), and they have been implemented in a number of cases. *See also* LEUENBERG AGREEMENT; *PORVOO COMMON STATEMENT*. [G.G.]

UNIVERSALISM (Lat *universalis*, "belonging to the whole"). In a general sense, the proposition that **God's grace** is so comprehensive and definitive of God's character that all people will be saved, no matter what their present situation of **sin** or belief is within a **tradition** other than Christianity. In a formal sense, universalism coheres with the older concept of apocatastasis (recapitulation) of the early Greek fathers (*see* PATRISTICS), which posits that God will gather up all history into the redeemed glory of the new creation. In a way, universalism is the implication of the Lutheran doctrine of single **predestination**—that God elects people to **salvation**—when taken to its logical end. However, there is little, if any, ground within the Lutheran confessions (*see* CONFESSIONS, LUTHERAN) themselves for holding universalism as a prescriptive or predictive claim as to what "will" happen in the future of God with humanity and **creation** (*see* ESCHATOLOGY). What God offers, sinful humans could yet reject.

What might appear to be universalistic claims, whether in the Lutheran confessions or in the Bible, Lutherans usually understand as descriptive predicates for the activity of God, primarily to underscore that God in Christ, with the **Holy Spirit** (*see* TRINITY, DOGMA OF) and no other, is the doer of salvation. A complementary claim to this emphasis on God's agency is that the **Gospel** has a universal scope; God's **love** applies to all things. Again, however, this is in the Lutheran tradition a predominately descriptive matter of how things are, as it were, in the present tense. **Lutheranism** is reticent to speak of the mysteries of God, except to proclaim the surety of the **promise** of salvation and the ease of **conscience** to those who have **faith**. [D.H.L.]

UNIVERSALITY OF THE CHURCH. *See* CATHOLICITY.

– V –

VATICAN COUNCIL I. The 20th general council in the Roman Catholic list of councils. Pope Pius IX convoked the First Vatican Council (1869–1870), which marked an extremely difficult moment in the history of the **Roman Catholic Church**. The apologetical, defensive attitude of Rome, provoked by the new reality of the **Reformation** churches, was increased steadily by reaction against internal pressures that demanded the national churches consent to papal decrees (the so-called Gallicanism in the 17th century). External threats and challenges came from the French revolution (1789), the **Enlightenment**, anticlerical intellectual Liberalism, loss of secular influence and power of the **papacy**, and so on. Many Catholic circles responded to these developments with the desire to strengthen papal authority and with a growing reverence for the person of the pope. He was seen as the center of stability and a bastion against the threats of modernity. Pius IX supported this so-called ultramontanist movement (Lat *ultra montes*, "beyond the mountains," referring to those who look beyond the Alps to Rome) and, in 1854, affirmed the papal claim to infallibility with the dogma of the immaculate conception of **Mary**.

Vatican I managed to adopt only two dogmatic constitutions before the council was suspended because of the Franco-Prussian War. The first document (*Dei Filius*) was on the nature and interconnection between religious knowledge, **faith**, **revelation**, and **reason**. The second and more famous one (*Pastor Aeternus*) decreed the full, ordinary, and immediate jurisdictional primacy of the pope over the whole **church**, and his gift of infallibility when he speaks *ex cathedra*, that is, in the exercise of his office when defining **doctrine** concerning faith or morals. Such definitions "are of themselves, and not by the consent of the Church, irreformable." Great tensions arose among the over 700 participants regarding this issue, and many did not agree with the decision or regarded it as inopportune. Vatican I was seen by the other churches as a further and important step towards widening the division within Christianity. *See also* VATICAN COUNCIL II. [G.G.]

VATICAN COUNCIL II. The 21st general council in the Roman Catholic list of councils. The Second Vatican Council had quite the opposite orientation and impact of **Vatican I**. Developments in the **Roman Catholic Church** since the end of the 19th century prepared a reversal of the road that had led to Vatican I. Such developments aimed at the recovery of a biblical-theological understanding of the **church**, its **worship**, the role of its **laity**, its relation to the modern world, and its social responsibility. There was also the growing influence of the **ecumenical movement**. At first, the Roman Catholic Church refused participation in this movement. The invitation of the **Faith and Order movement** to participate in its first world conference was rejected in 1919, and in 1928 the papal encyclical *Mortalium Animos* again excluded participation in ecumenical efforts and meetings with the same argument as in 1919, namely that Christian unity (*see* UNITY OF THE CHURCH) may be fostered only "by promoting the return to the one true Church of Christ of those who are separated from it."

A radical change of this polity, prepared by Roman Catholic ecumenical pioneers, came with Pope John XXIII who established in 1960 the (Vatican) Secretariat for Promoting Christian Unity. It was this pope who had announced a year before his intention to convoke a council that would serve the pastoral and theological renewal of the church and its *aggiornamento* (Ital "renewal, bringing up to date") in relation to the modern world. Vatican II began in 1962 and was continued in 1963 by Paul VI, the successor of John XXIII, until 1965. Between 2000 and 2500 bishops and other Catholic leaders took part, accompanied by many theological advisors. One hundred eighty-six officially invited ecumenical observers were present for varying periods as well.

Vatican II affirmed and received (*see* RECEPTION) the new developments in the Roman Catholic Church and formulated the results of the lively conciliar debates in 16 final documents. The most important one is the *Dogmatic Constitution on the Church* (*Lumen Gentium*). It reflects the new biblically based **ecclesiology** and begins, accordingly, with the dynamic concept of the church as mystery and as People of God before it comes to the traditional hierarchical structure of the church. Other important conciliar texts deal with *The Church in the Modern World*, *Divine Liturgy*, *Divine Revelation*, and *Religious Liberty*. For the non-Roman Catholic churches and the ecumenical movement, the *Decree on Ecumenism* (*Unitatis Redintegratio*) was and is of special interest and importance. This decree, by developing the implications of the *Dogmatic Constitution on the Church*'s full and partial recognition of the other churches and "ecclesiastical communities," announces the Roman Catholic participation in the ecumenical movement and outlines different forms of ecumenical activity.

The Lutheran churches and the **Lutheran World Federation** followed Vatican II with intensive interest and much hope, based on the great historical significance of Lutheran-Roman Catholic relations (*see* ROMAN CATHOLIC CHURCH AND LUTHERANISM). Since then, Lutherans and Roman Catholics have engaged in important theological dialogues (*see* LUTHERAN-ROMAN CATHOLIC DIALOGUE) and many other forms of ecumenical rapprochement. Vatican II, whose full implications are still being discussed within the Roman Catholic Church, has definitely inaugurated a new era in the history of this church and of its ecumenical relations. [G.G.]

VESTMENTS. The distinctive clothes worn by ministers (lay or ordained) since the fourth century to lead worship. While **Reformed** tradition forbade these as un-Biblical, Lutheran **tradition** saw them as **adiaphora**, unless required or forbidden by an authority outside the **church** (*see* INTERIM; *STATUS CON-FESSIONIS*). At the time of the **Reformation**, vestments included the alb, a long white tunic with full, narrow sleeves; the cincture, a rope that cinched the alb at the waist; the surplice, a fuller version of the alb; the stole, a scarf worn over the neck by presbyters and from the left shoulder to the right hip by deacons; the dalmatic, a long coat with short sleeves, worn by deacons and bishops; and the chasuble, a full cloak worn by the presider at the **eucharist**. Under these or as street dress, clergy might also wear: a cassock, a long black tunic; a gown, a black robe; a ruff, an elaborate ruffled collar; and bands or Ger *Beffchen*, two white pieces of linen connected at the throat.

Reformed influence, opposition to Roman Catholicism, a desire not to separate lay and clerical members, and economics led Lutherans to simplify medieval vestments. By the beginning of the 19th century a few towns such as Leipzig, along with Sweden, Finland, and Slovakia retained eucharistic vestments. Most German **pastors** preached and led worship in gown and bands. Many Norwegians and Danes wore the ruff over a cassock. In America, English-speaking Lutherans forswore distinctive vestments entirely, preferring to wear dark suits to lead worship. In the mid-19th century **Johann Konard Wilhelm Löhe** led a movement to return to liturgical ceremonial and dress. This movement was part of a larger aesthetic effort. Today, there exists in Lutheran churches a considerable variety of liturgical dress, the main forms being black or white preaching gown with bands, alb with stole, or eucharistic vestments. [M.O.]

VIOLENCE AND NONVIOLENCE. The ecumenical discussion on the use and nonuse of violence in sociopolitical conflicts. The issue of violence and nonviolence has been discussed in Christian history in relation to the use of power and **authority** of governments and rulers, the right of resistance against misuse of public power, the use of violence to overthrow the rule of a tyrant, and in other connections. For **Martin Luther**, there was no question that the state and its legitimate rulers had the right to use the sword in the service of **justice** and **peace** while the use of violent means for one's own aims was a denial of the will of **God**. When radical reformers like **Thomas Müntzer** justified theologically the use of violence in the **Peasants' War** for the sake of social justice, Luther protested vehemently. The subsequent Lutheran **tradition** tended to emphasize obedience to those in power and foresaw only passive resistance or suffering acceptance in cases of conflict with the state.

The issue of violence and nonviolence received new urgency in the 20th century. It was a deep cause of conscience for Christians who participated in the plot to kill Adolf Hitler in 1944 (*see* BONHOEFFER, DIETRICH). Twenty years later, a controversial debate arose in the **World Council of Churches** (WCC) about the use of violence in sociopolitical conflicts. The concept of "structural violence" on the side of those responsible for social injustice was introduced and the possibility of violent reactions was discussed, while at the same time the civil rights movement in the United States challenged the WCC to consider nonviolent means of social change. In the 1970s and 1980s the support by the WCC of liberation movements in Africa and Latin America, which had used violent means, provoked a heated debate in which no agreement was reached. WCC statements expressed a certain limited understanding for the use of violence as a last resort when all other efforts to change an oppressive and unjust system had failed. But the primary Christian attitude should be the support of nonviolent means of conflict resolution and social change. *See also* CHURCH AND STATE; LIBERATION THEOLOGY; QUIETISM. [G.G.]

VIRTUES (Lat *virtus*, "worth, moral strength"). Philosophical and theological ethical concept. Having its roots in Greek philosophy, the word "virtue" was taken over into Christian thinking, and has come to mean habits, attitudes, and qualities of character that are oriented towards positive moral behavior and action. **Augustine** accepted the four cardinal virtues of the Greeks: prudence, justice, temperance, and fortitude, but subordinated them to divine love (charity). **Thomas Aquinas**, in the framework of his **reception** of Aristotle, formed his medieval and later teachings on virtues. He distinguished between the four previously mentioned moral/natural/cardinal virtues and the theological/supernatural virtues of **faith**, **hope**, and **love**. The distinction and relationship between the two kinds of virtues corresponds to that of **nature** and **grace**. The acquired natural virtues are needed to develop the human powers and efforts towards a moral life. The infused supernatural virtues are needed to direct these powers and efforts toward their supernatural goal, **God**, enabling them to participate in the divine life. Thus, virtues are not only marked by an active orientation toward what is good, they are also actively involved in the cooperation between human nature and divine grace in the process leading up to **justification** and **sanctification**.

This meritorious role of virtues provoked the rejection of the medieval teaching on virtues by **Martin Luther** and the Lutheran **Reformation**. However, after the **ethics** of **conscience**, obligation, and moral law, as well as modern situation ethics have lost their influence, contemporary moral **theology** is reaffirming the positive meaning of virtues in the sense of basic moral orientations and attitudes of the moral subject. Many Lutherans will welcome the newly emphasized role of virtues in ethical reflection as long as virtues are not understood as part of the process of justification and **salvation**, but as components of Christian moral life that are a necessary consequence of justification. [G.G.]

VOCATION (Lat *vocare*, "to call"). Literally meaning "calling," this concept has often been limited to church-related occupations. Thus, a "crisis in vocations" refers to a shortage of clergy. More generally, though, and more faithfully, it refers to any occupation or office in which Christians live out their **baptism** within the created order. No single vocation is superior to other vocations. **Martin Luther**, for instance, affirmed parenthood as a vocation equally to be honored as **monasticism**, and called political rulers to account for the way in which they exercised their **stewardship** of the office to which they had been called. *See also* WORK. [M.O.]

– W –

WALTER, JOHANN (1496–1570). German Lutheran cantor, musician, composer, and reformer. A composer of competence, but not genius, Walter came to **Martin Luther's** attention as the publisher of the first Lutheran **hymnbook**, *Geystliche Gesangk Buchleyn*, in 1524, for which Luther wrote the preface. From that time, Walter served as the reformer's advisor in matters relating to **music**, and especially to congregational song. Because of Walter's modesty and Luther's silence, we have no way of knowing how many of the latter's **hymn** tunes were revised or even composed by the former. It is clear, however, that Walter provided direction in such matters as the chanting of the *Verba* in Luther's *German Mass* (*Deutsche Messe*). In 1526 Walter became head of the Torgau **Kantorei**, to which he dedicated most of the rest of his life. In that capacity, he trained the father of Michael Praetorius and the teacher of **Heinrich Schütz**, as well as many others. As a choral composer, he was very much in the tradition of Josquin des Prez, exploring the uses of counterpoint, but constantly subordinating the music to the texts. He was the first to set Luther's translation of the Bible to music, and his **chorale** preludes for **organ** on Luther's hymns are still played. There is no evidence that he ever composed anything but sacred, and in fact liturgical, music. [M.O.]

WALTHER, CARL FERDINAND WILHELM (1811–1887). Cofounder and first president of the **Lutheran Church-Missouri Synod**. After serving as **pastor** in a congregation in his home country, Germany, Walther immigrated in 1839 with a group of conservative Lutherans to North America. He became the spiritual leader of the German Lutherans in Perry County, Missouri, insisting on a strict adherence to the Lutheran confessions (*see* CONFESSIONS, LUTHERAN) and the teaching of **Martin Luther**. Soon after his arrival in the New World, he was from 1841 until his death (1887) the pastor of Trinity Church in St. Louis, Missouri, and later the chief pastor of four **congregations** there. He also became a professor of **theology** at the new Concordia Seminary (1850–1887). This institution was an ideal tool for him to shape generations of future **pastors** in the spirit and letter of Lutheran **Orthodoxy**, which combined a strong personal **piety**, solid theological learning, and unwavering doctrinal positions.

In 1847 Walther with like-minded colleagues founded the German Evangelical Lutheran Synod of Missouri, Ohio, and Other States, which came to be called the Lutheran Church-Missouri Synod a century later (1947). He became the first president of this church, which did not have a strong centralized structure because it granted congregations considerable independence. In 1872 Walther was able, after a series of Lutheran free conferences, to bring together a larger group of conservative Lutheran synods in the Evangelical Lutheran Conference, of which this equally competent theologian and administrator became the first president. Through his many activities, which included his editorship of the bimonthly *Der Lutheraner* (1844–1887) and the periodical *Lehre und Wehre* (founder and editor 1855–1864), Walther gave the German-speaking church its resolute doctrinal character that was unique in North American Christianity. [G.G.]

WAR. *See* JUST WAR.

WASA, ANNA (1568–1625). A Polish-Swedish princess who became a courageous Lutheran. Anna Wasa was the daughter of King John III of Sweden and his Polish wife Katarina Jagellonica. Though she was educated in a strict Catholic spirit by her devout Catholic mother and her father with his strong Catholic inclinations, Anna became a Lutheran after the death of her mother (1583). When her brother Sigismund, who retained the faith of their mother, was chosen to be king of Poland in 1587, she accompanied him to the Polish court. Disgusted by the extreme Catholicism at the court and the **persecution** of all non-Catholics, Anna left the court and moved to her estates in Pomerania, where she provided refuge for banished and persecuted **Protestants** from Poland and **refugees** from other countries. She also helped to advance science and the arts in Poland. Remaining a committed Lutheran throughout her life, this highly educated and compassionate princess protected all who had accepted the **evangelical faith**. [G.G.]

WESLEY, JOHN (1703–1791). English theologian, preacher, reformer, and writer. Son of religious parents, and rescued as a child from a burning building, John Wesley was early endowed with a sense of religious purpose. His course, from student to **priest** to tutor at Oxford, was one of increasing seriousness in matters of religion. A short and unsuccessful career as a missionary and colonial official in Georgia was followed, almost immediately upon his return to London, by his **conversion** experience on Wednesday, May 24, 1738, at Aldersgate Street. This experience, a deeply felt knowledge of his unmerited **salvation**, led to the formation of a society for inculcating such conviction. The method of **piety** was prescribed so clearly that the society was labeled "Methodism." While his itinerant preaching, some of his theological ideas, and his ordaining of preachers and **superintendents** for service in North America led to problems, he never left the Church of England.

Wesley's ties to **Lutheranism** were many. His shipmates on his trip to Georgia, who impressed him with their confidence and **hymn** singing, are usually identified as Moravians (*see* MORAVIAN CHURCH), but might have been Lutheran Salzburgers. The proximate cause for his conversion experience at Aldersgate was his reading of **Martin Luther**'s preface to his commentary on the Letter to the Romans. Wesley was one of the first translators of Lutheran **chorales** into English, usually to a different meter more attuned to the British ear, and always dramatically abridged. [M.O.]

WICHERN, JOHANN HINRICH (1808–1891). German Lutheran **pastor**, social reformer, and renewer of Christian **diakonia**. Born in Hamburg, Wichern studied theology at Göttingen and Berlin. Influenced by **Pietism** and the Lutheran **Awakening**, he began his career by teaching at a Sunday school in Hamburg. Deeply moved by the miserable living conditions of his pupils and their families, he decided to engage in social work. In 1833 he founded the Rauhe Haus, a home to rehabilitate and educate delinquent youth, which became a model for similar institutions. Wichern employed new pedagogical methods, and soon began to train helpers in what was to become (in 1844) the first school for deacons (*see* DIACONATE). In his flourishing institution, Wichern began in 1844 to publish a periodical and brochures that became major means to awaken social awareness in the church and beyond.

Wichern is regarded as one of the founders of the **Inner Mission** movement. In 1848 he was instrumental in the formation of the Central Committee for Inner Mission of the German Evangelical Church, whose aim was to organize and further Christian social work and **institutions**, as well as Christian **witness** among the de-Christianized working class. Wichern's Hamburg institutions and his untiring activity through lectures, publications, and correspondence served as a strong impulse for the establishment of social institutions and Inner Mission societies in several larger cities. He advised the Prussian king and government on prison reform and welfare work. In 1858 he founded the Johannesstift at Berlin, another training institution for deacons that eventually grew into a large diaconic center. A politically and theologically conservative Lutheran, but endowed with an ability to work with and for the poor and needy, and ahead of his time with his insistence on the connection between proclamation and social work, Wichern became the moving and organizing spirit of social and evangelistic work in the framework of the Inner Mission movement. [G.G.]

WITNESS. The demonstration, intentional or spontaneous, of the transforming power of the **Gospel**. It is no accident that *"martyria"* (Gk for "witness") has become the basis for the English word "martyr," since those who willingly offered their lives for the sake of the **faith** were seen as the most obvious and credible witnesses. Witness to **God's salvation** in Jesus Christ is an essential component in both **mission** and **evangelism**, as the risen Christ demonstrates in his commissioning of the **church** (e.g., Lk 24:48).

Witness by Lutherans has attempted to hold several dualities in tension. Such witness, to be both faithful and credible, must be corporate and personal, spoken and enacted, planned and spontaneous, orthodox and contemporary, joyous and cruciform. Different schools in **Lutheranism** have unbalanced some of these dualities, to the detriment of their witness. Lutheran **Orthodoxy**, for instance, often insists on obedience to established doctrinal formulae, giving less attention to the communication of the **truths** those formulae embody. **Pietism**, with its penchant for self-examination, often witnesses to the spiritual struggles of the believer rather than to the faith itself. Churches in bureaucratic cultures often transfer responsibility for enacted witness (such as care of the poor, sick, or imprisoned) to organizations. Witness to God's **love** and **justification** in Christ is, however, not only the central privilege and responsibility of the Christian (*see* PRIESTHOOD OF ALL BELIEVERS), but also the natural consequence of the gracious relationship established by God through the saving action of Jesus Christ and communicated by the **Holy Spirit**. The task of Christians from different churches to render a common witness in the modern world has been a major theme and goal in the **ecumenical movement**. [M.O.]

WITTENBERG. Cradle of the Lutheran **Reformation**. **Frederick III the Wise**, elector of Saxony, founded a university in 1502 in the small town of Wittenberg. He brought competent professors to his new university, among them several humanists (*see* HUMANISM). **Martin Luther** came to Wittenberg in the winter of 1508/9 and became a professor of biblical studies in 1512. In 1518 young **Philipp Melanchthon** joined the university as a professor of Greek. Both found a congenial atmosphere among their humanist colleagues for their exegetical work, and together with them, they reformed the university. The dominance of Aristotle, **Scholasticism**, and **canon law** was replaced by the study of the three ancient languages, history, practical experience, and, in addition, for theologians the Bible and the early church fathers (*see* PATRISTICS). The new spirit and curriculum of the university, as well as its becoming the center of the Lutheran Reformation, attracted an increasing number of students, so that it became the largest university in Germany. There were often more students in the town and vicinity than the approximately 2,500 inhabitants.

Luther and Melanchthon, as well as other important reformers like **Justus Jonas**, **Johannes Bugenhagen**, and **Georg Major** not only made this university the basis of their reforming activities, but also drew a large number of students, among them many foreigners and future leaders of the Lutheran movement in their countries. Between 1570 and 1590 the university saw struggles for influence between Lutherans and **Crypto-Calvinists**, and even Calvinists (*see* CALVIN, JOHN). In 1591 it became definitively Lutheran again and developed into the most important center of Lutheran Orthodoxy (*see* ORTHODOXY, LUTHERAN). In 1816 the university was united with the University of Halle. Parts of the former university buildings are today a **Protestant** seminary, a library, museum, and conference center. Luther and Melanchthon are buried side by side in the Castle Church (Schlosskirche), as is their protector, Frederick the Wise. [G.G.]

WOMEN IN THE CHURCH. The New Testament gives significant witness to the place and role of women in the **church** of the first generation. From Mary Magdalene, the apostle to the apostles, to the cadre of women whom Paul addressed as hosts and leaders of their communities, to the legion of anonymous women known only by their offices as deacons, widows, and virgins, it is obvious that women formed a large and influential portion of the apostolic church. While later generations excluded women from ordained leadership, they were influential as monastics, lay leaders, and patrons. During the Middle Ages, abbesses such as Hildegard of Bingen and mystics such as Margery Kempe wielded considerable power and influence.

The **Reformation** brought forth a few women as courageous Christian leaders, such as **Elizabeth of Braunschweig**, **Argula von Grumbach**, **Anna Wasa**, and **Katharina Zell**. The most prominent among them has become (more recently) **Katherina von Bora**, whose lauded characteristics were mostly domestic. This limitation set an example for the **Lutheran church**, and for many years exemplary women were confined in their sphere to home and **family**—certainly honorable and vital **vocations** but not the only ones possible for women. This situation began to change in the 19th century, in part because of the establishment of deaconess communities (*see* DIAKONIA), which perforce called on the gifts of women for leadership and mission in the church. The 19th century also saw a rise in feminist consciousness (*see* FEMINISM) and in social activism led by women. Women's organizations in the church became active in **education**, temperance, and, above all, overseas **missions**. Women missionaries from Europe and North America took on tasks and filled offices that were forbidden them at home, and the churches of Africa and Asia became models for the active and responsible inclusion of women in church life.

But it was only in the 20th century that the process of providing women with their appropriate place in the tasks and life of the church came closer to its goal. The **ordination of women** was an important step in this process, but it was neither the first nor the only way in which women received a place in the church that corresponds to their gifts and their status as equal members of the church of Jesus Christ. This process is still on its way. The **Lutheran World Federation** has played an active and pioneering role in furthering the place and coresponsibility of women in Lutheran churches through studies, advocacy, international exchange, and training seminars for future women leaders. [M.O.]

WORD OF GOD (Heb *dabar*, "word, event," Gk *logos*, "word"). Central theme of Lutheran **theology**, referring to the communication of **God's revelation** and **salvation**. While central to the Old Testament (where God creates by speaking, and where faithful prophecy is preceded by the formula, "Thus says the Lord"), the notion of the Word of God takes on new meaning in the New Testament where it refers primarily to the Christian message of salvation (Acts 4:31; Col 1:25; Heb 6:4–5). This message is inseparably linked to Jesus Christ, the *logos*, whose incarnation is the self-revelation of God (Joh 1:14), and whose message, **cross**, and **resurrection** (*see* CHRISTOLOGY) are the content of apostolic proclamation (e.g., 1 Cor 1:18; Col 3:16). The Word of God and the **Gospel** are, thus, synonymous. The occasional identification of the Word of God with Holy Scripture (e.g., Mk 7:13; Mt 15:1–6; Acts 4:25) is strengthened in the patristic period (*see* PATRISTICS), while in the Middle Ages the Word was closely linked to the **sacraments**, transforming the sacramental signs into efficacious signs. However, the concept of the living Word of God communicated through proclamation became more and more marginalized.

Against this neglect of the Word, as well as against the claim of the **Spiritualists** to having direct, divine inspiration without the outward Word, **Martin Luther** and the Lutheran confessions (*see* CONFESSIONS, LUTHERAN) emphasized that the Word of God, given in Scripture and to be proclaimed as **law and Gospel**, is the glorious divine **promise** of **grace**, salvation, and eternal life. Belief in the effectively proclaimed, living Word, enabled by the **Holy Spirit**, leads to the assurance of a life justified before God. It is the Word that makes water into **baptism**, bread and wine into the **Lord's Supper**, and human words into the **preaching** of the Gospel, which make such creaturely things able to accomplish the work of salvation. This Word, while never disconnected from the Bible, Luther rarely identifies with the Bible. Rather, the Word is the Gospel that is not only *about* Christ but that indeed *is* Christ, and which can norm even the Scriptures, whose duty and glory it is to bear Christ as the manger did. For Luther, the Word of God is always contextual. Therefore, the proclamation of the Scriptures in a particular situation, rather than simply their study *in vacuo*, is central. Finally, Luther was as radical as the evangelist in insisting that the Word was God. The key to his theology of the cross is the rejection of any other way to God than the way God chose to approach humanity—by the Word. In a culture that looked for God's identity and approval in mystical experience, ethical benevolence, or intellectual speculation, Luther rejected all these paths in favor of the Word.

The polemical climate of the generations after Luther made it impossible to preserve this understanding of the Word. Over and against Roman Catholic reliance on **tradition** and that of the enthusiasts on the "unmediated Spirit," it was Scripture as the Word of God on which Lutheran **Orthodoxy** relied. Thus was constructed on a scholastic basis a **doctrine** of the verbal inspiration and, thus, inerrancy and infallibility of the Bible (*see* BIBLE, INSPIRATION OF). **Pietism**, when it did not share this identification of Word and Scripture, tended to identify the Word instead with any cause that brought forth a religious or edifying effect—thus focusing on the faithful person, rather than on the gracious God or the **means of grace**.

After the **Enlightenment** and later **Liberalism** had tried to turn the Word of God into the communication of general truths of **reason** or of moral orientation, **dialectical theology** in the 20th century placed the Word of God, centered in Jesus Christ as the one Word and revelation of God, once again at the center of theology. This new emphasis has had a lasting impact that is still felt, where the relationship between the transcendence of God's Word and its communication through human words, in the Bible and in present proclamation, is discussed within a universal-historical interpretation of Christian revelation and **faith**, given in God's Word. [G.G.]/[M.O.]

WORK. The Lutheran understanding of work. It is difficult to establish from the New Testament an **evangelical** understanding of work. In fact, Jesus' peremptory calling of his disciples and Paul's view of the imminent eschaton (*see* ESCHATOLOGY) seem to lead to a denigration of labor, although many of Jesus' parables do depend on the working world. Such a denigration could not last, of course, and work became a part of the life of covenanted Christian communities, an understanding crystallized in the famous Benedictine slogan, *Ora et labora* ("pray and work"). The Middle Ages made work a part of the structure of society, with the honorable professions organized into guilds that were indeed societies themselves, providing order and security to their members.

Martin Luther criticized this order, which had in his time already partially disintegrated into individualism. For Luther, work was synonymous with **vocation**—one was called to a particular occupation as well as to a particular place in society as a way to honor **God** and to serve one's neighbors. All needful occupations were equally honorable, parenthood no less than

monasticism, and the office of the magistrate was as much one of divine ordination as that of the **pastor**. While this understanding of work was never
extinguished in **Lutheranism**, it was joined by other, less faithful understandings. Work has been understood as the defining identity of a person,
rather as one way in which that person lives out her or his baptismal identity. Work has been understood as a necessary evil, to be avoided as soon
and as often as possible, in order to dedicate oneself to "ministry," whether
that is seen as proclamation or benevolence. Certain groups of pietists (*see*
PIETISM) in particular have seen work as primarily a way of producing
profit, rather than as a part of God's preservation of **creation** and neighbor.
In the late 20th century a renewed respect for the ministry of the **laity** has
led to a reaffirmation of Luther's insight into the nature of work. [M.O.]

WORLD COUNCIL OF CHURCHES. The most important instrument of
the **ecumenical movement**. As early as 1919 Swedish Lutheran archbishop
Nathan Söderblom proposed to form an "ecumenical council of churches"
that would enable the churches to consider together their calling to unity
and to common **witness** and service in the world. In 1937 the movements
on **Faith and Order** and on **Life and Work** decided to unite and to set up
a more comprehensive ecumenical organization, the **World Council of
Churches** (WCC). In 1945 eight Lutheran churches in the United States requested that the membership of the proposed WCC should be on a confessional basis, that is, it should be a council of confessional families. A compromise provided for both a confessional and regional (individual churches)
representation. Finally, 90 churches came together in 1948 at Amsterdam
for the foundation of the WCC at its first assembly.

The WCC does not impinge on the autonomy of its member churches,
rather, it serves as the instrument of their "common calling." In 1961 the **International Missionary Council** (IMC) joined the WCC so that now the
three major ecumenical emphases are continued by the WCC: the theological efforts towards the **unity of the church** (Faith and Order), the common
study of and involvement in social and political issues (Life and Work), and
the common missionary task (IMC), together with questions relating to
Christian and theological **education**, **worship** and **spirituality**, **women**,
youth, the role of the **laity**, and **interreligious dialogue**. Today, over 330
churches belong to the WCC. They range from **Orthodox** to some Pentecostal and African independent churches and include the majority of
Lutheran churches. The **Roman Catholic Church** is not a member, but
since 1968 many forms of contact and cooperation have developed.
Through its eight assemblies to date, public statements and initiatives, consultations and publications, and studies and aid programs (*see* EMER-
GENCY AND DEVELOPMENT AID), the WCC has significantly con-

tributed to the radical change among churches from scandalous division to mutual respect, cooperation, and forms of **fellowship**. [G.G.]

WORMS, COLLOQUY OF (1540/41). Important conference aimed at theological agreement between Lutherans and **Roman Catholics**. Eleven theologians from both sides, led by **Philipp Melanchthon** and John Eck, respectively, met and discussed with each other in November 1540 and January 1541 at Worms, Germany. This was a second conference, after a first one at Hagenau in 1540 and was followed by a third one at Regensburg in 1541, called by Emperor Charles V in order to seek religious **reconciliation** in the empire. The altered *Augsburg Confession* of 1540 was used as the basis for the conversations, and an initial agreement on **original sin** was reached. But beyond this, further progress was not made and the colloquy was adjourned to Regensburg. *See also* REGENSBURG, COLLOQUY OF. [G.G.]

WORMS, DIET OF (1521). Diet of historical significance for the cause of the **Reformation** because of **Martin Luther's** stand and testimony for conscience's sake. It was the first diet, a kind of parliament, called by young Emperor Charles V in 1521 (January to May). Luther, who had been cited to appear before the diet, was under pressure to recant his writings and positions. On April 17 he was interrogated. On April 18 he defended his conviction and writings in a dramatic speech that included his famous statement: "Unless I am convinced by the testimony of the Scriptures or clear **reason** . . . I am bound by the Scriptures I have quoted and my **conscience** is captive to the **Word of God**, I cannot and will not retract anything, since it is neither safe nor right to go against conscience."

Immediately after the diet, Charles V issued the **Edict of Worms**, dated May 8 and published on May 26, 1521. It condemned Luther's teaching. He and his followers were banned (outlawed) within the whole empire. After the diet, Luther's (Catholic) protector **Frederick III the Wise** arranged a mock "kidnapping" of Luther on his return trip and his hiding. Over a period of 14 months at Wartburg Castle, he translated the New Testament into German and wrote several works. *See also* BIBLE, MARTIN LUTHER'S TRANSLATION. [G.G.]

WORMS, EDICT OF. *See* WORMS, DIET OF.

WORSHIP, HISTORY AND STRUCTURE. The development of worship in **Lutheranism**. By the beginning of the **Reformation**, the shape of the **Lord's Supper** in the West was set. It began with gathering (including a litany, **hymn**, and **prayer**). The lessons and responses followed, continuing a focus on the **Word** that the **church** had inherited from the Jewish synagogue. The meal itself, including the offertory, preface, eucharistic prayer, and communion, was followed by a dismissal with blessing. This structure was hidden, however, by an exclusive focus on the **priest**, making the **congregation** passive if it was present at all. Congregational involvement was limited to watching at critical moments (such as the elevation, to which a bell called attention) and, except for once a year, only the priest communed. **Martin Luther** kept the structure of the Western mass, while slashing from its content all indications of the mass as **sacrifice**. In practice, his great revolution was to return the mass to a public, participatory occasion, in which the **congregation** was involved (actively in singing, passively in attending to proclamation, and sacramentally in weekly communing in both kinds (bread and wine). Luther wrote two foundational service outlines. The first, the *Formula Missae*, which remained in Latin, envisioned a **choir** and was particularly well suited for sophisticated congregations. This format was used in Brandenburg-Nürnberg and much of Scandinavia and, during the Lutheran **Awakening**, in such repristinations of Reformation practice as **Johann Konrad Wilhelm Löhe's** *Agende* (service book) and the American *Common Service*. In Luther's more popular outline, the *German Mass*, the invariant portions of the service were sung by the congregation in hymn paraphrases, and the whole service was returned to the vernacular. Most other Lutheran services have been based on this outline.

During the 17th and 18th centuries Holy Communion came to be celebrated only quarterly, rather than on every **Sunday**. This change was due mostly to the influence of **Reformed** practice, to the antisacramental bias of the **Enlightenment**, to a **Pietism** that made preparation for Holy Communion so daunting that to frequently celebrate it was nearly impossible, and to such social disruptions as the **Thirty Years' War**. Outside of northern Europe, the frontier conditions of the Lutheran **diaspora** simply reaffirmed this now-normal practice. The normal Sunday assembly, then, had the **sermon** as its single focus in most of Lutheranism until the end of the 20th century.

Mission and immigrant churches continued the liturgical pattern of their homeland. In later generations, however, worship patterns and practices became more contextual, and therefore closer to those of their neighbors. In 19th-century North America, for instance, the older Lutheran churches followed a pattern of worship (a call to worship, hymns, offering, pastoral prayer, and preaching) that is shared with other **Protestants**. Many such bodies adopted American revivalism, finding it congenial to their brand of Pietism. Later in the century, however, these churches and the newer Lutheran churches of the Midwest participated in Romanticism's worldwide return to roots. This movement culminated in the almost universal adoption of the *Common Service*, which combined Reformation structure with the literary style of the Anglican *Book of Common Prayer*. The 20th century has seen a continuation of this contextualization. By their participation in the **liturgical movement**, Lutherans returned to the confessional standard of weekly communion and to the ideal of a knowledgeable, active assembly praying, praising, and proclaiming its way through the structure of the Western rite. Globally, churches are adapting traditional elements to liturgical use (*see* CHURCH MUSIC) and making clear the links between worship and matters of **peace**, **justice**, and care for the earth. *See also* CALENDAR, LITURGICAL; CHURCH YEAR; LECTIONARY; LITURGICAL RENEWAL; MINOR OFFICES; VESTMENTS; WORSHIP AND THE ARTS; WORSHIP, THEOLOGY OF. [M.O.]

WORSHIP, THEOLOGY OF. The theological understanding of Christian worship. While such understanding has varied almost as much as the practice of worship among Lutherans, all such variations share certain central understandings, most embodied in the *Augsburg Confession*. First, the definition of the **church**—the assembly of believers in which the **Gospel** is proclaimed and the **sacraments** administered in accordance with it—not only makes worship the church's central activity, but also demands that worship proclaim the Gospel with fidelity and clarity. Second, the business of proclamation and of the ordained **ministry** is to provide the forum wherein the **Holy Spirit** creates **faith** "when and where he pleases" (article 5). That is, the business of worship is not primarily to save souls, but to proclaim the **Word**. Finally, the notion of the sacrifice of the mass—that the **Lord's Supper** and by extension all worship is a propitiatory offering to **God**—is rejected. The sacraments and worship in general are primarily neither duty nor even human works, but rather the gift and offering of God to humans. All human action in worship, essential as it is, is in response to this divine initiative.

Within these general guidelines, Lutheran understanding of worship has varied considerably. The **theology** of the sacraments and the history of worship practice are treated in other entries of this dictionary. Lutheran **Orthodoxy**, for instance, tended to champion the notion of the church as an objective **institution** in which the Gospel was faithfully proclaimed and the individual's meditation on that Word led to **mystical union** with Christ. **Pietism** was more interested in the church as a covenanted **fellowship** of individuals, and the object of worship was the **conversion** and growth of the individual. The Lutheran **Awakening**, in its many forms, reaffirmed worship as primarily the activity of God, through both Word and sacrament— **Johann Konrad Wilhelm Löhe's** famous "twin peaks." In the 20th century Lutherans participated in the liturgical movement, with its understanding of community at worship as the Body of Christ. But in all of these movements, while worship might occasionally be seen as a means to a more important end—fellowship, **social action**, **education**, intimacy, or **mission**—it has more generally been understood as literally *Gottesdienst*, that is, God's own service to the beloved community and the community's response in worship

and life. *See also* LITURGICAL MOVEMENT; LITURGICAL RE-
NEWAL; WORSHIP, HISTORY AND STRUCTURE. [M.O.]

WORSHIP AND THE ARTS. The different **art** forms in Christian worship.
The **church** has never had a choice about using the **arts** in its worship.
While iconoclasts of various times and places have attempted to forbid pictorial representation, such representation forms only a small part of the art
involved in worship. Some arts may be eliminated, but others are simply unavoidable. Thus, once **congregations** set aside a place for worship, the concerns of architecture and design became important. It is clear, as Winston
Churchill noted, that we may shape our buildings, but then they shape us.
For instance, the development and dominance of the basilica as the normal
architectural shape of the church building, with its long, narrow aisles, and
separation of apse from nave, accompanied and reinforced the image of the
Christian life as a pilgrimage and the stratification of the community. On the
other hand, the design choice of giving prominence to pulpit or font may accompany and reinforce the prominence of **preaching** or **baptism** in the life
of the community. If the **Word** is to be proclaimed, then the art of rhetoric —
persuasive speech — is unavoidably practiced.

But there is an almost endless list of artistic forms that communities may
choose to use in worship. Certainly music — instrumental, choral, and congregational — has been a hallmark of most Christian worship since the New
Testament, and has found particularly wide expression among Lutherans.
Paintings and stained glass representations have been almost universal in
Lutheran usage, whether of biblical themes or characters from church history (e.g., images of **Martin Luther** and **Philipp Melanchthon**). Fabric art,
while more ephemeral than painting or carpentry, has been present in vestments, paraments, and banners. Dance and movement in general have been
far from unknown, particularly in African and African American communities in the late 20th century. The arts of bookbinding, calligraphy, and illumination have adorned Bibles, **lectionaries**, and service books. And printing has taken on new and more practical meaning as bulletins are designed
for ease of participation and produced by computers.

While it is clear that Lutheran congregations have used these and other arts
in worship over the centuries, it is less clear if there is a specifically Lutheran
perspective on worship and the arts. One general principle does, however, seem
to emerge. Artistic expression belongs to the **adiaphora**—something that is of
itself neither commanded nor forbidden. Thus, the questions Lutherans generally ask about such expression are "Does this expression proclaim the **Gospel**
in this time and place?" or "Does this aid the congregation to receive and proclaim the Word of God?" By this **evangelical** center, all matters of tradition,
taste, and familiarity must constantly be judged. *See also* MUSIC IN THE
LUTHERAN CHURCH; WORSHIP, HISTORY AND STRUCTURE. [M.O.]

– Y –

YOUTH. Youth work in Lutheran churches. Until the advent of **Pietism**, youth work in the church was limited to **education** in general and **catechesis** in particular. By the beginning of the 19th century, however, groups were established for youth to gather for Bible study, **prayer**, and support for foreign **missions**. By the 1840s these groups were joined by such newly established parachurch organizations as the Young Men's Christian Association, the Young Women's Christian Association, and the Student Christian Movement. In the United States, the first Lutheran youth group was founded by **Carl Ferdinand Wilhelm Walther** in 1848. By the beginning of the 20th century almost every Lutheran synod had a youth auxiliary. Two major exceptions were the General Synod and the General Council, whose congregational youth groups were organized into a single Luther League. Until the 1970s national American Lutheran youth groups were active in encouraging Bible study, sociability, development of leadership, and social as well as missionary involvement. During the 1970s it proved more and more difficult to involve youth on a national and state level, and most auxiliaries were disbanded, to be replaced by occasional large national gatherings.

Western missionaries (*see* MISSION HISTORY, LUTHERAN) carried with them a commitment to youth work. This commitment, however, has continued and been expanded as the younger churches organized themselves. Youth work has focused on study, **witness**, and service, as well as musical and other worship leadership, **justice** issues, and the impact of technological and social change on postcolonial societies. Here, as well as in North America and Europe, youth work has become more and more central to congregational life and the mission of the church. Many new forms of such work are tried out in order to help young people become responsible members of **church** and society. [M.O.]

– Z –

ZELL, KATHARINA (1497–1557). Active supporter of the **Reformation** in Strasbourg, Alsace. In 1523 Katharina Schütz married Matthias Zell, who was a **priest** at the Strasbourg Cathedral (Ger *Münster*) and eminent reformer of this city. When the bishop of Strasbourg tried to dismiss the married priest, Katharina wrote rather outspoken letters to the bishop in defense of clerical **marriage** and a biting critique of celibate priests. The town council confiscated one of her letters because of its "rough" style. Eventually, however, her husband was allowed to stay. Katharina supported his reforming work in many ways and considered herself a "church mother" because of her service to the poor, persecuted, and afflicted. The large parsonage of the cathedral became a haven for people in need or in search of security. During times of conflict or famine, there were often nearly one hundred people in her house. When 3,000 wives and children, survivors of the peasants slaughtered during the **Peasants' War,** fled to Strasbourg, she was one of the two main people who secured food and lodging for them.

She was instrumental in establishing a hostel for poor students, and she wrote a comforting pastoral epistle to the women of Kenzingen whose husbands were driven out of town by anti-Reformation military forces. Katharina corresponded with **Martin Luther**, and in 1538 traveled with her husband the 600 miles to **Wittenberg**. She entertained friendly contacts with the Swiss reformer **Ulrich Zwingli** and even defended **Anabaptists** and other radical reforming groups. In 1534 she put together a collection of **hymns**, wrote a preface for it, and published it in the form of little pamphlets. She delivered an address, after the eulogy of their friend **Martin Bucer**, at the funeral of her husband (1548). Before she died, this courageous and independent woman wrote in self-defense: "I have never mounted a pulpit, but I have done more than any minister in visiting those in misery." [G.G.]

ZIEGENBALG, BARTHOLOMÄUS (1682–1719). First and extraordinary German Lutheran missionary. Ziegenbalg studied under the pietist (*see* PIETISM) leader **August Hermann Francke** at Halle, Germany. In 1705 King Frederick IV of Denmark sent him through the Danish-Halle Mission to the Danish crown colony of Tranquebar, South India. Ziegenbalg and his comissionary Heinrich Plütschau arrived there in 1706. Ziegenbalg immediately started intensive mission activity and began with research on the Tamil language and the history of religion. He founded the first girls' school in India (1707) and other mission schools. He built a church, founded a seminary for the training of Indian assistants, and asked in 1709 for the authority to ordain indigenous **pastors**. When he was able to speak Tamil as good as he spoke his mother tongue, he published a Tamil **hymnbook**, translated **Martin Luther's** *Small Catechism*, the New Testament (1714), and parts of the Old Testament into this language. He did the groundwork for a Tamil dictionary and, during a European tour (1714–1716), he supervised the printing of his Tamil grammar (1716). The great value of his pioneering studies on South Indian Hinduism, culture, and society (*see* NON-CHRISTIAN RELIGIONS), and of his translations of Tamil texts was recognized only after his time. Ziegenbalg laid the foundations of a **church** that was both Lutheran and Indian. *See also* INCULTURATION; MISSION HISTORY; MISSION SOCIETIES. [G.G.]

ZWINGLI, ULRICH (1484–1531). Reformer of German-speaking Switzerland and parts of southwest Germany, and a "father" of the **Reformed/Presbyterian** wing of the **Reformation**. Born in the eastern part of Switzerland, Zwingli studied in Vienna and Basel from 1498–1506. Ordained a **priest** in 1506, he served at Glarus from 1506–1516 and Einsiedeln from 1516–1519 when he was elected to be the priest at the Great Minster in Zürich. Since his schooldays at Bern, Zwingli was attracted by **Humanism** and he later studied **Erasmus of Rotterdam** intensively (especially between 1513–1516) as well as the church fathers (*see* PATRISTICS) and scholastic theology (especially **Thomas Aquinas** and Duns Scotus). When he arrived in Zürich, he was a reform-oriented churchman in an Erasmian spirit. In Zürich he began to preach **sermons** based on the Bible, a new thing, and this led him (probably in 1519) to a Reformation stance: The Bible was a personal, decisive Word of **salvation** that included the **justification** of the sinner by **faith** alone and the focus on the crucified Christ as foundation and assurance of faith.

The reform movement in that city began with the open breaking of the **Lenten** fast by some people, supported by Zwingli, and was theologically introduced by Zwingli in 1523 in two disputations. The Bible was to be used as the sole authority and criterion concerning ceremonies, practices, and teachings (*see* BIBLE, AUTHORITY OF). The city council took over religious authority and ordered all priests to confine preaching to Holy Scripture. Zwingli became the leading reformer of the city. His listing of forms and concepts that he believed had no foundation in Scripture, a method similar to that of the English Puritans, led to a rather radical break with **tradition**: images were removed from Zürich churches in 1524, monastic houses were confiscated, the mass was abolished in 1525, the **liturgy** was very much simplified (with **hymns** and **organs** no longer used), the **sacraments** were conceived as signs and memorials, and the proclamation of the **Word of God** was given priority over the **Lord's Supper**, which was to be celebrated only three or four times per year.

Despite Zwingli's radical reforms, an even more radical opposition emerged at Zürich after 1523: the **Anabaptists**. They criticized the continuation of infant **baptism** and the close alliance of **church and state** at Zürich. Zwingli defended infant baptism by referring to its covenant significance as sign of allegiance and belonging both to the church and the state. Those who rejected infant baptism were, accordingly, also disloyal to the state, and the magistrate was entitled to punish or expel them from the city.

Even more far-reaching in its significance for the process of Reformation history was Zwingli's conflict with **Martin Luther**, especially concerning the understanding of the Lord's Supper. While Zwingli held that the risen Christ at the right hand of God cannot be present anywhere else and that, therefore, his body and blood cannot be present in the eucharist, Luther insisted on the real presence of the body and blood of Christ in the elements of bread and wine because the risen Christ, both divine and human, is not limited to a particular place. The attempt at the **Marburg Colloquy** of 1529 to overcome this difference failed because of the remaining difference about the bodily presence of Christ in the Lord's Supper. The unity of the **Protestant** Reformation could not be restored and secured.

From 1525–1530 Zwingli's ideas became influential in German-speaking Switzerland and in southern Germany up to Frankfurt and Strasbourg. The Catholic cantons of Switzerland, however, were not willing to allow the infiltration of Zwinglian ideas. They secured cantonal sovereignty to decide about and maintain one particular religion through a successful war against the Reformed cantons in 1531. Zwingli, who participated in the war as a chaplain, was killed. His successor at Zürich, the theologically more moderate Heinrich Bullinger (1504–1575), helped to bring together the Zwinglian and Calvinist (*see* CALVIN, JOHN) strands of Reformed/ Presbyterian Protestantism. [G.G.]

Appendix
List of Lutheran Churches

The following list contains all Lutheran churches, missions, and independent congregations in the world, together with their membership figures for 1999. The list is taken, with some modification, from *Lutheran World Information*, LWI, Geneva, No. 1-2/2000, January-February 2000. <http://www.lutheran world.org/Directory>

M	member churches of the Lutheran World Federation (LWF)
AM	associated member churches of the LWF
R	recognized congregations (of the LWF)
C	other Lutheran churches, missions, and independent congregations in infrequent contact with the LWF

GENERAL SUMMARY 1999

128 LWF member churches and 12 recognized congregations	59,457,737
Lutherans outside LWF constituency	3,677,061
TOTAL	63,134,798

	All Lutherans	LWF Membership	Other Contacts
Africa	9,749,818	9,695,395	54,423
Asia	6,647,733	6,524,226	123,507
Europe	37,053,291	37,012,532	40,759
Latin America	1,107,905	834,194	273,711
North America	8,576,051	5,391,390	3,184,661
TOTAL	63,134,798	59,457,737	3,677,061

Countries with More Than ½ Million Lutherans

Germany	13,927,262	Ethiopia	2,593,163
United States	8,288,352	Madagascar	1,500,000
Sweden	7,505,930	India	1,621,065
Finland	4,598,473	Brazil	915,983
Denmark	4,539,857	Papua New Guinea	910,000
Norway	3,821,060	South Africa	884,719
Indonesia	3,794,393	Namibia	740,000
Tanzania	2,500,000	Nigeria	800,000

Lutheran Churches with More Than ½ Million Members

Andhra Evangelical Lutheran Church [India]	700,000
Church of Norway	3,800,000
Church of Sweden	7,505,930
Ethiopian Evangelical Church Mekane Yesus	2,593,163
Evangelical Church in Württemberg [Germany]	2,450,000
Evangelical Church of the Lutheran Confession in Brazil	700,000
Evangelical Lutheran Church in America	5,178,225
Evangelical Lutheran Church in Bavaria [Germany]	2,746,708
Evangelical Lutheran Church in Denmark	4,539,857
Evangelical Lutheran Church in Namibia (ELCIN)	533,000
Evangelical Lutheran Church in Southern Africa [South Africa]	768,998
Evangelical Lutheran Church in Tanzania	2,500,000
Evangelical Lutheran Church in Thuringia [Germany]	534,500
Evangelical Lutheran Church of Finland	4,598,473
Evangelical Lutheran Church of Hanover [Germany]	3,293,241
Evangelical Lutheran Church of Papua New Guinea	815,000
Evangelical Lutheran Church of Saxony [Germany]	1,021,000
Lutheran Church—Missouri Synod [United States and Canada]	2,600,000
Lutheran Church of Christ in Nigeria	720,000
Malagasy Lutheran Church [Madagascar]	1,500,000
North Elbian Evangelical Lutheran Church [Germany]	2,353,816
Protestant Christian Batak Church [Indonesia]	2,905,316

MEMBERSHIP FIGURES

	Individual Churches	National
Africa		
Angola		23,000
Evangelical Lutheran Church of Angola (M)	*23,000*	

Botswana		18,000
Evangelical Lutheran Church in Botswana (M)	*18,000*	
Cameroon		206,030
Church of the Lutheran Brethren of Cameroon (M)	*81,672*	
Evangelical Lutheran Church of Cameroon (M)	*120,000*	
The Lutheran Church of Cameroon (C)	*4,358*	
Central African Republic		55,000
Evangelical Lutheran Church of the Central African Republic (M)	*55,000*	
Chad		21,305
Church of the Lutheran Brethren of Chad (C)	*21,305*	
Congo		750
Evangelical Lutheran Church of Congo (C)	*750*	
Democratic Republic of Congo		136,000
Evangelical Lutheran Church in Congo (M)	*136,000*	
Eritrea		12,000
Evangelical Church of Eritrea (M)	*12,000*	
Ethiopia		2,593,163
The Ethiopian Evangelical Church Mekane Yesus (M)	*2,593,163*	
Ghana		25,000
Evangelical Lutheran Church of Ghana (C)	*25,000*	
Kenya		78,357
Evangelical Lutheran Church in Kenya (M)	*55,000*	
Kenya Evangelical Lutheran Church (M)	*23,357*	
Liberia		35,000
Lutheran Church in Liberia (M)	*35,000*	
Madagascar		1,500,000
Malagasy Lutheran Church (M)	*1,500,000*	
Malawi		12,000
Evangelical Lutheran Church in Malawi (M)	*12,000*	
Mozambique		1,250
Evangelical Lutheran Church in Mozambique (M)	*1,250*	
Namibia		740,000
The Evangelical Lutheran Church in Namibia (M)	*533,000*	

Evangelical Lutheran Church in the Republic of Namibia (ELCRN) (M)	*200,000*	
Evangelical Lutheran Church in Namibia (GELC) (M)	*7,000*	
Nigeria		800,000
The Lutheran Church of Christ in Nigeria (M)	*720,000*	
The Lutheran Church of Nigeria (M)	*80,000*	
Senegal		3,100
The Lutheran Church of Senegal (M)	*3,100*	
Sierra Leone		2,134
Evangelical Lutheran Church in Sierra Leone (M)	*2,134*	
South Africa		884,719
Evangelical Lutheran Church in Southern Africa (M)	*768,998*	
Evangelical Lutheran Church in Southern Africa (Cape Church) (M)	*4,521*	
Evangelical Lutheran Church in Southern Africa (Natal-Transvaal) (M)	*11,000*	
Moravian Church in South Africa (M)	*100,200*	
Tanzania		2,500,000
Evangelical Lutheran Church in Tanzania (M)	*2,500,000*	
Zambia		3,010
Evangelical Lutheran Church in Zambia (C)	*3,010*	
Zimbabwe		100,000
Evangelical Lutheran Church in Zimbabwe (M)	*100,000*	

Asia

Australia		94,000
Lutheran Church of Australia (AM)	*94,000*	
Bangladesh		11,303
Bangladesh Lutheran Church (M)	*2,700*	
Bangladesh Northern Evangelical Lutheran Church (M)	*8,603*	
Hong Kong, China		41,785
The Chinese Rhenish Church, Hong Kong Synod (M)	*11,700*	
Hong Kong and Macau Lutheran Church (M)	*2,185*	

Lutheran Church, Hong Kong Synod (C)	*8,100*	
The Evangelical Lutheran Church of Hong Kong (M)	*12,800*	
Tsung Tsin Mission of Hong Kong (M)	*7,000*	
India		1,621,065
Andhra Evangelical Lutheran Church (M)	*700,000*	
Evangelical Lutheran Church in Madhya Pradesh (M)	*13,090*	
Gossner Ev. Luth. Church in Chotanagpur and Assam (M)	*361,520*	
India Evangelical Lutheran Church (M)	*56,493*	
Jeypore Evangelical Lutheran Church (M)	*140,000*	
North Western Gossner Evangelical Lutheran Church in Chotanagpur and Assam (C)	*100,022*	
Northern Evangelical Lutheran Church (M)	*80,000*	
South Andhra Lutheran Church—Telugu (M)	*31,155*	
The Arcot Lutheran Church (M)	*34,000*	
The Tamil Evangelical Lutheran Church (M)	*104,785*	
Indonesia		3,794,393
Batak Christian Community Church (M)	*20,000*	
Christian Protestant Angkola Church (M)	*27,000*	
Christian Protestant Church in Indonesia (M)	*255,601*	
The Indonesian Christian Church (M)	*350,000*	
Indonesian Christian Lutheran Church (M)	*16,895*	
Protestant Christian Batak Church (M)	*2,905,316*	
Protestant Christian Church in Mentawai (M)	*22,326*	
Simalungun Protestant Christian Church (M)	*197,255*	
Israel		135
Finnish Evangelical Lutheran Mission-Shalhevetyah Christian Center and Congregation (C)	*25*	
Lutheran Church in Israel (C)	*110*	
Japan		32,512
Japan Evangelical Lutheran Church (M)	*22,146*	
Japan Lutheran Brethren Church (C)	*1,256*	
Japan Lutheran Church (AM)	*3,040*	
Kinki Evangelical Lutheran Church (M)	*2,549*	
West Japan Evangelical Lutheran Church (C)	*3,521*	
Jordan		3,000
The Evangelical Lutheran Church in Jordan (M)	*3,000*	

Korea, Republic of South		3,125
Lutheran Church in Korea (M)	*3,125*	
Malaysia		84,764
Basel Christian Church of Malaysia (M)	*45,000*	
Evangelical Lutheran Church in Malaysia (M)	*3,000*	
Lutheran Church in Malaysia and Singapore		
(M)	*6,764*	
The Protestant Church in Sabah (M)	*30,000*	
Myanmar		1,525
Evangelical Lutheran Church in Myanmar		
(Lutheran Bethlehem Church) (C)	*1,525*	
Nepal		
Northern Evangelical Lutheran Church (M)		
(see India)		
New Zealand		1,802
Lutheran Church of New Zealand (C)	*1,802*	
(a district of the Lutheran Church of Australia)		
Papua New Guinea		910,000
Evangelical Lutheran Church of Papua		
New Guinea (M)	*815,000*	
Gutnius Lutheran Church—Papua New Guinea		
(M)	*95,000*	
Philippines		27,000
Lutheran Church in the Philippines (M)	*27,000*	
Singapore		3,000
Lutheran Church in Singapore (M)	*3,000*	
Sri Lanka		1,200
Lanka Lutheran Church (C)	*1,200*	
Taiwan (Republic of China)		15,010
China Evangelical Lutheran Church (C)	*2,621*	
China Lutheran Gospel Church (C)	*225*	
Chinese Lutheran Brethren Church (C)	*2,300*	
The Lutheran Church of Taiwan		
(Republic of China) (M)	*1,614*	
The Lutheran Church of the Republic of China		
(M)	*1,200*	
Taiwan Lutheran Church (M)	*7,050*	

Thailand   2,114
The Evangelical Lutheran Church in Thailand
   (M)   *1,314*
Lutheran Mission in Thailand (C)   *800*

Europe

Austria   336,992
Evangelical Church of the Augsburg Confession
   in Austria (M)   *336,992*

Belgium   274
Lutheran Church of Belgium: Arlon and
   Christian Mission in Brussels (R)   *274*

Croatia   7,500
Evangelical Church in Croatia (M)   *7,500*

Czech Republic   40,000
Silesian Evangelical Church of the Augsburg
   Confession in the Czech Republic (M)   *40,000*

Denmark (including Faroe Islands and
   Greenland)   4,539,85
Evangelical Lutheran Church in Denmark (M)   *4,539,857*

Estonia   200,000
Estonian Evangelical Lutheran Church (M)   *200,000*

Finland   4,598,473
Evangelical Lutheran Church of Finland (M)   *4,598,473*

France   258,000
Church of the Augsburg Confession of
   Alsace and Lorraine (M)   *210,000*
Evangelical Lutheran Church of France (M)   *40,000*
Malagasy Protestant Church in France (M)   *8,000*

Germany   13,927,262
Church of Lippe [Lutheran Section] (M)   *39,500*
Evangelical Church in Württemberg (M)   *2,450,000*
Evangelical Church of Pomerania (M)   *138,000*
Evangelical Lutheran Church in Baden (M)   *3,738*
Evangelical Lutheran Church in Bavaria (M)   *2,746,708*
Evangelical Lutheran Church in Brunswick (M)   *467,000*
Evangelical Lutheran Church in Oldenburg (M)   *493,000*

Evangelical Lutheran Church in Thuringia (M)	*534,500*	
Evangelical Lutheran Church of Hanover (M)	*3,293,241*	
Evangelical Lutheran Church of Mecklenburg (M)	*239,000*	
Evangelical Lutheran Church of Saxony (M)	*1,021,000*	
Evangelical Lutheran Church of Schaumburg-Lippe (M)	*67,000*	
Evangelical Lutheran Free Church in Germany (C)	*2,000*	
Independent Evangelical Lutheran Church (SELK) (C)	*38,759*	
Latvian Evangelical Lutheran Church Abroad (M)	*40,000*	
North Elbian Evangelical Lutheran Church (M)	*2,353,816*	
Greenland		
Evangelical Lutheran Church in Denmark (M) (see Denmark)		
Hungary		430,000
The Evangelical Lutheran Church in Hungary (M)	*430,000*	
Iceland		4,684
The Evangelical Lutheran Church of Iceland (M)	*244,684*	
Ireland		1,063
The Lutheran Church in Ireland (R)	*1,063*	
Italy		7,000
Evangelical Lutheran Church in Italy (M)	*7,000*	
Latvia		250,000
Evangelical Lutheran Church of Latvia (M)	*250,000*	
Liechtenstein (*see Switzerland*)		
Lithuania		30,000
Evangelical Lutheran Church of Lithuania (M)	*30,000*	
The Netherlands		17,500
Evangelical Lutheran Church in the Kingdom of the Netherlands (M)	*17,500*	
Norway		3,821,060
Church of Norway (M)	*3,800,000*	
The Evangelical Lutheran Free Church of Norway (AM)	*21,060*	

Poland		80,000
Evangelical Church of the Augsburg Confession in Poland (M)	*80,000*	
Romania		48,543
Evangelical Church of the Augsburg Confession in Romania (M)	*16,543*	
Evangelical Synodal Presbyterial Lutheran Church of the Augsburg Confession in Romania (M)	*32,000*	
Russian Federation and Commonwealth of Independent States		266,000
Evangelical Lutheran Church in Russia and other States (M)	*250,000*	
Evangelical Lutheran Church of Ingria in Russia (M)	*16,000*	
Slovak Republic		329,117
Evangelical Church of the Augsburg Confession in the Slovak Republic (M)	*329,117*	
Slovenia		19,000
Evangelical Church of the Augsburg Confession in Slovenia (M)	*19,000*	
Sweden		7,505,930
Church of Sweden (M)	*7,505,930*	
Switzerland		4,853
Federation of Evangelical Lutheran Churches in Switzerland and the Principality of Liechtenstein (M)	*4,853*	
United Kingdom		42,161
Lutheran Church in Great Britain (M)	*2,750*	
The Lutheran Council of Great Britain (R)	*39,411*	
Yugoslavia		48,022
Slovak Evangelical Church of the Augsburg Confession in SR Yugoslavia (M)	*48,022*	

Latin America

Argentina		97,215
Evangelical Church of the River Plate (M) (see Paraguay, Uruguay)	*47,000*	

Evangelical Lutheran Church of Argentina (C)
   (see Chile, Uruguay)   *29,755*
German Evangelical Lutheran Church
   Buenos Aires (C)   *7,500*
Protestant Congregation in Tandil (C)   *160*
Protestant Society in Southern Argentina -
Lutheran Church (C)   *3,800*
Protestant Society of the South-East (C)   *2,000*
United Evangelical Lutheran Church (M)   *7,000*

Bolivia   18,700
Bolivian Evangelical Lutheran Church (M) *18,000*
German-speaking Evangelical Lutheran
   Congregation in Bolivia (R)   *(250 families)*
Norwegian Lutheran Mission in Bolivia (C)   *70*

Brazil   915,983
Association of Free Lutheran Congregations (C) *983*
Evangelical Church of the Lutheran Confession
   in Brazil (M)   *700,000*
Evangelical Lutheran Church of Brazil (C) *215,000*

Chile   16,835
Evangelical Lutheran Association of the
Republic of Chile (C)   *135*
Evangelical Lutheran Church in Chile (M)   *3,000*
Evangelical Lutheran Church of Argentina (C)
   (see Argentina)
Lutheran Church in Chile (M)   *13,700*

Colombia   3,396
Evangelical Lutheran Church of Colombia (M) *3,000*
St. Martin's Congregation (R)   *(40 families)*
St. Matthew's Congregation (R)   *396*

Costa Rica   650
Evangelical Lutheran Church of Costa
   Rica, El Salvador, Honduras, Nicaragua and
   Panama (R)   *600*
Lutheran Church in Costa Rica (C)   *50*

Ecuador   2,020
Evangelical Lutheran Church in Ecuador
(includes the "El Adviento" Evangelical
   Lutheran Church in Quito, and

"The Saviour" Church in Guayaquil)
(R) — 520
Evangelical Lutheran Indigenous
Church of Ecuador (C) — 1,500

El Salvador — 12,000
Salvadoran Lutheran Synod (M) — 12,000

Guatemala — 850
Evangelical Lutheran Congregation La
Epifania (R) — 350
Augustinian Lutheran Church of Guatemala (C) — 500

Guyana — 11,000
Lutheran Church in Guyana (M) — 11,000

Honduras — 1,000
Christian Lutheran Church of Honduras (M) — 1,000

Mexico — 8,724
All Saints' Lutheran Church (C) — 191
Evangelical Lutheran Church of Mexico (C) — 3,000
German-speaking Evangelical Congregation
in Mexico (R) — 2,690
The Lutheran Church of the Good Shepherd (C) — 132
Lutheran Synod of Mexico (C) — 1,211
Mexican Lutheran Church (M) — 1,500

Nicaragua — 4,000
The Nicaraguan Lutheran Church of
Faith and Hope (M) — 4,000

Panama
Brotherhood of Popular Pastoral Action,
Lutheran Coordination (C) — *(no data)*

Paraguay — 3,800
Evangelical Church of the River Plate (M)
(see Argentina)
Evangelical Lutheran Church of Paraguay (C) — 3,800

Peru — 2,408
Evangelical Lutheran Church in Peru (R) — 140
Evangelical Lutheran Congregation "Cristo
Rey" (C) — 60
Norwegian Lutheran Mission (C) — 2,060
Peruvian Evangelical Lutheran Church (R) — 148

Suriname		4,000
Evangelical Lutheran Church in Suriname (M)	*4,000*	
Uruguay		190
Evangelical Church of the River Plate (M)		
(see Argentina)		
Evangelical Lutheran Church of Argentina (C)		
(see Argentina)		
Evangelical Lutheran Church in Uruguay (C)	*190*	
Venezuela		5,134
Evangelical Lutheran Church in Venezuela (M)	*4,150*	
Lutheran Church of Venezuela (C)	*984*	

North America

Canada		288,017
Estonian Evangelical Lutheran Church Abroad		
(M)	*12,000*	
The Evangelical Lutheran Church in Canada		
(M)	*196,165*	
Lutheran Church—Canada (C)	*79,852*	
United States of America		8,288,352
Apostolic Lutheran Church of America (C)	*7,707*	
Association of Free Lutheran Congregations (C)	*32,659*	
Church of the Lutheran Brethren of America (C)	*14,089*	
Church of the Lutheran Confession (C)	*8,768*	
Conservative Lutheran Association (C)	*994*	
Evangelical Lutheran Church in America (M)	*5,178,225*	
Evangelical Lutheran Synod (C)	*24,000*	
Fellowship of Lutheran Congregations (C)	*446*	
Lithuanian Evangelical Lutheran Church		
in Diaspora (M)	*5,000*	
Lutheran Church—Missouri Synod (C)	*2,600,000*	
Lutheran Churches of the Reformation (C)	*1,500*	
The Protestant Conference [Lutheran] (C)	*1,125*	
Wisconsin Evangelical Lutheran Synod (C)	*413,839*	

Bibliography

Innumerable publications on Lutheranism exist in many different languages. This bibliography is no more than a selection, which is further limited by the fact that, with very few exceptions, only English language titles are listed, and these only from the last 50 years. Still, it is hoped that the different and manifold facets of Lutheran past and present, life and work, and thinking and impact are represented by the long list that follows. [G.G.]

OUTLINE OF BIBLIOGRAPHY

I. GENERAL REFERENCE WORKS

A. Bibliographies

Bainton, Roland Herbert, and Gritsch, Eric W. *Bibliography of the Continental Reformation.* Hamden, Conn.: Archon, 1972.

Concordia Historical Institute. *Microfilm Index and Bibliography of the Concordia Historical Institute, the Department of Archives and History, the Lutheran Church-Missouri Synod, St. Louis, Missouri, 1954–1963.* St. Louis: Concordia Historical Institute, 1966.

——. *Microfilm Index and Bibliography of the Concordia Historical Institute, St. Louis, Missouri, 1964–1973.* Ed. August R. Suelflow. St. Louis: Concordia Historical Institute, 1978.

Daniel, David, and Arand, Charles, eds. *Bibliography of the Lutheran Confessions.* Sixteenth-century Bibliography 28. St. Louis: Center for Reformation Research, 1988.

DeBerg, Betty A. *Women and Women's Issues in North American Lutheranism: A Bibliography.* Minneapolis: Augsburg, 1992.

Historical Records Survey (New York). *Inventory of the Church Archives in New York City: The Lutherans.* Vol. 2. New York: The Historical Records Survey, 1940.

Huber, Donald L. *World Lutheranism: A Select Bibliography for English Readers.* Lanham, Md.: Scarecrow, 2000.

Kendrick, Alice M., and Knubel, Helen M., eds. *The Oral Collection of the Archives of Cooperative Lutheranism.* New York: Lutheran Council in the USA, 1984.

———. *The Oral History Collection of The American Lutheran Church, Association of Evangelical Lutheran Churches and Lutheran Church in America.* New York: Lutheran Council in the USA, 1987.

Lutheran World Federation, Department of Studies. *Documents and Publications of and Related to the Department of Studies (1970–1977).* Geneva: Lutheran World Federation, 1977.

Lutheran World Federation, Department of Theology. *Prehistory of the Lutheran World Federation: List of Material in Archives in Europe and the USA.* Geneva: Lutheran World Federation, 1968.

Petersen, Paul D., ed. *Luther and Lutheranism: A Bibliography Selected from the ATLA Religion Database.* Rev. ed. Chicago: American Theological Library Association, 1985.

Reichmann, Felix. *The Muhlenberg Family: A Bibliography Compiled from the Subject Union Catalog of Americana-Germanica of the Carl Schurz Memorial Foundation.* Philadelphia: Carl Schurz Memorial Foundation, 1943.

Whiting, Henry J. *The Churches Speak: A Bibliography of Official Social Statements and Study Reports.* New York: Lutheran Council in the USA, 1969.

B. Directories

Bachmann, Mercia Brenne, ed. *Lutheran Mission Directory.* 2nd ed. Geneva: Lutheran World Federation, 1982.

Directory: Evangelical Lutheran Church in America, Division for Global Mission. Minneapolis: Division for Global Mission, 1990.

Directory of the Lutheran Women in Graduate Studies, Teaching, or Other Positions. Division for Ministry, Evangelical Lutheran Church in America. Chicago: Division for Ministry, Evangelical Lutheran Church in America, 1994.

Directory of the Lutheran World Federation. Geneva: Lutheran World Federation, 2000.

Knubel, Helen M., ed. *An Introductory Guide to Lutheran Archives and Collections.* New York: Lutheran Council in the USA, 1981.

Lutheran Church Directory for the United States, 1988. Minneapolis: Evangelical Lutheran Church in America, 1988. A state listing of Lutheran churches.

Lutheran Higher Education Directory. Washington, D.C.: Lutheran Educational Conference of North America, 1989.

Working for Justice: A 1988 Directory of Lutheran Ministries. Chicago: Justice Network in the Lutheran Church, 1988.

C. Encyclopedias

Aland, Kurt, ed. *Luther Lexikon.* Stuttgart: Ernst Klotz Verlag, 1957.

Blackwell Encyclopedia of Modern Christian Thought. Ed. Alister E. McGrath. Oxford: Basil Blackwell, 1993.

Dictionary of the Ecumenical Movement. Ed. Nicholas Lossky et al. Grand Rapids, Mich.: Eerdmans; Geneva: WCC Publications, 1991.

Die Religion in Geschichte und Gegenwart: Handwörterbuch für Theologie und Religionswissenschaft (RGG). 3rd ed. Kurt Galling et al. Tübingen: J.C.B. Mohr, 1957–1965.

Die Religion in Geschichte und Gegenwart: Handwörterbuch für Theologie und Religionswissenschaft (RGG). 4th ed. Ed. Hans Dieter Betz et al. Tübingen: Mohr Siebeck, 1998ff.

Encyclopedia of Christianity. Ed. Erwin Fahlbusch et al. Grand Rapids, Mich.: Eerdmans; Leiden: Brill, 1999.

Encyclopedia of the Lutheran Church. 3 vols. Ed. Julius Bodensieck. Philadelphia: Fortress, 1965.

Hammack, Mary L. *A Dictionary of Women in Church History.* Chicago: Moody, 1984.

Historical Dictionary of Catholicism. William J. Collinge. Lanham, Md., and London: Scarecrow, 1997.

Historical Dictionary of Ecumenical Christianity. Ans J. Van der Bent. Metuchen, N.J., and London: Scarecrow, 1994.

Historical Dictionary of Methodism. Ed. Charles Yrigoyen and Susan E. Warrick. Lanham, Md., and London: Scarecrow, 1996.

Historical Dictionary of the Orthodox Church. Michael Prokurat, Michael D. Peterson, and Alexander Golitzin. Lanham, Md., and London: Scarecrow, 1996.

Historical Dictionary of the Reformation and Counter-Reformation. Hans J. Hillerbrand. Lanham, Md., and London: Scarecrow, 2000.

Historical Dictionary of Reformed Churches. Robert Benedetto, Darrell L. Guder, and Donald K. McKim. Lanham, Md., and London: Scarecrow, 1999.

Lutheran Cyclopedia. Rev. ed. Ed. Erwin L. Lueker. St. Louis: Concordia, 1975.

New Westminster Dictionary of Liturgy and Worship. Ed. J. G. Davies. Philadelphia: Westminster, 1986.

Oxford Dictionary of the Christian Church. 3rd ed. Ed. F. L. Cross and E. A. Livingstone. Oxford and New York: Oxford University Press, 1997.

Oxford Encyclopedia of the Reformation. 4 vols. Ed. Hans J. Hillerbrand. New York and Oxford: Oxford University Press, 1996.

Theologische Realenzyklopädie (TRE). Hauptherausgeber Gerhard Krause and Gerhard Müller. Berlin and New York: Walter de Gruyter, 1976ff.

Westminster Dictionary of Christian Ethics. Ed. John Macquarrie and James F. Childress. Philadelphia: Westminster, 1986.

Westminster Dictionary of Christian Spirituality. Ed. Gordon S. Wakefield. Philadelphia: Westminster, 1983.

Westminster Dictionary of Christian Theology. Ed. Alan Richardson and John Bowden. Philadelphia: Westminster, 1983.

Westminster Dictionary of Church History. Ed. Jerald C. Brauer. Philadelphia: Westminster, 1971.

II. SOURCES

Die Bekenntnisschriften der Evangelish-lutherischen Kirche. 6th ed. Göttingen: Vandenhoeck and Ruprecht, 1967.

Bente, Friedrich, ed. *Concordia Triglotta: The Symbolical Books of the Evangelical Lutheran Church*. St. Louis: Concordia, 1921.

Birmelé, André, and Lienhard, Marc. *La foi des églises luthériennes: Confessions et catéchismes*. Paris: Éditions du Cerf; Genève: Labor et Fides, 1991.

Book of Concord: The Confessions of the Evangelical Lutheran Church. Ed. and trans. Theodore G. Tappert. Philadelphia: Fortress, 1959.

Book of Concord: The Confessions of the Evangelical Lutheran Church. Ed. Robert Kolb and Timothy J. Wengert, and trans. Charles Arand et al. Minneapolis: Fortress, 2000.

D. Martin Luthers Werke. Kritische Gesamtausgabe. Over 100 vols. Weimar: Böhlau, 1883 ff.

Denzinger, H., and Schönmetzer, A., ed. *Enchiridion symbolorum definitionum et declarationum de rebus fidei et morum*. 36th ed. Freiburg im Breisgau: Herder, 1976.

Green, Lowell C., and Froelich, Charles D. *Melanchthon in English: New Translations into English with a Registry of Previous Translations*. St. Louis: Center for Reformation Research, 1982.

Gritsch, Eric W., ed. *Martin Luther: Faith in Christ and the Gospel—Selected Spiritual Writings*. New York: New City Press, 1996.

Hill, Charles L., trans. *Melanchthon: Selected Writings*. Minneapolis: Augsburg, 1962.

Hoffman, Bengt, ed. *Theologia Germanica of Martin Luther*. New York: Paulist, 1980.

Immenkötter, Herbert, ed. *Die Confutatio der Confessio Augustana vom 3. August 1530*. Rev. ed. Münster: Aschendorff, 1981.

Jacobs, Henry E., ed. *Book of Concord, or the Symbolical Books of the Evangelical Lutheran Church*. 2 vols. Philadelphia: General Council Publication Board, 1919.

Lull, Timothy F., ed. *Martin Luther's Basic Theological Writings*. Minneapolis: Fortress, 1989.

Luther, Martin. *D. Martin Luthers sämmtliche Schriften*. 23 vols. Ed. Johann Georg Walch. St. Louis: Gebauer, 1880–1910.

——. *Luther: Lectures on Romans*. Ed. and trans. Wilhelm Pauck. Library of Christian Classics 15. Philadelphia and London: Macmillan, 1961.

Luther and Calvin on Secular Authority. Ed. and trans. Harro Hopfl. Cambridge and New York: Cambridge University Press, 1991.

Lutheran Reformation: Sources, 1500–1650. Ed. William S. Maltby. Leiden: IDC, 1997.

Luther's Works, American Edition. 55 vols. Ed. Jaroslav Pelikan and Helmut T. Lehmann. St. Louis: Concordia; Philadelphia: Fortress, 1955–1986.

Melanchthon, Philipp. "Loci Communes Theologici." 1521. In *Melanchthon and Bucer*. Ed. Wilhelm Pauck, and trans. Lowell J. Satre. Philadelphia: Westminster, 1969.

——. *A Melanchthon Reader*. Ed. and trans. Ralph Keen. New York: Lang, 1988.

Melanchthon on Christian Doctrine: Loci Communes, 1555. Ed. and trans. Clyde Manschreck. Grand Rapids, Mich.: Baker, 1982.

Noll, Mark, ed. *Confessions and Catechisms of the Reformation*. Grand Rapids, Mich.: Baker, 1991.

Pauck, W., ed. *Melanchthon and Bucer*. Library of Christian Classics 19. Philadelphia: Westminster, 1969.

Reu, Michael J. *The Augsburg Confession: A Collection of Sources*. Chicago: Wartburg, 1930.

Sehling, Emil. *Die evangelischen Kirchenordnungen des XVI. Jahrhunderts.* Vols. 6ff. Tübingen: Mohr (Siebeck), 1955ff.

———. ed. *Die evangelischen Kirchenordnungen des XVI. Jahrhunderts.* Vols. 1–5. Leipzig: Reisland, 1902–1913.

Women of the Reformation. Reformation Texts with Translations (1350–1650). Milwaukee: Marquette University Press, 1996ff.

III. GENERAL WORKS ON LUTHERANISM

Arand, Charles P. *Testing the Boundaries: Windows to Lutheran Identity.* St. Louis: Concordia, 1995.

Arnold, Duane W., and Frey, C. George. *The Way, the Truth, and the Life: An Introduction to Lutheranism.* Grand Rapids, Mich.: Baker, 1983.

Bachmann, Theodore E., and Bachmann, Mercia B. *Lutheran Churches in the World: A Handbook.* Minneapolis: Augsburg, 1989.

Church in Fellowship. 2 vols. Ed. Vilmos Vajta and Paul E. Hofman. Minneapolis: Augsburg, 1963–1969.

Elert, Werner. *The Structure of Lutheranism.* 2nd ed. 2 vols. Trans. Walter A. Hansen. St. Louis: Concordia, 1962.

Gassmann, Günther. "Lutherische Kirchen." *Theologische Realenzyklopädie* 21:599–620.

Gritsch, Eric. *Fortress Introduction to Lutheranism.* Minneapolis: Fortress, 1994.

Institute for Ecumenical Research. *Lutheran Identity: Final Report of the Study Project "The Identity of the Lutheran Churches in the Context of the Challenges of Our Time."* Strasbourg: Institute for Ecumenical Research, 1977.

Krych, Margaret A. *Teaching about Lutheranism.* Minneapolis: Augsburg, 1993.

Lagerquist, DeAne L. *The Lutherans.* Westport, Conn.: Praeger, 1999.

Lutherans and the Challenge of Religious Pluralism. Ed. Frank W. Klos et al. Minneapolis: Augsburg, 1990.

Marty, Martin E. *Lutheranism: A Restatement in Question and Answer Form.* Royal Oak, Mich.: Cathedral, 1975.

Scherer, James A. *Mission and Unity in Lutheranism: A Study in Confession and Ecumenicity.* Philadelphia: Fortress, 1969.

Spitz, Lewis W., and Kolb, Robert. "Lutheranism." Vol. 2. In *Oxford Encyclopedia of the Reformation.* Ed. Hans J. Hillerbrand. New York and Oxford: Oxford University Press, 1996.

Swihart, Altman K. *Luther and the Lutheran Church, 1483–1960.* New York: Philosophical Library, 1960.

World Lutheranism of Today: A Tribute to Anders Nygren, 15 November 1950. Rock Island, Ill.: Augustana Book Concern, 1950.

IV. HISTORY OF LUTHERANISM

A. Lutheranism in General

Bergendoff, Conrad. *The Church of the Lutheran Reformation: A Historical Survey.* St. Louis: Concordia, 1967.

Lindberg, Carter. *The Third Reformation: Charismatic Movements and the Lutheran Tradition.* Macon, Ga.: Mercer University Press, 1983.

Nelson, Clifford E. *The Rise of World Lutheranism: An American Perspective.* Philadelphia: Fortress, 1982.

Swihart, Altmann K. *Luther and the Lutheran Church, 1483–1960.* New York: Philosophical Library, 1960.

Vajta, Vilmos, ed. *The Church and the Confessions: The Role of the Confessions in the Life and Doctrine of the Lutheran Churches.* Philadelphia: Fortress, 1963.

——, ed. *Lutheran Church Past and Present.* Minneapolis: Augsburg, 1977.

Wadensjö, Bengt. *Toward a World Lutheran Communion: Developments in Lutheran Cooperation up to 1929.* Uppsala: Universitet; Stockholm: Verbum, 1970.

Women in the Lutheran Tradition. Proceedings of the International Consultation of Lutheran Women Theologians, Karjaa, Finland, August 1991. Geneva: Lutheran World Federation, 1992.

B. Specific Periods and Places

1. Reformation

Bainton, Roland, H. *Women of the Reformation in Germany and Italy.* Boston: Beacon, 1974.

——. *Women of the Reformation, from Spain to Scandinavia.* Minneapolis: Augsburg, 1977.

——. *The Reformation of the 16th Century.* Boston: Beacon, 1985.

Braaten, Carl E., and Jenson, Robert W., eds. *The Catholicity of the Reformation.* Grand Rapids, Mich.; Cambridge, UK: Eerdmans, 1996.

Brady, Thomas A., Jr. *Protestant Politics: Jacob Sturm (1489–1553) and the German Reformation.* Atlantic Highlands, N.J.: Humanities, 1995.

Chadwick, Owen. *The Reformation.* New York: Penguin, 1972.

Chemnitz, Martin. *Examination of the Council of Trent.* Trans. Fred Kramer. St. Louis: Concordia, 1971.

Fletcher, Charles R. *Gustavus Adolphus and the Thirty Years' War.* New York: Capricorn, 1963.

Grimm, Harold J. *The Reformation Era, 1500–1650.* 2nd ed. New York: Macmillan, 1973.

Hendrix, Scott. *Tradition and Authority in the Reformation.* Brookfield, Vt., and Aldershot, UK: Ashgate (Variorum), 1996.

Immenkötter, Herbert. *Der Reichstag zu Augsburg und die Confutatio.* Münster: Aschendorff, 1979.

Jedin, Hubert. *A History of the Council of Trent.* 2 vols. Trans. Dom E. Graf. London: Nelson, 1954.

Kolb, Robert. *Nikolaus von Amsdorf (1483–1565): Popular Polemics in the Preservation of Luther's Legacy.* Nieuwkoop: De Graaf, 1978.

——. *Confessing the Faith: Reformers Define the Church, 1530–1580.* St. Louis: Concordia, 1991.

——. *Luther's Heirs Define His Legacy: Studies on Lutheran Confessionalization.* Brookfield, Vt., and Aldershot, UK: Ashgate (Variorum), 1996.

Lindberg, Carter. *Beyond Charity: Reformation Initiatives for the Poor*. Minneapolis: Fortress, 1993.

——. *The European Reformations*. Cambridge, Mass., and Oxford, UK: Blackwell, 1996.

Lortz, Joseph. *The Reformation in Germany*. 2 vols. Trans. Ronald Wals. New York: Herder and Herder, 1968.

Luther and Melanchthon in the History and Theology of the Reformation. Ed. Vilmos Vajta. Philadelphia: Muhlenberg, 1961.

McNally, Robert E. *The Council of Trent, the Spiritual Exercises, and Catholic Reform*. Philadelphia: Fortress, 1970.

Nischan, Bodo. *Prince, People, and Confession: The Second Reformation in Brandenburg*. Philadelphia: University of Pennsylvania Press, 1994.

Oberman, Heiko. *The Harvest of Medieval Theology*. Grand Rapids, Mich.: Eerdmans, 1967.

Ozment, Steven. *The Age of Reform, 1250–1550: An Intellectual and Religious History of Late Medieval and Reformation Europe*. New Haven and London: Yale University Press, 1980.

Pelikan, Jaroslav. *The Christian Tradition: A History of the Development of Doctrine*. Vol. 4, *Reformation of Church and Dogma*. Chicago: University of Chicago Press, 1983.

Rublack, Hans-Christoph, ed. *Die lutherische Konfessionalisierung in Deutschland*. Gütersloh: Gerd Mohn, 1992.

Schwiebert, Ernest G. *The Reformation*. Minneapolis: Fortress, 1996.

Spitz, Lewis W. *The Renaissance and Reformation Movements*. Chicago: Rand McNally, 1971.

——. *The Protestant Reformation, 1517–1559: The Rise of Modern Europe*. New York: Harper and Row, 1985.

——. *The Reformation: Education and History*. Brookfield, Vt., and Aldershot, Hampshire: Variorum, 1996.

Wicks, Jared. *Cajetan Responds: A Reader in Reformation Controversy*. Washington, D.C.: Catholic University of America Press, 1978.

——. "Abuses under Indictment at the Diet of Augsburg 1530." *Theological Studies* 41, no. 2 (1980): 253–301.

2. 17th to the 20th Centuries

Arndt, Johann. *True Christianity*. Trans. Peter Erb. New York: Paulist, 1979.

Bouman, Walter R. *The Unity of the Church in 19-century Confessional Lutheranism*. Th.D. diss., Ruprecht-Karl Universität, Heidelberg, 1962.

Brown, Dale W. *Understanding Pietism*. Grand Rapids, Mich.: Eerdmans, 1978.

Clouse, Robert G. *The Church in the Age of Orthodoxy and the Enlightenment: Consolidation and Challenge from 1600 to 1800*. St. Louis: Concordia, 1980.

Cragg, Gerald R. *The Church in the Age of Reason, 1648–1789*. New York and Harmondsworth, Middlesex: Penguin, 1970.

Erb, Peter C. *Pietists: Selected Writings*. New York: Paulist, 1983.

Frey, C. George, et al. *The Age of Lutheran Orthodoxy*. Fort Wayne, Ind.: Concordia Theological Seminary Press, 1979.

Gerhard, Johann. *Sacred Meditations*. Trans. C. W. Heisler. Philadelphia: Lutheran Publication Society, 1896.

Preus, Robert D. *The Theology of Post-Reformation Lutheranism*. 2 vols. St. Louis: Concordia, 1970–1972.

Schmid, Heinrich. *The Doctrinal Theology of the Evangelical Lutheran Church*. 3rd ed. Trans. Charles A. Hay and Henry E. Jacobs. Minneapolis: Augsburg, 1961.

Spener, Philip Jacob. *Pia Desideria*. Trans. Theodore G. Tappert. Philadelphia: Fortress, 1964.

Stoeffler, Ernest F. *The Rise of Evangelical Pietism*. Leiden: Brill, 1965.

———. *German Pietism during the Eighteenth Century*. Leiden: Brill, 1973.

Symposium on Seventeenth-century Lutheranism: Selected Papers. St. Louis: Symposium on Seventeenth-century Lutheranism, 1962.

Twentieth-century Theology in the Making. Ed. Jaroslav Pelikan, and trans. R. A. Wilson. London: Collins, 1969–1971.

Zundel, Friedrich. *The Awakening: One Man's Battles with Darkness* (on Johann Christoph Blumhardt). Farmington, Pa.: Plough, 1999.

V. WORLDWIDE LUTHERANISM

A. Lutheranism in Africa

All-Africa Lutheran Consultation, Gaborone, Botswana, 7–16 February 1977. Ed. Yvonne Lewer. Geneva: Department of Church Cooperation, Lutheran World Federation, 1977.

All-Africa Lutheran Consultation on Christian Theology and Christian Education in the African Context, Gaborone, Botswana. Geneva: Department of Church Cooperation, Lutheran World Federation, 1978.

All-Africa Lutheran Consultation on Christian Theology and Strategy for Mission: Monrovia, Liberia, April 1980. Geneva: Department of Church Cooperation, Lutheran World Federation, 1980.

Arèn, Gustav. *Evangelical Pioneers in Ethiopia: Origins of the Evangelical Church Mekane Yesus*. Addis Ababa: The Church, 1978.

Bakke, Johnny. *Christian Ministry: Patterns and Functions within the Ethiopian Evangelical Church Mekane Yesus*. Uppsala: Uppsala University Press, 1986.

Bockelman, Wilfred, and Bockelman, Eleanor. *An Exercise in Compassion: The Lutheran Church in South Africa*. Minneapolis: Augsburg, 1972.

———. *Ethiopia: Where Lutheran Is Spelled "Mekane Yesus."* Minneapolis: Augsburg, 1972.

Danielson, Elmer R. *Forty Years with Christ in Tanzania, 1928–1968*. New York: Lutheran Church in America, 1977.

East Africa Consultation on Women and Men As Partners in Development (1981: Arusha, Tanzania). Geneva: Department of World Service and Department of Studies, Lutheran World Federation, 1981.

Enquist, Roy J. *Namibia, Land of Tears, Land of Promise*. Selinsgrove, Pa.: Susquehanna University Press, 1990.

Farisani, Tshenuwani S. *In Transit: Between the Image of God and the Image of Man.* Grand Rapids, Mich.: Eerdmans, 1990.

Fleisch, Paul. *Lutheran Beginnings around Mt. Kilimanjaro: The First 40 Years.* Erlangen: Erlanger Verlag für Mission und Ökumene, 1998.

Hellberg, Carl J. *A Voice of the Voiceless: The Involvement of the Lutheran World Federation in Southern Africa, 1947–1977.* Stockholm: Skeab/Verbum, 1979.

———. *Mission, Colonialism, and Liberation: The Lutheran Church in Namibia, 1840–1966.* Windhoek, Namibia: New Namibia, 1997.

Kiel, Christel. *Christians in Maasailand: A Study of the History of Mission among the Maasai in the North Eastern Diocese of the Evangelical Lutheran Church in Tanzania.* Erlangen: Verlag der Ev.-Luth. Mission, 1997.

Lema, Anza A. *The Impact of the Leipzig Lutheran Mission on the People of Kilimanjaro, 1893–1920.* Ph.D. diss., University of Dar es Salaam, 1973.

Lindqvist, Ingmar. *Partners in Mission: A Case Study of the Missionary Practice of the Lutheran Foreign Mission Agency Involvement in Tanzania since the Early 1960s, Seen in a Historical and Theological Perspective.* Åbo, Finland: Research Institute of the Åbo Akademi Foundation, 1982.

Mtaita, Leonard A. *Wandering Shepherds and the Good Shepherd: Contextualization as the Way of Doing Mission with the Maasai in the Evangelical Lutheran Church in Tanzania.* Erlangen: Verlag für Mission und Ökumene, 1998.

Munga, Anneth Nyagawa. *Uamsho: A Theological Study of the Proclamation of the Revival Movement within the Evangelical Lutheran Church in Tanzania.* Lund: Lund University Press; Bromley, UK: Chartwell-Bratt, 1998.

Nambala, Shekutaamba V. *History of the Church in Namibia.* Milwaukee: Lutheran Quarterly, 1994.

Pederson, Pernie C. *Mission in South Africa: Studies in the Beginning and Development of the Indigenous Lutheran Church in the Union of South Africa.* Minneapolis: Augsburg, 1957.

Sahlberg, Carl-Erik. *From Krapf to Rugambwa: A Church History of Tanzania.* 2nd ed. Nairobi, Kenya: Evangel, 1987.

A Short History of the Lutheran Church of Nigeria, 1936–1986: 50th Anniversary Publication. Nigeria: The Church, 1986.

Söderström, Hugo. *God Gave Growth: The History of the Lutheran Church in Zimbabwe, 1903–1980.* Zimbabwe: The Church, 1984.

Stefano, Jesse A. *Missionary Work in the Church of Tanzania in the Past and in the Present.* Erlangen: Verlag der Ev.-Luth.Mission, 1990.

Syrdal, Rolf A. *Mission in Madagascar: Studies of Our Mission in Madagascar and the Beginnings and Development of the Malagasy Lutheran Church.* Minneapolis: Augsburg, 1957.

B. Lutheranism in Asia

Anderson, Gerald H., ed. *Asian Voices in Christian Theology.* New York: Orbis, 1976. Appendix has text of Batak Confession.

Burgess, Andrew S., ed. *Lutheran Churches in the Third World.* Minneapolis: Augsburg, 1970.

Carlberg, Gustav. *The Changing China Scene: The Story of the Lutheran Theological Seminary in its Church and Political Setting over a Period of 45 Years, 1913–1958.* Hong Kong: n.p., 1959.

Cooley, Frank L. *Indonesia: Church and Culture.* New York: Friendship, 1968.

Dolbeer, Martin Luther. *The Andhra Evangelical Lutheran Church: A Brief History.* Rajahmundry: Department of Religious Education of the Andhra Evangelical Lutheran Church, 1951.

Eastborn, S. *Luther-Lutheranism in the Indian Church: Some Essays on Luther and Lutheran Confessions in their Relation to Indian Christendom.* Madras: Diocesan, 1961.

Fugmann, Gernot, ed. *The Birth of an Indigenous Church: Letters, Reports, and Documents of Lutheran Christians of Papua New Guinea.* Goroka, Papua New Guinea: Melanesian Institute, 1986.

The Gospel and Asian Traditions: APATS Luther Studies Workshop. Lectures, Reports, Minutes, Hong Kong, March 1979. Geneva: Lutheran World Federation, 1979.

Huddle, Benjamin P. *History of the Lutheran Church in Japan.* New York: United Lutheran Church in America, 1958.

Jesudas, Martin. *India Evangelical Lutheran Church Growth, Expansion, and Mission: An Evaluation.* Pasadena, Calif.: Fuller Theological Seminary, 1976.

Ji, Won Yong. *A History of Lutheranism in Korea: A Personal Account.* St. Louis: Concordia Seminary, 1988.

Johnson, Jonas. *Lutheran Missions in a Time of Revolution: The China Experience, 1944–1951.* Uppsala: Tvåväga Förlags, 1972.

Kemmung, Numuc C. *Nareng-Gareng: A Principle for Mission in the Evangelical Lutheran Church of Papua New Guinea.* Erlangen: Verlag der Ev.-Luth.Mission, 1997.

Knudten, Arthur C. *The Forgotten Years and Beyond: Sketches in History, the Japan Evangelical Lutheran Church, 1942–1972.* N.p.: n.p., 1984.

Koschade, Alfred. *New Branches on the Vine: From Mission Field to Church in New Guinea.* Minneapolis: Augsburg, 1967.

Kretzmann, Herbert. *Lutheranism in the Philippines, 1952–1966.* St. Louis: Concordia, 1966.

Lehmann, Arno. *It Began at Tranquebar: The Story of the Tranquebar Mission and the Beginnings of Protestant Christianity in India. Published to Celebrate the 250th Anniversary of the Landing of the First Protestant Missionaries at Tranquebar in 1706.* Trans. M. J. Lutz. Madras: Christian Literature Society, 1956.

Lumbantobing, Andar. *The Lutheran Churches of North Sumatra.* Taipei, Taiwan: Asia Theological Association, 1980.

Manikam, Rajah B., ed. *Christianity and the Asian Revolution.* New York: Diocesan, 1955.

Pedersen, Paul. *Batak Blood and Protestant Soul: The Development of National Batak Churches in North Sumatra.* Grand Rapids, Mich.: Eerdmans, 1970.

Renck, Günther. *Contextualization of Christianity and Christianization of Language: A Case Study from the Highlands of Papua New Guinea.* Erlangen: Verlag der Ev.-Luth. Mission, 1990.

Sovik, Ruth, Fosmark, Aagoth, and Peterson, Clara. *Mission in Formosa and Hong Kong: Studies in the Beginning and Development of the Indigenous Lutheran Church in Formosa and Hong Kong.* Minneapolis: Augsburg, 1957.

Spruth, Erwin L. *And the Word of God Spread: A Brief History of the Gutnius Lutheran Church, Papua New Guinea*. D.Miss. diss., Fuller Theological Seminary, School of World Mission, 1981.

Swavely, Clarence H. *The Lutheran Enterprise in India, 1706–1952*. Madras: Federation of Evangelical Lutheran Churches in India, 1952.

Syrdal, Rolf A. *American Lutheran Mission Work in China*. Ph.D. diss., Drew University, 1942.

———. *Mission in Japan: Studies in the Beginning and Development of the Indigenous Lutheran Church in Japan*. Minneapolis: Augsburg, 1958.

United Evangelical Lutheran Churches of India. *Dreams and Visions of UELCI: Thine Is the Kingdom, the Power, and the Glory*. Madras: The Churches, 1988.

Vierow, Duain W. *A History of Lutheranism in Western Malaysia and Singapore*. New York: Board of World Missions, Lutheran Church in America, 1968.

Wagner, Herwig, and Reiner, Hermann, eds. *The Lutheran Church in Papua New Guinea: The First Hundred Years, 1886–1986*. Adelaide: Lutheran, 1987.

Zorn, H. M. *Bartholomaeus Ziegenbalg*. St. Louis: Concordia, 1933.

C. Lutheranism in Australia

Brauer, A. *Under the Southern Cross: History of the Evangelical Lutheran Church of Australia*. Adelaide: Lutheran, 1956.

Ey, Anna V. *Early Lutheran Congregations in South Australia*. Adelaide: A.P.H. Freud, 1986.

Hebart, Theodore. *The United Evangelical Lutheran Church in Australia: Its History, Activities, and Characteristics, 1839–1938*. North Adelaide: Lutheran Book Depot, 1938.

Iwan, Wilhelm. *Because of Their Beliefs: Emigration from Prussia to Australia*. Ed. and trans. David Schubert. Highgate, South Australia: Schubert, 1995.

Leske, Everard. *For Faith and Freedom: The Story of Lutherans and Lutheranism in Australia, 1838–1996*. Adelaide: Open Book, 1996.

Scherer, P. A. *Venture of Faith: An Epic in Australian Missionary History*. 2nd ed. Adelaide: Lutheran, 1971.

Schild, Maurice E., and Hughes, Philip J. *The Lutherans in Australia*. Canberra: Australian Government Publication Service, 1996.

Schubert, Helen. *A Pictorial History of the Lutheran Church in Australia*. Adelaide: Lutheran, 1988.

D. Lutheranism in Europe

Anderson, N. K. "The Reformation in Scandinavia and the Baltic Countries." In *The New Cambridge Modern History*. Vol. 2, *The Reformation, 1520–1559*. 2nd ed. Ed. G. R. Elton. Cambridge: Cambridge University Press, 1990.

Arden, Everett G. *Four Northern Lights: Men Who Shaped Scandinavian Churches*. Minneapolis: Augsburg, 1964.

Baranowski, Shelley. *The Confessing Church, Conservative Elites, and the Nazi State*. Lewiston, N.Y.: Mellen, 1986.

Barnett, Victoria. *For the Soul of the People: Protestant Protest against Hitler*. New York: Oxford University Press, 1992.

Bergendoff, Conrad. *Olavus Petri and the Ecclesiastical Transformation in Sweden*. Philadelphia: Fortress, 1965.

Betts, R. R. "Poland, Bohemia, and Hungary." In *The New Cambridge Modern History*. Vol. 2, *The Reformation, 1520–1559*. 2nd ed. Ed. G. R. Elton. Cambridge: Cambridge University Press, 1990.

Bilmanis, Alfred. *The Church in Latvia*. New York: Drauga Vests, 1945.

Bruhn, Verner. *A People and Its Church: The Lutheran Church in Denmark*. Copenhagen: Council on Inter-Church Relations, 1994.

Burgess, John P. *The East German Church and the End of Communism*. New York: Oxford University Press, 1997.

The Churches in Finland. Trans. Hans-Christian Daniel. Helsinki: Evangelical-Lutheran Church of Finland, 1992.

Church in Bondage. Stockholm: Estonian Evangelical Lutheran Church, 1979.

Church in Finland: The History, Present State, and Outlook for the Future of the Evangelical Lutheran Church of Finland. Helsinki: Church Council for Foreign Affairs Ecclesiastical Board, 1989.

Conway, John S. *The Nazi Persecution of the Church, 1933–1945*. New York: Basic, 1968.

Cuibe, Leons. *The Lutheran Church of Latvia in Chains*. Stockholm: Latvian Reporter in the Committee for Church Activities among the Baltic Peoples in Sweden, 1963.

Dercsényi, Balázs. *Lutheran Churches in Hungary*. Budapest: Hegyi, 1992.

Dickens, A. G. *The German Nation and Martin Luther*. New York: Harper and Row, 1974.

Drummond, Andrew L. *German Protestantism since Luther*. London: Epworth, 1951.

Duin, Edgar C. *Lutheranism under the Tsars and the Soviets*. 2 vols. Ann Arbor, Mich.: Xerox and University Microfilms, 1975.

Dunkley, E. H. *The Reformation in Denmark*. London: SPCK, 1948.

The Evangelical-Lutheran Church of France. Paris: La Mission Interieure, 1985.

The Evangelical-Lutheran Church in Finland. Helsinki: Information Center of the Evangelical-Lutheran Church of Finland, 1984.

Fabiny, Tibor. *Hope Preserved: The Past and Present of Hungarian Lutheranism*. Trans. Miklos Uszkay. Budapest: Nyomda, 1984.

Feige, Franz. *The Varieties of Protestantism in Nazi Germany: Five Theopolitical Positions*. Lewiston, N.Y.: Mellen, 1990.

Folke, Ellis I. *The Church in Sweden*. Solna, Sweden: Swedish Institute for Cultural Relations, 1960.

Forstman, Jack. *Christian Faith in Dark Times: Theological Conflicts in the Shadow of Hitler*. Louisville, Ky.: Westminster/John Knox, 1992.

Goeckel, Robert F. *The Lutheran Church and the East German State: Political Conflict and Change under Ulbricht and Honecker*. Ithaca, N.Y.: Cornell University Press, 1990.

Grell, Ole Peter. "Scandinavia." In *The Reformation in National Context*. Ed. R. Scribner, R. Porter, and M. Teich. Cambridge: Cambridge University Press, 1994.

———, ed. *The Scandinavian Reformation: From Evangelical Movement to Institutionalization of Reform*. Cambridge: Cambridge University Press, 1995.

Hale, Fredrick. *Norwegian Religious Pluralism: A Transatlantic Comparison.* Lewiston, N.Y.: Mellen, 1992.

Hark, Edgar. *The Estonian Evangelical Lutheran Church Today.* Trans. Ilmar Anvelt. Tallinn, Estonia: Perioodika, 1982.

Helmreich, Ernst. *The German Church under Hitler: Background, Struggle, Epilogue.* Detroit: Wayne State University Press, 1979.

Hoeye, Bjarne, Ager, Trygve, and Locke, Hubert G., ed. *The German Church Struggle and the Holocaust.* Detroit: Wayne State University Press, 1974.

Hope, Nicholas. *German and Scandinavian Protestantism, 1700–1918.* New York: Oxford University Press, 1995.

Höye, Bjarne, and Trygve, Ager M. *The Fight of the Norwegian Church against Nazism.* New York: Macmillan, 1943.

Hunter, Leslie S. *Scandinavian Churches: A Picture of the Development and Life of the Churches of Denmark, Finland, Iceland, Norway, and Sweden.* London: Faber and Faber, 1965.

Kauppinen, Juha. *An Evangelizing Revival Movement: A Study of the Members of the Finnish Lutheran Mission.* Tampere, Finland: Research Institute of the Lutheran Church in Finland, 1973.

Kjaer, Jens C. *History of the Church of Denmark: An Outline.* Blair, Nebr.: Lutheran, 1945.

Krueger, David. *Lutherans in Latvia and Estonia.* Lansing, Ill: David Krueger, 1984.

Littell, Franklin H. *The German Phoenix.* New York: Doubleday, 1960. Appendix: Texts of the Platform of German Christians (1932), the *Barmen Declaration* (1934), and the *Stuttgart Declaration* (1945).

Lutheran Council of Great Britain. *The Lutheran Council of Great Britain.* London: Lutheran Council of Great Britain, 1975.

Mauelshagen, Carl. *Salzburg Lutheran Expulsion and Its Impact.* New York: Vantage, 1962.

Molland, Einar. *Church Life in Norway, 1800–1950.* Trans. Harris Kaasa. Minneapolis: Augsburg, 1957.

Paananen, Martti. *The Church of the Finns.* Trans. Gregory Coogan. Helsinki: Department of Communications of the Evangelical-Lutheran Church of Finland, 1991.

Pearce, Edward G. *The Story of the Lutheran Church in Britain through Four Centuries of History.* London: Evangelical Lutheran Church of England, 1969.

Pinson, Koppel S. *Pietism As a Factor in the Rise of German Nationalism.* New York: Octagon, 1968.

Prelinger, Catherine M. *Charity, Challenge, and Change: Religious Dimensions of the Mid-Nineteenth-century Women's Movement in Germany.* New York: Greenwood, 1987.

Scholder, Klaus. *The Churches and the Third Reich.* 2 vols. Trans. John Bowden. Philadelphia: Fortress, 1988.

Sinnemäki, Maunu, ed., Wathen, Paula, trans. *No East nor West: The Foreign Relations and Mission of the Evangelical-Lutheran Church of Finland.* Helsinki: Evangelical-Lutheran Church of Finland Council for Foreign Affairs, 1988.

Skodacek, August A. *Lutherans in Slovakia.* N.p.: August Skodacek, 1982.

Stendahl, Brita K. *The Force of Tradition: A Case Study of Women Priests in Sweden.* Philadelphia: Fortress, 1985.

Stromberg, Peter G. *Symbols of Community: The Cultural System of a Swedish Church.* Tucson: University of Arizona Press, 1986.

These Ruins Accuse: A Record of Religious Suppression of the Evangelical Lutheran Church in Occupied Latvia. Stockholm: Latvian National Foundation, 1980.

Tokarczyk, Andrzej. *Five Centuries of Lutheranism in Poland.* Warsaw: Interpress, 1984.

Tyorinoja, Pirjo, ed. *The Evangelical Lutheran Church in Finnish Society.* Helsinki: Church Council for Foreign Affairs, 1994.

Viise, Michael G. *The Estonian Evangelical Lutheran Church During the Soviet Period.* Ph.D. diss., University of Virginia, 1995.

Ylonen, Katarina. *Religion and Ethnicity: The Renaissance of the Ingrian Church after the End of Communist Rule.* Trans. Michael Cox. Tampere: Research Institute of the Evangelical Lutheran Church of Finland, 1998.

E. Lutheranism in North America

Bengston, Gloria, ed. *Lutheran Women in Ordained Ministry, 1970–1995: Reflections and Perspectives.* Minneapolis: Augsburg, 1995.

Braaten, Carl E., ed. *The New Church Debate: Issues Facing American Lutheranism.* Philadelphia: Fortress, 1983.

Crews, Warren E. *Three Men, One Vision: Samuel Schmucker, John Nevin, William Muhlenberg, and a Church Evangelical and Catholic.* Ph.D. diss., University of Pennsylvania, 1958.

Danker, Frederick W. *No Room in the Brotherhood: The Preus-Otten Purge of Missouri.* St. Louis: Clayton, 1977.

Doctrinal Declarations: A Collection of Official Statements on the Doctrinal Position of Various Lutheran Bodies in America. 2nd ed. St. Louis: Concordia, 1957.

Evangelical Lutheran Church in America. *Twenty-five Years after the Ordination of Women: Participation of Women in the ELCA.* Chicago: Commission for Women, 1995.

Evenson, George O. *Adventuring for Christ: The Story of the Evangelical Lutheran Church of Canada.* Calgary: Foothills Lutheran Press, 1974.

Fendt, Edward C. *The Struggle for Lutheran Unity and Consolidation in the USA from the Late 1930s to the Early 1970s.* Minneapolis: Augsburg, 1980.

Fredrich, Edward C. *The Twentieth-century Shaping of United States Lutheranism.* Mequon: Wisconsin Lutheran Seminary Press, 1985.

Frost, Naomi. *Golden Visions, Broken Dreams: A Short History of the Lutheran Council in the USA.* New York: Lutheran Council, 1987.

Gustafson, David A. *Lutherans in Crisis: The Question of Identity in the American Republic.* Minneapolis: Fortress, 1993.

Haney, James L. *The Religious Heritage and Education of Samuel Simon Schmucker: A Study in the Rise of "American Lutheranism."* New Haven: n.p., 1968.

Heintzen, Eric H. *Love Leaves Home: Wilhelm Löhe and the Missouri Synod.* St. Louis: Concordia, 1973.

Henry Melchior Muhlenberg: The Roots of 250 Years of Organized Lutheranism in North America—Essays in Memory of Helmut T. Lehmann. Ed. John W. Kleiner. Lewiston, N.Y.: Mellen, 1998.

Johnson, Jeff G. *Black Christians: The Untold Lutheran Story.* St. Louis: Concordia, 1991.

Johnson, Lani L. *Led by the Spirit: A History of Lutheran Church Women.* Philadelphia: Lutheran Church Women, 1980.

Jorstad, Erling. *Bold in the Spirit: Lutheran Charismatic Renewal in America Today.* Minneapolis: Augsburg, 1974.

Klos, Frank W., Nakamura, Lynn, C., and Martensen, Daniel F., eds. *Lutherans and the Challenge of Religious Pluralism.* Minneapolis: Augsburg, 1990.

Koehler, John P. *The History of the Wisconsin Synod.* Ed. Leigh D. Jordahl. Mosinee, Wis.: Protestant Conference, 1970.

Kuenning, Paul P. *The Rise and Fall of American Lutheran Pietism: The Rejection of an Activist Heritage.* Macon, Ga.: Mercer, 1988.

Lagerquist, L. DeAne. *From Our Mother's Arms: A History of Women in the American Lutheran Church.* Minneapolis: Augsburg, 1987.

Levang, Joseph H. *The Church of the Lutheran Brethren, 1900–1975: A Believers' Fellowship—A Lutheran Alternative.* Fergus Falls, Minn.: Lutheran Brethren, 1980.

Lund, Henriette. *Of Eskimos and Missionaries: Lutheran Eskimo Missions in Alaska, 1894–1973.* Minneapolis: American Lutheran Church, 1974.

Lutheran Church-Missouri Synod. Commission on Theology and Church Relations. *Women in the Church: Scriptural Principles and Ecclesial Practice.* St. Louis: Concordia, 1985.

Marquart, Kurt E. *Anatomy of an Explosion: Missouri in Lutheran Perspective.* Fort Wayne, Ind.: Concordia Theological Seminary Press, 1977.

Meyer, Carl S. *A Brief Historical Sketch of the Lutheran Church-Missouri Synod.* St. Louis: Concordia, 1963.

——, ed. *Moving Frontiers: Readings in the History of the Lutheran Church-Missouri Synod.* St. Louis: Concordia, 1964.

Nelson, Clifford E. *Lutheranism in North America, 1914–1970.* Minneapolis: Augsburg, 1972.

——, ed. *The Lutherans in North America.* 2nd ed. Philadelphia: Fortress, 1980.

Noll, Mark. "Ethnic, American, or Lutheran? Dilemmas for a Historic Confession in the New World." *Lutheran Theological Seminary Bulletin* (Gettysburg) 71, no. 1 (Winter 1991): 31.

Reuss, Carl F. *Profiles of Lutherans in the USA: Who They Are, Where They Live, What They Believe, How They Participate in Church and Community.* Minneapolis: Augsburg, 1982.

Riforgiato, Leonard K. *Missionary of Moderation: Henry Melchior Muhlenberg and the Lutheran Church in English America.* Lewisburg: Bucknell University Press, 1980.

Rudnick, Milton L. *Fundamentalism and the Missouri Synod: A Historical Study of Their Interaction and Mutual Influence.* St. Louis: Concordia, 1966.

Schaaf, James L. *Wilhelm Löhe's Relations to the American Church: A Study in the History of Lutheran Mission.* Inaug. diss., Ruprecht-Karl University, Heidelberg, 1962.

Schmucker, Samuel. *Fraternal Appeal to the American Churches, with a Plea for Catholic Union on Apostolic Principles.* Ed. Frederick K. Wentz. Philadelphia: Fortress, 1965.

Strobel, Philip D. *The Salzburgers and Their Descendants.* Athens: University of Georgia Press, 1953.

Tappert, Theodore G., ed. *Lutheran Confessional Theology in America, 1840–1880.* New York: Oxford University Press, 1972.

Threinen, Norman J. *Fifty Years of Lutheran Convergence: The Canadian Case Study.* Dubuque: Brown, 1983.

——, ed. *In Search of Identity: A Look at Lutheran Identity in Canada.* Winnipeg: Lutheran Council in Canada, 1977.

Todd, Mary. *Authority Vested: A Story of Identity and Change in the Lutheran Church-Missouri Synod.* Grand Rapids, Mich.: Eerdmans, 2000.

Trexler, Edgar R. *Anatomy of a Merger: People, Dynamics, and Decisions That Shaped the ELCA.* Minneapolis: Augsburg, 1991.

Ward, Kenn. *This Evangelical Lutheran Church of Ours.* Winfield, British Columbia: Wood Lake, 1994.

Weiser, Frederick S. *To Serve the Lord and His People, 1884–1984: Celebrating the Heritage of a Century of Lutheran Deaconesses in America.* Gladwyne, Pa.: Deaconess Community of the Lutheran Church in America, 1984.

Wentz, Abdel R. *A Basic History of Lutheranism in America.* Rev. ed. Philadelphia: Fortress, 1964.

Wentz, Frederick K. *Lutherans in Concert: The Story of the National Lutheran Council, 1918–1966.* Minneapolis: Augsburg, 1968.

Wicke, Harold E. C. *The Catechism of Differences: A Popular Study of the Doctrine and Practice of the Various Lutheran Bodies in the United States.* Milwaukee: Northwestern, 1964.

Wiederaenders, Robert C., ed. *Historical Guide to Lutheran Church Bodies in North America.* St. Louis: Lutheran Historical Conference, 1998.

Wiederaenders, Robert C., and Tillmanns, Walter G. *The Synods of American Lutheranism.* St. Louis: Lutheran Historical Conference, 1968.

Wolf, Richard C., ed. *Documents of Lutheran Unity in America.* Philadelphia: Fortress, 1966.

F. Lutheranism in South America

Bachmann, Theodore E. *Lutherans in Brazil: A Story of Emerging Ecumenism.* Minneapolis: Augsburg, 1970.

Beatty, Paul B. *A History of the Lutheran Church in Guyana.* Georgetown: Daily Chronicle, 1970.

Brakemeier, G., and Altmann, W., eds. *Lutherans in Brazil, 1990: History, Theology, Perspectives.* São Leopoldo: IECLB, 1989.

Gómez, Medardo E. *Fire against Fire: Christian Ministry Face-to-Face with Persecution.* Trans. Mary M. Solberg. Minneapolis: Augsburg, 1990.

VI. BIOGRAPHIES AND AUTOBIOGRAPHIES

Aarflot, Andreas. *Hans Nielsen Hauge: His Life and Message.* Minneapolis: Augsburg, 1979.

Bethge, Eberhard. *Costly Grace: An Illustrated Biography of Dietrich Bonhoeffer.* Trans. Rosaleen Ockenden. New York: Harper and Row, 1979.

———. *Dietrich Bonhoeffer: A Biography.* Rev. ed. Ed. Victoria J. Barnett, and trans. Eric Mosbacher et al. under the editorship of Edwin Robertson. Minneapolis: Fortress, 1999.

Curtis, Charles J. *Söderblom: Ecumenical Pioneer.* Minneapolis: Augsburg, 1967.

Diehl, Carl G., and Bachmann, Theodore E. *Rajah Bushanam Manikam: A Biography.* Madras: Christian Literature Society, 1975.

Drevlow, A. H., Drickamer J. M., and Reichwald, G. E., eds. *C.F.W. Walther, the American Luther: Essays in Commemoration of the 100th Anniversary of Carl Walther's Death.* Mankato, Minn.: Walther, 1987.

Fischer, Robert H. *Franklin Clark Fry: A Palette for a Portrait.* Springfield, Ohio: Lutheran Quarterly, 1972.

Hauge, Hans N. *Autobiographical Writings.* Trans. Joel M. Njus. Minneapolis: Augsburg, 1954.

Johnson, Alex. *Eivind Berggrav, God's Man of Suspense.* Trans. Kjell Jordheim with Harriet L. Overholt. Minneapolis: Augsburg, 1960.

Koch, Hal. *Grundtvig.* Yellow Springs, Ohio: Antioch, 1952.

Larsson, Per. *Bishop Josiah Kibira of Bukoba: In an International Perspective.* Nairobi, Kenya: Uzima Press, 1992.

Lilje, Hanns. *The Valley of the Shadow.* Philadelphia: Muhlenberg, 1950.

McKee, Elsie Anne. *Katharina Schütz Zell.* Leiden and Boston: Brill, 1999.

Muhlenberg, Henry Melchior. *The Notebook of a Colonial Clergyman: Condensed from the Journals of Henry Melchior Muhlenberg.* Ed. and trans. Theodore G. Tappert and John W. Doberstein. Philadelphia: Fortress, 1959.

———. *The Journals of Henry Melchior Muhlenberg.* 3 vols. Trans. Theodore G. Tappert and John W. Doberstein. Philadelphia: Lutheran Historical Society, 1982.

———. *The Correspondence of Heinrich Melchior Muhlenberg.* Ed. and trans. John W. Kleiner and Helmut T. Lehmann. Camden, Maine: Picton, 1993.

Nothstein, Ira O. *Lutheran Makers of America: Brief Sketches of Sixty-eight Notable Early Americans.* Philadelphia: United Lutheran, 1930.

Riforgiato, Leonard R. *Missionary of Moderation: Henry Melchior Muhlenberg and the Lutheran Church in English America.* Lewisburg, Pa.: Bucknell University Press, 1980.

Robertson, Edwin H. *The Shame and the Sacrifice: The Life and Martyrdom of Dietrich Bonhoeffer.* New York: Macmillan, 1988.

Schober, Theodor. *Wilhelm Loehe: Witness of the Living Lutheran Church.* Trans. Bertha Mueller. N.p: n.p., 1965.

Spitz, Lewis W. *The Life of Dr. C.F.W. Walther.* St. Louis: Concordia, 1961.

Sundkler, Bengt. *Nathan Söderblom: His Life and Work.* Lund: Gleerup, 1968.

Terray, Laszlo G. *He Could Not Do Otherwise: Bishop Lajos Ordass, 1901–1978.* Trans. Eric W. Gritsch. Grand Rapids, Mich.: Eerdmans, 1997.

Trexler, Samuel G. *John A. Morehead Who Created World Lutheranism.* New York, and London: Putnam, 1938.

Wentz, Abdel Ross. *Pioneer in Christian Unity: Samuel Simon Schmucker.* Philadelphia: Fortress, 1967.

VII. LUTHERAN CONFESSIONS, HISTORY, AND INTERPRETATION

"450th Anniversary of the Augsburg Confession." *Sixteenth-century Journal* 11, no. 3 (1980).

Allbeck, Willard D. *Studies in the Lutheran Confessions*. Philadelphia: Muhlenberg, 1952.

Anderson, Niels K. *Confessio Hafniensis: Den Kobenhavnske Bekendelse af 1530*. Copenhagen: G.E.C. Gads, 1954.

Bente, Friedrich. *Historical Introductions to the Book of Concord*. St. Louis: Concordia, 1965.

Bishop, Sherman, and Yandala, Deborah. *I Believe It! Lutheran Confessions*. Minneapolis: Augsburg Fortress, 1995.

Brecht, Martin, and Schwarz, Reinhard. *Bekenntnis und Einheit der Kirche: Studien zum Konkordienbuch*. Stuttgart: Calwer, 1980.

Burgess, Joseph A. *The Role of the Augsburg Confession: Catholic and Lutheran Views*. Philadelphia: Fortress, 1980.

Cochrane, Arthur. "The Act of Confession-Confessing." *Sixteenth-century Journal* 8, no. 4 (1977): 61–83.

Concordance to the Book of Concord. Ed. Kenneth E. Larson. Milwaukee: Northwestern, 1989.

Daniel, David, and Arand, Charles, eds. *Bibliography of the Lutheran Confessions*. Sixteenth Century Bibliography 28. St. Louis: Center for Reformation Research, 1988.

Fagerberg, Holsten. *A New Look at the Lutheran Confessions, 1529–1537*. St. Louis: Concordia, 1972.

Forell, George W. *The Augsburg Confession: A Contemporary Commentary*. Minneapolis: Augsburg, 1968.

"Formula of Concord Quadricentenntial Essays." *Sixteenth-century Journal* 8, no. 4 (1977).

Gassmann, Günther, and Hendrix, Scott H. *Fortress Introduction to the Lutheran Confessions*. Minneapolis: Fortress, 1999.

Grane, Leif. *The Augsburg Confession*. Minneapolis: Fortress, 1987.

Jungkuntz, Theodore. *Formulators of the Formula of Concord*. St. Louis: Concordia, 1977.

Kolb, Robert. *Andreae and the Formula of Concord: Six Sermons on the Way to Lutheran Unity*. St. Louis: Concordia, 1977.

———. *Confessing the Faith: Reformers Define the Church, 1530–1580*. St. Louis: Concordia, 1991.

Lange, Lyle W. *Outline of the Book of Concord*. Milwaukee: Northwestern, 1994.

Maurer, Wilhelm. *Historical Commentary on the Augsburg Confession*. Philadelphia: Fortress, 1986.

Meyer, Harding, ed. *The Augsburg Confession in Ecumenical Perspective*. LWF Report 6/7. Geneva: Lutheran World Federation, 1980.

Mildenberger, Friedrich. *Theology of the Lutheran Confessions*. Philadelphia: Fortress, 1983.

Pöhlmann, Horst G., Austad, Torleif, and Krüger, Friedhelm. *Theologie der Lutherischen Bekenntnisschriften*. Munich: Chr. Kaiser; Gütersloh: Gütersloher Verlagshaus, 1996.

Russell, William R. *Luther's Theological Testament: The Schmalkald Articles.* Minneapolis: Fortress, 1995.

Schlink, Edmund. *Theology of the Lutheran Confessions.* Philadelphia: Muhlenberg, 1961.

Schmauk, Theodore E., and Benze, Theodore C. *The Confessional Principle and the Confessions of the Lutheran Church.* Philadelphia: General Council Publication Board, 1911.

Schmidt, John. *The Lutheran Confessions: Their Value and Meaning.* Ed. Arthur H. Getz. Philadelphia: Muhlenberg, 1957.

Spitz, Lewis W., and Lohff, Wenzel, ed. *Discord, Dialogue, and Concord: Studies in the Lutheran Reformation's Formula of Concord.* Philadelphia: Fortress, 1977.

Vajta, Vilmos, ed., and Lewis, David, trans. *Confessio Augustana, 1530–1980: Commemoration and Self-Examination.* Stuttgart: Lutheran World Federation, 1980.

Vajta, Vilmos, and Weissgerber, Hans, ed. *The Church and the Confessions: The Role of the Confessions in the Life and Doctrine of the Lutheran Churches.* Philadelphia: Fortress, 1963.

Wengert, Timothy J. "Wittenberg's Earliest Catechism." *Lutheran Quarterly* 7 (1993): 247–260.

Wenz, Gunther. *Theologie der Bekenntnisschriften der evangelisch-lutherischen Kirche.* 2 vols. New York and Berlin: Walter de Gruyter, 1996–1998.

VIII. MARTIN LUTHER, LIFE, AND THEOLOGY

Althaus, Paul. *The Theology of Martin Luther.* Trans. Robert C. Schultz. Philadelphia: Fortress, 1966.

——. *The Ethics of Martin Luther.* Trans. Robert C. Schultz. Philadelphia: Fortress, 1972.

Altmann, Walter. "Luther's Theology and Liberation Theology." In *Lutherans in Brazil, 1990: History, Theology, Perspectives.* Ed. Gottfried Brakemeier and Walter Altmann. São Leopoldo: Post-Graduate Institute of the IECLB, 1989.

——. *Luther and Liberation: A Latin American Perspective.* Trans. Mary M. Solberg. Minneapolis: Fortress, 1992.

Atkinson, James. *Martin Luther and the Birth of Protestantism.* Baltimore: Penguin, 1968.

Bainton, Roland. *Here I Stand: A Life of Martin Luther.* New York and Nashville: Abingdon, 1950.

Benne, Robert. "Luther, Martin (1483–1546)." In *Encyclopedia of Ethics.* Ed. Lawrence Becker and Charlotte B. Becker. New York: Garland, 1992.

Bielfeldt, Dennis D., and Schwarzwäller, Klaus, eds. *Freedom as Love in Martin Luther.* New York: Lang, 1995.

Bluhm, Heinz. *Luther Translator of Paul: Studies in Romans and Galatians.* New York: Lang, 1984.

Bornkamm, Heinrich. *Luther's Doctrine of the Two Kingdoms in the Context of His Theology.* Trans. Karl H. Hertz. Philadelphia: Fortress, 1966.

——. *Luther in Mid-career, 1521–1530.* Trans. E. Theodore Bachmann. Philadelphia: Fortress, 1983.

Braaten, Carl E., and Jenson, Robert W., eds. *Union with Christ: The New Finnish Interpretation of Luther.* Grand Rapids, Mich., and Cambridge, UK: Eerdmans, 1998.

Brecht, Martin. "Divine Right and Human Rights in Luther." In *Martin Luther and the Modern Mind: Freedom, Conscience, Toleration, Rights.* Ed. Manfred Hoffmann. Lewiston, N.Y.: Mellen, 1985.

——. *Martin Luther.* 3 vols. Trans. James L. Schaaf. Philadelphia and Minneapolis: Fortress, 1985–1993.

Brendler, Gerhard. *Martin Luther: Theology and Revolution.* Trans. Claude R. Foster. New York: Oxford University Press, 1991.

Cargill, Thompson, W.D.J. *The Political Thought of Martin Luther.* Ed. Philip Broadhead. Totowa, N.J.: Barnes and Noble, 1984.

Cranz, Edward F. *An Essay on the Development of Luther's Thought on Justice, Law, and Society.* Ed. Gerald Christianson and Thomas M. Izbicki. Mifflintown, Pa.: Sigler, 1997.

Croken, Robert C. *Luther's First Front: The Eucharist as Sacrifice.* Ottawa: University of Ottawa Press, 1990.

Dickens, Arthur G. *The German Nation and Martin Luther.* New York: Harper and Row, 1974.

Douglass, Jane Dempsey. "The Image of God in Women as Seen by Luther and Calvin." In *The Image of God: Gender Models in Judaeo-Christian Tradition.* Ed. Kari Elisabeth Borresen. Minneapolis: Fortress, 1995.

Ebeling, Gerhard. *Luther: An Introduction to His Thought.* Trans. R. A. Wilson. Philadelphia: Fortress, 1972.

Edwards, Mark U., Jr. *Luther and the False Brethren.* Stanford: Stanford University Press, 1975.

——. *Luther's Last Battles: Politics and Polemics, 1531–1546.* Ithaca and London: Cornell University Press, 1983.

Encounters with Luther: Lectures, Discussions, and Sermons at the Martin Luther Colloquia. 4 vols. Ed. Eric W. Gritsch. Gettysburg, Pa.: Institute for Luther Studies, Lutheran Theological Seminary, 1980–1990.

Erikson, Erik H. *Young Man Luther: A Study in Psychoanalysis and History.* New York: Norton, 1958.

Fischer, Robert H. "The Reasonable Luther." In *Reformation Studies: Essays in Honor of Roland H. Bainton.* Ed. Franklin Littell. Richmond, Va.: John Knox, 1962.

Forell, George W. *Martin Luther, Theologian of the Church: Collected Essays in Honor of his Seventy-fifth Birthday.* 2nd ed. Ed. William R. Russell. Word and World Supplement Series. St. Paul: Luther Seminary, 1994.

——. "Freedom As Love: Luther's Treatise on Good Works." In *Freedom As Love in Martin Luther.* Ed. Dennis D. Bielfeldt and Klaus Schwarzwäller. New York: Lang, 1995.

Gerrish, Brian A. *Grace and Reason: A Study in the Theology of Martin Luther.* Oxford: Oxford University Press, 1962.

Grislis, Egil. "The Foundation of Creative Freedom in Martin Luther's 'Von den Guten Werken (1520).'" In *Freedom As Love in Martin Luther.* Ed. Dennis D. Bielfeldt and Klaus Schwarzwäller. New York: Lang, 1995.

Gritsch, Eric W. *Martin—God's Court Jester: Luther in Retrospect*. 2nd ed. Ramsey, N.J.: Sigler, 1990.

Hagen, Kenneth. *A Theology of Testament in the Young Luther: The Lectures on Hebrews*. Leiden: Brill, 1974.

———. *Luther's Approach to Scripture as Seen in His "Commentaries" on Galatians, 1519–1538*. Tübingen: Mohr, 1993.

Hägglund, Bengt. *The Background of Luther's Doctrine of Justification in Late Medieval Theology*. Philadelphia: Fortress Facet, 1971.

Haile, H. G. *Luther: An Experiment in Biography*. Garden City, N.Y.: Doubleday, 1980.

Harran, Marilyn J. *Martin Luther: Learning for Life*. St. Louis: Concordia, 1997.

———, ed. *Luther and Learning: The Wittenberg University Luther Symposium*. Selinsgrove, Pa.: Susquehanna University Press; London and Toronto: Associated University Presses, 1985.

Headley, John. *Luther's View of Church History*. New Haven: Yale University Press, 1963.

Hendrix, Scott H. *Ecclesia in Via: Ecclesiological Developments in the Medieval Psalms Exegesis and the Dictata Super Psalterium (1513–1515) of Martin Luther*. Leiden: Brill, 1974.

———. *Luther and the Papacy: Stages in a Reformation Conflict*. Philadelphia: Fortress, 1981.

———. "Martin Luther's Reformation of Spirituality" *Lutheran Quarterly* 13 (1999): 249–270.

Hoffman, Bengt. *Luther and the Mystics*. Minneapolis: Augsburg, 1976.

———. "On the Relationship between Mystical Faith and Moral Life in Luther's Thought." In *Encounter with Luther*. Ed. Eric W. Gritsch. Gettysburg, Pa.: Institute for Luther Studies, 1980.

Hoffmann, Manfred, ed. *Martin Luther and the Modern Mind: Freedom, Conscience, Toleration, Rights*. Lewiston, N.Y.: Mellen, 1985.

Janz, Denis R. *Luther and Late Medieval Thomism: A Study in Theological Anthropology*. Waterloo, Ontario: Wilfrid Laurier University Press, 1983.

———. *Luther on Thomas Aquinas: The Angelic Doctor in the Thought of the Reformer*. Stuttgart: Franz Steiner, 1989.

Jüngel, Eberhard. *The Freedom of a Christian: Luther's Significance for Contemporary Theology*. Trans. Roy A. Harrisville. Minneapolis: Augsburg, 1988.

Kinder, Ernst. "Agape in Luther." In *The Philosophy and Theology of Anders Nygren*. Ed. Charles W. Kegley. Carbondale, Ill.: Southern Illinois University Press, 1970.

Kirst, Nelson, ed. *Rethinking Luther's Theology in the Contexts of the Third World*. Geneva: Lutheran World Federation, 1988.

Kittelson, James M. *Luther the Reformer: The Story of the Man and His Career*. Minneapolis: Augsburg, 1986.

———. "Luther the Theologian." In *Reformation Europe: A Guide to Research II*. 3rd ed. Reformation Guides to Research. Ed. William S. Maltby. St. Louis: Center for Reformation Research, 1992.

Kvam, Kristen E. "Honoring God's Handiwork: Challenges of Luther's Doctrine of Creation." In *A Reforming Church—Gift and Task: Essays from a Free Conference*. Ed. Charles P. Lutz. Minneapolis: Kirk House, 1995.

Lage, Dietmar. *Martin Luther's Christology and Ethics*. Lewiston, N.Y.: Mellen, 1990.

Lehmann, Hartmut. *Martin Luther in the American Imagination*. München: Wilhelm Fink Verlag, 1988.

Lienhard, Marc. *Martin Luther: Witness to Jesus Christ*. Minneapolis: Augsburg, 1982.

Lilje, Hans. *Luther and the Reformation: An Illustrated Review*. In collaboration with Karl F. Reinking. Philadelphia: Fortress, 1967.

Loewenich, Walter. *Luther's Theology of the Cross*. Minneapolis: Augsburg, 1976.

——. *Martin Luther: The Man and His Work*. Minneapolis: Augsburg, 1986.

Lohse, Bernhard. "Conscience and Authority in Luther." In *Luther and the Dawn of the Modern Era*. Ed. H. A. Oberman. Leiden: Brill, 1974.

——. *Martin Luther: An Introduction to His Life and Work*. Philadelphia: Fortress, 1986.

——. *Martin Luther's Theology: Its Historical and Systematic Development*. Minneapolis: Fortress, 1999.

Lull, Timothy F. *My Conversations with Martin Luther in which I Learn about God, Faith, Marriage, Sexuality, Education, War, Spirituality, Church Life, the Future, Ecumenism, Politics, Heaven and Hell, and Other Things, Too*. Minneapolis: Augsburg, 1999.

Luther and the Dawn of the Modern Era. Papers for the Fourth International Congress for Luther Research. Ed. Heiko A. Oberman. Leiden: Brill, 1974.

Marius, Richard. *Luther*. Philadelphia: Lippincott, 1974.

——. *Martin Luther: The Christian between God and Death*. Cambridge, Mass., and London: Harvard University Press, 1999.

Marty, Martin E. "Luther on Ethics: Man Free and Slave." In *Accents in Luther's Theology*. Ed. Heino O. Kadai. St. Louis: Concordia, 1968.

McDonough, Thomas M. *The Law and the Gospel in Luther: A Study of Martin Luther's Confessional Writings*. London: Oxford University Press, 1963.

McGrath, Alister. *Luther's Theology of the Cross: Martin Luther's Theological Breakthrough*. Oxford: Blackwell, 1985.

McSorley, Harry. *Luther: Right or Wrong? An Ecumenical-theological Study of Luther's Major Work "The Bondage of the Will."* New York and Minneapolis: Newman-Augsburg, 1969.

——. "Luther: Exemplar of Reform—or Doctor of the Church?" In *The Theology of Martin Luther*. Ed. Egil Grislis. Winfield, British Columbia: Wood Lake, 1985.

Montgomery, John Warwick. *In Defense of Martin Luther: Essays*. Milwaukee: Northwestern, 1970.

Nestingen, James A. *Martin Luther, His Life and Teachings*. Philadelphia: Fortress, 1982.

Nugent, Donald C. "What Has Wittenberg to Do with Avila? Martin Luther and St. Teresa." *Journal of Ecumenical Studies* 23 (1986): 650–658.

Oberman, Heiko A. *Luther: Man between God and the Devil*. Trans. Eileen Walliser-Schwarzbar. New Haven: Yale University Press, 1989.

Ozment, Steven. *Homo spiritualis: A Comparative Study of the Anthropology of Johannes Tauler, Jean Gerson, and Martin Luther (1509–16) in the Context of Their Theological Thought*. Leiden: Brill, 1969.

Pauck, Wilhelm. "Luther and Melanchthon." In *Luther and Melanchthon in the History and Theology of the Reformation*. Ed. Vilmos Vajta. Philadelphia: Muhlenberg, 1991.

Pelikan, Jaroslav. *Luther the Expositor: Introduction to the Reformer's Exegetical Writings.* St. Louis: Concordia, 1959.

——. *Obedient Rebels: Catholic Substance and Protestant Principle in Luther's Reformation.* New York: Harper and Row, 1964.

——. *Spirit versus Structure: Luther and the Institutions of the Church.* New York: Harper and Row, 1968.

——. ed. *Interpreters of Luther: Essays in Honor of Wilhelm Pauck.* Philadelphia: Fortress, 1968.

Pesch, Otto. *The God Question in Thomas Aquinas and Martin Luther.* Trans. Gottfried G. Krodel. Philadelphia: Fortress, 1972.

——. "Free by Faith: Luther's Contribution to a Theological Anthropology." In *Martin Luther and the Modern Mind: Freedom, Conscience, Toleration, Rights.* Ed. Manfred Hoffmann. Lewiston, N.Y.: Mellen, 1985.

Peterson, Pamela Honan. *Meet Martin Luther.* Minneapolis: Augsburg Fortress, 1995.

Pfürtner, Stephan. *Luther and Aquinas—A Conversation: Our Salvation, Its Certainty and Peril.* London: Darton, Longman, and Todd, 1964.

Pinomaa, Lennart. *Faith Victorious: An Introduction to Luther's Theology.* Trans. Walter J. Kukkonen. Philadelphia: Fortress, 1963.

Prenter, Regin. *Spiritus Creator: Luther's Concept of the Holy Spirit.* Trans. J. M. Jensen. Philadelphia: Muhlenberg, 1953.

Preus, Samuel J. *From Shadow to Promise: Old Testament Interpretation from Augustine to the Young Luther.* Cambridge, Mass.: Harvard University Press, 1969.

Reavis, Ralph. *The Meaning of Martin Luther for the Black Experience.* New York: Vantage, 1976.

Rupp, Gordon. *The Righteousness of God: Luther Studies.* London: Hodder and Stoughton, 1953.

Schneider, Carolyn. *The Connection between Christ and Christians in Athanasius and Luther.* Princeton, N.J.: Princeton Theological Seminary, 1999.

Schwarz, Hans. *True Faith in the True God: An Introduction to Luther's Life and Thought.* Trans. Mark William Worthing. Minneapolis: Augsburg Fortress, 1996.

Schwiebert, Ernst G. *Luther and His Times: The Reformation from a New Perspective.* St. Louis: Concordia, 1950.

Short, Ruth Gordon. *Meet Martin Luther: His Life and Teachings.* Grand Rapids, Mich.: Zondervan, 1959.

Siemon-Netto, Uwe. *The Fabricated Luther: The Rise and Fall of the Shriver Myth.* St. Louis: Concordia, 1993.

Simon, Edith. *Luther Alive: Martin Luther and the Making of the Reformation.* Garden City, N.Y.: Doubleday, 1968.

Smith, Ralph. *Luther, Ministry, and Ordination Rites in the Early Reformation Church.* New York: Lang, 1996.

Sockness, Brent W. "Luther's Two Kingdoms Revisited: A Response to Reinhold Niebuhr's Criticism of Luther." *Journal of Religious Ethics* 7 (1991): 93–110.

Spitz, Lewis W. "Luther in America: Reformation History since Philip Schaff." In *Luther in der Neuzeit.* Ed. Bernd Moeller. Gütersloh: Gerd Mohn 19, 1983.

———. *Luther and German Humanism*. Brookfield, Vt., and Aldershot, Hampshire: Variorum, 1996.

Steinmetz, David C. *Luther and Staupitz: An Essay in the Intellectual Origins of the Protestant Reformation*. Durham, N.C.: Duke University Press, 1980.

———. *Luther in Context*. Bloomington: Indiana University Press, 1986.

Strohl, Jane E. "Luther's Invocavit Sermons." In *Freedom as Love in Martin Luther*. Ed. Dennis D. Bielfeldt and Klaus Schwarzwäller. New York: Lang, 1995.

Stupperich, Robert. "Luther's Itio Spiritualis." In *The Bible, the Reformation, and the Church: Essays in Honor of James Atkinson*. Ed. W. P. Stephens. Sheffield: Sheffield Academic, 1995.

Tokuzen, Yoshikazu. "Luther's Contribution to an Asian Understanding of Nature and the Natural." In *Piety, Politics, and Ethics: Reformation Studies in Honor of George Wolfgang Forell*. Ed. Carter Lindberg. Kirksville, Mo.: Sixteenth-century Journal Publishers, 1984.

Tracy, James D., ed. *Luther and the Modern State in Germany*. Kirksville, Mo.: Sixteenth-century Journal Publishers, 1986.

Trigg, Jonathan D. *Baptism in the Theology of Martin Luther*. New York: Brill, 1994.

Vajta, Vilmos. *Luther on Worship*. Philadelphia: Fortress, 1958.

Watson, Philip S. *Let God Be God: An Introduction of the Theology of Martin Luther*. Philadelphia: Muhlenberg, 1950.

Westhelle, Vitor. "Luther and Liberation." *Dialog* 25, no. 1 (Winter 1986): 51–57.

Wicks, Jared. *Luther and His Spiritual Legacy*. Wilmington, Del.: Michael Glazier, 1983.

———. *Luther's Reform: Studies on Conversion and the Church*. Mainz: Verlag P. von Zabern, 1992.

———, ed. *Catholic Scholars Dialogue with Luther*. Chicago: Loyola University Press, 1970.

Wingren, Gustaf. *Luther on Vocation*. Philadelphia: Muhlenberg, 1957.

Wisløff, Carl F. *The Gift of Communion: Luther's Controversy with Rome on Eucharistic Sacrifice*. Trans. Joseph M. Shaw. Minneapolis: Augsburg, 1964.

Zachman, Randall C. *The Assurance of Faith: Conscience in the Theology of Martin Luther and John Calvin*. Minneapolis: Fortress, 1993.

Zeeden, Ernst W. *The Legacy of Luther: Martin Luther and the Reformation in the Estimation of the German Lutherans from Luther's Death to the Beginning of the Age of Goethe*. Trans. Ruth Mary Bethell. Westminster, Md.: Newman, 1954.

Ziemke, Donald C. *Love for the Neighbor in Luther's Theology: The Development of His Thought, 1512–1529*. Minneapolis: Augsburg, 1963.

IX. SIGNIFICANT LUTHERANS

Allen, Edgar C. *Kierkegaard: His Life and Thought*. London: Nott, 1935.

Bethge, Eberhard. *Dietrich Bonhoeffer: A Biography*. Rev. ed. Ed. Victoria J. Barnett. Minneapolis: Fortress, 1999.

Bonhoeffer, Dietrich. *The Cost of Discipleship.* Trans. Reginald H. Fuller and Irmgard Booth. New York: Macmillan, 1963.

———. *Letters and Papers from Prison.* Ed. Eberhard Bethge. New York: Macmillan, 1972.

———. *Works.* Ed. Gerhard L. Müller and Albrecht Schönherr, and trans. Daniel W. Bloesch and James H. Burtness, with new supplementary material by Geoffrey B. Kelly. Minneapolis: Fortress, 1996.

Chemnitz, Martin. *Examination of the Council of Trent.* Trans. Fred Kramer. St. Louis: Concordia, 1971.

———. *Loci Theologici.* Vol. 2. Trans. J.A.O. Preus. St. Louis: Concordia, 1989.

Curtis, Charles J. *Söderblom: Ecumenical Pioneer.* Minneapolis: Augsburg, 1971.

Diem, Hermann. *Kierkegaard: An Introduction.* Trans. David Green. Richmond: John Knox, 1966.

Feuerhahn, Ronald R. *Hermann Sasse: A Bibliography.* Metuchen, N.J., and London: Scarecrow, 1995.

Grundtvig, N.F.S. *Selected Writings of N.F.S. Grundtvig.* Ed. Johannes Knudsen. Philadelphia: Fortress, 1976.

Kelly, Geoffrey B., and Nelson, Burton F., eds. *A Testament to Freedom: The Essential Writings of Dietrich Bonhoeffer.* San Francisco: Harper, 1990.

Kierkegaard, Søren. "Fear and Trembling." In *Fear and Trembling* and *Repetition.* Ed. and trans. Howard V. Hong and Edna H. Hong. Princeton, N.J.: Princeton University Press, 1983.

———. *Either/Or.* 2 vols. Ed. and trans. Howard V. Hong and Edna H. Hong. Princeton, N.J.: Princeton University Press, 1987.

Kirmmse, Bruce H. *Kierkegaard in Golden-age Denmark.* Bloomington: Indiana University Press, 1990.

Knudsen, Johannes. *Danish Rebel: A Study of N.F.S. Grundtvig.* Philadelphia: Muhlenberg, 1955.

Philip Melanchthon—Then and Now (1497–1997): Essays Celebrating the 500th Anniversary of the Birth of Philip Melanchthon, Theologian, Teacher, and Reformer. Ed. Scott H. Hendrix and Timothy J. Wengert. Columbia, S.C.: Lutheran Theological Southern Seminary, 1999.

Preus, Jacob A. O. *The Second Martin: The Life and Theology of Martin Chemnitz.* St. Louis: Concordia, 1994.

Rasmussen, Larry. *Dietrich Bonhoeffer: His Significance for North Americans.* Trans. Geoffrey B. Kelly. Philadelphia: Fortress, 1990.

Sattler, Gary R. *God's Glory, Neighbor's Good: A Brief Introduction to the Life and Writings of August Hermann Francke.* Chicago: Covenant, 1982.

Scheible, Heinz. "Luther and Melanchthon." *LQ* 4 (1990): 317–339.

———. *Melanchthon: Eine Biographie.* Munich: Beck, 1997.

Spener, Philip Jacob. *Pia Desideria.* Ed. and trans. Theodore Tappert. Philadelphia: Fortress, 1964.

Stein, James K. *Philipp Jakob Spener: Pietist Patriarch.* Chicago: Covenant, 1986.

Sundkler, Bengt G. *Nathan Söderblom: His Life and Work.* Lund: Gleerup, 1968.

Thulstrup, Niels. *Kierkegaard and the Church in Denmark.* Trans. Frederick H. Cryer. Copenhagen: Reitzel, 1984.

Wengert, Timothy. "Luther and Melanchthon/Melanchthon and Luther." *Luther-jahrbuch* 66 (1999).

X. LUTHERAN DOCTRINE AND THEOLOGY

A. General Works

Anderson, Charles S. *Faith and Freedom. The Christian Faith According to the Lutheran Confessions.* Minneapolis: Augsburg, 1977.

Arand, Charles P. *Testing the Boundaries: Windows to Lutheran Identity.* St. Louis: Concordia, 1995.

Aulén, Gustaf. *The Faith of the Christian Church.* Trans. Eric H. Wahlstrom and G. Everett Arden. Philadelphia: Fortress, 1961.

Braaten, Carl E. *Principles of Lutheran Theology.* Philadelphia: Fortress, 1983.

Braaten, Carl E., and Jenson, Robert W. *The Catholicity of the Reformation.* Grand Rapids, Mich., and Cambridge, UK: Eerdmans, 1996.

———, eds. *Christian Dogmatics.* 2 vols. Philadelphia: Fortress, 1984.

The Function of Doctrine and Theology in Light of the Unity of the Church: A Report Plus 15 Papers from an Official Study Conducted by the Division of Theological Studies, Lutheran Council in the USA during 1972–1977. New York: Division of Theological Studies, Lutheran Council in the USA, 1978.

Gritsch, Eric W., and Jenson, Robert W. *Lutheranism: The Theological Movement and Its Confessional Writings.* Philadelphia: Fortress, 1976.

Keller, Paul F. *Studies in Lutheran Doctrine.* St. Louis: Concordia, 1960.

Kolb, Robert. *The Christian Faith: A Lutheran Exposition.* St. Louis: Concordia, 1993.

Lindbeck, George A. *The Nature of Doctrine: Religion and Theology in a Post-liberal Age.* Philadelphia: Westminster, 1984.

Montgomery, John Warwick. *Crisis in Lutheran Theology: The Validity and Relevance of Historic Lutheranism vs. Its Contemporary Rivals.* Grand Rapids, Mich.: Baker, 1967.

Pannenberg, Wolfhart. *Christianity in a Secularized World.* Trans. John Bowden. New York: Crossroad, 1989.

———. *Systematic Theology.* 3 vols. Trans. Geoffrey W. Bromiley. Grand Rapids, Mich.: Eerdmans, 1991.

Pero, Albert, and Moyo, Ambrose, eds. *Theology and the Black Experience: The Lutheran Heritage Interpreted by African and African-American Theologians.* Minneapolis: Augsburg, 1988.

Prenter, Regin. *The Church's Faith: A Primer of Christian Beliefs.* Trans. Theodor I. Jensen. Philadelphia: Fortress, 1968.

Sasse, Hermann. *Here We Stand: Nature and Character of the Lutheran Faith.* Trans. Theodore G. Tappert. New York: Harper, 1938.

Schmid, Heinrich. *The Doctrinal Theology of the Evangelical Lutheran Church.* Trans. Charles A. Hay and Henry E. Jacobs. Minneapolis: Augsburg, 1961.

Tradition in Lutheranism and Anglicanism. Ed. Günther Gassmann and Vilmos Vajta. Minneapolis: Augsburg, 1972.

B. History of Lutheran Theology

Cragg, Gerald R. *The Church and the Age of Reason, 1648–1789.* Grand Rapids, Mich.: Eerdmans, 1960.

Heick, Otto N. *A History of Christian Thought.* 2 vols. Philadelphia: Fortress, 1965.

Lohse, Bernhard. "Dogma und Bekenntnis in der Reformation: Von Luther bis zum Konkordienbuch." In *Handbuch der Dogmengeschichte.* 2nd ed. Vol. 2. Ed. Carl Andresen and Adolf Martin Ritter. Göttingen: Vandenhoeck and Ruprecht, 1998.

Mackintosh, Hugh R. *Types of Modern Theology.* New York: Scribner, 1937.

McGrath, Alister E. *Reformation Thought: An Introduction.* 2nd ed. Oxford: Basil Blackwell, 1994.

Pauck, Wilhelm. *From Luther to Tillich: The Reformers and Their Heirs.* Ed. Marion Pauck. San Francisco: Harper and Row, 1984.

Pelikan, Jaroslav. *From Luther to Kierkegaard: A Study in the History of Theology.* St. Louis: Concordia, 1950.

———. *Reformation of Church and Dogma (1300–1700).* Chicago: University of Chicago Press, 1984.

Preus, Robert D. *The Theology of Post-Reformation Lutheranism.* St. Louis: Concordia, 1978.

Raitt, Jill. *Shapers of Religious Traditions in Germany, Switzerland, and Poland, 1560–1600.* New Haven and London: Yale University Press, 1981.

Vajta, Vilmos, ed. *Luther and Melanchthon in the History and Theology of the Reformation.* Philadelphia: Muhlenberg, 1961.

Vidler, Alec R. *The Church in an Age of Revolution: 1789 to the Present Day.* Grand Rapids, Mich.: Eerdmans, 1961.

C. Specific Doctrinal Topics

Asheim, Ivar, and Gold, Victor R., eds. *Episcopacy in the Lutheran Church? Studies in the Development and Definition of the Office of Church Leadership.* Philadelphia: Fortress, 1969.

Aulén, Gustaf. *Eucharist and Sacrifice.* Trans. Eric H. Wahlstrom. Philadelphia: Muhlenberg; Edinburgh: Oliver and Boyd, 1958.

Baptism, Rites of Passage, and Culture. Ed. S. Anita Stauffer. Geneva: Lutheran World Federation, 1998.

Bergendoff, Conrad. *The Doctrine of the Church in American Lutheranism.* Philadelphia: Board of Publication of the United Lutheran Church in America, 1956.

Bonhoeffer, Dietrich. *Sanctorum Communio: A Dogmatic Inquiry into the Sociology of the Church.* London: Collins, 1963.

Braaten, Carl E. *Justification: The Article by Which the Church Stands and Falls.* Minneapolis: Fortress, 1990.

Brand, Eugene L. *Baptism: A Pastoral Perspective.* Minneapolis: Augsburg, 1975.

Called and Ordained: Lutheran Perspectives on the Office of the Ministry. Ed. Todd Nichol and Marc Kolden. Minneapolis: Fortress, 1990.

Categories of "Secular" and "Sacred" and their Implications for the Traditional Lutheran Categories of the Law/Gospel Dialectic and the Doctrine of the Two Kingdoms. New York: Division of Theological Studies, Lutheran Council in the USA, 1976.

Dantine, Wilhelm. *The Justification of the Ungodly*. Trans. Eric W. Gritsch and Ruth C. Gritsch. St. Louis: Concordia, 1968.

Elert, Werner. *Law and Gospel*. Trans. Edward H. Schroeder. Philadelphia: Fortress, 1967.

Farisani, Tshenuwani Simon. *In Transit: Between the Image of God and the Image of Man*. Grand Rapids, Mich.: Eerdmans; Trenton, N.J.: Africa World Press, 1990.

Forde, Gerhard O. *The Law-Gospel Debate: An Interpretation of Its Historical Development*. Minneapolis: Augsburg, 1969.

———. *Justification by Faith: A Matter of Death and Life*. Philadelphia: Fortress, 1982.

Fraenkel, Peter. *Testimonia Patrum: The Function of the Patristic Argument in the Theology of Philip Melanchthon*. Geneva: E. Droz, 1961.

Gensichen, Hans-Werner. *We Condemn: How Luther and 16th-century Lutheranism Condemned False Doctrine*. Trans. Herbert J. A. Bouman. St. Louis: Concordia, 1967.

Identity of the Church and Its Service to the Whole Human Being. 3 vols. Geneva: Lutheran World Federation, 1977.

Jeremias, Joachim. *Infant Baptism in the First Four Centuries*. Trans. D. Cairns. Philadelphia: Westminster, 1962.

———. *The Eucharistic Words of Jesus*. Trans. Norman Perrin. London: SCM Press, 1966.

Jüngel, Eberhard. *God as the Mystery of the World*. Trans. Darrell L. Guder. Grand Rapids, Mich.: Eerdmans, 1983.

Kähler, Martin. *The So-called Historical Jesus and the Historic Biblical Christ*. Trans. Carl E. Braaten. Philadelphia: Fortress, 1988.

Kantonen, Taito A. *Man in the Eyes of God: Human Existence in the Light of the Lutheran Confessions*. Lima, Ohio: CSS Publishing, 1972.

Käsemann, Ernst. *Essays on New Testament Themes*. Trans. W. J. Montague. London: SCM Press, 1964.

Knutson, Kent. *The Community of Faith and the Word: An Inquiry into the Concept of the Church in Contemporary Lutheranism*. Ann Arbor, Mich.: University Microfilms, 1961.

Larson, Duane H. *Times of the Trinity: A Proposal for Theistic Cosmology*. New York: Lang, 1995.

Löhe, Wilhelm. *Three Books about the Church*. Ed. and trans. James L. Schaaf. Philadelphia: Fortress, 1969.

Ordination of Women in Lutheran Churches: Analysis of an LWF Survey. Ed. Frances Maher. Stuttgart: Kreuz Verlag, 1984.

Pannenberg, Wolfhart. *Jesus, God, and Man*. Trans. Lewis L. Wilkins and Duane A. Priebe. Philadelphia: Westminster, 1977.

———. *The Church*. Trans. Keith Crim. Philadelphia: Westminster, 1983.

———. *Anthropology in Theological Perspective*. Trans. Matthew J. O'Connell. Philadelphia: Westminster, 1985.

———. *Toward a Theology of Nature: Essays on Science and Faith*. Ed. Ted Peters. Louisville, Ky.: Westminster/John Knox, 1993.

Peters, Ted. *God—the World's Future: Systematic Theology for a Postmodern Era*. Minneapolis: Fortress, 1992.

Pfnür, Vinzenz. *Einig in der Rechtfertigungslehre?* Wiesbaden: Fritz Steiner, 1970.

Pragman, James H. *Traditions of Ministry: A History of the Doctrine of the Ministry in Lutheran Theology*. St. Louis: Concordia, 1983.

Prenter, Regin. *Spiritus Creator.* Trans. John M. Jensen. Philadelphia: Fortress, 1953.

Preus, Robert D. *The Inspiration of Scripture: A Study of the Theology of the 17th-century Lutheran Dogmaticians.* Edinburgh: Oliver and Boyd, 1955.

Reumann, John H. P. *Ministries Examined: Laity, Clergy, Women, and Bishops in a Time of Change.* Minneapolis: Augsburg, 1987.

Sasse, Hermann. *This Is My Body: Luther's Contention for the Real Presence in the Sacrament of the Altar.* Minneapolis: Augsburg, 1959.

Schlink, Edmund. *The Coming Christ and the Coming Church.* Philadelphia: Fortress, 1968.

———, trans. *The Doctrine of Baptism.* St. Louis: Concordia, 1972.

Schweitzer, Albert. *The Quest of the Historical Jesus.* 3rd ed. Trans. W. Montgomery. London: Adam and Charles Black, 1954.

Senn, Frank C. "Structures of Penance and the Ministry of Reconciliation." *Lutheran Quarterly* 35 (1973): 270–283.

Serving the Word: Lutheran Women Consider Their Calling. Ed. Marilyn Preus. Minneapolis: Augsburg, 1988.

Sittler, Joseph, Jr. *The Doctrine of the Word in the Structure of Lutheran Theology.* Philadelphia: Board of Publication of the United Lutheran Church in America, 1948.

Together for Ministry: Final Report and Recommendations, Task Force on the Study of Ministry, 1988–1993. Chicago: Evangelical Lutheran Church in America, 1993.

Use of the Means of Grace: A Statement on the Practice of Word and Sacrament. Evangelical Lutheran Church in America. Minneapolis: Augsburg Fortress, 1997.

Welcome, Holy Spirit: A Study of Charismatic Renewal in the Church. Minneapolis: Augsburg, 1987.

Wengert, Timothy J. *Human Freedom, Christian Righteousness: Philip Melanchthon's Exegetical Disputes with Erasmus of Rotterdam.* New York: Harper and Row, 1960.

———. *Law and Gospel: Philip Melanchthon's Debate with John Agricola of Eisleben over Poenitentia.* Grand Rapids, Mich.: Baker, 1997.

Wisløff, Karl J. F. *The Gift of Communion.* Trans. Joseph M. Shaw. Minneapolis: Augsburg 1964.

XI. LUTHERAN WORSHIP, HISTORY, AND INTERPRETATION

Basic Principles for the Ordering of the Main Worship Service in the Evangelical Lutheran Church. Geneva: Lutheran World Federation, 1958.

Brand, Eugene L. *The Rite Thing.* Minneapolis: Augsburg, 1970.

———, ed. *Worship among Lutherans: Northfield Statement on Worship, 1983.* Tantur Report on Worship, 1981. Geneva: Lutheran World Federation, 1983.

Brunner, Peter. *Worship in the Name of Jesus.* Trans. M. H. Bertram. St. Louis: Concordia, 1968.

Bultmann, Rudolf. *Jesus and the Word.* Trans. Louise Smith and Erminie Lantero. New York: Scribner, 1934.

Encountering God: The Legacy of the Lutheran Book of Worship for the 21st Century. Ed. Ralph R. Van Loon. Minneapolis: Kirk, 1998.

Evanson, Charles J. *Evangelicalism and the Liturgical Movement and Their Effects on Lutheran Worship.* St. Louis: Morning Star, 1990.

Hahn, Ferdinand. *The Worship of the Early Church.* Trans. David E. Green. Philadelphia: Fortress, 1973.

Inside Out: Worship in an Age of Mission. Ed. Thomas H. Schattauer. Minneapolis: Fortress, 1999.

Kalb, Friedrich. *Theology of Worship in 17th-century Lutheranism.* St. Louis: Concordia, 1965.

Karant-Nunn, Susan C. *The Reformation of Ritual: An Interpretation of Early Modern Germany.* New York and London: Routledge, 1977.

Lang, Paul H. D. *Ceremony and Celebration.* St. Louis: Concordia, 1965.

Lathrop, Gordon W. *Holy Things: A Liturgical Theology.* Minneapolis: Fortress, 1993.

Leiturgia, Handbuch des evangelischen Gottesdienstes. 5 vols. Kassel: Johannes Stauda Verlag, 1954–1970.

Lietzmann, Hans. *Mass and Lord's Supper: A Study in the History of the Liturgy.* Trans. Dorthea H. G. Reeve. Leiden: Brill, 1979.

Lindemann, Herbert Fred. *The New Mood of Lutheran Worship.* Minneapolis: Augsburg, 1971.

Lutheran Book of Worship. Minneapolis: Augsburg; Philadelphia: Board of Publication of the Lutheran Church in America, 1978

Lutheran Worship: History and Practice. Ed. Fred L. Precht. Commission on Worship of the Lutheran Church-Missouri Synod. St. Louis: Concordia, 1993.

Occasional Services: Lutheran Book of Worship. Minneapolis: Augsburg; Philadelphia: Board of Publication, Lutheran Church in America, 1982.

Pfatteicher, Philip H. *Festivals and Commemorations: Handbook to the Calendar in the Lutheran Book of Worship.* Minneapolis: Augsburg, 1980.

——. *Commentary on the Occasional Services.* Philadelphia: Fortress, 1983.

——. *Commentary on the Lutheran Book of Worship: Lutheran Liturgy in Its Ecumenical Context.* Minneapolis: Augsburg, 1990.

Pfatteicher, Philip H., and Messerli, Carlos. *Manual on the Liturgy: Lutheran Book of Worship.* Minneapolis: Augsburg, 1979.

Piepkorn, Arthur C. *What the Symbolical Books of the Lutheran Church Have to Say about Worship and the Sacraments.* St. Louis: Concordia, 1952.

Precht, Fred L., ed. *Commentary on Lutheran Worship.* St. Louis: Concordia, 1992.

Quill, Timothy C. J. *The Impact of the Liturgical Movement on American Lutheranism.* Lanham, Md., and London: Scarecrow, 1997.

Reed, Luther D. *The Lutheran Liturgy.* 2nd ed. Philadelphia: Fortress, 1959.

Senn, Frank C. *The Pastor As Worship Leader: A Manual for Corporate Worship.* 2nd ed. Minneapolis: Augsburg, 1977.

——. *Luther's Liturgical Criteria and His Reform of the Canon of the Mass.* Grove Liturgical Study No. 30. Bramcote, Nottinghamshire: Grove, 1982.

——. *Christian Worship and Its Cultural Setting.* Philadelphia: Fortress, 1983.

——. *Christian Liturgy, Catholic and Evangelical.* Minneapolis: Fortress, 1997.

Sheppard, Lancelot, ed. *The People Worship: A History of the Liturgical Movement.* New York: Hawthorn, 1967.

Thompson, Bard. *Liturgies of the Western Church.* Cleveland: World, 1961.

Vajta, Vilmos. *Luther on Worship: An Interpretation.* Trans. Ulrich S. Leupold. Philadelphia: Muhlenberg, 1958.

Van Der Pol, G. J. *Martin Bucer's Liturgical Ideas.* Groningen: Van Gorcum, 1954.

Veal, David. *An Essential Unity: A Contemporary Look at Lutheran and Episcopal Liturgies.* Harrisburg, Pa.: Morehouse, 1997.

Worship and Culture in Dialogue: Reports of International Consultations, Cartigny, Switzerland, 1993, and Hong Kong, 1994. Ed. S. Anita Stauffer. Geneva: Department for Theology and Studies, Lutheran World Federation, 1994.

Worship and Ethics: Lutherans and Anglicans in Dialogue. Ed. Oswald Beyer and Alan Suggate. New York and Berlin: Walter de Gruyter, 1996.

XII. LUTHERAN ETHICS

Asheim, Ivar, ed. *Christ and Humanity: A Workshop in Christian Social Ethics.* Philadelphia: Fortress, 1970.

Atkinson, James. "Lutheranism." In *Dictionary of Ethics, Theology, and Society.* Ed. Paul Barry Clarke and Andrew Linzey. New York: Routledge, 1996.

Aulén, Gustaf. *Church, Law, and Society.* New York: Scribner, 1948.

Beach, Waldo, and Niebuhr, H. Richard, eds. *Christian Ethics: Sources of the Living Tradition.* 2nd ed. New York: Ronald, 1973.

Benne Robert. *The Paradoxical Vision: A Public Theology for the 21st Century.* Minneapolis: Fortress, 1995.

———. "The Calling of the Church in Economic Life." In *The Two Cities of God: The Church's Responsibilities for the Earthly City.* Ed. Carl E. Braaten and Robert W. Jenson. Grand Rapids, Mich.: Eerdmans, 1997.

Berggrav, Eivind. *Man and State.* Trans. George Aus. Philadelphia: Muhlenberg, 1951.

Bettenhausen, Elizabeth. "The Concept of Justice and a Feminist Lutheran Social Ethic." In *Annual of the Society of Christian Ethics, 1986.* Ed. Alan B. Anderson. Washington, D.C.: Georgetown University Press, 1987.

Bloomquist, Karen L. *Our Church and Social Issues.* Chicago: Commission for Church in Society, Evangelical Lutheran Church in America, 1989.

———. *The Dream Betrayed: Religious Challenges of the Working-class.* Minneapolis: Fortress, 1990.

Bloomquist, Karen L., and Stumme, John R., eds. *The Promise of Lutheran Ethics.* Minneapolis: Fortress, 1998.

Bonhoeffer, Dietrich. *Ethics.* Ed. Eberhard Bethge, and trans. Neville Horton Smith. New York: Simon & Schuster, 1995.

Braaten, Carl E. *Eschatology and Ethics: Essays on the Theology and Ethics of the Kingdom of God.* Minneapolis: Augsburg, 1974.

Brakenjhielm, Carl Reinhold. *Forgiveness.* Trans. Thor Mall. Minneapolis: Fortress, 1993.

Burtness, James H. *Shaping the Future: The Ethics of Dietrich Bonhoeffer.* Philadelphia: Fortress, 1985.

Buthelezi, Manas. "Theological Grounds for an Ethic of Hope." In *The Challenge of Black Theology in South Africa.* Ed. Basil Moore. Atlanta: John Knox, 1973.

———. "The Theological Meaning of True Humanity." In *The Challenge of Black Theology in South Africa*. Ed. Basil Moore. Atlanta: John Knox, 1973.

Childs, James M. *Faith, Formation, and Decision: Ethics in the Community of Promise*. Minneapolis: Fortress, 1992.

Church and State: A Lutheran Perspective. New York: Commission on Church and State Relations in a Pluralistic Society, Board of Social Ministry, Lutheran Church in America, 1963.

Cranz, Edward F. *An Essay on the Development of Luther's Thought on Justice, Law, and Society*. Ed. Gerald Christianson and Thomas M. Izbicki. Mifflintown, Pa.: Sigler, 1997.

Duchrow, Ulrich. *Two Kingdoms: The Use and Misuse of a Lutheran Theological Concept*. Geneva: Lutheran World Federation, 1977.

Elert, Werner. *The Christian Ethos*. Trans. Carl. J. Schindler. Philadelphia: Muhlenberg, 1957.

Ellingsen, Mark. *The Cutting Edge: How Churches Speak on Social Issues*. Grand Rapids, Mich.: Eerdmans, 1993.

Forell, George W. *Faith Active in Love: An Investigation of the Principles Underlying Luther's Social Ethics*. New York: American, 1954.

———. *Ethics of Decision: An Introduction to Christian Ethics*. Philadelphia: Muhlenberg, 1955.

———, ed. *Christian Social Teachings: A Reader in Christian Social Ethics from the Bible to the Present*. Garden City, N.Y.: Doubleday, 1966.

Frostin, Per. *Luther's Two Kingdoms Doctrine: A Critical Study*. Malmö: Lund University Press, 1994.

Gluchman, Vasil. *Slovak Lutheran Social Ethics*. Lewiston, N.Y.: Mellen, 1997.

Gomez, Medardo Ernesto. *And the Word Became History: Messages Forged in the Fires of Central American Conflict*. Trans. Robert F. Gussick. Minneapolis: Augsburg, 1992.

Hefner, Philip. *Theological Perspectives on Social Ministry*. New York: Board of Social Ministry, Lutheran Church in America, 1968

Hertz, Karl H., ed. *Two Kingdoms and One World: A Sourcebook in Christian Social Ethics*. Minneapolis: Augsburg, 1976.

Hoefer, Herbert E. *Church-State-Society: Issues of Mission in India from the Perspective of Luther's Two-kingdom Principle*. The Abraham Malpan Lectures, 1981. Madras: The Christian Literature Society, 1982.

Jacobsen, H. K. "Lutheran Ethics." In *New Dictionary of Christian Ethics and Pastoral Theology*. Ed. David J. Atkinson and David H. Field. Downers Grove, Ill: InterVarsity, 1995.

Jenson, Robert. *Essays in Theology of Culture*. Grand Rapids, Mich.: Eerdmans, 1995.

Jersild, Paul T. *Making Moral Decisions: A Christian Approach to Personal and Social Ethics*. Minneapolis: Fortress, 1990.

———. *Spirit Ethics: Scripture and the Moral Life*. Minneapolis: Fortress, 2000.

Jüngel, Eberhard. *Christ, Justice, and Peace: Toward a Theology of the State*. Trans. D. Bruce Hamill and Alan J. Torrance. Edinburgh: Clark, 1995.

Justification and Justice: A Meeting of Lutheran Theologians of the Americas. Minneapolis: American Lutheran Church, 1985.

Kersten, Lawrence K. *The Lutheran Ethic: The Impact of Religion on Laymen and Clergy*. Detroit: Wayne State University Press, 1970.

Klein, Christa, and Von Dehsen, Christian D. *Politics and Policy: The Genesis and Theology of Social Statements in the Lutheran Church in America.* Philadelphia: Fortress, 1989.

Lazareth, William H. *Luther on the Christian Home: An Application of the Social Ethics of the Reformation.* Philadelphia: Muhlenberg, 1960.

———. *A Theology of Politics.* New York: Board of Social Missions, Lutheran Church in America, 1960.

———. "Luther's Two Kingdoms Ethic Reconsidered." In *Christian Social Ethics in a Changing World.* Ed. John C. Bennett. New York: Association Press, 1966.

———. "Lutheran Ethics." In *The Westminster Dictionary of Christian Ethics.* Ed. James F. Childress and John Macquarrie. Philadelphia: Westminster, 1986.

Lazareth, William H., and Krodel, Gerhard A., eds. *The Left Hand of God: Essays on Discipleship and Patriotism.* Philadelphia: Fortress, 1976.

Lehmann, Paul L. *The Decalogue and a Human Future: The Meaning of the Commandments for Making and Keeping Human Life Human.* Grand Rapids, Mich.: Eerdmans, 1995.

Life and Death: Moral Implications of Biotechnology. Ed. Viggo Mortensen. Geneva: Published for the Lutheran World Federation by WCC Publications, 1995.

Lindbeck, George. "Modernity and Luther's Understanding of the Freedom of the Christian." In *Martin Luther and the Modern Mind: Freedom, Conscience, Toleration, Rights.* Ed. Manfred Hoffmann. Lewiston, N.Y.: Mellen, 1985.

Lindberg, Carter, ed. *Piety, Politics, and Ethics: Reformation Studies in Honor of George Wolfgang Forell.* 3rd ed. Sixteenth Century Essays and Studies. Kirksville, Mo.: SCJ Publishers, 1984.

———. *Beyond Charity: Reformation Initiatives for the Poor.* Minneapolis: Fortress, 1993.

Lissner, Jørgen, and Arne Sovik, eds. *A Lutheran Reader on Human Rights.* Geneva: Lutheran World Federation, 1978.

Løgstrup, Knud E. *The Ethical Demand.* Trans. Theodor I. Jensen. Philadelphia: Fortress, 1971.

Lønning, Per. *Creation—An Ecumenical Challenge? Reflections Issuing from a Study by the Institute for Ecumenical Research, Strasbourg, France.* Macon, Ga.: Mercer University Press, 1989.

Lorenz, Eckehart, ed. *How Christian Are Human Rights?* Geneva: Lutheran World Federation, 1980.

———, ed. *The Debate on Status Confessionis: Studies in Christian Political Theology.* Geneva: Lutheran World Federation, 1983.

Luecke, Richard. *New Meanings for New Beings.* Philadelphia: Fortress, 1964.

Lund, N. J. "Lutheran Ethics." In *Encyclopedia of Biblical and Christian Ethics.* Rev. ed. Ed. R. K. Harrison. Nashville: Thomas Nelson, 1992.

Lutheran Churches, Salt or Mirror of Society? Case Studies on the Theory and Practice of the Two Kingdoms Doctrine. Ed. Ulrich Duchrow, in collaboration with Dorothea Millwood. Geneva: Department of Studies, Lutheran World Federation, 1977.

Mortensen, Viggo, ed. *Justification and Justice.* Geneva: Lutheran World Federation, 1992.

———, ed. *Concern for Creation: Voices on the Theology of Creation.* Sweden: Svenska kyrkan, Forskningsrad, 1995.

Mühlen, Karl-Heinz zur. "Two Kingdoms." In *The Oxford Encyclopedia of the Reformation*. Ed. Hans J. Hillerbrand. New York: Oxford University Press, 1996.

Nolde, O. Frederick. *The Churches and the Nations*. Philadelphia: Fortress, 1970.

Nygren, Anders. *Agape and Eros*. Trans. Philip S. Watson. Philadelphia: Westminster, 1953.

Pannenberg, Wolfhart. "The Kingdom of God and the Foundation of Ethics." In *Theology and the Kingdom of God*. Ed. Richard John Neuhaus. Philadelphia: Westminster, 1969.

———. *Ethics*. Trans. Keith Crim. Philadelphia: Westminster, 1981.

Pasewark, Kyle A. *A Theology of Power: Being beyond Domination*. Minneapolis: Fortress, 1993.

Pelikan Jaroslav. "Justitia as Justice and Justitia as Righteousness." In *Law and Theology*. Ed. Andrew J. Buehner. St. Louis: Concordia Historical Institute, 1965.

Rasmussen, Larry L. "Moral Community and Moral Formation." In *Ecclesiology and Ethics: Costly Commitment*. Ed. Thomas F. Best and Martin Robra. Geneva: World Council of Churches, 1995.

———. *Earth Community, Earth Ethics*. Maryknoll: Orbis, 1996.

Rendtorff, Trutz. "Institutions as a Socio-ethical Problem." In *Faith and Society: Toward a Contemporary Social Ethics*. Supplement to *Lutheran World* 2 (1966): 34–47.

———. *Ethics 1: Basic Elements and Methodology in an Ethical Theology*. Vol. 2, *Applications of an Ethical Theology*. Trans. Keith Crim. Philadelphia: Fortress, 1986.

Reumann, John, and Lazareth, William. *Righteousness and Society: Ecumenical Dialog in a Revolutionary Age*. Philadelphia: Fortress, 1967.

Scharlemann, Martin H. *The Church's Social Responsibilities*. St. Louis: Concordia, 1971.

Schneider, Edward D. "Lutheran Theological Foundations for Social Ethics." *LWF Documentation* 29 (December 1990): 15–24.

Schroeder, Steven. *A Community and a Perspective: Lutheran Peace Fellowship and the Edge of the Church*. Lanham, Md.: University Press of America, 1993.

Sherman, Franklin. "The Church and the Proximate Goals of History." In *Christian Hope and the Future of Humanity*. Ed. Franklin Sherman. Minneapolis: Augsburg, 1969.

———. "Secular Calling and Social Ethical Thinking." In *The Lutheran Church Past and Present*. Ed. Vilmos Vajta. Minneapolis: Augsburg, 1977.

Sittler, Joseph. "Secularization as an Ethical Problem." In *Faith and Society: Toward a Contemporary Social Ethics*. Supplement to *Lutheran World* 2 (1966): 15–20.

———. *The Structure of Christian Ethics*. Louisville, Ky.: Westminster/John Knox, 1998.

Søe, Niels Hansen. "Natural Law and Social Ethics." In *Christian Social Ethics in a Changing World*. Ed. John C. Bennett. New York: Association Press, 1966.

Solberg, Richard W. *God and Caesar in East Germany: The Conflicts of Church and State in East Germany since 1945*. New York: Macmillan, 1961.

Stortz, Martha Ellen. "Ethics, Conservation, and Theology in Ecological Perspective." In *Covenant for a New Creation*. Ed. Carol S. Robb and Carl J. Casebolt. Maryknoll, N.Y.: Orbis, 1991.

Stumme, Wayne, ed. *Christians and the Many Faces of Marxism*. Minneapolis: Augsburg, 1984.

Thielicke, Helmut. *Theological Ethics*. 2 vols. Ed. William H. Lazareth. Philadelphia: Fortress, 1966, 1969.

Towards a Theology of Human Development. Delhi: Published for the Gurukul Lutheran Theological College and Research Institute by the Indian Society for Promoting Christian Knowledge, 1998.

Trillhaas, Wolfgang. "The Contribution of Lutheranism to Social Ethics Today: A Critique and a Program." In *Faith and Society: Toward a Contemporary Social Ethics.* Supplement to *Lutheran World* 2 (1966): 48–65.

Troeltsch, Ernst. *The Social Teaching of the Christian Churches.* Trans. Olive Wyon. New York: Harper and Row, 1960.

Two Cities of God: The Church's Responsibilities for the Earthly City. Ed. Carl E. Braaten and Robert W. Jenson. Grand Rapids, Mich.: Eerdmans, 1997.

Wee, Paul A. *Systemic Injustice and the Biblical Witness.* Geneva: Lutheran World Federation, 1984.

Wingren, Gustaf. *Luther on Vocation.* Philadelphia: Muhlenberg, 1957.

———. *Creation and Law.* Trans. Ross Mackenzie. Philadelphia: Muhlenberg, 1961.

XIII. MISSION AND EVANGELISM

Anderson, Oscar A. *Baptism and its Relation to Lutheran Evangelism.* Minneapolis: Augsburg, 1955.

Briese, Russel J. *Foundations of a Lutheran Theology of Evangelism.* New York and Frankfurt/Main: Lang, 1994.

Burgess, Andrew S., ed. *Lutheran Churches in the Third World.* Minneapolis: Augsburg, 1970.

China and Christian Mission: Three Papers and Summaries of Discussion from a Consultation on the Significance of the New China for Christian World Mission, Held in St. Paul, Minnesota, USA, May 31 to June 2, 1976. Ed. Arne Sovik. Geneva: Department of Studies, Lutheran World Federation, 1977.

The Continuing Frontier: Evangelism. New York: Division for World Mission and Ecumenism, Lutheran Church in America, 1984.

Currens, Gerald E. *Empowerment for Change: Strategy for Mission.* New York: Division for World Mission, Lutheran Church in America, 1986.

Empie, Paul C. *Christian World Mission in World Revolution.* New York: National Lutheran Council, 1962.

Gensichen, Hans-Werner. *Living Mission: The Test of Faith.* Philadelphia: Fortress, 1966.

Hedin, Arnold M., ed. *The Latin American Lutheran Mission: Pioneering in Colombia and Mexico.* N.p.: n.p., 1987.

Kolb, Robert. *Speaking the Gospel Today: A Theology for Evangelism.* Rev. ed. St. Louis: Concordia, 1995.

Lazareth, William H., and Rasolondraibe, Péri. *Lutheran Identity and Mission: Evangelical and Evangelistic?* Minneapolis: Fortress, 1994.

Luecke, David S. *Evangelical Style and Lutheran Substance: Facing America's Mission Challenge.* St. Louis: Concordia, 1988.

Mission Today: Challenges and Concerns. Ed. Abraham P. Athyal and Dorothy Yoder Nyce. Chennai: Gurukul Lutheran Theological College and Research Institute, 1998.

Neve, Herbert T. *Sources for Change: Searching for Flexible Church Structures. A Contribution to the Ecumenical Discussion on the Structures of the Missionary Congregation by the Commission on Stewardship and Evangelism of the Lutheran World Federation.* Geneva: World Council of Churches, 1968.

Scherer, James. *Mission and Unity in Lutheranism.* Philadelphia: Fortress, 1969.

——. *That the Gospel May Be Sincerely Preached throughout the World: A Lutheran Perspective on Mission and Evangelism in the 20th Century.* Stuttgart: Kreuz Verlag, 1982.

Scudieri, Robert L. *Apostolic Church: One, Holy, Catholic, and Missionary.* Fort Wayne, Ind.: Lutheran Society for Missiology, 1996.

Simensen, Jarle, ed. *Norwegian Missions in African History.* 2 vols. New York: Oxford University Press, 1986.

Spies, Karen B. *Visiting the Global Village. Evangelical Lutheran Church in America Global Mission.* Minneapolis: Augsburg Fortress, 1992.

Stavanger 1982. LWF Interregional Consultation on Mission and Evangelism. Geneva: Lutheran World Federation, 1983.

Thomsen, Mark W. *The Word and the Way of the Cross: Christian Witness among Muslim and Buddhist People.* Chicago: Division for Global Mission, Evangelical Lutheran Church in America, 1993.

Women in Global Mission: An Oral History. 34 vols. and supplement. Chicago: Evangelical Lutheran Church in America, 1993.

XIV. LUTHERANISM AND ECUMENISM

A. General

Braaten, Carl E. *Mother Church: Ecclesiology and Ecumenism.* Minneapolis: Fortress, 1998.

Burgess, Joseph A., ed. *In Search of Christian Unity: Basic Consensus, Basic Differences.* Minneapolis: Fortress, 1991.

Ecumenism, a Lutheran Commitment: An Official Statement of the Lutheran Church in America. New York: Division for World Mission and Ecumenism, Lutheran Church in America, 1982.

Elert, Werner. *Eucharist and Church Fellowship in the First Four Centuries.* Trans. Norman E. Nagel. St. Louis: Concordia, 1966.

Flesner, Dorris A. *American Lutherans Help Shape World Council: The Role of the Lutheran Churches of America in the Formation of the World Council of Churches.* St. Louis: Lutheran Historical Conference, 1981.

Function of Doctrine and Theology in Light of the Unity of the Church. A Report plus 15 Papers from an Official Study Conducted by the Division of Theological Studies, Lutheran Council in the USA, 1972–1977. New York: Division of Theological Studies, Lutheran Council in the USA, 1978.

Gritsch, Eric W., ed. "Luther, the Church and Christian Unity" and "Luther and the Christian Tradition." In *Encounters with Luther.* Vol. 3. Gettysburg: Institute for Luther Studies, 1986.

Growth in Ecumenical Commitment, Experiences and Perspectives: Report of the Consultation on the Ecumenical Orientation and Work of the LWF, 1983. Geneva: Lutheran World Federation, 1984.

International Consultation on Ecumenical Methodology (1976: Geneva). *Ecumenical Methodology: Documentation and Report.* Ed. Peder Højen. Geneva: Lutheran World Federation, 1978.

Ishida, Yoshiro, Meyer, Harding, and Perret, Edmond. *The History and Theological Concerns of World Confessional Families.* Stuttgart: Kreuz Verlag, 1979.

Rusch, William G. *Ecumenism: A Movement toward Church Unity.* Philadelphia: Fortress, 1985.

Seils, Michael. *Lutheran Convergence?: An Analysis of the Lutheran Responses to the Convergence Document "Baptism, Eucharist and Ministry" of the World Council of Churches Faith and Order Commission.* Geneva: Lutheran World Federation, 1988.

Skydsgaard, K. E. *One in Christ.* Trans. Axel C. Kildegaard. Philadelphia: Muhlenberg, 1957.

B. Lutheran World Federation

Assembly of the Lutheran World Federation. *The Proceedings of the (First) Lutheran World Federation Assembly, Lund, Sweden, June 30–July 6, 1947.* Philadelphia: United Lutheran Publication House, 1948.

——. *The Proceedings of the Second Assembly of the Lutheran World Federation, Hannover, Germany, July 25–August 3, 1952.* Geneva: Lutheran World Federation, 1952.

——. *The Proceedings of the Third Assembly of the Lutheran World Federation, Minneapolis, MN, August 15–25, 1957.* Minneapolis: Augsburg, 1958.

——. *Proceedings of the Fourth Assembly of the Lutheran World Federation, Helsinki, July 30–August 11, 1963.* Berlin: Lutherisches Verlagshaus, 1965.

——. *Sent into the World: The Proceedings of the Fifth Assembly of the Lutheran World Federation, Evian, France, July 14–24, 1970.* Minneapolis: Augsburg, 1971.

——. *In Christ, a New Community: The Proceedings of the Sixth Assembly of the Lutheran World Federation, Dar es Salaam, Tanzania, June 13–25, 1977.* Geneva: Lutheran World Federation, 1977.

——. *In Christ—Hope for the World: Official Proceedings of the Seventh Assembly of the Lutheran World Federation, Budapest, Hungary, July 22–August 5, 1984.* Geneva: Lutheran World Federation, 1985.

——. *I Have Heard the Cry of My People: Proceedings, the Eight Assembly, Lutheran World Federation, Curitiba, Brazil, January 29–February 8, 1990.* Geneva: Lutheran World Federation, 1990.

——. *In Christ—Called to Witness: Official Report of the Ninth Assembly of the Lutheran World Federation, Hong Kong, 8–16 July 1997.* Geneva: Lutheran World Federation, 1997.

Brand, Eugene. *Toward a Lutheran Communion: Pulpit and Altar Fellowship.* Geneva: Lutheran World Federation, 1988.

The Debate on Status Confessionis: Studies in Christian Political Theology. Ed. Eckehart Lorenz. Geneva: Department of Studies, Lutheran World Federation, 1983.

Duchrow, Ulrich. *Conflict over the Ecumenical Movement: Confessing Christ Today in the Universal Church.* Trans. David Lewis. Geneva: World Council of Churches, 1981.

From Federation to Communion: The History of the Lutheran World Federation. Ed. Jens Holger Schjørring, Prasanna Kumari, and Norman A. Hjelm. Minneapolis: Fortress, 1997.

Hellberg, Carl J. *A Voice of the Voiceless: The Involvement of the Lutheran World Federation in Southern Africa, 1947–1977.* Stockholm: Skeab/Verbum, 1979.

Holze, Heinrich, ed. *The Church as Communion: Lutheran Contributions to Ecclesiology.* Geneva: Lutheran World Federation, 1997.

Justification in the World's Context. (Most of the papers in this book were presented at a Lutheran World Federation consultation in Wittenberg, Germany, October 1998.) Lutheran World Federation Documentation No. 45. Ed. Wolfgang Greive. Geneva: Department for Theology and Studies, Lutheran World Federation, 2000.

Justification Today: Studies and Reports. Lutheran World. Supplement to No. 1. Geneva: Lutheran World Federation, 1965.

Lutheran Ecumenism on the Way. Lutheran World Federation Documentation 32. Institute for Ecumenical Research, Strasbourg. Geneva: Lutheran World Federation, 1993.

Lutz, Charles P. *Abounding in Hope: A Family of Faith at Work through the Lutheran World Federation.* Minneapolis: Augsburg, 1985.

Martensen, Daniel F. *The Federation and the World Council of Churches.* Stuttgart: Kreuz Verlag, 1978.

Prehistory of the Lutheran World Federation: List of Material in Archives in Europe and the USA. Geneva: Lutheran World Federation, 1968ff.

Self-understanding and Ecumenical Role of the Lutheran World Federation: Report of a Study Process 1979–1982. Geneva: Lutheran World Federation, 1984.

Thekaekava, Marie M. *Fireflies in the Night: Glimpses of the Lutheran World Service, 1975–1982.* Calcutta: Christ's Disciples' Media, 1983.

Vajta, Vilmos. *From Generation to Generation: The Lutheran World Federation, 1947–1982.* Ed. Gertraut Hobby and Frances Maher. Stuttgart: Kreuz Verlag, 1983.

C. Bilateral Dialogues and Relations

1. Dialogue Reports (Selection)

a. Lutheran-Anglican

Anglican-Lutheran Commission. *Anglican-Lutheran International Conversations: The Report of the Conversations, 1970–1972, Authorized by the Lambeth Conference and the Lutheran World Federation.* London: SPCK, 1973.

Anglican-Lutheran Dialogue: The Report of the Anglican-Lutheran European Regional Commission, Helsinki, August–September 1982. London: SPCK, 1983.

Anglican-Lutheran International Continuation Committee. *The Niagara Report: Report of the Anglican-Lutheran Consultation on Episcope, Niagara Falls, September, 1987.* London: Church, 1988.

Called to Common Mission: A Lutheran Proposal for a Revision of the Concordat of Agreement. Chicago: Evangelical Lutheran Church in America, 1998.

Church of England. Board for Missions and Unity. *On the Way to Visible Unity, Meissen, 1988: Relations between the Church of England, the Federation of the Evangelical Churches in the German Democratic Republic, and the Evangelical Church in Germany in the Federal Republic of Germany.* London: General Synod of the Church of England, 1988.

The Church of England and the Churches of Norway, Denmark, and Iceland: Report of the Committee Appointed by the Archbishop of Canterbury in 1951; in Pursuance of Resolution 72 of the Lambeth Conference 1948 on the Relations of the Churches of Norway, Denmark, and Iceland with the Anglican Communion; with Three Appendices. London: SPCK, 1952.

Lutheran-Episcopal Dialogue. *The Report of the Lutheran-Episcopal Dialogue, 2nd Series, 1976–1980.* Cincinnati: Forward Movement Publications, 1981.

Lutheran-Episcopal Dialogue (1983–1991). *Implications of the Gospel: Lutheran-Episcopal Dialogue, 3rd Series.* Ed. William A. Norgren and William G. Rusch. Minneapolis: Augsburg, 1988.

Lutheran-Episcopal Dialogue (1983–1991). *"Toward Full Communion" and "Concordat of Agreement": Lutheran-Episcopal Dialogue, 3rd Series.* Ed. William A. Norgren and William G. Rusch. Minneapolis: Augsburg, 1991.

Lutheran-Episcopal Dialogue: A Progress Report. Cincinnati: Forward Movement Publications, 1972.

Together in Mission and Ministry: The Porvoo Common Statement. London: Church, 1993.

b. Lutheran-Baptist

Baptist-Lutheran Joint Commission. *Baptists and Lutherans in Conversation: A Message to Our Churches.* Geneva: Baptist World Alliance and Lutheran World Federation, 1990.

c. Lutheran-Methodist

Lutheran-Methodist Joint Commission. *The Church: Community of Grace.* Geneva and Lake Junaluska: Lutheran World Federation and World Methodist Council, 1984.

Tuell, Jack M., and Fjeld, Roger W., eds. *Episcopacy: Lutheran-United Methodist Dialogue.* Minneapolis: Augsburg, 1991.

d. Lutheran-Orthodox

Finnish Lutheran-Orthodox Dialogue, 1989–1990. Helsinki: Church Council for Foreign Affairs, 1993.

Finnish Lutheran-Orthodox Dialogue: Conversations in 1991 and 1993. Helsinki: Church Council for Foreign Affairs, 1995.

Lutheran-Orthodox Joint Commission. *Agreed Statements, 1985–1989: Divine Revelation, Scripture and Tradition, Canon and Inspiration.* Geneva: Lutheran World Federation, 1992.

Salvation in Christ: A Lutheran-Orthodox Dialogue. Ed. John Meyendorff and Robert Tobias. Minneapolis: Augsburg, 1992.

e. Lutheran-Reformed

A Common Calling: The Report of the Lutheran-Reformed Committee for Theological Conversations, 1988–1992. Minneapolis: Augsburg, 1993.

Agreement between Reformation Churches in Europe (Leuenberg Agreement, 1973). Frankfurt/Main: Otto Lembeck, 1993.

Andrews, James E., and Burgess, Joseph A., eds. *An Invitation to Action: A Study of Ministry, Sacraments, and Recognition.* Philadelphia: Fortress, 1984.

Empie, Paul C., and McCord, James I., eds. *Marburg Revisited: A Reexamination of Lutheran and Reformed Traditions.* Minneapolis: Augsburg, 1966.

Lutheran-Reformed Joint Commission. *Toward Church Fellowship: Report of the Joint Commission.* Geneva: Lutheran World Federation and World Alliance of Reformed Churches, 1989.

f. Lutheran-Roman Catholic

Anderson, George H., Murphy, Austin T., and Burgess, Joseph A., eds. *Justification by Faith.* Minneapolis: Augsburg, 1985.

Anderson, George H., Stafford, Francis J., and Burgess, Joseph A., eds. *The One Mediator, the Saints, and Mary.* Minneapolis: Augsburg, 1992.

Burgess, Joseph A., et al., eds. *The Word of God: Scripture and Tradition.* Minneapolis: Augsburg, 1993.

Empie, Paul C., and Murphy, Austin T., eds. *Lutherans and Catholics in Dialogue.* 3 vols. Minneapolis: Augsburg, 1974.

——, eds. *Papal Primacy and the Universal Church.* Minneapolis: Augsburg, 1974.

Empie, Paul C., Murphy, Austin T., and Burgess, Joseph A., eds. *Teaching Authority and Infallibility in the Church.* Minneapolis: Augsburg, 1980.

Joint Declaration on the Doctrine of Justification by the Lutheran World Federation and the Catholic Church: Together with Official Common Statement and Annex to the Official Common Statement. Geneva: Lutheran World Federation, 1999.

Joint Lutheran/Roman Catholic Study Commission. *The Gospel and the Church.* Geneva: Lutheran World Federation, 1972.

Lutheran/Roman Catholic Joint Commission. *Church and Justification: Understanding the Church in the Light of the Doctrine of Justification.* Geneva: Lutheran World Federation, 1994.

Lutheran/Roman Catholic Joint Commission. *The Eucharist.* Geneva: Lutheran World Federation, 1980.

Roman Catholic/Lutheran Joint Commission. *Facing Unity: Models, Forms, and Phases of Catholic-Lutheran Church Fellowship.* Geneva: Lutheran World Federation, 1985.

Roman Catholic/Lutheran Joint Commission. *The Ministry in the Church.* Geneva: Lutheran World Federation, 1982.

Roman Catholic/Lutheran Joint Commission. *Ways to Community.* Geneva: Lutheran World Federation, 1981.

Scripture and Tradition. Ed. Harold C. Skillrud, F. Francis Stafford, Daniel F. Martensen. Minneapolis: Augsburg, 1995.

g. Other Dialogue Reports

Chandran, J. R. *The C.S.I.–Lutheran Theological Conversations, 1948–1959: A Selection of the Papers Read, Together with the Agreed Statements and an Introduction.* Madras: Christian Literature Society, 1964.

Following Our Shepherd to Full Communion: Report of the Lutheran-Moravian Dialogue with Recommendations for Full Communion in Worship, Fellowship, and Mission. Chicago: Evangelical Lutheran Church in America, 1998.

Rajaiah, Paul D., and Kumaresan, J. *Church of South India-Lutheran Conversations: A Historical Sketch.* Madras: Christian Literature Society, 1970.

Stages on the Way: Documents from the Bilateral Conversations between Churches in Australia. Ed. Raymond K. Willliamson. Melbourne: Joint Board of Christian Education, 1994 (with several Lutheran dialogue reports).

2. Publications about Dialogues and Relations

Anderson, George H., and Crumley, James R. Jr., eds. *Promoting Unity: Themes in Lutheran-Catholic Dialogue.* Minneapolis: Augsburg, 1989.

Anglican-Lutheran Relations: Report [of the] Anglican-Lutheran Joint Working Group, Cold Ash, Berkshire, England, 28 November–3 December 1983. Geneva: Lutheran World Federation, 1983.

Burgess, Joseph A., ed. *Lutherans in Ecumenical Dialogue: A Reappraisal.* Minneapolis: Augsburg, 1990.

Burgess, Joseph A., and Gros, Jeffrey, eds. *Growing Consensus: Church Dialogues in the United States, 1962–1991.* New York: Paulist, 1995.

Burgess, Joseph A., and Lindbeck, George, eds. *The Role of the Augsburg Confession: Catholic and Lutheran Views.* Philadelphia: Fortress, 1980.

Dialogue on the Way: Protestants Report from Rome on the Vatican Council. Ed. George A. Lindbeck. Minneapolis: Augsburg, 1965.

Ecumenical Relations of the Lutheran World Federation: Report of the Working Group on the Interrelations between the Various Bilateral Dialogues. Geneva: Lutheran World Federation, 1977.

Fackre, Gabriel J., and Root, Michael. *Affirmations and Admonitions: Lutheran Decisions and Dialogue with Reformed, Episcopal, and Roman Catholic Churches.* Grand Rapids, Mich.: Eerdmans, 1998.

Lehmann, Karl, ed. *Justification by Faith: Do the 16th-century Condemnations Still Apply?* Trans. Michael Root and William G. Rusch. New York: Continuum, 1996.

Lehmann, Karl, and Pannenberg, Wolfhart, eds. *The Condemnations of the Reformation Era: Do They Still Divide?* Trans. Margaret Kohl. Minneapolis: Fortress, 1990.

Lutheran-Catholic Quest for Visible Unity: Harvesting Thirty Years of Dialogue—An Educational Paper Prepared by the Lutheran-Roman Catholic Coordinating Committee. Washington, D.C.: United States Catholic Conference, 1998.

Martensen, Daniel F., ed. *Concordat of Agreement: Supporting Essays.* Minneapolis: Augsburg; Cincinnati: Forward Movement Publications, 1995.

Marty, Myron A. *Lutherans and Roman Catholicism: The Changing Conflict, 1917–1963.* Notre Dame: University of Notre Dame Press, 1968.

Meyer, Harding, ed. *Lutheran-Roman Catholic Discussion on the Augsburg Confession: Documents, 1977–1981.* Stuttgart: Kreuz Verlag, 1982.

O'Callaghan, Paul. *Fides Christi: The Justification Debate.* Dublin, Ireland, and Portland, Oreg.: Four Courts, 1997.

Radner, Ephraim, and Reno, R. R., eds. *Inhabiting Unity: Theological Perspectives on the Proposed Lutheran-Episcopal Concordat.* Grand Rapids, Mich.: Eerdmans, 1995.

Rusch, William G. *Reception: An Ecumenical Opportunity.* Geneva: Lutheran World Federation, 1988.

Rusch, William G., and Martensen, Daniel F., eds. *The Leuenberg Agreement and Lutheran-Reformed Relationships: Evaluations by North American and European Theologians.* Minneapolis: Augsburg, 1989.

Saarinen, Risto. *Faith and Holiness: Lutheran-Orthodox Dialogue, 1959–1994.* Göttingen: Vandenhoeck and Ruprecht, 1997.

Tobias, Robert. *Heaven on Earth: A Lutheran-Orthodox Odyssey.* Delhi, N.Y.: ALPB Books, 1996.

Turnquist, Arlynne C. *A Lutheran-Episcopal Vision and Practicum.* Saint Paul: Turnquist, 1997.

D. Dialogue and Relations with Other Religions

Christian-Muslim Dialogue: Theological and Practical Issues. Ed. Roland E. Miller and Hance A. O. Mwakabana. Geneva: Lutheran World Federation, 1999.

Christian Witness and the Jewish People: The Report of a Consultation Held under the Auspices of the Lutheran World Federation, Oslo, August 1975. Ed. Arne Sovik. Geneva: Department of Studies, Lutheran World Federation, 1976.

Ditmanson, Harold H., ed. *Stepping-stones to Further Jewish-Lutheran Relationships: Key Lutheran Statements.* Minneapolis: Augsburg, 1990.

Halpaerin, Jean, and Sovik, Arne, eds. *Luther, Lutheranism, and the Jews: A Record of the Second Consultation between Representatives of the International Jewish Committee for Interreligious Consultations and the Lutheran World Federation Held in Stockholm, Sweden, 11–13 July 1983.* Geneva: Lutheran World Federation, 1984.

Opsahl, Paul D., and Tanenbaum, Marc H., eds. *Speaking of God Today: Jews and Lutherans in Conversation.* Philadelphia: Fortress, 1974.

Rajashekar, Paul J., ed. *Christian-Muslim Relations in Eastern Africa: Report of a Seminar/Workshop Sponsored by the Lutheran World Federation and the Project for Christian-Muslim Relations in Africa, Nairobi, May 2–8, 1987.* Geneva: Lutheran World Federation, 1988.

Rajashekar, Paul J., and Wilson, H. S., eds. *Islam in Asia—Perspectives for Christian-Muslim Encounter: Report of a Consultation Sponsored by the Lutheran World Federation and the World Alliance of Reformed Churches, Bangkok, June 11–15, 1991.* Geneva: Lutheran World Federation, 1992.

The Significance of Judaism for the Life and Mission of the Church: Report of the Fourth International Consultation on the Church and the Jewish People, Held under the Auspices of the Lutheran World Federation, Division of Studies. Geneva: Lutheran World Federation, 1983.

Theological Perspectives on Other Faiths: Toward a Christian Theology of Religions. Lutheran World Federation Documentation No. 41. Geneva: Lutheran World Federation, 1997.

XV. THE CHRISTIAN LIFE

A. General

Avery, William O. *Empowered Laity: The Story of the Lutheran Laity Movement for Stewardship.* Minneapolis: Augsburg Fortress, 1997.

Benne, Robert. *Ordinary Saints: An Introduction to the Christian Life*. Philadelphia: Fortress, 1988.

Contemporary Reflections on the Faith of Our Mothers and Fathers. Ed. M. Mani Chacko. Madras: Gurukul Lutheran Theological College and Research Institute, 1994.

Erlander, Daniel. *Baptized We Live: Lutheranism as a Way of Life*. Chelan, Wash: Holden Village, 1981.

God's Woman for all Generations: A Report of the President's Commission on Women. Lutheran Church-Missouri Synod. St. Louis: President's Commission on Women, 1987.

In Search of a Round Table: Gender, Theology, and Church Leadership. Ed. Musimbi R. A. Kanyoro. Geneva: Published for the Lutheran World Federation by WCC Publications, 1997.

Kolb, Robert. *For All the Saints: Changing Perceptions of Martyrdom and Sainthood in the Lutheran Reformation*. Macon: Mercer University Press, 1987.

We Are Witnesses: Platform for Action from the LWF International Consultation on Women, 22–28 October 1995, Geneva, Switzerland. Geneva: Lutheran World Federation, 1995.

Wicks, Jared. *Luther and His Spiritual Legacy*. Wilmington, Del.: Glazier, 1983.

B. Piety/Spirituality

Antola, Markku. *Experience of Christ's Real Presence in Faith: An Analysis of the Christ-Presence-Motif in the Lutheran Charismatic Renewal*. Helsinki: Luther-Agricola-Society, 1998.

Arden, Gothard E. *Four Northern Lights: Men Who Shaped Scandinavian Churches*. Minneapolis: Augsburg, 1964.

Burgess, Faith. *Prayer and Piety*. Collegeville, Mich.: Institute for Spirituality, St. John's University, 1978.

Erb, Peter C., ed. *Pietists: Selected Writings*. Classics of Western Spirituality. New York: Paulist, 1983.

Hanson, Bradley. *A Graceful Life: Lutheran Spirituality for Today*. Minneapolis: Augsburg, 2000.

Hoffman, Bengt. "Lutheran Spirituality." In *Spiritual Traditions for the Contemporary Church*. Ed. R. Maas and G. O'Donnell. Nashville: Abingdon, 1990.

Koenig, John. *Charismata: God's Gifts for God's People*. Philadelphia: Westminster, 1978.

Lewis, Arthur J. *Zinzendorf, the Ecumenical Pioneer: A Study in the Moravian Contribution to Christian Mission and Unity*. Philadelphia: Westminster, 1962.

Longenecker, Stephen L. *Piety and Tolerance: Pennsylvania German Religion, 1700–1850*. Metuchen, N.J., and London: Scarecrow, 1994.

Lund, Eric. *Johann Arndt and the Development of a Lutheran Spiritual Tradition*. Ph.D. diss., Yale University, 1979.

McGrath, Alister E. *Roots That Refresh: A Celebration of Reformation Spirituality*. London: Hodder and Stoughton, 1992.

Nodtvedt, Magnus. *Rebirth of Norway's Peasantry: Folk Leader Hans Nielsen Hauge*. Tacoma: Pacific Lutheran University Press, 1965.

Ozment, Steven E. *Homo Spiritualis: A Comparative Study of the Anthropology of Johannes Tauler, Jean Gerson, and Martin Luther (1509–1516) in the Context of Their Theological Thought.* Leiden: Brill, 1969.

Pannenberg, Wolfhart. *Christian Spirituality.* Philadelphia: Westminster, 1983.

Sager, Allan H. *Gospel-centered Spirituality: An Introduction to Our Spiritual Journey.* Minneapolis: Augsburg, 1990.

Senn, Frank C. "Lutheran Spirituality." In *Protestant Spiritual Traditions.* Ed. Frank C. Senn. New York: Paulist, 1986.

———, ed. *Protestant Spiritual Traditions.* New York: Paulist, 1986.

Spener, Philip J. *Pia Desideria (Pious Desires).* Ed. and trans. Theodore G. Tappert. Philadelphia: Fortress, 1964.

Weckman, George. *My Brothers' Place: An American Lutheran Monastery.* Lawrenceville, Va.: Brunswick, 1992.

C. Diaconia and Social Work

Bachman, John, W. *Together in Hope: 50 Years of Lutheran World Relief.* Minneapolis: Kirk, 1995.

Bradfield, Margaret, ed. and trans. *The Good Samaritan: The Life and Work of Friedrich von Bodelschwingh.* London: Marshall, Morgan and Scott, 1960.

Christianson, Gerald. "J. H. Wichern and the Rise of the Lutheran Social Institution." *Lutheran Quarterly* 19 (1967): 357–370.

Freudenstein, Erich. *The Home Mission of the Evangelical Church in Germany: Facts and Features.* Trans. Friedrich Köhler. Hamburg: Agentur des Rauhen Hauses, 1949.

Larson, Duane H. *From Word and Sacrament: A Renewed Vision for Diaconal Ministry.* Chicago: Evangelical Lutheran Church in America, 1999.

Marty, Martin E. *Health and Medicine in the Lutheran Tradition: Being Well.* New York: Crossroad, 1983.

Olson, Jeannine E. *One Ministry, Many Roles: Deacons and Deaconesses through the Centuries.* St. Louis: Concordia, 1992.

Schober, Theodor. *Treasure Houses of the Church: The Formation of the Deaconate through the Lutherans Wilhelm Löhe, Hermann Bezzel, and Hans Lauerer.* Ed. Frederick S. Weiser, and trans. Bertha Moeller. Typescript, Gettysburg Lutheran Seminary Library.

Solberg, Richard W. *As between Brothers: The Story of Lutheran Response to World Need.* Minneapolis: Augsburg, 1957.

Weiser, Frederick S. *Love's Response: A Story of Lutheran Deaconesses in America.* Philadelphia: Board of Publication, United Lutheran Church in America, 1962.

———. *To Serve the Lord and His People, 1884–1984: Celebrating the Heritage of a Century of Lutheran Deaconesses in America.* Gladwyne, Pa.: Deaconess Community of the Lutheran Church in America, 1984.

Women and Children Living in Poverty: A Report to the Evangelical Lutheran Church in America with Recommendation for Action. Columbus, Ohio: Institute for Mission in the USA, 1989.

D. Education

Affirming the Origins and Value of Lutheran Higher Education: Papers and Proceedings of the 72nd Annual Meeting, Lutheran Educational Conference of North America, January 1986. Washington, D.C.: Lutheran Educational Conference of North America, 1986.

Bachmann, Theodore E. *Learning for Life: The Role of the Lutheran Church in America in Higher Education.* New York: Board of College Education and Church Vocations, 1963.

Confirmation: A Study Document. Prepared by the Commission of Education, Lutheran World Federation. Minneapolis: Augsburg, 1963.

Confirmation in the Lutheran Churches Today: Report of Studies on Confirmation in the LWF Member Churches in 1979–1986 by Riitta Virkunen. Geneva: Department of Studies, Lutheran World Federation, 1986.

Conrad, Robert L., et al. *Confirmation: Engaging Lutheran Foundations and Practices.* Minneapolis: Fortress, 1999.

Cooper, John C., ed. *The Future of Lutheran Higher Education.* Selinsgrove, Pa.: Susquehanna University, 1984.

Dishno, Richard W., ed. *American Lutheran History in Theological Education: 14 Seminary Profiles and a Report.* Chicago: Lutheran Historical Conference, 1990.

Faithful Leaders for a Changing World: Theological Education for Mission in the ELCA. Evangelical Lutheran Church in America Study of Theological Education. Chicago: Evangelical Lutheran Church in America, 1995.

The Future of Seminary Education in the Lutheran Church. A free conference on theological education held at the Trinity Lutheran Seminary, June 4–6, 1984. Columbus, Ohio: Trinity Seminary Review, 1984.

Handbook for Confirmation Ministry. Ed. Silvio Schneider. Geneva: Lutheran World Federation, 1998.

Jahsmann, Allan H. *What's Lutheran in Education? Exploration into Principles and Practices.* St. Louis: Concordia, 1960.

Lutheran Higher Education—Toward the 21st Century: Papers and Proceedings of the 76th Annual Meeting, Lutheran Educational Conference of North America, January 1990. Washington, D.C.: Lutheran Educational Conference of North America, 1990.

Solberg, Richard W. *Lutheran Higher Education in North America.* Minneapolis: Augsburg, 1985.

Wiencke, Gustav K., ed. *Christian Education in a Secular Society.* Philadelphia: Fortress, 1970.

E. Pastoral Theology

Bengston, Gloria E., ed. *Lutheran Women in Ordained Ministry, 1970–1995: Reflections and Perspectives.* Minneapolis: Augsburg, 1995.

Caemmerer, Richard R., et al. *The Pastor at Work.* St. Louis: Concordia, 1960.

Caemmerer, Richard R., and Lueker, Erwin L. *Church and Ministry in Transition: Application of Scripture and History to Current Questions.* St. Louis: Concordia, 1964.

Chilstrom, Herbert M., and Almen, Lowell G., eds. *The Many Faces of Pastoral Ministry: Perspectives by Bishops of the Evangelical Lutheran Church in America.* Minneapolis: Augsburg, 1989.

Kadel, Thomas E., ed. *Growth in Ministry.* Philadelphia: Fortress, 1980.

Marty, Martin E., et al. *Death and Birth of the Parish.* St. Louis: Concordia, 1964.

Reumann, John H. P. *Ministries Examined: Laity, Clergy, Women, and Bishops in a Time of Change.* Minneapolis: Augsburg, 1987.

XVI. MUSIC AND ART

Bajus, John. *The "Paul Gerhardt" of Slovakia: Lutheran Pastor and Hymnologist of the 18th Century, Samuel Hruskovic: A Tribute to His Memory in Commemoration of the Bicentenary of His Death.* Chicago: Zion Lutheran Church, 1949.

Bergmann, Leola M. *Music Master of the Middle West: The Story of F. Melius Christiansen and the St. Olaf Choir.* Minneapolis: University of Minnesota Press, 1944.

Blume, Friedrich, with Ludwig Finscher, Georg Feder, Adam Adrio, Walter Blankenburg, Torben Schousboe, Robert Stevenson, and Watkins Shaw. *Protestant Church Music: A History.* New York: Norton, 1974.

Cartford, Gerhard M. *Music in the Norwegian Lutheran Church: A Study of Its Development in Norway and Its Transfer to America, 1825–1917.* Ph.D. diss., University of Minnesota, 1961.

Christian Worship: A Lutheran Hymnal. Milwaukee: Northwestern, 1993.

Halter, Carl, and Schalk, Carl, eds. *A Handbook of Church Music.* St. Louis: Concordia, 1978.

Holborn, Hans L. *Bach and Pietism: The Relationship of Johann Sebastian Bach to Eighteenth-century Lutheran Orthodoxy and Pietism with Special Reference to the Saint Matthew Passion.* Ph.D. diss., Claremont School of Theology, 1976.

Leaver, Robin A. *The Liturgy and Music: A Study of the Use of the Hymn in Two Liturgical Traditions.* Bramcote, Nottinghamshire: Grove, 1976.

Milner, Scott C. *The "Blessed Death" in the Church Cantatas of Johann Sebastian Bach.* Ph.D. diss., Brandeis University, 1995.

Pelikan, Jaroslav J. *Bach among the Theologians.* Philadelphia: Fortress, 1986.

Rice, William C. *A Concise History of Church Music.* Nashville: Abingdon, 1964.

Schalk, Carl. *God's Song in a New Land: Lutheran Hymnals in America.* St. Louis: Concordia, 1995.

Sovik, E. A. *Architecture for Worship.* Minneapolis: Augsburg, 1973.

Stapert, Calvin. *My Only Comfort: Death, Deliverance, and Discipleship in the Music of Bach.* Grand Rapids, Mich.: Eerdmans, 2000.

Stiller, Günther. *Johann Sebastian Bach and Liturgical Life in Leipzig.* Ed. Robin A. Leaver, and trans. Herbert J. A. Bouman, Daniel F. Poellot, and Hilton C. Oswald. St. Louis: Concordia, 1984.

Stulken, Marilyn Kay. *Hymnal Companion to the Lutheran Book of Worship.* Philadelphia: Fortress, 1981.

Westermeyer, Paul. *The Church Musician.* Rev. ed. Minneapolis: Augsburg Fortress, 1997.

Winkworth, Catherine. *Christian Singers of Germany.* London: Macmillan, 1869.

About the Authors

Günther Gassmann is a visiting professor of the Lutheran Theological Seminary at Gettysburg, Pennsylvania, as well as of theological faculties in Tartu, Estonia; São Leopoldo, Brazil; Rostock, Germany; and Bratislava, Slovakia. He received his Doctor of Theology and Doctor of Theology-Habilitation from the University of Heidelberg, Germany—his home country. At the University of Heidelberg, he taught as an assistant professor (1964–1969). From 1969 to 1976 he served as a research professor at the Institute for Ecumenical Research in Strasbourg, France, and from 1977 to 1982 as the head of the central office of the Lutheran churches in (West) Germany at Hannover. In 1982 he joined the Lutheran World Federation at Geneva, Switzerland, as its ecumenical officer. His last employment before retirement in 1995 was with the World Council of Churches in Geneva, Switzerland, where he served as the director of the Commission on Faith and Order from 1984 to 1994. Dr. Gassmann has written over 180 articles for periodicals and encyclopedias and several books. His most recent book is the *Fortress Introduction to the Lutheran Confession* (1999, with Scott H. Hendrix).

Duane H. Larson is the president of the (Lutheran) Wartburg Theological Seminary at Dubuque, Iowa. A graduate of Pacific Lutheran University and Luther Northwestern Seminary at St. Paul, he received his doctorate from the Graduate Theological Union at Berkeley in 1993. He served as a pastor and from 1993 to 1999 taught systematic theology at the Lutheran Theological Seminary in Gettysburg before being called to his present position. Among his publications are *Times of the Trinity* (1995) and *From Word and Sacrament: A Renewed Vision of Diaconal Ministry* (1999). He has also written numerous articles on theology and science and ecumenical theology. He is the recipient of two Templeton awards in Science and Religion.

Mark W. Oldenburg is the professor of liturgics and chaplain of the Lutheran Theological Seminary in Gettysburg, Pennsylvania. A graduate of Gettysburg College and the Lutheran Theological Seminary at Philadelphia, he received his doctorate in liturgical studies from Drew University. Prior to coming to

Gettysburg Seminary in 1986, he served congregations in New Jersey and spent time as a synod staff member responsible for Evangelical Outreach. He has published hymns and sermons, as well as articles on the church year and the history of Lutheran worship in the United States.